Exploring Positive Identities and Organizations

Organization and Management Series

Series Editors
Arthur P. Brief
University of Utah

James P. Walsh
University of Michigan

Exploring Positive Identities and Organizations

Building a Theoretical and Research Foundation

Edited by **Laura Morgan Roberts**
and **Jane E. Dutton**

Routledge
Taylor & Francis Group
New York   London

Psychology Press
Taylor & Francis Group
270 Madison Avenue
New York, NY 10016

Psychology Press
Taylor & Francis Group
27 Church Road
Hove, East Sussex BN3 2FA

© 2009 by Taylor & Francis Group, LLC
Psychology Press is an imprint of Taylor & Francis Group, an Informa business

Printed in the United States of America on acid-free paper
10 9 8 7 6 5 4 3 2 1

International Standard Book Number-13: 978-1-84169-764-2 (Softcover)

Library of Congress Cataloging-in-Publication Data

Roberts, Laura Morgan.
    Exploring positive identities and organizations : building a theoretical and research
foundation / Laura Morgan Roberts, Jane E. Dutton. -- 1st ed.
        p. cm.
    ISBN 978-1-84169-763-5 (hardback) -- ISBN 978-1-84169-764-2 (pbk.)
    1. Positive psychology. 2. Identity (Psychology) 3. Organization. I. Dutton, Jane E. II.
Title.

BF204.6.R64 2008
302.3'5--dc22   2008044021

Visit the Taylor & Francis Web site at
http://www.taylorandfrancis.com

and the Psychology Press Web site at
http://www.psypress.com

Contents

PART I Introduction

PART II Identities and Individuals in Organizations

PART III Positive Identities and Relationships in Groups and Organizations

PART IV Positive Identities and Organizations and Communities

PART V   Conclusion

Series Foreword

Laura Morgan Roberts and Jane Dutton's book is bound to appeal broadly to organizational scholars. To those who believe our scholarship should be about producing positive outcomes in organizations, Laura, Jane, and their contributors' words will be reassuring. Alternatively, to those whose research aims are more descriptive and seemingly neutral, the book offers hope that the glass, in fact, is half full, that we at the same time can seek objectively (conceptually and methodologically) outcomes that are "beneficial, good, or generative...."

More specifically, Laura and Jane have collected a set of essays about positive identities in organizations that rest on three assumptions: (a) identity is central to organization studies; (b) identity is influenced by social context; and (c) individuals, groups, and organizations strive to construct positive identities. Resting on these assumptions, the 22 chapters comprising the book are wide ranging, dealing, for example, with sensemaking in posttraumatic growth, hope, leader identity, the motivation to mentor, and sustainably focused organizational identities. This breadth, as you would expect from Laura and Jane, is coupled with a set of provocative ideas that are sure to entice many organizational scholars.

We truly are pleased to add Laura and Jane's work to our series. The study of management and organizations keeps evolving, and this book represents a significant departure from the norm.

Arthur P. Brief
University of Utah

James Walsh
University of Michigan

Acknowledgments

This book grew and was strengthened from the efforts of many people whom we would like to thank. First, we thank Janet Max, who as the Administrative Leader of the Center for Positive Organizational Scholarship at Michigan attended to so many of the details and developed all of the relationships that created this book. Janet is a tour de force who did a fabulous job with our book-building conference, as well as a fantastic job managing the details for the book production from beginning to end. We also thank Jennifer Huntington, who came on board and managed the last leg of details and designed the cover for the book. We thank Anne Duffy from Psychology Press/Routledge at Taylor & Francis Group. Anne was the Senior Editor with us on the first book in this series on Positive Organizational Scholarship (*Exploring Positive Relationships at Work: Building a Theoretical and Research Foundation*, 2007), and she has been a guiding light and important supporter for this book as well. Jeff Bednar, who is a coauthor with us on our introductory and conclusion chapters, was a partner who helped us to understand and push the limits around the idea of positive identities and organizations. He has been a superb help throughout this project and added an amazing amount of intellectual content, especially considering we did this book during his first year in the doctoral program. We thank the terrific doctoral students who helped with the conference that launched this book, including Maria Farkas, ChakFu Lam, Vera Sacharin, and Lok-Sze Wong. In addition, Max Miller and Danya Dhanak were helpful in making sure the conference details and web site ran smoothly. We also thank Wayne Baker, Director of the Center for Positive Organizational Scholarship at the time we held the conference, for his gracious contributions, as well as the support of Kathie Sutcliffe and the Ross Business School (RBS) at the University of Michigan. The RBS continues to be a critical supporter of the Center for Positive Organizational Scholarship, and so much of the Center's outputs would not be possible without their financial and strategic investments. We thank the Harvard Business School for supporting the book-building conference and Laura Morgan Roberts' investment of time in cultivating these ideas on positive identities and organizations. We thank the J. Mack

Robinson School of Business at Georgia State University for providing the infrastructure for Laura Morgan Roberts to work on this book as a Visiting Scholar. On a personal note, we thank our families for their inspiration, support, and encouragement during this project. Special thanks to Anaiah Elizabeth for being such a cooperative and generous newborn. Lastly, we express our sincere appreciation to the authors involved in this book manuscript who met the deadlines, engaged the ideas, responded to feedback, and wrote dynamite chapters that are the core of this book project. We are proud to have had the opportunity to edit this volume.

Laura Morgan Roberts and Jane E. Dutton

Editors and Contributors

Laura Morgan Roberts is an assistant professor of organizational behavior at the Harvard Business School. She is a graduate of the University of Virginia (Bachelor of Arts, psychology) and the University of Michigan (master's and doctorate degrees, organizational psychology). Laura's research program examines positive identity processes in diverse organizational settings. She speaks to the role that leadership plays in creating work contexts where employees can engage authentically and contribute from a position of strength. She also investigates how employees of diverse professional and cultural backgrounds leverage their identities as strengths that create value, build connections, and foster personal fulfillment.

Jane E. Dutton is the Robert L. Kahn Distinguished University Professor of Business Administration and Psychology at the University of Michigan. She is currently the codirector of the Center of Positive Organizational Scholarship at the Ross School of Business (http://www.bus.umich.edu/Positive). She edited the book *Exploring Positive Relationships at Work* with Belle Ragins in 2007. Jane's research interests are on the processes that generate flourishing in work organizations. She studies positive identity, compassion at work, high quality connections, and job crafting.

Susan J. Ashford is the Michael and Susan Jandernoa Professor of Management and Organizations at the Stephen M. Ross School of Business, University of Michigan. She has been on the Ross School faculty since 1991 and taught previously at the Amos Tuck School of Business, Dartmouth College (1983–1991). Sue Ashford researches the experiences of people in organizations, focusing on how they attempt to enhance their own effectiveness, survival, and success proactively. She has published research in the areas of feedback seeking, proactivity, managerial effectiveness, issue selling, self-management, and organizational change. Her recent research is focused on proactivity, identity, and leadership (of self and others).

Blake E. Ashforth is the Rusty Lyon Chair in Business in the W. P. Carey School of Business, Arizona State University. He received his doctorate from the University of Toronto. His research concerns the ongoing dance between individuals and organizations, including identity and identification, socialization and newcomer work adjustment, and the links among individual-, group-, and organization-level phenomena. Regarding identity and identification, his current work focuses on multiple identities, dirty work identities, disidentification and ambivalent identification, and relational identities.

Brianna Barker Caza is an assistant professor of business administration at the University of Illinois at Urbana–Champaign. Her research interests fall into two distinct but interrelated streams. First, she studies how individuals perceive, experience, and react to adversity or setbacks in the workplace. This includes issues involving work crises, incivility, and organizational (in)justice. The second stream of research focuses on the nature, construction, and importance of work identity. Her current work combines these two research streams to look at the ways in which work identity shapes response to adversity at work.

Jeffrey Bednar is a doctoral student studying management and organizations at the Stephen M. Ross School of Business, University of Michigan. His current research focuses on identity and identity construction and maintenance processes, especially among professionals in professional service firms. Before entering his doctoral program, Jeff graduated from Brigham Young University with a Master of Accountancy degree.

Shelley L. Brickson is an associate professor at the University of Illinois at Chicago. She received her doctorate in organizational behavior at Harvard University. She was previously an assistant professor at London Business School. Shelley studies issues of identity at both the individual and organizational levels of analysis. Her work applies identity to such phenomena as stakeholder management, identification, and diversity management.

Arne Carlsen is a senior scientist at SINTEF Technology and Management in Norway. Much of his research has been linked to practical development processes in and with professional service organizations. He has published in journals, encyclopedias, and handbooks about knowledge management, organizational change, and identity formation at work. He is broadly interested in temporality, narrative theory, pragmatism, and positive psychology and is presently most curious about the various practices and motivational drivers of "idea work" in organizations.

Sandra E. Cha is an assistant professor of organizational behavior at McGill University. She earned a doctorate in organizational behavior from Harvard Business School and the Harvard Psychology Department. Professor Cha conducts research on leadership challenges in the 21st century: (a) leading through higher values and ideals and (b) professional image construction. Two of her publications—"When values backfire: Leadership, attribution, and disenchantment in a values-driven organization" (Cha & Edmondson, 2006) and "Leading by leveraging culture" (Chatman & Cha, 2003)—have been disseminated especially widely. "Leading by leveraging culture" received the 2004 Accenture Award and has entered the curricula at top business schools.

Lydia L. Chen is a doctoral student in cognitive psychology at the University of Michigan. She holds dual Bachelor of Arts degrees in psychology and applied mathematics from the University of California, Berkeley. As assistant technical staff at MIT Lincoln Laboratory's Sensor Systems Division, she specialized in mathematical and computational modeling and simulation, data analysis, and software and hardware development. Chen is a National Science Foundation Graduate Research Fellow and a past National Defense Science and Engineering Graduate Fellow. She investigates the roles of storytelling, coherence, and primacy effects in decision making and persuasion, especially in negotiation, law, and security affairs.

Kevin G. Corley is an assistant professor of management at the W. P. Carey School of Business, Arizona State University. He received his doctorate from The Pennsylvania State University. His research interests focus on organizational change, especially as it pertains to issues of organizational identity, image, reputation, identification, and knowledge.

Natalie C. Cotton is a joint doctoral student in management and organizations at the Stephen M. Ross School of Business, and sociology at the University of Michigan. She earned her Bachelor of Arts degree in international studies, Bachelor of Science degree in economics, Master of Business Administration degree in strategic management, and doctorate of law from the University of Pennsylvania. Her research interests include social networks and professional identity.

Gerald F. Davis is the Wilbur K. Pierpont Collegiate Professor of Management at the Stephen M. Ross School of Business, and a professor of sociology at the University of Michigan. He received his doctorate from the Graduate School of Business at Stanford University. He has published widely in management, sociology, and finance. He is currently Associate Editor of *Administrative Science Quarterly* and Co-Director of the Interdisciplinary Committee on Organization Studies (ICOS) at the University of Michigan.

D. Scott DeRue is an assistant professor of management and organizations at the Stephen M. Ross School of Business, University of Michigan. Scott's research and teaching interests are in the areas of leadership and teamwork. His research seeks to understand how leaders and teams in organizations adapt, learn, and develop over time. His research has been published in journals such as the *Academy of Management Journal, Journal of Applied Psychology, Leadership Quarterly,* and the *Human Resource Management Journal.* Before academia, Scott held leadership positions at the Monitor Group and Hinckley Yacht Company.

Amy C. Edmondson is the Novartis Professor of Leadership and Management at Harvard Business School. She received her master's in psychology and doctorate in organizational behavior from Harvard University. Her research focuses on understanding and improving processes through which organizations learn and innovate. She has investigated how teams learn and how their learning affects the organizations in which they work. Her previous work has explored the importance of a climate of psychological safety for enabling learning and innovation in teams in a variety of organizational contexts, ranging from health care delivery to space exploration.

Dennis A. Gioia is a professor of organizational behavior and chair of the Management and Organization Department in the Smeal College of Business, The Pennsylvania State University. He received his doctorate from Florida State University. Before his academic career he worked as an engineer for Boeing Aerospace at Cape Kennedy during the Apollo lunar program and for Ford Motor Company as corporate recall coordinator. Current research and writing interests focus primarily on the cognitive processes of organization members, especially the ways in which identity and image are involved in sensemaking, sensegiving, organizational change, and more recently, sustainability.

Phillip Glenn is a professor of communication studies at Emerson College, Boston. He received his doctorate from the University of Texas at Austin. His scholarly interests concern interaction in organizational and interpersonal contexts, especially negotiation, mediation, conflict, interviewing, and laughter. In 2008 he was a Visiting Scholar at the Program on Negotiation at Harvard Law School. He is the author of *Laughter in interaction* (Cambridge University Press, 2003), which received the Outstanding Scholarly Publication Award from the Language and Social Interaction Division of the National Communication Association. Along with Curtis LeBaron and Jenny Mandelbaum, he coedited *Studies in language and social interaction* (Erlbaum, 2003).

Mary Ann Glynn is the Joseph F. Cotter Professor of Organization Studies, Professor of Sociology (by courtesy), and Research Director for the Winston Center for Leadership and Ethics at Boston College. She is a Fellow of the Academy of Management and an executive officer of the Managerial and Organizational Cognition (MOC) Division. Mary Ann's research is centered on social cognition writ large, that is, organizational identity, learning, and creativity, as well as its embeddedness in larger systems of meaning arising from organizational fields, institutional systems, and cultural forces. Her approach to positive organizational scholarship focuses on the dynamics of generativity and resilience. Her research has been published in leading journals, including *Academy of Management Journal*, *Academy of Management Review*, *Organization Science*, *Strategic Management Journal*, *Journal of Applied Psychology*, *Journal of Management Studies*, and the *Journal of Marketing*, and numerous edited books.

Aimee Hamilton is a doctoral candidate in the Management and Organization Department of The Pennsylvania State University's Smeal College of Business. Her research interests include innovation, organizational identity, image and reputation, and sustainability. She holds a Bachelor of Arts degree, magna cum laude, from Harvard University and a Master of Business Administration degree from the Yale School of Management.

Spencer H. Harrison is a doctoral student at the W. P. Carey School of Business, Arizona State University. His research focuses on how organizations harness individual vitality, specifically focusing on organizing around passion and curiosity. He finds that research ideas often pop into his mind when he is 50 feet up on a cliff face.

Patricia F. Hewlin is an assistant professor of management and organizational behavior at the McDonough School of Business at Georgetown University. Dr. Hewlin studies the ways organization members express and suppress aspects of their identity, such as their personal values and beliefs at work. She also conducts research on organizational change and stigmatization and discrimination in the workplace. Dr. Hewlin's work is published in the *Academy of Management Review, Journal of Applied Psychology, Journal of Management Studies, Group and Organization Management Journal*, and *Research on Managing Groups and Teams*.

Shirli Kopelman is an assistant professor of management and organization at the Stephen M. Ross School of Business, University of Michigan. She received a doctorate in management and organizations from the Kellogg School of Management at Northwestern University and has a Bachelor of Arts degree in psychology from The Hebrew University of Jerusalem. Her research focuses on strategic display and response to emotions in social relationships, negotiation strategy, global resource-management negotiations, factors promoting cooperation in interdependent intraorganizational and interorganizational contexts, and cross-cultural conflict management and resolution.

Matthew S. Kraatz is an associate professor in the Department of Business Administration at the University of Illinois. His scholarly interests include organizational adaptation, governance, identity, leadership, and other institutional processes. His research has been published in the *Academy of Management Journal*, the *Strategic Management Journal, Organization Science*, and the *American Sociological Review*. He received his doctorate from the Kellogg Graduate School of Management at Northwestern University in 1994 and his Bachelor of Arts degree from Illinois College in 1989.

Glen E. Kreiner is an assistant professor of management and organization at the Smeal College of Business at The Pennsylvania State University. He received his doctorate from Arizona State University. His research areas include identity (positive and otherwise!), role transitions, dirty work/stigmatized jobs, emotions in the workplace, and organization identity change. Currently, he is engaging in a multimethod, long-term research project on identity and change studying the Episcopal Church. Researcher and teacher are not his only positive identities; he is also a husband to a wonderful wife and a father of three young, active, and delightful children.

Curtis D. LeBaron is an associate professor of organizational leadership and strategy at Brigham Young University, and a Warren Jones Fellow within the Marriott School of Management. He conducts video-based research on topics such as organizational knowledge and innovation, workplace identity, and organizational strategy as practice. His work has appeared in leading academic journals, such as *Journal of Communication* and *Human Studies*. His books include *Studies in Language and Social Interaction* (coedited with Phillip Glenn and Jenny Mandelbaum; Erlbaum, 2003) and *Multimodality and Human Interaction* (coedited with Charles Goodwin and Jürgen Streeck; Cambridge University Press, forthcoming).

Fiona Lee is a professor of psychology at the University of Michigan. She obtained her doctorate in social psychology from Harvard University and her Bachelor of Arts degree in economics and psychology from Scripps College in Claremont, California. Her research focuses on identity, power, and culture.

Grace Lemmon is a doctoral student in the College of Business Administration at the University of Illinois at Chicago. Her research interests include exploration of identity, exchange, and mutuality in the employer–employee relationship.

Lucy H. MacPhail is a doctoral candidate at Harvard University in the Health Policy, Management joint degree program at Harvard Business School and Harvard Graduate School of Arts and Sciences. Her research examines management coordination and adverse event in health care delivery organizations. Before pursuing her doctorate, she graduated from

Harvard College with a Bachelor of Arts degree in history and literature and worked as a health care research analyst at the Advisory Board Company in Washington, D.C.

Sally Maitlis is an associate professor of organizational behavior in the Sauder School of Business, University of British Columbia. Her research interests include the social processes of organizational sensemaking and decision making, and narrative and discursive approaches to the study of emotion in organizations. She is currently serving as Associate Editor for Non-Traditional Research at the *Journal of Management Inquiry*, and on the editorial boards of the *Academy of Management Journal, Academy of Management Review*, and *Organization Studies*.

Christopher Marquis is an assistant professor of organizational behavior at the Harvard Business School. He received his doctorate in sociology and business administration from the University of Michigan. His research addresses how firms' external environments influence their behavior, particularly focusing on geographic communities and the lasting influence of founding conditions. He has examined the effects of these processes in the context of community-based social networks, the history of 20th-century U.S. banking, and firms' corporate social responsibility activities.

Laurie P. Milton is an associate professor at the University of Calgary and a research professor at the University of Western Ontario. She studies interdependence, collaboration, and identity. She seeks to understand contexts within which people and groups thrive and work well together. She is especially interested in situations where they must integrate diverse perspectives and knowledge bases. Laurie earned her doctorate at the University of Texas at Austin, her Master of Business Administration degree at the University of Calgary, and her Bachelor and Master of Science degrees at the University of Alberta. Her interest in public policy reflects her history as a senior policy advisor in the Legislative Assembly of Alberta and in the Alberta Housing Ministry.

Tyrone Pitsis is a codirector of the Centre for Management and Organization Studies at the University of Technology, Sydney (UTS). He was awarded a doctorate from UTS in 2007 and an honors degree in psychology from the University of New South Wales. He has authored or coauthored several journal articles, book chapters, and books, and has been the recipient of a number of awards. He lectures in organizational behavior and leadership in the Executive MBA program at UTS, and his research interest is in human experience in projects. He has a gorgeous wife and two beautiful boys and in a former life was an executive chef.

Michael G. Pratt is a Winston Center Fellow and professor of organizational studies at Boston College. His current research interests include the role of identity (e.g., multiple identities, organizational identification) in organizations, with an emphasis on the role of sensemaking and emotion in identity-related processes. He is also doing research in the areas of intuition and work meaning in occupations. His work has appeared in various outlets, including the *Academy of Management Annual Review, Academy of Management Journal, Academy of Management Review*, and the *Administrative Science Quarterly*. He currently serves as an associate editor for the *Academy of Management Journal*.

Belle Rose Ragins is a professor of management at the University of Wisconsin–Milwaukee. Her research interests focus on mentoring, diversity, and positive relationships at work. She is coeditor or coauthor of *Exploring Positive Relationships at Work, Mentoring and Diversity: An International Perspective* and the *Handbook of Mentoring at Work*. Her research has been published in *Academy of Management Review, Academy of Management Journal, Psychological Bulletin*, and *Journal of Applied Psychology*. She is a Fellow of the Society for Industrial-Organizational Psychology, the American Psychological Society, the Society for the Psychology of Women, and the American Psychological Association.

Lakshmi Ramarajan is a Post-Doctoral Fellow at the Harvard Business School. Her research focuses on how individuals manage their multiple identities in organizations. Specifically, she examines the influence of conflict and compatibility among an individual's multiple identities on interpersonal problem solving.

Kathryn S. Roloff is a doctoral student in the Social-Organizational Psychology Program at Columbia University. She received her Bachelor of Arts degree in psychology and administrative science from Colby College and her Master of Arts degree in psychology from Boston University.

Before joining the program at Columbia, she worked as a research associate at Harvard Business School and as a research analyst at Boston University Medical School. Her research interests revolve around team processes such as learning, collaboration, and identity formation in diverse teams.

Nancy P. Rothbard is an associate professor of management at the Wharton School of the University of Pennsylvania. She received her Bachelor of Arts degree from Brown University and her doctorate in organizational behavior and human resource management from the University of Michigan. Her research focuses on the interplay between emotions, identity, engagement, and performance in multiple roles. She has examined these questions in the context of work and family roles and in the context of multiple tasks that people perform within the work role.

Jeffrey Sanchez-Burks is an assistant professor of management and organizations at the Ross School of Business. Dr. Sanchez-Burks received his doctorate in social psychology from the University of Michigan. His research focuses on cultural divides in a global marketplace: the relational dynamics likely to occur when people from different cultures work together, how these dynamics affect performance, and what individuals and organizations can do to address these issues. He currently serves on the Editorial Board of *Organization Science* and is a member of the Academy of Management, Society for Experimental Social Psychology, and the International Society for Research on Emotions.

Isis H. Settles is an assistant professor of social-personality psychology at Michigan State University. She received her Bachelor of Arts degree (psychology) from Harvard University, and her master's and doctorate degrees (personality psychology) from the University of Michigan. Isis studies the behavioral and psychological consequences of holding multiple identities. Additionally, she considers how members of devalued social groups, such as women and racial/ethnic minorities, perceive and cope with unfair treatment. In particular, Isis examines how people react and respond to negative treatment and difficult experiences in a manner that allows them to create new environments and more positive psychological outcomes for themselves.

Mathew L. Sheep is an assistant professor in the College of Business at Illinois State University. He received his doctorate in management and a Master of Arts degree in communication from the University of Cincinnati. His research interests include organizational identity and identification, organizational and individual creativity, ethical issues in workplace spirituality, work-home balance, and discourse analytic approaches to organization. With his colleagues, he has published award-winning articles in such journals as the *Academy of Management Journal, Human Relations,* and *Journal of Business Ethics.*

Joseph Shoshana is a clinical psychologist in private practice in Arlington Heights, Illinois and the greater Chicago area. He is also on staff at Northwest Community Hospital in Arlington Heights. Dr. Shoshana specializes in mood disorders and child and family treatment. He applies principles of cognitive behavioral psychology in his therapeutic approach and has enjoyed a high rate of success and positive outcome. Dr. Shoshana lectures widely on issues in his areas of expertise.

Michael P. Thompson is currently the Associate Dean of the Marriott School at Brigham Young University (BYU), where he has been a faculty member since 1988. He currently teaches graduate courses in leadership and knowledge management. Before joining the faculty at BYU, he was Executive Director of the Public Service Training Program for the State of New York. During its operation, this was the largest professional development program in the nation's public sector. Michael's research has focused primarily on the role of communication and social interaction in knowledge management and innovation. In addition to his publications in academic and practitioner journals, he is coauthor of *Becoming a master manager,* a management textbook used in many MBA programs internationally.

Ian J. Walsh is a doctoral candidate in organization studies at Boston College. His dissertation explores the role of deep structure identification in individuals' participation in organizing that sustains valued organizational elements following an organization's formal death. His study examines the experiences of 2700 former employees of two defunct technology companies. He was recently named the 2008–2009 Tomash Fellow in the History of Computing by the Charles Babbage Institute at the University of Minnesota. His research has been published in *Human Relations, Management and Organization Review,* and *Corporate Reputation Review.*

Marie Gee Wilson is academic dean and professor of management at Griffith University in Queensland, Australia. She received her PhD and JD at the University of Arizona in 1984 and took a position in the IT industry for seven years. She was on the faculty at the University of Auckland, New Zealand from 1991 to 2008 prior to joining Griffith Business School. Marie's research interests are in management of diversity and indigeneity and the processes that lead to professional commitment in contemporary workplaces. She studies employment discrimination, knowledge "nomads," citizenship behavior, and identity complexity. Her work has appeared in *Organizational Behavior and Human Decision Processes*, *Human Relations*, *Personnel Psychology*, and the *British Journal of Management*.

Part I

Introduction

1

Positive Identities and Organizations: An Introduction and Invitation

Jane E. Dutton, Laura Morgan Roberts, and Jeffrey Bednar

CONTENTS

When and how does applying a positive lens to the construct of identity generate new insights for organizational researchers? This is the broad question that unites the authors in this book as they attempt to jump-start an exciting new domain of scholarship in organizational studies that focuses on what we broadly call positive identity. Although the authors in this book use the term positive identity in different ways, they are all focused on illuminating and explaining identity content, identity processes, or outcomes that are beneficial, good, or generative in some way. This book forges a unique union among organizational scholars at the micro, meso, and macro levels interested in identity and positive organizational scholarship (Cameron, Dutton, & Quinn, 2003). This union opens up new research territory, reveals new theoretical insights, and blazes a trail for others to follow. We hope that the chapters in this book and the ideas and questions they inspire will impact organizational scholarship and the world of practice.

WHY THE TIME IS RIGHT FOR THIS BOOK

This book is timely for several compelling reasons. First, the current conversation about identity and identity processes in organizational studies is one of the fastest growing, most fertile, and perhaps most contested (e.g., Albert, Ashforth, & Dutton, 2000; Albert & Whetten, 1985; Alvesson, 1990; Ashforth & Mael, 1989; Bartel, Blader, & Wrzesniewski, 2007; Corley et al., 2006; Haslam, 2001; Hatch & Schultz, 2004; Whetten & Godfrey, 1998). The burgeoning literature on identity in organizational studies has been linked with "nearly everything: from mergers, motivation and meaning-making to ethnicity, entrepreneurship and emotions to politics, participation and project teams" (Alvesson, Ashcraft, & Thomas, 2008, p. 5). Identity is also a construct that is multilevel, giving it utility as a bridging construct in organizational studies (Ravasi & van Rekom, 2003). As a result, the ongoing conversation about identity permeates across levels of analysis and into numerous research domains in organizational studies.

The identity literature is founded on the basic assumption that individuals, dyads, and collectives are motivated to construct identities that are infused with positive meaning (Ashforth & Kreiner, 1999; Cornelissen, Halsam, & Balmer, 2007; Snow & Anderson, 1987; Tajfel & Turner, 1986; Whetten, 2006). However, researchers in this domain have spent a significant portion of their time focusing on how individuals, dyads, and collectives respond to identity discrepancies, deficiencies, or threats (i.e., situations where current identities are negative or inadequate in some way). Thus, we see a major opportunity to expand and develop the domain of scholarship on identity and organizations by seriously focusing on "positive" identity content, process, or outcomes. This focus on positive identity will deepen current knowledge about how individuals, dyads, and collectives navigate identity challenges to progress from "bad" (i.e., a negative or destructive state) to "good" (i.e., a more favorable state). Further, a positive identity lens can reveal exciting new insights into how entities reach beyond "good" to thrive, flourish, or become extraordinary in some way.

Second, individuals, dyads, and collectives face increasingly complex challenges in constructing and maintaining their identities (Blader, Wrzesniewski, & Bartel, 2007). Individuals are prone to work longer hours, in flexible arrangements, within several different organizations, and in multiple jobs or careers. In such a world of work, creating and maintaining a positive identity is consequential and yet more elusive. In a fast-paced, global society where organizational boundaries are becoming increasingly transparent, a deeper understanding of positive identity content and processes can reveal various ways organizations and their members can construct and maintain identities that are appropriately meaningful, legitimate, and stable yet also dynamic, flexible, and adaptable. A deeper understanding of positive identity processes can also uncover means that individuals, dyads, and collectives can deploy to sustain a sense of purpose, direction, and meaning in a world of flux.

Third, there is growing pressure on the field of organization studies and management to generate research with impact (e.g., Bennis & O'Toole, 2005; Hambrick, 2007). Impact means creating theories that stimulate thought, change understanding, generate actions, and/or produce valued outcomes. This book uncovers new theoretical insights that will inspire new questions about positive identity content and identity processes, deepen and change our understanding of theoretical mechanisms, motivate further exploration and research, and ultimately produce growth, authenticity, hope, well-being, trust, resilience, knowledge sharing, collaboration, and environmental sustainability for individuals, dyads, and collectives.

With these three motivations in mind, we designed this book to meet six goals.

1. To develop diverse perspectives on how individuals, dyads, and collectives can construct, sustain, and change positive identities
2. To provide individuals and collectives with ideas, concepts, and resources that will aid them as they strive to construct and to engage positive identities
3. To facilitate the integration of a positive identity perspective into new and established areas of organizational behavior and organizational theory

4. To establish positive identity as a multidisciplinary, multilevel field of inquiry and to facilitate and encourage cross-fertilization and interdisciplinary linkages

5. To offer a foundation for building a community of scholars in all stages of their careers and from various disciplines to pursue research that identifies antecedents, outcomes, processes, and mechanisms associated with positive identities

6. To bring positive identity to the forefront of organizational research by establishing, deepening, and broadening the link between the Positive Organizational Scholarship perspective and identity research

THREE KEY ASSUMPTIONS

As we enter this domain, we articulate three key assumptions that will provide some orienting ideas for the chapters that follow:

1. Identity is a core construct in organizational studies.

The concept of identity has a rich heritage in the social sciences (Gleason, 1983) and in organizational studies (e.g., Albert & Whetten, 1985; Bartel et al., 2007; Corley et al., 2006; Hatch & Schultz, 2004; Hogg & Terry, 2001; Whetten & Godfrey, 1998). Identity is a core construct used by organizational researchers in the micro, meso, and macro traditions that focuses on the meanings created and applied to an entity (Gecas, 1982), whether that entity is an individual (e.g., employee, customer, stakeholder), a dyad, a group, an organization, a profession, or a community. Identity is one way to capture an entity's self-knowledge (Kihlstrom & Klein, 1994) and capture the attributes, characteristics, and narratives that are claimed by or attributed to an entity, helping to define what the entity is and what it is not.

2. Identity is influenced by social context and interaction.

For organizational scholars, the idea of contextual embeddedness is key (Dacin, Ventresca, & Beal, 1999; Granovetter, 1985). When applied to the construct of identity, researchers must take into account the varying levels of the situation that enable, mold, shape, and alter the processes, structures, and contents of identities. The chapters in this book consider the influence of context in many different ways. For some chapters it is the local relational context that matters. For others it is the team, organization, community, industry, or broader cultural context that influences how the researchers are thinking about positive identity processes, structures, or contents. These different considerations of context enrich our understanding of positive identities and illuminate new research domains and questions for future research.

3. *Individuals, dyads, and collectives seek to construct positive identities.*

Research has shown that this drive to construct a positive identity is equivalent to and sometimes even exceeds our most basic physical needs. For example, Snow and Anderson (1987) found that people in homeless situations expend considerable work in constructing positive identities even though they are often deprived of the most basic human needs. In addition, Ashforth and Kreiner (1999) theorized about the tactics used by "dirty workers" to construct a positive work identity despite performing tasks that are "physically, socially, or morally tainted" (Hughes, 1958, p. 122). Elsbach and Kramer (1996) examined how members of top-20 business schools responded to the organizational identity threats of deflated *Business Week* rankings by justifying or excusing the ratings. This inherent drive to construct a positive identity is a basic tenet of many identity theories (Ashforth & Mael, 1989; Tajfel & Turner, 1986) and critical to organizational scholars seeking to understand how individuals, dyads, and collectives can construct identities that are positive in some way.

We assume that a focus on the positive in, of, and from identity unlocks new insights about identity and organizations. Although critiques of a positive perspective on organizational studies (e.g., Fineman, 2006; Hackman, 2008) remind scholars to be careful to define and place limits on the meaning of positive, we have tried to attend to this concern by having chapter authors be explicit about how they are defining and using the idea of positive identity. As we describe in the section below, the chapters address the idea of positive identity in several different ways.

APPROACHES TO POSITIVE IDENTITY

In designing this book we intentionally avoided specifying key criteria that authors should use to define "positive" as it relates to identity. Instead, we hoped that our open invitation would spark a rich dialogue between authors regarding which criteria were best suited for examining different identity-related content, processes, and outcomes at the individual, dyadic, and collective levels of analysis. Engagement with the conceptual and empirical studies in this book reveals several useful ways of approaching the idea of positive identity in organizational studies. As Ashforth suggests in his commentary, the variety of takes on positive identity as discussed in the various chapters indicate its generative potential. At the same time, this diversity of uses of positive identity puts necessary pressure on researchers to be clear about the "domain, boundaries and nomological network" of this construct (Ashforth, Chapter 8, p. 7). At a very general level, the chapters in this book focus on identity content, identity process, or identity-related outcomes (or some combination of the three) as means for seeing and understanding what is positive, valued, or beneficial about an identity as entity or process.

Identity Content Can Be Positive

Several authors make explicit claims regarding positive identity content—or the core characteristics of an identity content that make it "positive." A focus on identity content zooms in on the substance of an identity that distinguishes it as valuable, good, or beneficial. For example, Kreiner and Sheep (Chapter 2) specify five characteristics of a positive identity for individuals: competence, resilience, authenticity, transcendence, and holistic integration. Maitlis (Chapter 3) sees a positive identity as one that includes content that implies an individual's understanding of his or her "strength and resourcefulness in the face of extreme difficulty." MacPhail, Roloff, and Edmondson (Chapter 14) cast expert identity as a positive identity because it incorporates strengths, talents, and skills derived from education, work experience, functional background, and social memberships.

At the relational level, Kopelman, Chen, and Shoshana (Chapter 12) assert a positive relational identity is one where both parties in a relationship see the relationship as one that can overcome challenges and remain effective despite threats. MacPhail, Roloff, and Edmondson (Chapter 14) define a positive team identity as one in which members have accurate knowledge about one another's expertise and shared affective attachment to the team and its goals. DeRue, Ashford, and Cotton (Chapter 10) suggest that an internalized leader identity is a positive identity because leaders are often viewed favorably and that internalization is key for one to take on this positive identity. Ragins (Chapter 11) suggests that a mentor identity is a positive identity and explains how relationship experiences and social information can positively influence individuals' current and future conceptualization of themselves as a mentor and their desire to continue mentoring others.

At the more macro level, Hamilton and Gioia (Chapter 19) assert that an important form of a positive organizational identity is one that is focused on sustainability. They argue that it is critical to understand this type of positive organizational identity content because it allows us to better understand when and why organizations adopt and implement sustainability practices.

Another way of conceptualizing the content of a positive identity is by looking at its structure—the relationship among the various components of identity. In explaining how individuals and entities adopt multiple identities based on audience or stakeholder expectations and internal standards or goals, these chapters define a positive identity as one in which there are favorable or compatible relationships between an entity's different identities. Rothbard and Ramarajan (Chapter 6) propose that identity compatibility (i.e., synergy or complementarity among identities) is the means through which coactivation of work and nonwork identities benefits people at work. Caza and Wilson (Chapter 5) also specify that the compatibility among multiple identities is desirable for tapping into the cognitive, social, and instrumental resources of complex identity structures. Sanchez-Burks and Lee's (Chapter 15) commentary features several studies that show the positive impacts of identity compatibility for relationships and work teams.

Other chapters choose not to specify which identity content is indicative of positivity but instead claim that a positive identity equates to a favorable self-view. Roberts, Cha, Hewlin, and Settles (Chapter 7) adopt this perspective in their chapter, arguing that the process of becoming more authentic positively impacts identity by increasing feelings of self-regard. Milton also deploys this view of identity—she defines a positive relational identity as a relational identity that individuals view as desirable or positive descriptors of themselves. In their commentary, Glynn and Walsh (Chapter 21) remind us that "societies put expectations and pressures on organizations—to be authentic, to be socially responsible, to be meaningful—and, to the extent that organizations succeed in doing so, their identities may be judged by internal and external audiences, to be more 'positive'."

Identity Processes Can Be Positive

The chapters introduce several perspectives that articulate how identity-related processes can be positive, where positivity in the process is defined in varied ways. For example, LeBaron, Glenn, and Thompson (Chapter 9) use conversation analysis to illustrate how knowing and affiliating during boundary moments in interactions can be key practices for positive organizational identity work. Their analysis shows how the positivity of an identity may be accomplished through the processes and practices that create the identity, not merely through the contents or outcomes associated with the identity. Kopelman, Chen, and Shoshana (Chapter 12) also detail the positive processes in self-narration that affect relational identities when individuals are confronted with negative interpersonal encounters at work. Milton (Chapter 13) implies in her chapter that identity confirmation processes that affirm someone's worth are positive. Her approach extends to a focus on positive outcomes as she argues that identity affirmations create the desirable outcome of greater cooperative capacity in groups. Corley and Harrison (Chapter 16) focus on authenticity seeking as a positive (or in their words, generative) organizational change process. In their account of identity change at ACS (an employee-owned outdoor sports company specializing in the manufacture and distribution of climbing and skiing equipment), an authenticity-seeking process is positive in and of itself but also produces positive results that include in their terms "net positive returns in regards to emotional energy." Pratt and Kraatz (Chapter 17) direct us to the positivity in the process by which an organizational self is accomplished. In their view, an organizational self that can integrate in a true sense—making a whole while retaining the individual identities—is most likely to be generative for the organization. They also suggest that this accomplishment is likely transitory—needing to be reaccomplished over time. Carlsen and Pitsis (Chapter 4) map out a different form of positive identity process through their focus on hope. They help us to see the intertwinement of different kinds of hope with the identity construction process in ways that allow us to see how individuals construct a life of progress inside or outside of an organizational context.

Identity Outcomes Can Be Positive

A third approach to positive identity focuses on the positive outcomes associated with or produced by identity construction. A number of chapters address the idea that identity construction processes create outcomes that are valuable or beneficial in some way. For example, several chapters talk about identity content and identity processes that cultivate resilience. Maitlis' (Chapter 3) study of injured musicians illustrates how social sensemaking processes foster a resilient self-narrative that enables individuals to forge a new, positive identity and transcend pain in times of deep disappointment. Caza and Wilson's (Chapter 5) discussion of identity complexity explains how multiple identities can generate resources that enable resilience in the face of workplace challenges. By focusing on resilience as an outcome of identity construction, these chapters explain how experiences that may be construed initially as negative, traumatic, or painful can also generate opportunities for personal growth, relationship building, and workplace contributions.

Other chapters unearth beneficial outcomes that make an identity positive. DeRue, Ashford, and Cotton (Chapter 10) argue the internalization of a leader identity is associated with desirable individual-level (e.g., increased self-esteem), group-level (e.g., increased shared leadership), and organizational-level outcomes (e.g., greater capacity for change). At the more macro level, Marquis and Davis (Chapter 20) show through argument and example how a community's identity and image is shaped by local corporations' actions, and how this leads to positive outcomes such as the support and well-being of local nonprofits. Brickson and Lemmon's (Chapter 18) approach focuses on how different organizational identity types (individualistic, relational, and collectivist) produce different types of socially beneficial resources through what they call an identity-resourcing process. Their approach blends a focus on the process and a focus on the outcomes as positive or valuable in some way.

ROADMAP FOR THE BOOK

The book is divided into three major sections, each corresponding roughly to a different level of analysis. In the first section we begin with a focus on positive identity at the individual level and move progressively to more "macro" perspectives in the other sections. The second section of the book includes chapters that examine positive identity at the relational and group level. The third section includes chapters that focus on positive identity at the organizational and community level. Each of the three sections concludes with a commentary chapter authored by well-known identity scholars (Blake Ashforth—Individual Level; Jeffrey Sanchez-Burks and Fiona Lee—Relational/Group Level; Mary Ann Glynn and Ian Walsh—Organizational/Community Level). The commentary chapters illuminate emerging themes within each section and create additional insights about positive identity at a particular level of analysis. Our book concludes with a summary chapter that looks across the 21 chapters to identify core insights and map directions for future research.

CHAPTER SUMMARIES

Positive Identities and Individuals in Organizations

How can individuals transform identity challenges into opportunities for identity growth? Glen Kreiner and Matthew Sheep (Chapter 2) introduce five identity work tactics that promote the development of identities that are more competent, resilient, authentic, transcendent, and holistic. Each cognitive, affective, and behavioral tactic enhances one's sense of agency, self-awareness, and growth as discrepancies between real and ideal selves are reduced. Kreiner and Sheep spark future research by pointing to ways that individuals can conscientiously pursue identity growth rather than becoming passive targets of identity challenges.

Think for a moment about something that you love to do ... something that really defines you as a person. What would you do if a traumatic experience severely interrupted this activity? Sally Maitlis (Chapter 3) invokes the transformational power of identity in providing a pathway toward growth following work-related trauma. She writes of how musicians with career-altering injuries engage in a social sensemaking process that helps them to renarrate themselves in expanded and empowering ways that promote professional and personal growth. This chapter offers an inspiring view of how even the most traumatic experiences can open up new possibilities for enjoyment and contribution.

How does hope intersect with identity construction to propel people and organizations forward? Arne Carlsen and Tyrone Pitsis (Chapter 4) invite researchers to explore the interplay between identity and hope—a future-oriented quality of experiencing that infuses one's current existence with positive expectancies. They write of how hope emerges from identity narratives of discovery, transformation, and expectations of becoming stronger in some way. They encourage scholars to pursue identity research that highlights various dimensions of hope (e.g., hoping to achieve goals, hoping to expand possibilities, or hoping to move away from hardship) and that potentially benefits individuals and collectives in various ways (e.g., personal growth, legacy building, organizational vitality).

How does the complexity of one's identity as a professional foster resilience and other desirable outcomes? Brianna Barker Caza and Marie Gee Wilson (Chapter 5) explain how the possession of multiple social and role identities can generate cognitive, social, and behavioral resources that foster resilience to work stress, responsiveness to others' needs, and citizenship behaviors in routine and challenging work environments. Specifically, they show how identity complexity enables people to draw on their identity-based knowledge, relationships, and routines to promote well-being and performance. They also show how complex social and role identities are linked with high levels of novel, beneficial, and discretionary behavior among professionals that can generate positive outcomes for individuals and their organizations.

Can work and family identities really align in ways that create beneficial outcomes? How do individuals and organizations affect this process? Nancy Rothbard and Lakshmi Ramarajan (Chapter 6) invite researchers to consider how individuals form and maintain positive relationships between their work and nonwork identities. They challenge the assumption that multiple identities lead to negative tension and competing demands. Using a positive identity lens, they explain how two identities that are coactivated (i.e., salient at the same time, in the same domain) can be compatible (i.e., positively related) when people have control over coactivation or experience coactivation frequently. This chapter points to the process by which "bringing one's whole self to work" can positively impact interrelationships between one's identities.

What does it take to be authentic at work, and how does this process contribute to positive identity? In their chapter, Laura Morgan Roberts, Sandra Cha, Patricia Hewlin, and Isis Settles (Chapter 7) feature the process of being authentic at work as an important contributor to the construction of a positive identity. The chapter offers a description of two major ways through which authenticity affects levels of self-regard. They also describe three critical pathways through which individuals can become more authentic in work organizations: (a) deepening self-awareness; (b) peeling off masks that conceal who one really is; and (c) authentication (having others see oneself as authentic). The chapter suggests a variety of new research opportunities opened by focusing on what enables authenticity as opposed to what prohibits it.

The *Positive Identities and Individuals in Organizations* section concludes with a commentary by Blake Ashforth (Chapter 8). Ashforth draws out several themes that emerge from the discussions of positive identity: the dynamic, contextualized, socially constructed, and narrative characterizations of identity; the role of agency in developing and enacting positive identities; and the ways that singular and multiple identities form a resource pool that is valuable in and of itself, and that also promotes positive action. He then raises important questions and encourages rigorous scientific inquiry into relationships among facets of positivity, relationships between positivity and negativity, and relationships between conceptions of identity at multiple levels of analysis.

Positive Identities and Relationships and Groups in Organizations

How and why do boundary moments in conversation matter in constructing positive identities? Curtis LeBaron, Phillip Glenn, and Michael Thompson (Chapter 9) examine audio and video recordings of what they call "identity in the wild." Their analysis reveals moment-by-moment moves in interaction through which individuals constitute positive identities. They show through empirical examples how positive identities emerge together as "mutually constitutive, reflexive, actions" through micromoves in interaction. Their chapter opens up substantive possibilities for enriching understanding of identity work in organizations through careful and detailed analyses of the talk and visible behaviors that are part of the ordinary interactions that compose life in organizations.

What are the interpersonal dynamics that enable you to begin to view yourself as a leader? What does it mean to internalize the idea of leader into your personal identity? Scott DeRue, Sue Ashford, and Natalie Cotton (Chapter 10) invite researchers to consider the process by which leaders incorporate the quality of "leader" as part of their personal identity given the ambiguity of what it means to be a leader. Their process model of leader identity internalization includes self and other comparison processes that prompt and motivate self-inquiry into whether one is a leader. At the heart of their model is the identity work involving one person's claiming the identity of leader and others' granting this quality, which can lead to a positive or negative spiral of identity development. Their chapter opens up new domains of inquiry about leadership development and positive identity construction that take place through claiming and granting actions.

How do you take on the identity of mentor in a way that is generative for yourself and for others? Belle Rose Ragins (Chapter 11) describes a process of positive identity development that involves developing clear and positive mentoring self-schemas, drawing on schemas to form positive visions of oneself as a mentor, entering into a mentoring relationship, and leveraging experiences in mentoring relationships to refine one's mentoring identity. Her model shows how positive experiences in relationships spark positive identity cycles that reinforce mentors' capability and commitment to mentoring. This chapter points to new research avenues for examining how the full range of self-structures and relationship experiences influence the development of positive relational identities at work for both parties in a relationship, even after the relationship has terminated.

How can individuals at work respond to relational threats in ways that allow them to construct themselves together as a relationship that is able to overcome challenges and remain effective? Shirli Kopelman, Lydia L. Chen, and Joseph Shoshana (Chapter 12) import ideas from cognitive-behavioral therapy and narrative identity literature to build the argument that individuals can respond to relational threats in resilient ways, helping to foster a more positive relational identity. Their chapter outlines how counterproductive emotions in the workforce can be met with self-narration as a form of strategic responding that mitigates threats and restores or affirms a positive relational identity. This self-narration process engages a person in mindful observation, mindful description, and mindful participation, all of which allow a person to authentically manage his or her emotions in a way that preserves or increases a positive relational identity.

How do positive identity processes become embedded in the norms, routines, and social networks of work groups and enhance their cooperative capacities? Laurie Milton (Chapter 13) elucidates how cooperation in work groups is fostered by confirmation of positive relational identities among group members. She presents a self-regenerating cycle of positive relational identities and cooperation, in which identity confirmation (a subjective state that exists when an individual's social environment is aligned with his or her identities) is a critical mechanism for enhancing relationships within groups, developing the cooperative capacity of groups, promoting cooperation, and fostering optimal achievement of work groups and their members. Groups confirm members' identities by validating and valuing these within the group. At the core of this process lies members' experience of the work group context as a social environment that supports the existence and expression of their authentic selves. Her research uses the positive identity lens to bridge two prominent theories of self in relation, self-enhancement theory and self-verification theory, and opens up new avenues of research.

In a world of diverse teams, how can team members contribute to the construction of a positive team identity, as well as foster collaboration and learning? Lucy MacPhail, Kathryn Roloff, and Amy Edmondson (Chapter 14) explore how diverse teams benefit from the shared recognition of and appreciation for members' expert identities (i.e., strengths and contributions). They introduce the construct "reciprocal expertise affirmation" to capture the shared experience of verification and affirmation of members' expertise. MacPhail, Roloff, and Edmondson explain how reciprocal expertise affirmation fosters psychological safety and, by consequence, promotes knowledge sharing, collaboration, and the formation of a positive team identity. This chapter illuminates how an individual's experience of being understood and affirmed benefits the identity of his or her team, thus bridging the individual and group levels of analysis.

The *Positive Identities and Relationships and Groups in Organizations* concludes with a commentary by Jeffrey Sanchez-Burks and Fiona Lee (Chapter 15), who undertake the "elusive search for a positive identity." They explore four core questions that are raised in these chapters on relational and group identities: Who am I in relation to others? How do my identities affect the groups to which I belong? How do my relationships affect my behavior? How do my individual identities relate to my relational and team identities? They draw on several empirical studies that highlight positive aspects of identity that have elsewhere been construed as negative. They explain how having multiple, conflicting identities does not necessarily lead to fragmentation, but instead can promote psychological and relational well-being. They also question whether inauthenticity is indicative of a negative identity by discussing situations in which inauthentic facework can preserve interpersonal relationships, whereas authenticity may damage these relationships. To conclude, they invite readers to consider whether positive identities are best construed in relation with or in isolation from others.

Positive Identities and Organizations and Communities

How does an organization accomplish identity change through the process of seeking authenticity? Kevin Corley and Spencer Harrison (Chapter 16) introduce us to ACS, an employee-owned outdoor sports company specializing in the manufacture and distribution of climbing and skiing equipment, as a venue for understanding a generative identity change process. Corley and Harrison describe how ACS engages in a process of authenticity seeking as a means of continuous identity change. They argue that ACS is in constant pursuit of answering the question of "What does it mean to be who we are?" This process of authenticity searching is enabled through action and reflection practices that keep the organization and its members in a state of impermanence that is generative. This organizational process of searching for its authentic self creates a new way of theorizing about organizational identity change processes that locates positivity in the process of searching for authenticity as an ongoing organizational accomplishment.

What if we think about an organizational self as a way to conceptualize how organizations function with multiple identities? Mike Pratt and Matt Kraatz (Chapter 17) invite us to use the metaphor of organizational self to address three core questions in organizational identity theory that have, at their heart, the coexistence of contradictory ideas about organizational identities as: (a) unique and internally developed versus categorical and externally ascribed; (b) fonts of purposive action versus sources of social constraint; and (c) shared and integrative versus pluralistic and fragmented. Their chapter elaborates the theoretical possibilities generated by integrating ideas from symbolic interaction theory (Mead, 1934) into models of organization identity that allow researchers to consider multiple organizational identities and a whole organizational self at the same time. They conclude that "considerations of an organizational self infuses identity conversations with notions about how organizations can be more agentic, more distinctive, and more unified while at the same time recognizing their fundamentally pluralistic and institutionally constrained nature."

How does an organization's relationship with its stakeholders unlock a process that creates social goods? Shelley Brickson and Grace Lemmon (Chapter 18) set out to answer this question by proposing a process model of what they call stakeholder resourcing. The core idea in their model is that an organization's identity, and particularly its identity orientation (i.e., how members see the organization in relation to its stakeholders), elicits different organizational goals and actions, which generate different positive resources for both internal and external stakeholders. Their chapter provides a new way of seeing how organizations can contribute to society through this resourcing process that is enabled by an organization's identity.

How can an organization cultivate an identity of sustainability and what difference would it make? Aimee Hamilton and Dennis Gioia (Chapter 19) focus on how sustainability is integrated into an organization's identity. They argue that sustainability-focused identities are positive because of the identity content and the beneficial outcomes this kind of identity produces (e.g., "contributing to sustainability of the global social, economic, and natural environment"). Their chapter identifies a range of internal organizational enablers and external pressures that contribute to sustainability-focused identity change. Their chapter outlines four exciting areas in which new research could be done that opens up organizational identity theory and connects it to the important conversation about sustainability.

What difference do corporations make in the construction of a positive identity for a community? Chris Marquis and Jerry Davis (Chapter 20) open up the black box of positive community identity, asking how and why local corporations and nonprofits make a difference in creating and sustaining a positive community identity and reputation. They are interested in explaining why geographically bounded places like Minneapolis-St. Paul become known as places that are defined by positive social features such as social cohesion, generalized trust, and reciprocity. They point to the role of "hardware" (the networks, norms, or social infrastructure) and "software" (roles as instruments for community involvement) in organizations for creating and maintaining a positive community identity. Their chapter raises new possibilities for linking organizational action and community identities in ways that are generative for both.

The Positive Identities and Organizations and Communities section concludes with a Commentary by Mary Ann Glynn and Ian Walsh (Chapter 21). Glynn and Walsh help us find the positive in positive organizational identities. Their commentary points to positive identity attributes revealed through the chapters (e.g., identities as inspirational, generative, authentic, and adaptive). Their chapter also opens up consideration of positive collective identity processes, focusing on the three process themes of resourcing, relationship building, and meaning making. They summarize the positive identity outcomes revealed in the chapter, including tangible and intangible beneficial organizational, community, and societal outcomes. Finally, they add their own provocative propositions about the power of a positive collective identity lens and invite future research to take seriously the organization-in-society lens when considering positive identity attributes, processes, and outcomes.

THE INVITATION

As the chapter overviews suggest, the chapters provide a rich foundation for building a vibrant research domain on positive identities. The multidisciplinary roots and multilevel coverage of this topic provides fertile soil for cultivating new research streams. Our hope is that new and more seasoned organizational scholars alike will join in the tilling of this new ground with the hope of high-impact research yield.

REFERENCES

Albert, S., Ashforth, B. E., & Dutton, J. E. (2000). Organizational identity and identification: Charting new waters and building new bridges. *Academy of Management Review, 25,* 13–17.

Albert, S., & Whetten, D. A. (1985). Organizational identity. In L. L. Cummings & B. M. Staw (Eds.), *Research in organizational behavior* (263–295). Greenwich, CT: JAI Press.

Alvesson, M. (1990). Organization: From substance to image? *Organization Studies, 11,* 373–394.

Alvesson, M., Ashcraft, K. L., & Thomas, R. (2008). Identity matters: Reflections on the construction of identity scholarship in organization studies. *Organization, 15,* 15–28.

Ashforth, B. E., & Kreiner, G. E. (1999). "How can you do it?" Dirty work and the challenge of constructing a positive identity. *Academy of Management Review, 24,* 413–434.

Ashforth, B. E., & Mael, F. A. (1989). Social identity theory and the organization. *Academy of Management Review, 14,* 20–39.

Bartel, C., Blader, S., & Wrzesniewski, A. (2007). *Identity and the modern organization.* Mahwah, NJ: Lawrence Erlbaum Associates.

Blader, S. L., Wrzesniewski A., & Bartel, C. (2007). Identity and the modern organization. In C. Bartel, S. Blader, & A. Wrzesniewski (Eds.), *Identity and the modern organization* (pp. 3–13). Mahwah, NJ: Lawrence Erlbaum Associates.

Bennis, W., & O'Toole, J. (2005). How business schools lost their way. *Harvard Business Review, 83,* 96–124.

Cameron, K., Dutton, J., & Quinn, R. E. (2003). *Positive organizational scholarship: foundations of a new discipline.* San Francisco, CA: Berrett-Koehler Publishers.

Corley, K., Harquail, C., Pratt, M., Glynn, M., Fiol, C., & Hatch, M. (2006). Guiding organizational identity through aged adolescence. *Journal of Management Inquiry, 15,* 95–99.

Cornelissen, J. P., Halsam, S. A., & Balmer, J. M. T. (2007). Social identity, organizational identity and corporate identity: Towards an integrated understanding of processes, patternings and products. *British Journal of Management, 18,* S1–S16.

Dacin, T., Ventresca, M. J., & Beal, B. (1999). The embeddedness of organizations: Dialogue and directions. *Journal of Management, 25,* 317–356.

Fineman, S. (2006). On being positive: Concerns and counterpoints. *Academy of Management Review, 31,* 270–291.

Gecas, V. (1982). The self-concept. *The Annual Review of Sociology, 8,* 1–33.

Gleason, P. (1983). Identifying identity: A semantic history. *Journal of American History, 69,* 910–931.

Granovetter, M. (1985). Economic action and social structure: The problem of embeddedness. *American Journal of Sociology, 91,* 481–510.

Hackman, J. R. (2008). The perils of positivity: "Counterpoint" of point-counterpoint section. *Journal of Organizational Behavior,* forthcoming.

Hambrick, D. (2007). The field of management's devotion to theory: Too much of a good thing? *Academy of Management Journal, 50,* 1346–1352.

Haslam, S. A. (2001). *Psychology in organizations: the social identity approach.* London: Sage.

Hatch, M. J., & Schultz, M. (2004). *Organizational identity: a reader.* New York: Oxford University Press.

Hogg, M. A., & Terry, D. J. (2001). *Social identity processes in organizational contexts.* Philadelphia: Psychology Press.

Hughes, E. C. 1958. *Men and their work.* Glencoe, IL: Free Press.

Kihlstrom, J. F., & Klein, S. B. (1994). The self as a knowledge structure. In R. S. Wyer Jr., & T. K. Srull (Eds.), *Handbook of social cognition: Vol. 1. Basic processes* (2nd ed., pp. 153–208). Hillside, NJ: Lawrence Erlbaum Associates.

Mead, G. H. (1934). *Mind, self and society.* Chicago: University of Chicago Press.

Ravasi, D., & van Rekom, J. (2003). Key issues in organizational identity and identification theory. *Corporate Reputation Review, 6,* 118–132.

Snow, D. A., & Anderson, L. (1987). Identity work among the homeless: The verbal construction and avowal of personal identities. *The American Journal of Sociology, 92,* 1336–1371.

Tajfel, H., & Turner, J. C. (1986). The social identity theory of intergroup behavior. In S. Worchel & W. G. Austin (Eds.), *The psychology of intergroup relations* (2nd ed., p. 24). Chicago: Nelson-Hall.

Whetten, D. A. (2006). Albert and Whetten revisited: Strengthening the concept of organizational identity. *Journal of Management Inquiry, 15,* 219–235.

Whetten, D. A., & Godfrey, P. C. (1998). *Identity in organizations: building theory through conversations.* Thousand Oaks, CA: Sage Publications.

Part II

Identities and Individuals in Organizations

2

Growing Pains and Gains: Framing Identity Dynamics as Opportunities for Identity Growth

Glen E. Kreiner and Mathew L. Sheep

CONTENTS

If you quit growing, you've died. I mean, I cannot think of a greater species of hell than being like the same as I was twenty-five years ago.

People who have come to some clarity about what they really want to do and what their gifts enable them to and have found a way to do that, then you can just go ahead and be who you are, feel what you feel and operate with some degree of integration and integrity and not be pulled apart in so many ways.

—Both quotes from Episcopal priests[1]

---

[1] Although this chapter is *not* built on our other work with Episcopal clergy (Kreiner, Hollensbe, & Sheep, 2006a; Kreiner, Hollensbe, & Sheep, in press), we do draw from our qualitative database in a few instances to better explicate our major arguments. We thank our dear colleague, Elaine Hollensbe, for her work with us on those projects.

INTRODUCTION

It has been said that the only constant is change. Our philosophy with this chapter is that individuals can be purposeful in the changes in their identities such that identity growth is achieved. We link identity with growth and review several themes that serve as a bridge between the two. Specifically, we will explore five types of "identity work"—processes that can be undertaken by individuals to create, sustain, and present healthy individual identities. Our overall goal is to inform the reader of several interesting developments in identity research streams that can be applied to the positively focused notion of "identity growth." In other words, we are focusing on how existing themes in identity research might be adjusted for an intentional, agential *positive* identity development. This growth has positive effects not only for the individual but also for workplace relationships and the employing organizations.

To ensure we are on the same page, we begin with some brief definitions of our key constructs. We define a *positive identity* as one that is competent, resilient, authentic, transcendent, and holistically integrated. We define *identity growth* as progressive increases in the competence, resilience, authenticity, transcendence, and holistic integration of one's self-concept, coupled with a decrease in perceptual discrepancies between real and ideal selves. We chose these characteristics as definitive of *positive* identity growth because, taken together, they describe an idealized state of self-concept toward which individuals may strive, consistent with the assumptions of positive psychology and positive organizational behavior—i.e., that benefits derive from a concept of self focused on developing personal strengths in harmony with one's environment rather than only "fixing" pathologies or weaknesses of the self (Luthans, 2002; Seligman & Csikszentmihalyi, 2000).[2] These definitional aspects will be more specifically addressed as they are applied in the identity work tactics in the sections that follow.

Finally, we define *identity work* as the cognitive, affective, and/or behavioral tactics undertaken by individuals to "create, present, and sustain

---

[2] Thus, positive identity does not strictly mean (in our context) the opposite of negative. It does not connote a "prestigious" identity so much as one that enables the individual to function efficaciously in the world as an integrated, whole, coherent, competent individual—thereby experiencing greater life satisfaction and happiness.

personal identities that are congruent with and supportive of the self-concept" (Snow & Anderson, 1987, p. 1348). We note, too, that there are two types of identity issues inherent in our definitions, and this chapter addresses both of them: (a) those that involve closing the gap between the "real" and "ideal" (both as perceived by the self) and (b) those that involve closing the gap between self-perception and other-perception.

Identity work toward growth is distinguishable from other "garden variety" cognitive mechanisms that do not inherently imply growth, such as cognitive dissonance reduction processes or impression management. Identity work tactics are examples of "agentic work behaviors" that lead to thriving at work (Spreitzer et al., 2005). A key assumption underlying our chapter is the notion that individuals can be proactive rather than passive when it comes to shaping their identity (cf., self-determination theory, Ryan & Deci, 2000). This shaping can occur via identity work, which can reduce the gap between the expected/ideal and perceived/real identity and stimulate identity growth (Kreiner, Hollensbe, & Sheep, 2006b). A reduction in this gap/tension translates to growth and achieving a desired identity that is more positive. As Csikszentmihalyi & Csikszentmihalyi (2006, p. 141) expressed:

> We do not depend for our happiness on good luck or inherited resources—whether genetic or financial. The measure of freedom and autonomy that our complex brains afford—whether we like it or not—makes it possible for each person to carve out a life worth living, despite the most dire circumstances. Being able to approach one's lot with optimism, savoring the moment instead of ruminating about what could have been, is a first step. After that, a commitment to realistic yet ambitious, unselfish, nonmaterial goals helps to give meaning to one's actions and leads to a richer life.

Hence, we argue herein that individuals need not merely accept their circumstances or rely on such "good luck or inherited resources," but rather can be proactive in shaping and crafting their identities to "carve out a life worth living." Specifically, in the subsequent sections, we provide further details on five identity work tactics that we argue can be used for this positive identity growth—developing spiritual identity, searching for optimal balance, transforming identity threats, experimenting with possible selves, and leveraging (in)congruence. First, however, we briefly posit how the tactics relate to one another and return again in the future research section to their interrelations. We believe that each tactic can be classified in terms of its primary and secondary functions. Tactics can vary along a continuum between those having a primarily ongoing/continuous orientation or those having a more episodic/sporadic orientation. That is, some tactics tend toward long-term processes, whereas others are more typically invoked as shorter-term processes. Further, within the episodic functions, we believe it is useful to specify whether the tactic is primarily used in a reactionary or a proactive manner. This will help identify with greater precision the underlying mechanisms of the tactic, as well to more accurately predict enabling conditions for their enactment. A *reactionary* approach is typically invoked in response to some stimulus (e.g., an identity threat, a workplace that is counter to one's values), whereas a *proactive* approach is generated without a negative stimulus. Our use of the term "reactionary" comes with the following caveat: although the tactic occurs in *reaction* to some stimulus, that reaction is in fact coupled with the *agential choice* to enact the specific identity work tactic. See Table 2.1 for the classification scheme of the tactics.

We believe that first two tactics (developing spiritual identity and searching for optimal balance) are best characterized as typically ongoing and continuous processes. Indeed, we argue that the search for spirituality and optimal balance provides an ongoing foundation that can facilitate the other three tactics. That is, as individuals strive to develop a spiritual identity at work and search for optimal identity balance, they are better enabled to invoke the more responsive and episodic tactics appropriately. We also note that although we use the word "tactic" to emphasize that individuals can use these tools proactively, we also acknowledge that these processes often occur unintentionally. That is, individuals can somewhat "naturally" engage in these processes as a response to such stimuli as identity threats, significant life changes, or particularly salient opportunities.

IDENTITY WORK TACTIC 1: DEVELOPING SPIRITUAL IDENTITY AT WORK

The first identity work tactic we present is an ongoing life process that has begun to receive scholarly attention in the emerging research stream of workplace spirituality. This tactic suggests that developing a spiritual identity in the context of the workplace can play a pivotal role in enabling

TABLE 2.1

Identity Work Tactics Toward Identity Growth

Tactic	Positive Identity Characteristics Targeted	Typical Motivations for Tactic Usage	Nature of Tactic		
			Ongoing	Episodic: Reactionary	Episodic: Proactive
Developing spiritual identity	Holistic integration Transcendence	Finding meaningfulness Development of inner life	Primary	Secondary	Secondary
Searching for optimal balance	Holistic integration Competence Authenticity	Balancing need for inclusion and need for distinctiveness	Primary	Secondary	Secondary
Transforming identity threats	Resilience	Protection Safety Improving relationships	Secondary	Primary	Secondary
Experimenting with possible selves	Decreasing gap between real and ideal selves Authenticity Holistic integration Resilience	Change Frustration with current identity	Secondary	Secondary	Primary
Leveraging (in)congruence	Holistic integration Competence	Adaptation to environment	Secondary	Primary (for incongruence)	Primary (for congruence)

Primary denotes the tactic's most common manifestation, whereas *secondary* denotes a possible but less common manifestation.

an individual to link the workplace to his or her broader identity growth goals and opportunities. Although the conceptualization of workplace spirituality is still a work in progress, emergent themes or dimensions repeatedly surface in the literature: (a) integration of the "whole self" in the context of work; (b) meaningfulness in work; (c) transcendence of self toward a greater whole; and (d) development of one's inner life at work (Ashforth & Pratt, 2003; Ashmos & Duchon, 2000; Pfeffer, 2003; Pratt & Ashforth, 2003; Sheep, 2006).

The social scientific study of spirituality spans multiple disciplines, but none so related to identity growth as that of developmental psychology. From that perspective, spiritual identity development is typically defined as

> the process of growing the intrinsic human capacity for self-transcendence, in which the self is embedded in something greater than the self, including the sacred. It is the developmental "engine" that propels the search for connectedness, meaning, purpose, and contribution. It is shaped both within and outside of religious traditions, beliefs, and practices. (Benson, Roehlkepartain, & Rude, 2003, pp. 205–206)

In other words, a sense of "who I am" is shaped by my views (whatever they may be) of how the world is ordered, of how I approach connections with others or "other," and of what matters most in life (Sheep & Foreman, 2007). Two mechanisms for positive identity growth germane to the workplace are suggested from this view: holistic integration and transcendence. We note for the reader that both of these are definitional elements of positive identity that we introduced earlier, and we now discuss them further.

First, *holistic integration* can be further subdivided into two dimensions, being realized as individuals seek growth toward a self-concept progressively marked by (a) identity integration (coherence) and (b) wholeness (completeness). Of course, this idea is not altogether new. For example, Erikson (1964, p. 92) described the individual quest for identity as a search for "wholeness"—which he defined as "a sound, organic, progressive mutuality between diversified … parts." What is new is the notion that individuals should be enabled, even encouraged, to bring all of these "diversified parts"—the "whole self" (cognitive, physical, affective, and spiritual)—into the *workplace*. Such integration enables one to infuse work with meaning and purpose *in harmony* with one's overall beliefs about life's meaning and purpose (Dehler & Welsh, 2003; Mirvis, 1997; Pfeffer, 2003). The work environment, rather than fragmenting the self-concept, thus becomes a context in which growth toward a more positive, holistically integrated identity is facilitated. As one of the clergy we interviewed for another project noted, people "want a consistency between their life and their work. They want something that has a sense of wholeness to them."

Second, *transcendence* of self-identity is facilitated when individuals view their work as "a web of relationships … in a larger context that makes it meaningful" (Mirvis, 1997, p. 199). Such relationships provide "high quality connections" externally that have been linked both to human growth generally and to the coconstruction of valued identities (Dutton & Heaphy, 2003).

As spiritual identity development is viewed as an ongoing quest for transcendence, then the developmental path toward a positive identity (growth) proceeds toward an identity that is increasingly self-defined in terms of something greater than oneself (Ashforth & Pratt, 2003)—that is, in terms of a collective, the greater good, a social cause, or the ultimate source of one's beliefs. Paradoxically, loosening the grip on self-interest to embrace larger interests is seen as enhancing self-concept and developing a more positive identity rather than detracting from it.

The spiritual dimension of one's identity—progressively marked by internal integration as well as a connecting transcendence "to something greater than oneself" (Ashforth & Pratt, 2003, p. 93)—thus functions as a powerful frame within which an overall positive identity can develop.

IDENTITY WORK TACTIC 2: SEARCHING FOR OPTIMAL BALANCE

Our second tactic, like developing one's spiritual identity, is also primarily an ongoing process, although it can also be used episodically (e.g., as a result of particularly jarring or eye-opening events). This tactic suggests that attention to the delicate balance between personal and social identities is needed to avoid identity dysfunctions (Kreiner, 2007) and is indeed rewarding for personal growth. Individuals search for ways to maintain and express individuality while simultaneously wanting to belong to something greater than themselves (Ashforth & Mael, 1989; Brewer &

Pickett, 1999; Dutton, Dukerich, & Harquail, 1994). Hence, individual identities comprise two basic human needs that are in tension with one another: a need for inclusion ("How am I similar to others?") and a need for uniqueness ("How am I different from others?") (Brewer, 1991, 2003). The consequences of imbalance are considerable: too much uniqueness can yield isolation and loneliness, yet too much sameness can depersonalize an individual and a loss of self. A critical function of identity work, then, is to search for an "optimal balance" in identity—"a state of being neither too distinct/independent nor too inclusive/dependent in relation to a given social identity" (Kreiner, Hollensbe, & Sheep, 2006b, p. 1033).

In our previous work (with our colleague Elaine Hollensbe), we demonstrated that individuals have at their disposal a wide variety of identity work tactics that promote optimal balance (Kreiner et al., 2006b). Whereas other research has addressed threats to *group* distinctiveness along with tactics employed to preserve social identity and self-esteem (e.g., outgroup derogation, increased self-stereotyping, and "other forms of collective resistance") (Branscombe, Ellemers, Spears, & Doosjie, 1999, p. 48), our findings, through a positive identity lens, reveal a broader spectrum of growth-promoting tactics. Specifically, we found evidence that identity work tactics can be successfully invoked to bring an individual closer in line with their ideal blend of personal and social identities—consistent with the definitional elements of holistic integration, competence, and authenticity. We classified three broad categories of tactics: integration tactics, differentiation tactics, and dual-purpose tactics, which we now briefly describe.

Integration tactics are used to merge social and personal identity and bring a person closer to others via membership in a social group (e.g., other team, organizational, or occupational members). Individuals can infuse aspects of themselves (e.g., personality, skills, abilities, life history) into their work, can cast themselves as an emblem of their role, and can merge the more task-oriented parts of their work with their identity. *Differentiation tactics*, by contrast, separate the personal identity from the social identity and bring a person more toward uniqueness. Individuals can set limits regarding the degree to which they will allow the role to affect their lives; create an identity hierarchy to separate, prioritize, and control self-aspects; enact ephemeral roles to "escape" the social identity for a time and immerse in another; and what we called "flip the on/off switch" to consciously choose *when* a given social identity would be enacted or not. Finally, *dual-purpose tactics* could be used for either integration or differentiation. For example, individuals can seek refreshment from a social identity or personal demands, involve other people in their identity work as a resource, or tap spiritual resources such as prayer or meditation.

The upshot of our research on optimal balance and these tactics is that individuals need not merely be passive recipients of identity challenges but rather are able to consciously navigate the often turbulent waters of identity work. Indeed, we argue that searching for optimal balance—and being conscious and purposeful in this process—can lead to identity growth. As an individual perceives imbalance and subsequently invokes identity work tactics to rebalance identity, opportunities for learning, increased self-knowledge, and growth present themselves. Our previous research also showed that being consciously attuned to these matters helped our interviewees learn more about themselves, gain a greater sense of control, and develop over time (Kreiner et al, 2006b). Therefore, we suggest that the *conscious* search for optimal balance is itself an important identity work tactic that can serve a foundational role for identity growth. Because individuals and contexts are continually changing, the need to search for optimal balance is ongoing. By engaging in the tactics necessary for optimal balance, individuals can grow into improved identities.

IDENTITY WORK TACTIC 3: TRANSFORMING IDENTITY THREATS

Whereas the first two tactics we discussed are primarily of an ongoing nature, the final three tactics tend to be manifested in a more episodic manner. The first of these is "transforming identity threats." Our basic premise with this tactic is that as individuals learn to reframe threats into opportunities; they are better able to grow from them rather than be defeated by them—a key competence related to the positive identity definitional element of *resilience*—the ability to adapt, cope, and grow in beneficial ways through adverse circumstances. Following Sutcliffe and Vogus (2003, pp. 96–97), we believe that resilience can be developed by individuals as they progressively learn through experiences of confronting adverse circumstances, including identity threats. Individuals face identity threats when their sense of self is called into question. This can occur at a global level ("Am I who I think I am?"; "Am I of value?") or a facet level ("Is this really a part of me?"; "Is this part of me of value?") (Ethier & Deaux, 1994). The debilitating effects and negative potential of identity threats have been well-documented in previous work (e.g., Blanz, Mummendey, Mielke, & Klink, 1998; Breakwell, 1983, 1986; Elsbach, 2003).

Typically, identity threat research focuses on coping or minimizing threat. That is, the more typical question in this line of research is, "how can an individual *minimize harm* from identity threat?" We suggest that the other side of the coin be examined in the context of identity growth—namely, instead of coping with or minimizing the threat, an individual can transform the identity threat into a growth opportunity—more in line with the concept of resilience. That is, we posit the question, "how can an individual *maximize benefit* from identity threat?"

We provide an overall answer to this question within what we call "identity threat jujitsu," a term we coined to conjure the imagery of using the very power of the threat as the thrust toward positive change. In kung fu, an art of self-defense practiced anciently in China and throughout the modern world, an individual uses the forces of the attacker to his or her own advantage rather than merely responding with equal force. Previous invocations of the jujitsu imagery in organizational literature have included treatments on "tempered radicals" and on emotional discipline (Manz, 2003; Meyerson, 2003). We apply this principle to identity threats to suggest that individuals can strategically use the force of the threat itself as a catalyst for increased self-awareness and positive change. Or, as Manz (2003, p. 70) put it, "rather than resisting an emotional attack, we can use its energy to work toward a solution." We argue that identity threat jujitsu is manifest through at least two mechanisms, both of which enable individuals to transform identity threats into opportunities for growth: (a) reframing identity threats, and (b) improving relationships with those individuals who pose threats.

Reframing Identity Threats

Individuals can learn and grow from identity threats. For example, Ely and Roberts (2008) explain how people can learn from experiences reacting to stereotypes and power imbalances in teams. We also refer the reader to Sally Maitlis' Chapter 3 on sensemaking in posttraumatic situations for a vivid example of growth from threat. Reframing refers to the act of transforming the meaning of a stimulus or, more simply, looking at something in a new way. Two forms of reframing have been identified previously: neutralizing and infusing (Ashforth & Kreiner, 1999). *Neutralizing* diminishes the negative value of a stimulus and is the kind of response more typically associated with advice given to individuals facing identity threats. The premise is that by neutralizing the threat, the identity of the individual is no longer threatened but preserved. Although an effective tactic in terms of *coping*, we argue that neutralizing identity threat is essentially ineffective for identity growth. This is because neutralizing the threat negates the opportunity for serious self-reflection and the chance for change and growth based on that reflection. If the individual neutralizes the threat, there is no need for introspection, hence, no basis for change.

By contrast, the other response to threat, *infusing*, offers more opportunity for positive change. Infusing injects a stimulus with positive value to recast it in a different light. Individuals can draw on a repertoire of resources for infusing identity threats with positive value, such as spiritual or religious belief systems, occupational or other group-based ideologies, or past successful identity threat reframing experiences. In essence, the individual examines the identity threat and then reframes it with a positive lens as an opportunity; this is accomplished by infusing it with a positive element drawn from past experience or looking toward the future. Herein, then, lies an opportunity for individuals to reframe identity threats in a way that is generative, positive, and forward-thinking.

Improving Relationships With Individuals Who Pose Threats

In workplace interactions and relationships, identity threats can take such forms as negative feedback, stereotypes, or values discrepancies. Often, the response to the identity threat is simple dismissal or denial (Goldsmith, 2007). Other times, however, a person's natural instinct on identity threat is to "condemn the condemners" (Ashforth & Kreiner, 1999), that is, to devalue or attack the source of the identity threat. This typically leads to short- or long-term decreases in association, contact, and/or trust with the individual(s) who are the source of the threat. This can occur at the individual level (such as a subordinate distancing himself or herself from a superior) or the group level (such as stigmatized groups casting aspersions on nonstigmatized groups) (Ashforth, Kreiner, Clark, & Fugate, 2007). Put another way, an identity threat often cues the classic "fight or flight" syndrome (Selye, 1974). Either choice has important consequences—an individual who chooses "fight" may create an adversarial role with the perceived source of the threat, whereas an individual who chooses "flight" may lose intimacy and closeness with the perceived source of the threat. In either case, the opportunity for growth through challenge is severely diminished or lost entirely. Hence, we suggest that a specific tactic that can be employed in response to an identity threat is neither fight nor flight, but the attempt to *improve* relations—rather than harm them—with the source of the threat. As Roberts (2007, p. 33) notes, positive relationships "provide the psychosocial support and inspiration required for identity change and growth."

As an overall caveat to our discussion of identity threats, we note that identity threats may not always fall into an episodic: reactive tactic category (see Table 2.1). At times, individuals may instead *proactively* self-scrutinize and challenge their own identity (in a sense, threaten its current formulation) if it is not producing desired outcomes. This overlaps, of course, with the process of experimenting with possible selves but is conceptually distinct. Rather than trying a new "self" per se, it may take the form of "stepping outside one's comfort zone" or putting oneself at risk to grow, even though it threatens the current self-concept. Thus, although tactics are primarily reactive to external threats, those stimuli may also be proactively, intrapersonally induced.

IDENTITY WORK TACTIC 4: EXPERIMENTING WITH POSSIBLE SELVES

This tactic is linked with the ongoing process of our first tactic—spiritual identity development—in that one definition of spirituality conceives it as an individual quest for what one considers to be the "sacred" or ultimate (Hill & Pargament, 2003, p. 68). Such a quest dynamically shapes individual values that both enable and constrain how one approaches the fundamental question of "who should I become?"—the driving question that motivates experimenting with possible or provisional selves (Ibarra, 1999).

Markus and Nurius (1986, p. 954) define possible selves as "cognitive components of hopes, fears, goals, and threats" that "function as incentives for future behavior ... and ... provide an evaluative and interpretive context for the current view of self." Important components of that definition include the notion that possible selves are oriented toward a future state and linked to behaviors related to the attainment of the future identity. Additionally, possible selves "provide the essential link between the self-concept and motivation." The impetus for human growth toward a more positive identity is certainly implied in "motivation" that is linked to self-concept. Thus, possible selves provide the cognitive categories that comprise idealized or aspirational identities toward which one is striving (growing).

Individuals are able to test out potential selves as a path to positive growth, as well as to take risk through "experimenting with identity" (Ibarra, 1999, 2003). Ibarra (1999) found that individuals create a repertoire of possible selves by observing desirable role models (role prototyping) and comparing or contrasting the prototype with themselves (identity matching). In the matching process—and particularly when there is a large gap between one's perception of current identity vis-à-vis that of a *hoped-for* provisional self—intrinsic motivation looms large to make changes (e.g., attitudinally, behaviorally, vocationally) necessary to grow toward the more valued identity. Such changes may also be motivated by a confirming perception that a *feared* provisional self (undesirable future identity) is becoming an increasing possibility (Hoyle & Sherrill, 2006; Ibarra, 1999). In our previous research, an interviewee referred to this as "playfulness" and discussed how she had tried different manifestations of her role (e.g., clothing, demeanor, openness) over time to find what helped her "feel pretty integrated."

Of course, simply making a cognitive comparison does not in itself bring about a new identity or identity growth. Instead, it is a necessary (but not sufficient) condition for positive identity growth that would additionally require experimentation by acquiring new behaviors associated with the provisional self. This process is carried out in a dialectic tension of imitating exemplary role models while yet remaining true to one's self— i.e., not stepping outside of the categories that one perceives as his or her "authentic" self (Ibarra, 1999, p. 778).[3] As one of our interviewees reflected on navigating this tension, he described that in "the old days," he "was trying to go by other people's expectations and the image. As I've discovered, God really calls me to be me." Thus, experimenting with "possible selves" is definitely not a "fake it 'til you make it" strategy for growth. On the contrary, only as members favorably evaluate the new identity does it become added to the "new repertoire" of self-concept (Ibarra, 1999, p. 782).

Thus, in terms of definitional components of positive identity, experimenting with possible selves is most associated with decreasing perceptual discrepancies between real and ideal selves, as well as actualizing an authentic self. In addition, a comparison is noted between possible selves and spiritual development. Although both are dynamic works in progress, both are ultimately working toward (teleologically proceeding toward) an integrated or holistic identity. However, because life situations and roles are more often in a state of flux, neither of these tactics arrives permanently at an end state but is always in process (as long as the person lives). This dynamic produces what Lifton (1993) called the "protean self," or one who is competent and adaptable to experiment resiliently with a variety of identities and roles in ways that embrace and "seek change as an affirmation of self" rather than seeing change as a threat (Ashforth, 2007, p. 93). Or, as Ibarra (1999, p. 782) put it, "Over time, with feedback loops among tasks, people expand and refine their repertoires and eventually attain a negotiated adaptation that is neither conformity to rigid role requirements nor changing role requirements to fit a stable, unitary self."

Finally, even though hoped-for possible selves are oriented toward a desired future state, they may yet have desirable effects not confined to future realization. Merely adopting the perceived future identity as that toward which one is presently striving may positively impact current behaviors and motivation related to the attainment of that identity—i.e.,

---

[3] Within the conceptual framework of experimenting with possible selves, we adhere to a definition of "authentic self" as an individual's assessment of *alignment* or congruence between his or her internal experiences/perceptions vis-à-vis external expressions of the various aspects of self-concept (Ibarra, 1999; Roberts, et al., this volume). Thus, if one cannot eventually move beyond "faking" the provisional self—even though initiated in an experimental sense—it is ultimately seen as a violation of the authentic self that cannot be sustained as a viable new identity. We also assume that authenticity is a *process* of being or becoming authentic—or maintaining authenticity—rather than a stable trait that one "possesses" a priori (Corley & Harrison, this volume). Thus, as individuals experiment with provisional selves, the dialectical process of maintaining the internal/external alignment of the authentic self while experimenting with novel aspects of the self is scrutinized reflexively by the individual.

positive identity growth. Attitudinally, there are also benefits. Mental schemata of future selves arouse attitudes of *optimism* and *hope* for desired future states of a more positive identity, increasing those two dimensions of psychological capital that an individual is able to contribute to the organization (Luthans, Youssef, & Avolio, 2007, p. 10), even though the future identity is still (and, in some degree, always) a work in progress. We also refer readers to Carlsen and Pitsis' Chapter 4, which illuminates the linkages between hope and future identity.

IDENTITY WORK TACTIC 5: LEVERAGING (IN)CONGRUENCE

The person-environment fit literature primarily focuses on the issues of (in) congruence between an individual and situational factors and (in)congruence's direct effects on the individual (Kristof, 1996). The basic premise that a match between an individual and his or her environment will yield healthy results has a long history, not merely in organizational studies, but in early philosophers' writings as well (Ostroff & Schulte, 2007). An identity that is congruent with one's environment relates closely to our definitional elements of holistic integration and competence—i.e., a positive identity is one that enables the individual to function efficaciously and harmoniously in his or her social world as an integrated, whole, coherent, competent individual.

There are numerous permutations of fit, including variations on the "who" (e.g., person-organization, person-job, person-group), the "what" (e.g., dimensions of congruence such as values, characteristics, personality/culture), and the "so what" (e.g., positive outcomes of fit such as satisfaction, commitment, reduced stress). Generally, person-environment fit theory argues that congruence is good for the individual, whereas incongruence is harmful. In this section we will articulate the potential for growth under *both* circumstances. Specifically, we will show how individuals can leverage either situation for identity growth: congruence provides safety for some types of growth within a safe harbor (fosters growth), whereas incongruence provides opportunity for dynamic tension to spur growth (springboard for adaptation, change, growth) (Kreiner, Hollensbe, & Sheep, 2006a).

The effects of congruence between the individual and workplace are well-documented, and we refer the interested reader to some recent works that further articulate the details of this relationship (e.g., Kristof-Brown, Zimmerman, & Johnson, 2005; Ostroff & Judge, 2007). For our purposes, however, we wish to look beyond the rather static situation in which congruence simply means less conflict and toward the way in which an individual can *maximize* that state of congruence. To do this, it is useful to first draw the distinction between complementary and supplementary fit.

Complementary fit occurs when the individual has some aspect that is necessary but lacking from the group or organization (Kristof, 1996). This often takes the form of a skill, talent, or ability. Under complementary conditions, the individual is the proverbial "odd man out," *but* is highly valued because he or she is bringing to the table something that the group did not previously have. (This value added distinguishes complementary fit from incongruence, in which the person is still "odd man out" but not valued—an important difference.) In a complementary fit situation, the growth opportunity lies in the ability to learn from others in the group that have skills and abilities that are not currently held by the individual. This could occur with technical skills (e.g., mastering new software), functional skills (e.g., accounting, finance), or process skills (e.g., teamwork, decision making). Similarly, the diversity literature is replete with examples of how diverse perspectives and backgrounds provide complementary fit (e.g., Ely & Thomas, 2001). This growth can be tied to identity in various ways, such that the newly acquired skills actually change (and improve) identity, or relationships are improved and relational identification is increased with those giving/receiving the skills.

Unlike complementary fit, *supplementary fit* occurs when the individual has some aspect that is redundant and compatible with group members (Kristof, 1996). This usually takes the form of an attitude, a personality dimension, or value. The opportunity for growth—identity or otherwise—is perhaps more difficult to perceive in this context, as we tend to see growth as stemming from challenges or adversity. But we argue that in the context of general supplementary fit, the individual has an opportunity to work from a "safe haven" perspective to enact other identity work tactics we have described in this chapter. That is, because of the generally safe condition of being with like-minded company, the individual can (a) have a more sure foundation for developing spirituality and searching for optimal balance, (b) "afford" to take risks through experimenting with possible selves, and (c) better weather the storms of identity threats. For example, because a person feels safer in a congruence situation, he or she might be more likely to take the risk of "trying on" the possible selves mentioned above, whereas under more turbulent conditions he or she would not feel safe enough to take such a risk. Similarly, the workplace spirituality literature as a whole (and our tactic of developing spirituality in particular) would suggest that these psychologically safe climates can spur identity development because they provide more fertile ground for growth via transcending past selves and increasing the integration of the whole self in the work context.

Finally, we consider states of *incongruence*, which occur when the values of the individual do not align with those of the group or organization. Incongruence is conceptually distinct from, but sometimes related to, the previously explored issue of identity threat. Incongruence is a fairly stable state within a particular situation that results from the mismatch between a person and some facet of the environment (e.g., group, occupation, organization). An individual will have varying levels of awareness or concern over this state, but there are not necessarily identity threat implications of incongruence. Incongruence *does* become a "threat," however, when the individual not only becomes conscious or concerned over the incongruence but also perceives its potential effects on identity. For example, an individual can "live with" a state of incongruence at work without perceiving identity threat until he or she learns that they might be fired because they do not fit in; loss of identity as a member of the specific organization and/or the unwanted identity of "unemployed" can then cue identity threat. Meyerson (2003) provides a vivid illustration of using value incongruence to lead positive change in organizations. Her notion of "tempered radicals" is those people who want their organizations to succeed yet are at odds with the predominant organizational culture. These individuals work through formal and/or informal channels to effectuate positive, generative change, often despite the accompanying personal setbacks.

We argue that the state of incongruence offers the opportunity for identity growth via two potential processes, what we call "adaptation-staying" and "learning-exiting." (Precursor to both processes is the individual recognizing the incongruence.) These processes are somewhat akin to the classic exit-voice-loyalty-neglect typology (Hirschman, 1970; Turnley & Feldman, 1999) but with an eye toward how these choices are made in the context of identity growth opportunities. In the *adaptation-staying* process, the individual changes to fit with his or her environment and therefore, after adapting, stays with the organization. In this process, the opportunity for identity growth mirrors the complementary fit scenario above, wherein the individual can grow by adopting new skills or attitudes. For example, a priest we interviewed in our previous work told us how when she first arrived at her parish, she did not fit well with the lay leaders in the congregation, leading to contentious meetings; but that over the years "there has been movement and growth" among them. Another interviewee, who was a self-described introvert "had to do a lot of growing in order to grow into the sort of gregarious role that … people expect from their clergy." In seeking to adapt certain aspects of their identity to be congruent with the expectations of their professional identity (clergy), these priests have engaged in a process similar to that of *identity customization*, or "changes in identity made to fit work demands" (Pratt, Rockman, & Kaufmann, 2006, p. 246). In doing so, they may be more apt not only to stay in the current context but also to thrive in it as enabled by a more congruent (competent and integrated) exercise of "who one is" in that particular context.

By contrast, sometimes adaptation is not a viable option, or, as one of our clergy member interviewees told us, trying to change too much is "like squeezing blood out of a turnip. I'm trying. It just doesn't work because that's not who I am." Therefore, in the *learning-exiting* process, the individual decides to exit the organization because of the incongruence experienced but has the opportunity to learn about oneself from the process (e.g., through the contrast effects with others in the organization, through self-reflection about mistakes made in joining the organization). Of course, individuals perhaps more typically deny themselves said opportunity, instead blaming the situation or other individuals involved. This provides another example of how the underlying tactics of increasing spirituality at work and searching for optimal balance would provide a foundation that primes the individual to capitalize on such a growth opportunity.

In sum, we believe that our basic premise has an important implication for the positive organizational scholarship movement. Namely, regardless of the situation—incongruence or congruence—an individual has the opportunity to leverage it for identity growth. This enables individuals to frame either kind of situation as a growth opportunity.

LOOKING FORWARD: FUTURE RESEARCH ON IDENTITY GROWTH

In this chapter, we have covered but a few of the myriad topics that can be linked to identity growth, yet other parameters of identity growth can be articulated. Therefore, we briefly consider some potential bridges to future research. First, we wonder what role *learning* plays in identity growth. How does learning capacity help translate into a more positive identity and influence how (effectively) individuals approach the tactics? Which tactics are preferred for what reasons related to prior learning? We suspect that an encouraging learning cycle could develop in which individuals increase their capacity for the future as they engage in identity growth tactics.

Second, how might we consider the implications for the *temporal nature* of identity growth? For example, how might a hierarchical or sequential approach to growth differ? Or, as some have argued, the "end" is never fully realized in growth, and we are always a work in progress. Similarly, growth can be cyclical rather than linear, and the effects of growth may have a decay effect over time if not nurtured, maintained, or reinforced.

Third, we are curious to bump up the level of analysis and apply the notion of identity growth to dyads, groups, and organizations. How might these processes play out in similar and different ways at different levels, and what additional tactics might be discovered at different levels of analysis? Future research can also consider various ways in which an organization might provide a context in which the individual can experience identity growth. For that, we suggest as a starting point Ashforth and Pratt's (2003) three-way typology of organizational orientations toward spirituality—enabling, partnering, and directing—that vary along a continuum from high individual control to high organizational control. As Ashforth and Pratt (2003, p. 96) suggested, this typology can be applied more broadly to varying organizational orientations toward a number of other issues that have been traditionally regarded as an "unwarranted intrusion of the personal sphere into the proprietary"—e.g., work-family balance issues and spiritual identity development (Sheep & Foreman, 2007).

By extension, then, we suggest that these three types could also exist according to the degree of organizational support and/or control for positive identity growth. *Enabling* organizations, although assuming a facilitating, nonthreatening posture, are generally passive in regard to identity growth, deferring such issues to individual control. *Directing* organizations usurp or co-opt individual efforts at identity growth by exercising a high degree of organizational control, essentially mandating the specific types and processes of growth. *Partnering* organizations represent a middle ground between enabling and directing organizations, where both individuals and the organization have a high degree of control over identity development and growth. Although organizations in this category would be proactive in promoting identity growth, it is nevertheless a mutually shared coconstruction with members. We would also add a fourth possibility to the typology—*impeding*, in which the organization actively hinders or inhibits an individual's identity growth. Future research, then, can consider these types of organizational environments and explore their roles on individual identity growth. Indeed, it would be useful to consider how certain environments would be more or less conducive to each of the five identity tactics we explored in this chapter. For example, one environment might enable optimal distinctiveness but direct or impede spirituality.

Fourth, we suspect that a very fruitful path can be followed by exploring the roles of individual differences in identity growth. Clearly, individuals frame stimuli differently (e.g., as threat or opportunity) and respond to them in vastly different ways (Bryant, 1989). How might identity growth stem from a trait-like state in which people frame challenges as positive opportunities? How might this be related to—or distinct from—such constructs as positive affect or optimism? How might identity growth relate to self-esteem? How might we better understand that whereas some people respond to identity threats by accepting a challenge and growing, others simply self-affirm or rationalize and deny the growth potential?

Finally, as we have noted, our list of identity work tactics is meant to be suggestive rather than exhaustive—a "starter's yeast" for future work. Other tactics can be identified—either through theorizing or empirical work. Other streams within identity research can be infused with our major premise of framing identity challenges as growth opportunities. Further, although we acknowledge that all five of the identity work tactics have their own relatively independent research streams, an overall model of positive identity growth that integrates them (along with others) as interdependent tactics at the individual level could be the ultimate goal of our research agenda. Although a propositional model is beyond the scope and limits of this chapter, we can readily envision potential linkages that may emerge, such as the individual's spiritual orientation (that may or may not be framed as religious—Emmons, 2006) serving as the evaluative/interpretive framework for the construction of possible selves—both intrapersonally and interpersonally through connection with others. Spiritual identity development may also especially shape what the individual considers to be optimally balanced extents of uniqueness (individuality) versus inclusion (connectedness to a greater whole).

CONCLUSION

As a concluding thought, we offer a practical caveat. As stated in the introduction, we assume a highly agential and intentional approach to positive identity development. Whether the five identity work tactics presented in this chapter are ongoing or episodic, reactive or proactive, their implementation involves transforming an identity pain (problem) into an identity gain (growth). This positive "jujitsu" often requires a good deal of cognitive and emotional energy and, in some cases, no small amount of risk. Ironically, then, these efforts could have an unintended effect of being a pathologically stressful series of activities if carried to obsessive extremes.

Thus, we close with a prescription for that ever-elusive state of "balance." In our interviews with Episcopal priests, we asked more senior church leaders what they would recommend to leaders who were new to the priesthood—early in their journey of identity growth in that calling. Interestingly, items of advice most frequently offered were to develop effective social support networks and outside interests—and not to take oneself "too seriously." Thus, a balanced approach to positive identity development becomes one that is paradoxically marked by diligent effort and contemplative reflection toward an authentic self—while at the same time conducted in the spirit of an adventure, even playful experimentation, with potential for a competent, resilient, authentic, transcendent, and holistically integrated self.

REFERENCES

Ashforth, B. E. (2007). Identity: The elastic concept. In C. A. Bartel, S. Blader, & A. Wrzensniewski (Eds.), *Identity and the modern organization* (pp. 85–96). Mahwah, NJ: Lawrence Erlbaum Associates.

Ashforth, B. E., & Kreiner, G. E. (1999). "How can you do it?": Dirty work and the challenge of constructing a positive identity. *Academy of Management Review, 24,* 413–434.

Ashforth, B. E., Kreiner, G. E., Clark, M. A., & Fugate, M. (2007). Normalizing dirty work: Managerial tactics for countering occupational taint. *Academy of Management Journal, 50,* 149–174.

Ashforth, B. E., & Mael, F. A. (1989). Social identity theory and the organization. *Academy of Management Review, 14,* 20–39.

Ashforth, B. E., & Pratt, M. G. (2003). Institutionalized spirituality: An oxymoron? In R. A. Giacalone, & C. L. Jurkiewicz (Eds.), *Handbook of workplace spirituality and organizational performance* (pp. 93–107). Armonk, NY: M. E. Sharpe.

Ashmos, D., & Duchon, D. (2000). Spirituality at work: A conceptualization and measure. *Journal of Management Inquiry, 9,* 134–145.

Benson, P. L., Roehlkepartain, E. C., & Rude, S. P. (2003). Spiritual development in childhood and adolescence: Toward a field of inquiry. *Applied Developmental Science, 7,* 205–213.

Blanz, M., Mummendey, A., Mielke, R., & Klink, A. (1998). Responding to negative social identity: A taxonomy of identity management strategies. *European Journal of Social Psychology, 28,* 697–729.

Branscombe, N. R., Ellemers, N., Spears, R., & Doosjie, B. (1999). The content and context of social identity threat. In N. Ellemers, R. Spears, & B. Doosjie (Eds.), *Social identity: Context, commitment, content* (pp. 35–58). Oxford, England: Blackwell Science.

Breakwell, G. M. (1983). *Threatened identities.* New York: John Wiley & Sons.

Breakwell, G. M. (1986). *Coping with threatened identities.* London: Methuen.

Brewer, M. B. (1991). The social self: On being the same and different at the same time. *Personality and Social Psychology Bulletin, 17,* 475–482.

Brewer, M. B. (2003). Optimal distinctiveness, social identity, and the self. In M. R. Leary & J. P. Tangney (Eds.), *Handbook of self and identity* (pp. 480–491). New York: Guilford Press.

Brewer, M. B., & Pickett, C. L. (1999). Distinctiveness motives as a source of the social self. In T. R. Tyler, R. M. Kramer, & O. P. John (Eds.), *The psychology of the social self* (pp. 71–87). Mahwah, NJ: Lawrence Erlbaum Associates.

Bryant, F. B. (1989). A four-factor model of perceived control: Avoiding, coping, obtaining, and savoring. *Journal of Personality, 57,* 773–797.

Csikszentmihalyi, M., & Csikszentmihalyi, I. S. (2006). *A life worth living: Contributions to positive psychology.* New York: Oxford University Press.

Dehler, G. E., & Welsh, M. A. (2003). The experience of work: Spirituality and the new workplace. In R. A. Giacalone, & C. L. Jurkiewicz (Eds.), *Handbook of workplace spirituality and organizational performance* (pp. 108–122). Armonk, NY: M. E. Sharpe.

Dutton, J. E., Dukerich, J. M., & Harquail, C. V. (1994). Organizational images and member identification. *Administrative Science Quarterly, 39,* 239–263.

Dutton, J. E., & Heaphy, E. D. (2003). The power of high quality connections. In K. S. Cameron, J. E. Dutton, & R. E. Quinn (Eds.), *Positive organizational scholarship: Foundations of a new discipline* (pp. 263–278). San Francisco: Berrett-Koehler Publishers, Inc.

Elsbach, K. D. (2003). Relating physical environment to self-categorizations: Identity threat and affirmation in a non-territorial office space. *Administrative Science Quarterly, 48,* 622–654.

Ely, R. J., & Roberts, L. M. (2008). Shifting frames in team-diversity research: From difference to relationships. In A. P. Brief (Ed.), *Diversity at work* (pp. 175–201). Cambridge, England: Cambridge University Press.

Ely, R. J., & Thomas, D. A. (2001). Cultural diversity at work: The effects of diversity perspectives on work group processes and outcomes. *Administrative Science Quarterly, 46,* 229–273.

Emmons, R. A. (2006). Spirituality: Recent progress. In M. Csikszentmihalyi, & I. S. Csikszentmihalyi (Eds.), *A life worth living: Contributions to positive psychology* (pp. 62–81). New York: Oxford University Press.

Erikson, E. H. (1964). *Insight and responsibility: Lectures on the ethical implications of psychoanalytic insight.* New York: W. W. Norton & Company, Inc.

Ethier, K. A., & Deaux, K. (1994). Negotiating social identity when contexts change: Maintaining identification and responding to threat. *Journal of Personality and Social Psychology, 67,* 241–251.

Goldsmith, M. (2007). *What got you here won't get you there: How successful people become even more successful.* New York: Hyperion Books.

Hill, P. C., & Pargament, K. I. (2003). Advances in the conceptualization and measurement of religion and spirituality. *American Psychologist, 58,* 64–74.

Hirschman, A. O. (1970). *Exit, voice, and loyalty: Responses to decline in firms, organizations, and states.* Cambridge, MA: Harvard University Press.

Hoyle, R. H., & Sherrill, M. R. (2006). Future orientation in the self-system: Possible selves, self-regulation, and behavior. *Journal of Personality, 74,* 1673–1696.

Ibarra, H. (1999). Provisional selves: Experimenting with image and identity in professional adaptation. *Administrative Science Quarterly, 44,* 764–791.

Ibarra, H. (2003). *Working identity: Unconventional strategies for reinventing your career.* Boston: Harvard Business School Press.

Kreiner, G. E. (2007). The struggle of the self: Identity dysfunctions in the contemporary workplace. In J. Langan-Fox, C. L. Cooper, & R. J. Klimoski (Eds.), *Research companion to the dysfunctional workplace: Management challenges and symptoms* (pp. 75–89). Cheltenham, England: Edward Elgar Publishing Ltd.

Kreiner, G. E., Hollensbe, E. C., & Sheep, M. L. (2006a). On the edge of identity: Boundary dynamics at the interface of individual and organizational identities. *Human Relations, 59,* 1315–1341.

Kreiner, G. E., Hollensbe, E. C., & Sheep, M. L. (2006b). Where is the "Me" among the "We"? Identity work and the search for optimal balance. *Academy of Management Journal, 49,* 1031–1057.

Kreiner, G. E., Hollensbe, E. C., & Sheep, M. L. (in press). Do I build a bridge or secure the border? Negotiating the work-home interface via boundary work tactics. *Academy of Management Journal.*

Kristof, A. L. (1996). Person-organization fit: An integrative review of its conceptualizations, measurement, and implications. *Personnel Psychology, 49,* 1–49.

Kristof-Brown, A. L., Zimmerman, R. D., & Johnson, E. C. (2005). Consequences of individuals' fit at work: A meta-analysis of person-job, person-organization, and person-supervisor fit. *Personnel Psychology, 58,* 281–342.

Lifton, R. J. (1993). *The protean self: Human resilience in an age of fragmentation.* New York: Basic Books.

Luthans, F. (2002). The need for and meaning of positive organizational behavior. *Journal of Organizational Behavior, 23,* 695–706.

Luthans, F., Youssef, C. M., & Avolio, B. J. (2007). Psychological capital: Investing and developing positive organizational behavior. In D. L. Nelson, & C. L. Cooper (Eds.), *Positive organizational behavior* (pp. 9–24). Thousand Oaks, CA: Sage.

Manz, C. C. (2003). *Emotional discipline: The power to choose how you feel.* San Francisco: Berrett-Koehler Publishers, Inc.

Markus, H., & Nurius, P. (1986). Possible selves. *American Psychologist, 41,* 954–969.

Meyerson, D. E. (2003). *Tempered radicals: How everyday leaders inspire change at work.* Boston: Harvard Business School Press.

Mirvis, P. H. (1997). "Soul work" in organizations. *Organization Science, 8,* 193–206.

Ostroff, C. & Judge, T. A. (2007). *Perspectives on organizational fit.* Mahwah, NJ: Lawrence Erlbaum Associates.

Ostroff, C., & Schulte, M. (2007). Multiple perspectives of fit in organizations across levels of analysis. In C. Ostroff & T. A. Judge (Eds.), *Perspectives on organizational fit* (pp. 3–69). Mahwah, NJ: Lawrence Erlbaum Associates.

Pfeffer, J. (2003). Business and the spirit. In R. A. Giacalone, & C. L. Jurkiewicz (Eds.), *Handbook of workplace spirituality and organizational performance* (pp. 29–45). Armonk, NY: M. E. Sharpe.

Pratt, M. G., & Ashforth, B. E. (2003). Fostering meaningfulness in working and at work. In K. S. Cameron, J. E. Dutton, & R. E. Quinn (Eds.), *Positive organizational scholarship: Foundations of a new discipline* (pp. 309–327). San Francisco: Berrett-Koehler Publishers, Inc.

Pratt, M. G., Rockman, K. W., & Kaufmann, J. B. (2006). Constructing professional identity: The role of work and identity learning cycles in the customization of identity among medical residents. *Academy of Management Journal, 49,* 235–262.

Roberts, L. M. (2007). From proving to becoming: How positive relationships create a context for self-discovery and self-actualization. In J. E. Dutton, & B. R. Ragins (Eds.) *Exploring positive relationships at work: Building a theoretical and research foundation* (pp. 29–45). Mahwah, NJ: Lawrence Erlbaum Associates.

Ryan, R. M., & Deci, E. L. (2000). Self-determination theory and the facilitation of intrinsic motivation, social development, and well-being. *American Psychologist, 55,* 68–78.

Seligman, M. E. P., & Csikszentmihalyi, M. (2000). Positive psychology: An introduction. *American Psychologist, 55,* 5–14.

Selye, H. (1974). *Stress without distress.* New York: J. P. Lippincott.

Sheep, M. L. (2006). Nurturing the whole person: The ethics of workplace spirituality in a society of organizations. *Journal of Business Ethics, 66,* 357–375.

Sheep, M. L., & Foreman, P. O. (2007). *A marriage made in heaven? Exploring the relationships of organizational identity and spirituality.* Paper presented at the 67th Annual Academy of Management Meeting, Philadelphia.

Snow, D. A., & Anderson, L. (1987). Identity work among the homeless: The verbal construction and avowal of personal identities. *American Journal of Sociology, 92,* 1336–1371.

Spreitzer, G., Sutcliffe, K., Dutton, J., Sonenshein, S., & Grant, A. M. (2005). A socially embedded model of thriving at work. *Organization Science, 16,* 537–549.

Sutcliffe, K. M., & Vogus, T. J. (2003). Organizing for resilience. In K. S. Cameron, J. E. Dutton, & R. E. Quinn (Eds.) *Positive organizational scholarship: Foundations of a new discipline* (pp. 94–110). San Francisco: Berrett-Koehler Publishers, Inc.

Turnley, W. H., & Feldman, D. C. (1999). The impact of psychological contract violations on exit, voice, loyalty, and neglect. *Human Relations, 52,* 895–922.

3

Who Am I Now? Sensemaking and Identity in Posttraumatic Growth

Sally Maitlis

CONTENTS

One of the amazing things to come to grips with is the identity crisis of who on earth you are if you're no longer a cellist, having wrapped yourself in that cover for so long.

—Matthew the cellist

In a relatively minor skiing accident, Matthew, a professional cellist, damaged two tendons in his shoulder. Although it did not seem significant at the time, in the months that followed he found it almost impossible to play without pain. This was an extremely distressing time for him, when he felt "a kind of total emptiness and utter exhaustion that really was literally sapping my will to live." At the center of this emptiness lay the question, "Who am I now?" This chapter is about musicians such as Matthew and what happens to their identities after a trauma—an injury that affects their ability to do the work that is core to their self-understanding.

Trauma typically triggers a variety of distressing emotions, such as anxiety, sadness, guilt, and anger (Herman, 1997). Recent research, however, suggests that trauma can also act as a catalyst for transformational positive change—posttraumatic growth—that is manifest in an increased appreciation for life, more meaningful interpersonal relationships, and a greater sense of personal strength (Calhoun & Tedeschi, 2001; Joseph & Linley, 2008). This chapter focuses on the sensemaking processes that underpin posttraumatic growth, paying particular attention to the new understandings that individuals develop about themselves. Research on posttraumatic growth suggests a variety of different strategies that can help victims of trauma come to terms with their losses, reframe their experiences, and even find the silver lining in what has happened to them (Davis, Nolen-Hoeksma, & Larson, 1998; Pennebaker, 2000; Thornton & Perez, 2006). However, this work overlooks a potentially critical aspect of posttrauma sensemaking: the central role played by identity (Janoff-Bulman, 1992). Drawing on studies of meaning making after loss (Davis et al., 1998; Neimeyer, 2000) and work in the narrative tradition that examines trauma as a turning point in individuals' self-narratives (McAdams, 1993; McAdams et al., 2001), this chapter will examine the role of identity in the sensemaking that follows a work-related trauma, as well as explore how people construct new, positive identities, which form a central part of the process of psychological growth.

This topic is important for two main reasons. First, although there is a growing literature that shows that the phenomenon of posttraumatic growth occurs, it offers only partial explanation of how it does so. This chapter highlights and explores a central element of the growth process that previous studies have largely overlooked: positive identity. I define positive identity as an expanded identity that incorporates an understanding of one's strength and resourcefulness in the face of extreme difficulty, and an appreciation of one's ability to transcend deep pain, including the ability to do so again in the future. Second, as one of the first explorations of posttraumatic growth that examines work-related trauma, this study increases our understanding of trauma and growth at work. These are extremely powerful experiences that are highly consequential for individuals, occupational groups, and organizations, but ones about which our knowledge is still very limited.

TRAUMA AS AN OCCASION FOR SENSEMAKING

Trauma can be understood as an extremely upsetting event that "at least temporarily overwhelms the individual's resources" (Briere & Scott, 2006, p. 4), and one that presents "significant challenges to individuals' ways of understanding the world and their place in it" (Tedeschi & Calhoun, 2004, p. 1). Traumas challenge the assumptions that guide action and often disrupt the meanings that people have made of their lives (Wigren, 1994). Sensemaking—as the process of social construction through which we attempt to explain surprising or confusing events—offers an important way of dealing with trauma (Solomon, 2004). A traumatic event provides a "jolt" to our routines (Meyer, 1982) that creates an "occasion for sensemaking" (Weick, 1995), interrupting existing ways of thinking and triggering an emotional reaction that prompts sensemaking about what is happening and what it means (Roberts, Dutton, Spreitzer, Heaphy, & Quinn, 2005; Weick, Sutcliffe, & Obstfeld, 2005).

TRAUMA, SENSEMAKING, AND IDENTITY

One of the reasons that trauma is so devastating is because of its impact on individuals' beliefs about who they are and who they can become. The negative emotion generated by a trauma signals the loss of or damage to a significant aspect of self (Pals & McAdams, 2004). This threat to self triggers sensemaking, a process that is fundamentally concerned with identity (Weick, 1995). Writing about the sensemaking process that follows a significant bereavement, Neimeyer, Prigerson, and Davies (2002, p. 236) note a person's need to maintain a "continuity with *who they have been* while also integrating the reality of a changed world into their conception of *who they must now be*" (italics added). Thus, in the struggle to come to terms with the new reality that follows a trauma, people are forced to give up certain assumptions and goals and to work to create new meanings and a new understanding of the world and of themselves in that world. This process is both confusing and painful but contains the opportunity for significant change. Ibarra (2003), in her analysis of professional career change decisions, identifies the importance of "alert intermissions," the moments when pivotal events catalyze change. During these times, people notice new things and perceive old things in different ways, often provoking insights that enable different ways of being. These disruptive moments, Ibarra argues, thus provide individuals with the opportunity to rework and reassemble their experiences, and thus to reinvent themselves.

In this chapter, I draw on an understanding of identity as socially constructed, produced in and through language (Ainsworth & Hardy, 2004; Kärreman & Alvesson, 2001). Of particular importance in this process is the story or narrative, which provides the central means through which people construct, describe, and understand their experiences, and, through this, their identities (Lieblich, Tuvel-Mashiach, & Zilber, 1998; McAdams, 1993). Identities are formed through efforts to develop a coherent, continuous biography, where a person's "life story" is the sensible result of a series of related events or cohesive themes (Gergen, 1994; McAdams, 2001). Because identities are constituted in social interaction, they must be negotiated in a social context to be accepted as legitimate (Gergen, 1999; Riessman, 1993). From this perspective, we can understand identity as a dynamic process or set of practices rather than a static state or entity, and as constantly being confirmed and modified in negotiation with others.

SENSEMAKING AND POSTTRAUMATIC GROWTH

Posttraumatic growth has been defined as "the experience of positive change that occurs as a result of the struggle with highly challenging life crises" (Tedeschi & Calhoun, 2004, p. 1), and much existing research has focused on domains of growth such as an increased appreciation for life, a greater sense of personal strength, and a radically changed sense of priorities (Calhoun

& Tedeschi, 2001; Tedeschi & Calhoun, 2004). It is important to note that posttraumatic growth does not occur in place of pain. Those experiencing growth are unlikely to view the trauma itself as a desirable or positive event but do believe that good has come from having to deal with it.

From the growing body of work on posttraumatic growth, we have an understanding of certain cognitive strategies that may contribute to growth. Some scholars have explored the value of deliberate or reflective rumination, which involves reminiscing, problem solving, and trying to make sense of what has happened (Calhoun & Tedeschi, 2006; Martin & Tesser, 1996; Nolen-Hoeksema & Davis, 2004;), whereas others have focused specifically on positive meaning making, identifying several tactics such as accepting, reframing, and benefit finding (e.g., Davis et al., 1998; Pennebaker, 2000; Thornton & Perez, 2006). Taking a slightly different perspective, narrative scholars have examined how individuals story their experience following a trauma (McAdams, 1993; Neimeyer, 2000; Pals, 2006; Pals & McAdams, 2004), identifying key processes that seem to lead to growth. This research suggests the importance of acknowledging the trauma's emotional impact, analyzing its effect on and meaning for the self, and constructing a positive ending that explains how the self has been transformed (Pals, 2006; Pals & McAdams, 2004).

POSITIVE IDENTITY IN POSTTRAUMATIC GROWTH

More than other researchers, writers in the narrative tradition see posttraumatic growth as inherently concerned with changes in people's understandings of themselves (Neimeyer, 2004; Pals, 2006; Pals & McAdams, 2004). Pals and McAdams (2004, p. 66) propose that growth may best be revealed by analyzing "how people go about narrating the traumatic event and making sense of its impact on the self." From this perspective, growth is evidenced in themes of strength, interpersonal connection, appreciation for life, and so on, in individuals' narratives. Neimeyer (2000, 2004), who has written extensively on bereavement as a "narrative disrupting event," examines how different forms of narrative disruption trigger the affective, cognitive, and social processes that "enlarge and deepen" the survivor's identity to enable growth. Some kinds of narrative disruption lead to evolutionary changes to identity, achieved through an elaboration of a preloss narrative, whereas others produce more radical identity change, as new capacities are constructed that allow individuals to live in ways richer than before. Whether incremental or revolutionary, such changes in self-understanding are positive for the trauma survivor, enabling a greater appreciation for life, and a new sense of what is important.

Individuals who achieve this "positive identity" are more likely to be agential in their own and in others' lives, and, significantly, to understand themselves as able to cope with, and even transcend, the destructive and seemingly debilitating events that they are now painfully aware can unexpectedly occur. Indeed, this growth is believed to come as a result of incorporating the traumatic event into one's understanding of oneself in the world (Janoff-Bulman, 1992). Furthermore, because this new self-understanding contains the idea that "I can withstand one of life's most painful experiences," it is likely to be more resilient than identities available before the trauma. Thus, positive identity can be understood as a central element of a growth story.

Although positive identities may be enabled by the disruption trauma creates, a trauma does not itself create a positive identity. From research on identity change, we know that individuals engage in a variety of different kinds of identity work as they negotiate new selves, including using role models, experimenting with "provisional selves," and customizing their existing identities in various ways (Ebaugh, 1988; Ibarra, 1999, 2003; Pratt, Rockmann, & Kaufmann, 2006; Snow & Anderson, 1987). We also know that identities are not constructed in isolation but are socially negotiated using a variety of relational resources (Dutton, 2003; Roberts et al., 2005). We do not yet, however, understand very much about how identities, and especially how positive identities, are constructed following a trauma.

In this chapter, I examine the sensemaking processes that follow an identity-challenging trauma and explore how some individuals come to negotiate new, positive identities for themselves. Drawing on interviews conducted with musicians who can no longer play professionally, I present the stories of their lives before and after a life-altering injury, and explore the processes through which they have constructed expanded self-understandings that incorporate their resourcefulness in the face of extreme difficulty. All but one of the musicians was interviewed in 2007 or 2008 as part of a study of sensemaking following a work-related trauma. Agnès' story comes from interviews conducted in 1994 and reported in Richer, Giasson, and Lapierre (2007). In each case, the story is recounted up to the time of the interview, which took place at a different life stage for each person. As is always the case, the sensemaking that makes up these narratives is retrospective (Weick, 1995), shaped by the speaker's current place in the world.

MUSICIANS—IDENTITY AND INJURY

Although work is understood to play a central role in many people's identities, this is perhaps especially true for those who regard work as a "calling" rather than a job or career, working for the fulfillment that doing the work brings (Wrzesniewski, 2003). Musicians often see music as a calling and feel compelled to play, even in discouraging circumstances. The vast majority of professional musicians have trained from early childhood, believing since adolescence or earlier that they will work in music. It is not unusual for musicians to dismiss the idea of an alternative career with the question "What else can I do?" which may reflect both their intense training and their confidence in doing something else. Typically, these individuals see their profession not simply as what they do but as who they are. For this reason, having an injury that forces them to change their work—although not uncommon in this profession (Zaza, 1998)—presents a major challenge both to their work identity and to their self-understanding more broadly. Therefore, musicians represent a population for whom identity is likely to be especially significant in the sensemaking that follows work-related trauma.

MEETING THE MUSICIANS

Brian the Horn Player

Brian was about 4 when he began playing piano, subsequently moving to the trumpet and then to the French horn. While at university, he played part time with the local symphony orchestra, and although his first job after graduating was teaching music in a high school, he soon felt the pull back to performing. As he explained, "I figured, 'you know, I really want to get back into professional playing' ... I really wanted to play the horn. Yeah, it pulled me back."

An opening came up in the orchestra, which he auditioned for and won. He described how his life had been as an orchestral musician and what it meant to him to be one:

> You're doing the orchestra music, plus either woodwind quintet or a brass quintet, or you're going off and doing radio and television commercials; you're doing film work; you're playing for ice shows … and Broadway shows coming through…. You couldn't put the instrument down; you couldn't get enough of it.

As he commented, "I really did define my whole life by this piece of metal and what I can do with it." Not only did it define who he was but also how he lived. Brian explained, "It's just such a hard taskmaster; even if you go away on a holiday you have to take a mouthpiece along, so you can do buzzing routines to keep things going."

After playing for several years with the orchestra, Brian noticed something was wrong:

> I started to have occasions when I couldn't feel this (the third) finger and know whether I was pushing that valve down all the way. Sometimes the finger would not move; it was not getting a neurological response to move it.

This was at first disconcerting, and, as the condition worsened, very disturbing. "It felt like, at that time, I was really coming to an end of being able to do anything … 'oh it's gone, I can't do this at all anymore.' "

Although physiotherapy helped to extend his career, it could not solve the neurological condition. Over the last few years, and with the support of the orchestra management, he has eased himself out of his role, playing part time in a different position, and is soon to take early retirement. He explained how he felt he had reached his "best before" date:

> It's sort of like you go to the refrigerator and you see a tub of sour cream or salsa, and you look at the "best before" date on it…. I've reached it. You open it up, you may have to scrape a little something off the top, but you stir it up and you still use it for a while. It doesn't mean that it's no good anymore. It's still usable. But there's also something else called an "expiry date" and I think I want to get out of here before I reach that. I feel like I'm at my "best before."

Although this was not a choice he would have made without the injury, he does not feel negative about leaving. Using the metaphor of an "albatross" to describe his orchestral work, he explained:

> It's a constant in your life that you can't turn off. Even quite often the music goes around and around in your head. If I have a particularly onerous

concert coming up, I know for several days before it I can't turn off the muzak going in my head of the problem spots. Once the concert's over, usually it's gone. But up until that point it really is such a horrible—horrible, there I said it—a horrible constant in your life. Playing the concert is almost a relief. So in terms of a lifelong thing, knowing that I'm retiring from it and I can turn off that level of constant preparation, of being at a standard that you can't let slide too much, yeah, I can let go of that.

Sometimes he goes to the orchestra as a member of the audience, which he described as, "Okay ... especially when it's a particularly hard piece. I'll be thinking, 'Boy, glad it's not me up there. You're welcome to that part!' "

He also reflected on how it is to know he will never play certain pieces of music again:

It's a bit of a bittersweet feeling, but it's good to ... say good-bye to some to these pieces, and I sometimes do that when we stand up for the bow and the piece is there and I just sort of wave "bye" to it and then close the book. It doesn't feel bad, especially if I've done a good performance. If I've played a bad one, then, yeah, maybe I'd like another crack at it. But no, it's good. It's time.

Saying good-bye to his colleagues does not feel difficult. He feels much less connected to them than he did earlier in his career, seeing himself as a father or grandfather figure in an orchestra that is now made up of mostly much younger players. He has begun thinking about his retirement, and what he will—and will not—do.

I think I don't want to play the horn at all anymore.... They're asking me to play in the community amateur orchestra because they know I'm a professional and they want me to play. I'm not going to do that. I don't want to play horn at that level.

As he explained, "In my head I have a concept of what I want to do, how I want to be able to play this instrument, and if I can't do that ... then I don't want to make those sounds."

Instead, he says:

I started out on trumpet, so I think I'll play in a community band on trumpet. That's what I want to go back to. Whenever people say, "what do you want to do with your music?" I say, "I'm not going to play horn." I'd love to go back to playing trumpet.

But playing the trumpet in an orchestra (rather than a band) does not appeal: "I don't want to play trumpet in an orchestra because that's, again, been my professional life. I want to make a real change from it."

His other plans include doing more teaching and spending more time traveling and visiting family, especially his grandchildren. Brian sees this partly as creating a distraction, saying of himself and his wife, who will also be retiring as a professional musician, "Both of us are sort of distracting ourselves from our performance—and seeing what else there is for us."

Overall, he expresses appreciation for how the injury has broadened the way he thinks of himself:

> It has allowed me to move to a better mental idea of what I am or who am I, and I'm not necessarily "that horn player." I'm Brian, who has other opportunities, other things that I can do.

Exploring Brian's Identities

Music was clearly a calling for Brian, an occupation that pulled him in and that then completely consumed and defined him. The injury significantly challenged his identity, leaving him feeling lost and unable to do what mattered most. However, although he initially believed he had come "to an end of being able to do anything," he found ways to manage his condition and continued to play, revising his self-understanding to that of a musician with an injury. He was now aware, though, of the fragility of this identity, and over time became keen to preempt it spoiling in his or his colleagues' minds, being seen as an "expired" musician who had gone past his best. In contemplating alternative futures, he began to disidentify with his former self, rehearsing the benefits of leaving professional musical life—shedding the albatross of perpetual high standards, experiencing relief at not having to play the hard parts, and leaving colleagues who no longer felt like friends. He was clear that he would not continue to play horn, that "performing horn player" is not an identity he wishes to maintain in a casual or amateur way. Rather, his intention is to experiment with new identities, some connected to music and others not: horn teacher, community band trumpeter, and grandfather. Happy to be beginning a new chapter at the same time as his wife, he positively anticipates constructing a broader self, taking pleasure in no longer being "that horn player," but "Brian, who has other opportunities, other things that I can do."

Linda the Bassoon Player

Linda began playing the flute at age 9. Her family life was quite difficult, and music offered "a way for me to feel like I was good at something. And I was always just gifted with it.... It was just something that made me feel really good."

Encouraged and assisted by her high school band teacher, she went on to study music at university. She soon switched from flute to bassoon, an instrument for which she felt an overwhelming compulsion. By her third year at university, she had won the concerto competition, and after graduating, she went on to spend a year at a specialist center for performing arts. This was a wonderful time for Linda. "I knew it was something I really was good at. And I liked to do." Although she did not have a real sense of what the professional life was like, she believed this was her future.

> I was winning things. I was not as polished technically as some other people, but I still felt really good about who I was as a bassoon player. I felt I really had a career. I was receiving wonderful complements from famous musicians.

After graduating with a master's degree from Yale University, Linda spent a year spent working part time to earn some money, while at the same time practicing hard, freelancing, and putting on a recital series. This was a demanding existence, and her teacher warned her, "You just want it too bad. You're too intense about your playing." Eventually, Linda decided that this exhausting life was not tenable long term and decided to pursue a Doctorate of Musical Arts (DMA) degree, which would allow her to pursue her love of chamber music while also learning to teach.

The day of her first DMA recital that fall, she was hit by a car while on her bike. The impact caused nerve damage to her arm and hip, as well as a bulging disk in her neck. Describing the significance of the instant the accident occurred, she explained:

> The moment I was hit by that car it was like I became aware of everything I was thinking ... my anxiety about everything—what am I doing with my life, including this next concert? Really, when I was still on the pavement.

I don't how fast or slow the thoughts were but I was like, "Okay I have to change something. I really do because this is not good.".... I really felt like I needed to find a better way to live.

Over the Christmas break that followed, she did not play at all. This was a very difficult time for Linda in many ways:

It was the only time in my life where I felt, you know, suicidal. I was just laying there. I was in pain. I had no support, no friends. I knew it was a big change, but I didn't know where it was going. It was really painful.... I felt like I had nothing ... and it wasn't enough anymore to be talented. You know, it wasn't enough that I could play really well, because I knew I could.

Although she returned to playing in January, things were not the same. The physical effects of the injury were constantly with her, "You know when you hit your funny bone, you get that nerve pain? I had that running all the time." She still played well, but:

The joy was gone.... When I unpacked my instrument, it was still a beautiful instrument. It still sounded good. But, I just didn't, you know, it was a burden to play it. It just felt like a burden.

Linda continued to play for the next 2 years, but she also started to read as she had never done before, and to learn how to teach writing.

Through that I learned—and through reading more—my world started opening. A lot. And I started finding out I had ideas and interesting things to say.... I kept playing and it was, you know, it was painful and I was confused and all of that. But I still, like I say, I still sounded good. But I wasn't sure anymore what my career would be. And the teaching writing opened up a window for me that wasn't there before.

On a whim, she sold her bassoon, bought a car, and drove west, where she taught writing for 3 years. She missed playing, but the teaching was wonderful, and straightforward:

Teaching writing was fun. It kept me busy, and it was lower stress. I didn't freak out about anything. I just went in, had a great time. Relaxed on the weekends. Even if I was really busy, I didn't get upset. And so for me it was a real break from the stress of being a musician.

Eventually, she returned to her hometown and started to teach writing there. A few years ago, she bought a new bassoon, encouraged by her partner. This came after several conversations in which her passion for the instrument was apparent: "Every time we talked about the instrument my eyes would light up, and he was like, 'You need another one.'" As she explained:

> That began a process of me relearning the instrument, relearning myself as well, and that's been the most interesting part of it. Coming back to learn the instrument again, all of my bad habits were really out in front of my face. All of the negative thoughts—all of the patterns that were so stressful. And I had a chance to learn the instrument again without those, or at least look at them and say, "I don't want to think that way. I don't have to do that anymore. You know what I do, I do differently." And that's been a really amazing process.

She has recently finished an interdisciplinary doctorate degree that pulls together her interests in musical performance and in learning. "I've come to realize that I enjoy writing more than playing bassoon, even though I love playing bassoon." Her thesis research drew considerably on her own experiences as a musician:

> My playing became an important role in my research. So my journaling about playing and thinking about the ideas and findings in the context of practice was an important part of my study. So I found a way to bring my playing into the research as well.

She would like to continue to combine research and music in her future career:

> I'd like to have a job as a professor. I'd like to be able to do research, ideally in a music program where I could still make music as part of my job. And do research on music making and teach courses in social and cognitive science and music performance. That's what I would like to do.

And she still feels very positive about herself as a musician:

> I feel pretty good as a bassoonist, even though right now I'm not doing a lot of playing. I seem to only get better, you know… I mean better in the sense of more composed as a musician…. I don't have the same fast fingers that I had, but I think I'm a better musician.

Reflecting back on her life to date:

> I don't regret any of my experiences, really any of them except being hit by a car…. But again, it did shape, it made me realize, it led me to a path of realizing that, you know, I can do a lot more with research than I ever could have done as a bassoonist.

By this she means that she can have "a much larger impact on teaching younger people and shaping the way music is made, and the way people think about how music can be made."

And, with intense feeling, she says, "It isn't really just platitudes that music is an international language. I think there's something really important to be learned there, that I didn't necessarily learn the first time around."

As she concludes her story, Linda reiterates:

> The accident really has played a very large role in my narrative, in the way I think about myself … at that moment all of it just sort of came right in front of my face. It was like "this isn't working. You know, I'm really stressed and I can't handle this. What's wrong with this picture?" And my thesis is sort of like this is how we can study what's wrong with this picture.

Exploring Linda's Identities

Music became important to Linda early on, providing an arena of strength and passion for an underconfident girl who was uncertain about much in life. Guided by supportive teachers and mentors, she moved very successfully through her training and became increasingly sure that she would become a professional bassoonist. Even when experiencing the harsh realities that face most musicians after graduate school, Linda still saw herself as a performer, although she now planned to teach alongside. Throughout these years, she had an intense approach to playing and to life, wanting desperately to be a professional musician and striving hard to get there. The car accident was a pivotal point for her, not only injuring her in ways that made playing painful but also causing her to reevaluate how she was living. During this anguished period, she felt she had nothing: the joy of playing was gone, and it was not clear what else lay ahead. Turning to books and then to teaching writing, a new world opened up for her. She began to see herself not just as "Linda the bassoon player," but as someone with "ideas and interesting things to say." In the years that followed, she missed playing but loved her new work and the feeling of freedom that came with it. Now, through her doctoral research, and with the support of her partner, she has found a way to integrate her loves of music making, teaching, and writing. She sees herself continuing in this direction, hoping to become a professor, and feeling positive both about her new researcher self and herself as a "more composed musician."

Gordon the Trombone Player

Like Brian, Gordon is an orchestral musician who has an ongoing neurological condition that significantly affected his playing. As he explained:

> Around the age of 40, I started having these physical problems with a tremor. And the tremor started coming in—well, I started noticing it—one day I'll never forget it—we were doing the Mozart Requiem and I was playing the—this there's a big trombone solo in the Mozart Requiem—in the Tuba Mirum movement. And it just went great in the rehearsals, and then in the dress rehearsal, my arm started shaking like a leaf.

This was frightening and also very confusing for Gordon: "My colleague, a trumpet player, says 'What's wrong?' I said, 'I don't know what's wrong. I guess I'm nervous or something.' "

On the suggestion of a fellow musician, he took beta blockers to get through the concert, but still:

> I was just petrified, and I'd never been that petrified playing a solo before because I played it so well in rehearsals. It was quite an effort to get through that solo. And that was sort of like the event that was the introduction of this part of my career.

A significant effect of the condition was that it undermined his understanding of himself. "I started losing confidence in myself, that maybe my nerves are going, you know, because I'd been playing for so many years now. Maybe the conductor's getting to me."

This was compounded by some of his colleagues, "who were definitely giving me the guilt feeling that I was a weak individual and that I was just sort of a nervous guy." One day, he noticed his hand shaking while he was eating and realized, "Wait a second. My buddies are telling me this is nerves. I'm not nervous eating a chip at McDonald's. There's something not right here." He went to see a specialist and, given the alternative explanations he had been carrying, was relieved to receive the diagnosis of an incurable neurological condition. The medication he received gave him some control over it, but much of the pleasure of playing had gone. "For a lot of the notes I play on my instrument, my main concentration now isn't how to make this phrase more beautiful … it's how do I keep this instrument from shaking?"

He began to think about leaving the orchestra, keen not to be judged by others. "I don't want to overstay like this guy and that guy and this guy. And just people whispering behind my back, you know, 'I'd wish he'd leave.'"

He also wanted to retain a positive sense of himself in his own eyes: "If I can't sound good to myself and I have to struggle to play and … what do I need it for?" He felt it was critically important that he take some control, explaining, "I've been determined and stubborn that I'm not going to let this end my career. *I'm* going to end the career."

Gordon recently decided to take early retirement and was helped to do so in a dignified way by the orchestral management. At first, retiring did not feel easy because playing trombone was pretty much everything that he knew. But he gradually became aware of the constraints his profession had been putting on his life, as well as the time he could share with his wife.

"I realized our whole careers, starting from 1st September till the end of June, I know exactly what I'm doing every minute of the day. My career—my time is set for me."

He also began to weigh the costs up against the rewards.

> I don't get medals sitting on the stage of the [Concert Hall] playing, you know, the Russian Sailors' Dance, which I've played 500 times. It's a neat piece and I love it, but I've done it and when I play it for that moment, I love it. But I want to do something else in my life.

Looking ahead to the future, he explained that he was seeking a real change. "I think I won't play the trombone after that (retirement). I'm thinking more and more I'll just make a clean cut … one day I think I'll just stop practicing."

He then spoke about the business that he had started a few years earlier:

> Things just seem to work out … I just didn't think I was going to have a music publishing business. I did a few arrangements and I sent them to a friend who did have a music publishing business. And he just never got back to me. After about 4 or 5 years of trying to get his attention, I figured, "to hell with this, I'll just start selling stuff on eBay," and stuff started selling. "Wow. Hey. Maybe I can get a web site. Maybe I can start selling to dealers." And now people are starting to come to me, so now I have not just catalogues of my arrangements, but catalogues of about 80% to 90% of other people's arrangements.… This has fallen in perfectly for me.

He also wants to return to being more of a music listener again.

> I loved music before I played the trombone. And I know when I'm not playing in the orchestra, I don't really miss the orchestra too much.… I miss the music. So I'll go back to my original love, which was listening to music … I'll just go back to being a dedicated listener.

He sees his life in extremely positive terms, even the current time as he prepares for retirement: "I don't see this as a difficult period right now. This is just—I'm just sort of winding things down. And I'm trying to have as good a time as possible with it." And he compares himself to others who have had much more debilitating injuries, observing, "I'm so blessed in my life with this career and everything. So, what if I have this? This is nothing."

Exploring Gordon's Identities

Gordon's injury not only severely affected his playing but also how he understood himself as a person. With no other available explanations, he and his colleagues interpreted his shake as nerves, perhaps a result of being too long in the job or triggered by a demanding conductor. Gordon no longer saw himself as a reliable professional, but as a weak and nervous individual who could not meet the challenges of the job. His medical diagnosis allowed him to revise this disturbing identity, and, although playing could no longer be the pleasure it once was, he was able to stop thinking of himself as a person with psychological problems. The meaning of his work had changed, though, from making musical phrases more beautiful to trying to stop his instrument from shaking. He still played well in the concerts but had to regularly medicate to do so. He, like Brian, was keen to leave the orchestra before he and others felt he had stayed too long and was determined to take control in ending his career before it ended him. As Gordon thought about what he might do afterward, the constraints under which he had been living for so long moved into the foreground, and he became excited about taking on other roles, spending more time with his wife, running his business, and returning to a former passion as a dedicated listener of music. Looking back, he celebrates the wonderful career he has had and the exciting new paths that lie ahead.

Agnès the Pianist and Conductor

Agnès' injury forced her to end her promising performing career just a few years after it began (Richer et al., 2007).[1] Born to two professional musicians, Agnès knew from a very early age that she wanted to play the piano: "The piano had been my life forever. I had always wanted to play the piano. It was my passion. It was already clear to me when I was 3 years old. It was my dream." From early on, she showed great talent and received extensive training. After graduating, she immediately began to give concerts and tour widely, soon receiving a prestigious prize for her interpretations. The piano meant everything to her: "The piano is like a world in itself, a world apart, whose color of sound casts a spell on me.... It's the mirror of my inner life, the loyal friend who frees the language of love in me."

Very early in her career she experienced some discomfort in one of her fingers. It was diagnosed as a nodule on a tendon, and a small operation followed quickly. Weeks later, however, Agnès could still not lift her finger. There followed, "2 years of agony, but also 2 years in which I learned a great deal." Consulting with specialists all over the world, she did physiotherapy exercises for several hours a day in an attempt to heal. It was an extremely difficult time:

> For those 2 years, I lived on a wire, like a tightrope walker in the circus, suspended between hope and despair.... Every day, I had to reactivate the strength and hope to balance on that wire, but at the same time I had to

---

[1] These excerpts are taken from an interview conducted with Agnès Grossmann by the authors in 1994 and are reported in Richer, Giasson & Lapierre (2007). My thanks to Veronika Kisfalvi for bringing this work to my attention.

learn that it might not work. Staying up on that wire … I was hopeful for a year. But I only got temporary results—never results that would have allowed me to play as before.

The first year was particularly brutal: "I needed to learn how to renew myself. I needed to gather my strength and inner energy. The first months of the first year, I wanted to die."

Struggling to find meaning in her altered life, Agnès got great support and inspiration from her mother. She also read widely and immersed herself in religion and its rituals. She explains, "I survived, and I think that's a miracle. It was a miracle to find meaning in my life without that instrument."

Although she began to come to terms with her loss, she knew that she could not leave music behind altogether: "I had to make music. I had to have a musical language." Seeking a new way of expressing herself through music, and greatly supported by a conductor friend who later became her husband, Agnès began to learn conducting. However, she only gradually came to terms with the new medium of the conductor's baton: "It happened very slowly, and even after a few years as a conductor it still wasn't settled in my mind."

She now works full time as a conductor, directing major orchestras and choirs in Canada and beyond. She does not, however, think it is something to which she would have been drawn, were it not for her injury:

> I had never wanted to direct before, to become a conductor. I'd seen my father direct choirs and orchestras, but I didn't want to do that. It was really the accident—the problem with my third finger—that led me to make that decision.

But the piano, and her identification with it, has stayed with her: "The piano is still there today. It no longer has an active role. The piano watches." Her identification is strongest when she is working with a pianist. As she declares, "I become a pianist once again." However, she explains, "The piano is no longer a necessity. It is content no longer being used. It's not really painful anymore either. It's like another life."

Looking at the unexpected direction her life has taken, Agnès observes, "I really began a new life with this new musical activity, and I learned that if something doesn't work, it's not a calamity." Moreover, she began to understand that:

The value of a human being does not depend just on his or her external achievements, but above all on his or her ability to experience life. Loving life for itself is more important than calculating its failures and successes.

Exploring Agnès' Identities

Agnès identified very strongly as a pianist and struggled enormously with the threat to her life's core meaning that came with the injury, to the point of wanting to die. For the 2 years it took for it to become clear that she would not perform again, she teetered between hope and despair. As she searched for new meaning, she realized that she needed music to communicate in the world and turned toward conducting. This was not something to which she had previously been drawn, and she was slow to truly connect to it and to take it on as her language. As she moved gradually into the world of conducting, the piano and her self-understanding as a pianist stayed with her, reminding her who she once was and who, in some way, she still was. The pain associated with this lost identity has largely gone, though, and she sees herself as having started a new life and a new self with her conducting career. Moreover, she appreciates the new experiences that have come as a result of her life-changing injury, the relationships that helped her through her painful times, and the lessons she has learned about living life to the fullest.

ACHIEVING POSITIVE IDENTITY FOLLOWING A WORK-RELATED TRAUMA

In this section, I look across these musicians' narratives to explore how identities are revised, reconstructed, and radically expanded following an injury that forces a change in one's life's work. First, I consider the nature of the individuals' identities before the trauma, and then the immediate and unfolding impacts of the trauma on these identities. Following this, I examine how individuals iterate between their old and new identities as they gradually take on new ways of being and of understanding themselves. Finally, I explore the nature of the emergent constructed identities, investigating how they are positive and how they contribute to the growth that the musicians express in their stories. These ideas are illustrated in Figure 3.1.

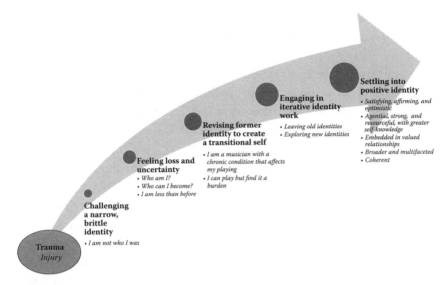

FIGURE 3.1
Constructing positive identities in posttraumatic growth.

The individuals studied here begin with strong and restrictive identities, understanding themselves and engaging in their lives as musicians above all else. For some, such as Linda, this identity allows them to be somebody in the absence of other resources; for others, it subsumes other possible selves, as they focus everything they have and could be into the intense, demanding, and highly competitive world of professional music. Although powerful, the narrow and brittle nature of this identity makes it very vulnerable to external shocks.

The effect of a serious injury is significant. The musicians find not only that they are unable to play as before but also that they no longer know who they are. This drives an intense and painful search for meaning. The experience is made harder by the ambiguity that surrounds the musicians' conditions and prognoses. Agnès' "2 years of agony" passed as she worked to see if she might heal and play the piano as before; Brian first believes "it's gone" before gradually finding ways to work around his condition. For Gordon, his misinterpretation of his symptoms rapidly turns him from a seasoned professional into a "weak individual." Interestingly, whereas one might expect a work-related trauma to have a smaller impact on individuals than events such as bereavement, divorce, or a serious illness, the negative effect of these injuries on the musicians' identities was clearly very great.

In the case of these musicians, but similarly for anyone whose occupation provides a "master status" (Merton, 1957)—a role around which other identities are organized—a trauma that prevents them from doing their work is likely to have a significant effect on their self-understanding.

As the facts of the injury and the reality of the situation become clearer, the musicians again revise their identities, this time in a more enabling direction. Now Brian and Gordon see themselves as musicians with a permanent neurological condition—not a positive identity but certainly more heartening than being "nothing" or a "nervous guy." Agnès studies conducting and very gradually begins to think of herself as making music once again. However, work does not mean the same as it did before: for Linda, playing has become a "burden," and Gordon's priority is now keeping the notes from shaking, rather than making beautiful music. Still, this transitional way of being is manageable, gives some pleasure, and is certainly better than they first feared. But it is transitional. Over time, Brian and Gordon anticipate a decline, and it becomes important to pre-empt a negative identity of the expired musician who has overstayed his welcome.

As the musicians confront the future, they become as agential as they have ever been. Agnès and Linda read voraciously and begin to learn an entirely new skill; Brian and Gordon think about how they might retire on their own terms. In moving forward, the musicians are often supported by key relationships—with a parent, a partner, a teacher, a conductor. For example, Brian and Gordon find that their orchestral management is happy to help create a way forward that is positive for everyone; Agnès takes strength from her mother, who helps her see that there are many ways to live. Each individual now focuses on the core of what matters most: Agnès has to make music; Linda needs to express her newly forming ideas; Brian prefers not to play horn and wants to spend more time with his grandchildren; and Gordon is keen to have more flexibility with his schedule and enjoy the next stage of life with his wife.

In the process of constructing these new identities, the musicians begin to separate and disassociate from their former selves. This is not a simple or discrete process, and they shift back and forth: Brian is sometimes in the orchestra, sometimes in the audience; Agnès is a conductor who becomes a pianist again when accompanying one. They help detach themselves from who they have been by focusing on the attractions of the new possibilities ahead; they also disidentify with their former selves, reflecting on the costs of their previous lives and creating distance from what once mattered so much.

Out of this process of flux, this moving between the old and new, the more and less known, these individuals begin to expand their self-understandings. They will always be musicians, but they may not continue to make music or to make it in the same way. They do not deny who they have been and how they have spent an important part of their lives, but now this is just a piece of themselves and their story. Each musician claims more identities, and each enjoys the breadth this creates in his or her self-understanding and in the eyes of others. For some, such as Linda, the integration of these identities is immensely satisfying; for others, such as Brian and Gordon, value lies in the clear boundaries they will draw between these different selves.

To conclude, there are many differences between these individuals, the nature and impact of their injuries, and the stories they tell. In each case, however, we see a trauma that seriously affected someone's ability to do what he or she loved best, and the ensuing struggle to understand what life would be and who he or she could become. Whatever the specific nature of the injury, the sensemaking process that followed was long and circuitous but led, eventually, to the construction of new identities—positive identities—that are fulfilling and enabling to the individuals in question.

What makes these new identities positive, and these stories ones of growth? First, although none of the musicians was shy to speak of the intense pain they had experienced along the way, they all narrated stories with optimistic endings that involved the enactment of affirming identities: each expressed satisfaction, gratitude, and excitement about the person they were becoming. Second, the musicians all conveyed strongly agentic approaches to the development of their new identities. This involved both preempting negative constructions and exploring new roles for themselves, which together liberated them from future selves they feared, such as a musician past his prime or an amateur player making an amateur sound. Contained in this sense of agency was the idea that they were strong and resourceful in ways that they had not previously known, and an appreciation that this self-knowledge would serve them well in the future. Third, they described how these new identities were connected to and embedded in important relationships, making them more robust and durable. Not only was each musician's new identity developed in interaction with key others, but their significant relationships also played a major role in the future life developing around this identity. Fourth, they took pride in the greater number and variety of identities they now had, seeing this as an indication of their engagement with a fuller range of life's possibilities. At the same time, they all achieved coherence in their narratives, woven around the thread of music, a thread central to their identities before, during, and after their injuries. Thus, we see the highly agential construction of satisfying, affirming, and broadened identities, which are embedded in valued relationships and which, although multifaceted, retain a central theme that enables coherence in each individual's story. These, then, are positive identities, which are core to the growth these individuals experienced.

CONCLUSION

This chapter, although exploratory, makes several contributions to the literatures on identity in positive organizational scholarship and sense-making in posttraumatic growth. From writing on positive organizational scholarship, we understand that positive identity can be shaped by appreciative, developmental experiences, which provide jolts that challenge or affirm an individual's sense of self (Roberts et al., 2005). These authors argue that, in the context of such a jolt, the construction of positive identity is enabled by access to certain positive resources, including positive affect, a sense of relational connection, and personal agency. The narratives presented in this chapter add to these ideas by suggesting that positive identity can be constructed not only from supportive experiences that trigger positive affect but also out of very negative life experiences that may leave people feeling lost, alone, and even suicidal. As I hope to have made clear, these circumstances do not *in themselves* enable positive identity, but they do create conditions that compel people to search for new meaning and to act in ways that can be positively transformative for their self-understandings.

One of these conditions is the intense demand for identity change in situations in which trauma has severely damaged identity. In contrast to many identity transitions where a key challenge is daring to jump (Bridges, 2004; Ibarra, 2003), the triggers for change in the present study are nonvolitional. These individuals had little choice but to change, and yet they were in a physical and psychological state that was hardly conducive to a positive transition. Whereas we might expect them to have been paralyzed by what had happened to them, or to make the smallest changes necessary to move on, we see instead the proactive creation of identities that allowed them to live broadened, multidimensional lives while retaining at their core a connection to what had always mattered to them—music. This may have been because they were less preoccupied by what they stood to lose than those who voluntarily engage in identity transitions, or perhaps the sheer inability to carry on as before drove actions that had unexpectedly positive outcomes. These unexpected positive outcomes, in turn, especially in the context of others who supported and encouraged different ways of being, seem to have enabled individuals to construct themselves in new and positive ways. No one would wish for trauma in their lives, but we see that such experiences can be highly generative.

This work also adds to our understanding of the role of sensemaking in posttraumatic growth by highlighting the value of identity as a sensemaking target. To date, little attention has been paid to the role of identity in the sensemaking of those who have experienced a major life crisis (Pals, 2006). This chapter places identity center stage, revealing how individuals' self-understandings can become a compelling focus for sensemaking after a work-related trauma and showing the importance of identity in narratives of posttraumatic growth. Previous research has found a complex relationship between individuals' attributions and their posttrauma recovery, some studies suggesting that even irrational internal attributions can provide meaning makers with a valuable sense of control (Janoff-Bulman, 1992), whereas others find that whether a trauma is attributed to internal or external causes makes no difference to recovery (Landsman, 2002). Interestingly, none of the narratives in this chapter contained a rhetoric of blame: none of the musicians engaged in either self- or other-recrimination; no one described what had happened using explanations such as "if only I hadn't" or "they should never have." Therefore, one reason why sensemaking about identity may enable growth in these circumstances is because it allows individuals to move beyond destructive ruminations and explanations about the trauma that keep them rooted in the past, such as "why this?" and "why me?", and to focus their attention on more constructive, future-oriented thoughts and actions, such as "who can I become?"

and "how shall I live?". This focus may have been critical in allowing people to move forward positively instead of becoming stuck in a reproachful, fearful, and repeating cycle of "if only."

This chapter also adds to our understanding of posttraumatic growth more generally by examining trauma and growth in the context of "ordinary" work. Most research in this area has looked at individuals' reactions to non-work-related traumas, such as bereavement (e.g., Lehman et al., 1993), cancer (e.g., Collins, Taylor, & Slokan, 1990), and sexual assault and abuse (e.g., Frazier, Conlon, & Glaser, 2001). Although there are a small number of studies of traumas occurring in the service of certain occupations, such as combat and disaster work (e.g., Britt, Adler, & Bartone, 2001; Linley & Joseph, 2006), these are in jobs in which, by their very nature, encountering trauma would be expected. In general, however, very little attention has been paid to posttraumatic growth at work, and still less to it in professions that do not ordinarily involve exposure to traumatic events. One reason for this may be an assumption that work-related trauma is somehow less significant, indeed, less traumatizing, than those traumas that have more commonly been studied. However, work-related trauma that may at first appear relatively minor, such as an injury that leaves the victim almost fully functioning, can—through its impact on identity—have a very significant effect on those involved. By showing how both trauma and growth can occur in the context of ordinary work, this chapter suggests that posttraumatic growth may occur in a variety of occupations.

IMPLICATIONS FOR RESEARCH

This chapter has several implications for future research. Through its examination of the impact of work-related trauma on individuals' identities, and by investigating the link between sensemaking, positive identity, and posttraumatic growth, this research is some of the first to bring the posttraumatic growth construct into the study of work and organizational behavior. In so doing, it opens the door for research on many common work-related traumas, such as demotion, job loss, and abusive supervision, which, although apparently relatively minor, may have profound effects on individuals' understandings of themselves and so hold the potential for positive identity transformation and psychological growth. Therefore, much may be learned by examining the various kinds of traumas, identity changes, and growth trajectories that occur in different work contexts.

Notably, although examining a work-related trauma, this chapter focused on members of an occupation where professionals are often not part of formal organizations, indeed, where organizational membership may not even play a significant role in their musician identity. This suggests that the role of the organization and the role of colleagues may have been underplayed in the present account and leaves unanswered many important questions about the parts that organizations and those within them can play in sensemaking and positive identity construction following work-related trauma. This is a critical avenue for future research in the area. It also raises questions about the relationship between trauma, identity, and growth at the collective level. Although this chapter takes as its focus the experience of individuals, trauma can affect groups (Frost, 2003) and even entire organizations (e.g., Dutton, Frost, Worline, & Lilius, 2002). As a social process, sensemaking will be key to the construction of collective positive identities and to moving teams and organizations toward trajectories of growth. Therefore, examining how shared narratives develop in teams and organizations following a trauma, as well as the mechanisms through which positive identities are shaped, offers another exciting path for future research.

A further question concerns how the nature of the trauma, as well as the nature of individuals' pretrauma identities, shapes their sensemaking, identity construction, and ultimate growth. Because of its corporeal and seemingly tangible nature, one might think the meaning of this trauma was perhaps less open to contestation. However, as the musicians so clearly convey, the significance and meaning of their injuries were uncertain and remained so long after they occurred. Thus, this chapter examined a trauma that was chronic and ambiguous in ways similar to nonphysical traumas, such as ongoing victimization at work, the gradual breakdown of a relationship, or time spent in a war zone. These attributes of the trauma, without doubt, had important implications for the kinds of sensemaking and identity work in which the individuals engaged, perhaps resulting in processes that were less goal directed, more gradual, and more oscillating than would occur following an acute trauma, or a trauma with more immediately obvious effects. For example, the chronic nature of the trauma in this study, as well as its uncertain effect on the individuals' identities, may have allowed the musicians to move back and forth between an old identity as musician and various new selves in a way that would not have been possible had the injury instantaneously prevented them from ever playing again (e.g., an accident resulting in quadriplegia). Such a trauma might have immediately shattered their self-understanding as a performing musician and led to different sensemaking processes, as well as the development of different identities. On the other hand, we see here how music, whether played, listened to, published, or researched, remained a central part of each person's new identity, despite the broad and multifaceted nature of their new selves. This raises the question of whether some identities or key parts of identities have a durability that transcends even the most profound trauma, offering still further compelling directions for future research on sensemaking, identity, and posttraumatic growth.

ACKNOWLEDGMENTS

My gratitude goes to all the musicians who have shared their stories so openly with me, and to Laura Morgan Roberts, Jane Dutton, Richard Hackman, Tom Lawrence, Kathy Scalzo, and members of the May Meaning Meeting, for their support and helpful comments as these ideas have been developing.

REFERENCES

Ainsworth, S., & Hardy, C. (2004). Discourse and identity. In D. Grant, C. Hardy, C. Oswick, & L. Putnam (Eds.), *Handbook of organizational discourse* (pp. 153–174). London: Sage.

Bridges, W. (2004). *Transitions: Making sense of life's changes* (2nd ed.). New York: De Capo Lifelong Books.

Briere, J., & Scott, C. (2006). *Principles of trauma therapy*. Thousand Oaks, CA: Sage.

Britt, T., Adler, A., & Bartone, P. (2001). Deriving benefits from stressful events: The role of engagement in meaningful work and hardiness. *Journal of Occupational Health Psychology, 6,* 53–63.

Calhoun, L., & Tedeschi, R. (2001). Posttraumatic growth: The positive lessons of loss. In R. A. Neimeyer (Ed.), *Meaning reconstruction and the meaning of loss* (pp. 157–172). Washington, DC: American Psychological Association.

Calhoun, L., & Tedeschi, R. (2006). *Handbook of posttraumatic growth: Research and practice.* Mahwah, NJ: Lawrence Erlbaum Associates.

Collins, R., Taylor, S., & Slokan, L. (1990). A better world or a shattered vision? Changes in life perspectives following victimization. *Social Cognition, 8,* 263–285.

Davis, C., Nolen-Hoeksma, S., & Larson, J. (1998). Making sense of loss and benefiting from the experience: Two construals of meaning. *Journal of Personality and Social Psychology, 75,* 561–574.

Dutton, J. (2003). *Energize your workplace: How to create and sustain high-quality connections at work.* San Francisco: Jossey-Bass.

Dutton, J., Frost, P., Worline, M., & Lilius, J. (2002). Leading in times of trauma. *Harvard Business Review, 80,* 54–61.

Ebaugh, H. (1988). *Becoming an ex.* Chicago: University of Chicago Press.

Frazier, P., Conlon, A., & Glaser, T. (2001). Positive and negative life changes following sexual assault. *Journal of Consulting and Clinical Psychology, 69,* 1048–1055.

Frost, P. (2003). *Toxic emotions at work: How compassionate managers handle pain and conflict.* Boston: HBS Press.

Gergen, K. (1994). *Realities and relationships: Soundings in social construction.* Cambridge, MA: Harvard University Press.

Gergen, K. (1999). *An invitation to social construction.* Thousand Oaks, CA: Sage.

Herman, J. (1997). *Trauma and recovery* (2nd ed.). New York: Basic Books.

Ibarra, H. (1999). Provisional selves: Experimenting with image and identity in professional adaptation. *Administrative Science Quarterly, 44,* 764–791.

Ibarra, H. (2003). *Working identity: Unconventional strategies for reinventing your career.* Boston: HBS Press.

Janoff-Bulman, R. (1992). *Shattered assumptions: Towards a new psychology of trauma.* New York: Free Press.

Joseph, S., & Linley, P. (2008). Trauma, recovery, and growth. *Positive psychological perspectives on posttraumatic stress.* Hoboken, NJ: Wiley.

Kärreman, D., & Alvesson, M. (2001). Making newsmakers: Conversational identity at work. *Organization Studies, 22,* 59–90.

Landsman, I. (2002). Crises of meaning in trauma and loss. In J. Kauffmann (Ed.), *Loss of the assumptive world.* New York: Brunner-Routledge.

Lehman, D., Davis, C., Delongis, A., Wortmann, C., Bluck, S., Mandel, D., & Ellard, J. (1993). Positive and negative life changes following bereavement and their relations to adjustment. *Journal of Social and Clinical Psychology, 12,* 90–112.

Lieblich, A., Tuvel-Mashiach, R., & Zilber, T. (1998). *Narrative research: Reading, analysis, and interpretation.* London: Sage.

Linley, P. A., & Joseph, S. (2006). Positive and negative aspects of disaster work. *Journal of Loss and Trauma, 11,* 229–245.

Martin, L., & Tesser, A. (1996). Some ruminative thoughts. In R. S. Wyer (Ed.), *Advances in social cognition* (Vol. 9, pp. 1–47). Hillsdale, NJ: Lawrence Erlbaum Associates.

McAdams, D. (1993). *The stories we live by: Personal myths and the making of the self.* New York: Morrow.

McAdams, D., Reynolds, J., Lewis, M., Patten, A., & Bowman, P. (2001). When bad things turn good and good things turn bad: Sequences of redemption and contamination in life narrative and their relation to psychosocial adaptation in midlife adults and in students. *Personality and Social Psychology Bulletin, 27,* 474–485.

Merton, R. (1957). *Social theory and social structure.* New York: Free Press.

Meyer, A. (1982). Adapting to environmental jolts. *Administrative Science Quarterly, 27,* 515–537.

Neimeyer, R. (2000). Searching for the meaning of meaning: Grief therapy and the process of reconstruction. *Death Studies, 24,* 541–557.

Neimeyer, R. (2004). Fostering posttraumatic growth: A narrative contribution. *Psychological Inquiry, 15,* 53–59.

Neimeyer, R., Prigerson, H., & Davies, B. (2002). Mourning and meaning. *American Behavioral Scientist, 46,* 235–251.

Nolen-Hoeksema, S., & Davis, C. (2004). Theoretical and methodological issues in the assessment and interpretation of posttraumatic growth. *Psychological Inquiry, 15,* 60–64.

Pals, J. (2006). Authoring a second chance in life: Emotion and transformational processing within narrative identity. *Research in Human Development, 3,* 101–120.

Pals, J., & McAdams, D. (2004). The transformed self: A narrative understanding of post-traumatic growth. *Psychological Inquiry, 15,* 65–69.

Pennebaker, J. W. (2000). Telling stories: The health benefits of narrative. *Literature and Medicine, 19,* 3–18.

Pratt, M., Rockmann, K., & Kaufmann, J. (2006). Constructing professional identity: The role of work and identity learning cycles in the customization of identity among medical residents. *Academy of Management Journal, 49,* 235–262.

Richer, F., Giasson, F., & Lapierre, L. (2007). *Agnès Grossmann: Transmitting her own sound without touching an instrument* (K. Larsen, Trans.). Montreal, Quebec, Canada: Centre de cas, HEC Montréal.

Riessman, C. (1993). *Narrative analysis.* London: Sage.

Roberts, L. M., Dutton, J. E., Spreitzer, G., Heaphy, E., & Quinn, R. E. (2005). Composing the reflected best-self portrait: Building pathways for becoming extraordinary in work organizations. *Academy of Management Review, 30,* 712–736.

Snow, D., & Anderson, L. (1987). Identity work among the homeless: The verbal construction and avowal of personal identities. *American Journal of Sociology, 92,* 1336–1371.

Solomon, J. (2004). Modes of thought and meaning making: The aftermath of trauma. *Journal of Humanistic Psychology, 44,* 299–319.

Tedeschi, R., & Calhoun, L. (2004). Posttraumatic growth: Conceptual foundations and empirical evidence. *Psychological Inquiry, 15,* 1–18.

Thornton, A., & Perez, M. (2006). Posttraumatic growth in prostate cancer survivors and their partners. *Psycho-oncology, 15,* 285–296.

Weick, K. (1995). *Sensemaking in organizations.* Thousand Oaks, CA: Sage.

Weick, K., Sutcliffe, K., & Obstfeld, D. (2005). Organizing and the process of sensemaking. *Organization Science, 16,* 409–421.

Wigren, J. (1994). Narrative completion in the treatment of trauma. *Psychotherapy: Theory, research, practice, training, 31,* 415–423.

Wrzesniewski, A. (2003). Finding positive meaning in work. In K. Cameron, J. Dutton, & R. Quinn (Eds.), *Positive organizational scholarship: Foundations of a new discipline* (pp. 296–308). San Francisco: Berrett-Kohler.

Zaza, C. (1998). Playing-related musculoskeletal disorders in musicians: a systematic review of incidence and prevalence. *Canadian Medical Association Journal, 158,* 1019–1025.

4

Experiencing Hope in Organizational Lives

Arne Carlsen and Tyrone Pitsis

CONTENTS

> You know, none of this that you see here—this building, all these people working here, today's workshop—none of it matters without us having *faith* in there being oil in the Barents Sea. It is all about having faith. It is the single most important thing in everything we do, to really believe that somewhere in this vast area there is oil waiting to be found ... the reason I quit working in [a competitor] was that [a top manager] had no faith in there being significant discoveries to be made within the area. Then it all collapses, then there's no point.
>
> —*Uttered with intensity by a senior geologist of an oil company during a workshop break in 2005*

It was a very tired school. The wear had come from a decision to close it down. When deciding to close down a school, you are abandoned by God and human beings alike.... I told them that we would start to build it up again, all the teachers sat there and then they just slid somewhat down in their chairs and smiled a funny little smile, you now the song; "we've heard it all before."... The facade had fallen off ... the windows ... it looked like Beirut.... The two first years, seriously, I hoped for a small heart attack so that I could say that I had to quit ... it was slum.... We had to stand there in the schoolyard and face the gang members ... to this day I still cannot even think to drive a BMW.... [I displayed] that naive enthusiasm, I called it the Davey Crockett method, smiling when facing the grizzly... it was like I had sleepwalked to the closet and had the clothes hanger stuffed upside down in my mouth, because I just went around smiling "now it's coming, this will be good, we are on our way, it's coming."

—*From an interview with a headmaster accredited the transformation of a vocational school located in the gangland of a Scandinavian capital*

HOPE AS A QUALITY OF EXPERIENCING

Organizations offer people participation in goal-directed value-creating activities, in self-adventures ranging from mundane projects to enduring strivings, in the unforeseen and naked terrains of possibility. A potentially defining feature of these participations is hope. Hope, in turn, is a quality of experiencing that may unleash powers of creativity, bring life to transformations, and shape that part of people's experiencing that deeply concerns how they see their lives. For some people, exploring for oil or attending to the duties of being a headmaster is just that, a job, a way of making income that is of little passion and modest consequence for their sense of self. For others, the promise of venturing into an untamed geological area, or the alluring danger of turning around the most hopeless of schools, represents not just what is deeply meaningful to them but forms the very horizon of their expectations.

The overall aim of this chapter is to take a few steps toward establishing an approach to a fairly large research question: *What is the role of hope as a motive of positive identity construction in organizations?* This is a field of inquiry that has received little attention as previous identity research has been primarily occupied with questions of differentiating qualities, continuity, coherence, and maintaining status quo. We aim to provide the skeleton of an integrative framework for streams of organizational research that emphasizes forward-looking identity motives—thus to provide a "vocabulary of hope" (Ludema, Wilmot, & Srivastava, 1997) for identity research, and from this outlook point to new avenues for inquiry.

Along with previous research we acknowledge hope as a positively charged emotion that is directed toward the future and a generative force in people's lives. Key contributors in hope theory (e.g., Stotland, 1969; Snyder, 2000a) emphasize hope as forms of positive expectation for goal attainment that may include agency, pathway thinking, and affective resources (Snyder, 2000b, 2002). We recognize that use of the term hope will sometimes inevitably overlap with "belief" and "faith," but hold that hope is a wider concept that penetrates more fully into the future, may be linked to fantasies of projected acts (Schütz, 1970), and is less tied to specific outcomes or ascriptions to ways of seeing (Crapanzano, 2003). We also acknowledge the potential overlap between hope and self-efficacy (Bandura, 1997) but hold that hope can be based on goal thoughts that are cross-situational and enduring (Snyder, 2000b), as well as on open-endedness.

Following tenets of theorizing in pragmatism—in particular the work of William James and George Herbert Mead—and the pragmatic phenomenology of Alfred Schütz, we shall explore the notion of hope as a *future-oriented quality of experiencing*. Our conception acknowledges the fundamental nature of present future temporality in all experiencing and highlights its importance in positive identity construction. Central to this inquiry is to understand the *addressivity* of hope: to what is hope directed, hope for *what*? The idea of hope in identity construction should not be conceived as being linked to goal attainment alone. Also, the experiencing of hope transcends levels of analysis, from individual lives to collective lives, sometimes beyond organizational borders. We shall start with a conceptual map. The opening quotes will serve as thinking devices along the way.

WHAT HAS HOPE GOT TO DO WITH POSITIVE IDENTITY CONSTRUCTION?

Linking hope to identity inevitably forces a more focused approach than a casual use of the term, which may refer to almost any set of action-motive in everyday life, like "hoping to see a movie tonight" or "hoping the plane is on schedule." By contrast, we associate hope in identity construction with a selective process of perceiving experience and attributing experience to selves, a process where most mundane events are not likely to enter. The function of hope in positive identity construction cannot be fully understood without acknowledging the role of experience and agency. We propose that three analytical aspects of identity are fruitful and necessary for that purpose: (a) self as object (hope as a defining characteristic), (b) self as subject (hope as a quality of experiencing), and (c) self as evolving life stories (hope as that particular quality of experiencing that is associated with favorable progression in life stories). Although not negating the relevance of the first of these three dimensions, we shall emphasize the two latter.

Self as Object and Self as Subject

Let us start with self as object. One could say, for example, that a key distinguishing characteristic of the geologist in our first opening quote is that he is a hoping person—or that the exploration collective in question, whether a team or a whole assembly of teams, is a hoping collective. One could go further and uphold this characteristic of hoping as central, enduring, and differentiating as perceived by organization members—compared with organizations that have given up on exploring the area for oil—thus assigning hoping a status on par with such characteristics attended to in the usual definitions of organizational identity (Albert & Whetten, 1985). Likewise, one could characterize the vocational school in the second opening quote as an organization devoid of hoping during a certain stretch of time and uphold this characteristic as key to school identity (again in comparison with other schools). Going further, we can assign the first set of characterizations a positive value (given that there was more oil to be found, which was proven in the years after the statement was made), and the second a negative one (given that a well-functioning school could be built in that neighborhood, which is what eventually unfolded).

The little exercise done so far is meant to illustrate that linking hope to identity in the sense of one of the defining characteristics of self as object is indeed possible. However, taken alone this is an insufficient conception. It is derived of notions of experience, agency, and temporality and is incapable of shedding much light on the functions of hope in positive identity construction. Confining hope to self as object would amount to studying buckets of water when one should inquire about the flows of a river. To attain a fuller understanding, it is necessary to bring to life the concept of self as subject, central to the writings of William James (1890/1950, chap. 10) and George Herbert Mead (1934/2000). James and Mead are often used to establish that people's identities—in the sense of self as object—are many and depend on interaction in various social contexts. However, they both conceived that as only half the picture as they differentiated between the self as object, a "me" (or a "we"), and the self as subject, an "I." The me self is the object of one's knowledge, a *content* aspect of self, whereas the I self is the knower, a *process* aspect of self. For both James and Mead the I and the me presuppose one another. The me's do not have independent existence outside the stream of constitutive acts, and each act of the I toward the me passes onto a next me (along with constitutive acts of others). The self as subject is necessary to account for initiative, emergence, and novelty, whereas the self as object is necessary to account for social reflexivity and the conditioning power of the succession of responses and attitudes of others.

It was James who first launched the decisive argument in this stream of theorizing. James basically did away with the soul as a valuable concept for empirical investigation by casting the I self (self as subject) as an event in the flow of time, a judging thought in passing, recollective of previous thoughts, and (James, 1890/1950, vol. 1, p. 369): "the only thinker which the facts require." Rather than attributing people souls independent of experience, James saw the processes of self as subject as having functions of self-awareness, self-continuity, and self-agency in relation to the self as object. By this move, James placed identity and agency firmly in the flow of ongoing experience (Carlsen, 2009). In a superb introduction to James's work, McDermott (2000) has shown how the personal experience of emerging from suicidal depression colors James' entire scholarship and underpins his conception of the self and his radical theory of experience. When James decided he would have the will to believe, it was really a will to hope for current thoughts and actions to be fruitful in future experience, and for his sense of self to be not destroyed but enhanced by future experience. On the dark evening in his life, at the edge of the abyss, painfully aware of the vulnerability of his sense of self, James grabbed the will to hope.

Returning to our two empirical snippets in the opening, what we may induce from them are two basic observations. First, behind the mere characteristic of a hoping individual or collective must lay a succession of acts. Hope understood in the sense of self as subject, as this succession of acts, amounts to a process. This process, still following James, should be understood as a subset in the stream of experience in which people find themselves immersed. Thus, to understand hope in positive identity construction, one must understand the processes that constitute hope, not as something outside identity, but integral to it: how the experiencing of hope in oil exploration is sustained or threatened, how and why the experiencing of hopelessness in the vocational school eventually is turned around by a succession of acts that create hope.

Second, acts of hoping are acts of will and may be considered the very foundation of agency. Where James grabbed the will to hope for a favorable future, others may grab the will to hope for oil discoveries or the will to hope for a turnaround of a school. Being immersed in a steady stream of hope-generating acts is likely to be different from having to face circumstances where many have given up and the installment of hope requires a leap in one's outlook for the future. All such shades of hope are manifestations of the projective capacities of human agencies, but the intensities and functions of hoping will depend on the directionality of hope (emerging from depression, getting away from hopelessness, attaining a discovery) and the particulars of the sequences of events that form contexts for acts of hoping (the life of James, the history of the school, the circumstances of the exploration team, and the geological area in question). This brings us to the third dimension of self: the mediating role of life stories.

Self as Evolving Life Stories

People use a wide variety of words, images, gestures, or other symbols to signal or endorse accounts of me's or we's. Stories inevitably form part of this repertoire for constituting self as objects. However, the primary significance of using narrative theory to understand identity construction does lie elsewhere. It lies in the widely accepted suggestion that narratives are basic cultural forms to render sequences of human experiences and intentions meaningful through time (MacIntyre, 1981; Sarbin, 1986; White, 1973) and in the stronger assertion that narratives are necessary for people to achieve some semblance of continuity and purpose among the variety of situationally determined me's. According to the latter view, people experience their lives through evolving life stories that they continuously construct and reconstruct to make sense of their past and anticipate their future (Bruner, 1990; Crites, 1971; McAdams 1995, 1999; Polkinghorne, 1988). Life stories are reflexively achieved, socially endorsed, and continually experienced within the flow of time, the ongoing present of things past and future. It is from this perspective we shall speak of hope in organizational lives. Whether hope concerns identity is a matter of whether it has some salience in the particular form of experiencing that concerns how people see their life stories evolving. More precisely, *we understand the role of hope in positive identity construction as being linked to some kind of favorable progression in the life stories of individuals and collectives.* By this we do not rule out the relevance of retrospective coherence, ontological security, or differentiation versus salient others as important motives for identity construction. Rather, we acknowledge that hope is first a temporal construct that pertains to the future. Maintaining and producing the experience of hope may be considered a metamotive in identity construction, a present future equivalent of present past coherence. Following St. Augustine's (397–400/1998, p. 235) notion of the threefold present, Crites (1971) talks about three modes of experiencing interior to the experiencing of self: the present of things past, the present of things present, and the present of things future. Hope is inherent in the experience of self in the present of things future. It is a quality of experience that can never be fully brought out of experiencing or considered a separate distinct thing. As propagated in pragmatism, in particular by James (who uses the term "belief") and Rorty (1990) (who talks of hope), hope may be seen as the ultimate addressee of all claims to reality and truth. Correspondingly, we suggest investigating hope as the ultimate addressee of all future-oriented claims to identity.

"Favorable progression" in life stories can obviously mean many things. Motives for enrichment of life stories in terms of bettering their prospective qualities range from purpose (Blasi, 1988; Bruner, 1990; McAdams, 1997) to challenge (Csikszentmihalyi, 1985), unpredictability (MacIntyre, 1981; Turner, 1980), openness (McAdams, 1993), generativity (McAdams, 2006), and drama (Carlsen, 2008; Mattingly, 1998; Scheibe, 1986). By this we can deduce that hope as a prospective quality of experiencing will surely be related to goal-directed pursuits and purpose but not exclusively so. Hope will also be linked to opening up for unforeseen possibility or escaping from forces of entrapment. One may also ask whether there are aspects of hope that fall outside narrative emplotment. Following Schütz (1967), one could say that hope is constituted by rays of anticipated possibilities as projects for action, conditioned by agents' habitual beliefs and interests (all this being conducive to narrative analysis), but *also* that it includes shocks in experience that open up new possibility, thus the notion of "possibilities of new possibilities." By this, hope must be seen both as a narratively shaped field of desire in the present future and as a quality of undirected open-endedness that stands against a closedness one may bring to lived experience. Consequently, hope needs to be investigated not only as a *generative force* in identity construction, within established or projected trajectories of action, but also as a *subversive force* that opposes closedness.

Shades of Hope—Teleological and Relational Addressivity[1]

It follows from what has been said so far that one needs to take into account the multiple addressees of hope to understand its role in positive identity construction. When speaking of hope in organizational lives, *what* is hope directed to, and hope for *whom*? To unpack this we introduce the concepts of *teleological* and *relational addressivity*. Teleological addressivity denotes the directionality of hope in terms of creating progression in life story: *hope for what?* We shall, for analytical purposes, distinguish between three forms of teleological addressivity in what follows: *attainment hope, opening-up hope,* and *away-from hope.*

Relational addressivity denotes the directionality of hope in terms of whose life story is being involved: are we talking about a *me hope*, hope that primarily concerns oneself; a *we hope*, hope for some collective that one is part of (whether a team, an organization, or some interorganizational group); or an *other hope* that is primarily directed to some (group of) outside beneficiaries? These distinctions are more blurred than distinctions of teleological addressivity. In their thorough review of hope literature, Ludema et al. (1997) dwell on the enduring qualities of hope processes that are intensely relational, both in how they are born, sustained, and in their functions. Hope is enlivened in the personal and professional relationship.

---

[1] Our use of the term "addressivity" here acknowledges a debt to the work of the Russian linguist and philosopher Mikhail Bakhtin (1981), who emphasized the dialogical quality of all experiencing and the way people use language to make sense of experience. Bakhtin resisted the (1981, p. 274) "dungeons of the single context" and elaborated in great detail on how people borrow words from many contexts, purposes, genres, and situations in their everyday meaning making. We pay homage to this more elaborate philosophical stance by indicating the multiple directions and relational ties that goes into the experiencing of hope.

Hope may prosper when one places oneself in service to others, and hope may be a binding force in a community or even society at large. In his famous discussion of utopia, Ernst Bloch (1959/1995) saw hope as a fundamental generative force behind all human creation. Rorty (2000) has advocated that we see hope for a better human future as the final addressee of all scientific inquiry. As we shall demonstrate, a sharp analytical distinction between individual and collective hope is just that, an analytical distinction made for certain purposes that will often mean a reduction of the plurality of motives at work in real events. Doing the upstream shifter from a mere focus on self as object to self as subject enables us to see that the processes of attributing experiences to selves are seldom entirely pure, seldom addressed to only a "me" or a "we." More often than not, life stories are embedded in each other and gain significance for that very reason. So, no, there is no 3 × 3 matrix of teleological versus relational addressivity to be drawn here because the latter set of categories seldom arises in some distinct isolation. Thus, we shall refer to the relational addressivity of hope in our treatment of each of the three categories of teleological addressivity.

Attainment Hope

Attainment hope is directed toward desired outcomes of goal-directed pursuits (situational or more enduring) that deeply concern a me or a we and engender lived experience with a sense of purpose. The need for forms of purpose in life is a recurring theme in the social sciences and in narrative identity literature, although with few accounts so far in organizational identity theory. We shall illustrate some of the varieties of attainment hope by speculating around the identity motives of our geologist: What kinds of attainment hope could his statement in the opening quote signify, and which functions would various shades of hope have relative to his evolving life stories?

Beginning at an individual level outlook, we can imagine that the hope for discoveries in the Barents Sea was primarily a hope for the geologist's own knowledge and previous experience to come to fruition. The geologist could have superior regional knowledge or have well-grounded hunches about specific hydrocarbon prospects that would need corporate backing for further qualification and eventual drilling. Further engagement in exploration in the area could have amounted to one of his key personal project pursuits (Little, Salmela-Aro, & Phillips, 2007), a dedication to finding oil where many had given up. A discovery could have represented a nuclear experience in the geologist's life story (McAdams, 1993) or at least represent a jolt in experience that could result in what Roberts, Dutton, Spreitzer, Heaphy, and Quinn (2005) have called an improved "reflected best self portrait," and thus set the geologist on pathways for achieving new possible selves. In all these interpretations, hope would primarily be directly toward progression in personal life story.

Alternatively, and not necessarily at odds with the first version of hoping, the geologist could have tied his hoping to a more collectively oriented pursuit, seeing further exploration as a chance to be involved in a life-enriching positive drama (Carlsen, 2008): enacted self-adventures formed in relation to the specifics of what is at stake. Positive dramas are stories lived as much as they are stories told, lived-in realms of interpretation that enrich the way people attend to experience. Positive dramas are determinants of the teleological addressivity of hoping. In this case one could conjure strong elements of a Mystery theme (to solve and discover) and a Treasure Hunt theme (finding and seizing valuable resources) in the positive drama. Positive dramas are formed and reformed in relation to distinct value-creating activities (be it oil exploration, teaching, construction work, etc.) and represent nested manifestations of human agency (Carlsen, 2008). Thus, this form of hoping would be tied to grabbing a narrative plot where the geologist could emphasize the pursuit of the collective as primary and consider himself one of several protagonists. Furthermore, his hoping could be tied to a specific time-bound cycle such as the new round of tendering for geological areas to explore and developing prospects, or a more open-ended quest spanning decades of future exploration efforts.

The geologist's hoping for goal attainment could also be addressed to one or more "others" beyond the organization of which he was part. He could see future exploration in the Barents Sea as a potentially powerful vehicle of industrial development for the entire northern region, thus hope for thousands of new jobs and bustling activity in the years to come. This other hope could of course be linked back to a me hope. Following McAdams, Diamond, de St. Aubin, and Mansfield (1997), one could say that the identity motive of generativity—leaving a legacy behind that is valuable for future generations—could be at work here, meaning that the geologist hoped to leave behind the legacy of having revitalized exploration in a large geological area. In its grandest version, one could see such hoping as addressing a possible legendary status in the region, on par with great discoverers.

Opening-Up Hope

Opening-up hope is oriented toward new possibilities and the open-ended qualities of experience: the unforeseen, the break with the past, the new day. Its function in the life story is to maintain openness and prevent stagnation caused by a determining past or the imposing constraints of others. Eclea Bosi (1979) (as referred to in Scheibe, 1986, p. 145) has remarked on the pleasure with which old people she interviewed about their lives remembered their youths, despite having gone though periods of poverty, deprivation, and limitation of freedom. In retrospect, the old persons viewed what many would describe as miserable childhoods with "great pleasure and warm nostalgia," as quoted by Scheibe (1986, p. 145):

> Bosi remarks that the reason for this historical foreshortening has to do with the character of youthful perceptions of the world—perceptions that are fresh and full of adventure. No matter how hard the external conditions, the playful gathering in of fresh perceptions of the world comprise essential features—the fundaments—of the life story as it is to develop.

The point here is not that remembering brings hope to the present for these folks, more so that they remembered how important opening-up hope used to be in their lives. One may regard openness in life story an inevitable quality of youth that is primarily located in early stages of a life cycle where experimentation dominates and decisions of which pathways to follow in life have yet to be made (Erikson, 1959/1994). We suggest the need to maintain opening-up hope is more fundamental than that. Hope itself implies an openness toward the future that "precedes and anticipates a coherent image of the future" (Ludema et al., 1997), an openness toward life as becoming that is also much in need in today's organizations. Ibarra (1999, 2003, pp. 91–111) has shown how experiments with provisional selves, ranging from small projects to singular acts of doing something new, highlight the opening-up function in identity construction. A related strategy revolves around telling stories of one's professional experiences in ways that open up and qualify several future possible selves and development paths (Ibarra, 2003, p. 133–158; Ibarra & Lineback, 2005). Likewise, the notions of "jolts in experience" (Roberts et al., 2005) and "instantiating" (Carlsen, 2006) can be regarded as seeding opening-up hope. In both contributions, a breach in experience is made significant, by individuals or a collective, as opening-up new growth patterns, whether possible selves (Roberts et al.,

2005) or identity salient new trajectories of practice (Carlsen, 2006). In the latter case, two relatively small and insignificant projects were projected as ideal exemplars of future practice of the firm and revitalized the life story of the organization. In the eyes of organizational members, the projects represented, "...just the kind of work we really wanted to do" (Carlsen, 2006, p. 140). Thus, we may speak of a synergistic function of opening-up hope, as charging breaches in experience with identity potential, and attainment hope, as setting people on the pathways that have been opened up. Chapter 3 by Maitlis in this volume demonstrates this beautifully: In the process of making sense of traumas that threatened or undermined musicians' sense of self, they report from a deep-seated experiencing of opening up by discovering new roles and pathways.

Opening-up hope may also be regarded as having a necessary regulatory function in relation to attainment hope. To illustrate this, let us consider the metaphor of the adventure-seeking proclivities of the Arthurian Knights (in Steinbeck's version), first used by Scheibe (1986), to illustrate a basic human need for adventure. In Steinbeck's (1982) story, Sir Lancelot is increasingly frustrated by postwar idleness. The tranquility of peace brings restlessness and boredom as there are no new struggles in sight. Sir Lancelot eventually finds his new Quest in upholding the King's Peace and embarks on a series of new (although smaller) adventures. One may see this as an upholding of attainment hope by a series of continued dramas bringing purpose, excitement, and possibility to Sir Lancelot's life. Reading on in the novel, there is a different story to be heard. Sir Lancelot also finds himself somehow caught: weary of the violence caused by the obligation of his oaths to the King and all despairing damsels, trapped by his idealized love for Queen Guinevere, really a character derived of hope. He is the participant in a form of social practice that brings closedness and despair to his life. At no time does Sir Lancelot attempt to go back and confront the assumptions that have created the succession of dramas he imposes on himself. Dramas may not only be life enriching but also life entrapping.

A direct parallel to Sir Lancelot's entrapment can be found in the growth process of an IT consulting firm, where the enactment of a powerful organizational drama charged people with attainment hope and led to growth but also had effects of constraining development through idealization, denial of problems, and underestimating learning needs (Carlsen, 2006). In this case, a process of reframing of the organizational drama instigated two deeply emotionally charged sets of reactions. The first was an open display of despair caused by a loss of faith in the once celebrated dream of the company, thus loss of attainment hope. This stream of reaction was most evident for a group of strong believers who had expectations that the firm could become a world leader in applied expert systems technology. The second set of reactions was a display of relief from having shed the burden of what many saw as an entrapping vision and a related accumulation of undiscussables. Here an opening up toward new pathways of services and ways of functioning resulted, a clear gain of opening-up hope. Sir Lancelot's path to discovering his own freedom could have been equally painful. Our geologist could have been trapped in a futile hope that hindered successful endeavors in other areas. Hoping is not an absolute good.

Away-From Hope

Away-from hope signifies hope that is primarily directed toward circumstances, forces, and structures that one wants to subvert, counter, or escape from, not necessarily knowing where such countering or escape may lead. Hoping to escape from several illnesses, like cancer, is a typical example of this that is often treated in hope literature,[1] and, interestingly, a hope that may be central to both patients and health personnel (Crapanzano, 2003). In her book about healing dramas of occupational therapy, Mattingly (1998) pointed to a similar mechanism—by instilling hope in the lives of their patients and their patients' next of kin, therapists also find deep sources of hope in their own lives.

Another example of away-from hope is hope for escape and survival from captivity. Tales from Holocaust survivors often emphasize hope as a generative force that was necessary to escape death and the watershed differentiator between those who managed to struggle on and those who gave up (e.g., Bratteli, 1980; Sachnowitz, 1976). These tales typically also emphasize something beyond mere survival as the source for hoping: to be able to tell the story and leave behind a legacy that would prevent similar atrocities from happening again. Thus, one may speak of a blend of away-from hope and attainment hope.

---

[1] Snyder (2002) considers hope to escape cancer a variation of attainment hope, as it is tied to deterring specific negative goal outcomes. We recognize that conception as logical in and of itself but hold that the notion of away-from hope covers a larger class of phenomena as it does not assume locating hope to some concrete condition or specific ailment. Away-from hope may also pertain to getting out of some ill-defined vague standstill or ambiguous barrier that people experience in their lives.

Finally, the importance of away-from hope can also be illustrated through the story of the transformation of the vocational school, from which a snippet is given in our second opening quote. This school, we shall call it River Hill, is located in a part of a Scandinavian capital that used to be a worn-down neighborhood with high crime rates. In the mid-1990s, the school faced shut down and was stripped of educational programs and resources. Following a decision to rebuild the school, a new headmaster was appointed, generally accredited with starting a major turnaround process. The headmaster describes a situation where hopelessness reigns. The decision to rebuild the school seems to be overshadowed by the remembering of previous failures, the burden of the physical decay, and the everyday experience of being situated in a gangland neighborhood. What happens next may be viewed as the slow growth of a timid away-from hope, a blind faith in the possibility of improvement not knowing where it may lead. As time passes, this away-from hope gradually gives way to an attainment hope, spurred by a call to battle for school resources by the headmaster (see Carlsen, 2008) and reinforced by a series of subsequent achievements. Many years later, as the school emerges as the uncontested winner of the annual competition for student applications (decisive for allocation of public resources), the headmaster recognizes a dilemma of having attained a major goal: "It's a bit like Bob Beamon having made that jump, walking back and forth staring at the pitch in disbelief, knowing he would never surpass it—what's next?" In the wake of temporary emptying attainment hope, a search for new ventures necessitates acts of installing opening-up hope. Furthermore, the production of hope at River Hill can be viewed primarily as a we hope, fueled by shades of other hope (for students, for the neighborhood) and working back at me hopes (the headmaster and teachers).

TOWARD A RESEARCH AGENDA FOR IDENTITY HOPE

We have argued that the hope in positive identity construction should be primarily viewed as a quality of experience associated with some kind of progression in life story. We have further provided tenets of an analytical grid—the forms of teleological and relational addressivity—for studying production of such identity hope at work. From these discussions it can be concluded that hope may be considered a metamotive in positive identity construction, pointing to basic human needs for finding purpose, escaping entrapment, and living with undirected openness. Furthermore, hope is manifested in a narratively shaped field of desire in the present future, a field of desire that will often resist distinct location at individual or organizational levels of analysis. What people hope for may be mediated by nested narratives, and understanding more of how the different relational addressivities of hope feed into each other is in itself an important area for further research.

It follows from our overall conception of identity and hope that we advocate a phenomenological approach where one follows people in their work settings over time and tries to capture the functions of hope in positive identity construction as part of change efforts and everyday work. The term "as part of" is key here. Activating and sustaining identity hope in organizations should not be considered some kind of outside, independent activity of storytelling set apart from accomplishment of everyday tasks. Both James and Schütz underlined that mere good intentions are not enough. Intentions must be *acted* on to have effect on character (James, 1890/1950, chap. 4). Projects must be *acted* on to realize their projective powers (Schütz, 1967). Sustaining hope over time requires that expectations are acted on by people doing specific moves into the future. The larger issue here is whether we think about identity hope as something that is thrown on people passively awaiting a better outlook or as something that people actively pursue and try to produce. Certainly, the second of our opening quotes is open to interpretation by both sets of views. The wedding of identity hope to agency may be key to move beyond a mere acknowledgement of hope as a fundamental motive in identity construction to seeing it as an energizing force in organizational life. An agentic approach to identity hope means fully acknowledging the active processes of self as subject in grabbing authorship and creating more positive future states.

To a research agenda on identity hope we voice a word of caution against an overly functional approach. Our knowledge of hope in positive identity construction is still limited, and hope is potentially so powerful and fundamental in people's lives that it must be treated with humility and held above organizational ends. With those words, let us point to two sets of questions for further research on hope in positive identity construction.

Experiencing Hope in Change Efforts

How is people's hoping shaping and taking shape from change efforts in organizations? Activation of identity hope in change efforts may be seen as a main road to create intrinsic motivation, where involvement of self is regarded the key (Ryan & Deci, 2000). Protruding from our discussion so far is a need to understand the balancing between attainment hope, opening-up hope, and away-from hope in change processes. An indication of the power of hope in such efforts, as well as the interplay between teleological addressivities of hope, may be the case of repeated use of "future perfect thinking" in a project to clean the Sydney harbor within 2 years and in time for the Olympics, a time frame all independent assessors and experts claimed was impossible (Pitsis, Clegg, Marosszeky, & Rura-Polley, 2003). Future perfect thinking refers to the narrative act of projecting one's present fantasies into the future and speaking of them as if they exist in the past tense (Pitsis et al., 2003; Schütz, 1967). As one of the alliance leadership team members stated in an interview in 1999:

> Our team, from the guys in the tunnels all the way to the ones in Artarmon [head office] know this is something different.... They know that they will do things differently and when the last bit of concrete dries and the last person turns out the lights, they will know they were part of something innovative. When all is said and done, they are working in something alien to many of them. It is going to change how they do things, it's changed how I do things, and I mean in a really good way, you will see!

Such narratives were common place in this unique project, so much so that although the research team was originally investigating quality management, it was the future perfect strategy that eventually became the focus of investigation because it dominated the project storytelling and leadership sensemaking (see Pitsis et al., 2003 for more examples and discussion of future perfect strategy).

For Alfred Schütz, such acts are important breaks from the reality of the present, as well as an act of opening up possible futures. In the Sydney Waterworks project, future perfect thinking in terms of imagining a successful end result became a recurrent project management practice that allowed for less disagreement on contractual issues. The aim of the project was to construct a 20-km tunnel meandering underneath the properties of some of the world's most expensive real estate, without the opportunity for any scoping work (geological testing). One large public organization and four private companies entered into a shared risk and reward alliance. Against great odds, political power plays, and expert opinion that the project could not be achieved in 2 years, the project performed surprisingly well in all its objectives. Attaining the goals remarkably well, the project also had an opening-up function. Carlsen and Pitsis (2008) discuss how the project built narrative capital and opened up possibilities for the organizations involved to foster positive change; most importantly, it enabled a large and old public bureaucracy to completely turn around its operations. Consider the following quotes from an Alliance Leadership Team meeting in November 1999 and from interviews conducted in 2002:

Alliance project director (from Sydney Water Board):

> What we have achieved is remarkable. We, as a team, set the standards high. Higher than any industry benchmark in many ways, and we said "let's do it! Let's do what's best for project." You guys have to realize that only a few years ago we would never have done this as an alliance. This alliance and what we are doing has changed the way Sydney Water will do things.

Alliance Leadership Team Member 1 (from private organization):

> Trust me, it's changed me too. Some of the ideas that we have got out of this have changed how I want to do things at Transfield. It's been exhausting but I can't wait for the next one [alliance].

Alliance Leadership Team Member 2 (private organization):

> What is interesting is how people are telling me that they don't know how they are going to go back to the way they used to work when they leave here [the alliance].

The case can be read as a two-stage drama: The first stage revolves around a charging of the members of the project alliance with attainment hope, mainly on behalf of the project. The next stage is driven by opening-up hope, seeding both personal and corporate expectations for future alliance work by replicating what seemingly worked so well in new projects. One could imagine less fortunate developments from the same case, in particular that the first set of achievements (from stage one) would be so idealized that they were in effect used to impose the past on the future in project circumstances not fitting the new approach and eventually close down hope, amounting to a narrative strategy of hoping for that which really should be remembered (Crites, 1986). Thus, understanding the processes by which past experiences are made to open up or close down hope is a key research issue here.

Experiencing Hope in Everyday Work

How is identity hope produced in everyday work? One inroad to that question is job design theory. Inquiring into identity hope may mean possible detailing (or resurrection) of a classical psychological job design criteria: the need for seeing one's work as part of a meaningful future (Emery & Thorsrud, 1976). What are the strongest enablers of identity hope in different kinds of work practice in terms of such issues as opportunities for career experiments (Ibarra, 1999) or perceived autonomy (Ryan & Deci, 2000)? A key question here is whether identity hope is instilled by some managerial effort of job design, or if one should rather regard it as resulting from active job crafting by workers being allowed space for doing so, or indeed, both. Wrzesniewski and Dutton (2001) have identified key job crafting moves as changing cognitive task boundaries and shaping interactions with beneficiaries at work. Grant (2007) points to the centrality of the identity motive of making a difference in other people's lives through relational design of jobs, certainly what one could regard a potentially important source of identity hope in work (Mattingly, 1998). A parallel discussion is offered by Kreiner and Sheep in this volume: People at work may seek to embrace larger interests to enhance their "spiritual identities." One could also investigate how acts of job crafting and the experiencing of identity hope feed into each other in cycles of mutual generation.

Focusing on job design and job crafting in production of identity hope is a specific instance of a more general recognition of the importance of practice in identity production. Shotter and Cunliffe (2002) have written evocatively about how leaders can produce meaning from within ambiguous everyday experience by forms of "practical authoring." Included here is seeing how leaders on an everyday basis are able to provide a sense of direction, open up new discursive space, and point to new landscapes of possibility. Carlsen (2006, 2008) has conceptualized how practice is imagined as representing promising development paths or framed as belonging to various forms of identity salient positive dramas. A related line of inquiry would be to approach production of identity hope in everyday work from looking at the specific set of work practices that produces and selects ideas. Oil exploration, for example, typifies a form of work dominated by symbolic analytic problem solving and demand for novelty through combining known information and earlier experiences in new ways. It is a form of work where ideas are the main input, content, and deliverable—akin to work in, for example, legal services, architecture work, advanced engineering, or research. James saw ideas as part of what could bring people out of their habituated standstill and energize them to function on a higher level of power (James, 1907/1977). If we accept that identity is as much a prospective as a retrospective phenomenon, people's engagement in ideas—whether we consider those ideas embryos for hydrocarbon prospects, scientific papers, or architectural projects—must matter considerably for what they hope for, and by implication, who they are. Ideas are likely to be generators of hope and sources of vitality, long before work unfolds into full-fledged positive dramas. Small how-to ideas may represent openings of the new long before they are wedded to why ideas. For a person engaged in exploration of oil, a new idea of interpreting old data into a new model may mean a play opener with vast consequences—or, more often, a pleasant little puzzle to dwell on for a few days. What kinds of ideas, at what level of development instigate hope in peoples' lives? After all, is not the combination of new ideas and hope exactly what people at work need to bring with them when being creative and venturing forth?

EXIT

In a thoughtful recent article, Webb (2007) has argued for talking about different modes of hope rather than hope as an undifferentiated experience. The overall approach taken in this chapter follows that line of argument in the sense that the experiencing of hope in organizational lives is likely to be as diverse and multifaceted as the streams of experience in which people find themselves immersed. Indeed, the analytical grid offered here, with teleological and relational addressivities of hope, reflects that observation. The experiencing of hope may be directed to goal attainment, to getting away from that which binds, or to opening up for new pathways. It is an experiencing that will often have improvement of individual lives as its referent but development of organizational lives as its context and the betterment of lives of others as its horizon.

In another sense, focusing on the experiencing of hope reveals a more radical conjecture, one easily lost from view if we downplay what James and Mead conceived as self as subject. Hope will always be directed toward the future and thrive on the new, the unforeseeable, and the will to move forward. Whether we focus on change efforts or everyday work, understanding hope in people's lives means acknowledging that positive identity construction is a potentially powerful force in social change.

ACKNOWLEDGMENTS

We thank the editors for their helpful suggestions to previous versions of this chapter. We also thank the people in our case organizations for their openness and unrestricted access—both the people of the two cases held anonymous and the people of Sydney Water Corporation through the North Side Tunnel Alliance and the Priority Sewerage Program Alliance. The writing of this chapter was sponsored by grant 187952/I40 of the Norwegian Research Council and Linkage grant LP0348816 of the Australian Research Council.

REFERENCES

Albert, S., & Whetten, D. (1985). Organizational identity. In L. L. Cummings & B. M. Staw (Eds.), *Research in Organizational Behavior, 7,* 263–295.

Augustine, St. (1998). *Confessions.* In H. Chadwick (Ed.), *Oxford world's classics.* Oxford, England: Oxford University Press. (Original work published ca. 397–400)

Bakhtin, M. (1981). *The dialogic imagination.* M. Holquist (Ed.), Austin, TX: University of Texas Press.

Bloch, E. (1995). *The principle of hope: Vol. 2.* (N. Plaice, S. Plaice, & P. Knight, Trans.). Cambridge, MA: MIT Press. (Original work published 1959)

Bandura, A. (1997). *Self-efficacy: The exercise of control.* New York: W. H. Freeman and Company.

Blasi, A. (1998). Identity and the development of the self. In D. K. Lepsley & F. C. Power (Eds.), *Self, ego and identity. Integrative approaches* (pp. 226–242). New York: Springer-Verlag.

Bosi, E. (1979). *Memoria a sociedade.* Sao Paolo, Brazil: T.A. Queiroz.

Bratteli, T. (1980). *Fange i natt og take* [Captive in night and fog, a paraphrase over the German 'Nacht und Nebel]. Oslo: Tiden Norsk forlag.

Bruner, J. (1990). *Acts of meaning.* Cambridge, MA: Harvard University Press.

Carlsen, A. (2006). Organizational becoming as dialogic imagination of practice. The case of the indomitable Gauls. *Organization Science, 17,* 132–149.

Carlsen, A. (2008). Positive dramas. Enacting self-adventures in organizations. *Journal of Positive Psychology, 3,* 55–71.

Carlsen, A., & Pitsis, T. S. (2008). Projects for life: Building narrative capital for positive organizational change. In S. R. Clegg & C. L. Cooper (Eds.), *The handbook of macro-organizational behavior.* London: Sage.

Carlsen, A. (2009). After James on identity. In P. S. Adler (Ed.), *Oxford handbook of sociology and organization studies: Classical foundations* (pp. 421–443). New York: Oxford University.

Crapanzano, V. (2003). Reflections on hope as a category of social and psychological analysis. *Cultural Anthropology, 18,* 3–32.

Crites, S. (1971). The narrative quality of experience. *Journal of the American Academy of Religion, 39,* 291–311.

Crites, S. (1986). Storytime: Recollecting the past and projecting the future. In T. R. Sarbin (Ed.), *Narrative psychology* (pp. 152–173). Westport, CT: Praeger Publishers.

Csikszentmihalyi, M. (1985). Emergent motivation and the evolution of the self. *Advances in Motivation and Achievement, 4,* 93–119.

Emery, F., & Thorsrud, E. (Eds.). (1976). *Democracy at work: The report of the Norwegian industrial democracy program.* Leiden; The Netherlands: Martin Nijhoff Social Sciences Division.

Emirbayer, M., & Mische, A. (1998). What is agency? *American Journal of Sociology, 104,* 962–1023.

Erikson, E. (1994). *Identity and the life cycle.* New York: Norton. (Original work published 1959)

Grant, A. M. (2007). Relational job design and the motivation to make a prosocial difference. *Academy of Management Review, 32,* 393–417.

Ibarra, H. (1999). Provisional selves: Experimenting with image and identity in professional adaptation. *Administrative Science Quarterly, 44,* 764–792.

Ibarra, H. (2003). *Working identity: Unconventional strategies for reinventing your career.* Boston: Harvard Business School Press.

Ibarra, H., & Lineback, L. K. (2005). What's your story? *Harvard Business Review, 83/1,* 64–71.

James, W. (1950). *Principles of psychology.* New York: Dover. (Original work published 1890)

James, W. (1977). The energies of men. In J. J. McDermott (Ed.), *The writings of William James. A comprehensive edition* (pp. 671–683). Chicago: The University of Chicago Press. (Original work published 1907)

Little, B. R., Salmela-Aro, K., & Phillips, S. D. (2007). *Personal project pursuit. Goals, action and human flourishing.* London: Lawrence Erbaum.

Ludema, J. D., Wilmot, T. B., & Srivastva, S. (1997). Organizational hope: Reaffirming the constructive task of social and organizational inquiry. *Human Relations, 50,* 1015–1053.

MacIntyre, A. (1981). *After virtue.* London: Duckworth Press.

Mattingly, C. F. (1998). *Healing dramas and clinical plots. The narrative structure of experience.* Cambridge, UK: Cambridge University Press.

McAdams, D. P. (1993). *The stories we live by.* New York: William Morrow.

McAdams, D. P. (1995). Introduction: Narrative construction of emotional life—commentary. *Journal of Narrative Life Histories, 5/3,* 207–221.

McAdams, D. P. (1997). The case for unity in the (post)modern self: A modest proposal. In R. D. Ashmore, & L. Jussim (Eds.), *Self and identity. Fundamental issues* (pp. 46–78). New York: Oxford University Press.

McAdams, D. P. (1999). Personal narratives and the life story. In A. Pervin, & O. P. John (Eds.), *Handbook of personality. Theory and research* (2nd ed., pp. 478–500). New York: Guilford Press.

McAdams, D. P. (2006). *The redemptive self: Stories Americans live by.* New York: Oxford University Press.

McAdams, D. P., Diamond, A., de St. Aubin, E., & Mansfield, E. (1997). Stories of commitment: The psychosocial construction of generative lives. *Journal of Personality and Social Psychology, 72*, 678–694.

McDermott, J. J. (2000). William James. Introduction. In J. Stuhr (Ed.), *Pragmatism and classical American philosophy. Essential readings and interpretive essays.* (2nd ed., pp. 140–151). New York: Oxford University Press.

Mead, G. H. (2000). The "I" and the "Me". In J. Stuhr (Ed.) *Pragmatism and classical American philosophy. Essential readings and interpretive essays.* (2nd ed., pp. 589–591). New York: Oxford University Press. (Original work published 1934)

Pitsis, T. S., Clegg, S., Marosszeky, M., & Rura-Polley, T. (2003). Constructing the Olympic dream: A future perfect strategy of project management. *Organization Science, 14,* 574–590.

Polkinghorne, D. E. (1988). *Narrative knowing and the human sciences.* Albany, NY: State University of New York Press.

Roberts, L. M., Dutton, J. E., Spreitzer, G., Heaphy, E., & Quinn, R. E. (2005). Composing the reflected best self portrait. Building pathways for becoming extraordinary in organizations. *Academy of Management Review, 30,* 712–736.

Rorty, R. (2000). *Philosophy and social hope.* New York: Penguin.

Ryan, R. M., & Deci, E. L. (2000). Self-determination theory and the facilitation of intrinsic motivation, social development, and well-being. *American Psychologist, 55,* 68–78.

Sachnowitz, H. (1976). *Det angår også deg* [It also concerns you]. Told to Arnold Jacoby. Oslo: Cappelen.

Sarbin, T. R. (1986). The narrative as a root metaphor for psychology. In T. R. Sarbin (Ed.), *Narrative psychology* (pp. 3–21). Westpost: Praeger Publishers.

Scheibe, K. E. (1986). Self-narratives and adventure. In T. R. Sarbin (Ed.), *Narrative psychology* (pp. 129–151). Westpost, CT: Praeger Publishers.

Schütz, A. (1967). *The phenomenology of the social world.* (G. Walsh & F. Lehnert, Trans.). Evanston, IL: Northwestern U. Press.

Schütz, A. (1970). *Reflections on the problem of relevance.* R. M. Zaner (Ed.). New Haven, CT: Yale University Press.

Shotter J., & Cunliffe, A. (2003). Managers as practical authors: Everyday conversations for action. In D. Holman & R. Thorpe (Eds.), *Management and language* (pp. 15–37). London: Sage.

Snyder, C. R. (Ed.). (2000a). *Handbook of hope.* San Diego: Academic Press.

Snyder, C. R. (2000b). Hypothesis: there is hope. In C. R. Snyder (Ed.). *Handbook of hope* (pp. 3–21). San Diego, CA: Academic Press.

Snyder, C. R. (2002). Hope theory: Rainbows in the mind. *Psychological Inquiry, 13,* 249–279.

Steinbeck, J. (1982). *The acts of King Arthur and his noble knights.* New York: Avenel Books.

Stotland, E. (1969). *The psychology of hope.* San Francisco: Jossey-Bass.

Turner, V. (1980). Social dramas and stories about them. In W. J. T. Mitchell (Ed.), *On narrative* (pp. 137–164). Chicago: The University of Chicago Press.

Webb, D. (2007). Modes of hoping. *History of the Human Sciences, 20,* 65–83.

White, H. V. (1973). *Metahistory: The historical imagination in nineteenth-century Europe.* Baltimore: Johns Hopkins University Press.

Wrzesniewski, A., & Dutton, J. E. (2001). Crafting a job: Revisioning employees as active crafters of their work. *Academy of Management Reviews, 26,* 179–201.

5

Me, Myself, and I: The Benefits of Work-Identity Complexity

Brianna Barker Caza and Marie Gee Wilson

CONTENTS

Work is an important source of meaning for adults (Collin & Young, 1992), and it is a primary way in which adults define their identity as a person (Gini, 1998). Yet, despite its centrality in modern life, self-definition within work organizations is a complex and multifaceted concept (Blader, 2007). Identity is not a simple or even a stable state; rather, one's sense of self is a time- and situation-bound composite of personal identities, social identities, and role identities that emerge within social structures and social interactions (Brewer & Gardner, 1996). As such, individuals have multiple ways of attaching meaning to their selves (James, 1890; Mead, 1934; Stryker, 1980, 1987), even within a single domain such as work.

Identity within the work domain has the potential to be particularly complex as individuals have multiple targets and levels for identification with their work (Albert & Whetten, 1985; Ashforth, Harrison, & Corley, 2008; Ashforth & Mael, 1996; Pratt & Foreman, 2000; Pratt & Rafaeli, 1997). Moreover, individuals must choose how much of their personal identities (e.g., hardworking, intelligent) or other nonwork social identities (e.g., gender, race) to bring into their work, which may further complicate the picture. For example, when focusing on identity at work, we, the authors, are simultaneously members of a profession, a discipline, a department, and a university. In addition, we can define ourselves at work as teachers, researchers, mentors, colleagues, and/or supervisors or subordinates. Lastly, we may further specify who we are by describing ourselves as hardworking female professors.

As this simple example illustrates, one's identity at work can be a complex phenomenon, with potential for both positive and negative outcomes. The complexity is derived from the numerous social and role-based ways of assigning meaning to the self at work and the high likelihood for coactivation of these various identities. This potential, as well as its impact, is a springboard for this chapter. Both social identity theory and role-identity theory have acknowledged that each individual can have multiple group memberships and occupy numerous roles simultaneously, and that understanding the implications of these multiple memberships and roles is important (Milkie & Peltola, 1999; Roccas & Brewer, 2002; Thoits, 1986; Voydanoff & Donnelly, 1999). Understanding how individuals react to complexity is an important step toward understanding the nature and impact of identity in work organizations. Although there is the potential for identity complexity at work in almost any occupation, the degree to which an individual defines their identity in a complex way is an individual difference. Specifically, the degree of identity complexity depends on the way in which an individual subjectively structures his or her perceptions of his or her work group memberships or work roles. As Roccas and Brewer (2002, p. 93) explain, "Complexity involves understanding what people mean when they say I am both 'A' and 'B.' "

The aim of this chapter is to detail the positive outcomes associated with work-identity complexity. Whereas many of the other chapters in this book are focused on the positivity of a particular identity, we are more interested in the positive outcomes of complex work-identity structures (i.e., interrelationships among identities). Identity complexity is a relative term. In the academic example above, we list 11 identities that we engage as academics when we are at work. However, the number of possible identities is not the source of complexity; identity complexity is a function of how individuals cognitively organize their various identities. Low complexity occurs when an individual does not differentiate between identities, focuses only on their intersection, or allows one identity to dominate another. Higher complexity requires the individual to focus on both integration and differentiation (Ashforth et al., 2008).

Much of previous research on identity complexity at work has focused on the problems associated with multiple identities (e.g., Gouldner, 1957), with the most extensive investigation regarding conflict between work and family role identities (e.g., Halpern & Murphy, 2005; Voydanoff & Donnelly, 1999). We extend and complement this research by providing a new perspective: the ways in which work-identity complexity can be a resource for increased positive functioning in contemporary organizational environments (Ashforth et al., 2008; Caza & Bagozzi, 2008).

The chapter is organized in five parts. First, we discuss the assumptions of work identity that are the basis for our definition and conceptualization of work-identity complexity in this chapter. Then, in the second section, we provide a brief review of the literature relating to work-identity complexity. In the third section, we present an organizing framework that articulates the beneficial outcomes associated with increased work-identity complexity. Specifically, we will talk about the complementary positive mechanisms of social identity-based work-identity complexity (cognitive buffering and increase in resource availability) and the positive mechanisms of role-based identity complexity (increased behavioral repertoire). In the fourth section, we provide evidence from two different field studies demonstrating how identity complexity can be a resource in the modern workplace and detailing the mechanisms we discussed in section three, as well as the positive outcomes associated with these mechanisms. Finally, in the last section, we outline a research agenda based on our model of work-identity complexity.

WORK-IDENTITY COMPLEXITY

Work identities are the various meanings an individual attaches to his or her self at work. They can be either social-based, role-based, or a combination of the two. Much of the current research on work identities has focused on social identities (Ashforth et al., 2008; Blader, 2007), or how individuals define themselves as members of a particular group at work (Ashforth & Mael, 1989; Tajfel, 1978). Although most of this work has focused on either demographically derived group identities or organizational identification (e.g., Ashforth & Mael, 1989; Ely, 1994; Tajfel, 1978), social identities can also derive from membership in occupational groups or other work subgroups (Alderfer & Smith, 1982; Hogg & Terry, 2000; Van Maanen & Barley, 1984).

Other sources of self-definition are the various roles individuals play at work. Role-identity theory, a derivative of symbolic interactionism, posits that the self-concept is a function of hierarchically structured role identities drawn from the extant social structure (Burke, 1980; McCall & Simmons, 1978; Stryker, 1980). Role identity refers to the characteristics and expectations that simultaneously create meaning an individual derives from his or her self in specific roles (Stryker, 1980) and defines social position in a community (Charng, Piliavin, & Callero, 1988). Whereas some identities are clearly either social or role identities, other types of work identities can be classified as both social and role identities. For example, an individual's professional identity as a nurse denotes not only her membership in a particular occupational group (social identity) but also her role as a caregiver (role identity).

Previous research has demonstrated that different identities are made salient in various roles and contexts (Ashforth & Johnson, 2001; Serpe & Stryker, 1987). However, more than one identity may be salient at the same time, a phenomenon termed coactivation (Blader, 2007). Coactivation increases the potential for complexity by simultaneously invoking more than one identity, their schemas, and associated actions, such that a broader array of resources and actions are available and can be cognitively integrated. In their chapter in this book, Rothbard and Ramarajan (Chapter 6) talk more extensively about the circumstances that lead to coactivation, the potential for conflict, and the ways to manage this coactivation to generate compatibility between multiple identities. In this chapter, we highlight that identities in the same domain, such as work, have a greater likelihood of coactivation because similar cues will make these identities salient, and that this coactivation can lead to greater complexity. To illustrate the common coactivation of multiple work identities, take, for example, a lawyer who is likely to be aware of both her organizational (law firm), community (membership in a political or activist group), and professional (lawyer) identities simultaneously when she makes a public submission on proposed legislation. The degree of identity complexity this lawyer will experience depends on how she reacts to this coactivation of multiple work identities and her cognitive integration of these diverse requirements and resources. For example, her roles as both community activist and lawyer may be integrated for an increased repertoire of advocacy behaviors.

Linville (1985, 1987) defines self-complexity as the structure of one's self-knowledge or the subjective organization of one's personal attributes. Building on this, identity complexity is defined as the degree of overlap an individual perceives to exist between his or her identity memberships (Roccas & Brewer, 2002). To have a complex identity structure, an individual must acknowledge and accept that memberships in multiple groups and roles may not be convergent or overlapping (Roccas & Brewer, 2002). Specifically, complexity involves distinctiveness and cognitive separation of identities. Therefore, although all individuals have multiple work group memberships and occupy various roles at work, the degree of their work-identity complexity depends on their individual cognitive representation of these memberships and roles. It is important to note that there is no implicit valence associated with complexity; the degree of overlap is not inherently negative or positive. Instead, it is how people perceive and react to complexity, or the lack of complexity, that is of interest.

IMPACT OF WORK-IDENTITY COMPLEXITY: A REVIEW OF THE LITERATURE

Given the attributes of work identities reviewed above, there is great potential for conflict *and* for complementarity of work identities (Ashforth & Kreiner, 1999; Halpern & Murphy, 2005; Stryker & Serpe, 1994). Yet to date, the majority of previous research on multiple identities at work has been primarily concerned with the incidence, impact, and management of identity conflicts, often at the level of role (e.g., Greenhaus & Beutell, 1985; Merton, 1957). Ashforth et al. (2008, p. 56) define an identity conflict as "an inconsistency between the contents of two or more identities, such as a clash of values, goals or norms." Identity conflicts at work can be divided into two broad categories: conflicts between work and work identities (e.g., conflicts between professional and organizational identities) and conflicts between work and nonwork identities (e.g., work-family conflict). Below, we provide a brief overview of these two literatures.

For the past half a century, organizational researchers have struggled to understand how professional workers manage their multiple organizational and professional role and social identities. Gouldner (1957) was one of the first to problematize professionals' multiple loci of work identification. He theorized that professionals had two bases for identification: their profession and their organization, and that this bilateral identification could lead to conflict. He argued that as a result professionals will identify with one at the expense of the other. As such, professionals could either be classified as "'cosmopolitans," who identified with their occupation, or "locals," who identified with their organization. Although more recent research has acknowledged that individuals can identify with both their occupation and organization simultaneously, the overall sense of conflict between the two still exists. For example, Ashforth et al. (2008) give an example of a lawyer who has to balance the demands of professional standards with her employer's financial interests. This example assumes a conflict between these interests, consistent with Freidson's (2001) argument that managerial or bureaucratic "logics" threatened the "soul" of professionals and professionalism.

Another body of literature that has predominantly focused on the conflictual side of work-identity complexity is work-family conflict. Research in this area has detailed mechanisms that contribute to the negative outcomes of complexity. Role conflict researchers have discussed the problem of complexity as being the result of one role putting undue strain on another (role strain) (Merton, 1957). This argument is consistent with findings that the possession of multiple identities may exacerbate the negative effect of adversity on psychological health (Biddle, 1986). Based on the depletion argument of identity complexity, researchers suggest that engagement in multiple, and often conflicting, roles can lead to a drain of psychological and physiological resources (Edwards & Rothbard, 2000; Greenhaus & Beutell, 1985; Rothbard, 2001). Therefore, the greater number of roles or identities an individual has, the greater the potential for role conflict and overload, as well as resource depletion (Goode, 1960; Merton, 1957). The assumption behind this argument is that individuals have a fixed amount of cognitive resources available, and when these resources are spread between too many roles or used for resolving conflicts between roles, it reduces the resources available for cognitive, affective, and behavioral health, resulting in poor outcomes for the individual and the organization. This is most commonly framed in work-family scenarios that position parents (usually mothers) as stressed and overloaded in the intersection of primary caregiver and worker (Halpern & Murphy, 2002; Kossek & Ozeki, 1998; Waring & Fouché, 2007).

Research has also focused on the potential negative impact of multiple social identities. The dominant perspective in psychological research on multiracial identities is the "marginal man" theory (Shih & Sanchez, 2005). As Shih and Sanchez (2005, p. 570) describe, a "marginal man was thought to be an individual caught between two cultures but who, in reality, was not a member of either world." This theory focuses on the deficits and problems of multiple racial identities and/or complex self-structure. For example, research indicates that the multiracial identity construction process is more difficult, increasing the possibility of poor psychological adjustment for the multiracial individual (Lyles, Yancey, Grace, & Carter, 1985). Transferred to the workplace, this research suggests that the more complex an individual's work identity is, the more "marginal" the individual may become in the workplace and the less supported he or she may feel with reduced personal and social resources.

In each of these research trajectories—cosmopolitan-local, work-family, and multiracial—the primary underlying focus has been on the negative consequences of identity complexity, particularly the division of energy and resources as a consequence of identity conflict. This dominant focus on the negative paints a fairly grim, but incomplete, picture of work-identity complexity. The identity conflict literature assumes that individuals have a fixed amount of resources available to them, and that multiple role identities require balancing that is likely to result in overload and strain (Marks, 1977; Rothbard, 2001). Yet, a growing body of literature challenges this assumption by highlighting instances in which identity complexity is not inherently problematic and may have positive consequences (Rothbard, 2001; Thoits, 1983, 1986).

For example, even the cosmopolitan-local "conflict" has been disputed by more recent work. Berger and Grimes (1973) demonstrated that the structure of Gouldner's (1957) argument was not robust, and subsequent research established that the professional and organizational identities could be reconciled with professional values and behaviors (Goldberg, 1976) were not inherently in conflict (Glaser, 1963) and could lead to both enhanced cognitive and behavioral outcomes (Glaser, 1963; Li, 2008), as well as enhanced commitment to multiple, complex role identities (Dukerich, Golden, & Shortell, 2002).

Similarly, a growing amount of research in work-family conflict also sheds light on the potential for complementarity of identities. For example, Rothbard (2001) tested and found support for the enrichment hypothesis, which is when engagement in one role leads to engagement in another. Rothbard's thesis is also consistent with Thoits' (1986) study of multiple-role identities and their positive relationship to reduced distress in a population of working adults.

Research in social psychology has also begun to uncover the positive aspects of identity complexity, which can be extended to demonstrate the positive potential of work-identity complexity. For example, research on self-complexity has demonstrated that individuals often effectively organize their self-concept in ways that simultaneously promote self-unity, allow them to maintain high self-complexity, and reduce fragmentation of the self (Linville, 1985; Showers, 1992; Showers & Zeigler-Hill, 2003). Further, research on multiracial identities has demonstrated psychological benefits to having a complex identity (Shih & Sanchez, 2005). In contrast to the depletion argument, these perspectives assume that individuals do not have fixed resources but instead have an expandable amount of emotional and psychological energy (Marks, 1977).

These positive consequences are not just limited to individuals. There is evidence that these benefits may have a spillover effect on the organizations in which they work. For instance, in the discretionary performance literature, Coyle-Shapiro, Kessler, and Purcell (2004) have found that "citizenship" behaviors are best explained by an expansion of roles linked to positive individual, group, and organizational consequences.

As noted above, research increasingly takes a contingent or contextual approach to identity complexity; complexity is not inherently positive or negative; rather, an individual's reaction to this complexity is what determines the valence of the outcomes (Rothbard, 2001). As previous research has indicated, work-identity complexity may indeed be negative where coactivated identities evoke irreconcilable cognitive and/or behavioral repertoires, either through the nature of the requirement (e.g., opposite actions would be required) or temporal competition (even if not functionally inconsistent, time permits only one type of response). The possibility of conflict is potentially exacerbated by identity across multiple domains (e.g., work and family). For example, a parental caregiver may experience temporal inconsistencies when he or she has to choose between finishing a required report or attending a PTA meeting, as well as role conflict (between caregiver and professional, between parent and employee). However, in other circumstances, possession of multiple identities at work may lead to positive and profoundly functional outcomes for individuals and organizations (see Halpern & Murphy, 2005; Rothbard, 2001). In particular, identity complexity within a single domain, such as work, may provide less dissonance and greater opportunity for positive outcomes, including enhanced performance and psychological resilience. As the professional identity literature demonstrates, many role-identity requirements are reconcilable and positive (Goldberg, 1976; Li, 2008), and nonoppositional differences provide opportunities for creative adaptation (Caza & Bagozzi, 2008; Pratt, Rockmann, & Kaufmann, 2006) and repertoire expansion (Coyle-Shapiro et al., 2004; Marks & Scholarios, 2007).

WORK-IDENTITY COMPLEXITY AS RESOURCE

In this section, we build on the mounting body of research on the positive outcomes of work-identity complexity, extending it to propose that work-identity complexity can be a resource for individuals in organizations. Then, we present a framework detailing mechanisms and consequences associated with social identity complexity and role-identity complexity, respectively. Specifically, we draw on work by Hobfoll (1989) and Callero (1994) in defining work-identity complexity as a resource. Hobfoll's (1989) Conservation of Resource theory (COR) is based on the idea that individuals will strive to retain, protect, and build resources at all times.

According to Hobfoll's theory, there are various categories of resources. Energy resources are objects, personal characteristics, or conditions that can be used to help gain other resources, such as money or social competence (Hobfoll, 1988, p. 26). Identity complexity can be considered an energy resource in that it can also be used to attain other needed resources, such as direct or social support. Research by Callero and colleagues has demonstrated the utility of conceptualizing identities as resources for both individuals and organizations (Callero, 1986, 1994, 1998; Piliavin, Callero, & Grube, 2002). Callero (1994) built on Baker and Faulkner's (1991) concept of role identity as a resource and argued that roles are structures that can be used to help establish routines and pattern work in organizations.[1] Further, he pointed out that human agency is expressed through the use of roles as resources. Callero (1994) demonstrated that roles can be used by individuals for thinking, for acting, for creating structures, and for political ends. Therefore, work-identity complexity could increase integration and cognitive availability of roles to individuals, and therefore the potential resources available.

Positive Mechanisms of a Work-Identity Complexity

As we pointed out earlier, various work identities can be categorized as social identities, role identities, or both. Although both social and role-based components of work-identity complexity can be beneficial and a resource for individuals, they may operate through slightly different, yet complementary, mechanisms. Specifically, drawing from social identity theory, we propose that complex social identities (a) present cognitive resources that help buffer individuals psychologically from potential work conflicts, and (b) provide important direct and social resources. Building on role-identity theory, we propose that complex role identities increase positive functioning through enhanced availability and use of behavioral resources.

Complex Social Identities and Increased Cognitive Resources

Emerging psychological research on multiracial identities suggests that possessing complex social identities may increase individuals' psychological health and ability to withstand adversity (e.g., Shih & Sanchez, 2005). Specifically, empirical research in the area of self-complexity has found support for the cognitive buffering hypothesis (e.g., Linville, 1987; Shih, 2004; Thoits, 1986). The basic logic behind this hypothesis is that greater self-complexity provides a buffer against the adverse consequences of stress and will therefore moderate the negative psychological and physical effects of stressful events (Linville, 1987). Having a greater number

---

[1] Although there are some conceptual differences between roles and identities, these differences are inconsequential to the current argument. Callero (1994, p. 239) points out, "When roles are used as a resource to define self and other, I believe it is conceptually appropriate to refer to such roles as identities." Therefore, the use of "roles" in this section refers to what we have discussed as "role identities."

of self-representations that are distinct protects individuals from negative affective reactions to experienced stress by allowing them to contain negative thoughts and feelings to only one part of their self-representation, buffering other aspects of the self and thereby decreasing the incidence of physical reactions such as illness and depression.

LaFromboise, Coleman, and Gerton (1993) also find psychological benefits in possessing complex social identities through buffering individuals psychologically and behaviorally from adversity. Further, they argue that bicultural individuals may be better at negotiating conflict because of the experience they have had in balancing the competing demands of two cultures. Therefore, they are better prepared psychologically to respond to complex social situations. This research suggests that individuals who have more than one socially derived work identity may possess greater cognitive resources to both address the complexity that their work environment demands and extend themselves into diverse environments.

Complex Social Identity and Increases in Social and Instrumental Resources

Multiple and complex work group memberships are also beneficial as they increase the potential sources of social and instrumental support available for individuals. Each work group with which an individual identifies (e.g., organizational, professional, departmental) is another source of social identification and membership (Tajfel, 1978; Tajfel & Turner, 1986). As a result of membership in these groups, the individual will have social resources from which to draw. Both experimental and field research demonstrate that individuals perceive, provide, and receive more social support from in-group members (e.g., Levine, Prosser, Evans, & Reicher, 2005; Reicher, Cassidy, Wolpert, Hopkins, & Levine, 2006).

Increased social resources are linked to a host of positive outcomes for individuals. For example, social support has been linked to resilience in the face of adversity (e.g., Luthar, Cicchetti, & Becker, 2000; Masten & Reed, 2002; Rutter, 1985, 1987). Research also indicates that the social support provided by identification with work groups protects individuals from burning out (Haslam, O'Brien, Jetten, Vormedal, & Penna, 2005). Additionally, increased social resources lead to better adjustment to new situations (Swanson & Power, 2001). Increased social resources not only help individuals to feel affectively supported but also provide direct instrumental resources such as information and advice. Individuals with multiple social identities are more likely to have networks composed of multiple weak ties, which will better allow them to bridge structural holes and allow them to draw on a wider pool of resources from others (Granovetter, 1973).

Complex Role Identities and Increased Behavioral Repertoire

In addition to aiding individuals by increasing the availability of important cognitive, social, and instrumental resources, increased work-identity complexity may make individuals better able to respond to a variety of situations (Hoelter, 1985). The theoretical basis for this argument lies in role theory. Identities provide schemas[2] that guide behavior and action in organizations (Callero, 1994). When individuals identify with multiple roles within their work, they will have a wider range of behavioral "scripts" or "schemas" available for their use; therefore, their options to act and react to a variety of situations increases.

Complexity can also increase the skills underlying behaviors; possessing more than one identity may increase competence in multiple domains (LaFromboise et al., 1993). Greater work-identity complexity can lead to greater potential for novel and perhaps even creative responses during times of adversity. Just as bilingualism may increase the ability to negotiate complex social settings, those with complex work identities may be also fluent in more than one work practice. For example, a certified nurse midwife (CNM) who is both a nurse and a midwife may understand both the "language" and work practices of nurses, as well as those of midwives (Caza & Bagozzi, 2008). Moreover, this CNM will have enhanced resources in any work situation as she can draw on either schema when the situation calls for it (Hoelter, 1985).

---

[2] A schema is "a cognitive structure that represents organized knowledge about a given concept or type of stimulus. A schema contains both the attributes of the concept and the relationships among the attributes" (Fiske & Taylor, 1984, p. 140). By work practice schemas, we refer to individuals' internalized scripts for how they should carry out their work. The values of a profession as depicted in a code of ethics will provide guidelines for interaction with individuals of other professions, as well as recommendations for methods of interacting with patients. Each of these schemas provides individuals with a script for action (Fiske & Taylor, 1984). Therefore, the possession of a number of different professional self-schemas should enable the individual to have a broader repertoire of work practices to employ during any given time in an organization.

Individuals may also be able to combine elements of different schemas to create new and novel responses. Pratt and colleagues' (2006) study of professional identity formation in residents demonstrated how individuals employ identity customization techniques to change how they view their work. Individuals drew from other identities to enhance, patch, or split their current identity and expand their behavioral range during a period of uncertainty. By extension, identity customization and combinatorial processes are likely to increase individuals' ability to creatively respond when faced with adversity by increasing their discretion to act in a given situation (Caza, 2008). Individuals who have the ability to add complexity to their work identity not only can employ a variety of practice schemas but also can create new ones when the situation requires it.

Below, we draw from our fieldwork to link the resources derived from complex work identities to two positive outcomes. In the first project reported, we explore the contribution of complex work identity to increased resilience in the face of adversity, providing rich examples of increased cognitive, social, and instrumental resources from complex social identities, as well as increased behavioral repertoires from role-identity complexity. In the second study, we examine how complex work identity leads to increased organizational citizenship behavior, illustrating how role complexity interacts with social identity complexity to increase the behavioral repertoire with regard to positive, discretionary behaviors.

FIELD RESEARCH 1: RESILIENCE IN THE FACE OF CHALLENGING WORK SITUATIONS

Increased work-identity complexity helps individuals to operate functionally in times of uncertainty. In a survey of 227 CNMs who faced a significant critical adversity at work, Caza and Bagozzi (2008) found that increased work-identity complexity was negatively associated with burnout and positively associated with resilience at work. Resilience at work is displayed when individuals not only avoid the negative consequences of stress (e.g., burnout) but also emerge from stressful situations with more knowledge and competence, thereby allowing their professional careers to follow a positive developmental trajectory (Caza & Bagozzi, 2008). Exploring the connection between work-identity complexity and functioning in the face of adversity more deeply, interviews with CNMs revealed that work-identity complexity increased CNM's ability to react positively to both small and large workplace challenges. As one CNM explains:

> When I first began [in this profession], I had a straightforward view of who a midwife is. And, I was strict about staying within those lines; I did things by the book. But that was hard because not everyone appreciated it. Now, I can wear many different hats. If she wants a natural birth, I am a midwife. If she wants a painless birth, I will get her epidural and be her nurse. It can be tiring, you know, playing so many parts, but, it is the only way to do my job well.
> —CNM6, university hospital

The CNM quoted in this passage talks about the multiple identities that are all a part of her work identity. In this passage, she admits that a complex work identity can be tiring but emphasizes that it is beneficial in allowing a greater range of behavioral responses in any situation. This echoes similar findings in research conducted by Thoits (1983, 1986) about the benefits of holding multiple identities outweighing the costs associated with them. Additionally, this passage suggests that greater complexity increases the CNM's ability to customize her care to her patient's needs, suggesting it helps her do her job better. Other CNMs further expanded on this idea by explaining that increased identity complexity allowed them to provide more "patient-centered" care, a hallmark of midwifery practice (Rooks, 1997). In her words:

> I have lots of different roles within midwifery. In fact, I define it differently all the time because I really teach to my audience. I like to think that my practice changes with every patient I care for.
> —CNM2, birth center

Another way increased identity complexity served as a resource for CNMs was through increasing the scope of their practice. CNMs reported that the complexity of their identity allowed them to engage in more varied work activities. As one describes:

> My job is not an easy one to understand because I don't fit neatly into any particular category. And, I am okay with that because it means that I am able to be flexible in my care regimen. Although I prefer women to be able to trust their bodies and have a natural birth, I am perfectly capable of getting them important medical interventions if something is going wrong.
> —CNM5, big hospital

In addition to allowing a broader range of behavioral options in any given situation, increased identity complexity seemed to play an important role in helping CNMs respond cognitively, affectively, and behaviorally with unexpected critical incidents in the workplace. One way this occurred was through social support. In the following passage, a CNM describes how her diverse social network derived from multiple work-identity memberships helped her to cope with a tragic situation in which a baby died during birth:

> It was one of the dark times in my career because no one wants to lose a patient, especially a baby. But, it was during that time that I realize how great the people are that I work with. I got calls from nurse-midwives across the state offering me condolences, advice, and support. And, the doctors I worked with helped reassure me that I did everything correctly and it was just one of those things that are out of our control.
>
> —CNM8, city hospital

In this passage, it is notable that the CNM mentioned the social support she gained from individuals within her organizational group and within her occupational group, demonstrating the diversity of her network. In another interview, a CNM explained how relying on her complex work identity provided her with behavioral resources that enabled her to respond quickly to an unexpected critical situation with a patient:

> I walked into the room and I knew immediately that something was wrong. And, honestly I just went on autopilot. Normally, I do not advocate for medical interventions, but I was a nurse for 10 years before becoming a midwife, and I am still a nurse in many ways—I do know how to get an IV line going. So, I walked in, and did what I needed to get her prepped and called my back-up doctor for surgery because I knew that baby needed to come out immediately. But, at the same time, I was able to stay by her side, and be there psychologically, supporting her as a midwife should even though I could not catch the baby.
>
> —CNM12, university hospital

Both of these CNMs talked about the critical role their work-identity complexity played in helping them to be resilient in the face of critical workplace adversities. CNM8 explained how the social resources she derived from her complex social identities (various group memberships) helped her to psychologically deal with the trauma she endured.

Additionally, she noted that this support helped her to learn important lessons about her work that she can use in the future. CNM12 described an incident in which her complex work identity helped her to form a positive behavioral response in the face of adversity. She was able to combine the work-practice schemas derived from her various role identities to act resiliently in the face of a critical work incident.

FIELD RESEARCH 2: ORGANIZATIONAL CITIZENSHIP BEHAVIORS

In a project investigating organizational citizenship behaviors (OCBs; Organ, 1988) among professionals, we conducted a dyadic survey of professional employees and their supervisors to determine levels of OCB. We then interviewed 129 high and 91 low OCB employees to elicit their rationales for engaging in positive discretionary behaviors. Open coding of interview responses yielded consistent relationships between citizenship behaviors and complex work identities; more than 70% of all responses linked social and/or role identities to citizenship behaviors. Complex social identities played a particularly large role in explaining OCB; three fourths (76%) of the participants stated that they engaged in some of the OCB activities because of diverse coworker expectations of social exchange and intergroup reciprocity, as well as their profession, juxtaposing professional role identity, with multiple (social) team identities.

> Well, it's good for the team, keeps us all together . . . we expect of it each other . . . I am able to balance everyone's expectations of me with who I am as a [lawyer].
>
> —Attorney, commercial firm

Based on frequency of mention, repetition, and emphasis, coworker and team member expectations of in-group exchange and actions—reflecting social identities—far outweighed supervisory expectations or job requirements in explaining positive, discretionary actions for all participants (both high and low OCB). However, there was one important difference in the way that high- and low-OCB participants discussed their behavior, and that was in reference to both "role" and "professionalism" (both

role-identity[3] markers). Whereas only 18 (20%) of the 91 low-OCB participants mentioned professional roles and practice, all of the 129 high-OCB
participants mentioned them. Professional role issues were ubiquitous
among the high-OCB participants' responses; they discussed "how I see
this role" (92% of high-OCB), "role expectations" (81%), and "being a
professional role model or mentor" (85%) in addition to social identity-
based expectations. Thus, high-OCB participants linked the ideas of role
identity, social identity, and discretionary behavior consistently (95%) and
with great emphasis. Moreover, the more complex and multifaceted the
references to both social and role identities, the greater and more elaborate
the discretionary, positive behaviors displayed. Both low- and high-OCB
employees described complex social identities and the resources these provided, in terms of team exchanges, reciprocity, and support. Only high-
OCB employees, however, also included complex role identities, moving
beyond simple exchanges to high levels of novel, beneficial, and discretionary behavior. The example below of a chef in a busy cafe details one such
narrative, outlining the multiple identities invoked, their coactivation and
interrelationship, and the subsequent mechanisms and consequences:

> during service, I am all things to all people. I am a chef ... [and] team leader
> creating a smooth-running "back of house" ... and mentor developing my
> sous chef toward sole-charge ... and [for] the owner, ensuring nothing is
> wasted, portions are cost-effective.... I am always carrying my [being a
> chef] with me, but I have to include the other ingredients, these other parts
> of what I am.... I can act in so many ways ... that is what makes the job so
> interesting.

We can see that both social and role identities are in play throughout
his experience of work through both personal expectations and those of
various stakeholders. This complexity results not only in the positive affect
and interaction but also an increased behavioral repertoire, including citizenship behaviors, that is, both "helping" behaviors to support and assist
other members of the kitchen and restaurant staff, and "conscientiousness"
behaviors that enable higher levels of integrated performance of both individuals and the kitchen overall.

---

[3] References to the profession could also be seen as social identification; however, the participants
tied these statements strongly to role identifiers, both the use of the term "role" or "role model"
and a high level of abstraction of expectations.

> Being a professional, I pull this together for my team.... I can be and act like a dozen different people.... I can adapt and blend what I do.... To help others, to go "above and beyond" any job description.
>
> —Architect, property development firm

> Because I wear multiple hats, I am not constrained.... I can be creative in how I act, and those actions often far exceed the boundaries of what the "job" is.... I think I have a lot more room to maneuver when I can be both engineer and designer at the same.
>
> —Civil engineer, construction company

In particular, the complex work identity combining both complex social and role-based identities has led to the incorporation of a wide array of discretionary helping behaviors (including OCBs) that allow the role-based behavioral repertoire to leverage the cognitive and social resources gained through complex social identities.

IMPLICATIONS FOR THEORY AND PRACTICE

In this chapter, we have described and illustrated a resource-based view of work-identity complexity in organizations. Because work identities span both social and role-based identities, we drew on research in both social identity theory and role-identity theory to explain how work-identity complexity can be seen as a resource for individuals in modern organizations. Specifically, we argued that membership in multiple social work-identity groups can lead to increased cognitive and social resources. Second, we posited that a greater number of role identities can lead to an increase in behavioral resources. In turn, we proposed that these increased cognitive, social, and behavioral resources derived from work-identity complexity can lead to positive individual functioning in workplaces, in both common-place and exceptionally challenging situations. We demonstrated how these mechanisms played out in the context of two specific categories of positive functioning: resilience at work and OCBs.

The exemplar below, from our fieldwork, illustrates the potential for work-identity complexity as a resource for effective cognitive, social, and behavioral functioning in both routine and challenging work situations.

Mike is a research nurse, managing research projects in a large, urban, inpatient mental health unit. As part of his portfolio, he manages the quality improvement process. On a day-to-day basis, Mike operates as a researcher and nurse, as well as a quality consultant, and views these as distinct and somewhat divergent roles. He does not view this as problematic; rather, they allow him both an enlarged scope of activities and access to knowledge and social networks. Indeed, he sees himself as making "best use of strategic ambiguity" by crafting his job to optimize the range of responsibilities. He operates in a way that clearly exceeds any individual job description and contributes positively to the organization: a recognized organizational "citizen." When a suicide occurred in the unit, the complexity also afforded him with cognitive and behavioral options—to assess the contributing quality issues in existing committees, to research similar clinical events, or to integrate the new experience through reflection into his clinical practice. The complexity also allowed reframing of the death. As a nurse, suicide is a cause for deep professional concern and personal distress, but this is moderated by review of the research to contextualize the event (reframing), and working with the quality committee to establish initiatives that increase support and monitoring for patients at risk (using social networks).

Drawing from a complex work identity, Mike accrues myriad resources from both the social and role bases of this complexity, including cognitive buffering, social resources, and increased behavioral scope in a challenging situation, as well as an increased behavioral repertoire and opportunity for social exchange in day-to-day working. Although complexity is positive for Mike in the example given, we have acknowledged that identity complexity is not inherently positive or negative. Instead, we suggested that positive outcomes are the result of complex, coactivated identities that are complementary or at least reconcilable in creative, adaptive ways. Whether any particular identity structure is experienced as simple or complex, conflictual or competing, or enriching rather than depleting is a fruitful direction for future research.

Future research may address the influence of individual differences and the organizational context. Identity formation is a cognitive process, and as such the complexity of one's identity is subject to individual differences in preferences, perception, and cognition. Individuals have varying needs and preferences for identity complexity (Roccas & Brewer, 2002). Research should examine how these individual differences in preferences for identity complexity impact the strategies individuals use to manage their various work group memberships and work roles, as well as the implications of these management strategies. Other individual difference variables that may play a role in shaping how individuals respond to identity complexity may include individual creativity and tolerance for ambiguity.

Another important area for future research is to understand how individuals' perceptual framing (e.g., how compatible individuals perceive their identities to be) may explain why some experience overload where others find resilience. As previously mentioned, different individuals may perceive the same combination of work identities in dramatically different ways. Understanding why some individuals perceive compatibility and complementarity when others perceive conflict would be an important element in understanding how individuals react to their experienced complexity.

At a practical level, organizations may do a number of things structurally and culturally that have the potential to influence people's ability to use their identity complexity as a resource. First, organizations may influence employees' perceptions of the benefits (or drawbacks) to work-identity complexity. An organization that standardizes behavioral protocols or generates strong role-based behavioral norms may restrict complexity. On the other hand, an organization in which diversity of background, identity, and/or perspective is specifically encouraged and in which novel behaviors and/or views are valued may stimulate both more complex self-meaning and creative responding.

An organization may also influence the types of multiple identity management techniques that individuals use. As we mentioned earlier, work-identity complexity can be a resource when these identities have the potential for complementarity and are coactivated. If an organization encourages segmentation of social or role identities at work, the resources of work-identity complexity may not be actualized. For example, if a chef is only seen as "'hired hands," those engaged in the workplace may suppress more complex aspects of identity, and their cognitive, affective, and behavioral work repertoire. This aspect of organizational framing might also have similar impact on work/nonwork-identity complexity.

Similarly, organizations may influence the degree to which individuals see their multiple identities as complementary or conflicting. Nurse-midwives often note that organizations are critical to seeing the two roles—nurse and midwife—as complementary or as antithetical. Similarly, physicians who also practice naturopathy, osteopathy, or other less traditional forms of medicine may be marginalized in some clinical settings and welcomed in others.

Finally, organizations can reward positive behavior associated with increased identity complexity and in doing so increase the likelihood that individuals will use their identity complexity as a resource. For example, one of the CNMs quoted above talked about how she combined her roles to act resiliently when faced with a patient crisis. The organization could have viewed her behavior as being in conflict with standard hospital practice procedures, in which case she may have even been reprimanded for her resilient behavior. In contrast, the hospital she works for complimented her on "thinking outside the box" (her words) and being able to respond in the face of a potential disaster. In doing so, they provided an incentive for her to find ways to continue to use her work-identity complexity as a resource in the future. Thus, the potential for positive multiple identities challenge us, as well, to "think outside the box" and engage with the model of positive complexity and its interaction across levels of analysis.

REFERENCES

Albert, S., & Whetten, D. (1985). Organizational identity. In L. L. Cummings, & B. M. Staw (Eds.) *Research in organizational behavior* (Vol. 7, 263–295). Greenwich, CT: JAI Press.

Alderfer, C. P., & Smith, K. K. (1982). Studying intergroup relations embedded in organizations. *Administrative Science Quarterly, 27,* 17–40.

Ashforth, B., & Mael, F. (1989). Social identity theory and the organization. *Academy of Management Review, 14,* 20–39.

Ashforth, B. E., Harrison, S. H., & Corley, K. (2008). Identification in organizations: An examination of four fundamental questions. *Journal of Management, 34,* 325–374.

Ashforth, B. E., & Johnson, S. A. (2001). Which hat to wear? The relative salience of multiple identities in organizational contexts. In A. Hogg, & D. J. Terry (Eds.), *Social identity processes in organizational contexts.* Sussex, England: Psychology Press.

Ashforth, B. E., & Kreiner, G. E. (1999). How can you do it? Dirty work and the challenge of constructing a positive identity. *Academy of Management Review, 24,* 413–434.

Ashforth, B. E., & Mael, F. (1996). Organizational identity and strategy as a context for the individual. In J. A. C. Baum, & J. E. Dutton (Eds.), *Advances in strategic management* (Vol. 13) (pp. 19–64). Greenwich, CT: JAI Press.

Baker, W. E., & Faulkner, R. R. (1991). Role as a resource in the Hollywood film industry. *American Journal of Sociology, 97,* 279–309.

Berger, P. K., & Grimes, A. J. (1973). Cosmopolitan-local: A factor analysis of the construct. *Administrative Science Quarterly, 18,* 223–235.

Biddle, B. J. (1986). Recent developments in role theory. *Annual Review of Sociology, 26,* 183–193.

Blader, S. L. (2007). Let's not forget the "Me" in "Team": Investigating the interface of individual and collective identity. In C. Bartel, S. L. Blader, & A. Wrzesniewski, (Eds.), *Identity and modern organization* (pp. 63–84). London: Routledge.

Brewer, M. B., & Gardner, W. (1996). Who is this "we"? Levels of collective identity and self representations. *Journal of Personality and Social Psychology, 71,* 83–93.

Burke, P. J. (1980). The self: Measurement requirements from an interactionist perspective. *Social Psychology Quarterly, 43,* 18–29.

Callero, P. L. (1986). Toward a median conceptualization of role. *Sociological Quarterly, 27,* 343–358.

Callero, P. L. (1994). From role-playing to role-using: Understanding role as a resource. *Social Psychology Quarterly, 57* (special issue on conceptualizing structure), 228–243.

Callero, P. L. (1998). Crisis and reform in the classroom. *Social Psychology Newsletter.* Fall.

Caza, B. B. (2008). *Individual functioning in the face of adversity at work: An identity-based perspective.* Manuscript in preparation.

Caza, B. B., & Bagozzi, R. (2008). *Individual functioning in the face of adversity at work.* Manuscript in preparation.

Charng, H.-W., Piliavin, J. A., & Callero, P. L. (1988). Role identity and reasoned action in the prediction of repeated behavior. *Social Psychology Quarterly, 51,* 303–317.

Collin, A., & Young, R. A. (1992). Constructing career through narrative and context. In R. A. Young, & A. Collins (Eds.), *Interpreting career: Hermeneutical studies of lives* (pp. 1–12). Westpost, CT: Praeger.

Coyle-Shapiro, J. A.-M., Kessler, I., & Purcell, J. (2004). Exploring organizationally directed citizenship behaviour: Reciprocity or "It's my job"? *Journal of Management Studies, 41,* 85–106.

Dukerich, J. M., Golden, B. R., & Shortell, S. M. (2002). Beauty is in the eye of the beholder: The impact of organizational identification, identity, and image on the cooperative behaviors of physicians. *Administrative Science Quarterly, 47,* 507–533.

Edwards, J. R., & Rothbard, N. P. (2000). Mechanisms linking work and family: Clarifying the relationship between work and family constructs. *Academy of Management Review, 25,* 178–199.

Ely, R. J. (1994). The effects of organizational demographics and social identity on relationships among professional women. *Administrative Science Quarterly, 39,* 203–238.

Freidson, E. P. (2001). *The third logic.* Chicago: The University of Chicago Press.

Gini, A. (1998). Work, identity and self: How we are formed by the work we do. *Journal of Business Ethics, 17,* 707–714.

Glaser, B. G. (1963). The local-cosmopolitan scientist. *The American Journal of Sociology, 69,* 249–259.

Goldberg, A. I. (1976). The relevance of cosmopolitan/local orientations to professional values and behavior. *Work and Occupations, 3,* 331–356.

Goode, A. W. (1960). *Medicine, science and the law.* London: Street & Maxwell.

Gouldner, A. W. (1957). Cosmopolitans and locals: Toward an analysis of latent social roles—I. *Administrative Science Quarterly, 2,* 281–306.

Granovetter, M. (1973). The strength of weak ties. *American Journal of Sociology, 78,* 1360–1380.

Greenhaus, J. H., & Beutell, N. J. (1985). Sources of conflict between work and family roles. *Academy of Management Review, 10*, 76–88.

Halpern, D. F., and Murphy, S. E. (2002). *From work-family balance to work-family interaction: Changing the metaphor.* New York: Routledge.

Haslam, S. A., O'Brien, A., Jetten, J., Vormedal, K., & Penna, S. (2005). Taking the strain: Social identity, social support and the experience of stress. *British Journal of Social Psychology, 44*, 355–370.

Hobfoll, S. E. (1988). *The ecology of stress.* New York: Hemisphere.

Hobfoll, S. E. (1989). Conservation of resources: A new attempt at conceptualizing stress. *American Psychologist, 44*, 513–524.

Hoelter, J. W. (1985). The structure of self-conception: Conceptualization and measurement. *Journal of Personality and Social Psychology, 49*, 1392–1407.

Hogg, M. A., & Terry, D. J. (2000). Social identity and self-categorization processes in organizational contexts. *Academy of Management Review, 25*, 121–140.

James, W. (1890). *The principles of psychology.* New York: Henry Holt.

Kossek, E. E., & Ozeki, C. (1998). Work-family conflict, policies, and the job-life satisfaction relationship: A review and directions for organizational behavior-human resources research. *Journal of Applied Psychology, 83*, 139–149.

LaFromboise, T., Coleman, H. L. K., & Gerton, J. (1993). Psychological impact of biculturalism: Evidence and theory. *Psychological Bulletin, 114*, 395–412.

Levine, R. M., Prosser, A., Evans, D., & Reicher, S. D. (2005). Identity and emergency intervention: How social group membership and inclusiveness of group boundaries shape helping behavior. *Personality and Social Psychology Bulletin, 31*, 443–453.

Li, L. (2008). *Entrepreneurial professionalism in academia.* Unpublished doctoral dissertation, The University of Auckland, Auckland, New Zealand.

Linville, P. W. (1985). Self-complexity and affective extremity: Don't put all of your eggs in one cognitive basket. *Social Cognition, 3*, 94–120.

Linville, P. W. (1987). Self-complexity as a cognitive buffer against stress-related illness and depression. *Journal of Personality and Social Psychology, 52*, 663–676.

Luthar, S. S., Cicchetti, D., & Becker, B. (2000). The construct of resilience: A critical evaluation and guidelines for future work. *Child Development, 71*, 543–562.

Lyles, M. R., Yancey, A., Grace, C., & Carter, J. H. (1985). Racial identity and self-esteem: Problems peculiar to biracial children. *Journal of the American Academy of Child Psychiatry, 24*, 150–153.

Marks, A., & Scholarios, D. (2007). Revisiting technical workers: Professional and organizational identities in the software industry. *New Technology, Work, and Employment, 22*, 98–117.

Marks, S. R. (1977). Multiple roles and role strain: Some notes on human energy, time and commitment. *American Sociological Review, 42*, 921–936.

Masten, A. S., & Reed., M. J. (2002). Resilience in development. In C. R. Snyder, & S. J. Lopez, (Eds.), *The handbook of positive psychology* (pp. 74–88). Oxford, England: Oxford University Press.

McCall, J. G., & Simmons, J. L. (1978). *Identities and interactions.* New York: Free Press.

Mead, G. H. (1934). *Mind, self, and society: From the standpoint of a social behaviorist.* Chicago: University of Chicago Press.

Merton, R. K. (1957). *Social theory and social structure.* Glencoe, IL, Free Press.

Milkie, M. A., & Peltola, P. (1999). Playing all the roles: Gender and work-family balancing act. *Journal of Marriage and the Family, 61*, 476–490.

Organ, D. W. (1988). *Organizational citizenship behavior: The good soldier syndrome.* Lexington, MA: Lexington Books.

Piliavin, P. L., Callero, P. L., & Grube, J. (2002). Role as a resource for action in public service. *Journal of Social Issues, 58,* 469–485.

Pratt, M. G., & Foreman, P. O. (2000). Classifying managerial responses to multiple organizational identities. *Academy of Management Review, 25,* 18–42.

Pratt, M. G., & Rafaeli, A. (1997). Organizational dress as a symbol of multilayered social identities. *Academy of Management Journal, 40,* 862–898.

Pratt, M. G., Rockmann, K. W., & Kaufmann, J. B. (2006). Constructing professional identity: The role of work and identity learning cycles in the customization of identity among medical residents. *Academy of Management Journal, 49,* 235–262.

Reicher, S., Cassidy, C., Wolpert, I., Hopkins, N., & Levine, M. (2006). Saving Bulgaria's Jews: An analysis of social identity and the mobilisation of social solidarity. *European Journal of Social Psychology, 36,* 49–72.

Roccas, S., & Brewer, M. (2002). Social identity complexity. *Personality and Social Psychology Review, 6,* 88–106.

Rooks, J. P. (1997). *Midwifery and childbirth in America.* New York: Temple University Press.

Rothbard, N. P. (2001). Enriching or depleting? The dynamics of engagement in work and family roles. *Administrative Science Quarterly, 46,* 655–684.

Rutter, M. (1985). Resilience in the face of adversity: Protective factors and resistance to psychiatric disorder. *British Journal of Psychiatry, 147,* 598–611.

Rutter, M. (1987). Psychosocial resilience and protective mechanisms. *American Journal of Orthopsychiatry, 57,* 316–331.

Serpe, R. T., & Stryker, S. (1987). The construction of self and the reconstruction of social relationships. *Advances in Group Processes, 4,* 41–66.

Shih, M. (2004). Positive stigma: Resilience and empowerment in overcoming stigma. *The Annals of the American Academy, 571,* 175–185.

Shih, M., & Sanchez., D.T. (2005). Perspectives and research on the positive and negative implications of having multiple racial identities. *Psychological Bulletin, 131,* 569–591.

Showers, C. (1992). Evaluatively integrative thinking about characteristics of the self. *Personality and Social Psychology Bulletin, 18,* 719–729.

Showers, C., & Zeigler-Hill, V. (2003). Organization of self-knowledge: Features, functions, and flexibility. In M. Leary, G. MacDonald, & J. Price Tangney (Eds.), *Handbook of self and identity* (pp. 47–67). London: Guilford Press.

Stryker, S. (1980). *Symbolic interactionism: A social structure version.* Menlo Park, CA: Benjamin/Cummings.

Stryker, S. (1987). Identity theory: Developments and extensions. In K. Yardley, & T. Honess (Eds.), *Self and identity: Psychosocial perspectives* (pp. 89–103). London: John Wiley & Sons Ltd.

Stryker, S., & Serpe, R. T. (1994). Identity salience and psychological centrality: Equivalent, overlapping, or complementary concepts. *Social Psychology Quarterly, 57,* 16–35.

Swanson, V., & Power, K. G. (2001). Employees' perceptions of organizational restructuring: The role of social support. *Work and Stress, 15,* 161–178.

Tajfel, H. (1978). Social categorization, social identity, and social comparison. In H. Tajfel (Ed.). *Differentiation between social groups: Studies in the social psychology of intergroup relations* (pp. 61–76). London: Academic Press.

Tajfel, H., & Turner, J. C. (1986). The social identity theory of intergroup behavior. In S. Worchel, & W. G. Austin (Eds.) *Psychology of intergroup relations* (pp. 2–24). Monterey, CA: Brooks/Cole.

Thoits, P. A. (1983). Multiple identities and psychological well-being: A reformulation and test of the social isolation hypothesis. *American Sociological Review 48,* 174–187.

Thoits, P. A. (1986). Multiple identities: Examining gender and marital status differences in distress. *American Sociological Review, 51,* 259–272.

Van Maanen, J. V. B., & Barley, S. R. (1984). Occupational communities: Culture and control in organizations. In B. M. Staw, & L. L. Cummings (Eds.) *Research in organizational behavior* (Vol. 6, pp. 287–365). Greenwich, CT: JAI Press, Inc.

Voydanoff, P., & Donnelly, B. W. (1999). Multiple roles and psychological distress: The intersection of the paid worker, spouse and parent roles with the adult child. *Journal of Marriage and the Family, 61,* 725–738.

Waring, M., & Fouché, C. (2007). *Managing mayhem: Work-life balance in New Zealand.* Wellington, New Zealand: Dunsmore Press.

6

Checking Your Identities at the Door? Positive Relationships Between Nonwork and Work Identities

Nancy P. Rothbard and Lakshmi Ramarajan

CONTENTS

A woman, a mother, a manager, a team member—individuals often have several identities, both in and outside of the workplace, that are important to them (James, 1890; Roccas & Brewer, 2002; Rosenberg, 1997). Typically, one assumes that although individuals have many identities, identities are often triggered or activated one at a time in relevant domains. For example, one's work identity may be activated while at work, and one's parent identity may be activated at home. However, research also suggests that identities often spill over (Rothbard, 2001; Rothbard & Edwards, 2003) or are intermingled (Ashforth, Kreiner, & Fugate, 2000) across domains. Thus, getting a telephone call about a child while at work might trigger an employee's family identity while his or her work identity is already activated. Given the existence of multiple identities, it is important to understand how coactivation, the activation of more than one identity at a time, occurs and is managed by individuals, particularly because the ensuing relationship between identities may be positive or negative. Having positive relationships between coactivated identities is important because it can lead to beneficial outcomes for individuals such as enrichment through the generation of positive emotion (Rothbard, 2001), greater integrative complexity and problem-solving ability (Ramarajan, 2008), and greater effectiveness and resilience (Caza & Wilson, Chapter 5, this volume) or innovation (Cheng, Sanchez-Burks, & Lee, 2008). Thus, our focal question is, "under what conditions do individuals experience simultaneously activated identities positively?"

Individuals can experience identities that are simultaneously activated negatively or positively. A negative coactivation is experienced as *conflicting*, that is, identities are experienced in opposition or tension with one another. A positive coactivation is experienced as *compatible*, that is, identities are experienced as complementary or synergistic with one another (Ramarajan, 2008). In the above example of the telephone call regarding a child while at work, the employee may feel that the identity of being a parent and an employee are in contradiction with one another, or conversely that these two identities can be mutually enhancing. Although conflict between identities has been extensively studied (Greenhaus & Beutell, 1985), positive relationships between identities have been less investigated. The notion of compatibility between multiple identities builds on research on enrichment between multiple roles, which suggests that positive affect and synergistic information from one role or identity can spill over and be accessed in another role (Greenhaus & Powell, 2006; Rothbard, 2001). In this chapter on positive identities, we specifically focus on compatibility between an individual's multiple identities, that is, *positive relationships between identities* when more than one identity is activated.

More specifically, in this chapter we examine factors that can enable individuals to experience positive relationships or compatibility between coactivated identities. We argue that factors such as status, respect, and temporal control that allow for greater control over whether and when identities are coactivated, as well as factors such as cognitive routines for managing multiple identities simultaneously, can lead individuals to experience greater compatibility between multiple coactivated identities. In other words, we suggest that identity compatibility is influenced by (a) the extent to which individuals can control the coactivation of identities, and by (b) the routinization of identity coactivation, which arises as individuals cope with situations in which coactivation occurs frequently.

Although the definition of a positive identity is a question that recurs throughout this book, in this chapter, we do not examine whether identities themselves are positive or negative in content. Similarly, we do not examine the positive effects of identities. Rather, we examine individuals' experience of *positive relationships* between their many identities (i.e., coactivated identities that are experienced compatibly as complementary or amenable to synthesis).

DEFINITIONS OF POSITIVE IDENTITY AND RELATED CONCEPTS

Our explanation of compatibility among identities relies on several core concepts. We define these core concepts starting with the definition of identity itself. We next discuss the following concepts: identity activation, the existence of multiple identities and coactivation of identities, and relationships of conflict or compatibility among identities. These core concepts underlie our model of positive identity relationships.

Identity

We rely on a definition of identity as a set of subjective knowledge about the self that is considered to mean "I am" (Kihlstrom & Klein, 1994). It is how an individual defines himself or herself. Research in psychology shows that people can define themselves as members of groups (collective or group identity), as partners in close relationships (relational or role identities), and in terms of personal aspects and traits (personal or individual identities) (Brewer & Gardner, 1996). For example, individuals may define themselves based on membership in both their organization and their profession (Johnson, Morgeson, Ilgen, Meyer, & Lloyd, 2006). Similarly, individuals may define themselves based on multiple roles such as work and family (Lobel, 1991; Rothbard & Edwards, 2003). In this chapter, we treat personal, social, and role identities as equivalent to the extent that individuals psychologically define themselves based on these various characteristics.

Activation

Because identities are a type of knowledge (knowledge about oneself), identities can be activated. Activation is the level of excitation of knowledge in the brain (Cronin, 2004; Higgins, 1991, 1996). Identity activation occurs when individuals are thinking about who they are. Activation is associated with identity salience in that salience relates to how cognitively accessible a particular identity is to the individual (Ashmore, Deaux, & McLaughlin-Volpe, 2004; Stryker & Serpe, 1994). Identities are often activated by the situation, that is, particular conditions may activate a relevant identity (Bargh, Chen, & Burrows, 1996). For example, talking to one's parents or a telephone call about one's children may activate one's family identity. Identities may also be chronically activated, that is, individuals may often define themselves in a particular way, such as "woman," regardless of whether a particular situational cue, which activates one's female identity, is present.

Coactivation of Multiple Identities

As noted above, individuals often have multiple identities that are important to them (Rosenberg, 1997); indeed, individuals often hold up to five to seven important identities in general (Roccas & Brewer, 2002), although they may all be at various states of activation at a given time. Previous literature on both role and social identities has proposed that individuals primarily enact one identity at a time. For example, the role identity literature proposes the notion of a salience hierarchy, where specific situations trigger the prominence of a particular identity such that as one identity becomes activated and rises in the hierarchy in a specific situation, the level of activation of other identities falls (Stryker & Serpe, 1994). Likewise, in the social identity literature, the notion of functional antagonism conveys a similar idea; a particular situation may trigger or activate one identity, whereas other identities are consequently suppressed (Turner et al., 1987). Because of the prominence of ideas like salience hierarchy and functional antagonism, the identity literature does not focus on the notion of coactivation, the simultaneous salience or activation of more than one identity. Coactivation builds on the logic of associative networks in cognitive psychology in which multiple knowledge nodes (in this case—identities) can be activated simultaneously. Furthermore, in contrast to identity research, which builds on the notion that one identity is activated at a time depending on a particular situation or domain, we focus on situations in which boundaries such as those between work and nonwork domains are being crossed and multiple identities are activated together. That is, in many situations, more than one identity may be activated simultaneously (Blader, 2007). For example, an individual may have a strong identity as a gay/lesbian employee but also work for an institution such as the military, and this professional identity may also be important. Clearly, both of these identities could be activated at the same time in the work domain.

As multiple identities can be activated by the situation or be chronically activated, it is likely there is also an interaction between chronic and situational activation. Whereas identities at high levels of chronic activation mean that a person's identities are activated regardless of the situation, identities at low levels of chronic activation may become more salient in a particular situation. For example, for a woman whose female identity is chronically activated, being in a work meeting with all male senior executives may make this female identity even more salient to her in this situation and may simultaneously coactivate her organizational identity.

One question that arises when considering the coactivation of identities is under what conditions are we more likely to experience coactivation of work and nonwork identities? Opportunities for coactivation may be most likely to occur when the boundaries between identities are relatively permeable. Research on boundary theory suggests that individuals cognitively and behaviorally demarcate physical, temporal, and social arenas as a way to order and organize their environment (Nippert-Eng, 1995), creating domains such as "home" and "work." Further, boundary theory suggests that individuals can separate or *segment* identities in terms of time, place, and behavior, such that there are few opportunities for values and beliefs associated with one role or identity to influence another role or identity (Ashforth et al., 2000; Nippert-Eng, 1995; Rothbard, Phillips, & Dumas, 2005). Boundary theory also suggests that individuals can *integrate* identities, such that identities intermingle and can be enacted across different times and places (Ashforth et al., 2000; Nippert-Eng, 1995; Rothbard et al., 2005).

We argue that coactivation of work and nonwork identities occurs when identities are integrated and the boundaries between identities are relatively permeable. Here, given our interest in coactivated identities, we explore only situations of integration. The definition of integration does not necessarily mean that coactivated identities need to be related to one another positively, in a compatible way. In fact, such coactivated, integrated identities could just as easily be related negatively, such that they are conflicting. Our key point is that coactivation whether it is experienced as compatible or conflicting requires integration. Without integration of identities (for instance, if identities are segmented), there is no potential for coactivation.

Another important distinction is that, in contrast to work on boundary theory and identity integration that examines role *transitions*, defined as "the psychological movement between roles, including disengagement in one role and engagement in another" (Ashforth et al., 2000, p. 472), we examine identity *coactivation*. For example, a role identity transition would entail deactivating the work identity when receiving a call from home while at work. Whereas transitioning between identities entails disengaging from an initial identity when engaging in another identity, coactivation involves adding onto or engaging in a second, third, or fourth identity while other identities remain activated.

Conflict and Compatibility Between Identities

A second question that arises when considering coactivation of more than one identity simultaneously is *how* do we experience the coactivation of identities, that is, positively or negatively? In research on work-family and bicultural identities, two identities can be related to one another in terms of either conflict or compatibility. Much previous work on identities focuses on tension or opposition between identities. For instance, work-family research has examined how work and family identities may often collide (Greenhaus & Powell, 2003; Lambert, 1990; Lobel, 1991; Rothbard & Edwards, 2003), whereas studies of immigrant acculturation discuss conflict between cultural identities (Benet-Martinez & Haritatos, 2005; Berry, 1997). Building on this literature, identity conflict occurs when the information associated with one identity acts as a constraint or is antithetical to another identity (Ramarajan, 2008). For example, when two identities such as parent and worker intermingle in the workplace, one may feel conflict because one is torn between being a parent and worker. When two identities are coactivated and conflicting, often we may suppress one of the opposing cognitions, or we may experience negative affect, stress, and tension because of opposing cognitions (Festinger, 1957). Research indicates that negative affect restricts an individual's cognitive capacity and inhibits accessible cognitions and motivation to pursue and approach multiple goals (Aarts, Custers, & Holland, 2007; Clore & Huntsinger, 2007; Isen, 1990; Staw & Barsade, 1993). In either case, individuals experiencing identity conflict are restricting their access to the full complexity of their multiple identities.

More recently, research has begun to examine how identities can relate to one another positively. Consistent with this idea is the notion that identification with and engagement in a role can be enriching to other roles and identities (Greenhaus & Powell, 2006; Rothbard, 2001). Building on this literature, identity compatibility occurs when information associated with one identity is complementary or amenable to synthesis with another identity (Ramarajan, 2008). In the earlier example of the intermingling of parental and worker identities in the workplace, one may instead feel compatibility because these identities are complementary to one another. For example, it may be that a lawyer brings in a new client to the practice through his involvement in his child's school functions. When coactivated identities are experienced as compatible, individuals are likely to feel positive emotion (Greenhaus & Powell, 2006; Rothbard, 2001). Positive emotion has been shown to be associated with a broadening and exploratory approach in terms of one's cognitive capacity, accessible cognitions, and one's actions (Clore & Huntsinger, 2007; Fredrickson, 2001; Isen, 1990). Thus, individuals experiencing identity compatibility are maintaining access to the full complexity of their multiple identities.

Boundary Crossover

As we note above, the integration of identities makes it more likely that individuals will experience simultaneously coactivated identities.

However, Ashforth et al. (2000) propose that one of the costs of integration is greater undesired interruptions (i.e., boundary violations, and these interruptions are seen as potentially detrimental, giving rise to conflict between one's identities). In fact, although the terms "boundary violation" and "interruption" seem to inherently presume a negative consequence, that is, identity conflict, it is also possible that individuals can experience multiple coactivated identities as compatible. Hence, we propose the term *boundary crossover* as a more neutral term to allow for the possibility of both identity conflict and identity compatibility. Boundary crossovers are a specific case of coactivation of identities in which the two or more coactivated identities cross a boundary such as work-family or professional-personal roles.

In sum, individuals may experience the coactivation of work and nonwork identities when these identities are integrated across work and nonwork boundaries (see Figure 6.1). Moreover, such coactivations can be experienced not just as conflicting but also as compatible.

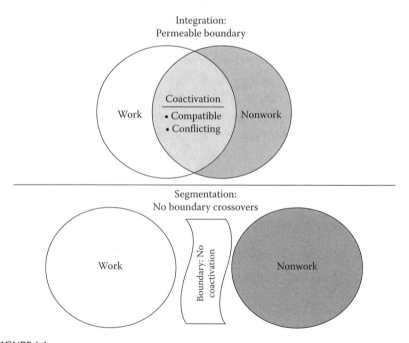

FIGURE 6.1

Boundary crossovers, integration, and coactivation between work and nonwork identities.

COMPATIBLE IDENTITY COACTIVATION

Given that individuals can experience both conflict and compatibility among their coactivated identities, we now turn our focus to compatibility. To reiterate, our research question is, "when is compatibility between coactivated identities likely to be experienced?" We propose two factors: (a) whether one has control over the coactivation of identities, and (b) whether the coactivation of the particular identities is routinized. We predict that when individuals do not have control over their environment (and thus the choice of when or which identities are activated) and the identities that are coactivated are not habitually activated together, they would experience the lowest levels of compatibility between identities. Whereas when they are in control of their environment and the coactivation of identities is routinized, they will have the highest levels of compatibility between identities (see Figure 6.2).

Control Over the Activation of Identities

The importance of agency and control over one's environment is well studied in psychology (Skinner, 1996). An individual's sense of control over

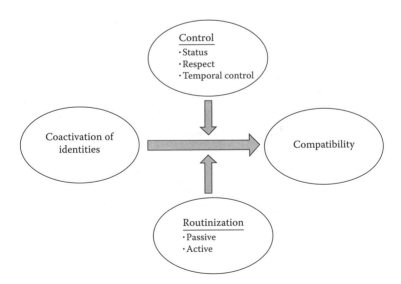

FIGURE 6.2
The relationship between coactivated identities and compatibility.

his or her own fate has been implicated in a variety of positive work outcomes, including well-being and motivation (Ng, Sorensen, & Eby, 2006). In Karasek's demand-control model for instance, high demands and high control lead to positive energy and health outcomes, not stress (1979). Likewise, to the extent that the individual experiences control over boundary crossovers, there may be potential for compatibility in situations of identity integration. This is an area of research on which boundary theory currently does not focus, but where we believe there is an opportunity for much future work. Several factors may allow individuals to experience more agency and control over the coactivation of multiple identities. Here we explore three examples of such factors that are likely to lead to greater psychological control for the individual—status, respect, and temporal control—and discuss how and why they may influence compatibility.

Status

Recent work has defined status as the respect, deference, and influence individuals have in the eyes of others (Anderson, John, Keltner, & Kring, 2001; Anderson, Srivastava, Beer, Spataro, & Chatman, 2006; Berger, Cohen, & Zelditch, 1972; Goldhamer & Shils, 1939; Ridgeway & Walker, 1995). From a multiple identity perspective, status is an important factor to consider because higher status individuals often have more flexibility with fulfilling identity and role expectations than lower status individuals (Ridgeway, 1982). For example, a higher status person, such as a more experienced team member, may be more able to respond to a telephone call about a sick child (and experience these two identities as compatible) than a newcomer to the team, who may experience the telephone call as representing a choice between his work and family identities. Thus, higher status individuals may have the ability to act and behave in ways that create greater identity compatibility because they have more idiosyncrasy credits that allow for their behavior to be interpreted more positively by others. This freedom from fear about the negative interpretation of boundary crossovers may allow higher status individuals more positive or compatible experiences of coactivated identities.

Respect

Respect and identity are closely intertwined. An individual's identity is often an internalized reflection of the approval and recognition that is gained from others (Mead, 1934). Individuals feel respected when they perceive they are being treated with care for their identity and positive self-regard (Ramarajan, Barsade, & Burack, 2008). Respect for one's identities is important in part because individuals have a powerful desire to have their self views verified by others (Polzer, Milton, & Swann, 2002; Swann, Milton, & Polzer, 2000). In contrast, when individuals feel disrespected, it can cause a person's self-concept to collapse (Honneth, 1992, p. 189). Status and respect are also closely related, as the definition of status above indicates. Indeed, Tyler and colleagues have argued that respect for a person is often communicated as one's status within one's group and enhances one's group identity (de Cremer & Tyler, 2005; Smith & Tyler, 1997; Tyler, 1999; Tyler & Blader, 2001). Like status, respect may also increase one's control or perceived control over the situation, increasing compatibility between identities. However, respect differs from status in that an organization might instill a culture of respect that applies broadly regardless of status distinctions (Phillips, Rothbard, & Dumas, in press). Such a culture of respect could make up for the lack of control individuals feel in low-status positions.

Moreover, although respect is a reflected appraisal based on others' responses to an individual, feeling respected may increase one's sense of control over one's identity (i.e., who one is or can be) in a given situation. Specifically, in terms of identities, research shows that respect for an individual's identities is important and influences their desire to be part of a group (Barretto and Ellemers, 2002; Tyler & Blader, 2001). For example, Barretto and Ellemers (2002) conducted an experiment in which they showed that if an individual chose a particular group identity (categorized herself in a certain group) and this choice of identity was respected, she would also be more likely to identify with *an additional* group that she had not chosen, when compared with an individual whose choice of identity was disrespected. In the above example, it seems likely that respecting individuals' important identities not only may have acted as an indicator of status but also perhaps increased individuals' feelings of control over "who they were" in a given setting, whereas disrespecting important identities reduced their sense of control. Therefore, by positively influencing one's self-perceptions, respect may enable one to enact multiple nonwork identities in the workplace rather than suppress them.

Because respecting individuals' nonwork identities can increase their sense of control in organizations, respect can provide an important buffer when organizational and nonorganizational identities are coactivated. For example, in organizations that outsource many of their functions to overseas call centers, call center employees are often forced to take on organizational identities that imply they belong to the organization's home country as opposed to their own country. In this example, the boundary crossover occurs when one's preexisting national identity is invoked in the workplace along with an organizational identity. In such situations, if managers respected the employee's national identity, it is possible that employees would feel greater compatibility between their own preexisting identities and the various organizational identities they were asked to enact.

Temporal Control

Time also affects the extent to which a boundary crossover may be experienced as desirable or as a boundary violation and has the potential to increase one's sense of control over coactivation of identities. In the work-family literature, time-based conflict is one aspect of conflict between work and family roles (Greenhaus & Beutell, 1985). However, far from simple constraints on the physical amount of time one spends enacting one's identities, time-based conflict can also be psychological; that is, a person can be enacting one identity (such as employee) physically but be consumed by thoughts of family while at work (Cardenas et al., 2004; Carlson & Frone, 2003; Friedman & Greenhaus, 2000). However, there is potential for such boundary crossovers to lead to experiences of compatibility rather than conflict between identities to the extent that there is control over when identities are coactivated. For example, in a qualitative study of working mothers, Morehead (2001) examined a sample of nurses who were also mothers and found that they temporally synchronized both their work and mother roles, such that they mothered at work and vice versa. Specifically, they could be thinking about a work project while at home or considering their family obligations while at work, and this synchronization allowed them to fulfill both these important identities simultaneously.

Similarly, in Hackman and Oldham's (1980) job design model, job autonomy specifically refers to the ability to schedule the pace and timing of one's tasks. Individuals with the ability to exert control over when boundary crossovers occur, for instance, by scheduling tasks and activities that require activating another identity may thus experience compatibility. For example, scheduling regular check-ins with one's childcare provider allows one to choose when to coactivate identities; as one mother in Morehead's (2001) study notes, this checking-in allows her to be a better worker as it relieves her of worry (p. 366).

In considering temporal control and its effects on the compatibility or conflict experienced between multiple identities, an important analogy can be drawn to research on task interruptions (Jett & George, 2003). Jett and George (2003) note that various types of interruptions, such as intrusions, breaks, and distractions, can have positive and negative effects on individuals and organizations. Intrusions, which are unexpected interruptions of work flow that bring one's activities to a temporary halt, could result in a sense of time pressure and disrupt the individual's focus (negative consequence) but could also result in information sharing and feedback from the source of the interruption that could enhance one's work performance (positive consequence). Just as with these task-related interruptions, temporal control over when the boundary is breached (i.e., when coactivation occurs) is likely to enhance compatibility and lead to positive performance outcomes, such as greater information sharing and incubation of creative ideas. For example, recent work indicates that compatibility between identities can result in greater integrative complexity of thought and greater problem solving (Ramarajan, 2008).

In understanding the effects of control on compatibility between multiple identities, we note that all three factors—status, respect, and temporal control—can work in concert with one another, and all are ways and means by which individuals can gain or exhibit control in organizations, although they operate somewhat differently. For example, temporal control is different from status because one could be in a type of job where one has control over time (job autonomy) but low status based on the nature of the work, for example, a junior software programmer in an organization. On the other hand, status can afford individuals greater temporal control as they have more decision latitude around how they perform their work (Karasek, 1979). Moreover, as noted above, respect can be a marker of status or a substitute for status in conferring a sense of control.

Routine Coactivation of Identities

Whereas control over coactivation is one way in which individuals may experience compatibility among multiple identities, the routinization of coactivation of identities can also have an effect on compatibility. For example, a person might often have a dual role as a father and manager in a family business. Although initially this boundary crossover might be difficult to manage as these two identities have the potential for conflict, over time the person might become accustomed to enacting both the father and manager roles simultaneously, thus routinizing a coactivation of identities. Research on cognitive processing suggests that over time individuals develop automatic processing, that is, "the activation of a learned sequence of elements in long-term memory that is initiated by appropriate inputs and then proceeds automatically—without subject control, without stressing the capacity limitations of the system, and without necessarily demanding attention" (Schneider & Shiffrin, 1977, p. 1). Below, we examine the effect of routine coactivation, defined as expected and familiar coactivation of particular identities, on compatibility among identities and vice versa, the initial experience of compatibility among identities which may lead to more routinized coactivations.

As identities are coactivated and boundary crossovers occur, the individual may experience these coactivations as either positive (compatible) and/or negative (conflicting). According to psychological research on behavioral activation (approach) and behavioral inhibition (avoidance) systems, individuals are motivated to seek and approach positive stimuli and affect and withdraw from negative stimuli and affect (Carver & White, 1994; Gray, 1990; Taylor, 1991). For example, research on the "positivity offset" suggests that individuals' approach systems react more strongly than their avoidance system in neutral environments, and that this might be because of evolutionary reasons, that is, those who responded with approach motivations to neutral environments were better able to explore and learn and hence survive (Cacioppo & Gardner, 1999). Another more proximal reason for seeking compatibility between identities is that positive emotion and experience is inherently rewarding (Fredrickson, 1998). Thus, over time individuals will keep seeking and hence repeating the sequence of coactivation that leads to compatibility. Eventually, as a result of repetition, specific coactivations get embedded in individuals' long-term memory and become automatically executed (Schneider & Shiffrin, 1977; Smith, 1984; Smith & Lerner, 1988). On the other hand, to the extent that individuals are motivated to avoid negative stimuli and affect, identity coactivations that frequently result in conflict are likely to become suppressed or avoided.

The literature on behavioral scripts (Gioia & Poole, 1984, p. 450), that is, "a knowledge structure that fits predictable, conventional or frequently encountered situations" also supports the idea that a script can be acquired through the repetition of experience and that rewards and reinforcement are important for solidifying a particular sequence of actions into a script.[1] An evolutionary model of mental processes also suggests a similar outcome; mental processes, which meet a selection criterion (in this case, the experience of compatibility), are most likely to be retained (Campbell, 1965; Weick, 1979) and become routinized (Nelson & Winter, 1982), whereas those that do not meet the selection criteria (such as coactivations that result in conflict) are likely never to become routinized and will be experienced as nonroutinized effortful processing. Overall then, through the mechanisms of reinforcement and selection based on individuals' preference for positive affect and stimuli, a particular coactivation is more likely to be repeated, and hence more likely to be routinized, the more it is associated with experiences of identity compatibility rather than identity conflict. Importantly, because these routines evolve over time, the relationship between routines and compatibility is likely to be reciprocal, whereby compatibility fosters the development of routinized coactivation, and routinized coactivation can in turn enhance compatibility.[2]

Passive Adaptation

The relationship between compatibility and routinized coactivation can occur in two ways. On the one hand, there is a passive adaptation process, whereby individuals may be exposed to numerous situations over time where they receive feedback through which they "learn" (Carver & Scheier, 1981; Schneider & Shiffrin, 1977) which coactivations are most likely to result in compatibility versus those coactivations that are most likely to result in conflict. As individuals are motivated to seek positive experiences and affect (Carver & White, 1994; Gray, 1990; Taylor, 1991),

---

[1] Similarly, in boundary theory, when discussing transitions between roles (disengagement in one role and engagement in another), Ashforth et al. (2000) discuss routinized role transitions in terms of transition scripts. Through experience over time and repeated execution of a role transition, individuals develop a transition script or routine that becomes relatively automatically executed.

[2] Routinized coactivation occurs when coactivated identities require limited cognitive processing. Chronic coactivation occurs when coactivated identities are readily accessible. Therefore, it is possible for both temporarily and chronically coactivated identities to be routinely coactivated. Thus, chronic coactivation and routine coactivation are distinct constructs.

the coactivations that result in compatibility are likely to be repeatedly evoked. Thus, over time through this selection process the individual develops a routine or automatic coactivation of identities that are experienced as compatible. In the example of the family business above, if the person frequently experiences his father and manager identities as compatible, then to the extent that individuals seek and maintain positive stimuli, the individual will be drawn to opportunities to experience his father and manager identities simultaneously, and so the coactivation of these identities is likely to become habituated and routinized. Thus, routinized coactivation and subsequent identity compatibility can occur through a passive adaptation to environmental influences.

Active Adaptation

A second way in which routinely coactivated identities may be compatible involves a more active adaptation process whereby individuals may "create" compatibility between identities. Once compatibility is established, individuals will keep seeking and repeating the coactivation of the identities that were made compatible, thus laying the groundwork for the development of a routine.

When and how might individuals actively create compatibility between identities? Although individuals may create compatibility between any identities that are likely to be coactivated, chronically activated identities in particular may pose a compelling reason for creating compatibility. As we note above, chronically activated identities are those identities that remain activated across situations. By definition, they are frequently activated and are not easily discarded. Thus, repeated coactivations of chronically activated identities with other chronically or situationally activated identities are likely to occur. This means the potential for both identity conflict and identity compatibility may be high with chronically activated identities. To avoid conflict between one's chronically activated identities and other identities, individuals may resort to creating compatibility as a coping strategy.

One way in which individuals may create compatibility is by cognitively *reframing* one's identities to emphasize features that are congruent or reframe the identity dimensions in ways that are valued (Derks, van Laar, & Ellemers, 2006, 2007; Lazarus & Folkman, 1984). For example, consider a boundary crossover when a female leader has both her female and leader identities coactivated while at work. When confronted with the stereotype of leaders having masculine characteristics such as being directive and task oriented, female leaders may choose to emphasize features of leadership that are more stereotypically feminine, such as being participative and relational (see Eagly & Johnson, 1990). Thus, a female leader could cognitively reframe her nonwork identity (in this case being a woman) to be compatible with her leader identity as a way to avoid negative affect and stimuli every time her female identity is activated at work. As an example, Roberts (2007) describes the case of Jeannette Clough, CEO of Mount Auburn Hospital, who authentically drew on multiple identities such as her nursing background to lead a dramatic turnaround at the hospital. In this case, Clough may have cognitively reframed her low-status gendered nursing identity to be more compatible with her identity as CEO. Specifically, she may have reframed for herself how her nursing identity was compatible and even enriching to her leadership identity because it gave her insight into marshaling resources in a hospital environment and provided a deep understanding of decisions about patient care.

A second way in which individuals may create compatibility between a chronically activated identity and other identities is by *choosing* to enact only those identities that are complementary or synergistic to the chronically activated identity they cannot discard. Recent work on the low number of women in the computer science profession suggests that women actively choose not to take on "computer scientist" as a professional identity because the prototype of the computer scientist as a "geek" does not fit their self-image as a woman (Cheryan, Plaut, Davies, & Steele, 2007). Consider the career choice facing an Asian student. On the one hand, this student could choose to be a doctor or an engineer, to the extent that Asian families tend to value these professions and Asian children tend to choose these professions (Fouad et al., 2008; Tang, 2002; Tang, Fouad, & Smith, 1999). On the other hand, the student could choose to be an artist or an actor. The professional identities presented by the latter career choices (artist, actor) may have much greater potential to raise identity conflicts, whereas the former career choices (doctor, engineer) may have much greater potential to raise identity compatibility when the person's Asian and professional identities are coactivated. Over time, given their basic tendency to seek positive affect and stimuli, individuals may be more likely to choose professional identities that are more likely to lead to identity compatibility when work and nonwork identities are coactivated. That is, the boundary crossover of professional and ethnic identities is carefully chosen. Thus, identity compatibility and the subsequent routinized coactivation can also occur through an agentic process of reframing or choosing identities.

In sum, both passive and active adaptation rely on basic psychological processes such as the selection and reinforcement of positive stimuli and affect that result in routinization of identity coactivations that are experienced as compatible. Thus, over time, a strong relationship between compatibility and routinized coactivation is likely to develop.

DISCUSSION

We proposed a model of the conditions under which and how compatibility between coactivated work and nonwork identities is likely to occur by reviewing particular examples of factors that may enable people to experience coactivated identities in a compatible way. Specifically, we discussed two mechanisms, control and routinization, that may account for how individuals experience compatibility when their work and nonwork identities are coactivated.

Our model has implications for several fields of research. For scholarship on multiple identities, we add to the discussion on positive relationships *between* identities that are implicit in constructs such as enrichment, enhancement, and compatibility and broaden our understanding of the conditions under which compatibility can occur. By positing that role integration can entail either conflict or compatibility between the identities that are simultaneously activated, we also add to research on boundary theory. Specifically, we introduce the term boundary crossover, rather than boundary violation. We believe that such an affectively neutral term will allow scholars more facility in examining the potential for both positive and negative experiences when studying identities and the spillover across such boundaries. Last, our two mechanisms of control and routinization provide explanations about what factors can influence compatibility between work and nonwork identities. To fully illustrate how these mechanisms foster compatibility, we integrate research from numerous areas of organizational behavior, including status, respect, time, and the development of cognitive routines.

Our theoretical approach to multiple identities considers that positive relationships between multiple identities are important to investigate and understand in and of themselves. However, given the scope of this book, a relevant question to consider for future research is to what extent are the *outcomes* of compatibility between identities also likely to be positive? Research in related areas suggests the potential for future work to address this question in the following ways. First, there is the outcome of positive emotion. Research on role enrichment suggests that positive emotion is a critical factor in enrichment processes (Rothbard, 2001). Similarly, to the extent that coactivated sets of knowledge about the self are compatible, that is, are seen as complementary or synergistic, individuals may feel positively about themselves and generally experience positive emotion as they approach and embrace their multiple identities.

A second important outcome of compatible identities is increased productivity. Ashforth et al. (2000) suggest that identity integration may often lead to confusion and anxiety over enacting different identities, and this may then translate into a loss of productivity. However, it is possible that anxiety and confusion are byproducts of identity conflict. Conversely, identity compatibility may not have a negative effect on productivity. Future research should investigate to what degree productivity gains or losses may occur when identities are compatible versus conflicting. Addressing this question may also have managerial implications. For example, whereas managers may consider employees' preoccupation with family matters while at work a distraction and try to assert their own control over the temporal boundary between work and home (Perlow, 1998), it is also possible that leaving temporal control in the hands of workers enhances their ability to do their job. That is, the boundary crossover can operate in favor of the organization, too, that is, employees who ponder work while at home.

Another outcome of compatible identities is improved interpersonal problem solving. Recent research examining the effects of compatibility between identities finds that compatibility between identities leads individuals to be more cooperatively oriented toward one another. Moreover, they are more likely to resolve problems with others through integrative problem solving and using greater integrative complexity (Ramarajan, 2008).

In contrast to current research, common wisdom, and managerial practice that suggest individuals should check their nonwork identities at the door when entering the workplace, both for their own good and the good of the organization, this chapter seeks to explain how coactivated work and nonwork identities may be experienced as compatible. Factors such as control over and routinization of coactivation of identities can influence the extent to which employees feel their work and nonwork identities are compatible. For individuals and organizations that struggle with managing multiple identities that cross the organizational boundary, this chapter highlights mechanisms that create compatibility and the potential for positive outcomes that can arise from embracing rather than rejecting the whole person while at work.

REFERENCES

Aarts, H., Custers, R., & Holland, R. W. (2007). The nonconscious cessation of goal pursuit: When goals and negative affect are coactivated. *Journal of Personality and Social Psychology, 92,* 165–178.

Anderson, C., John, O. P., Keltner, D., & Kring, A. M. (2001). Who attains social status? Effects of personality and physical attractiveness in social groups. *Journal of Personality and Social Psychology, 81, 116–132.*

Anderson, C., Srivastava, S., Beer, J. S, Spataro, S. E., & Chatman, J. A. (2006). Knowing your place: Self-perceptions of status in face-to-face groups. *Journal of Personality and Social Psychology, 91, 1094–1110.*

Ashforth, B. E., Kreiner, G., & Fugate, M. (2000). All in a day's work: Boundaries and micro role transitions. *Academy of Management Review, 25,* 472–491.

Ashmore, R. D., Deaux, K., & McLaughlin-Volpe, T. (2004). An organizing framework for collective identity: Articulation and significance of multidimensionality. *Psychological Bulletin, 130,* 80–114.

Bargh, J. A., Chen, M., & Burrows, L. (1996). Automaticity of social behavior: Direct effects of trait construct and stereotype activation on action. *Journal of Personality and Social Psychology, 71,* 230–244.

Barreto, M., & Ellemers, N. (2002). The impact of respect versus neglect of self-identities on identification and group loyalty. *Personality and Social Psychology Bulletin, 28,* 629–639.

Benet-Martinez, V., & Haritatos, J. (2005). Bicultural identity integration (BII): Components and psychosocial antecedents. *Journal of Personality, 73,* 1015.

Berger, J., Cohen, B. P., & Zelditch, M., Jr. (1972). Status characteristics and social interaction. *American Sociological Review, 37,* 241–255.

Berry, J. W. (1997). Immigration, acculturation and adaptation. *Applied Psychology: An International Review, 46,* 5–34.

Blader, S. (2007). Let's not forget the "me" in "team": Investigating the interface of individual and collective identities. In C. Bartel, S. Blader, & A. Wrzesniewski (Ed). *Identity and the modern organization.* Mahwah, NJ: Lawrence Erlbaum Associates.

Brewer, M. B., & Gardner, W. (1996). Who is this we? Levels of collective identity and self representations. *Journal of Personality and Social Psychology, 71,* 83–93.

Cacioppo, J. T., & Gardner, W. L. (1999). Emotions. *Annual Review of Psychology, 50,* 191–214.

Campbell, D. T. (1965). Variation and selective retention in socio-cultural evolution. In H. R. Barringer, G. I. Blanksten, & R. Mack (Eds.), *Social change in developing areas* (pp. 19–49). Cambridge, MA: Schenkman.

Cardenas, R. A., Major, D. A., & Bernas, K. H. (2004). Exploring work and family distractions: Antecedents and outcomes. *International Journal of Stress Management, 11,* 346–365.

Carlson, D. S., & Frone, M. R. (2003). Relation of behavioral and psychological involvement to a new four-factor conceptualization of the work–family interference. *Journal of Business and Psychology, 17,* 515–535.

Carver, C. S., & Scheier, M. F. (1981). *Attention and self-regulation: A control theory approach to human behavior.* New York: Springer-Verlag.

Carver, C. S., & White, T. L. (1994). Behavioral inhibition, behavioral activation, and affective responses to impending reward and punishment: The BIS/BAS scales. *Journal of Personality and Social Psychology, 67,* 319–333.

Caza, B. B., & Wilson, M. (2009). Me, myself, and I: The benefits of multiple work identities. In L. M. Roberts & J. E. Dutton (Eds). *Exploring positive identities and organizations: Building a theoretical and research foundation.* Boca Raton, FL: Taylor & Francis.

Cheng, C. Y., Sanchez-Burks, J., & Lee, F. (2008). Taking advantage of differences: Increasing team innovation through identity integration. In K. W. Phillips, E. Mannix, & M. A. Neale (Eds.), *Research on managing groups and teams: Diversity in groups* (Vol. 11, pp. 55–73). Bingley, United Kingdom: JAI Press.

Cheryan, S., Plaut, V., Davies, P., & Steele, C. (2008). Detecting belonging: How stereotypical environments impact gender participation in computer science. Unpublished work.

Clore, G. L., & Huntsinger, J. R. (2007). How emotions inform judgment and regulate thought. *Trends in Cognitive Sciences, 11,* 393–399.

Cronin, M. A. (2004). A model of knowledge activation and insight in problem solving. *Complexity, 9,* 17–24.

De Cremer, D., & Tyler, T. R. (2005). Am I respected or not? Inclusion and reputation as issues in group membership. *Social Justice Research, 18,* 121–153.

Derks, B., van Laar, C., & Ellemers, N. (2006). Striving for success in outgroup settings: Effects of contextually emphasizing ingroup dimensions on stigmatized group members? Social identity and performance styles. *Personality and Social Psychology Bulletin, 32,* 576–588.

Derks, B., van Laar, C., & Ellemers, N. (2007). Social creativity strikes back: Improving motivated performance of low status group members by valuing ingroup dimensions. *European Journal of Social Psychology, 37,* 490–493.

Eagly, A. H., & Johnson, B. T. (1990). Gender and leadership style: A meta-analysis. *Psychological Bulletin, 108,* 233–256.

Festinger, L. (1957). *A theory of cognitive dissonance.* Oxford, England: Row, Peterson.

Fouad, N. A., Kantamneni, N., Smothers, M. K., Chen, Y., Fitzpatrick, M., & Terry, S. (2008). Asian American career development: A qualitative analysis. *Journal of Vocational Behavior, 72,* 43–59.

Fredrickson, B. L. (1998). What good are positive emotions? *Review of General Psychology. Special Issue: New Directions in Research on Emotion, 2,* 300–319.

Fredrickson, B. L. (2001). The role of positive emotions in positive psychology: The broaden-and-build theory of positive emotions. *American Psychologist, 56,* 218–226.

Friedman, S. D., & Greenhaus, J. H. (2000). *Work and family—Allies or enemies?* New York: Oxford University Press.

Gioia, D. A., & Poole, P. P. (1984). Scripts in organizational behavior. *Academy of Management Review, 9,* 449–459.

Goldhamer, H, & Shils, E. A. (1939). Types of power and status. *American Journal of Sociology, 45,* 171–182.

Gray, J. A. (1990). Brain systems that mediate both emotion and cognition. *Cognition & Emotion, 4,* 269–288.

Greenhaus, J. H., & Beutell, N. J. (1985). Sources of conflict between work and family roles. *Academy of Management Review, 10,* 76–88.

Greenhaus J. H. & Powell, G. N. (2003). When work and family collide: Deciding between competing role demands. *Organizational Behavior and Human Decision Processes, 90,* 291–303.

Greenhaus, J. H. & Powell, G. N. (2006). When work and family are allies: A theory of work-family enrichment. *Academy of Management Review, 3,* 72–92.

Hackman, J. R., & Oldham, G. R. (1980) *Work redesign.* Reading, MA: Addison-Wesley.

Higgins, E. T. (1991) Expanding the law of cognitive structure activation: The role of knowledge applicability. *Psychological Inquiry, 2,* 192–193.

Higgins, E. T. (1996). Knowledge activation: Accessibility, applicability, and salience. In E. T. Higgins, & A. W. Kruglanski (Eds.), *Social psychology: Handbook of basic principles* (pp. 133–168). New York: Guilford Press.

Honneth, A. (1992). Integrity and disrespect: Principles of a conception of morality based on the theory of recognition. *Political Theory, 20,* 187–201.

Isen, A.M. (1990). The influence of positive and negative affect on cognitive organization: Implications for development. In N. Stein, B. Leventhal, & T. Trabasso (Eds.), *Psychological and biological processes in the development of emotion.* Hillsdale, NJ: Lawrence Erlbaum Associates.

James, W. (1890). The consciousness of self. *The principles of psychology* (Vol I., pp. 291–401). Cambridge, MA: Harvard University Press.

Jett, Q., & George, J. M. (2003). Time interrupted: A closer look at the role of interruptions in organizational life. *Academy of Management Review, 28,* 494–407.

Johnson, M. D., Morgeson, F. P., Ilgen, D. R., Meyer, C. J., & Lloyd, J. W. (2006). Multiple professional identities: Examining differences in identification across work-related targets. *Journal of Applied Psychology, 91,* 498–506.

Karasek, R. A. (1979). Job demands, job decision latitude, and mental strain: Implications for job redesign. *Administrative Science Quarterly, 24,* 285–308.

Kihlstrom, J. F., & Klein, S. B. (1994). The self as a knowledge structure. In R. S. Wyer, Jr., & T. K. Srull (Eds.), *Handbook of social cognition.* Mahwah, NJ: Lawrence Erlbaum Associates.

Lambert, S. 1990. Processes linking work and family: A critical review and research agenda. *Human Relations, 43,* 239–257.

Lazarus, R. S., & Folkman, S. (1984). *Stress, appraisal, and coping.* New York: Springer.

Lobel, S. A. (1991). Allocation of investment in work and family roles: Alternative theories and implications for research. *Academy of Management Review, 16,* 507–521.

Mead, G. H. (1934). *Mind, self and society.* Chicago: University of Chicago Press.

Morehead, A. (2001). Synchronizing time for work and family: Preliminary insights from qualitative research with mothers. *Journal of Sociology, 37,* 355–369.

Nelson, R. R., & Winter, S. G. (1982). *An evolutionary theory of economic change.* Cambridge, MA: Harvard University Press.

Ng, T. W. H., Sorensen, K. L., & Eby, L. T. (2006). Locus of control at work: A meta-analysis. *Journal of Organizational Behavior, 27,* 1057–1087.

Nippert-Eng, C. E. (1995). *Home and work: Negotiating boundaries through everyday life.* Chicago: The University of Chicago Press.

Perlow, L. A. (1998). Boundary control: The social ordering of work and family time in a high-tech corporation. *Administrative Science Quarterly, 43,* 328–357.

Phillips, K. W., Rothbard, N. P., & Dumas, T. L. (in press). To disclose or not to disclose? Status distance and self-disclosure in diverse environments. *Academy of Management Review.*

Polzer, J. T., Milton, L. P., & Swann, W. B., Jr. (2002). Capitalizing on diversity: Interpersonal congruence in small work groups. *Administrative Science Quarterly, 47,* 296–324.

Ramarajan, L. (2008). The diversity in your head: The influence of multiple intrapersonal identities on interpersonal problem solving. Unpublished work.

Ramarajan, L., Barsade, S., & Burack, O. (2008). The influence of organizational respect on emotional exhaustion in the human services. *Journal of Positive Psychology, 3,* 4–18.

Ridgeway, C. L. (1982). Status in groups: The importance of motivation. *American Sociological Review, 47,* 76–88.

Ridgeway, C. L., & Walker, H. (1995). Status structures. In K. Cook, G. Fine, & J. House (Eds.), *Sociological perspectives on social psychology* (pp. 281–310). New York: Allyn and Bacon.

Roberts, L. M. (2007). Bringing your whole self to work: Lessons in authentic engagement from women leaders. In B. Kellerman, & D. L. Rhode (Eds.), *Women and leadership: The state of play and strategies for change* (pp. 329–360). San Francisco: Jossey-Bass.

Roccas, S., & Brewer, M. B. (2002). Social identity complexity. *Personality and Social Psychology Review, 6,* 88–106.

Rosenberg, S. (1997). Multiplicity of selves. In R. D. Ashmore, & L. J. Jussim (Eds.), *Self and identity: Fundamental issues* (Vol. 1, pp. 23–45). New York: Oxford University Press.

Rothbard, N. P. (2001) Enriching or depleting? The dynamics of engagement in work and family roles. *Administrative Science Quarterly, 46,* 655–684.

Rothbard, N. P., & Edwards, J. R. (2003). Investment in work and family roles: A test of identity and utilitarian motives. *Personnel Psychology, 56,* 699–730.

Rothbard, N. P., Phillips, K. W., & Dumas, T. L. (2005). Managing multiple roles: Work-family policies and individuals' desires for segmentation. *Organization Science, 16,* 243–258.

Schneider, W., & Shiffrin, R. M. (1977). Controlled and automatic human information processing: Detection, search, and attention. *Psychological Review, 84,* 1–66.

Skinner, E. A. (1996). A guide to constructs of control. *Journal of Personality and Social Psychology, 71,* 549–570.

Smith, E. R. (1984). Model of social inference processes. *Psychological Review, 91,* 392–413.

Smith, E. R., & Lerner, M. (1986). Development of automatism of social judgments. *Journal of Personality and Social Psychology, 50,* 246–259.

Smith, H. J., & Tyler, T. R. (1997). Choosing the right pond: The impact of group membership on self-esteem and group-oriented behavior. *Journal of Experimental Social Psychology, 33,* 146–170.

Staw, B. M., & Barsade, S. G. (1993). Affect and managerial performance: A test of the sadder-but-wiser vs. happier-and-smarter hypotheses. *Administrative Science Quarterly, 38,* 304–331.

Stryker, S., & Serpe, R. T. (1994). Identity salience and psychological centrality: Equivalent, overlapping, or complementary concepts? *Social Psychology Quarterly, 57,* 16–35.

Swann, W. B., Jr., Milton, L. P., & Polzer, J. T. (2000). Should we create a niche or fall in line? *Journal of Personality and Social Psychology, 79,* 238–250.

Tang, M. (2002). A comparison of Asian American, Caucasian American, and Chinese college students: An initial report. *Journal of Multicultural Counseling and Development, 30,* 124–134.

Tang, M., Fouad, N. A., & Smith, P. L. (1999). Asian Americans' career choices: A path model to examine factors influencing their career choices. *Journal of Vocational Behavior, 54,* 142–157.

Taylor, S. E. (1991). Asymmetrical effects of positive and negative events: The mobilization-minimization hypothesis. *Psychological Bulletin, 110,* 67–85.

Turner, J. C., Hogg, M. A., Oakes, P. J., Reicher, S. D., & Wetherell, M. S. (1987). *Rediscovering the social group: A self-categorization theory.* Oxford, England: Blackwell.

Tyler, T. R. (1999). Why people cooperate with organizations: An identity-based perspective. *Research Organizational Behavior, 21,* 201–246.

Tyler, T. R., & Blader, S. L. (2001). Identity and cooperative behavior in groups. *Group Processes & Intergroup Relations, 4,* 207–226.

Weick, K. E. (1979). *The social psychology of organizing.* Reading, MA: Addison-Wesley.

7

Bringing the Inside Out: Enhancing Authenticity and Positive Identity in Organizations

Laura Morgan Roberts, Sandra E. Cha,
Patricia F. Hewlin, and Isis H. Settles

CONTENTS

Authenticity is an ideal that Western culture has recently embraced with unprecedented force (Liedtka, 2008; Trilling, 2006). Exhortations by classical Greek philosophers to "Know thyself" and "To thine own self be true" imply that authenticity is beneficial for individuals and society. Research supports these claims, in that authenticity has been associated with fewer physical and depressive symptoms, lower anxiety, lower stress, and greater subjective vitality (e.g., Lopez & Rice, 2006; Ryan, LaGuardia, & Rawsthorne, 2005).

In the 21st century, a growing number of organizational scholars have joined with philosophers, sociologists, and psychologists to examine the nature and benefits of authenticity. Much of this research is early-stage, conceptual work. Empirical work on authenticity in organizations is scant, and definitions of authenticity are broad and varied. The bulk of conceptual and empirical research related to authenticity in organizations has focused on the *lack* of authenticity rather than ways in which authenticity is manifested and supported. This focus on the "false self" rather than the "true self" has led scholars to address the negative consequences associated with inauthenticity. As a result, much remains to be understood about authentic experiences in organizations.

To fill this gap in the literature, our chapter has three goals. First, we offer our conceptualization of authenticity and delineate the assumptions of our definition. Second, we review previous research on authenticity in organizations and articulate the value of additional research on greater authenticity for individuals in the workplace. Third, we propose a model that highlights both the potential benefits of authenticity and the process through which individuals may become more authentic. Specifically, we explicate two ways in which becoming more authentic can enable positive identities and propose three pathways through which individuals can become more authentic at work. By offering this model, we seek to deepen understanding of the antecedents and consequences of authenticity in organizations. This focus on defining and enhancing authenticity illuminates how people develop more positive identities in organizations. We conclude the chapter by highlighting ideas for future research on becoming more authentic in organizations.

DEFINITION AND CORE ASSUMPTIONS ABOUT AUTHENTICITY

Despite its limited presence in organizational studies, authenticity has been a topic of discussion among philosophers, literary scholars, sociologists, and psychologists for centuries. Most discussions of authenticity deal, at least in part, with the understanding, embracing, and enactment of self-defining characteristics. Yet, scholars hold differing assumptions about the nature of authenticity. Whereas some scholars consider authenticity a moral virtue or set of character strengths that individuals possess (George, 2003; Peterson & Seligman, 2004), others view authenticity as an optimal psychological state that people should pursue (Goffee & Jones, 2006). Moreover, scholars differ in the extent to which they consider authenticity to be an intrapersonal versus relational construct. Those with an intrapersonal perspective define authenticity as the extent to which a person is true to himself or herself, in terms of living up to the moral standards that he or she endorses, absent considerations of others' experiences of him or her (Erikson, 1995). Others construe authenticity as fundamentally relational—determined by the extent to which two parties are true to the relationship. Specifically, authenticity is achieved when two parties experience one another as engaging with transparency and mutual commitment to understanding and appreciating one another's strengths, limitations, and unique social location (Eagly, 2005; Gardner, Avolio, Luthans, May, & Walumbwa, 2005; Goldman & Kernis, 2002; Lopez & Rice, 2006; Smircich & Chesser, 1981).

In this chapter, we define authenticity as the subjective experience of alignment between one's internal experiences and external expressions (see Harter, 2002; Kahn, 1992; Roberts, 2007). By internal experiences, we mean thoughts, feelings, values, and behavioral preferences; by external expressions, we mean outward behavior, including verbal disclosures and nonverbal behavior, as well as displays such as attire and office décor. This definition is based on several key assumptions regarding the experience of authenticity. First, we adopt a phenomenological stance that privileges the actor's experience of authenticity. The authentic experience is determined by an individual's gestalt or overall feeling of having sufficiently communicated and acted on his or her genuine internal experiences in the workplace (Liedtka, 2008). Accordingly, our stance assumes that individuals are capable of reflecting on and assessing the congruence between their experiences and expressions.

Second, we view authenticity as a variable state rather than an individual trait; that is, we do not differentiate between authentic versus inauthentic individuals but instead examine where people stand on a spectrum of experiences that range from inauthenticity to authenticity at any particular moment in time. Some underlying factors may need to be present across situations for a given individual to characterize his or her experiences as authentic; however, the specific aspect of internal self that is expressed cross-situationally, as well as the way in which internal experiences are communicated, may vary (Avolio & Gardner, 2005; Endrissat, Müller, & Kaudela-Baum, 2007; Erikson, 1995). For example, a professor need not express himself or herself in exactly the same way with undergraduate business students as with a group of senior executives or with academic colleagues to characterize those experiences as highly authentic. What matters in each circumstance is whether the professor expresses those thoughts, feelings, values, and preferences that he or she considers important and relevant in each relational context.

Third, it is important to note that our phenomenological stance also leaves the content of one's authentic self undetermined. In contrast to other scholars (e.g., Avolio & Gardner, 2005; Gardner et al., 2005; George, 2003; May, Chan, Hodges, & Avolio, 2003), we do not make a priori assumptions regarding the specific character strengths, virtues, or skills that represent the "authentic self." However, we do assume that people are active agents who, under certain conditions, will attempt to "become more authentic" by increasing the alignment between their internal experiences and external expressions (Avolio & Gardner, 2005; Erikson, 1995).

REVIEW OF RESEARCH ON AUTHENTICITY IN ORGANIZATIONS

Some limited research has explored the benefits of authenticity for organizational stakeholders. Specifically, scholars have discussed the value of "strategic authenticity," in which organizations construct authentic experiences for others by pulling out the desirable aspects of real experiences (see Liedtka, 2008 for a summary). Examples of this approach to marketing authenticity can be found in the tourist industry, in which consumers seek to "authentically" experience other cultures via historical tours, performances, art, and cuisine (Peterson, 2005). This approach can also be found in media productions, in which reality TV viewers are intrigued by watching "authentic" interactions between people in social, romantic, athletic, and professional contexts (Pine & Gilmore, 1999; Rose & Wood, 2005). Aside from this work, however, there has been little empirical study of authenticity in organizational settings.

In contrast to the sparse body of work on creating authenticity within organizations, a substantial literature has examined the emotional and productivity costs of inauthenticity for individuals, work groups, and organizations (Bell & Nkomo, 2001; Ely & Thomas, 2001; Hewlin, 2003; Roberts, 2005). For example, Hochschild's (1983) study of emotional labor described the pressures that flight attendants face to behave inauthentically (by suppressing negative emotions) to meet customer demands. Other studies emphasize the strong pressure individuals often feel, in groups of all kinds, to conform to the views and expectations they believe are held by the majority (Hackman, 1992). As a consequence, individuals often engage in self-censorship, suppressing their ideas and opinions because they perceive that others in their environment hold different or less controversial views (Avery & Steingard, 2008; Milliken, Morrison, & Hewlin, 2003; Morrison & Milliken, 2000; Van Dyne, Ang, & Botero, 2003). In these cases, authenticity is curtailed because internal experiences (i.e., thoughts) are not aligned with external expressions (i.e., verbal statements). Moreover, when organizational members suppress their divergent ideas, values, and beliefs, they may limit creativity, innovation, and group learning (Argyris & Schön, 1978; Milliken et al., 2003; Morrison & Milliken, 2000).

Inauthenticity can also impose psychological stress on organizational members. People who feel that they must behave inauthentically (i.e., suppressing ideas, values, or behavioral preferences) to conform to social expectations may experience identity conflict or feelings of dissonance and distress (Bell, 1990; Bell & Nkomo, 2001; Hewlin, 2003; Higgins, 1989; Settles, 2006; Settles, Sellers, & Damas, Jr., 2002; Tunnel, 1984). Identity conflict is especially likely to occur when the identities being negotiated are important to the individual (Settles, 2004). "Identity work" to reduce identity conflict requires cognitive resources (Fried, Ben-David, Tiegs, Avital, & Yeverechyahu, 1998) that might otherwise be directed toward work-related tasks.

All of this work suggests that inauthenticity is costly for individuals and organizations. In comparison, research that documents the benefits of authenticity in organizations is scant. Nevertheless, research on the value of authenticity is timely for conceptual and practical reasons. A growing interest among researchers in positive organizational scholarship encourages scholars to focus on generative dynamics and potential rather than deficits and dysfunction within organizations to identify pathways toward building extraordinary organizations (Cameron, Dutton, & Quinn, 2003). Along these lines, we can learn a great deal about the possibilities for individual and organizational well-being and growth by focusing on authenticity rather than inauthenticity. First, learning about enhancing authenticity can help individuals and organizations to avoid the documented psychological and organizational costs of inauthenticity. Second, in the age of the nonlinear, self-guided career, many adults are seeking to enhance their experiences of authenticity at work (Sullivan & Maniero, 2007). Research on authenticity in organizations can promote career satisfaction by helping individuals and their employers to increase alignment between internal experiences and external expressions. Third, corporate scandals point to a lack of authenticity on the part of some organizational leaders, several of whom have deceived shareholders and employees for personal, financial gain. Leadership scholars have already begun to place a strong emphasis on developing "authentic leaders" who are willing and able to act with integrity to build more ethical organizations (for examples, see *The Leadership Quarterly*'s special issue on Authentic Leadership development with an introduction by Avolio & Gardner, 2005).

LINKS BETWEEN AUTHENTICITY AND POSITIVE IDENTITY

We stated earlier that one of our chapter goals is to deepen understanding of the antecedents and consequences of authenticity in organizations. We begin by developing theory on potential consequences of authenticity. Specifically, in this section we explicate the positive links between authenticity and individual identity. By identity, we refer to the various meanings that an individual attaches to individual, relational, and collective components of his or her self-concept (Ashmore, Deaux, & McLaughlin-Volpe, 2004; Gecas, 1982). We acknowledge that there are various ways to construe the positivity of an identity in the workplace based on whether one focuses on the content, structure, functionality, development, or regard of one's self-concept (Dutton, Roberts, & Bednar, 2008). In this chapter, we define a positive individual identity in terms of private regard, the evaluative dimension of identity. Private regard reflects the extent to which one feels favorably about an aspect of one's self-concept (Ashmore, Deaux, & McLaughlin-Volpe, 2004). We suggest that authenticity promotes the construction of more positive identities by increasing private regard (i.e., how positively people feel about themselves).

Next, we present a process model of becoming more authentic in organizations. A core aim of this chapter is to consider the generative potential of increasing authenticity in organizations. Hence, our emphasis is on the flow of action and how each step in the model creates conditions that can give rise to the next step (see Mohr, 1982)—that is, how actions taken by individuals can lead to increased authenticity, which can lead in turn to more positive identities. This analysis is not meant to suggest that all individuals who embark on the three pathways will be successful in achieving more positive identities. In the final section of our chapter, we identify several key contingencies that may increase or decrease the chances of our proposed process unfolding, and we invite scholars to test our model by investigating the conditions under which these relationships will hold true.

The model involves two primary components that explain the positive relationship between authenticity and identity. First, we propose that the experience of increased authenticity likely increases private regard through one's self-construal as an authentic person and/or through the experience of eudaimonia. Second, we propose three pathways that increase the likelihood that one will become more authentic: deepening self-awareness, peeling off masks, and authentication. Figure 7.1 depicts this model.

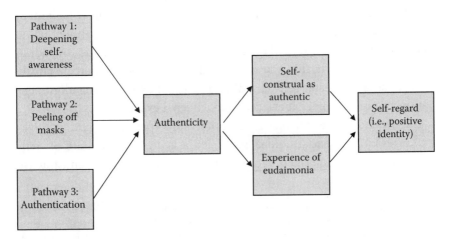

FIGURE 7.1
Process model of becoming more authentic in organizations.

AUTHENTICITY AND PRIVATE REGARD

As noted above, we propose two routes by which authenticity increases private regard: (a) via the self-construal as an authentic person, and (b) via the experience of eudaimonia. The first route is more cognitive and conscious, whereas the second route is more affective and less conscious.

To describe the first proposed route, we draw on Bem's (1982) self-perception theory, which focuses on how a person's outward behavior influences his or her self-concept. Bem proposed that people observe their own behavior and then draw inferences about who they are. Because individuals are likely to make dispositional attributions for their behavior, they will tend to conclude that their actions reflect their internal traits and dispositions. For example, a person who behaves in an anxious manner is likely to conclude that he or she is a dispositionally anxious person. (A similar process occurs when others observe one's behavior; they tend to attribute an individual's outward behavior to stable internal traits.) Thus, if one behaves authentically (engages in the outward expression of genuine internal experiences), one is likely to conclude that one is a dispositionally authentic person. In this way, engaging in authentic behavior helps to build a self-construal as authentic ("I am an authentic person because I observed myself behave authentically.").

The self-construal as an authentic person will lead to positive regard because current societal norms hold that being an authentic person is an aspect of virtuousness and worth[1] (Argyris, 1969; Peterson & Seligman, 2004). Because of the strength of these norms, the modal individual is likely to hold in high regard anyone who is seen as authentic (including himself or herself). In this way, one is likely to view oneself more positively (i.e., experience greater self-regard) as a result of experiencing alignment between one's internal experiences and external expressions.

The second route between authenticity and private regard involves the experience of eudaimonia. Eudaimonia is an optimal state of well-being that is characterized by feelings of happiness, enjoyment, intense

---

[1] Peterson and Seligman identify authenticity as a virtue that is embraced across cultures. However, Western cultures may place more emphasis than do Eastern cultures on behavioral consistency across situations and over time when evaluating authenticity. Research supports that Eastern cultures value behavioral and self-concept consistency within relationships but are more comfortable with dynamism and contradictions across contexts (English & Chen, 2007).

personal meaning, and direction in life that result from living in accord with one's daimon—one's true, optimal self (Ryff, 1989; Ryff & Keyes, 1995; Waterman, 1993). When one behaves authentically, one's external expressions are aligned with internal experiences, and one is likely to feel as though one is living in accordance with the daimon (Ilies, Morgeson, & Nahrgang, 2005). Specifically, by enabling people to own and express their thoughts, feelings, and values that can benefit others, authenticity can create a pathway through which people are able to embrace and realize their potential to create value for themselves and for the world (Roberts, 2007). On the other hand, suppressing or deceiving others about one's internal experiences can inhibit one's ability to embrace and express his or her daimon. Living in accord with one's daimon can increase positive evaluations of oneself and one's past (Maslow, 1968; Ryff, 1989; Ryff & Keyes, 1995). The positive feelings associated with eudaimonia can enable one to develop a clearer and more expansive view of one's "best-self" (Roberts, Dutton, Spreitzer, Heaphy, & Quinn, 2005) and can promote feelings of self-acceptance (Ryff & Keyes, 1995), both of which are likely to increase private regard.

BECOMING MORE AUTHENTIC

We have described how authenticity is important for constructing more positive identities in organizations. How, then, can individuals become more authentic or enhance their experience of authenticity? On the surface, the answer to this question seems rather straightforward—"just be yourself." However, becoming more authentic in work organizations can be challenging. Being oneself requires a certain measure of self-awareness— one must know oneself to be oneself. Being oneself also requires a certain measure of courage—one must be willing to counter his or her tendencies to suppress counternormative thoughts, feelings, values, and behaviors. Being oneself is also challenging for people who face stereotypical expectations about how they should think, feel, and behave. In this section, we describe three pathways through which an individual can deal with these challenges and become more authentic: (a) deepening self-awareness, (b) peeling off masks, and (c) authentication. An individual may follow a single pathway or multiple pathways in concert to become more authentic.

Pathway 1: Deepening Self-Awareness

Deepening self-awareness involves two activities: the creation of narrative accounts and individuation. First, deepening self-awareness involves a narrative project of making sense of the connections between one's own past, present, and future. As Heidegger (1962) states, "Authenticity is the loyalty of one's self to its own past, heritage and ethos" (p. 117). The narrative project involves constructing a coherent story of one's life that weaves together disparate actions, feelings, and motivations of life events (McAdams, 1990; Sparrowe, 2005). Through short narrative accounts, people create causal links between life experiences and make sense of change, contradiction, and surprises. Narrative accounts enable people to develop a clearer and more coherent understanding of their recurring internal experiences in the context of their personal history.

Second, deepening self-awareness also involves critical participation in life—understanding the context, questioning contradictions inherent in that context, and then owning one's values and beliefs because they reflect one's personal experience, not because they are socially or politically appropriate (Heidegger, 1962; Shamir & Eilam, 2005). Developmental psychologists have made similar claims about the evolution of identity, theorizing that adults reach the highest or most mature stages of identity development when they have questioned their parents', peers', or society's values and practices and then internalized those that resonate with their experience as an autonomous agent in their social world (see Schwartz, 2001 for a summary; see also Erikson, 1980; Kegan, 1982; Phinney, 1990). Therefore, deepening self-awareness involves examining how one's internal experiences differ from others' expectations of thoughts, feelings, values, and preferences. In the process of individuating ourselves, we become more aware of our recurring internal experiences that differentiate us from other people. Through individuation, therefore, we develop greater clarity about our recurring internal experiences.

In sum, in both activities of creating narrative accounts and individuation, deepening self-awareness thus involves producing greater understanding of, or greater clarity with respect to, one's recurring internal experiences. That is, deeper self-awareness involves greater understanding of patterns among one's internal experiences, i.e., the thoughts, feelings, values, and behavioral inclinations that occur repeatedly. As a result of greater clarity about one's recurring internal experiences (one's internal experience "patterns"), one should by extension be able to express these internal experience patterns more clearly and accurately to others. Thus, the alignment between one's internal experiences and external expressions should be tighter. In this way, we propose that deepening self-awareness can increase authenticity.

Pathway 2: Peeling Off Masks, or Revealing More of the "True Self"

The second path to becoming more authentic is based on the assumption that individuals are capable of putting on masks or public personae that deny their own internal experiences or deceive others about their thoughts, feelings, values, or behavioral preferences to increase their stature, protect their image, or avoid conflict in relationships (Hewlin, 2003; Kahn, 1992; Neff & Harter, 2002; Roberts, 2005; Smircich & Chesser, 1981). Becoming more authentic often requires an individual to peel off such masks to reveal more of the true self.

Peeling off masks can be challenging for individuals who feel pressured to suppress aspects of internal experience to conform to others' norms and expectations, which distances the public persona from the private self. Peeling off masks involves countering suppression—adjusting external expressions to reveal previously suppressed internal experiences, even if these expressions defy social norms in a particular context. As noted earlier, people often engage in self-censorship, withholding their opinions because they perceive others in their surroundings to hold views that differ from, and are less controversial than, their own (Avery & Steingard, 2008; Milliken et al., 2003; Morrison & Milliken, 2000; Van Dyne, Ang, & Botero, 2003). After discovering how one differs from the crowd, becoming more authentic involves standing apart from the crowd to voice personal thoughts, feelings, values, and beliefs. For example, the emerging literature on authentic leadership emphasizes leaders' moral responsibility to stand apart (and even rise above) the rash of high-profile corporate scandals by engaging in ethical decision-making and providing honest, transparent disclosures about their company's financial transactions (e.g., Cooper, Scandura, & Schriesheim, 2005; George, 2003; Goffee & Jones, 2006).

Another important component of peeling off masks is the willingness to display aspects of one's cultural heritage, even when they do not conform to mainstream stylistic preferences. This facet of becoming more authentic is especially relevant for women and racial minorities, who often perceive a devaluation of the diversity they bring into the workplace (Settles, 2006). As a consequence of this devaluation, women and minorities often feel unable to be authentic, and many conceal aspects of their personal lives that are not consistent with what is most acceptable within their organizations (Hewlin, 2003; Roberts, 2005). For women and minorities, social acceptance and career success are partially determined by how well they assimilate and conform to their work environments by adopting the behaviors of white men (Bell, 1990; Bell & Nkomo, 2001; Kanter, 1977). In these circumstances, becoming more authentic means finding ways to integrate one's gendered and cultural experiences into the values and practices of their work environment, perhaps even drawing on such aspects of one's background as a source of strength that enhances the quality of one's work and relationships (Bell & Nkomo, 2001; Cha & Roberts, 2008; Roberts, 2007).

Pathway 3: Authentication

In this section, we build the argument that input from other people regarding their perceptions of one's alignment influences an individual's subjective experience of authenticity. As such, becoming more authentic may also mean negotiating perceptions of one's authenticity (Goffee & Jones, 2006).

Authentic experience is socially constructed, in that one's identity claims are accepted or rejected by others (Peterson, 2005). When valued and self-defining characteristics are recognized and affirmed by others, people are more certain of their place and purpose in the social world, and interactions with others unfold more smoothly (Swann, 1985; Swann, De La Ronde, & Hickson, 1994). However, social feedback that challenges the veracity and legitimacy of one's public expressions can create problems for one's social interactions. For example, Eagly (2005) discusses how followers play a critical role in legitimizing leaders' expressions of values and authority. Those leaders who belong to social groups that have not traditionally held positions of power may not possess the legitimacy to inspire follower identification, despite their public expression of internal experiences (Eagly, 2005). Shamir and Eilam (2005) similarly describe how followers authenticate leaders by judging a leader's claim for leadership as driven by personal values rather than the desire for status or power, as well as by judging the leader's behaviors as consistent with the leader's stated beliefs. When leaders are perceived as behaving in ways that are inconsistent with espoused values, followers no longer perceive leaders as being authentic; instead, they often attribute such inconsistencies to hypocrisy, and leaders' attempts to inspire and mobilize employees are less effective (Cha & Edmondson, 2006; Simons, Friedman, Liu, & McLean Parks, 2007; Simons & McLean Parks, 2000).

We acknowledge that the consideration of "authentication," or the degree to which people view others' behavior as genuine and appropriate and affirm internally aligned self-expressions, pushes the limits of our phenomenological stance. Authenticity, as we define it, is the subjective sense of alignment between one's own internal experiences and external expressions. However, becoming more authentic via "being true to oneself" is a social process whereby people rely on reflected appraisals to understand and assess their own values, preferences, and actions. As such, social feedback regarding others' perceptions of one's alignment (or "sincerity" as Erikson, 1995, and Trilling, 2006, conceptualize it) indirectly influences a person's beliefs about whether he or she is being true to himself or herself. People come to associate self-verifying evaluations with feelings of authenticity (Swann et al., 1994). Thus, the process of becoming more authentic may involve reshaping others' understanding of one's internal experiences or their acceptance of one's external expressions.

In this vein, becoming more authentic often requires an individual to defy or complicate other people's stereotypic, simplistic, and/or restrictive expectations of his or her role or group membership. For instance, leaders are highly visible figures who are scrutinized intensely by organization members (Tyler & Lind, 1995). They are also subject to heroic, possibly unattainable, expectations—of strength, altruism, and the ability to meet followers' needs (Cha & Edmondson, 2006; Rioch, 1975). Leaders may feel torn between wanting to meet heroic, but stereotypic, expectations and the desire to be authentic, especially when this requires them to reveal their limitations and vulnerability. Becoming more authentic would involve countering others' idealized images of leadership and revealing more of their humanity through public expressions (see Dutton, Frost, Worline, Lilius, & Kanov, 2002; see also Avolio & Gardner's [2005] discussion of how inauthenticity results from being overly compliant with stereotypes of the leader role). As an example, Mayor Rudy Giuliani publicly displayed grief in the wake of the tragedies on September 11, 2001, which opened the avenues for other New Yorkers to express their pain (Dutton et al.,

2002). Giuliani's emotional display was authenticated (seen as genuine and appropriate, and was welcomed) by the public, and as a result, he was evaluated more favorably as a leader during this time of national crisis.

Women and underrepresented minorities may also face authentication challenges with perceivers because they are often construed in stereotypical terms that do not reflect the diversity and strengths that exist within groups (Cox, 1993; Kanter, 1977). In this case, becoming more authentic may involve displaying aspects of one's gender, culture, or other identities that challenge group stereotypes. For example, African American medical students and women scientists may attempt to educate others about the inaccuracies of group stereotypes or differentiate themselves from stereotypes that do not reflect their personal characteristics (Roberts, Settles, & Jellison, 2008). Strategically displaying these positive aspects of one's racial or gender identity can enhance one's own experience of authenticity and can also help others to appreciate one's experiences as a member of a social identity group (Roberts, 2005). In this way, countering stereotypes can increase the likelihood of authentication and thus can further enhance one's experience of alignment between external expressions and internal thoughts, feelings, values, and preferences.

AVENUES FOR FUTURE RESEARCH: COMPLICATING THE MODEL

In this chapter, we highlighted three individual processes ("pathways") that can lead to enhanced authenticity in organizations. We also explicated how enhanced authenticity can lead, in turn, to more positive individual identities. However, the three pathways to becoming more authentic that we describe are by no means the only ones.

To complement our focus on individual-level processes, future research may wish to consider how the organizational context and organizational leaders can create conditions that facilitate the process of becoming more authentic. Organizational practices play a critical role in the process of members' bringing more of their selves into the work environment (Kahn, 1992). For example, over the past two decades, organizations have emphasized creating diverse work environments through initiatives that have centered on diversity-based attraction and selection processes, reward systems, and socialization practices (Dass & Parker, 1999; Ely & Thomas, 2001; Kirton & Greene, 2005). These practices are intended to communicate a clear message in words and actions that "difference" is not a liability and that authentic expression of self is needed for the overall well-being of organizational members. As organizations earnestly create environments that foster authenticity, women and minorities may be more readily inclined to peel off their masks and leverage their uniqueness for the betterment of the organization.

In addition to expanding the pathways included in the model, future research may wish to further address the complexity associated with one's journey toward becoming more authentic by exploring key contingencies. We highlight several such important contingencies that should be explored. First, how does the content of one's authentically expressed thoughts, feelings, values, or behavioral preferences influence the impact of such expression on self-regard? That is, does the authentic expression of weakness or less favorable characteristics have the same positive impact on self-regard as does the expression of strengths or virtues? For example, one might construe oneself as authentic because one has fully displayed weaknesses and limitations. The increased positive regard created by an authentic self-construal may be counterbalanced by the decreased self-regard created by a focus on the weaknesses one has expressed.

Moreover, sharing thoughts and emotions relevant to work tasks can facilitate organizational effectiveness (Argyris, 1969), but full disclosure of all of one's internal experiences to all of one's colleagues is likely to interfere with organizational efficiency and create extreme vulnerability for the individual. Hence, tempering age-old exhortations, employees may find that "bounded authenticity" is a more functional approach for navigating the complex intrapsychic, interpersonal, and organizational dynamics involved in bringing one's "whole" self to work. Future research may wish to examine how individuals can become more authentic at work while also bounding their authenticity to maximize positive outcomes for themselves and their organizations.

Second, what motivates individuals to deliberately seek to become more authentic? Our process model assumes intentionality, in contrast to a person who unconsciously increases his or her degree of "just being himself or herself" over time. Future research on this topic should examine catalyzing events that prompt individuals to become more authentic. For instance, one person may seek to become more authentic after receiving feedback from significant others that her external expressions appear inconsistent with internal experiences. Another person may seek to experience more authenticity in his daily work experiences because he believes it will enable him to contribute more fully to his organization. Corley & Harrison (this volume) examine this question from the organizational level of analysis as they study how and why organizations pursue authenticity through a never-ending process of action, reflection, and evolution. Research that spans levels of analysis may reveal similar processes for individuals and collectives who earnestly pursue authenticity.

Third, how might the lack of authentication by others influence feelings of authenticity and the process of one becoming more authentic? Although becoming more authentic can facilitate the development of transparent, growth-enhancing relationships (Kahn, 1992), authentic self-expressions may be met with resistance by other people. Others may judge one's behavior and reject those self-expressions that are deemed socially undesirable or inappropriate because they deviate from situational norms or status expectations. Further, the audience may be more likely to authenticate one's behavioral expressions if they are perceived as being consistent with one's previous behavior and personality. Future research could explore how individuals achieve authenticity when their behaviors are not authenticated by others.

Fourth, future research might explore the generalizability of our proposed model. Certain aspects of the model may be more relevant to certain groups, especially those facing distinctive challenges in becoming more authentic in organizations. For example, leaders and members of underrepresented social identity groups have in common a heightened visibility that may result in a greater likelihood of their being negatively scrutinized by others (Kanter, 1977; Tyler & Lind, 1995). As a result, leaders and minorities may find it more difficult to become more authentic via authentication (i.e., for external audiences to see their internally aligned self-expressions as genuine, appropriate, and of value) than less visible organization members because they face the challenge of countering others' stereotypical expectations that may be inconsistent with their internal experiences. In contrast, prototypical organizational members may face very few challenges to becoming authentic and thus may more easily reap the rewards of authenticity for positive identity construction.

CONCLUSION

This chapter sought to address the increasing interest in supporting authenticity in organizations by offering a clear definition of authenticity and a process model of pathways to authenticity and subsequent self-regard. This model is particularly important for uncovering new research questions on positive identities, given that authenticity often emerges as an idealized trait or state in discussions of identity and identity formation for individuals, teams, and organizations. Even in this volume, our colleagues point to authenticity as an important dimension of personal growth (Kreiner & Sheep, 2009), relationship formation, and team collaboration (MacPhail, Roloff & Edmondson, 2009; Milton, 2009), as well as generative organizational identity evolution (Corley & Harrison, 2009). As we discussed, becoming more authentic in work organizations can be challenging, particularly for organizational members whose "true selves" are counternormative. Despite these potential difficulties, our chapter suggests that individuals and organizations may benefit substantially from an increase in authenticity in the workplace. The question of how individuals and organizations can promote greater authenticity at work represents an important avenue for future research.

REFERENCES

Argyris, C. (1969). The incompleteness of social psychological theory: Examples from small group, cognitive consistency, and attribution research. *American Psychologist, 24,* 893–908.

Argyris, C., & Schön, D. (1978). *Organizational learning: A theory of action perspective.* Reading, MA: Addison-Wesley.

Ashmore, R. D., Deaux, K., & McLaughlin-Volpe, T. (2004). An organizing framework for collective identity: Articulation and significance of multidimensionality. *Psychological Bulletin, 130,* 80–114.

Avery, D., & Steingard, D. (2008). Achieving political trans-correctness: Integrating sensitivity and authenticity in diversity management education. *Journal of Management Education, 32,* 269–293.

Avolio, B., & Gardner, W. (2005). Authentic leadership development: Getting to the root of positive forms of leadership. *The Leadership Quarterly, 16,* 315–338.

Bell, E. L. (1990). The bicultural life experience of career-oriented black women. *Journal of Organizational Behavior, 11,* 459–477.

Bell, E. L., & Nkomo, S. M. (2001). *Our separate ways: Black and white women and the struggle for professional identity.* Boston: Harvard Business School Press.

Bem, D. (1982). Self-perception theory. In L. Berkowitz (Ed.), *Advances in experimental social psychology* (Vol. 6). New York: Academic Press.

Cameron, K. S., Dutton, J. E., & Quinn, R. E. (Eds.). (2003). *Positive organizational scholarship: Foundations of a new discipline.* San Francisco: Berrett-Koehler.

Cha, S. E., & Edmondson, A. C. (2006). When values backfire: Leadership, attribution, and disenchantment in a values-driven organization. *The Leadership Quarterly, 17,* 57–78.

Cha, S. E., & Roberts, L. M. (2008). *Steering identity: Mobilizing a multivalent identity as a resource in organizations.* Unpublished manuscript, McGill University and Harvard Business School.

Cooper, C. D., Scandura, T. A., & Schriesheim, C. A. (2005). Looking forward but learning from our past: Potential challenges to developing authentic leadership theory and authentic leaders. *The Leadership Quarterly, 16,* 475–493.

Corley, K., & Harrison, S. (2009). Generative organizational identity change: Approaching organizational authenticity as a process. In L. M. Roberts & J. Dutton (Eds.), *Exploring positive identities and organizations: Building a theoretical and research foundation.* New York: Psychology Press, Taylor & Francis Group.

Cox, T. (1993). *Cultural diversity in organizations: Theory, research, and practice.* San Francisco: Berrett-Kochler.

Dass, P., & Parker, B. (1999). Strategies for managing human resource diversity: From resistance to learning. *Academy of Management Executive, 13,* 68–80.

Dutton, J., Frost, P., Worline, M., Kanov, J., & Lilius, J. (2002, January). Leading in times of trauma. *Harvard Business Review,* 54–61.

Dutton, J. E., Roberts, L. M., & Bednar, J. (2008). Positive work-related identities and why they matter: A prism for understanding. Unpublished manuscript, University of Michigan and Harvard Business School.

Eagly, A. H. (2005). Achieving relational authenticity in leadership: Does gender matter? *The Leadership Quarterly, 16,* 459–474.

Ely, R. J., & Thomas, D. A. (2001). Cultural diversity at work: The effects of diversity perspectives on work group processes and outcomes. *Administrative Science Quarterly, 46,* 229–273.

Endrissat, N., Müller, W., & Kaudela-Baum, S. (2007). En route to an empirically-based understanding of authentic leadership. *European Management Journal, 25,* 207–220.

English, T., & Chen, S. (2007). Culture and self-concept stability: Consistency across and within contexts among Asian Americans and European Americans. *Journal of Personality and Social Psychology, 93,* 478–490.

Erikson, E. H. (1980). *Identity and the life cycle.* New York: Norton.

Erikson, R. (1995). The importance of authenticity for self and society. *Symbolic Interaction, 18,* 121–144.

Fried, Y., Ben-David, H. A., Tiegs, R. B., Avital, N., & Yeverechyahu, U. (1998). The interactive effect of role conflict and role ambiguity on job performance. *Journal of Occupational and Organizational Psychology, 71,* 19–27.

Gardner, W., Avolio, B., Luthans, F., May, D., & Walumbwa, F. (2005). Can you see the real me? A self based model of authentic leader and follower development. *The Leadership Quarterly, 16,* 343–372.

Gecas, V. (1982). The self-concept. *Annual Review of Sociology, 8*, 1–33.

George, B. (2003). *Authentic leadership: Rediscovering the secrets to creating lasting value.* San Francisco: Jossey-Bass.

Goffee, R., & Jones, G. (2006). *Why should anyone be led by you? What it takes to be an authentic leader.* Boston: Harvard Business School Press.

Goldman, B., & Kernis, M. (2002). The role of authenticity in healthy psychological functioning and subjective well-being. *Annals of the American Psychotherapy Association, 5*, 18–20.

Hackman, J. R. (1992). Group influences on individuals in organizations. In M. D. Dunnette & L. M. Hough (Eds.), *Handbook of industrial and organizational psychology* (Vol. 3, pp. 199–268). Palo Alto, CA: Consulting Psychologists Press.

Harter, S. (2002). Authenticity. In C. R. Snyder & S. Lopez (Eds.), *Handbook of positive psychology* (pp. 382–394). London: Oxford University Press.

Heidegger, M. (1962). *Being and time* (J. MacQuarrie & E. Robinson, Trans.). London: SCM Press.

Hewlin, P. F. (2003). And the award for best actor goes to…: Facades of conformity in organizational settings. *Academy of Management Review, 28*, 633–656.

Higgins, E. T. (1989). Self-discrepancy theory: What patterns of self-beliefs cause people to suffer? In L. Berkowitz (Ed.), *Advances in experimental social psychology* (Vol. 22, pp. 93–136). San Diego, CA: Academic Press.

Hochschild, A. R. (1983). *The managed heart.* Berkeley, CA: University of California Press.

Ilies, R., Morgeson, F., & Nahrgang, J. (2005). Authentic leadership and eudaemonic well-being: Understanding leader-follower outcomes. *The Leadership Quarterly, 16*, 373–394.

Kahn, W. A. (1992). To be fully there: Psychological presence at work. *Human Relations, 45*, 321–349.

Kanter, R. M. (1977). *Men and women of the corporation.* New York: Basic Books.

Kegan, R. (1982). *The evolving self: Problem and process in human development.* Cambridge, MA: Harvard University Press.

Kirton, G., & Greene, A. (2005). *The dynamics of managing diversity. A critical approach (2nd ed.).* Oxford, England: Elsevier Butterworth-Heinemann.

Kreiner, G., & Sheep, M. (2009). Growing pains and growing gains: Framing identity dynamics as opportunities for identity growth. In L. M. Roberts & J. Dutton (Eds.), *Exploring positive identities and organizations: Building a theoretical and research foundation.* New York: Psychology Press, Taylor & Francis Group.

Liedtka, J. (2008). Strategy-making and the search for authenticity. *Journal of Business Ethics, 80*, 237–248.

Lopez, F., & Rice, K. (2006). Preliminary development and validation of a measure of relationship authenticity. *Journal of Counseling Psychology, 53*, 362–371.

MacPhail, L., Roloff, K., & Edmondson, A. (2009). Collaboration across knowledge boundaries within diverse teams: Reciprocal expertise affirmation as an enabling condition. In L. M. Roberts & J. Dutton (Eds.), *Exploring positive identities and organizations: Building a theoretical and research foundation.* New York: Psychology Press, Taylor & Francis Group.

Maslow, A. (1968). *Motivation and personality* (3rd ed.). New York: Harper.

May, D. R., Chan, A. Y. L., Hodges, T. D., & Avolio, B. J. (2003). Developing the moral component of authentic leadership. *Organizational Dynamics, 32*, 247–260.

McAdams, D. P. (1990). Unity and purpose in human lives: The emergence of identity as a life-story. In A. I. Robin, R. A. Zucker, R. A. Emmons, & S. Frank (Eds.), *Studying persons and lives* (pp. 148–200). New York: Springer.

Milliken, F. J., Morrison, E. W., & Hewlin, P. F. (2003). An exploratory study of employee silence: Issues that employees don't communicate upward and why. *Journal of Management Studies, 40*, 1453–1476.

Milton, L. (2009). Catalysts of cooperation and optimal achievement in groups: Positive relational identities, identity confirmation, authenticity and cooperative capacity. In L. M. Roberts & J. Dutton (Eds.), *Exploring positive identities and organizations: Building a theoretical and research foundation*. New York: Psychology Press, Taylor & Francis Group.

Mohr, X. (1982). Approaches to explanation: Variance theory and process theory. In L. B. Mohr (Ed.), *Explaining organizational behavior* (pp. 35–70). San Francisco: Jossey-Bass.

Morrison, E. W., & Milliken, F. J. (2000). Organizational silence: A barrier to change and development in a pluralistic world. *Academy of Management Review, 25*, 706–731.

Neff, K., & Harter, S. (2002). The authenticity of conflict resolutions among adult couples: Does women's other-oriented behavior reflect their true selves? *Sex Roles, 47*, 403–417.

Peterson, C., & Seligman, M. E. P. (2004). *Character strengths and virtues: A handbook and classification*. New York: Oxford University Press.

Peterson, R. (2005). In search of authenticity. *Journal of Management Studies, 42*, 1083–1098.

Phinney, J. S. (1990). Ethnic identity in adolescents and adults: A review of research. *Psychological Bulletin, 180*, 499–514.

Pine, B., & Gilmore, J. (1999). *The experience economy: Work is theater & every business a stage*. Boston: Harvard Business School Press.

Rioch, M. J. (1975). The work of Wilfred Bion on groups. In A. D. Colman & W. H. Bexton (Eds.), *Group relations reader* (pp. 21–33). Sausalito, CA: GREX.

Roberts, L. M. (2005). Changing faces: Professional image construction in diverse organizational settings. *Academy of Management Review, 30*, 685–711.

Roberts, L. M. (2007). Bringing your whole self to work: Lessons in authentic engagement from women leaders. In B. Kellerman & D. L. Rhode (Eds.), *Women and leadership: The state of play and strategies for change* (pp. 329–360). San Francisco: Jossey-Bass.

Roberts, L. M., Dutton, J. E., Spreitzer, G. M., Heaphy, E. D., & Quinn, R. E. (2005). Composing the reflected best-self portrait: Building pathways for becoming extraordinary in work organizations. *Academy of Management Review, 30*, 712–736.

Roberts, L. M., Settles, I. H., & Jellison, W. (2008). Predicting the strategic identity management of gender and race. *Identity, 8*, 269–306.

Rose, R., & Wood, S. (2005). Paradox and the consumption of authenticity through reality television. *Journal of Consumer Research, 32*, 284–297.

Ryan, R., LaGuardia, J., & Rawsthorne, L. (2005). Self-complexity and the authenticity of self-aspects: Effects on well being and resilience to stressful events. *North American Journal of Psychology, 7*, 431–448.

Ryff, C. (1989). Happiness is everything, or is it? Explorations on the meaning of psychological well-being. *Journal of Personality and Social Psychology, 57*, 1069–1081.

Ryff, C., & Keyes, C. (1995). The structure of psychological well-being revisited. *Journal of Personality and Social Psychology, 60*, 719–727.

Schwartz, S. (2001). The evolution of Eriksonian and Neo-Eriksonian identity theory and research: A review and integration. *Identity: An interdisciplinary journal of theory and research, 1,* 7–58.

Settles, I. H. (2004). When multiple identities interfere: The role of identity centrality. *Personality and Social Psychology Bulletin, 30,* 487–500.

Settles, I. H. (2006). Use of an intersectional framework to understand Black women's racial and gender identities. *Sex Roles, 54,* 589–601.

Settles, I. H., Sellers, R. M., & Damas, A., Jr. (2002). One role or two? The function of psychological separation in role conflict. *Journal of Applied Psychology, 87,* 574–582.

Shamir, B., & Eilam, G. (2005). "What's your story?" A life-stories approach to authentic leadership development. *The Leadership Quarterly, 16,* 395–417.

Simons, T., Friedman, R., Liu, L. A., & McLean Parks, J. (2007). Racial differences in sensitivity to behavioral integrity: Attitudinal consequences, in-group effects, and "trickle down" among Black and non-Black employees. *Journal of Applied Psychology, 92,* 650–665.

Simons, T., & McLean Parks, J. (2000, August). *The sequential impact of behavioral integrity on trust, commitment, discretionary service behavior, customer satisfaction, and profitability.* Paper presented at the annual meeting of the Academy of Management, Toronto, Ontario, Canada.

Smircich, L., & Chesser, R. (1981). Superiors' and subordinates' perceptions of performance: Beyond disagreement. *Academy of Management Journal, 24,* 198–205.

Sparrowe, R. N. (2005). Authenticity and the narrative self. *The Leadership Quarterly, 16,* 419–439.

Sullivan, S., & Maniero, L. (2007). Kaleidoscope careers: Benchmarking ideas for fostering family-friendly workplaces. *Organizational Dynamics, 36,* 45–62.

Swann, W. B., Jr. (1985). The self as architect of social reality. In B. Schlenker (Ed.), *The self and social life* (pp. 100–125). New York: McGraw-Hill.

Swann, W., De La Ronde, C., & Hixon, J. G. (1994). Authenticity and positivity strivings in marriage and courtship. *Journal of Personality and Social Psychology, 66,* 857–869.

Trilling, L. (2006). *Sincerity and authenticity (the Charles Eliot Norton Lectures)* (New edition edition). Cambridge, MA: Harvard University Press.

Tunnel, G. (1984). The discrepancy between private and public selves: Public self-consciousness and its correlates. *Journal of Personality Assessment, 48,* 549–555.

Tyler, T. R., & Lind, E. A. (1995). A relational model of authority in groups. *Advances in experimental social psychology* (Vol. 25, pp. 115–191). New York: Academic Press.

Van Dyne, L., Ang, S., & Botero, I. C. (2003). Conceptualizing employee silence and employee voice as multidimensional constructs. *Journal of Management Studies, 40,* 1359–1392.

Waterman, A. S. (1993). Two conceptions of happiness: Contrasts of personal expressiveness (eudaimonia) and hedonic enjoyment. *Journal of Personality and Social Psychology, 64,* 678–691.

8

Commentary: Positive Identities and the Individual

Blake E. Ashforth

CONTENTS

Positive identity. It sounds like an easy term to define. "Positive" suggests a value connotation, where something is good, desirable, and beneficial. "Identity" suggests how an actor is defined (Who am I? Who are we?). So pairing "positive" with "identity" suggests a good, desirable, and beneficial self-definition. But what does *that* really mean? After some false starts at answering this question, it struck me that perhaps this definitional issue is not something that we should try to address at the start of our conversation—which is, after all, what this book represents—but something that should be allowed to emerge naturally *from* the conversation; something the conversation should play with and savor. When the destination is only roughly known, the journey has license to meander, and our conversation will be richer for it.

Let me begin this commentary by examining how each of the authors in this section on positive identities and the individual chose to pair the notions of positive and identity. After briefly recapping the chapters, I will draw out some common themes. I will then offer some questions for future research that these pairings—considered as a loosely coupled set—seem to suggest. Finally, I will close with two cautionary notes about positive identity as a field of inquiry—cautionary notes that I think also apply to the broader field of positive organizational scholarship (POS).

HOW DID OUR AUTHORS PAIR "POSITIVE" AND "IDENTITY"?

Glen E. Kreiner and Mathew L. Sheep (Chapter 2) tackle the role of *identity growth* in fostering a positive identity, that is, "one that is competent, resilient, authentic, transcendent, and holistically integrated." Individuals strive to close the gaps between their perceptions of their real and ideal selves and between their self-perceptions and the perceptions of others. This is accomplished through a mix of identity work tactics, including developing a spiritual identity (which fosters holistic integration [i.e., coherence and completeness] and transcendence [i.e., a self-defining connection to something greater than oneself]), searching for optimal balance between one's personal and social identities (holistic integration, competence, and authenticity), transforming identity threats by reframing them and improving relations with those posing the threats (resilience), experimenting with possible selves (holistic integration, authenticity, and resilience), and leveraging both congruence and incongruence between oneself and one's environment (holistic integration and competence). The notion of identity growth suggests that a given identity is forever a "work in progress," spurred not just by a lack of fit with one's surroundings but by the "safe haven" afforded by fitting in well.

Sally Maitlis (Chapter 3) continues the theme of growth, asking what happens to a musician's identity when faced with an injury that affects his or her ability to perform. Drawing from a larger study, she relates the experiences of four musicians who avoided self-pity and displayed post-traumatic growth. The musicians indicated that the injury threatened their understanding of self, prompting an "intense and painful search for meaning" made more difficult by the chronic but ambiguous nature of the injury (e.g., Will I be able to regain my form?). The interviewees gradually, haltingly, formed varied transitional identities (e.g., I am a musician with a neurological condition) and found reasons to disidentify with their former identity (e.g., the standards are too high), which helped ease their shift away from their previously untrammeled calling of professional musician. Ultimately, they reconstructed their identities in a manner that respected their past while being firmly rooted in the opportunities of the present: "They will always be musicians, but they may not continue to make music, or to make it in the same way." The personal journeys are remarkable, as pain was used as a catalyst to explore and enact related identities, and each musician "expressed satisfaction, gratitude, and excitement about the person they were becoming."

Starting from the premise that "identity is as much a prospective as a retrospective phenomenon," Arne Carlsen and Tyrone Pitsis (Chapter 4) explore the nature of *hope* in organizations—"a *future-oriented quality of experiencing*" (their emphasis). Hope can be directed at attaining a goal, at "opening up" to new possibilities, and at escaping from unwanted circumstances. Thus, hope is a driver of identity construction and a strong theme in the narratives individuals formulate about themselves, conferring a sense of possibility, purpose, and progress to their lives. Simultaneously, hope is a "meta-motive in positive identity construction," as individuals *seek* to feel hopeful. The notion of open-ended possibilities is particularly intriguing, as it suggests that surprises, novel experiences, chance encounters, and so on may prompt epiphanies and thus serve as fulcrums for "new trajectories of practice" (see Carlsen, 2006; Roberts, Dutton, Spreitzer, Heaphy, & Quinn, 2005).

The way that individuals cognitively organize their various identities, as well as the impact this has in the work domain, is the subject of Brianna Barker Caza and Marie Gee Wilson's Chapter 5. Specifically, although a differentiated identity map—*work-identity complexity*—has traditionally been argued to be a source of between-identity conflict for the individual, complexity can also be a highly beneficial resource. When identities are complementary and coactivated, complexity can cognitively buffer individuals from potential problems, facilitate instrumental and social support, and provide a greater behavioral repertoire for managing problems. Caza and Wilson illustrate these arguments with two studies. One focused on certified nurse midwives (CNM), who combine the identities of nurse and midwife, enabling them to customize their care to a patient's particular needs and use a broader range of capabilities to solve problems. Said one CNM:

> I walked into the room and I knew immediately that something was wrong ... [I] did what I needed to get her prepped [for surgery] and called my back-up doctor.... But, at the same time, I was able to ... be there psychologically, supporting her as a midwife.

In sum, identities not only connect an individual to personally meaningful groups, roles, and social categories (e.g., gender) but also are potential resources for coping with the inevitable challenges of living in a complex and dynamic organization.

Continuing the theme of multiple identities, Nancy P. Rothbard and Lakshmi Ramarajan (Chapter 6) propose several conditions under which coactivated identities—specifically, work and nonwork identities—are more likely to be experienced as *compatible*. The first condition is control: the greater the status of the individual, the respect the identities garner, and the individual's temporal control over the coactivation, the greater the perceived compatibility. The second condition is routinization: the more "expected and familiar" the coactivation, the greater the perceived compatibility. Individuals choose, where possible, to coactivate identities that are compatible and are reinforced for doing so by positive affect. Further, because compatible identities are mutually reinforcing, they tend to become cognitively yoked such that compatibility in turn fosters greater routinization. Why does this matter? Coactivated compatible identities are likely to promote not only positive affect but also integrative problem solving, productivity, and interpersonal cooperation. Together with Caza and Wilson, Rothbard and Ramarajan's work offers an important corrective to the traditional emphasis on identities as singly activated and typically incompatible.

Finally, Laura Morgan Roberts, Sandra E. Cha, Patricia F. Hewlin, and Isis H. Settles (Chapter 7) focus on a construct touched on by Kreiner and Sheep (Chapter 2), *authenticity*, "the subjective experience of alignment between one's internal experiences and external expressions." The pathways to authenticity include "deepening self-awareness" (via individuating oneself from others and their expectations, and crafting a coherent narrative of oneself), "peeling off [socially prescribed] masks" to reveal one's true self, and receiving "authentication" or social affirmation of oneself. Authenticity, in turn, promotes the experience of "eudaimonia"—"an optimal state of well-being"—and a self-construal of oneself as an authentic person. These twinned states foster a positive identity, that is, "private regard" for oneself. A particularly interesting argument was that leaders and minorities may find authentication more challenging than less visible organizational members because they may need to buck others' stereotypical expectations of them—but doing so is precisely what helps organizations realize the promise of diversity.

Between the Lines

Clearly, our authors have offered varied takes on "positive identity." This speaks less, I think, to the novelty of the construct than to its great generative potential. In short, the variety is a healthy indicator of the vitality of the construct. Competence, resilience, authenticity, transcendence, integration, growth, learning, meaning, hope, identity complementarity/compatibility, self-awareness, social affirmation, and private regard are all considered. As a set, these takes are not meant to be exhaustive; I am confident our authors would have no quarrel adding belonging, enjoyability, redemption, and a raft of other edifying constructs to the list. Inductively, the roster of positive attributes suggests not particular content per se (such as the specific goals, skills, beliefs, and time horizons of, say, a mechanical engineer or a receptionist), but generic qualities (competence, resilience, authenticity, meaning, hope, identity complementarity/compatibility, private regard) and processes (growth, learning, social affirmation)—and perhaps both at once (transcendence, integration, self-awareness). This suggests that there are many ways of instantiating a "positive" identity and that there are many routes to these instantiations. Indeed, perhaps any given identity can be positive, depending on the qualities one imputes to it (such as the optimism a layoff victim holds for a fresh start) and how one enacts it (such as the integrity-affirming efforts of a bankrupt entrepreneur to make good on her debts to family and friends).

What is unclear at this early stage of theorizing is what qualities and processes are part and parcel of positive identity itself and what qualities and processes are better understood as antecedents, covariates, moderators, mediators, or outcomes. For example, positive relationships and a willingness to experiment are mentioned as antecedents of positivity, and yet it would not be too difficult to argue that these are also aspects of a positive identity. After all, as definitions of self, identities are naturally rich and diverse and a given identity (e.g., female manager) can be construed in idiosyncratic ways. Thus, it is important to establish the domain, boundaries, and nomological network of positive identity.

What *is* at least clear is that a positive identity is not only instrumental to organizational effectiveness—in these chapters, through organizational citizenship behaviors, creative problem solving, and organizational change, to name a few—but also is desirable as an end in itself. In organizational studies, we are accustomed to the so-what logic of instrumentality, with turnover and performance being two of our classic dependent variables. But organizational studies are skittish about ultimate ends. As an applied discipline, organizational studies justifiably embrace the idea of relativism, that there are few absolutes and that much depends on context. These chapters, however, remind us that there are inherently good, universally regarded qualities and processes that are desirable for the edification of self and others that they provide.

What Identity Themes Cross-Cut the Chapters?

Despite the different foci of the chapters, certain themes percolate throughout (indicated below by italics). One common theme is that identities are *dynamic*, whether in terms of the emergence and initial construction of an identity (e.g., the relatively new career of CNM), the construction of the individual as a member of the group holding the identity (e.g., the socialization of a new CNM), or the ongoing adaptation of both the group and its individual members to the inherent turbulence and challenges of organizational life. Concepts such as identity experimentation, playfulness, provisional selves, and identity customization speak to this dynamism (e.g., Ibarra, 1999; Pratt, Rockmann, & Kaufmann, 2006). The upshot is that individuals and groups are constantly in a state of becoming.

This sense of becoming is conveyed through identity *narratives* that individuals and groups "construct and reconstruct to make sense of their past" in the context of their present and their preferences for the future—"the ongoing present of things past and future," as Carlsen and Pitsis (Chapter 4) eloquently put it. Thus, narratives provide a sense of continuity and progress, fostering momentum. Shamir and Eilam (2005, p. 402) go so far as to say that identity *is* a story "created, told, revised and retold throughout life." As motivated stories in progress, identity narratives are less literal depictions of history than selectively crafted tales—tales that often follow storytelling conventions (e.g., plot, antagonist, crisis, resolution).

Whereas narratives are open-ended, Kreiner and Sheep (Chapter 2) note that "the effects of growth may ... decay ... over time if not nurtured, maintained, or reinforced." I am reminded of a junior faculty workshop at the Academy of Management annual meeting where Jane Dutton likened scholarship to gardening. A scholar plants and nurtures ideas, and as the ideas develop and blossom, she trims and weeds the garden to shape its growth and create an overall holism. The same can be said of identities. Identities are precious and often fragile things; in addition to nurturing, they often require active tending through an openness to feedback, a willingness to reflect and self-question, and a desire to not only hone who one is but also to play and experiment with alternate ways of doing and being. In the absence of ongoing gardening, it is all too easy for identities to decay, to drift into irrelevance, or to ossify into a caricature.

Identities are not only *socially constructed* and reconstructed, but they also need to be *socially validated* or affirmed through the responses of others. For example, Maitlis's (Chapter 3) rich descriptions of how musicians recalibrated their identities in the wake of disruptive injuries indicates the importance of peers, mentors, family, and friends for actively supporting attempts to change one's identity and for validating the emergent identity claims. Identities that remain unvalidated are likely to remain tenuous and lose their psychological grip over time. Indeed, Roberts et al. (Chapter 7) offer the intriguing argument that even "authentic experience is socially constructed" because "'being true to oneself' is a social process whereby people rely on reflected appraisals to understand and assess their own values, preferences, and actions" (see also Sparrowe, 2005).

Perhaps the strongest theme cross-cutting the chapters is the role of *agency* in developing and enacting an identity. For instance, agency is central to Rothbard and Ramarajan's (Chapter 6) model, as they posit that control over the coactivation and framing of work and nonwork identities is critical to realizing any synergies. Similarly, Kreiner and Sheep (Chapter 2) view proactivity as a "key assumption" underlying the very notion of identity work, and Roberts and her colleagues (Chapter 7) discuss how authenticity is forged through "critical participation in life," "owning one's values and beliefs," and "standing apart from the crowd." So important is agency or control that it is frequently regarded as a fundamental psychological need. As Gecas (1986, p. 140, his emphasis) wrote, "the *experience* of agency ... seems to lie at the very heart of the experience of self."

As Caza and Wilson (Chapter 5) and Rothbard and Ramarajan (Chapter 6) make clear, individuals have *multiple identities,* spanning many levels of self (e.g., person, partner, group, and organization) and many categories of self within a given level. Thus, the issues of identity compatibility and identity complexity—how one "subjective structures" (Caza & Wilson, Chapter 5) his or her identities—become very important. The discussions of these issues suggest that positivity lies not just in the qualities and processes associated with a given identity but also at the interface and even the totality or gestalt of multiple identities. Further, the interaction of multiple identities likely speaks volumes about how much one psychologically invests oneself in each identity, that is, how much one identifies with each. For example, an accounting clerk I know chooses to define himself primarily in terms of the prestigious organization he works for rather than his occupation.

A relatively tacit theme in the chapters is the notion of an identity as a *resource pool.* Caza and Wilson (Chapter 5) are the most explicit, discussing identity complexity as a source of instrumental, social, and cognitive resources. More generally, identities are situated personas, such as what it means to be a female surgeon in a particular hospital or a rookie on a university football team. In situating individuals in a given social domain, identities provide (or deny) access to a variety of tangible and intangible resources, from legitimacy to specific ways of thinking, feeling, and acting, as well as from social networks to socially desirable career paths. The notion of identity as a resource pool is undoubtedly relevant to what makes one identity more attractive than another, to the latitude permitted for agency, and to the narratives that individuals craft to explicate who they are.

Finally, another relatively tacit theme is the importance of *context.* Heath and Sitkin (2001) argue that the central focus and core competence of the field of organizational behavior should be explicating the process of *organizing.* Identity, as the definition of an actor, is a "root construct" (Albert, Ashforth, & Dutton, 2000, p. 13) for diverse organizational phenomena and thus scores well on Heath and Sitkin's central focus criterion. Identity is fundamentally about organizing, namely, organizing the sense that individuals make of the organization—the groupings of occupations, dyads, workgroups, demographic groups, cliques, and so on, the web of relationships among these entities and how they connect to the whole, and of themselves as members of these entities. Identity, in short, helps constitute the context for the individual even as an individual's identity is likewise constituted by the context (cf. social architecting, Roberts et al., 2005).

More conventionally, context can be viewed as an exogenous force that facilitates the development and expression of identities. Kreiner and Sheep (Chapter 2), for example, discuss the varied orientations of organizations to identity growth, from impeding to passive enabling, to more proactive partnering and outright directing. Additionally, Caza and Wilson (Chapter 5) note how some organizations view the roles of nurse and midwife as antithetical rather than complementary, thus drastically affecting how the CNM enacts her identity.

Although our focus here is on positive identities, I suspect that these themes are true of identities in general, and not only at all levels of self (i.e., the individual as a unique person, a role occupant, a partner, a group member, an organizational member, an industry member) but also at all levels of analysis (i.e., the identity of a workgroup, an occupation, an organization, an industry). This suggests that these themes are neither inherently "positive" nor focused on a specific level of self or analysis. Rather, they speak to the scaffolding and tools (context, agency, resource pool, narratives, social construction, and validation) from which all forms of identity are fashioned and to the very nature of identity in contemporary organizations (dynamic, multiple). This begs the very important question of how a given set of scaffolding and tools may give rise to positive rather than negative qualities and processes—to, say, learning rather than willful ignorance, private regard rather than hubris, meaning rather than anomie, transcendence rather than self-absorption.

WHAT RESEARCH QUESTIONS DO THE CHAPTERS RAISE?

The hallmark of a good article is that it does not just answer a research question, it sparks further questions. In that respect, our six chapters are very good indeed, as the following sampler of research questions suggests.

What Are the Relationships Among the Facets of Positivity?

The chapters generally considered singular facets of positivity, begging the question of how the facets might be linked. The default assumption—at this early stage of theorizing in the field—seems to be that the facets are *additive*, such that, say, authenticity plus hope equals "two units" of positivity. If positivity is simply the sum of the parts, then each facet can be safely studied in isolation from the rest.

I strongly suspect, though, that more complex relationships are the norm. Some facets may be *compensatory*. For example, if growth is difficult to discern because the objective situation is impassive, then hope may provide an alternative segue to well-being. What I find most intriguing about the literature on hope is that it does, as the saying goes, "spring eternal" even in the most bleak of circumstances (e.g., terminal illness) (e.g., Snyder, 2000).

Some facets may be *hierarchical*. As Kreiner and Sheep's Chapter 2 suggests, one's spiritual orientation may provide a framework for constructing other identities and instantiating the facets of positivity. The notion of hierarchy quickly prompts related questions: Are particular facets necessary or foundational for the rest? Are there common temporal orderings for the construction of a hierarchy? Under what conditions is a top-down construction more likely than a bottom-up? Might the facets be better arrayed as a network, replete with central nodes and structural holes?

More generally, the facets are likely *interactive* such that there are synergies to be realized. Maitlis's (Chapter 3) musicians drew heavily on identity resources (e.g., social support) and hope to reframe and broaden their original identities in a manner that preserved the musicians' authenticity. The questions prompted by the general notion of interaction are equally legion: Which facets are most likely to serve as catalysts for the realization of synergies? Which facets are most likely to interact? Might some interactions among otherwise positive facets prove negative (e.g., a quest for identity compatibility impeding growth and necessary differentiation)?

Must Positivity and Negativity Exist on a Single Continuum?

Research suggests that the opposite of identifying with one's organization is *not* disidentifying (Elsbach, 1999; Kreiner & Ashforth, 2004). To identify means to define oneself in terms of an entity (I am a Democrat); the opposite is simply to not identify with the entity. A lack of identification means there is no resonance between the person and the entity. Conversely, to disidentify is to actively define oneself as *not* a member of the entity (I am not a Republican); the opposite is to not disidentify. Thus, identification is a qualitatively different phenomenon than disidentification; it is not simply a case of reversing the signs on a 1 to 7 scale. One's self-conception becomes the "constellation" (Elsbach, 1998) of identifications and disidentifications. To further complicate matters, one can simultaneously identify with some aspects of a given entity even as one disidentifies with others.

Analogously, as Kreiner and Sheep (Chapter 2) hint, perhaps certain positive qualities and processes associated with identity are not simply the absence or opposite of negative qualities and processes. As noted, Caza and Wilson (Chapter 5) discuss how an identity can serve as a resource. The absence or opposite is that the identity does not serve as a resource. I would argue that this absence/opposite reflects low positivity, not negativity. Negativity would occur when the identity serves as an impediment or resource drain. The literature on burnout, for example, indicates that many service providers find the identity of caregiver to be emotionally exhausting (e.g., Maslach, 1982). The etiology, experience, and trajectory of this negativity are very different than for positivity. Similarly, Maitlis (Chapter 3) and Kreiner and Sheep (Chapter 2) describe how an identity can be a spur to growth. The absence or opposite is that an identity is not a spur to growth. However, negativity would be evident if an identity is a spur to regression. For instance, Kelman's (1961, p. 63) notion of classic identification involves suppressing one's own individuality "to be like or actually to *be* the other person."

This issue of two continua is very important because it suggests that understanding how to achieve a positive identity does not mean that we simultaneously understand how to thwart a negative identity—and vice versa. Uncharted negativity may undermine positivity, even if all the enablers of positivity are evident. For instance, a very supportive context, chock-full of engaging tasks and enthusiastic peers, may have little effect on a newcomer if he or she has been rendered deeply cynical by repeated disappointments in former jobs (e.g., Fein, 1990). Negativity is often a learned defense, a means of preserving oneself in the face of corrosive forces. Under such circumstances, daring to be positive is more than many can muster.

What Are the Relationships Between the Levels of Self and Between the Levels of Analysis?

In organizational studies, we tend to focus on discrete levels of self (e.g., individual, partner, group member, organizational member) and discrete levels of analysis (e.g., individual, group, organization), but much of the "action" in organizations and many of the most provocative and practically significant questions occur at the interface of multiple levels—between the vertical rather than horizontal links. This is no less true when we consider the qualities and processes that typify positive identities.

Maitlis (Chapter 3), Carlsen and Pitsis (Chapter 4), and Kreiner and Sheep (Chapter 2) note that trauma, hope, and growth apply to levels of analysis beyond the individual. I think the same can be said for the focus of each chapter—and not only for the levels of analysis but also for the levels of self. Further, as suggested earlier, all of the identity themes—dynamism, narratives, social construction and validation, agency, multiplicity, resource pools, context—likely apply to each level of self and to each level of analysis as well. This raises a host of intriguing research questions. Let me offer just a few.

To what extent are the positive qualities and processes isomorphic across levels of self and across levels of analysis (cf., House, Rousseau, & Thomas-Hunt, 1995)? For example, do resilience and authenticity mean the same things at the individual and organizational levels (see Corley & Harrison's Chapter 16 on organizational authenticity)? Do groups "learn" in much the same way as dyads? Is trauma doubled at the team level because of contagion effects among team members, or is it halved because of social support? How do the pros and cons of identity complexity for an individual differ for an organization (see Pratt & Kraatz's Chapter 17 on organizational self)?

How might positive qualities and processes at one level affect those at higher and lower levels (Cameron, Dutton, Quinn, & Wrzesniewski, 2003)? For instance, what factors enable the dissemination of positivity, and what factors impede it? Can one level compensate for the failings of another (e.g., positive regard for one's department atoning for negative regard for one's employer; a nurturing middle manager compensating for the overbearing style of a supervisor)? Might some forms of positivity travel up the organizational hierarchy better than they travel down? How might positive qualities and processes at one level become nested and entrained in another? For example, Carlsen and Pitsis (Chapter 4) note that the hope that a geologist has for discovering oil may be tied to the organization's tendering period for exploring a new area.

What are the various mechanisms through which positive qualities and processes become suffused throughout an organization? Although the importance of organization development, transformational leadership, newcomer socialization, mentors, and so on are staples in the organizational literature, what about less institutionalized mechanisms? For example, some positive qualities and processes may form a contagion of sorts, such as where actors "catch" the hope of others, and tempered radicals (Meyerson & Scully, 1995) may quietly demonstrate the efficacy of more humanistic ways of doing business.

CAUTIONARY NOTES

Let me close by sounding two cautionary notes that pertain as much to the nascent field of POS as to the present chapters on positive identity.

Be Careful What You Wish For

Positive identity has tremendous potential, but as the cliché has it, be careful what you wish for, lest it come true. Two examples will suffice. First, the literature on authenticity in organizations, and particularly authentic leadership, tends to assume that individuals have more or less unique, socially desirable inner selves such that authentically displaying those selves results more or less automatically in positive outcomes for the individual and organization (e.g., Liedtka, 2008; Walumbwa, Avolio, Gardner, Wernsing, & Peterson, 2008).[1] However, authenticity may impose real costs on individuals and organizations. As Roberts and her colleagues note (Chapter 7), full disclosure of one's thoughts and feelings, as well as expressions of weakness and unfavorable attributes, may have problematic effects. Similarly, whistleblowers,

---

[1] It should be noted that the chapter in this volume by Roberts et al. explicitly does *not* make this assumption.

iconoclasts, and even "positive deviants" (Spreitzer & Sonenshein, 2004) are routinely sacrificed on the altar of organizational conformity. What if one's authentic self is abusive, unethical, willfully ignorant, or otherwise destructive to the social and economic fabric of the organization? Although "authentic" implies one's *actual* self, many scholars seem to tacitly invoke more of an idealized or *aspirational* self—as if we all naturally channel an inner Gandhi. Unfortunately, for every Jim Sinegal (CEO of Costco) running an organization, there is a smattering of Jeffrey Skillings (former CEO of Enron).

Second, the literature on hope clearly indicates the salutary impact of hope on individuals (e.g., Snyder, 2000; Youssef & Luthans, 2007). Hope can help one cope with difficult circumstances and provide a strong beacon for action. Indeed, hope is so important that Stern, Dhanda, and Hazuda (2001) found that a sense of hopelessness predicts mortality. However, the desire for hope can lead one to seize on false hopes—to "clutch at straws" —that is, brighter futures that are highly unrealistic. False hopes can lead one to engage in ultimately futile action, perhaps forestalling more efficacious action. Indeed, hope that is vested in a *deus ex machina* (e.g., God will provide) may discourage concrete problem solving altogether. For example, Illes (1996) chronicles how some victims of an impending plant closing clung to the irrational hope that the closing would be averted and took little or no action to secure their own futures until it was too late. In short, as Carlsen and Pitsis (Chapter 4) put it, individuals can become "entrapped" by their hopes and the narratives they spin to make sense of their past and present.

More generally, regardless of whether positivity and negativity exist on a single continuum, as one reaches the heights of positivity, weird things often happen: linear relations turn curvilinear, tipping points occur, feedback loops kick in, vicious cycles (and, fortunately, virtuous cycles) get tripped, and the inevitably gray world of equivocality, complexity, and dynamism becomes redefined and frozen into black and white. As a direct result, many bad things have occurred in the name of good, albeit often unintentionally. Indeed, "evil" per se is seldom the problem in organizations; the evil, say, of a supervisor who feels powerful by abusing his subordinates is relatively easy to spot and therefore root out. Instead, it is the good idea viewed uncritically or taken too far that organizations have to be most wary about. For instance, the history of management is littered with examples of managers seizing on seemingly promising fads only to discover that there are no universal panaceas for complex problems (Collins, 2000). Thus, managers and scholars alike need to be vigilant about the zone of optimality, that is, how far they can push a particular form of positivity before it may become self-defeating.

A large part of the problem, I suspect, is pushing any one positive quality or process in isolation from others. Returning to the notion of synergies, when the qualities and processes are considered as a constellation, positiveness may inhere not in the individual facets but in their interaction—not just as catalysts, but in the checks and balances they mutually impose.

Guarding Against the Kumbaya Effect

Years ago, I immersed myself in the literature on the role of spirituality in work organizations. I came away feeling like I had eaten five pounds of cotton candy. Instead of rich conceptual frameworks, nuanced theorizing, and rigorous qualitative and quantitative research, I found—with some notable exceptions—a slew of cloying bromides. It was a literal case of preaching to the choir. Call it the kumbaya effect: In the flush of discovering an apparently important phenomenon, there is a strong temptation among early adherents to sing its praises and gloss over the necessary but hard questions about its inner workings, boundaries, and potential drawbacks. The major problem with the kumbaya effect is that it is inherently polarizing: Whereas it draws its adherents into a tighter circle, it tends to put off "outsiders" who might otherwise be intrigued by the rich potential of the phenomenon.

Given the positive orientation of POS, of which this book is an example, POS is also potentially susceptible to the kumbaya effect. An orientation to positivity may tempt one to discount the limits and trade-offs that inhere in all complex and dynamic phenomena. However, the chapters in this section show the great promise of POS generally, as well as positive identities specifically, when we approach these constructs not with the dewy-eyed boosterism of the disciple, but with the disciplined rigor of the social scientists that we are and need to remain.

REFERENCES

Albert, S., Ashforth, B. E., & Dutton, J. E. (2000). Organizational identity and identification: Charting new waters and building new bridges. *Academy of Management Review, 25,* 13–17.

Cameron, K. S., Dutton, J. E., Quinn, R. E., & Wrzesniewski, A. (2003). Developing a discipline of positive organizational scholarship. In K. S. Cameron, J. E. Dutton, & R. E. Quinn (Eds.), *Positive organizational scholarship: Foundations of a new discipline* (pp. 361–370). San Francisco: Berrett-Koehler.

Carlsen, A. (2006). Organizational becoming as dialogic imagination of practice: The case of the indomitable Gauls. *Organization Science, 17,* 132–149.

Collins, D. (2000). *Management fads and buzzwords: Critical-practices perspective.* London: Routledge.

Elsbach, K. D. (1998). The process of social identification: With what do we identify? In D. A. Whetten & P. C. Godfrey (Eds.), *Identity in organizations: Building theory through conversations* (pp. 232–237). Thousand Oaks, CA: Sage.

Elsbach, K. D. (1999). An expanded model of organizational identification. *Research in Organizational Behavior, 21,* 163–200.

Fein, M. L. (1990). *Role change: A resocialization perspective.* New York: Praeger.

Gecas, V. (1986). The motivational significance of self-concept for socialization theory. *Advances in Group Processes, 3,* 131–156.

Heath, C., & Sitkin, S. B. (2001). Big-B versus Big-O: What is *organizational* about organizational behavior? *Journal of Organizational Behavior, 22,* 43–58.

House, R., Rousseau, D. M., & Thomas-Hunt, M. (1995). The meso paradigm: A framework for the integration of micro and macro organizational behavior. *Research in Organizational Behavior, 17,* 71–114.

Ibarra, H. (1999). Provisional selves: Experimenting with image and identity in professional adaptation. *Administrative Science Quarterly, 44,* 764–791.

Illes, L. M. (1996). *Sizing down: Chronicle of a plant closing.* Ithaca, NY: ILR Press.

Kelman, H. C. (1961). Processes of opinion change. *Public Opinion Quarterly, 25,* 57–78.

Kreiner, G. E., & Ashforth, B. E. (2004). Evidence toward an expanded model of organizational identification. *Journal of Organizational Behavior, 25,* 1–27.

Liedtka, J. (2008). Strategy making and the search for authenticity. *Journal of Business Ethics, 80,* 237–248.

Maslach, C. (1982). *Burnout: The cost of caring.* Englewood Cliffs, NJ: Prentice-Hall.

Meyerson, D. E., & Scully, M. A. (1995). Tempered radicalism and the politics of ambivalence and change. *Organization Science, 6,* 585–600.

Pratt, M. G., Rockmann, K. W., & Kaufmann, J. B. (2006). Constructing professional identity: The role of work and identity learning cycles in the customization of identity among medical residents. *Academy of Management Journal, 49,* 235–262.

Roberts, L. M., Dutton, J. E., Spreitzer, G. M., Heaphy, E. D., & Quinn, R. E. (2005). Composing the reflected best-self portrait: Building pathways for becoming extraordinary in work organizations. *Academy of Management Review, 30,* 712–736.

Shamir, B., & Eilam, G. (2005). "What's your story?" A life-stories approach to authentic leadership development. *Leadership Quarterly, 16,* 395–417.

Snyder, C. R. (Ed.) (2000). *Handbook of hope: Theory, measures, & applications.* San Diego, CA: Academic Press.

Sparrowe, R. T. (2005). Authentic leadership and the narrative self. *Leadership Quarterly, 16,* 419–439.

Spreitzer, G. M., & Sonenshein, S. (2004). Toward the construct definition of positive deviance. *American Behavioral Scientist, 47,* 828–847.

Stern, S. L., Dhanda, R., & Hazuda, H. P. (2001). Hopelessness predicts mortality in older Mexican and European Americans. *Psychosomatic Medicine, 63,* 344–351.

Walumbwa, F. O., Avolio, B. J., Gardner, W. L., Wernsing, T. S., & Peterson, S. J. (2008). Authentic leadership: Development and validation of a theory-based measure. *Journal of Management, 34,* 89–126.

Youssef, C. M., & Luthans, F. (2007). Positive organizational behavior in the workplace: The impact of hope, optimism, and resilience. *Journal of Management, 33,* 774–800.

Part III

Positive Identities and Relationships in Groups and Organizations

9

Identity Work During Boundary Moments: Managing Positive Identities Through Talk and Embodied Interaction

Curtis D. LeBaron, Phillip Glenn, and Michael P. Thompson

CONTENTS

In a famous sketch by M. C. Escher, entitled "Drawing Hands," two hands are holding pencils so that each draws the other into existence as they jointly emerge from the blank page. In this chapter, we regard identity as something that people do together, as a way of jointly coming into being. We notice that when positive identities emerge within organizations, they do so jointly in interaction. If they happen, they co-occur.

Our approach is to look at identity "in the wild" (Hutchins, 1995). By carefully examining audio and video recordings of people in real conversations at work, we show how "small" verbal and nonverbal behaviors may have "big" consequences for *who people are* relative to one another and their organizations. A variety of interrelated observations stem from our field work, including:

- *Identities are prominent during boundary moments.* Like the greens that grow in the cracks, identities spring to life at the boundaries of conversations (such as when coworkers meet and greet) and at the boundaries of careers (such as during employment interviews). Transitions are fertile places for doing—and for noticing—the identities of people within organizations.

- *Identities, including positive ones, are interactive accomplishments.* No one creates an identity alone. Rather, identities are deeply and inescapably social, and positive identities may take a lot of social work. When positive identities emerge within our data, people seem rather busy: Their voices are animated with variation in volume, pitch, and rate; their bodies are engaged with other people and things through spatial maneuvers, facial expressions, and hand gestures; they show recognition, give appreciation, and ask questions; they play with language, laugh in overlap, and talk at length.

- *Positive identities involve knowing and relating.* To locate positive identities within our data is to find people who show knowledge of and affiliation with each other. Organizations sometimes make a distinction between knowledge work and relationship building, but within the boundary moments that we examine, the same behaviors often do both. For example, our data show that interviewers enact (and interviewees ratify) a positive identity by both (a) being knowledgeable about applicants' file information, and (b) being helpful in how they pose questions that draw on that information.

By looking at identity "in the wild," we can point to specific behaviors and patterns of human interaction that foster positive identity. While we assume that our site-specific findings have relevance beyond the situations that we analyze, generalizability is not our goal. Rather, we have selected a handful of "virtuoso moments," or episodes that "strike the observer as being carried out in a particularly felicitous manner" (ten Have, 1999, p. 40), the analysis of which reveals potential resources for human interaction and organizational work. We agree with Sacks (1984), who said that a "detailed study of small phenomena may give an enormous understanding of the way humans do things and the kinds of objects they use to construct and order their affairs" (p. 24).

What is *positive* identity? One answer is: Positive identity is what people constitute it to be in the moment. This answer is not a dodge—rather, it is an ontological and epistemological commitment. Our approach is to look at what actors themselves constitute and treat as positive, which brings empirical rigor to our methods for identifying positive practices, moving analysis away from the researchers' subjective assessments and toward descriptions of the participants' intersubjective practices. Within the recordings that we examine, people manage positive identities in the moment by showing that they know and relate to each other. Such identity work may profit organizations, as when displays of knowing foster workplace efficiencies, or when displays of relating enable people to be candid or creative. In this chapter, we share both our data and our reasoning, inviting readers to scrutinize and corroborate our claims.

In this chapter, we also use *positive identity* as an umbrella term. We recognize that a conversation or interaction may simultaneously index and inform various identity domains, both individual and institutional. For example, when an interviewer shows that she is knowing and affiliating, the interaction may be in the service of her individual identity ("a smart and friendly person"), her role identity ("a well-prepared and personable recruiter"), her organizational identity ("a manager who is intelligent and diplomatic"), her organization's identity ("a firm that values its employees"), and more. We use the term *positive identity* to imply any or all of these, depending on the situated and constitutive work of the participants themselves.

POSITIVE IDENTITIES—SOMETHING THAT PEOPLE DO TOGETHER

Research on identity within organizations has been conducted at various altitudes. At a macro level, identity refers to the central, distinctive, and enduring attributes of the entire organization (e.g., Albert & Whetten, 1985; Corley, et al, 2006). At a micro level, individuals derive a sense of identity as they view themselves as individuals in relation to the larger collective or organization (e.g., Ashforth & Johnson, 2001; Kreiner & Sheep, 2006). At a meso level, identity is rooted in interpersonal relationships, as when people compare their traits, abilities, goals, and performance within supervisor-subordinate or coworker-coworker relationships (Brewer & Gardner, 1996; Sluss & Ashforth, 2007). Resonant with symbolic interactionism (Mead, 1934), notions of identity in relationship emphasize "the *situation* as the context in which identities are established and maintained through the process of negotiation" (Gecas, 1982, p. 10).

We contribute to meso-level understandings by analyzing the *identity work* of people who are engaged in conversations. Snow and Anderson (1987) defined identity work rather loosely, as the "range of activities individuals engage in to create, present, and sustain personal identities." We regard identity work more specifically, as the moment-to-moment behaviors whereby identities within organizations are interactively managed. Conversations within organizations are unavoidably situated within the social, material, and temporal unfolding of organizational activities. When people converse, they draw on their social and material surroundings to create, present, and sustain the identities of participants—including themselves. Furthermore, identity work is a bridge between macro and micro conceptions of identity: The individual identities that people interactively negotiate may also reflect on the organizations that they represent (Antaki & Widdicombe, 1998).

Meso-level views of identity relate closely to the notion of self or selves. Within organization studies, researchers have made different assumptions about self, depending on their positivist or constructionist leanings. On one hand, much of the organizational assimilation literature has assumed a stable self undergoing recruitment, socialization, and assimilation into an organization (see, e.g., Jablin, 2001). On the other hand, dramaturgical work in the tradition of Goffman (1959) does not assume a stable self but characterizes people as social actors who manage impressions and facework across situations (e.g., Dillard, Browning, Sitkin, & Sutcliffe, 2000). An early challenge to a monolithic view of self was Harre's (1984) observation that within organizations people exist both in person and on paper, which he distinguished as a "real self" and "file self." A poststructuralist view depicts "a discursively constituted self, a self subjected to and by discourses of power in an increasingly complex, destabilized, and multi-vocal world" (Tracy & Trethewey, 2005, p. 171). In this chapter, we use the term "identity work" to describe how selves may be brought into play, toward the social constitution of individual identities, with organizational identities following in the wake. We regard selves as performed (Goffman, 1959), variable (Tracy & Trethewey, 2005), material (Harre, 1984), relational (Gergen, 1991), temporary (Ibarra 1999), and possible (Markus & Nurius, 1986). We see identities as a product of social interaction, a "relatively stable and enduring constellation of attributes, beliefs, values, motives, and experiences in terms of which people define themselves in a professional role" (e.g., Ibarra, 1999, pp. 764–765).

When positive identities emerge within an organization, they emerge together. As people interact in positive ways, the identity work of one person invokes and indexes the selves of others, with positive identities emerging in mutually constitutive, reflexive communicative action. Positive identities emerge not only from *what* people say, but also *when* and *how* they say it. Through the content of talk, people may treat or cast each other as recognizable, likeable and competent. Through the unfolding structure of interaction, people may create opportunities for each other to perform and to succeed. While identity work is something that people continually do, it is especially salient at the boundaries of conversations (e.g., openings, closings, and transitions within activities) and at the boundaries of careers (e.g., hirings, firings, and job appraisals). We call these *boundary moments*, when people's identities hang in the balance or when identities are particularly consequential to what is going on.

Thus, our claims about positivity are grounded, not in some external measure such as organizational effectiveness, but in the displayed orientations and situated practices of people who constitute positivity. Consistent with the research agenda of ethnomethodology (Garfinkel, 1967), we can claim that positive identities are happening because we can explicate social actors' methods for doing them. That is, we treat positive identities as performed, and we document how people go about displaying and responding to each others' behaviors in ways that mutually ratify positive (or negative) identity. They display to each other—and us as overhearers. Therefore, we regard organizational behavior as a kind of social chess, looking at the moves that people make but remaining agnostic about what they may be thinking or feeling.

RESEARCH METHODS—LOOKING AT IDENTITY WORK

Our theoretical claims about identity work are supported by our research methodology: an empirical, qualitative approach, best known as conversation analysis (CA). With roots in ethnomethodology (Heritage, 1984),

CA assumes that human interaction is orderly. What a particular behavior "means" must be understood contextually—that is, it accomplishes social action not only through its content but also through its placement or location within unfolding sequences of situated interaction. In other words, behavior is not inherently meaningful, but is made meaningful as people act in concert; what a particular utterance or gesture means or does depends on what others do in relation to it, such as before and after. Analysts routinely create detailed transcripts that highlight structural features of interaction, showing not only *what* words were spoken, but also *when* and *how* they were spoken (see Appendix).

In this chapter, we examine excerpts from recorded conversations to show how positive identities may be interactively managed. First, we analyze telephone conversations that illustrate how identity work is especially salient and evident at the boundaries of communication events, such as openings and closings. Second, we analyze excerpts from videotaped employment interviews to show how identity work involves not only talk but also embodied forms of interaction such as posture, gesture, facial expressions, and the situated use of material objects and artifacts.

Our data samples demonstrate at least a couple of trends in CA research. First, many conversation analysts have turned their attention from "everyday" conversation (Atkinson & Heritage, 1984) to organizational or "institutional" interaction (Drew & Heritage, 1992). CA enables researchers to address so-called "big" organizational issues (the macro) through careful analysis of "small" moments of human activity (the micro). Second, while conversation analysts have traditionally focused on talk such as telephone conversations (e.g., Drew, 2005), they are increasingly looking at embodied forms of interaction such as those that can be captured on videotape. Our analysis illustrates a growing recognition that "body parts are the first mediating elements in our interaction with the people and objects around us" (Duranti, 1997, p. 322); that "human action is built through the simultaneous deployment of a range of quite different kinds of semiotic resources" (Goodwin, 2000, p. 1489); and that "when people talk, they also locate their bodies, assume various postures, direct their eyes, perhaps move their hands, altogether behaving in ways that constitute an interactive event" (Jones & LeBaron, 2002, p. 499).

Our research procedures may be summarized as four interrelated steps (adapted from LeBaron, 2005; Pomerantz & Fehr, 1997):

1. Collect the data. Researchers who are interested in identity may select a site where identity work is prominent and then record interaction as unobtrusively as possible. The employment interviews that we examine were recorded between 2001 and 2006 at two locations in the United States. We anticipated that when interviewers and applicants come into a room, meeting and talking for the first time, they would need to quickly establish who they are relative to one another and their organizations, with identities emerging in the wake. When writing this chapter, we drew additional examples of identity work from our digital collection of naturally occurring interaction—that is, interaction that would have occurred whether or not it was recorded.

2. Prepare to analyze the data. We listened and watched the recordings carefully and repeatedly, selecting moments where identity work was being done. We made detailed transcripts of those moments. Within our recorded telephone conversations, we could see identity work especially at the openings and closings of the calls. When we looked at employment interviews, we soon became interested in "challenging questions"—that is, when an interviewer calls on an applicant to account for a "problem" in his or her resume. Such moments are challenging because applicants must manage, impromptu, the discursive relationship between their file and their embodied performance in interaction with the interviewer.

3. Analyze the data. We identified social actions, described the packaging of those actions, and explicated how people's actions accomplish relative status, roles, relationships, attitudes, knowledge states, and other aspects of identity within organizations. For example, when interviewers ask challenging questions, they talk and gesture in ways that locate a "problem" in either the file on the table or the applicant across the table. How the interviewer asks a challenging question has consequences—not only for the applicant's subsequent answer but also for the identities that they are jointly negotiating.

4. Report research findings. Reports may highlight recurring patterns of behavior across moments, or document the complexities of a single case. Our purpose is to analyze a handful of excerpts that illustrate how positive identities within organizations may be interactively constituted through unfolding sequences of vocal and visible behavior.

Through these steps, CA claims can be grounded in the empirical details of actual behavior that are recorded and made available to a scrutinizing audience. Although conversation analysts may avoid explicit claims about the generalizability of site-specific findings, they assume that patterns and practices found in one place will have relevance elsewhere, as part of what Goffman (1959) called the "interaction order" of social and organizational life.

IDENTITY WORK AT THE BOUNDARIES OF CONVERSATIONS

Our examination of boundary moments begins with *openings*. The onset of an activity or communicative event is typically (perhaps necessarily) rich with information about the participants, their identities, and who they are in relation to one another. Such social "realities" are not preexistent and independent of openings; rather, they are invoked, brought into play and established through the subtle behaviors that interactively constitute openings. Kendon (1990) observed:

> It is by way of a greeting that friends acknowledge, and so confirm and continue their friendship. In the manner in which the greeting is performed, the greeters signal to each other their respective social status, their degree of familiarity, their degree of liking for one another, and also, very often, what roles they will play in the encounter that is about to begin (p. 154).

Through such interaction at the opening of an encounter or activity, participants quickly negotiate a way of being together. Their identity work is, of course, performed for each other's view, which makes it possible for researchers to record and analyze it.

For example, when people begin a telephone conversation, they quickly participate in a cultural routine that has been well documented by conversation analysts. The openings of telephone conversations involve turn sequences that signal availability (or not), display mutual recognition (or not), offer greetings (or not), make initial inquiries (or not), and move to a first topic (Schegloff, 1968, 1979). Through small adjustments to the details of an opening, or through deviations from the cultural routine, participants can do identity work—indicating that they are intimates or strangers, that they have an organizational affiliation or not, that their call is casual or urgent, and so forth, all within the first few seconds (Hopper, 1992; Schegloff, 1986). To illustrate, consider the following transcription of a telephone opening between two people ("Matt" and "Dale"),[1] members of the same organization who quickly negotiate and display their friendship (see Appendix for transcription conventions).

Excerpt 1: "My Buddy"

1		((Ring))
2	Matt:	Hello
3	Dale:	Hey
4	Matt:	↑He:y
5	Dale:	He:y
6	Matt:	What's happening
7	Dale:	Hey buddy↑
8	Matt:	Is this my buddy↑
9	Dale:	He:y you ain't got no bud ⌈dies
10	Matt:	⌊What's happening
11	Dale:	Hey
12	Matt:	He:y
13	Dale:	Did u::h
14	Matt:	You ready for Thanksgiving?

Within seconds, the men enact friendship as each shows the other to be familiar, likeable, and engaging. When Dale says "Hey" (Line 3), he signals that he recognizes Matt's voice and thereby skips the identification sequence that is found in the typical telephone opening. In response, Matt also says "Hey" (Line 4), showing that he recognizes Dale's voice (after only one syllable from Dale), strongly corroborating their mutual familiarity. At the same time, Matt raises his vocal pitch, increases his volume, and stretches his utterance (Line 4), which marks his enthusiasm for the conversation. As their telephone opening unfolds, the men playfully exaggerate their mutual regard by recycling the greeting "hey" (Lines 5, 7, 9, 11, and 12), by repeatedly using the word "buddy" (Lines 7, 8, and 9), and by marking their voice with enthusiasm. Although Dale initiates the telephone call, the first topic is introduced by Matt (Line 14),

---

[1] All names and identifiers in our data have been replaced by pseudonyms.

which also deviates from the norm and further demonstrates—or rather accomplishes—their informality and shared history. Thus, through the content and structure of their telephone opening, the men do positive identity work: They interactively demonstrate enthusiasm for their relationship, jointly casting each other as memorable, likeable, and engaging.

We emphasize that positive identities are an interactive accomplishment. They do *not* exist before and independent of interaction, nor are they a causal outcome of conditions or circumstances. Even when possibilities for negativity abound within an organization, leaders and members may nevertheless do positive identity work.

For example, consider another telephone conversation involving two people from different organizations. "David" is a vice president at "Retail Inc," a multibillion-dollar corporation; "Neal" is the owner of "Sports Inc," an external supplier of sports paraphernalia. After placing a large order for merchandise, David did not hear back from Sports Inc as promised. Then one morning, David repeatedly called Sports Inc, trying to confirm delivery of his order. That afternoon, David received not just one call, but multiple calls from representatives of Sports Inc who seemed unaware of each other's activities, including a call from Neal, the owner himself.

Rather than complain about missed promises, wasted time, and redundant responses, David engaged in positive identity work with Neal. The opening of their telephone conversation is transcribed as follows:

Excerpt 2(a): "Double-Teamed"

1		((Ring))
2	David:	This is David
3	Neal:	David this is Neal from Sports Inc how you doing
4	David:	<u>Hey</u> Neal fine thank you
5	Neal:	What's going on buddy?

The participants quickly enact a professional and friendly relationship. Evidently not familiar with each other's voice, they take turns identifying themselves and repeating each other's names (Lines 2–4). However, their process of mutual identification is wrapped in a friendly inquiry ("how you doing" at Line 3) and a response ("fine thank you" at Line 4). Moreover, David acknowledges Neal with an enthusiastic "<u>Hey</u>" (Line 4).

From that point until the end of the conversation, Neal refers to David as "buddy" (starting in Line 5), repeatedly indexing the friendly opening of their conversation.

By gingerly moving toward a first topic, David and Neal manage the potential awkwardness of their conversation. Neal's question, "What's going on buddy?" (Line 5), is ambiguous because of its location: The question creates an opportunity for David to either extend their telephone opening (i.e., continue friendly small talk) or to introduce a first topic (e.g., a complaint about the poor service of Sports Inc). David does the former by giving the turn back to Neal, allowing him to introduce the first topic and articulate the reason for their conversation. Their exchange unfolds as follows:

Excerpt 2(b): "Double-Teamed"

5	Neal:	What's going on buddy?
6	David:	Not- not much
7	Neal:	You got a second ⌐or you in the middle something
8	David:	⌐Yes I do
9	Neal:	Okay I just want to touch base. I know we haven't
10		spoken in a little bit

With the words "not much" (Line 6) and "Yes I do" (Line 8), David makes himself available for a conversation and gives Neal an opportunity to introduce the first topic. In this way, David casts Neal into the role of the initiator rather than the respondent, as someone who is reaching out to serve a client, rather than someone who is reacting to a customer's prior call. Neal engages accordingly. He says, "I just want to touch base. I know we haven't spoken in a little bit" (Lines 9 and 10), which avoids any explicit reference to poor service and depicts his telephone call as self-initiated. Thus, despite arguably negative circumstances, the participants do positive identity work at the opening of their conversation in a way that supports their relative roles.

As the telephone conversation continues, Neal learns that David's problems have already been solved. Other representatives from Sports Inc have already called, and the delivery of merchandise is already underway. Essentially, David informs Neal about what has been happening within Neal's own organization. Potentially, the owner's telephone call could be regarded as not only late and redundant but also uninformed.

Nevertheless, the closing of their telephone conversation features positive identity work. By invoking a sports metaphor, David explicitly frames Neal's telephone call in a way that casts both participants in a positive light. When it becomes clear that David's needs have already been "covered" (Lines 22 and 23), he immediately suggests that he is being "double-teamed" (Lines 25 and 27), which depicts Neal's telephone call as attentive and flattering—*not* as redundant and distracting. The moment unfolds as follows:

Excerpt 2(c): "Double-Teamed"

```
22    Neal:    So you're covered ⌈then
23    David:                       ⌊We're- we're- we're covered
24    Neal:    Okay   buddy
25    David:   But I- but I appreciate this, uh, double-teamed
26    Neal:    I just wanted to follow up, man
27    David:   ⌈I love to be double-teamed
28    Neal:    ⌊I didn't even have uh
29    David:   That means I'm a big player
30    Neal:    I can't not ca:ll
31    Neal:    Cause then I don't feel like I'm doing my job-
```

David validates Neal's telephone call, claiming that it is something he appreciates (Line 25), even loves (Line 27). Whether the sports metaphor resonates deeply with the owner of Sports Inc, Neal embraces the positive identity that David's metaphor proffers. Neal plays the part of an attentive businessman by asserting, "I can't not ca:ll" (Line 30), and by explaining, "Cause then I don't feel like I'm doing my job" (Line 31). Of course, by embracing the positive identity that David makes available, Neal also alter-casts David as "a big player" (Line 29), as someone who needs to be double-teamed. Through their interaction, they demonstrate how positive identities are something that people do together. They both win, jointly, at the same time.

The conversation concludes much as it began, with the participants interactively doing a professional and friendly relationship. Neal invites David to call him if he ever needs something in the future (Lines 33–35), which illustrates the advantages that positive identity work can engender for an organization. Immediately after Neal is interactively cast in the role of an attentive business man who is just trying to do his job, he announces that he is ready to act accordingly (Lines 33–35):

Excerpt 2(d): "Double-Teamed"

33	Neal:	Well listen, if you can neve- if you can't get
34		him or something or you ever need something
35		just give me a call
36	David:	I'll do it
37	Neal:	Alright bud⌐dy
38	David:	└Uh he- he's uh
39	Neal:	So you guys are on the right track, you're all set
40	David:	You bet
41	Neal:	Alright man
42	David:	Yup
43	Neal:	David have a good weekend
44	David:	Thanks Neal
45	Neal:	Alright buddy
46	David:	See ya
47	Neal:	Bye

The pattern of their interaction is consistent with the cultural routine for closing a telephone conversation (Schegloff & Sacks, 1973). That is, they project some future or next conversation (Lines 33–36); they briefly revisit their initial topic and formulate the outcome (Lines 39 and 40); and they take a series of short speaking turns to notify and acknowledge that their conversation is coming to a close (Lines 41–47). What is important for the purposes of this study is that this mundane cultural routine is used in the service of positive work identities. Neal repeatedly calls David his "buddy" (Lines 37 and 45), who in turn expresses appreciation for Neal (Line 44), as they interactively sustain a mutual regard that brings out the best in both of them.

Notice that the boundaries of conversations point backward and forward. Through the openings of conversations, participants may negotiate and display a relational history as a basis for current identities. During the closings of conversations, participants may negotiate and display a relational future as a basis for current identities. Thus, conversations enact a relationship that continues, with identities instantiated as though they are enduring.

IDENTITY WORK AT THE BOUNDARIES OF CAREERS

Within organizations, people exist as various selves. A living presence or "embodied self" can hear, see, move, initiate conversation, extemporaneously elaborate and passionately argue—but this embodied self can occupy only one physical location at a time. A paper presence or "file self" (Harre, 1984) may be an application, resume, letter, or some combination of documents that can be copied and distributed to influence multiple activities simultaneously—but a file self is mute until read, passive and impotent until regarded.

When organizations bring selves together, important identity work usually happens. During courtroom testimony, a witness who is on the stand and under oath (an embodied self) may be confronted with his or her written deposition (a file self), a dramatic moment in which the identities of both the examining attorney and the witness may hang in the balance. Within a doctor's office, a patient on the examination table (an embodied self) may receive test results (a file self), with the possibility of an identity-changing diagnosis such as "Alzheimer's," from a physician whose reputation depends on accurate diagnoses. During employment interviews, an applicant sitting in a chair (an embodied self) may be asked to account for details in his or her resume (a file self), by an interviewer whose professional identity is also in flux. We emphasize that identities emerge jointly, through conversations that unfold interactively.

For example, consider a brief excerpt from a videotaped interview that goes badly—for both applicant and interviewer. Midway through the interview, after the applicant has rambled somewhat incoherently for more than a minute, the interviewer interjects and explicitly critiques the applicant's performance. The interaction is transcribed as follows:

Excerpt 3: "Just Say I Don't Know"

1	Applicant:	▲...core co̲mpetencies you wanna be able
2		to use (.)
3	Interviewer:	((Figure 9.1A)) Do you ⌈kno:w
4	Applicant:	⌊s:ki:lls (.) that
5	Interviewer:	Do you know the answer to this question?
6		(1.4)
7	Applicant:	I fe̲e̲l like (.) I feel like I know, uh I-

8		⌈I have an understanding
9	Interviewer:	⌊You haven't given me the an-
10	Interviewer:	You haven't given me the answer yet
11	Applicant:	Okay
12	Interviewer:	But if you don't <u>know</u> (.) then the best thing
13		to do is just say I don't know. ((Figure 9.1B))

Without waiting for the applicant to finish his answer, the interviewer questions *aloud* whether the applicant knows what he is talking about (Lines 3 and 5). After a moment of silence (Line 6), the applicant begins to assert an understanding (Lines 7 and 8), but the interviewer talks over him and rejects his claim, saying, "You haven't given me the answer yet" (Lines 9 and 10). Then the scope of the interviewer's critique expands: He generalizes beyond the current conversation to suggest a general rule—that the applicant should confess his ignorance when he does not know the answer to an interview question (Lines 9 and 10). Throughout his critique, the

FIGURE 9.1A

FIGURE 9.1B

interviewer looks directly at the embodied self of the applicant (Figures 9.1A and 9.1B), making him the location of the "problem" and the focus of critique—not the file self. Without hesitation, qualification, or mitigation, the interviewer regards and casts the applicant as deficient.

Because organizational identities emerge jointly, through conversation that unfolds interactively, this unfortunate moment may have negative consequences for both participants. Obviously the applicant's identity suffers to the extent that others regard him as deficient, uninformed, or unqualified. But negative identity work cuts both ways. The interviewer's identity is also affected because his critique does more than give information—it *gives off* information (Goffman, 1959). The content and structure of his critique communicates something about the way that he engages with other people. By interrupting to say, "You haven't given me the answer yet" (Lines 9 and 10), the interviewer ironically cuts off the applicant's opportunity to do so. In his rush to talk about the applicant's knowledge deficiencies, the interviewer demonstrates his own relational ones.

In our examination of employment interviews, we find that positive identity work involves both a *knowing stance* and *relating stance*. "Stance" refers to a speaker's outward display of what is presumed to be (and often is) his or her internal state, both epistemic and affective (e.g., Tracy, 2002). Interviewers can show that they know the file self: that they are familiar with an applicant's history and prepared for the work at hand. They can also show that they relate with the embodied self, that they are aware of an applicant's circumstance and ready to empathize with it. Stance indicators may be particular words or phrases, tone of voice, silence during conversation, and so forth. We agree with Ochs (1993), who argued that "speakers attempt to establish the social identities of themselves and others through verbally performing certain social acts and verbally displaying certain stances" (p. 288). Our videotaped data also include visible stance indicators such as hand gestures, facial expressions, and eye gaze.

For example, consider an excerpt from a videotaped interview that demonstrates positive identity work. Like an attorney during cross-examination, the interviewer takes information from the applicant's resume and asks him to account for a non sequitur or "disconnect" (Line 12) in his professional history. By bringing the applicant's file self and embodied self jointly into play, the interviewer creates a challenging question that may have consequences for the applicant's identity. However, as the interviewer asks for information from the applicant, he also gives off information about himself. His challenging question is mitigated by displays of knowing and relating: He shows that he is both familiar with the documents on the table and empathetic with the person in the chair. His question comes off as an opportunity for the applicant to tell his story, rather than as a judgment against his qualifications. The vocal and visible features of this interaction are transcribed as follows:

Excerpt 4: "Bridge the Gap"

1	Interviewer:	I was looking over your resume ((Figure 9.2A))
2	Applicant:	S<u>u</u>re
3		(0.4)
4	Interviewer:	▼ ((Figure 9.2B)) And noticed that you have a ▲
5		(.) a really strong PR background ((Figure 9.2C))
6		(0.2)
7	Applicant:	Okay
8	Interviewer:	▼ You know, <u>but</u> (.) it says that ▲ you're
9		in school for a finance track ⌐you know
10	Applicant:	└Right
11	Interviewer:	I've- I've had the same problem a little di- (.)
12		disconnect in my background ▼ I was just
13		wondering if you could ▲ kind of bridge the gap
14		for me between public relations and finance
15	Applicant:	S<u>u</u>re (.) be happy to do that . . .

The interviewer's knowing is claimed, demonstrated, and embodied. He claims knowledge of the file by saying that he was "looking" at it (Line 1) and that he "noticed" certain details (Line 4). He demonstrates knowledge of the file by describing its contents, such as when he says "you have a really strong PR background" (Lines 4 and 5) and "you're in school for a finance track" (Lines 8 and 9). He embodies knowledge through the coordination of talk, gaze, and gesture. By looking down at the file *after* his question is already underway (Line 4, Figure 9.2B), he makes it likely that the applicant will be watching (Goodwin, 1980) and that his shifting gaze will be a public performance. His downward glance is coordinated with the word "noticed" (Line 4), which invites the applicant to see his glance as pointing and not perusing, as explanation and not examination. While the interviewer talks, the file is in constant motion: He holds it in his hand

FIGURE 9.2A

FIGURE 9.2B

FIGURE 9.2C

and beats the paper emphatically, consonant with the rhythm of his voice, making it all the more visible but temporarily unreadable. Soon, the interviewer looks back up and at the applicant (Line 4, Figure 9.2C). By looking down only briefly—too short to examine the file, but long enough for the applicant to notice—the interviewer makes the file relevant to the conversation without making it the primary object of his attention. In this way, the interviewer looks at the file, not to glean information, but to locate it as the source of information already gleaned. The interviewer embodies a knowing stance.

The interviewer's relating is both vocal and visible. Although he explicitly labels the applicant's history as a "problem" (Line 11), he affiliates by acknowledging a similar "disconnect" in his own background (Line 12). While his question is challenging, it is wrapped in the positive assessment, "you have a really strong PR background" (Lines 4 and 5). He also mitigates his request with words such as "little" (Line 11), "just wondering" (Lines 12 and 13), and "kind of" (Line 13), which function to soften his challenging question, while at the same time marking the moment as potentially challenging for the applicant. By looking down at the file (e.g., Line 4, Figure 9.2B), the interviewer invites the applicant to join him in regarding the file, treating it as the location of the "problem" that they are discussing. In this way, his orientation to the file mitigates the potential face threat of his question, altogether marking his relational stance as empathetic, diplomatic, and helpful.

Notice that the same behaviors can do both knowing and relating (see Cross & Sproull, 2004, who also find a co-occurrence of organizational knowledge and relationships.). When the interviewer says, "You have a really strong PR background" (Lines 4 and 5), he is both demonstrating his knowledge of the file and blunting the sharpness of his challenging question. Similarly, when he briefly glances down at the file (Line 4, Figure 9.2C), he locates the source of information already gleaned, *and* he locates the problem or "disconnect" within the file self rather than the embodied self, which makes his challenging question less face threatening. Within organizations, knowledge work and relationship work may be mutually reinforcing and inseparable.

In summary, applicants and interviewers must quickly negotiate who they are (and who they will be) relative to one another. When interviewers ask questions, they also give off information. In other words, interviewers manage *their own* identities at the same time that they create opportunities for applicants. We have focused on challenging questions, when interviewers bring an applicant's file self and embodied self jointly into play, through vocal and visible behaviors that show interviewers to be knowing (or not) and affiliating (or not). Positive identities may emerge as interviewers spontaneously interlace acts and gestures of both knowing and affiliating. While demonstrating familiarity with the applicant's file self, an interviewer may also relate to the applicant's embodied self. Further, we have shown that positive identity work is accomplished, among other ways, by drawing on the file self as the source of a challenging question.

DISCUSSION AND CONCLUSION

In various ways, our study expands and strengthens Snow and Anderson's (1987) notion of "identity work." Most obviously, we bring new research methods to the table. Whereas Snow and Anderson relied on observations and field notes, we have collected audio and video recordings that enable us to observe repeatedly and analyze carefully. Our conversation analytic methods feature transcriptions and descriptions of specific behaviors, providing more detail and complexity than the ethnographic and discourse analytic methods used by Snow and Anderson. Whereas they were able to identify a few "generic patterns of identity talk," we show how talk and *visible* behaviors may be orchestrated in identity work, including the use of material objects and artifacts. Whereas they oriented toward people's overt and explicit "avowals of personal identity," we document the more subtle actions and even the silent displays of participants. Thus, our conversation analytic approach expands the phenomenological range and strengthens the empirical grounding of research on identity work.

Our methodological difference gives rise to an important theoretical one: interactivity. Snow and Anderson (1987) observed individual actors, focusing on their monologic discourse, treating identity work as a unilateral or solo accomplishment. In contrast, we study dyadic and face-to-face encounters, focusing on the dialogic and embodied engagement of interlocutors, treating identity work as coaccomplished through unfolding turns of interaction. We show how identities emerge jointly, through negotiation-like processes inherent to social interaction. For example, our examination of telephone openings illustrates how people quickly and interactively negotiate who they are relative to one another and their task at hand. In Excerpt 1 ("My Buddy"), Matt and Dale deviated from the typical or canonical telephone opening to cast each other as memorable (e.g., through immediate voice recognition), likeable (e.g., through vocal emphasis and variation), and engaging (e.g., through playful repetition). In this way, their positive organizational identities were interactively instantiated before they turned to other kinds of work.

When researchers look for interactivity, they assume a social constructionist view of the world, which is friendly to the agenda of positive organizational scholarship (POS) (e.g., Dutton & Ragins, 2007). If people largely or partly constitute the "realities" of their organization—such as their organizational identities—then POS offers ways for people to improve their lives. In Excerpt 2 ("Double-Teamed"), David and Neal negotiated positive organizational identities despite rather negative circumstances. Their achievement involved a set of discursive markers and mechanisms, employed at both the opening and closing of their conversation, including terms of address (e.g., "buddy"), turn taking (e.g., who introduces first topic), role negotiation (e.g., who is taking the initiative), and framing (e.g., "I love to be double-teamed"). In addition to whatever fun or good feelings David and Neal may have experienced, their positive identities improved the circumstances of their work: Their difficulties were resolved rather than protracted; their relative roles were clarified rather than complicated; and they encouraged rather than discouraged future conversation. In contrast, Excerpt 3 ("Just Say I Don't Know") shows an employment interview going badly. The interviewer interrupted the applicant and accused him of being ignorant, which ironically prevented him from demonstrating otherwise. Through this interaction, negative identities jointly emerged, which adversely affected their immediate circumstance and probably the organization's ability to recruit top talent in the future.

Our claims about positivity are empirically grounded. Consistent with the ethnomethodological roots of conversation analysis, we avoid imposing external norms on our data, as we argue for a situated understanding of positivity. In other words, positive identity is what people constitute it to be in the moment. When we look at our data, we see that positive identity work is associated with *knowing* and *affiliating*. In Excerpt 1 ("My Buddy"), Matt and Dale quickly established positive identities through mutual recognition (a kind of knowing) and vocal repetition (a way of affiliating or being together). Additionally, they marked their interaction as positive through laughter, play, and mutual regard. In Excerpt 4 ("Bridge the Gap"), the interviewer and applicant managed positive identities, even during challenging circumstances, through displays of knowing and affiliating. For example, when the interviewer asked the applicant to account for a "disconnect" in his professional history, he mitigated his challenging question with a positive assessment of the applicant's resume ("a really strong PR background"), showing both knowledge of the resume (file self) and approval of the candidate (embodied self). The applicant marked the question as positive by saying, "Sure (.) be happy to do that." On one hand, the interviewer was interactively cast as a well-prepared and diplomatic professional. On the other hand, the applicant was given an opportunity to take the stage, to go beyond the information in his file (because this information was already "known") and to talk about himself within a supportive (or affiliating) environment. The moment was positive for the participants and for their organization.

While knowing and affiliating are about *how* positive identities may be done, we have coined the term *boundary moments* to emphasize *where* they may be done. Although identity work pervades interaction, it is especially prominent at the openings, closings, and transitions of conversations and careers. During the openings and closing of telephone conversations, people use and adapt cultural routines in ways that quickly and interactively show who they are relative to one another and their organizations. Positive identities do not exist before and independent of conversation; rather, they are invoked and brought into play through the subtle behaviors that constitute openings and closings. The boundaries of conversations point backward and forward. Through the openings of conversations, participants may negotiate and display a relational history as a basis for current identities. During the closings of conversations, participants may negotiate and display a relational future as a basis for current identities. Thus, conversations enact a relationship that continues, with identities performed as though they are enduring. However, we suggest that identities are not inherently enduring but are performed to seem enduring. Both practitioners and researchers should attend to boundary moments as opportunities to do and to see positive identity work.

In conclusion, identities are negotiated and instantiated, moment to moment and day to day, through interaction within social and material environments. Most research on identity within organizations relies on surveys and questionnaires that report participants' perceptions of their relationships to other persons and/or their organization. While insightful, such approaches risk reifying identity and may overlook how it comes to be consequential at particular moments within organizations. By looking at identity "in the wild" (Hutchins, 1995), by carefully analyzing audio and video recordings, researchers can identify and explicate the multimodal resources and social practices associated with identity work. From an ethnomethodological perspective, identity is an accomplishment, something that people do. By studying situated behavior, researchers can better understand how positive identities are interactively created and how they are consequential within organizations.

Our study raises a variety of opportunities for future research on positive identity work. First, we invite researchers to confirm or dispute the importance of knowing and affiliating as practices of identity work within organizations. Second, we have examined only four episodes—two telephone conversations and two employment interviews—which is a relatively small sample. Conversation analysts often work with large collections so that they can argue that their qualitative findings have widespread relevance (a surrogate for generalizability). We encourage large-scale CA studies that examine identity work within organizational settings. Third, we call for more multimodal studies of identity work. Overwhelmingly, research on identity work has focused on talk (usually monologue) and has ignored the embodied and material world, which is primordial and unavoidable. Finally, we urge researchers to find compelling evidence for the connection between "small" situated behaviors and "big" organizational outcomes.

APPENDIX: TRANSCRIPTION CONVENTIONS

Our transcription conventions, listed below, have been adapted from a transcription system developed by Gail Jefferson (see Atkinson & Heritage, 1984; Ochs, Schegloff, & Thompson, 1996).

Symbol	Name	Description
Yes	Underline	Vocal stress or emphasis through increased volume
he::y	Colons	Vocal emphasis through sound stretching
↑	Up arrow	Vocal emphasis through raised pitch
-	Hyphen	Halting, abrupt cut off of sound
(0.8)	Timed silence	Length of pause by tenths of a second
(.)	Micropause	Short pause, less than 0.2 seconds
[	Brackets	Overlapping talk, precisely located
(( ))	Double parentheses	Visible behaviors; transcriber's comments
▼	Down arrow	Interviewer looks down at file
▲	Up arrow	Interviewer looks up at applicant

REFERENCES

Albert, S., & Whetten, D. (1985). Organizational identity. In L. Cummings & B. Staw (Eds.), *Research in organizational behavior* (Vol. 7, pp. 263–295). Greenwich, CT: JAI Press.

Antaki, C., & Widdicombe, S. (1998). Identity as an achievement and as a tool. In C. Antaki & S. Widdicombe (Eds.), *Identities in talk* (pp. 1–14). London: Sage.

Ashforth, B., & Johnson, S. (2001). Which hat to wear? The relative salience of multiple identities in organizational contexts. In M. Hogg & D. Terry (Eds.), *Social identity processes in organizational contexts* (pp. 31–48). Philadelphia: Psychology Press.

Atkinson, J., & Heritage, J. (1984). *Structures of social action.* Cambridge, England: Cambridge University Press.

Brewer, M., & Gardner, W. (1996). Who is the 'we'?: Levels of collective identity and self representations. *Journal of Personality and Social Psychology, 71,* 83–93.

Corley, K., Harquail, C., Pratt, M., Glynn, M., Fiol, C., & Hatch, M. (2006). Guiding organizational identity through aged adolescence. *Journal of Management Inquiry, 15,* 85–99.

Cross, R., & Sproull, L. (2004). More than an answer: Information relationships for actionable knowledge. *Organization Science, 15,* 446–462.

Dillard, C., Browning, L., Sitkin, S., & Sutcliffe, K. (2000). Impression management and the use of procedures at the Ritz-Carlton: Moral standards and dramaturgical discipline. *Communication Studies, 51,* 404–414.

Drew, P. (2005). Conversation analysis. In K. Fitch & R. Sanders (Eds.), *Handbook of language and social interaction* (pp. 71–102). Mahwah, NJ: Lawrence Erlbaum Associates.

Drew, P., & Heritage, J. (Eds.) (1992). *Talk at work: Interaction in institutional settings.* Cambridge, England: Cambridge University Press.

Duranti, A. (1997). *Linguistic anthropology.* Cambridge, England: Cambridge University Press.

Dutton, J., & Ragins, B. (Eds.) (2007). *Exploring positive relationships at work.* Mahwah, NJ: Lawrence Erlbaum Associates.

Garfinkel, H. (1967). *Studies in ethnomethodology.* Englewood Cliffs, NJ: Prentice-Hall.

Gecas, V. (1982). The self-concept. *The Annual Review of Sociology, 8,* 1–33.

Gergen, K. (1991). *The saturated self: Dilemmas of identity in contemporary life.* New York: Basic Books.

Goffman, E. (1959). *The presentation of self in everyday life.* Harmondsworth, England: Penguin.

Goodwin, C. (1980). Restarts, pauses, and the achievement of a state of mutual gaze at turn-beginning. *Sociological Inquiry, 50,* 277–302.

Goodwin, C. (2000). Practices of color classification. *Mind, Culture, and Activity, 7,* 19–36.

Harre, R. (1984). *Personal being: A theory for individual psychology.* Cambridge, MA: Harvard University Press.

Heritage, J. (1984). *Garfinkel and ethnomethodology.* Cambridge, England: Polity Press.

Hopper, R. (1992). *Telephone conversation.* Bloomington, IN: Indiana University Press.

Hutchins, E. (1995). *Cognition in the wild.* Cambridge, MA: MIT Press.

Ibarra, H. (1999). Provisional selves: Experimenting with image and identity in professional adaptation. *Administrative Science Quarterly, 44,* 764–791.

Jablin, F. (2001). Organizational entry, assimilation, and disengagement/exit. In F. Jablin & L. Putnam (Eds.), *The new handbook of organizational communication: Advances in theory, research, and methods* (pp. 732–818). Thousand Oaks, CA: Sage.

Jones, S., & LeBaron, C. (2002). Research on the relationship between verbal and nonverbal communication: Emerging integrations. *Journal of Communication, 52,* 499–521.

Kendon, A., (1990). *Conducting interaction: Patterns of behavior in focused encounters.* Cambridge, England: Cambridge University Press.

Kreiner, G., & Sheep, M. (2006). Where is the "me" among the "we"? Identity work and the search for optimal balance. *Academy of Management Journal, 49,* 1031–1057.

LeBaron, C. (2005). Considering the social and material surround: Toward microethnographic understandings of nonverbal behavior. In V. Manusov (Ed.), *The sourcebook of nonverbal measures* (pp. 493–506). Mahwah, NJ: Lawrence Erlbaum Associates.

Markus, H., & Nurius, P. (1986). Possible selves. *American Psychologist, 41,* 954–969.

Mead, G. H. (1934). *Mind, self, and society: From the standpoint of a social behaviorist.* Chicago: University of Chicago Press.

Ochs, E. (1993). Constructing social identity: A language socialization perspective. *Research on Language and Social Interaction, 26,* 3.

Ochs, E., Schegloff, E., & Thompson, S. (1996). *Interaction and grammar.* Cambridge, England: Cambridge University Press.

Pomerantz, A., & Fehr, B. (1997): Conversation analysis: An approach to the study of social action as sense making practices. In T. van Dijk (Ed.), *Discourse as social interaction* (pp. 64–91). London: Sage.

Sacks, H. (1984). Notes on methodology. In J. M. Atkinson & J. Heritage (Eds.), *Structures of social interaction* (pp. 21–27). Cambridge, England: Cambridge University Press.

Schegloff, E. (1968). Sequencing in conversational openings. *American Anthropologist, 70,* 1075–1095.

Schegloff, E. (1979). Identification and recognition in telephone conversation openings. In G. Psathas (Ed.), *Everyday language: Studies in ethnomethodology* (pp. 23–78). New York: Irvington Press.

Schegloff, E. A. (1986). The routine as achievement. *Human Studies, 9,* 111–152.

Schegloff, E. A., & Sacks, H. (1973). Opening up closings. *Semiotica, 7,* 289–327.

Sluss, D., & Ashforth, B. (2007). Relational identity and identification: Defining ourselves through work relationships. *Academy of Management Review, 32,* 9–32.

Snow, D., & Anderson, L. (1987). Identity work among the homeless: The verbal construction and avowal of personal identities. *The American Journal of Sociology, 92,* 1336–1371.

ten Have, P. (1999). *Doing conversation analysis: A practical guide.* London: Sage.

Tracy, K. (2002). *Everyday talk: Building and reflecting identities.* New York: Guilford Press.

Tracy, S., & Trethewey, A. (2005). Fracturing the real-self ← → fake-self dichotomy: Moving toward "crystallized" organizational discourses and identities. *Communicaton Theory, 15,* 168–195.

10

Assuming the Mantle: Unpacking the Process by Which Individuals Internalize a Leader Identity

D. Scott DeRue, Susan J. Ashford, and Natalie C. Cotton

CONTENTS

The way we perceive ourselves, our identity, can have profound effects on the way we feel, think, and act, as well as on what we strive to achieve in life (James, 1892; Leary & Tangney, 2003). Individuals' self-perceptions are thought to encompass social and role identities, representing the groups and roles they feel tied to, and also a personal identity. Personal identity refers to "a sense of self built up over time as the person embarks on and pursues projects or goals...." (Hewitt, 1997, p. 93). A personal identity is based on a set of attributes that individuals believe differentiate them from other individuals, and thus reflects their "true self" (Sedikides & Brewer, 2001). We experience our personal identity as a set of dispositional traits or behavioral tendencies that are considered "core" to ourselves (Thoits & Virshup, 1997). Examples may include single attributes such as smart or kind, or more complex constellations of traits and tendencies such as environmentalist or good corporate citizen. In this way, personal identity is a set of labels that individuals come to internalize as descriptive of the self. The designation or attribution of these personal attributes to the self, which we refer to as internalization, is often embedded in a particular social context and asserted during the course of social interaction (Deaux, 1996; Snow & Anderson, 1987). Thus, whereas personal identity is a cognitive representation of oneself, the process by which any particular personal identity comes to be internalized is decidedly social.

The two most prominent theories on identity, identity theory and social identity theory, discuss the idea of personal identity but primarily to differentiate it from other forms of identity (Stets & Burke, 2000). In identity theory (Stryker & Burke, 2000), one's identity is thought to be tied to hierarchically structured roles that become salient as situations call for a particular role. In this sense, one's identity is based on the properties of a particular role and does not necessarily reflect anything unique about the individual. Likewise, social identity theory (Hogg & Abrams, 1988; Tajfel & Turner, 1985) treats identity as a function of one's membership in various social collectives and focuses primarily on the commonalities between people in different groups, not what differentiates individuals from each other (Hogg, 2001). In this sense, neither identity theory nor social identity theory explains how individuals develop personal identities.

Another limitation of identity theory and social identity theory in explaining the development of personal identities is related to the degree of clarity versus ambiguity of one's personal identity. In both identity theory and social identity theory, one's identity is based on a clear referent (i.e., a formal role, a social collective, or category) that is external to the self and offers social cues regarding characteristics of the identity. In contrast, the basis for one's personal identity can be much less clear. Aspects of personal identity (e.g., leader, good citizen, nurturing person) are often based on multiple personal attributes that are sometimes ambiguous in meaning (Hitlin, 2003). Indeed, the meaning of individual traits and behavioral tendencies can be vague (e.g., what does it mean to be nurturing?), dynamic (e.g., what nurturing means changes over time and situation), and socially constructed (e.g., others give one signals about what is and is not nurturing from their perspective). As a result, there is significant ambiguity in assessing and determining whether one does or does not embody a particular personal identity. Consequently, how one best exhibits a particular attribute in specific contexts is also often unclear. Considering the potential ambiguity underlying one's personal identity, current theories of identity development do not sufficiently explain why some individuals internalize a specific personal identity and other individuals do not. Therefore, our objective in this chapter is to describe the processes and underlying mechanisms by which individuals develop personal identities when the identity itself is ambiguous and socially constructed.

To achieve this objective, we focus on "leader" as an ambiguous personal identity that some, but not all, people come to internalize as part of their self concept. The leader personal identity provides a theoretically interesting and appropriate backdrop for several reasons. First, there is no objective measurement of whether one "is" or "is not" a leader, making leader an especially ambiguous personal identity that one may internalize or not. Second, leadership can be a social exchange process that can be independent of any formal role (e.g., people can lead in groups with no assigned leader), depends on reciprocity, and holds the potential for two-way, mutual influence (Hollander, 1978). Thus, it is likely that one's personal identity as a leader is subject to social cues, thereby providing a useful context for examining the relational processes that lead to the internalization of ambiguous personal identities. Given that individuals often aim to resolve identity ambiguity through social interactions (Bartel & Dutton, 2001), the decidedly social process of leadership makes it an apt choice to examine the internalization process for personal identities. Finally, scholars often cite the development of a leader identity as one of the most important predictors of effective leadership and career development (Day & Harrison, 2007; Hall, 2004). The internalization of a leader identity is thought to be a positive, generative process that empowers people to assume the mantle of leader and thereby more effectively engage in leadership processes that facilitate the accomplishment of organizational goals (Hall, 2004). Thus, not only is "leader" an ambiguous personal identity that is socially constructed and theoretically interesting, but it also is a personal identity that holds positive value for individuals and organizations. Given the tangible and symbolic rewards for thinking of oneself as a leader or being seen as a leader, the process by which individuals internalize this identity is worthy of study. Leader is a positive personal identity and social designation in most contexts. Individuals have an interest in developing their leadership capabilities, and organizations often see the development of leaders within their ranks as key to their vitality and success. Thus, the study of how individuals come to internalize this positive personal identity is important.

In articulating the processes by which individuals come to internalize a leader personal identity, this chapter makes several important contributions to our understanding of identity-related processes in organizations. Although a processual interactionist perspective is not new to theories of identity (e.g., Blumer, 1969; Goffman, 1959), social interaction processes have not played a central role in the current literature on personal identity. Yet, it is likely through social interaction that ambiguous personal identities such as a leader are negotiated and internalized. Given the positive consequences of this internalization for both individuals and organizations, understanding and articulating the social processes that prompt internalization become important. To begin understanding this process, we generalize a concept invoked in Bartel and Dutton's (2001) work on ambiguous organizational membership to the larger question of how individuals come to internalize particular personal identities. Specifically, we explore how the personal identity of leader is constituted through interactions with others in the form of claiming and granting acts (Bartel & Dutton, 2001). Claiming entails the behaviors that individuals engage in to assert an identity, in particular the verbal or nonverbal acts intended to reflect the characteristics that are unique and essential to a particular personal identity. In the case of leader, claiming acts might include taking the seat at the head of a meeting table or asserting one's expertise in a particular domain. Granting refers to the behaviors that others in a social interaction engage in to assert their own opinions of that person's identity. Granting involves verbal or nonverbal acts that are intended to affirm that an individual personifies the characteristics that signify a particular identity. In the case of leader, granting acts might include deferring to the claimer's opinion or seeking out his or her help and expertise. Together, claiming and granting behaviors constitute the joint work that leads to personal identity growth. This claiming-granting framework constitutes the social interactions that become the inputs to the process of internalizing an ambiguous personal identity such as leader. Thus, we emphasize that the internalization of leader as a personal identity is not simply an intrapersonal, cognitive act but also a social process of mutual claiming and granting through word and deed that gets enacted over time. In this sense, our chapter draws attention to the social processes by which people come to internalize the positive personal identity of leader.

We present our theory as follows. First, we articulate a conceptual definition of ambiguous identities and specify why leader is a particularly ambiguous personal identity. Next, we elaborate the process by which individuals come to internalize leader as a personal identity. Our emphasis on the process of internalizing a leader identity also yields a broader understanding of the possible boundary conditions associated with the process. Thus, we go on to posit that personal and contextual factors can constrain or enhance one's ability or willingness to claim a personal identity or grant it to others.

WHAT IS AN AMBIGUOUS IDENTITY?

Some identities are unambiguous. A person is or is not a female, or is or is not a mother. In the area of personal identities, things are less clear. A personal identity is especially *ambiguous* when it meets the following criteria. First, identities that are composed of multiple attributes can be especially ambiguous. For example, the personal identity of "punctual" is less ambiguous because it is one attribute; by contrast, a personal identity of "good corporate citizen" is more ambiguous. Being a "good corporate citizen" may entail being helpful to others, raising concerns on behalf of the organization, and/or supporting organizational values, rules, and regulations (Organ, 1988). Second, personal identities are ambiguous when the relationship between the personal attributes within the particular personal identity or their relative importance is unclear, contextually bound, and socially constructed. To use the same example of "good corporate citizen," the relative importance of raising concerns to others versus obeying organizational rules and regulations in any particular social context is ambiguous and may vary across people. Finally, just how one should enact some identities is ambiguous, as some identities have less consistency and social consensus about how they should be enacted in particular contexts than do others. In other words, when the appropriate behavior associated with a particular identity is vague, uncertain, variable across contexts, and/or dynamic, there is likely to be greater difficulty in concluding that the identity is descriptive of oneself (and therefore internalizing the identity).

Based on these criteria, a leader identity seems particularly ambiguous. As noted earlier, there are no objective measures or indicators of whether one is or is not a leader. Rather, multiple traits and behavioral tendencies are associated with leadership, and there is often disagreement as to the relative importance of these attributes for defining just what a leader is. Although individuals often have implicit theories and schemas for what personal attributes are prototypical of effective leaders (Lord, 1985), how individuals should enact leadership in any given context is often unclear. In any single situation, scholars and laypeople alike often have different cognitive representations or schemas about what leadership behaviors and actions are appropriate. These differing views about what leaders should do and what behaviors are appropriate, along with the fact that leadership occurs in the context of relationships and involves social exchange and influence processes, make the leader identity particularly ambiguous and susceptible to social construction. In the next section, we specify how one's schema of leadership influences the interpersonal processes that then facilitate the internalization of the ambiguous personal identity of leader.

PROCESS OF INTERNALIZING A LEADER IDENTITY

Recent literature has begun to explore the process by which individuals actively shape their identities (Bartel & Dutton, 2001; Pratt, Rockmann, & Kaufmann, 2006; Snow & Anderson, 1987). Drawing on social interactionism (Blumer, 1969; Goffman, 1959) and reflecting an emphasis on personal agency, the broader concept of identity work "refers to people being engaged in forming, repairing, maintaining, strengthening or revising the constructions that are productive of a sense of coherence and distinctiveness" (Sveningsson & Alvesson, 2003, p. 1165). This notion of identity work reinforces the symbolic interactionist idea that the meaning of the self is dynamic and negotiated through interactions with others (Goffman, 1959).

Past research in this area has addressed how people engage in activities to create, present, and sustain identities that are positive despite troublesome social conditions, such as among the homeless (Snow & Anderson, 1987), and how identity work can cleanse a "dirty" occupation of its negative social meaning (Ashforth & Kreiner, 1999). Identity work also describes how individuals negotiate among different identities, such as between the personal and social identities (Kreiner, Hollensbe, & Sheep, 2006), or how individuals customize an identity to fit their evolving understanding of a setting (Pratt et al., 2006).

Our perspective draws from this previous research. It takes an interactionist perspective regarding how identities are formed in social contexts. This perspective is similar to one taken by Bartel and Dutton (2001), who developed a picture of identity work in situations where membership in an organization is ambiguous. They applied Goffman's idea of "working consensus" to the example of temporary workers whose status as organizational members is not always clear and cannot be taken for granted. In this work, Bartel and Dutton proposed that whether these workers would be seen as organizational members is developed through an active and relational process of claiming and granting. The moves and acts that temporary workers undertake to establish themselves as legitimate members of the organization (claiming) are met by responses from others (granting), which resolve the ambiguity of membership.

We propose that this claiming-granting process not only occurs when situations or social group memberships are ambiguous (e.g., as in the case of organizational membership for some) but also when the identity itself is ambiguous (as in the case for many personal identities, including a leader identity). Figure 10.1 and the following sections provide a description of how this process unfolds with respect to leader as a personal identity. As shown in Figure 10.1, our depiction of how a leader identity comes to be internalized (a cognitive outcome) is inherently interpersonal and iterative. In this model, we posit that individuals engage in claiming a leadership identity and others engage in granting (or not granting) a leader identity to the individual. Through this iterative process, the individual comes to internalize "leader" as a personal identity.

Claiming

Our depiction of the process begins with an assumption that people have at least a perspective on what leaders "look like" and what leadership entails. This sense is developed over time through personal experience (e.g., with family, school or church leaders), historical accounts (e.g.,

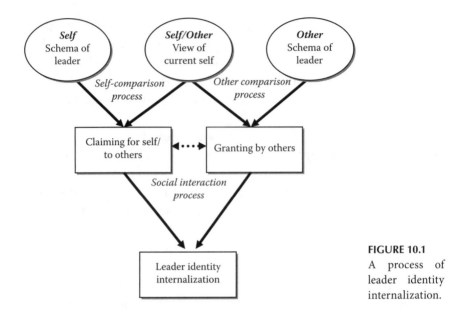

FIGURE 10.1

A process of leader identity internalization.

military and political leaders), culture (e.g., social and artistic leaders), and media (e.g., accounts of business or world leaders). Over time, individuals integrate these various cultural vocabularies (Weick, 1995) to form a loose schema for what leadership is (i.e., what it means to be a leader in terms of attributes and behaviors). When individuals first think about the question of whether they are a leader, they compare their self-view of their own personal attributes (e.g., traits, behaviors, skills) to their own cognitive schema of leadership (Kenney, Schwartz-Kenney, & Blascovich, 1996). Based on this *internal-to-self* comparison process, individuals choose whether to assert a leader identity in social interactions. Their subsequent acts in a particular social context, which are intended to display characteristics that they see as embodying attributes of a leader, are claiming behaviors.

At times, this choice to claim a leader identity will be fairly automatic based on a perceived match of the individual's attributes and those attributes specified within his or her leadership schema. However, this comparison process could also be the result of a deliberate and conscious process whereby the individual thinks through whether the attributes of a leader are self-descriptive. If the self-view corresponds to the individual's schema of leadership, this match should encourage an individual to claim a leader identity. In other words, if people see themselves as leaders, they are more likely to exhibit leader-like qualities and engage in behaviors and actions that are consistent with their views of leadership. Individuals engage in schema-consistent behavior because they are motivated to act in accordance with their self-view as a way of expressing their true self (Foote, 1951), especially when the personal identity, like leader, is positively valued in society.

Claiming can also occur when there is discrepancy between the self-view and one's schema of a leader. In this case, the individual may become motivated to experiment with or "try out" a possible rendition of the self that is compatible with his or her view of leadership. Through this process, individuals claim a leader identity within their social environment. Thus, we expect that individuals may claim a personal identity of leader for one of at least three reasons. First, individuals are motivated to act in accordance with their view of self (Foote, 1951) and to bring others in line with their self-view (Swann & Read, 1981). Second, being leader-like and being seen as a leader is socially valued in many organizational settings. Based on research by Higgins (1987) and Markus and Nurius (1986), we expect that individuals will experiment with such rewarded and socially valued "ideal selves." Finally, people may have multiple conceptions of what it means to be a leader based on their life experiences and observations of various role models. For example, one schema of leadership may emphasize authoritarian attributes, another may emphasize democratic or participative attributes, and another might highlight more servant-leader ideals. An individual aware of multiple possible schemas of leadership might invoke any of these schemas in their internal-to-self comparison process and choose to experiment with one or another as a possible identity. Consistent with Ibarra's (1999) research on how individuals experiment with "provisional selves," we propose that by taking small steps to act *like* a leader, individuals can explore where they stand with respect to a leader personal identity in their particular social context. We extend this idea of identity experimentation to emphasize that the "trying on" of a personal identity is also an interpersonal process; it involves both claiming by the self and granting by others.

Beyond the reasons for why one might claim a leader identity, there is also a question of how one would claim this ambiguous personal identity. Literature on the broader construct of identity work, which explores how people shape their identities, provides some insight into various context-specific tactics for claiming an identity. Examples include "identity patching" for new medical residents (Pratt et al., 2006) or "inquiring" for those with ambiguous organizational memberships (Bartel & Dutton, 2001). At a more molar level, the literature also offers a distinction between verbal acts of claiming (e.g., making statements that one is a leader or statements consistent with being a leader) and nonverbal or behavioral acts such as managing one's appearance or dress to convey a personal identity (Snow & Anderson, 1987). Another example related to a leader identity would be employing physical artifacts associated with leadership (e.g., hanging a picture of a famous leader in one's office, use of space in a way that claims a leader-like position). Behavioral claiming might also include the display of relational claims such as noticing or demonstrating closeness with recognized authorities. This is similar to Snow and Anderson's (1987) notion of "associational embracement" or "distancing" behaviors. Given that the aim of this chapter is to describe the overall process of developing a leader identity, we stop short of developing an organizing framework of these specific claiming tactics, but this would be a worthy target of future research. This research could leverage previous research on how new medical residents (Pratt et al., 2006) construct their identities and temporary workers negotiate their membership status in the organization (Bartel & Dutton, 2001).

We note that one contribution that our model implies for the investigation of specific claiming tactics—and identity work more generally—is that assertions of identity should not be seen as simple impression management (Kreiner, Hollensbe, & Sheep, 2006), but as actions that can reflect *both* the expression of one's own self-perceptions and attempts to shape others' perceptions. Our core propositions related to claiming are that individuals will engage in claiming acts under three different conditions: (a) when individuals desire to express an already internalized leader personal identity, (b) when there is extrinsic value in being seen as a leader in a particular context, and (c) when they are uncertain as to whether they are a leader.

Granting

Comparable with how the focal individual goes through an internal-to-self comparison process that results in claiming, others within the social environment go through a similar cognitive comparison process of their own. They have their own schema for what it means to be a leader based on their own background and experiences. We propose that they compare the focal person's attributes in terms of traits, skills, and behaviors to this schema and, based on this comparison process, choose to either grant or not grant the focal individual a leader identity in their social interaction. Granting behaviors are actions that express how others perceive the focal individual. Their actions either affirm or disaffirm whether that person is seen as a leader. Granting acts, or the lack thereof, will help shape whether the focal individual internalizes leader as part of his or her personal identity.

Except under conditions that we will discuss later, we theorize that others will grant the focal individual a leader identity when their attribute-to-schema comparison process results in a match. In other words, according to the perceiver, the focal individual looks like, seems like, and acts like a leader. This matching process and the recognition of leadership likely depend on how well the focal person corresponds to the perceiver's implicit theory or schema of leadership (Lord & Maher, 1991). This cognitive process, which like claiming can be conscious or unconscious, shapes and is shaped by the highly contextual and social processes of claiming and granting and is the central focus of our attention.

Although granting in the presence of and in response to claiming acts is more likely, we expect that granting can occur without a previous claim by the focal person. For example, the schemas used by the focal person and others may or may not be similar, and so others may see something in the focal person (e.g., leader attributes) that he or she does not yet see. Thus, the process of internalizing a personal identity as a leader may begin with a granting act (such as unexpectedly designating someone as the leader of a group or task force). It is also possible that on some occasions, even when there is a discrepancy between what others observe of the focal person's attributes and their leadership schemas, granting may also occur based on other intentions or motives. For example, mentors might choose to grant a leader identity to mentees in the hopes of spurring the internalization of the mentee's leader identity and subsequent leader behaviors. The mentor's granting behaviors construct and affirm the mentee as a leader in their interactions, helping the mentee to think of him or herself as a leader.

Similar to the claiming process, granting can include both verbal and nonverbal acts. Others in the social context might grant an individual a leader identity via verbally affirming ("you are our leader") and/or behaving *as if* the individual is a leader (e.g., consulting the individual's opinion and deferring to his or her wishes). Likewise, granting might occur via the use of physical space; an example might be when an individual is given a prominent position at the meeting table. Granting may also be accomplished via the manipulation of artifacts, as when giving someone the dry erase marker in a brainstorming meeting.

Internalization of Personal Identity

When the focal person claims a leader identity and others in the social environment grant the leader identity to this person, together they accomplish the social achievement of a leader identity for the individual. Specifically, as others in the social environment validate the individual's leader claims through granting, the individual comes to see the leader identity as reflective of his or her true self and internalizes it. In this sense, the leader identity becomes part of a "working consensus" (Goffman, 1959) that the focal person is a leader in this particular context, resulting in the leader identity becoming a stronger and more salient part of one's personal identity.

Conversely, others not granting the individual a leader identity may begin to call into question the focal individual's claims of a leader identity. Ungranted claims signal to individuals that others do not perceive them in a way that is consistent with their self-view. For example, if a member of a consulting team sees himself as a leader, consequently petitions to lead an upcoming client presentation, and that claiming act is met with resistance from other team members, the focal individual may begin to question whether he truly is a leader in this team. This discrepancy between claiming and granting acts likely causes individuals to adjust their self-view to reduce the inconsistency, leading to fewer subsequent leader identity claims. Alternatively, if individuals are deeply interested in seeing themselves as a leader, or are in situations where a leader identity is particularly valuable for extrinsic reasons, they may engage in stronger subsequent efforts to claim a leader identity and attempt to change others' perceptions.

We propose that this claiming-granting process is iterative and developmental over time. As more claims and grants are made, the personal identity of "leader" becomes a more salient and central part of one's self-concept. As noted, the process need not begin with an initial claim. Rather, the process may begin with an initial grant as others perceive the individual to match their schemas of leadership before the individual has made any claims for this personal identity. The granting itself in this case can be the stimulus for the individual to make the internal-to-self comparison, thus inviting the question of "Who me? Am I a leader?" The comparison work stimulated by this initial grant may cause the focal individual to reevaluate his or her self-view and/or leadership schema, further illustrating how social interactions and cognitive processes together shape individuals' personal identities.

Positive and Negative Spirals

The iterative nature of the claiming-granting process suggests two possible spirals of identity development. When individuals claim the leader identity and others grant the identity, a positive spiral ensues. Because grants from others not only convey how they see the focal individual but also signal what is valued in the social environment, the grant of leader identity not only strengthens the identity in the focal individual's self-concept but also may leave the individual more motivated to value the identity. Thus, grants from others increase both the salience and valence of the personal identity. Further, the identity grant may lead to the individual feeling more empowered to act in accordance with his or her leadership schema. Being seen as a leader by others may affect a person's efficacy beliefs with respect to leadership. Both of these effects directly lead to more leader identity claims being engaged in with greater confidence. If others then continue to grant in response, these more frequent and confident claims lead to a positive spiral.

Alternatively, a negative spiral can emerge when the individual is not granted a leader identity. One likely response is for the focal individual to engage in fewer or weaker claiming behaviors. If these leader identity claims also remain ungranted, the individual further reduces the number and/or strength of future claims. There are several reasons for the emergence of this negative spiral. First, a long history of research on motivational processes concludes that behaviors not positively reinforced are less likely to be repeated in the future (Ferster & Skinner, 1957). Second, when claiming acts are not met with mutually reinforcing grants, it is likely that individuals will begin to question or doubt their leadership capabilities and thus revise their self view to be less inclusive of a leader personal identity. In addition, the lack of a "working consensus" signified by claiming acts not followed by granting causes uncertainty about the claimer's status within the group, which may lead the person to withdraw from the social environment. The negative spiral based on these three mechanisms occurs unless there is a particular motive to be seen as a leader, thus leading to claiming behavior in the absence of granting by others. However, it is most likely that accumulating ungranted claims over time results in the individual coming to see the leader identity as not self-descriptive.

In addition to positive or negative spirals, we also propose that personal identity development is not a smooth or linear process. Drawing from stage theories of human development (e.g., Kegan, 1982; Levinson, Darrow, Klein, Levinson, & McKee, 1978), we posit that individuals will initially develop a leader identity in relation to specific situations. As claiming and granting occurs in one context, the leader identity will be specific to that context, such as "I am a leader on the new product development team." However, through repeated claiming-granting processes across situations and over time, we posit that this situation-specific and socially affirmed leader identity will begin to transcend across situations and grow stronger. This evolution of the leader identity requires that the individual draw connections across leadership situations, which may look very different and involve different behaviors. This process is akin to Sluss and Ashforth's (2007) notion of moving from specific to generalized identities. As the individual begins to make this transition, various context-specific leader identities should cohere into a single, clear, and strong identity as a leader ("I am a leader"). In this sense, the identity "leader" would come to play a larger cross-contextual role in the content and structure of the individual's personal identity.

BOUNDARY CONDITIONS OF CLAIMING AND GRANTING

We have highlighted an integrated social and cognitive process in which individuals first match their perceptions of their personal attributes to their schema of leadership, claim a leader identity in their social worlds, and are granted that identity by others. However, it is also likely that various contextual and personal factors influence this process. In particular, these factors can constrain or enable the individual's ability or willingness to claim a leader identity, as well as others' ability or willingness to grant a leader identity.

In terms of the social context, one factor that likely influences the claiming of a leader identity is whether the focal individual holds a formal supervisory role in a particular group or setting. The endorsement represented by a formal supervisory role reflects a "granting" of leadership, if not by the current group members, then by a formal social structure that all group members operate within and to some extent endorse. Roles are made up of sets of activities or behaviors expected "to be performed, at least approximately, by any person who occupies that office" (Katz & Kahn, 1966, p. 173). Thus, it is likely that others hold expectations of a supervisory role that are indicative of leadership. When this is the case, others are more likely to grant that individual a leader identity unless that individual is ineffective or acts in ways that are considerably inconsistent with existing schemas of leadership. We also expect that individuals in formal supervisory roles will feel particularly free to try "leader-like" acts, which should facilitate further granting of a leader identity. Indeed such behaviors, in that they are likely aligned with the expectations of role senders, will be reinforced and affirmed by those role senders, creating greater freedom to experiment in the leadership domain over time (Tsui & Ashford, 1994; Tsui, Ashford, St. Clair, & Xin, 1995). Thus, it is likely that a person's leader identity will be enhanced over time by being placed in formal supervisory roles.

On the other hand, in self-managing groups where there is no hierarchical role differentiation among members, individuals may be less certain about whether they should (or could) lead. In contexts where formal role differentiation does not exist, claims to the leader identity may be met with only ambiguous social feedback as to their efficacy (i.e., tentative or unclear grants). This should be especially true in contexts where the competition for leadership is high. If members of a self-managing group all covet a leader identity, the simultaneous claiming of the leader identity could lead to effective sharing of leadership or to conflict over personal identities. If members of the group share an aversion to the leader identity, however, this might produce a void of leadership in the group.

Another feature of the social environment that likely influences the claiming-granting process proposed here is the degree to which the environment provides an opportunity to experiment with a provisional leader identity. In some organizational or cultural contexts, taking on leadership responsibilities in a group might be encouraged (e.g., empowered, decentralized organizational cultures). In other contexts, acts of leadership might be discouraged for those who are not appointed formal hierarchical roles. This idea is evident in research showing that the emergence of informal leaders in social contexts can be constrained by factors present in that context (Lord, Brown, Harvey, & Hall, 2001; Neubert & Taggar, 2004). We expect the more opportunity there is to experiment with leading, the more willing and able the focal individual will be to experiment with various leadership acts. When these leadership acts are met with granting by others, the leader identity will be reinforced. In contexts where experimenting with leadership is not available, the claiming-granting process is interrupted. Thus, it is important that attention be given to the social environments within a group. Groups with norms that encourage personal risk taking, tolerate failure, and view experimentation as learning opportunities seem like particularly fertile ground for the development of leader identities. Beyond these informal cultural influences, organizations might also take explicit steps to give individuals more opportunity to experiment with a leader identity by, for example, redesigning jobs or implementing leadership rotational programs.

In addition to social context factors, features of the claimer and grantor also likely influence the claiming-granting process. For example, a lack of self-awareness may constrain a person's interest in, willingness, or ability to claim a leader identity. Individuals may not know that they possess the personal attributes that are viewed by others as prototypical of leadership. Moreover, people may hold a schema of leadership that is so idealized and elevated that they cannot see how the identity of leader could apply to them. In this way, a lack of self-awareness is a constraint on the development of a leader identity. For these individuals, the process of developing a leader identity would likely be initiated by a grant from others (e.g., a promotion, assignment to a supervisory role, or an assignment to head a task force). Organizations, of course, can take steps to reduce this constraint. Organizations can develop training and feedback mechanisms that enhance individuals' self-awareness about what leadership means in a particular context and how the individual is seen along those defined dimensions. For example, one way of building this self-awareness would be to give individuals greater access to effective leader role models.

Thus far, we have presented the granting process as an affirmative response to a person's claim to a leader identity, assuming they enact related behaviors effectively. That is, grants are offered when the individual's personal attributes match the schema for leadership held by others. Although we expect this to be the dominant process associated with developing such an identity, we recognize that there may be things about the grantor or the relationship between the claimer and granter that shape one's willingness or ability to grant a leader identity. For example, there are several reasons why others might grant a leader identity regardless of the outcome of their schema comparison process. The leader identity may be granted to a person not because he or she seems to embody leadership, but because he or she seems to want it. That is, others may do such granting for affective or political reasons. Affectively, such grants may be offered because of simple liking of the other person. From a political perspective, group members may be more than happy to grant someone else the leader identity to avoid any personal risk stemming from leadership. Likewise, based on theories of social exchange (Foa & Foa, 1974; Homans, 1961; Kelley & Thibaut, 1977), it seems likely that people may grant a leader identity because of that person's ability to provide resources or favors in return at some later point. Conversely, others may not grant a claim for leadership because they do not like the claimer, do not want him or her to reap the rewards of leadership, or because they want to claim it for themselves.

DIRECTIONS FOR FUTURE RESEARCH

We have put forth a variety of ideas about the process of developing ambiguous personal identities such as leader. In addition to empirical tests of the ideas proposed in this chapter, there are several additional directions for future research that could enhance our understanding of the personal identity development process.

Are there regularities in who tends to claim and not claim a leader identity (and who gets granted the identity)? We have articulated a claiming-granting process that explains how individuals develop a leader identity, but we have done so with little attention to individual differences beyond cognitive schemas and self-awareness. We expect individual differences beyond these will impact the process. For example, do men tend to claim a leader identity more than women, or vice versa, and if so why? Do those who fit the societal norms or "great man" theories of leadership tend to make leader identity claims more often in group settings than those who do not? As new leadership styles emerge, will new claims be forthcoming? Will these claims be more successful?

To what extent and how does history matter? If one person grants a leader identity to another person in one context, how does this grant shape future claiming and granting processes among the same individuals but in different contexts? Future research that examines how and to what extent claims and grants from one context carryover to different contexts would be particularly helpful extensions of the ideas presented in this chapter.

What does granting imply for the grantor? When one member of a work group grants a leader identity to another person, does this mean that he or she is implicitly (or explicitly) claiming a "follower" identity? Moreover, under what conditions might an individual grant a leader identity to another person and at the same time claim a leader identity for himself or herself?

What happens when there are multiple claims? Especially in a new situation or in a situation with no appointed leader, several individuals may be interested in claiming this identity for themselves and having others grant it to them. Current theory, including this chapter, does not speak to what happens when multiple people in a single context (e.g., team) claim a leader identity.

CONCLUDING REMARKS

This chapter articulates a process by which individuals come to see themselves as a leader. This process comprises interplay between intrapersonal, cognitive processes and interpersonal, claiming-granting processes that together facilitate the internalization of leader as part of one's personal identity. Although not all people will assume the mantle and internalize a leader personal identity, this chapter provides insight into how and under what conditions people will come to believe: "Yes, I am a leader."

REFERENCES

Ashforth, B. E., & Kreiner, G. E. (1999). "How can you do it?": Dirty work and the challenge of constructing a positive identity. *Academy of Management Review, 24,* 413–434.

Bartel, C., & Dutton, J. (2001). Ambiguous organizational memberships: Constructing organizational identities in interactions with others. In M. A. Hogg & D. J. Terry

(Ed.), *Social identity processes in organizational contexts* (pp. 115–130). Philadelphia: Psychology Press.

Blumer, H. (1969). *Symbolic interactionism; perspective and method.* Englewood Cliffs, NJ: Prentice-Hall.

Day, D. V., & Harrison, M. M. (2007). A multilevel, identity-based approach to leadership development. *Human Resource Management Review, 17,* 360–373.

Deaux, K. (1996). Social identification. In E. T. Higgins, & A. W. Kruglanski (Eds.), *Social psychology: handbook of basic principles* (pp. 777–798). New York: Guilford Press.

Ferster, C. B., & Skinner, B. F. (1957). *Schedules of reinforcement.* New York: Appleton-Century-Crofts.

Foa, U. G., & Foa, E. B. (1974). *Societal structures of the mind.* Springfield, IL: Thomas.

Foote, N. N. (1951). Identification as the basis for a theory of motivation. *American Sociological Review, 16,* 14–21.

Goffman, E. (1959). *The presentation of self in everyday life.* Garden City, NY: Doubleday.

Hall, D. T. (2004). Self-awareness, identity, and leader development. In D. V. Day, S. J. Zaccaro, & S. M. Halpin (Eds.), *Leader development for transforming organizations* (pp. 153–176). Mahwah, NJ: Lawrence Erlbaum Associates.

Hewitt, J. P. (1997). *Self and society: a symbolic interactionist social psychology* (7th ed.). Boston: Allyn and Bacon.

Higgins, E. T. (1987). Self-discrepancy—a theory relating self and affect. *Psychological Review, 94,* 319–340.

Hitlin, S. (2003). Values as the core of personal identity: drawing links between two theories of self. *Social Psychology Quarterly, 66,* 118–137.

Hogg, M. A. (2001). Social identity and the sovereignty of the group. In C. Sedikides, & M. B. Brewer (Eds.), *Individual self, relational self, collective self* (pp. 123–143). Philadelphia: Psychology Press.

Hogg, M. A., & Abrams, D. (1988). *Social identifications: a social psychology of intergroup relations and group processes.* London, New York: Routledge.

Hollander, E. P. (1978). *Leadership dynamics: A practical guide to effective relations.* New York: Free Press.

Homans, G. (1961). *Social behavior.* New York: Harcourt Brace.

Ibarra, H. (1999). Provisional selves: Experimenting with image and identity in professional adaptation. *Administrative Science Quarterly, 44,* 764–791.

James, W. (1892). *Psychology.* New York: H. Holt and Company.

Katz, D., & Kahn, R. (1966). *The social psychology of organizations,* New York: John Wiley & Sons.

Kegan, R. (1982). *The evolving self: Problem and process in human development.* Cambridge, MA: Harvard University Press.

Kelley, H. H., & Thibaut, J. W. (1977). *Interpersonal relations: a theory of interdependence.* New York: Wiley.

Kenney, R. A., Schwartz-Kenney, B. M., & Blascovich, J. (1996). Implicit leadership theories: Defining leaders described as worthy of influence. *Pers Soc Psychol Bull, 22,* 1128–1143.

Kreiner, G. E., Hollensbe, E. C., & Sheep, M. L. (2006). Where is the "me" among the "we"? Identity work and the search for optimal balance. *Academy of Management Journal, 49,* 1031–1057.

Leary, M. R., & Tangney, J. P. (2003). *Handbook of self and identity.* New York: Guilford Press.

Levinson, D. J., Darrow, C. N., Klein, E. B., Levinson, M. H., & McKee, B. (1978). *The seasons of a man's life.* New York: Knopf.

Lord, R. G. (1985). An information processing approach to social perceptions, leadership perceptions, and behavioral measurement in organizational settings. In B. M. Staw, & L. L. Cummings (Eds.), *Research in organizational behavior* (Vol. 7, pp. 87–128). Greenwich, CT: JAI Press.

Lord, R. G., Brown, D. J., Harvey, J. L., & Hall, R. J. (2001). Contextual constraints on prototype generation and their multilevel consequences for leadership perceptions. *Leadership Quarterly, 12,* 311–338.

Lord, R. G., & Maher, K. J. (1991). *Leadership and information processing: linking perceptions and performance.* Boston: Unwin Hyman.

Markus, H., & Nurius, P. (1986). Possible selves. *American Psychologist, 41,* 954–969.

Neubert, M. J., & Taggar, S. (2004). Pathways to informal leadership: The moderating role of gender on the relationship of individual differences and team member network centrality to informal leadership emergence. *The Leadership Quarterly, 15,* 175–194.

Organ, D. W. (1988). *Organizational citizenship behavior: The good soldier syndrome.* Lexington, MA: Lexington Books.

Pratt, M. G., Rockmann, K. W., & Kaufmann, J. B. (2006). Constructing professional identity: The role of work and identity learning cycles in the customization of identity among medical residents. *Academy of Management Journal, 49,* 235–262.

Sedikides, C., & Brewer, M. B. (2001). *Individual self, relational self, collective self.* Philadelphia: Psychology Press.

Sluss, D. M., & Ashforth, B. E. (2007). Relational identity and identification: Defining ourselves through work relationships. *Academy of Management Review, 32,* 9–32.

Snow, D. A., & Anderson, L. (1987). Identity work among the homeless: The verbal construction and avowal of personal identities. *The American Journal of Sociology, 92,* 1336–1371.

Stets, J. E., & Burke, P. J. (2000). Identity theory and social identity theory. *Social Psychology Quarterly, 63,* 224–237.

Stryker, S., & Burke, P. J. (2000). The past, present, and future of an identity theory. *Social Psychology Quarterly, 63,* 284–297.

Sveningsson, S. F., & Alvesson, M. (2003). Managing managerial identities: Organizational fragmentation, discourse and identity struggle. *Human Relations, 56,* 1163–1193.

Swann, W. B., & Read, S. J. (1981). Acquiring self-knowledge: The search for feedback that fits. *Journal of Personality and Social Psychology, 41,* 1119–1128.

Tajfel, H., & Turner, J. C. (1985). The social identity theory of intergroup behavior. In S. Worchel, & W. G. Austin (Eds.), *Psychology of intergroup relations* (Vol. 2, pp. 7–24). Chicago: Nelson-Hall.

Thoits, P. A., & Virshup, L. K. (1997). Me's and we's: Forms and functions of social identities. In R. D. Ashmore, & L. J. Jussim (Eds.), *Self and identity: fundamental issues* (pp. 106–133). New York: Oxford University Press.

Tsui, A. S., Ashford, S. J., St. Clair, L., and Xin, C. (1995). Dealing with discrepant expectations: Response strategies and managerial effectiveness, *Academy of Management Journal, 38,* 1515–1540.

Tsui, A. S., & Ashford, S. J. (1994) Adaptive self-regulation: A process view of effectiveness. *Journal of Management, 20,* 93–121.

Weick, K. E. (1995). *Sensemaking in organizations.* Thousands Oaks, CA: Sage.

11

Positive Identities in Action: A Model of Mentoring Self-Structures and the Motivation to Mentor

Belle Rose Ragins

CONTENTS

The benefits of mentoring relationships have been clearly documented in the empirical literature over the past 20 years (Allen & Eby, 2007; Ragins & Kram, 2007b). Mentoring contributes to the growth and development of both mentors and protégés and is associated with a wide range of positive work attitudes and career outcomes (Allen, Eby, Poteet, Lentz, & Lima, 2004; Underhill, 2006; Wanberg, Welsh, & Hezlett, 2003). In fact, at its best mentoring exemplifies one of the most positive types of workplace relationships (Ragins & Verbos, 2007).

Although mentoring is important, mentoring scholars lack a contemporary theoretical foundation for understanding why individuals choose to become mentors initially and throughout their careers. There has been quite a bit of research on antecedents to becoming a mentor (cf., Allen, 2003, 2007; Allen, Poteet, & Burroughs, 1997; Ragins & Cotton, 1993), but we lack an understanding of *why* individuals are motivated to mentor. Despite massive changes in the nature and functions of careers (cf., Ragins & Kram, 2007a), theory in this area has not advanced substantively over the past 30 years. Existing research still relies on developmental and life stage theories (e.g., Erikson, 1963; Levinson, Darrow, Klein, Levinson, & McKee, 1978), which hold that individuals are motivated to become mentors as a consequence of mid-life transitions that spark questions about the meaning and value of their lives. Although these developmental stage theories may explain the initial motivation to become a mentor, they fail to explain why individuals *continue* to mentor over the course of their lives—even as they move beyond mid-life stages that are held to be responsible for their motivation to mentor. More pressing is the fact that these perspectives fail to take into account how the *experience of being in a relationship* influences and changes the mentor. A consistent finding in the literature is that individuals are more likely to become a mentor when they have had previous experience in a mentoring relationship (Allen, Poteet, Russell, & Dobbins, 1997; Ragins & Cotton, 1993; Ragins & Scandura, 1994), but the theoretical mechanism driving this finding has not been explored or articulated.

So what motivates mentors to initiate, develop, and sustain their mentoring relationships? In this chapter, I draw on the identity literature to explain the motivation to mentor. In particular, I integrate identity theory with social cognition theory to explore how mentors develop positive self-structures that fuel and maintain their motivation to mentor. I then offer a model that explains how positive mentoring identities, one type of self-structure, are developed from experiences in mentoring relationships, and how these identities in turn influence mentoring relationships and the motivation to mentor.

This chapter, then, has two primary purposes. The first is to broaden the theoretical base for understanding the motivation to mentor, as well as other behaviors in the mentoring relationship. Accordingly, theoretical perspectives from the relational identity, self-construal, and social cognition literatures are integrated (Anderson & Chen, 2002; Brewer & Gardner, 1996; Chen, Boucher, & Tapias, 2006; Cross, Bacon, & Morris, 2000; Markus, 1977; Markus & Nurius, 1986; Sluss & Ashforth, 2007) to identify three self-structures that influence mentoring relationships: mentoring schemas, mentoring as possible selves, and mentoring identities. As described later, these three self-structures reflect different aspects of the self in relation to mentoring. Mentoring self-schemas reflect knowledge structures of what mentoring relationships look like (i.e., "What is a mentor?") that may include the mentor's role in the relationship (i.e., "What does a mentor do?"). Mentoring as a possible self represents the self in the future (i.e., "Who will I be in the future?"), which may include a sense of self-efficacy (i.e., "Can I be a mentor?"), whereas mentoring identity reflects the current state of the relational self (i.e., "Do I define myself in terms of my relationship to others?"). For the purpose of this volume, I pay particular attention to the self-structure of mentoring identity, defined as the degree to which mentors define themselves in terms of their mentoring relationships.

The second purpose of this chapter is to contribute to the positive organizational scholarship literature (e.g., Cameron, Dutton, & Quinn, 2003; Dutton & Ragins, 2007; Luthans, Youssef, & Avolio, 2007; Nelson & Cooper, 2007) by using mentoring relationships as an anchor for examining how positive identities create and influence the development of positive relationships at work. By offering a theoretical marriage of the mentoring and identity literatures, this chapter seeks to accomplish the dual objectives of (a) illuminating the processes underlying the motivation to mentor, and

(b) elucidating how positive identities are developed, enacted, and shaped by relationships at work. Because I seek to reach two different audiences in this chapter—mentoring and identity scholars—particular care will be provided to offer a clear foundation for both audiences.

With these goals in mind, the chapter is organized as follows. It begins with offering the reader foundational insights into mentoring relationships, as well as constructs of self, identity, and positive identity that will be applied later in the chapter. These constructs are used to identify three core self-structures that influence mentoring relationships: mentoring self-schemas, mentoring as possible selves, and mentoring identities. A self-structure of mentoring model is then presented that illuminates how these self-structures of mentoring combine to influence behaviors, expectations, and experiences in mentoring relationships. The model illustrates how positive identities are formed within mentoring relationships, and how relationship experiences and self-structures combine to influence the motivation to mentor. The chapter concludes with implications and an agenda for future research that offers new insights into how self-structures and relationship experiences combine to influence the development of positive identities at work.

MENTORING RELATIONSHIPS

Let us begin by defining mentoring and situating it within the constellation of other relationships at work. This section also provides a foundation for understanding how mentoring identities are developed and how identity structures influence the motivation to mentor.

What Is Mentoring?

Mentoring is traditionally defined as a relationship between an older, more experienced mentor and a younger, less experienced protégé for the purpose of developing and helping the protégé's career (Kram, 1985; Ragins, 1989). Newer relational perspectives on mentoring focus on the interdependence and capacity for mutual growth in the relationship and define mentoring as a developmental relationship that involves mutual growth, learning, and development in personal, professional, and career domains (Ragins & Verbos, 2007).

Mentors offer two primary types of functions for their protégés (Kram, 1985): career functions and psychosocial functions. Career functions help protégés "learn the ropes" and facilitate their advancement. For example, mentors may coach their protégés, sponsor their advancement, and increase their protégé's positive exposure and visibility in the organization. Psychosocial functions enhance the protégé's professional and personal growth. Examples of psychosocial functions include providing counseling, friendship, acceptance, confirmation, and role modeling. Mentors may provide some or all of these behaviors, and the provision of these functions may vary across time and relationships.

There are three key aspects of the mentoring experience that, as we will discover later, influence the development of mentoring identities. First, like other relationships, some mentoring relationships entail positive experiences, whereas others have the capacity to become negative or even dysfunctional (Eby, 2007; Ragins, Cotton, & Miller, 2000; Ragins & Verbos, 2007). Second, mentors may have multiple relationships over the course of their careers, and mentors may be in more than one relationship at the same time (e.g., Higgins & Thomas, 2001; van Emmerik, 2004). It is important to keep in mind that no two mentoring relationships are the same, so at a given point in time a mentor may have both positive and negative experiences from different mentoring relationships. As we see later, experiences both within and across mentoring relationships influence the development of mentoring identities. Finally, some mentoring relationships develop informally or spontaneously, whereas others are formal relationships that are developed by the organization—usually by voluntary assignment that involves the matching of mentors and protégés (Ragins & Cotton, 1999). Formal relationships are shorter in duration than informal relationships and often involve mentoring contracts that focus on achieving organizational rather than individual goals. Because formal and informal relationships differ in significant ways (cf., Underhill, 2006), as discussed later, some of the processes described in this chapter vary by relationship type.

How Do Mentoring Relationships Differ From Other Relationships at Work?

As we explore the interface of identity and relationships at work, a key question that comes to mind is whether and how mentoring differs from other work relationships. Although mentoring relationships often occur in the workplace, they differ from other work relationships in three primary ways. First, unlike managerial or leadership relationships, mentors may or may not be in the protégé's chain of command, or be employed in the same organization as their protégés.

Second, mentoring relationships focus on role relationships and functions that are situated within the *career context*. Although learning, growth, and development may occur in other work relationships, the primary focus of mentoring relationships is meeting the career and developmental needs of its members. Unlike managerial or leader-subordinate relationships, where the focus is on work and organizational outcomes, mentoring relationships focus primarily on meeting members' developmental needs. In some cases, allegiance to the protégé may even outweigh allegiance to the organization. For example, a mentor may advise a high-performing protégé to leave the organization to pursue career opportunities that are not available within the firm. It is important to note here that although leaders and managers may engage in mentoring behaviors (e.g., coaching, counseling), this does not necessarily mean that either member of the relationship considers the relationship a mentoring relationship (Fletcher & Ragins, 2007; Ragins, 1999). To distinguish these processes, short-term interactions are called mentoring episodes (Fletcher & Ragins, 2007).

The third difference between mentoring and other work relationships is that mentoring relationships evolve through distinct phases of development that eventually result in the termination or redefinition of the relationship (Kram, 1985). For example, after progressing through initiation and cultivation phases, the protégé may no longer need the mentor, or members may geographically move to other organizations or regions. The separation phase, which occurs 2 to 5 years into the relationship, may result in the termination of the relationship or may lead to a redefinition phase in which the mentor and protégé become peers.

What Is the Motivation to Mentor?

The motivation to mentor, also called willingness to mentor, is one of the "black boxes" in the field of mentoring. Mentoring scholars have examined prosocial personality variables (i.e., empathy, helpfulness) as predictors of willingness to mentor (e.g., Aryee, Chay, & Chew, 1996; Allen, 2003), and although personality captures some of the variance, it does not offer a complete theoretical account of how individuals develop the motivation to mentor, nor does it recognize the impact of relationships on motivation and behavior (Berscheid, 1994, 1999). In fact, a consistent empirical finding is that individuals report greater willingness to mentor when they have been in mentoring relationships in the past—either as mentors or as protégés (Allen, Poteet, Russell, & Dobbins, 1997; Ragins & Cotton, 1993; Ragins & Scandura, 1994). Although this suggests that the experience of being in a mentoring relationship sparks key processes that influence future decisions to mentor, this idea has not been explored in the mentoring literature.

Increasingly, management scholars are applying the rich theoretical tradition of social cognition and identity theory to the workplace and have used these perspectives to understand how identity influences workplace behaviors and relationships (e.g., Flynn, 2005; Gelfand, Major, Raver, Nishii, & O'Brien, 2006; Lord, Brown, & Freiberg, 1999; Sluss & Ashforth, 2007). As described next, these perspectives offer a rich theoretical base for understanding why individuals may be motivated to develop mentoring relationships. Moreover, by examining how the experience of mentoring shapes, creates, and refines a mentoring identity, we can also gain broader insights into how positive identities can be developed through positive relationships at work.

IDENTITY AND SELF

In this section, I first define positive identity and then briefly review key constructs on identity and self. These constructs are then applied to the mentoring arena by exploring how mentors develop positive self-representations that fuel and maintain their motivation to enter, maintain, and sustain effective mentoring relationships.

A Definition of Positive Identity

Although identity has been defined in various ways (see review by Leary & Tangney, 2003), the working definition used in this chapter is that identity is one's definition of self. In essence, identity answers the question "Who am I?" and positive identity answers this question in a way that entails positive self-cognition, self-affirmation, and affect. By "positive" I mean a beneficial state or experience that includes both current experiences and future expectations. Within the organizational context, positive identity allows employees to achieve states of growth and generativity in the workplace (Cameron, Dutton, & Quinn, 2003), and as described later, can enable the development of positive relationships at work (Dutton & Ragins, 2007).

Identity and the Self

Psychologists have grappled with the nature of self and identity for the past 50 years (cf., Leary & Tangney, 2003; Markus & Wurf, 1987). Although there are many controversies in the field, a few relationships are apparent. Identity is a major component of the self, and the self has been used as an organizing construct for understanding identity (Leary & Tangney, 2003; Markus & Wurf, 1987). In fact, self and identity are terms that are often used interchangeably in the literature. Individuals have multiple identities (Stryker, 1980) that are socially constructed through relationships with others (e.g., Cooley, 1902; Goffman, 1959; Mead, 1934). These multiple selves reflect the past, the present, and the future (Harter & Marold, 1991; Higgins, Klein, & Strauman, 1987; Markus & Nurius, 1986; Markus & Wurf, 1987). Individuals manage their multiple identities through working self-concepts that govern which identity regulates behavior in a given social interaction (Markus & Kunda, 1986; Markus & Nurius, 1986). Therefore, self-structures are multidimensional, multifaceted, dynamic, and activated by situational cues (Markus & Wurf, 1987).

Levels of Identity and the Relational Self

Although various terms are employed, identity and self-scholars generally concur that identity operates at three primary levels: individual, relational, and collective (Brewer & Gardner, 1996; Leary & Tangney, 2003). Individual identity, also called personal identity or independent self-construal (Brewer & Gardner, 1996; Markus & Kitayama, 1991), reflects self-definitions that distinguish oneself from others, such as one's unique traits, abilities, interests, or goals. Collective identity, also called social identity or self-categorization (Hogg & Abrams, 1988; Tajfel & Turner, 1986), operates at the group level and involves defining oneself in terms of group membership. Relational identity, also called the relational self (Chen et al., 2006) or interdependent self-construal (Cross, Morris, & Gore, 2002; Markus & Kitayama, 1991), involves defining oneself in relation to others. As applied to the workplace, Sluss & Ashforth (2007) define relational identity as one's role relationships at work and use the term relational identification to refer to the extent to which one defines oneself in terms of a role relationship.

A key concept that will be used later in this chapter is that people have multiple relational identities that exist at various levels of specificity. Chen et al. (2006) explain that the relational self may be particular to a given relationship or may be generalized to represent a relational self that exists within the context of multiple relationships or roles. A similar perspective is offered by Sluss and Ashforth (2007) in their discussion of particularized and generalized relational identities in the workplace. Applying this idea to the mentoring arena, individuals may define themselves in terms of a particular relationship (e.g., "Who am I? I am Suzie's mentor.") and may also use more generic relational identities (e.g., "Who am I? I am a mentor."). Now that we have established this foundation, let us explore how these constructs operate in creating positive mentoring identities and relationships.

THE SELF-STRUCTURES OF MENTORING FRAMEWORK

Applying self and identity theory to mentoring relationships offers the idea that the motivation to mentor and the ultimate ability to develop effective mentoring relationships are influenced by three interconnected self-structures: mentoring self-schemas, mentoring as possible selves, and mentoring identities. As we will see, these three self-structures of mentoring vary along a continuum ranging from positive to negative, with positive self-structures playing a key role in the development of positive mentoring relationships.

It is important to remember that self-schemas, possible selves, and identity are all intricately connected in an overall self-system that motivates and regulates behaviors in relationships (Leary & Tangney, 2003; Markus & Wurf, 1987). Schemas and possible selves both determine and are determined by identities, so an understanding of positive identity within the context of mentoring relationships requires an understanding of the interplay of these three self-structures as they emerge from and are influenced by mentoring relationships. As will be illustrated later, positive mentoring identities are influenced by these other components of the self-system, as well as by the mentoring relationship itself. A key proposition offered here is that mentoring may become internalized into the mentor's self-structure through self-schemas, possible selves, and identity processes, and that this process ultimately influences the quality of the mentoring relationship and the motivation to pursue future mentoring relationships.

Mentoring Self-Schemas

Mentoring schemas are defined as "fluid cognitive maps derived from past experiences and relationships that guide mentor's and protégé's perceptions, expectations, and behaviors in mentoring relationships." (Ragins & Verbos, 2007, p. 101). Drawing on social cognition theory (Fiske, 1992; Markus, 1977; Markus & Zajonc, 1985) and relational schema theory (Baldwin, 1992; Planalp, 1985, 1987), mentoring schema theory holds that individuals have mental maps of mentoring that frame their experiences, shape their expectations, and motivate their behaviors in mentoring relationships (Ragins & Verbos, 2007). Essentially, mentoring schemas are knowledge structures of what mentoring relationships "look like." These cognitive schemas influence expectations, behaviors, and how information is processed from social experiences and relationships (cf., Markus, 1977). Although mentors and protégés hold mentoring schemas for both themselves and their partners, here we will focus on the mentor's side of the relationship.

As discussed earlier, cognitive structures vary on the dimension of specificity. As applied to mentoring relationships, mentors may have generic self-schemas that reflect their knowledge about the general role of being a mentor, as well as particularistic schemas that reflect knowledge about a specific role in a relationship. For example, a mentor may hold a generic self-schema that reflects general role expectations and knowledge about what it means to be a mentor (i.e., "Mentors open doors for their protégés"), as well as a particularistic self-schema for a given relationship (i.e., "As Patty's mentor, my role is to help her develop self-confidence.").

Mentoring self-schemas may also vary along a continuum of clarity. According to Markus (1977), individuals who have clear self-structures of knowledge in a given domain are schematic and may pay close attention to and favor information from that domain, whereas individuals who are aschematic lack self-schemas for a particular ability domain and may not be motivated to pursue activities related to that domain. As discussed later, both clarity and specificity of mentoring self-schemas play a key role in the decision to mentor and the shaping of mentoring identities in the relationship.

Finally, it should be noted that although the mental maps of mentoring often reflect visions of positive or ideal relationships, mentoring schemas may also reflect negative aspects of the relationship because schemas reflect the full range of experiences (Fiske & Taylor, 1984). As we see later, those who have clear, positive mentoring schemas should be more likely to enter mentoring relationships than those who are aschematic or those who view mentoring relationships through the lens of negative mentoring schemas.

Mentoring as Possible Selves

Possible selves represent the self in future states and include both positive possible selves, or the selves we would like to become, as well as negative possible selves, or the selves we fear becoming (Markus & Nurius, 1986). For example, at any given point in time we have possible selves that are hoped for (e.g., the successful self, the happy self, and the fit self), as well as possible selves that are feared (e.g., the incompetent self, the miserable self, and the decrepit self). Possible selves involve the self we want, the self we fear, and the self we think we can become. These visions of our future selves are derived from our current and past selves, but help us interpret and evaluate our current and past sense of self (Markus & Wurf, 1987). Possible selves direct, self-regulate, and motivate current and future behavior (cf., Hoyle & Sherrill, 2006) and offer a critical link between self-structure and motivation (Markus & Nurius, 1986).

Although self-schemas and possible selves are both part of the multifaceted self-concept (cf., Markus & Wurf, 1987), they are distinguished by the fact that self-schemas are knowledge structures that provide form, content, and structure to our experience, whereas possible selves are compelling visions that give our current experiences meaning (Erikson, 2007).

Cross and Markus (1994) point out that self-schemas lead to possible selves. They observe that our knowledge structure about a given domain influence whether and how we view ourselves as able to act on that domain in the future.

The construct of possible selves has traditionally been viewed from an individual level of the self, but the emergence of new perspectives on relational selves (i.e., Brewer & Gardner, 1996; Chen et al., 2006) offers a new and important lens for viewing this construct. Seen from a relational vantage point, possible selves involve not only personal, trait-based identities but also may include relational, role-based identities. For example, a new bride could have a positive possible relational self of "beloved spouse" or a negative possible relational self as "bitter divorcee." Similarly, a new manager could have a positive possible relational self of "great boss" or fear that he will become a "little dictator" in his new work relationships.

Applying this theoretical lens to the mentoring arena offers the idea that individuals may incorporate mentoring as a possible self into their self-structures. Mentoring as a possible self is defined here as a future-oriented representation of oneself in a mentoring relationship. Although it should be noted that mentoring as a possible self could include perceptions of self as a future mentor or as a future protégé, this chapter will focus just on the mentor's side of the relationship.

Like mentoring schemas, mentoring as a future self may vary by level of specificity. Self-representations of mentoring as a future self may be generic and relate to the general role of being a mentor in the future (i.e., "I can be a mentor to others in the future.") or may reflect a specific role or relationship (i.e., "I can mentor graduate students." or "I can be Sydney's mentor.").

The possible selves of mentoring may range from positive to negative, reflecting the best and the worst visions of the future self as a mentor. Given the multifaceted nature of the self, individuals have more than one possible self at a time (Markus & Nurius, 1986) and may therefore entertain both positive and negative views of what they would be like as a mentor. In balancing these different visions of the future self, it is reasonable to expect that those who hold more positive visions of their possible self as a mentor will be more motivated to mentor, as well as be more likely to develop a mentoring relationship, than those who hold more negative visions of themselves as future mentors.

This social cognitive perspective helps to explain why individuals who have been mentors in the past report stronger intentions to mentor in the future than those lacking mentoring experience (Allen, Poteet, Russell, & Dobbins, 1997; Ragins & Cotton, 1993; Ragins & Scandura, 1994). Because past selves influence the development of the future self (Markus & Nurius, 1986), individuals who were mentors in the past may be more likely to have mentoring as a possible self than those lacking mentoring experience. Therefore, experience as a mentor may create and solidify the past self as a mentor, which then supports and reinforces the vision of future self as a mentor. However, a key factor that needs to be included in this equation is the degree to which previous relationships were positive, and as discussed below, the extent to which the individual incorporates a mentoring identity into his or her self-structure as a consequence of the mentoring experience.

Mentoring Identities

Mentoring identities are a type of relational identity (cf., Brewer & Gardner, 1996) and represent the degree to which individuals define themselves in terms of their mentoring relationships. As discussed earlier, relational identities may reflect generic roles ("I am a mentor") and particular relationships ("I am Joe's mentor") (cf., Sluss & Ashforth, 2007). Generic and particularistic mentoring identities may fall along a continuum ranging from positive to negative. Drawing on the definition of positive identity provided earlier, positive mentoring identities involve states of positive self-cognition, affect, and self-affirmation ("As Joe's mentor, I am a good mentor, I do the right thing, and this gives me a sense of satisfaction."). Individuals with negative mentoring identities also define themselves in terms of a mentoring relationship but in a negative way ("As Joe's mentor, I am ineffective and inadequate, which gives me a sense of sadness and loss."). Individuals with a positive mentoring identity may be more likely to view mentoring as playing a greater role in their overall self-concept: They may be more psychologically attached to the identity; they may be more likely to self-categorize themselves in that identity group; and they may have more positive emotional and cognitive outcomes associated with these processes (cf., Ashmore, Deaux, & McLaughlin-Volpe, 2004).

Like the other self-structures, mentors may have multiple mentoring identities. Mentors with multiple protégés may have multiple particularistic identities that reflect these different relationships. This offers the possibility that mentors may have both positive and negative mentoring identities occurring at the same time, which may create states of identity congruence or conflict. For example, a mentor with multiple positive mentoring relationships may hold positive particularistic identities reflecting these relationships, as well as an overall positive generic identity of her role as a mentor. In contrast, a mentor who has both negative and positive mentoring relationships may face a state of identity conflict as consequence of these different experiences. Although a discussion of mentoring identity conflict goes beyond this chapter, it is clear that identity conflict may fall on a continuum that is determined not only by current mentoring experiences but also by past experiences and self-structures reflecting mentoring schemas and possible selves. The negotiation of multiple mentoring identities may also be influenced by the strength of these self-structures, as discussed next.

Strength of Self-Structures

Social cognitive theory suggests that three dimensions influence the strength of mentoring self-structures: clarity, salience, and valence. Clarity refers to the degree to which individuals define and articulate a self-structure. For example, individuals may hold schematic or aschematic self-schemas that reflect various degrees of knowledge about a domain (Markus, 1977), and their possible selves may vary in the degree of elaboration (Markus & Nurius, 1986). Individuals with strong clarity in their mentoring self-structures may have a detailed and specific understanding of what mentors do, their role as a mentor, and the role mentoring plays in their self-representation of their current and future selves.

Salience refers to the importance of mentoring relative to other identities, selves, and roles in the self-structure. According to social cognition theory, individuals have multiple identities and self-structures that become more or less important relative to other aspects of self and employ working self-concepts to manage these different identities in social interactions (Markus & Wurf, 1987). Drawing on the idea of salient identities (cf., Stryker, 1968, 1980) and the relative importance of a given identity relative to the individual's collective identity structure (Ashmore et al., 2004), individuals with salient mentoring identities may view mentoring as a big part of their working self-concept and overall identity structure.

Along similar lines, the strength of mentoring self-schemas and mentoring possible selves may also be determined by the salience of these self-structures.

Valence taps the affective component of self-structures and involves the anticipated or experienced affective experience that is associated with a mentoring self-structure. Markus and Nurius (1986) view the self-concept as a system of cognitive-affective structures and propose that possible selves vary in valence and that each identity or self-conception has a particular affect that is attached to it. Applied to the mentoring arena, strong mentoring self-structures may reflect strong positive, or negative, associations. In sum, strong mentoring self-structures are clear, salient, and have strong affective associations.

Finally, the strength of one self-structure may solidify and increase the strength of another. For example, individuals with strong mentoring self-schemas (e.g., those with precise, clear, and salient mental maps that guide their behaviors in the relationship) may be more likely to develop strong self-structures of possible selves and identities than those with weak self-schemas. Along similar lines, those with strong mentoring identities may also be more likely to develop strong mentoring self-schemas and possible selves.

Summary of the Self-Structures of Mentoring Framework

As summarized in Figure 11.1, individuals hold three primary types of self-structures that may influence their current and future experiences in mentoring relationships: mentoring self-schemas, mentoring as possible selves, and mentoring identities. These self-structures vary from positive to negative and also vary in terms of specificity; some structures are generic and apply to the general role of being a mentor, whereas other self-structures apply to specific mentoring relationships. Self-structures vary in strength, which can be assessed by three dimensions: clarity, salience, and valence. Finally, although this chapter focuses on the mentor's side of the relationship, it is important to keep in mind that both mentors and protégés hold these self-structures of mentoring. Moreover, as we will see next, experiences in the relationship shape and create these self-structures, and these experiences are driven by cognitive processes in both mentors and protégés.

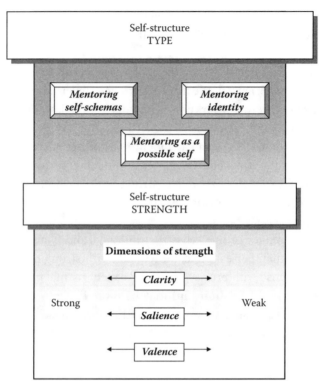

FIGURE 11.1
The self-structures of mentoring: type and dimensions of strength.

MENTORING SELF-STRUCTURES IN ACTION: A MODEL OF THE MOTIVATION TO MENTOR

In this section, I apply the self-structures of mentoring framework to explain the cognitive processes underlying the motivation to mentor. This social cognitive perspective offers an identity-based lens for understanding why mentors are motivated to mentor, and also offers new insights into how self-structures and relationship experiences combine to influence the development of positive identities in the workplace.

Overview of the Model

The purpose of the model is to explicate the dynamic processes involved in the creation of a mentoring identity and to explain the underlying psychological mechanisms that motivate people to mentor. The model is displayed in Figure 11.2. As described below, the three self-structures of mentoring interact in creating and sustaining the motivation to mentor. Mentors develop mentoring identities from their experiences in the relationship, and mentoring identities in turn influence the motivation to mentor, as well as the other self-structures of mentoring. A key proposition of this model is that positive mentoring identities are formed and shaped as a consequence of a cyclical process involving positive experiences in the relationship. Let us now examine these processes in more detail.

Self-Schemas, Possible Selves, and the Motivation to Mentor

As shown in Figure 11.2, the process begins when individuals develop generic mentoring schemas that represent general knowledge and expectations of who a mentor is and what a mentor does in a mentoring relationship (Ragins & Verbos, 2007). In brief, these mental maps of mentoring are developed through direct and indirect experiences with mentoring

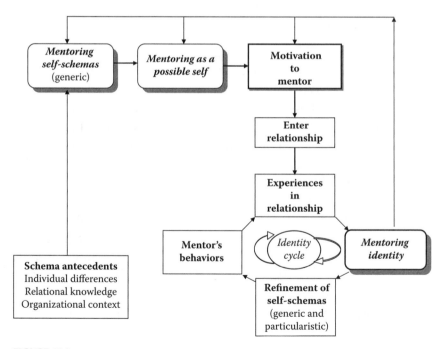

FIGURE 11.2
Mentoring self-structures and the motivation to mentor.

relationships, and are influenced by organizational factors (e.g., mentoring climate and formal mentoring programs) and individual differences (e.g., interdependent self-construals, attachment styles). Individuals are likely to develop mentoring schemas when they have had past experiences in mentoring relationships, when they work in an organization that values mentoring and is explicit about the mentoring role, and when they have self-construals and attachment styles that make relationships central to their sense of self.

As discussed earlier, mentoring schemas influence the development of mentoring as a possible self (cf., Cross & Markus, 1994). A clear conception of mentoring allows individuals to visualize themselves as a mentor in the future, which in turn influences their motivation to enter a mentoring relationship. Therefore, mentoring as a possible self mediates the relationship between the general knowledge of what a mentor is and the motivation to mentor. As we see next, once individuals are in a mentoring relationship, their experiences in the relationship create and shape the development of a mentoring identity through an identity cycle.

The Identity Cycle

As displayed in Figure 11.2, mentoring identities are developed through a cyclical process. Let us use Joan as an example. Her experience of being a mentor in a relationship creates and shapes her generic and particularistic mentoring identities. These identities help her develop and refine her particularistic mentoring schemas, which shape her expectations for her roles in the relationship. Because self-schemas drive behaviors (Markus & Wurf, 1987), her particularistic self-schemas guide her behaviors in this particular relationship. In turn these behaviors influence her overall experience, which creates a feedback loop that can solidify and strengthen both her particularistic (relationship specific) and generic (general) mentoring identities. Her mentoring identities influence her general expectations about what a mentor does, her perceptions of herself as a future mentor, and her motivation to become a mentor again in the future.

Two other factors influence this cycle: the protégé's behavior and the organizational context. Given space constrictions, these factors are not illustrated in Figure 11.2, but a depiction of this process would reflect a three-dimensional model. As mentioned earlier, protégés also develop relational identities and self-schemas that reflect their role as protégés. So even as Joan's mentor's identity is created and shaped by her experiences in the relationship, so are similar processes occurring for her protégé. The protégé's experiences both influence and are influenced by Joan's mentoring behaviors.

All of this occurs within the organizational context, which influences the behaviors, processes, and experiences of mentoring relationships (cf., Eby, Lockwood, & Butts, 2006). Organizations prescribe a more limited base of behaviors and roles for formal mentors in that they are usually advised to constrain their behaviors to job-coaching functions (Ragins & Cotton, 1999). This restriction may not only influence mentoring schemas but also may affect the mentor's experiences in the relationship and the strength of their mentoring identity. As a consequence, formal mentors may be less likely to incorporate mentoring into their self-structures, and may therefore have less motivation to mentor than informal mentors. This may explain the finding that formal mentoring generally produces lower quality relationships than informal mentoring (cf., Underhill, 2006); formal mentors may be less likely than informal mentors to develop strong mentoring identities, which may further perpetuate differences in relational quality and the self-structures of mentoring.

Positive Mentoring Identities

Positive mentoring identities are a relational identity that entails positive self-cognition, self-affirmation, and affect. The model illustrates how positive mentoring identities are derived from experiences in mentoring relationships and how these identities shape relationships. It is proposed here that mentors are most likely to develop positive mentoring identities when they have had positive experiences in their relationships, i.e., when their mentoring experiences engender a positive affective or cognitive state. In turn, positive mentoring identities increase the probability that mentors will become more committed to their relationships, have more positive expectations about their roles in their relationships, and will behave in ways that create future positive experiences in mentoring relationships.

Although the relationship is the primary driver, other factors may also influence the development of positive mentoring identities. For example, because mentors may have multiple relationships, their particularistic and generic identities may be influenced by their constellation of current and past relationships. As discussed earlier, the development of a positive mentoring identity in one relationship may be weakened by negative experiences in another. Moreover, even if the mentor engages in positive behaviors in a given relationship, negative behaviors by their protégé may weaken the mentor's ability to develop positive mentoring identities. Finally, the ability of mentors to develop positive mentoring identities may be facilitated or tempered by organizational influences; positive mentoring identities should be more likely to develop in organizations that value, support, and reward mentoring relationships.

Mentoring Identity and the Motivation to Mentor

The final link in the model involves a feedback loop in which mentoring identities influence the motivation to mentor, as well as the other self-structures of mentoring. Specifically, individuals with strong positive mentoring identities should be more motivated to mentor again in the future and should have stronger and more positive generic self-schemas and perceptions of mentoring as a possible self. In essence, by engaging in a relationship that yields a strong and positive mentoring identity, individuals should be able to develop clearer and more positive expectations about the general role of the mentor and more concrete positive visions of themselves as a future mentor.

To illustrate how the positive dynamic unfolds in this model, let us revisit Joan. Joan's general expectation of what a mentor is shapes her view of herself as a future mentor, which in turn influences her motivation to become a mentor. Let us say she becomes a mentor and has an initial positive experience in the relationship. As a consequence of this experience, she may be more likely to define herself not only in terms of being a mentor but also being a particular person's mentor. This may increase her sense of pride, commitment, and dedication to the mentoring role, and she should also become more cognizant and aware of her roles and behaviors in the relationship. In essence, the mentoring relationship becomes more important to her in part because she has incorporated it into her sense of self through identity and self-schema processes. Her positive mentoring identity refines and strengthens her generic mentoring schemas, her view of herself as a future mentor, and her motivation to mentor others in the future. In contrast, consider Jim, who has had a negative experience in his mentoring relationship. Jim may be less likely than Joan to incorporate mentoring into his relational identity, and he may develop negative or ambivalent expectations about mentoring relationships in general and this relationship in particular. These schemas influence his commitment and behaviors in the relationship, which in turn affect his experience in the relationship, his self-structures of mentoring, and his motivation to enter a mentoring role again in the future. However, Jim may be in more than one mentoring relationship, and his experiences in other relationships may offset or amplify these psychological processes. In addition, if he is in a formal mentoring relationship, his organization can nip these negative processes in the bud by offering interventions and triage that create more positive mentoring experiences and, ultimately, self-structures.

SUMMARY

As revealed in this chapter, mentoring identities are not static but instead reflect dynamic and evolving processes that are reciprocally influenced by experiences in mentoring relationships and the other self-structures of mentoring. Mentoring relationships not only influence the formation of mentoring identities but they also serve as a setting for the self-structures of mentoring to interact in ways that create and sustain the motivation to mentor.

Therefore, the motivation to mentor is more than just a function of the individual's developmental stage (e.g., Erikson, 1963; Levinson et al., 1978); it is also a product of mentoring self-structures that emerge, shape, and change as consequence of the individual's cumulative experiences in mentoring relationships. This longitudinal perspective explains the finding of greater willingness to mentor among those with experience in mentoring relationships (Allen, Poteet, Russell, & Dobbins, 1997; Ragins & Cotton, 1993; Ragins & Scandura, 1994). A key point is that it is not the experience in the relationship per se that creates the motivation to mentor as much as it is the change in self-structures that emerge as a *consequence* of the experience.

In sum, the key propositions advanced here are that individuals become more motivated to mentor when they have clear knowledge of what a mentor is and does, a concrete perception of mentoring as a possible self, and when they incorporate mentoring into their identity structure as a consequence of their direct experience in the relationship. Mentoring identities, in turn, further clarify, strengthen, and solidify the other self-structures of mentoring, which creates a generative cycle that produces and reinforces the motivation to mentor. However, a key prerequisite to this process is positive experiences in relationships; negative experiences may weaken the self-structures of mentoring and ultimately attenuate the willingness to mentor.

IMPLICATIONS AND FUTURE RESEARCH

The self-structure of mentoring model has significant implications for both the field of mentoring and for the emerging domain of positive identities at work.

Implications for the Field of Mentoring

The model presented here explains not only the motivation to mentor but also can be used to explain other behaviors, motivations, and outcomes of mentoring relationships. Future research could test this model and expand it to incorporate the protégé's side of the relationship. As discussed earlier, protégés also have self-structures of mentoring, and dyadic research could examine how these self-structures interact in the relationship and the conditions under which optimal outcomes are obtained for both members of the relationship.

A second key area for future research is the comparison of self-structures in formal and informal mentoring relationships. As mentioned earlier, formal mentoring relationships may be less effective than informal relationships because of differences in schemas, possible selves, and mentoring identities that create differences in relationship quality that perpetuates differences in self-structures. Formal mentoring relationships vary in quality (Ragins, Cotton, & Miller, 2000), and future research could examine the conditions under which members of formal mentoring relationships develop self-structures that yield high quality formal relationships. Because the organization plays a key role in formal mentoring, it would be interesting to examine the types of organizations and mentoring programs that promote and sustain the development of positive mentoring self-structures for formal mentors and their protégés.

Future research should examine the impact of diversity on these processes. Gender may play a key role here, as women are more likely than men to have interdependent self-construals (Cross & Madson, 1997) and define themselves in terms of their relationships with others (Miller & Stiver, 1997). Although women and men generally report equivalent willingness to mentor (Ragins & Scandura, 1994), the sources of their motivation may differ by gender (cf., Fletcher & Ragins, 2007). Drawing on Stone Center Relational Cultural Theory, women may be motivated to develop relationships to establish connection and interdependency with others, whereas men's motivation for developing relationships may be grounded in establishing status and independence from others (Miller, 1976; Miller & Stiver, 1997). This suggests that mentoring identities may differ by gender in subtle but important ways; men and women may both define themselves in terms of their mentoring relationships but for different reasons and outcomes. This offers fascinating possibilities for future research.

Finally, future research needs to examine the effects of cumulative experiences of mentoring relationships on behaviors, processes, and the motivation to mentor. At least two promising areas of inquiry come to mind. First, how do individuals develop positive mentoring identities in the face of mixed experiences in their relationships? Would one bad relationship attenuate a positive mentoring identity, or can individuals develop a type of identity resilience that buffers them from negative experiences? Second, do mentoring identities transcend work and nonwork boundaries? Mentoring relationships occur not only in workplaces but also in schools, communities, and places of worship (cf., Allen & Eby, 2007). Future research could assess how, and under what conditions, mentoring experiences in one setting spill over to another. For example, mentors in the Big Brothers Big Sisters program may develop strong identities as consequence of positive experiences in these relationships. Are these individuals more motivated to mentor in the workplace than those lacking this experience, or are mentoring identities compartmentalized by role and place?

Implications for the Field of Positive Identity

By using mentoring relationships to explore identity processes, this chapter uncovered three insights that may be useful to the emerging field of positive identities at work. First, an application of social cognitive perspectives to relationships suggests that positive identities may develop from, as well as guide the development of, relationships in the workplace. As illustrated in this chapter, identities are immersed within relationships and are also connected to other structures of the self, so future research and theory on positive identities should include the full range of self-structures.

Second, this chapter illustrates how positive identities develop from positive relationships at work, and therefore situates positive identities within the emerging literature on positive relationships in the workplace (Dutton & Ragins, 2007). Because positive relationships are influenced by group, organizational, and community factors, a multilevel approach can and should be used to examine how other positive identities (e.g., leader, manager) emerge from relationships in the workplace.

Finally, the interface between identity and relationships does not happen in a vacuum but is nested in a constellation of current and past relationships that are situated within organizations, professions, and communities. Therefore, holistic perspectives are needed that examine the cumulative impact of these experiences on the development of positive identities in the workplace.

In conclusion, although there is nothing quite as slippery as the dual constructs of identity and relationships, mapping the terrain of their interface offers solid footing for future theory and research on mentoring and positive identities at work.

REFERENCES

Allen, T. D. (2003). Mentoring others: A dispositional and motivational approach. *Journal of Vocational Behavior, 62,* 134–154.

Allen, T. D. (2007). Mentoring relationships from the perspective of the mentor. In B. R. Ragins, & K. E. Kram (Eds.). *The handbook of mentoring at work: Theory, research and practice* (pp. 123–148). Thousand Oaks, CA: Sage Publications.

Allen, T. D., & Eby, L. T. (Eds.) (2007). *Blackwell handbook of mentoring: A multiple perspectives approach.* Oxford, England: Blackwell.

Allen, T. D., Eby, L. T., Poteet, M. L., Lentz, E., & Lima, L. (2004). Career benefits associated with mentoring for protégés: A meta-analysis. *Journal of Applied Psychology, 89,* 127–136.

Allen, T. D., Poteet, M. L., & Burroughs, S. M. (1997). The mentor's perspective: A qualitative inquiry and future research agenda. *Journal of Vocational Behavior, 51,* 70–89.

Allen, T. D., Poteet, M. L., Russell, J. E. A., & Dobbins, G. H. (1997). A field study of factors related to supervisors' willingness to mentor others. *Journal of Vocational Behavior, 50,* 1–22.

Anderson, S. M., & Chen, S. (2002). The relational self: An interpersonal social-cognitive framework. *Psychological Review, 109,* 619–645.

Aryee, S., Chay, Y. W., & Chew, J. (1996). The motivation to mentor among managerial employees: An interactionist approach. *Group & Organization Management, 21,* 261–277.

Ashmore, R. D., Deaux, K., & McLaughlin-Volpe, T. (2004). An organizing framework for collective identity: Articulation and significance of multidimensionality. *Psychological Bulletin, 130,* 80–114.

Baldwin, M. W. (1992). Relational schemas and the processing of social information. *Psychological Bulletin, 112,* 461–484.

Berscheid, E. (1994). Interpersonal relationships. *Annual Review of Psychology, 45,* 79–129.

Berscheid, E. (1999). The greening of relationship science. *American Psychologist, 54,* 260–266.

Brewer, M. B., & Gardner, W. (1996). Who is this "we"? Levels of collective identity and self representations. *Journal of Personality and Social Psychology, 71,* 83–93.

Cameron, K. S., Dutton, J. E., & Quinn, R. E. (Eds.). (2003). *Positive organizational scholarship: Foundations of a new discipline.* San Francisco: Berrett-Koehler Publishers, Inc.

Chen, S., Boucher, H. C., & Tapias, M. P. (2006). The relational self revealed: Integrative conceptualization and implications for interpersonal life. *Psychological Bulletin, 132,* 151–179.

Cooley, C. H. (1902). *Human nature and the social order.* New York: Scribner's Sons.

Cross, S. E., Bacon, P. L., & Morris, M. L. (2000). The relational-interdependent self-construal and relationships. *Journal of Personality and Social Psychology, 78,* 791–808.

Cross, S. E., & Madson, L. (1997). Models of the self: Self-construals and gender. *Psychological Bulletin, 122,* 5–37.

Cross, S. E., & Markus, H. R. (1994). Self-schemas, possible selves, and competent performance. *Journal of Educational Psychology, 86,* 423–438.

Cross, S. E., Morris, M. L., & Gore, J. S. (2002). Thinking about oneself and others: The relational-interdependent self-construal and social cognition. *Journal of Personality and Social Psychology, 82,* 399–418.

Dutton, J., & Ragins, B. R. (Eds.). (2007). *Exploring positive relationships at work: Building a theoretical and research foundation.* Mahwah, NJ: Lawrence Erlbaum Associates.

Erikson, E. H. (1963). *Childhood and society* (2nd ed.). New York: Norton.

Erikson, M. G. (2007). The meaning of the future: Toward a more specific definition of possible selves. *Review of General Psychology, 11,* 348–358.

Eby, L. T. (2007). Understanding relational problems in mentoring. In B. R. Ragins, & K. E. Kram. (Eds.) *The handbook of mentoring at work: Theory, research and practice* (pp. 323–344). Thousand Oaks, CA: Sage Publications.

Eby, L. T., Lockwood, A. L., & Butts, M. (2006). Perceived support for mentoring: A multiple perspectives approach. *Journal of Vocational Behavior, 68,* 267–291.

Fiske, A. P. (1992). The four elementary forms of sociality: Framework for a unified theory of social relations. *Psychological Review, 99,* 689–723.

Fiske, S. T., & Taylor, S. E. (1984). *Social cognition.* New York: Random House.

Fletcher, J. K., & Ragins, B. R. (2007). Stone Center Relational Cultural Theory: A window on relational mentoring. In B. R. Ragins, & K. E. Kram (Eds.). *The handbook of mentoring at work: Theory, research and practice* (pp. 373–399). Thousand Oaks, CA: Sage.

Flynn, F. J. (2005). Identity orientations and forms of social exchange in organizations. *Academy of Management Review, 30,* 737–750.

Gelfand, M. J., Major, V. S., Raver, J. L., Nishii, L. H., & O'Brien, K. (2006). Negotiating relationally: The dynamics of the relational self in negotiations. *Academy of Management Review, 31,* 427–451.

Goffman, E. (1959). *The presentation of self in everyday life.* Garden City, NY: Doubleday Anchor Books.

Harter, S., & Marold, D. B. (1991). A model of the determinants and mediational role of self-worth: Implications for adolescent depression and suicidal ideation. In J. Strauss, & G. R. Goethals (Eds.). *The self: Interdisciplinary approaches* (pp. 66–92). New York: Springer-Verlag.

Higgins, E. T., Klein, R. L., & Strauman, T. J. (1987). Self-discrepancies: Distinguishing among self-states, self-state conflict, and emotional vulnerabilities. In K. Yardley, & T. Honess (Eds.). *Self and identity.* Chichester, England: Wiley.

Higgins, M. C., & Thomas, D. A. (2001). Constellations and careers: Toward understanding the effects of multiple developmental relationships. *Journal of Organizational Behavior, 22,* 223–247.

Hogg, M. A., & Abrams, D. (1988). *Social identifications: A social psychology of intergroup relations and group processes.* London: Routledge.

Hoyle, R. H., & Sherrill, M. R. (2006). Future orientation in the self-system: Possible selves, self-regulation and behavior. *Journal of Personality, 74,* 1673–1696.

Kram, K. (1985). *Mentoring at work: Developmental relationships in organizational life.* Glenview, IL: Scott, Foresman.

Leary, M. R., & Tangney, J. P. (Eds.) (2003). *Handbook of self and identity.* New York: Guilford Press.

Levinson, D. J., Darrow, C. N., Klein, E. B., Levinson, M. H., & McKee, B. (1978). *The seasons of a man's life.* New York: Alfred A. Knopf.

Lord, R. E., Brown, D. J., & Freiberg, S. J. (1999). Understanding the dynamics of leadership: The role of follower self-concepts in the leader/follower relationship. *Organizational Behavior and Human Decision Processes, 78,* 167–203.

Luthans, F., Youssef, C. M. & Avolio, B. J. (2007). *Psychological capital: Developing the human competitive edge.* New York: Oxford University Press.

Markus, H. (1977). Self-schemata and processing information about the self. *Journal of Personality and Social Psychology, 35,* 63–78.

Markus, H., & Kunda, Z. (1986). Stability and malleability of the self-concept. *Journal of Personality and Social Psychology, 51,* 858–866.

Markus, H., & Nurius, P. (1986). Possible selves. *American Psychologist, 41,* 954–969.

Markus, H., & Wurf, E. (1987). The dynamic self-concept: A social psychological perspective. *Annual Review of Psychology, 38,* 299–337.

Markus, H., & Zajonc, R. B. (1985). The cognitive perspective in social psychology. In G. Lindzey, & E. Aronson (Eds.), *Handbook of social psychology* (Vol. 1, 3rd ed., pp. 137–230). New York: Random House.

Markus, H. R., & Kitayama, S. (1991). Culture and the self: Implications for cognition, emotion, and motivation. *Psychological Review, 98,* 224–253.

Mead, G. H. (1934). *Mind, self and society.* Chicago: University of Chicago Press.

Miller, J. B. (1976). *Toward a new psychology of women.* Boston: Beacon Press.

Miller, J. B., & Stiver, I. (1997). *The healing connection.* Boston: Beacon Press.

Nelson, D. L., & Cooper C. L. (Eds.) (2007). Positive organizational behavior: Accentuating the positive at work. London: Sage.

Planalp, S. (1985). Relational schemata: A test of alternative forms of relational knowledge as guides to communication. *Human Communication Research, 12,* 3–29.

Planalp, S. (1987). Interplay between relational knowledge and events. In R. Burnett, P. McGhee, & D. Clarke (Eds.), *Accounting for relationships: Explanation, representation, & knowledge.* New York: Methuen.

Ragins, B. R. (1989). Barriers to mentoring: The female manager's dilemma. *Human Relations, 42,* 1–22.

Ragins, B. R. (1999). Where do we go from here and how do we get there? Methodological issues in conducting research on diversity and mentoring relationships. In A. Murrell, F. J. Crosby, and R. Ely (Eds.), *Mentoring dilemmas: Developmental relationships within multicultural organizations* (pp. 227–247). Mahwah, NJ: Lawrence Erlbaum Associates.

Ragins, B. R., & Cotton, J. (1993). Gender and willingness to mentor in organizations. *Journal of Management, 19,* 97–111.

Ragins, B. R., & Cotton, J. L. (1999). Mentor functions and outcomes: A comparison of men and women in formal and informal mentoring relationships. *Journal of Applied Psychology, 84,* 529–550.

Ragins, B. R., Cotton, J. L., & Miller, J. S. (2000). Marginal mentoring: The effects of type of mentor, quality of relationship, and program design on work and career attitudes. *Academy of Management Journal, 43,* 1177–1194.

Ragins, B. R., & Kram, K. (2007a). The roots and meaning of mentoring. In B. R. Ragins, & K. E. Kram (Eds.), *The handbook of mentoring at work: Theory, research and practice* (pp. 3–15). Thousand Oaks, CA: Sage Publications.

Ragins, B. R., & Kram, K. E. (2007b) *The handbook of mentoring at work: Theory, research and practice.* Thousand Oaks, CA: Sage Publications.

Ragins, B. R., & Scandura, T.A. (1994) Gender differences in expected outcomes of mentoring relationships. *Academy of Management Journal, 37,* 957–971.

Ragins, B. R., & Verbos, A. K. (2007). Positive relationships in action: Relational mentoring and mentoring schemas in the workplace. In J. Dutton, & B. R. Ragins (Eds.), *Exploring positive relationships at work: Building a theoretical and research foundation.* (pp. 91–116). Mahwah, NJ: Lawrence Erlbaum Associates.

Sluss, D., & Ashforth, B. E. (2007). Relational identity and identification: Defining ourselves through others. *Academy of Management Review, 32,* 9–32.

Stryker, S. (1968). Identity salience and role performance. *Journal of Marriage and the Family, 30,* 558–564.

Stryker, S. (1980). *Symbolic interactionism: A social structural version.* Menlo Park, CA: Benjamin/Cummings.

Tajfel, H., & Turner, J. C. (1986). The social identity theory of intergroup behavior. In S. Worchel, & W. G. Austin (Eds.), *The psychology of intergroup relations* (2nd ed., pp. 24). Chicago: Nelson-Hall.

Underhill, C. M. (2006). The effectiveness of mentoring programs in corporate settings: A meta-analytical review of the literature. *Journal of Vocational Behavior, 68,* 292–307.

van Emmerik, I. J. H. (2004). The more you can get the better: Mentoring constellations and intrinsic career success. *Career Development International, 9,* 578–594.

Wanberg, C. R., Welsh, E. T., & Hezlett, S. A. (2003). Mentoring research: A review and dynamic process model. *Research in Personnel and Human Resources Management, 22,* 39–124.

12

Renarrating Positive Relational Identities in Organizations: Self-Narration as a Mechanism for Strategic Emotion Management in Interpersonal Interactions

Shirli Kopelman, Lydia L. Chen, and Joseph Shoshana

CONTENTS

This chapter explores the impact of emotions on identity. In organizational settings, displays of negative (e.g., anger or sadness) and positive (e.g., happiness or joy) emotions, whether authentic or feigned, can be counterproductive to both task and relational outcomes (e.g., Allred, Mallozzi, Matsui, & Raia, 1997; Côté, 2005; Hochschild, 1983; Pillutla & Murnighan, 1996). Strategic response to counterproductive emotional displays impact the responder's experienced emotions and subsequent behavior (Kopelman, Gewurz, & Sacharin, 2008). We suggest that emotion management—strategic response and display of emotions—will not only lead to improved interdependent outcomes (Barry, 1999; Frank, 1988; Kopelman, Gewurz, & Sacharin, 2008; Kopelman, Rosette, & Thompson, 2006) but also will influence the social construction and reconstruction of interpersonal relational identities. Adopting a framework that conceptualizes identity as narrative (Gergen, 1991; McAdams, 1985; Omer & Strenger, 1992; Spence, 1982), a relational identity (Sluss & Ashforth, 2007) is a shared narrative that emerges from both parties' self-narration of the social interaction (see Figure 12.1). When relational threats such as a counterproductive display of a positive or negative emotion are strategically managed, people in interdependent role relationships can cocreate, renarrate, and maintain positive relational identities.

This chapter focuses on the theoretical antecedents of positive relational identities (see Figure 12.2). The dependent variable in our theoretical model is the positive relational identity. We define a *positive relational identity* as a coherent and constructive shared narrative, in which both parties in a role relationship view their relationship as one that is likely to overcome future relational challenges and remain effective despite threats to the relationship. The exogenous variable in our theoretical model is a particular type of relational threat: a party's counterproductive emotional display in the context of an interpersonal relationship. The mechanism is the responding party's individual-level process of emotion management via *self-narration*. Self-narration is conceptualized as a resilient—in contrast to a rigid—response to a relational threat (Sutcliffe & Vogus, 2003). Paradoxically, self-narration involves a detached observing capacity that enables the responder to fully engage in the relationship more authentically and more effectively.

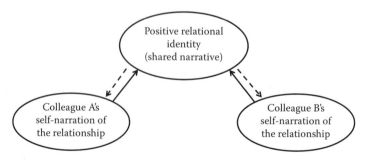

FIGURE 12.1
Positive relational identity as a shared narrative.

We begin by conceptualizing a relational identity as a narrative identity and define a *positive* relational identity as a coherent narrative that emerges from resilient responses to relational threats. We then provide a brief review of the literature on emotional displays in organizational settings, identifying situations where positive or negative emotions may present relational threats. Finally, we integrate the emotion management and identity literatures and build on research in clinical and social psychology to conceptualize the process of self-narration as a mechanism that develops, maintains, and repairs relational identities. We conclude by discussing theoretical and empirical implications for the study of identity and positive organizing.

RELATIONAL IDENTITIES AS NARRATIVE IDENTITIES

Relational identities refer to one's role relationship with interdependent others (Sluss & Ashforth, 2007) and are conceptualized at the interpersonal level, in contrast to the individual or collective levels of the self (Brewer & Gardner, 1996). For example, two coworkers may have a relational identity (e.g., colleagues), alongside each one's autonomous individual (e.g., ambitious/meticulous) and collective social (e.g., gender/professional) identities. Relational identities—unlike individual or collective identities—define the self in relation to others (Sluss & Ashforth, 2007; Stryker, 1980). Relational identities include both hierarchical occupational relationships such as manager-employee, as well as egalitarian relationships such as colleagues or teammates. In an organizational setting, a relational identity may refer

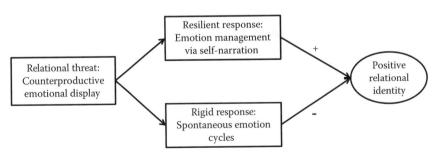

FIGURE 12.2
The emotion response process: building resilience.

to a dyadic or a small group level of analysis. For ease of explanation, this chapter focuses on dyadic interactions. Likewise, we focus on role relationships with a specific other (e.g., Mary and John in a specific manager and subordinate relationship), which is referred to as *particularized relational identities*, in contrast to *generalized relational identities* (e.g., Mary as a manager; Sluss & Ashforth, 2007).

A narrative framework views stories as a critical means by which people make themselves intelligible within the social world. The narrative identity framework (Gergen, 1991; McAdams, 1985; Omer & Strenger, 1992; Spence, 1982) conceptualizes identity as a story that is developed and refined, complete with settings, scenes, characters, plots, and themes. A *narrative* refers to an individual's account of self-relevant life events that lends coherence to those events (Gergen & Gergen, 1984). Thus, narratives can apply to individual, interpersonal, and collective identities. "In order to exist in the social world with a comfortable sense of being a good, socially proper, and stable person, an individual needs to have a coherent, acceptable, and constantly revised life story" (Linde, 1993, p. 3). Because people have a continual need to form and maintain relationships (Baumeister & Leary, 1995), they are likely to construct and reconstruct narratives about interpersonal relationships—that is, relational narrative identities—just as they do with their individual identities. Thus, not only do people tell their lives to themselves as stories, but also their relationships with each other are lived out in narrative form.

Integrating a theoretical framework that conceptualizes identity as narrative with Sluss and Ashforth's (2007) definition of a relational identity, we suggest that a relational identity is a shared narrative that emerges from both parties' self-narration of the relationship (see Figure 12.1). In this context, a narrative identity is a self-account of one's role relationship with interdependent others. These are "social constructions that undergo continuous alteration as interactions progress" (Gergen & Gergen, 1988, p. 19) and are explicitly or implicitly communicated. For example, suppose Mary perceives her relationship with John as a "mentor-mentee" relationship and tries to instruct him as such. If John perceives their relationship as a "bully-subordinate" one, though, he would not take her instruction well. Therefore, it is to Mary's benefit (as well as the benefit of the organization) to have John agree with her on their relational identity. To have John accept the role of "mentee" to her "mentor" would help maintain the appropriate hierarchy and facilitate interaction between them. Sluss and

Ashforth (2007) suggest that "parties in a role-relationship tend to come to a mutual understanding of their relational identity, and this shared meaning facilitates the coordinated interaction that is the hallmark of effective role-relationships" (p. 13). A narrative approach to relational identities helps illuminate this social construction process.

As narratives, relational identities are products of social accounts or discourse. Language and interpersonal relationships have a bidirectional association (Botella & Herrero, 2000). On the one hand, language is a product of shared action; on the other hand, relationships and interactions are mediated via conversations. Communicating one's narrative of a relationship to others in the relationship can be advantageous because relational identities help structure relationships, provide ground rules for interaction, and facilitate communication. Furthermore, the fluidity of characters within this *interpersonal field* (termed by Botella & Herrero, 2000) allows multiple interpretations on the part of the narrator. For example, suppose Mary is making requests and suggestions to John. Narrating their relational identity to himself as "a bully lording it over a subordinate" is one way for John to assimilate and assign meaning to the interactions. Narrating the relational identity to himself as "a mentor showing a mentee the ropes," however, yields different connotations. Narration allows the narrator to "try out" the various characters in different roles to see which roles fit the facts better. For instance, John may try out the "bully" story, only to realize that Mary's kindness toward him fits a "mentor" story better. Note that each party in the interaction may have a different view of the relational identity. For example, Mary (unbeknownst to him) may harbor romantic feelings for John and may be narrating their relational identity to herself as that of a "woman trying to get his attention." Thus, narratives can be construed as meaning bridges between the narrator's beliefs and the declarations of other people.

POSITIVE RELATIONAL IDENTITIES AND RESILIENCE

Relational identities are continually negotiated among people in a relationship. People are especially likely to revise accounts of life experiences in the face of unexpected or adverse events so as to maintain coherence, continuity, and meaning (Gergen & Gergen, 1986). In response to adversity, relationships may be formed (narrated) or renarrated. Likewise, adversity may lead to a positive or negative adjustment to the relational identity. We suggest that positive relational identities emerge from resilient responses to relational threats.

Resilience refers to a "dynamic process encompassing positive adaptation within the context of significant adversity" (Luthar, Cicchetti, & Becker, 2000, p. 543). The concept of resilience as a dynamic developmental process differs from a personality characteristic called ego resiliency (Block & Block, 1980), in that (a) it is not a trait of the individual, and (b) it necessitates exposure to adversity. Adversity may stem from an internal or external threat. Threats can lead to rigid (e.g., Staw, Sandelands, & Dutton, 1981) or resilient responses, which respectively lead to negative versus positive adjustment. Rigid responses are characterized by maladaptive processes such as narrow information processing and tightening of control, whereas resilient responses rely on broad information processing and flexibility (Sutcliffe & Vogus, 2003). According to Sutcliffe and Vogus (2003), resilience, which can be conceptualized at the individual, group, and organizational levels of analysis, is "the capacity to rebound from adversity strengthened and more resourceful. That is why it is at the heart of positive organizing" (p. 97).

Identity, whether at the individual, relational, or collective level, plays a role in understanding resilience. An identity-based approach for understanding response to adversity at work examines how identity processes may play an important role in shaping how individuals experience and respond to adversity at work (Caza, 2007). For example, recent empirical research suggests that the strength of professional identification and complexity are positively associated with resilience in the face of adversity (Caza & Bagozzi, 2008). Building on Caza's identity-based approach, we explore how a person's response to adversity may shape identity. We focus on the impact of relational threats on identity. Specifically, we focus on how a resilient/rigid response to a counterproductive emotional display (relational threat) will respectively lead to a positive/negative adjustment to the interpersonal level identity (see Figure 12.2). Following our theoretical model, resilient responses to relational threats lead to a positive adjustment to the relational identity, that is, a positive relational identity.

Thus, a positive relational identity is a coherent and constructive shared narrative according to which both parties in a role relationship view their specific relationship (e.g., colleagues) as one that is flexible, adaptive, and likely to overcome future threats and remain effective despite adversity. For example, if Mary believes that she and John are good colleagues, their relational identity may be threatened when he enters her office yelling at the top of his voice. His display of anger is likely to make Mary angry (emotional contagion; e.g., Hatfield, Cacioppo, & Rapson, 1992) and lead her to respond angrily (emotion cycle; Hareli & Rafaeli, 2008), which may lead to a conflict spiral and a prolonged dispute. Mary may renarrate their relational identity as "a temperamental worker who is disrespecting my position as boss," whereas John renarrates their relational identity as "an obstinate boss who is being unresponsive to my concerns." Such a spontaneous process of emotional contagion is characterized by narrow information processing and represents a rigid response to adversity, which therefore leads to negative adjustment to the relational identity (or a deteriorated relational identity). As an alternative to responding in the moment by reciprocating anger, a resilient response involving broader information processing and flexibility such as necessitated by strategic emotion management would lead to positive adjustment, that is, a more positive relational identity. If Mary can respond to John's counterproductive display of anger by engaging in strategic emotion management that leads to problem solving, Mary and John will be more likely to share a relational identity that enables them to strategically manage future interpersonal threats to productive ends. Such resilient responses will beget future resilient responses. Thus, a positive relational identity is poised to respond resiliently to future threats.

COUNTERPRODUCTIVE EMOTIONS AS RELATIONAL THREATS

In the context of positive relational identities and resilience, we focus on a specific threat to relational identities: display of counterproductive emotions. An emotional display by party B is considered counterproductive if it impacts the other party in the role relationship, party A (the responder), in such a way as to adversely influence task and relational outcomes. To better understand counterproductive emotions, we define emotions, differentiate counterproductive from productive emotional displays, and subsequently distinguish between rigid and resilient responses to a counterproductive emotional threat to the relational identity.

Emotions are relatively short-lived affective episodes. A key feature that differentiates emotions from other affective processes (e.g., mood) is that emotions include behavioral response tendencies (Frijda, 1986). Emotions arise when a person attends to a situation and perceives it as relevant to enduring or transient goals. These situations give rise to appraisals that constitute a person's assessment of the situation's characteristics such as valence and value relevance (Ellsworth & Scherer, 2003) and are associated with physiological changes (Mauss, Levenson, McCarter, Wilhelm, & Gross, 2005). In contrast to moods (which are more general, stable, and diffuse), emotions are either triggered by an identifiable event or brought on as a means to achieve an aspired end (e.g., Barry, 1999; Schwarz & Clore, 1996). Generally, in social interactions, emotional displays serve to communicate to others and/or to motivate behavior (Blair, 2003; Horstmann, 2003). According to the *emotions as social information* (EASI) model (Van Kleef, 2008), communicated emotions serve as important cues for strategic information gathering and processing in interpersonal exchanges (Van Kleef, De Dreu, & Manstead, 2004b). Emotional displays also serve as a means of persuasion and influence the cognitions, emotions, and behavior of others (e.g., Forgas, 2001; Frank, 1988; Kopelman et al., 2006). Thus, they may constitute an influence tactic that leads the responder to think, feel, and/or behave in a manner that otherwise would not have been a first choice.

The norm that emotions should be "checked at the door" in organizations is grounded in beliefs that emotions lead people to stray from rationality and are inappropriate at the workplace. These beliefs are more prevalent in some cultures than others (Sanchez-Burks, 2002), but emotions and emotion regulation are often a part of day-to-day organizational life and work roles (e.g., Barsade & Gibson, 2007; Côté, 2005; Rafaeli & Sutton, 1987). Research suggests that people across cultures recognize six basic facial displays of emotions: anger, disgust, fear, sadness, surprise, and happiness (Ekman, Friesen, & Ellsworth, 1972), but other discrete experienced and displayed emotions such as hate, shame, guilt, jealousy, love, and joy may be influenced by cultural socialization processes that begin in early child development (e.g., Cole, Bruschi, & Tamang, 2002). The ability to recognize one's own experienced and others' displayed positive and negative emotions is considered an evolutionary adaptive human characteristic

(Ekman, 1993), which can have strategic implications for social interactions. For example, empirical findings suggest that people convincingly display both positive and negative emotions in interpersonal interactions, such as negotiations (Kopelman et al., 2006; Sinaceur & Tiedens, 2006), and that such displays influence both task and relational outcomes (for reviews, see Barry, Fulmer, & Goates, 2006; Li & Roloff, 2006).

Empirical research has begun to map out when emotional displays might be beneficial versus counterproductive. Positive affect has been shown to improve decisions (see Isen, 1987 for a review), increase cooperation (e.g., Forgas, 1998), signal optimal individual functioning (Fredrickson, 2003), and facilitate individual and joint gains in negotiated outcomes (e.g., Baron, 1990; Carnevale & Isen, 1986; Kopelman et al., 2006). In some situations, deliberate display of positive emotion increases the likelihood of closing a deal, gaining concessions on price, and developing a long-term business relationship following a dispute (Kopelman et al.). However, display of negative emotion can also be effective. For example, negative emotional display is advantageous in specific role relationships such as the role of a criminal investigator or a bill collector (Rafaeli & Sutton, 1991), perhaps because negative emotions are normative and considered culturally appropriate (Kopelman & Rosette, 2008). Furthermore, in negotiations the display of anger by one party can lead to increased concession making by lower-power parties (Sinaceur & Tiedens, 2006; Van Kleef, De Dreu, & Manstead, 2004a). Finally, negative emotions such as guilt and embarrassment may have positive relational consequences when they provoke efforts to repair relationships (e.g., Bagozzi, 2003).

However, displaying emotions, whether positive or negative, can be risky. For example, happiness (as well as anger) leads to poor information processing (Bodenhausen, Sheppard, & Kramer, 1994; Forgas, 1992; Tiedens, 2001), which can be counterproductive when deep processing is necessary. Because happiness can lead to heuristic behavior associated with a fixed pie perception (Thompson & Hastie, 1990) or *satisficing*—being satisfied with less than what is optimal (Simon, 1955)—the display of positive emotion can be detrimental to organizational processes and outcomes. Furthermore, given that emotions are contagious (Hatfield, Cacioppo, & Rapson, 1992), this effect can cascade if both parties are "happy go lucky" or angry when deep processing is necessary. Likewise, because of emotional contagion, displays of anger can generate a retaliatory response from the other party that leads to conflict spirals (Ury, Brett, & Goldberg, 1993), worse outcomes for both parties (Allred et al., 1997), as well as decreased resolution rates when disputant parties turn to third-party mediation (Friedman et al., 2004).

Thus, counterproductive emotions may range from inappropriate positive or negative emotions to potentially violent emotional outbursts that constitute significant challenges to task and relational outcomes. It is important to note that both positive and negative emotional displays can be counterproductive in organizational settings. Moreover, positive emotions do not necessarily lead to positive relational identities themselves; rather, it is the response to counterproductive positive and negative emotional displays that influences the relational identity.

RESILIENT VERSUS RIGID RESPONSES TO COUNTERPRODUCTIVE EMOTIONAL THREATS

The modal model of emotions suggests four sequential and iterative stages of party A's emotional response. It begins with a *situation* (in this case the emotional display of party B) that compels *attention*, has particular meaning represented by a person's *appraisal*, and results in a multisystem *physiological manifestation* (Gross & Thompson, 2007).[1] If the emotional display of party B is perceived by party A as appropriate and productive, a spontaneous emotional response such as positive emotional contagion in groups (Barsade, 2002) will likely lead to desired outcomes and will not threaten the relational identity. However, if an emotional display is perceived as counterproductive, we suggest that a spontaneous, narrow, and rigid response such as emotional contagion (Hatfield, Cacioppo, & Rapson, 1992) would create emotional cycles (Hareli & Rafaeli, 2008) and escalate the emotional threat. In general, to successfully handle emotion-related conflicts, a person must engage in critical thinking, openness, emotional regulation, and flexibility (Matsumoto, Yoo, & LeRoux, 2007). Strategic emotion management enables such a resilient response to an emotional

---

[1] In the emotion regulation literature (for a review, see Gross & Thompson, 2007), the physiological manifestation of an emotion (e.g., increased heart rate and avoidance behavior) is called the "behavioral response tendency." In this chapter we call it "physiological manifestation" of emotion to differentiate the behavioral response tendency stage of the "modal model" of emotions from the more general strategic response to a relational threat.

threat. Specifically, if party B displays a counterproductive emotion in the context of the relationship, party A will need to strategically manage her own emotional response. Strategic emotion management includes not only emotion regulation but also mindfulness.

SELF-NARRATION AS A RESILIENT RESPONSE

Building on and integrating principles of cognitive-behavioral therapy (for a review, see Beck, 1995)—and more specifically, dialectical behavioral therapy (DBT) (Linehan, 1993a, 1993b; Linehan, Bohus, & Lynch, 2007)— with the modal model of emotions and emotion regulation research (for a review, see Gross & Thompson, 2007), we suggest that *self-narration* functions as a form of strategic emotion management. We define self-narration as a sequential and iterative process of *mindful* emotion regulation as one (a) *observes*, (b) *describes*, and (c) *participates* in social interactions (see Figure 12.3). *Mindfulness* (Linehan, 1993a, 1993b) enables a responder to process the relational threat (counterproductive emotional display of the other party) in a nonjudgmental and holistic manner because mindfulness authentically integrates the responder's logical and emotional response. *Emotion regulation* (Gross & Thompson, 2007) may occur at multiple stages of an emotional response (attention, appraisal, or physiological manifestation) to the given situation (e.g., relational threat). Self-narration may also occur in the absence of emotional threats to the

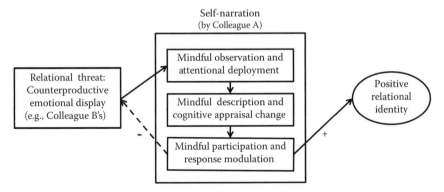

FIGURE 12.3
Emotion management via self-narration: (re)narrating a positive relational identity.

relationship, in which case the emotional regulation dimension of the self-narration process would be deemphasized. However, in a potentially emotional social interaction, self-narration requires mindfulness and emotion regulation. Self-narration serves as a mechanism that facilitates positive relational identities by mitigating threats to role relationships, such as counterproductive emotional displays.

Self-narration is rooted in core mindfulness skills developed in the context of DBT (Linehan, 1993a, 1993b). DBT is grounded in Hegel's philosophical perspective that focuses on integrating and transforming two seemingly contradictory thoughts (Hegel, 1910; Houlgate, 2005). For example, in DBT, therapists and clients work to balance acceptance with acknowledgment of the need for change. With regard to strategic emotion management, this implies that one needs to both accept one's spontaneous emotional reaction as real and legitimate *and* engage in thoughtful emotion regulation, which transforms both into a more adaptive and goal-congruent response.

In the context of DBT skill training, Linehan (1993a, 1993b) distinguishes between three states of mind: *reasonable, emotional,* and *wise*. A person in a state of reasonable mind approaches a situation intellectually, thinks rationally and logically, attends to facts, and plans his or her behavior with a purpose. In contrast, when the emotional mind is dominant, thinking and behavior are controlled primarily by a person's current emotional state. The emotional mind suppresses cognitions, reasoning, and logical thinking, distorts perceptions to make them fit with current affect, and makes behaviors congruent with the current emotional state. A wise mind represents the integration of both the emotional and reasonable minds, and thus represents the transformation of dialectical opposites into a more adaptive state of mind. Mindfulness skills are considered the vehicles for integrating the emotional and reasonable minds to achieve a wise mind.

Strategically responding to a counterproductive emotion rather than spontaneously reacting rests on the assumption that in the moment one can achieve a wise mind (Linehan, 1993b), regulate one's own emotions (for a review, see Gross & Thompson, 2007), and respond appropriately. Sometimes this may not be practical, and a *cooling-off* period may be recommended, especially during heated conflict (Ury, Brett, & Goldberg, 1993). However, expertise in strategic emotion management can be developed (Potworowski & Kopelman, 2008). One can develop skills to strategically respond in the moment and allow one's *wise mind* to lead the way (Linehan 1993b). Because strategic emotion management requires the integration of one's emotional and reasonable mind (to achieve a wise mind) and the alignment of one's revised experienced emotion with one's display of emotion, strategic emotion management through the process of self-narration is an authentic response (for a discussion on authenticity, see Roberts et al., Chapter 7 of this volume).

As a concrete illustration of strategic emotion management through self-narration, suppose that John is happy and telling jokes instead of completing a task. John's manager, Mary, notices John's display of happiness (attention stage) and perceives it as counterproductive—John is stalling on an important task (appraisal stage). Her instinctive reaction is to frown (physiological manifestation) and call out "Hey, can you get back to work, and tell jokes on your own time?" (rigid response). However, she may stop herself short of yelling at John and reconsider either what she noticed (appraisal), how she interpreted it (appraisal), and/or her physiological response. For instance, she may notice the clock and realize that John is telling jokes at 4:30 p.m. on a Friday afternoon. This revised observation may lead to a different appraisal of the situation as Mary remembers that John has worked hard all week and achieved an important milestone that was completed earlier that day, thus deserving a few moments of comic relief. Furthermore, the task he is currently working on, although important and complicated, can wait until Monday. Mary physiologically relaxes, smiles, and responds with a joke of her own. If she had followed her instinctive, rigid response, she might have fostered bad feeling between herself and John; their relational identity would have suffered. Instead, Mary's response strengthens the camaraderie between herself and John, who then sees her as supportive of him and renarrates their relational identity as resilient in the face of potential relational conflict (e.g., an inappropriate display of positive emotion at the workplace). As she ruminates about this, Mary realizes how important it is to wisely differentiate and know when to discipline a subordinate, when to let go of her need to maximize task efficiency of her team, and when to simply socialize. John also leaves the office thinking to himself that Mary is an understanding manager. Given this social interaction, and potentially others like it, Mary and John are likely to have a positive relational identity as manager and employee that is characterized by mutual respect and a belief that they can flexibly overcome relational threats.

Integrating and building on mindfulness and emotion regulation, we conceptualize self-narration as an authentic yet strategic emotion management response to a counterproductive emotional display (a relational threat) that includes three sequential and cyclical stages of mindfulness and emotion regulation as one observes, describes, and participates in a social interaction (see Figure 12.3).

Self-narration requires a person to temporarily disengage himself or herself from the spontaneous emotional cycle by engaging a mindful observing capacity that facilitates more authentic and fully engaged participation in the social relationship. In this sense, the person becomes a narrator of the interaction while also being a participant. For example, as Mary listens to John's jokes she self-reflects and feels as though she is both watching the scene develop and narrating her response. Thus, she is narrating her relationship with John. Learning to form stories is crucial to developing a coherent "emotional life" (Mancuso & Sarbin, 1998). According to Linehan (1993b), the key to achieving mindfulness and engaging a wise mind is the propensity to take a nonjudgmental stance, to focus on one thing in the moment, and to be effective (Linehan, 1993b). In Linehan's skills-training framework, these are considered the "how" mindfulness skills. The "what" mindfulness skills require wise observation, description, and participation (Linehan, 1993a, 1993b). Observation, description, and participation correspond to emotion regulation at three stages of the modal model of emotions: attention to, appraisal of, and physiological manifestation. Emotion regulation at each of these stages is called *attentional deployment* (refocusing one's attention to factual information), *cognitive appraisal change* (reframing one's interpretation of the attended information), and *response modulation* (changing one's behavioral response) (Gross & Thompson, 2007).

Mindful Observation and Attentional Deployment

Mindful observation corresponds to the *attention* (perception) stage of the modal model of emotions (Gross & Thompson, 2007). Without changing the situation, individuals can direct their attention within a given situation to influence their emotions. Emotional regulation at the *attention* stage of the modal model of emotions is referred to as *attentional deployment* (Gross & Thompson, 2007). Attentional deployment is one of the first emotion regulation processes to appear in child development (Rothbart,

Ziaie, & O'Boyle, 1992). Attentional deployment may take different forms, such as physical withdrawal of attention (e.g., covering one's eyes and ears). It may also involve *distraction*, which works by focusing attention on different aspects of the situation (Gross & Thompson, 2007). For example, drawing on therapeutic findings (Philippot, Baeyens, Douilliez, & Francart, 2004), people can redirect attention toward elements that are incongruent with their negative interpretations to develop a more balanced and objective view of the situation.

Thus, emotion regulation at the attention stage requires objective and flexible reassessment of the perceived social interaction. For example, one can attend to the situation without necessarily trying to terminate it when it is painful or to prolong it when it is pleasant. One can notice and experience the situation as it is unfolding with awareness, without jumping to the emotional appraisal stage. This focus on "experiencing the moment" is based on Eastern philosophical approaches, as well as on Western notions of exposure without positive or negative reinforcement, as a method to extinguish automatic avoidance and fear responses (Linehan, 1993b). Linehan, in her skills training manual, provides tips for mindfully observing, for example: "(a) Just notice the experience: Notice without getting caught in the experience; experience without reaction; (b) Have a 'Teflon mind': Let experiences, feelings, and thoughts come into your mind and slip right out; (c) Control your attention, but not what you see; push away nothing; cling to nothing; (d) Notice what comes through your senses: your eyes, ears, nose, skin, and tongue; see others' actions and expressions" (Linehan, 1993b, p. 111). While mindfully accepting and broadening the scope of what one observes, one also strategically regulates through attentional deployment what information is subsequently appraised.

Mindful Description and Cognitive Appraisal Change

Mindful description corresponds to the appraisal stage of the modal model of emotions (Gross & Thompson, 2007). Describing of events and personal responses in words refers to the ability to apply verbal labels to behavioral and environmental events, which is essential for both communication and self-control (Beck, 1995). Mindful description requires an acknowledgement that a person's emotions and thoughts are not literal reflections of environmental events, but rather parts of a personal, subjective interpretation of the environment. For example, feeling afraid does not necessarily mean that a situation is life-threatening (Linehan, 1993b). Mindful describing involves assessing and reassessing the association of thoughts and feelings with their corresponding environmental events and teasing them apart. For example, if Mary is yelling at John, he may experience fear or anger. As he describes to himself in words what is happening, he may think to himself: "Mary is yelling at me, my stomach muscles are in knots, and I feel angry about her rudeness...." Putting words on the experience and putting experiences into words helps people become aware of their own appraisal of the observed situation. Studies have shown that having people write or talk about their negative personal experiences in the form of stories improves their mental and physical health (for a review, see Pennebaker, 2000). Both empirical analyses and descriptive comments of participants in these studies indicated that storying benefits people by forcing them to think things out, organize their thoughts and feelings, and take an outside perspective on themselves.

Emotion regulation at the appraisal state of the process involves *cognitive change* (Gross & Thompson, 2007). It allows people to examine multiple appraisals and chose one they deem most appropriate to their strategic goals. How one reappraises an observed situation may alter its emotional significance. Reappraisal may require shifting from a positional- to an interest-based mindset (Fisher, Ury, & Patton, 1991; Ury, Brett, & Goldberg, 1993). For example, disputants facing counterproductive emotional displays often need to let go of "being right" (e.g., "I need and deserve the private office with the nice windows because it was promised to me!") in favor of achieving underlying interests (e.g., "I only want the office for its natural sunlight, whereas you only want it for the privacy, so I can take the cubicle next to the window, and you can take the private office."). Likewise, reappraisal may shift cause-and-effect interpretations and attributions (e.g., "Mary is yelling because John did not complete his task" versus "Mary is yelling because she has a short temper when she is hungry"). Pennebaker (2000) found that people who benefited from describing their negative experience in the form of a story tended to use more positive emotion words than negative emotion words at first, followed by the gradual replacement of emotional words with less affective, cognitive words. Such storying may involve going back to the observation stage to "check the facts" to distinguish assumptions, interpretations, ruminative thoughts, and worries from occurrences during the situation (Linehan, 1993a).

Mindful Participation and Response Modulation

Participation entails fully entering into ongoing events and interactions of the moment. The action is usually spontaneous and mindless, like driving a car while relying on habit. However, mindful participation requires alertness and awareness as one responds (Linehan, 1993b), such as that of a skilled line worker who simultaneously juggles several tasks with acute attention. For example, in the moment during an interpersonal emotional interaction, Mary is aware that she is responding to John's anger by yelling back. Emotion regulation at this stage—response modulation—occurs after physiological emotional response tendencies have been initiated. Participating while engaging in an action that opposes or is inconsistent with the behavioral experience and/or expression of emotion may help regulate and mitigate it. This is called "opposite action all the way" (Linehan, 1993a). Responses could be physiological, experiential, or behavioral. Mindful participation targets the entire range of physical responses that accompany action, including visceral responses, body postures, and facial expression, as well as movements. For example, if Mary senses that her behavioral response is anxiety ridden, she can take a deep breath or tense a limb momentarily and then relax it; both would lead to a reduction in generalized physical tension and allow her to alter her response as it is unfolding. Altering one's physical state alters one's emotional state (Philippot et al., 2004) and enables more effective participation. It may loop back and lead to attending to different facts or reappraising the situation.

Mindful participation is key to the social interaction because at this stage of self-narration, the other party can observe the behavioral response tendency. Thus, party A's response to party B's initial counterproductive emotional display influences party B's subsequent response, which then influences party A's next response. Each response may in turn be rigid or resilient. We suggest that the benefits of self-narration increase if both parties in the relationship reciprocally engage in emotion management via self-narration.

CONCLUSIONS

Integrating a narrative framework of identity with the emotion management literature in clinical and social psychology, we have developed the concept of self-narration as a mechanism for building resilience in the face of relational threats. Self-narration requires an individual-level observing capacity that engages a process of mindfulness and emotion regulation during a potentially counterproductive social interaction. This enables more authentic and effective participation in the moment. It is conceptualized as a resilient, in contrast to a rigid, response to relational adversity that leads to the development of a positive relational identity—a coherent and constructive shared narrative according to which both parties in a role relationship view their relationship not only as meaningful and effective but also flexible, adaptive, and likely to prevent or overcome future relational threats.

This chapter contributes to the literature on relational identities by integrating a narrative perspective that proposes an individual-level process by which relational identities can become shared at a dyadic level by mutual negotiation and renarration. Thus, relational identities are dynamic, socially constructed narratives. It contributes to the literature on positive organizational scholarship (POS) (Cameron, Dutton, & Quinn, 2003) by integrating resilience into the process of identity formation and repair. Furthermore, it contributes to both the identity and POS literatures by examining the effects of emotion on relational identities and of authentic emotion management on resilience building. Like other chapters, we assume the role of agency in developing positive relational identities. This chapter complements other chapters in this book by highlighting the importance of emotional dynamics, by examining the antecedents of a positive relational identity, and by linking these two to a developmental process of resilience.

The model put forth in this chapter opens the door to empirical research on the links between strategic response to emotional displays and positive relational identities. Research has shown that narrating emotional dimensions of personal and interpersonal life leads to positive adaptation in therapeutic contexts (Angus, Lewin, Bouffard, & Rotondi-Trevisan, 2004; Greenberg & Angus, 2004; White & Epston, 1990). Such research needs to be extended to examine how narrating personal relationships in organizational contexts can similarly lead to positive adaptation in relational identities. Likewise, mindfulness skills and emotion regulation proven effective in clinical psychology (Linehan et al., 2007) also need to be tested in organizational contexts. On the one hand, they may have benefits, such as development of resilience; on the other hand, there may be costs, given people's limited cognitive resources (e.g., Muraven & Baumeister, 2000).

Furthermore, it would be interesting to explore who might be more likely to engage in self-narration. Would people in positions of power be more likely to do so? Are charismatic leaders who empower followers (Kark, Shamir, & Chen, 2003) more likely to engage in self-narration? Are there individual or cultural differences (e.g., Asians tend to think more dialectically; e.g., Peng & Nisbett, 1999) that facilitate mindfulness and enhance self-narration? Given the emphasis on the relational self in organizational life and negotiating relationally (e.g., Gelfand, Major, Raver, Nishii, & O'Brien, 2006), we hope that our chapter will spur empirical research on the links between mindful (authentic) emotion regulation and positive relational identities.

REFERENCES

Allred, K. G., Mallozzi J. S., Matsui F., & Raia C. P. (1997). The influence of anger and compassion on negotiation performance. *Organizational Behavior & Human Decision Processes, 70,* 175–187.

Angus, L. E., Lewin, J., Bouffard, B., & Rotondi-Trevisan, D. (2004). "What's the story?": Working with narrative in experiential psychotherapy. In L. E. Angus & J. McLeod (Eds.), *The handbook of narrative and psychotherapy* (pp. 331–350). Thousand Oaks, CA: Sage Publications.

Bagozzi, R. P. (2003). Positive and negative emotions in organizations. In K. S. Cameron, J. E. Dutton, & R. E. Quinn (Eds.), *Positive organizational scholarship: Foundations of a new discipline.* San Francisco: Berrett-Koehler Publishers.

Baron, R. A. (1990). Environmentally induced positive affect: Its impact on self-efficacy, task performance, negotiation, and conflict. *Journal of Applied Social Psychology, 20,* 368–384

Barry, B. (1999). The tactical use of emotion in negotiation. In R. J. Bies & R. J. Lewicki (Eds.), *Research in negotiation in organizations* (pp. 93–121). Stamford, CT: JAI Press.

Barry, B., Fulmer, I., & Goates, N. (2006). Bargaining with feeling: Emotionality in and around negotiation. In L. L. Thompson (Ed.), *Negotiation theory and research* (pp. 99–127). Madison, CT: Psychosocial Press.

Barsade, S. G. (2002). The ripple effect: Emotional contagion and its influence on group behavior. *Administrative Science Quarterly, 47,* 644–675.

Barsade, S. G., & Gibson, D. E. (2007, February). Why does affect matter in organizations? *Academy of Management Perspectives,* 36–59.

Baumeister, R. F., & Leary, M. R. (1995). The need to belong: Desire for interpersonal attachments as a fundamental human motivation. *Psychological Bulletin, 117,* 497–529.

Beck, J. S. (1995). *Cognitive therapy: Basic and beyond.* New York: Guildford Press.

Blair, R. J. (2003). Facial expressions, their communicatory functions and neuro-cognitive substrates. *Philosophical Transactions of the Royal Society of London, B, Biological Sciences, 358,* 561–572.

Block, J., & Block, J. H. (1980). The role of ego-control and ego-resiliency in the organization of behavior. In W. A. Collings (Ed.), *The Minnesota symposia on child psychology* (Vol. 13, pp. 39–101). Hillsdale, NJ: Lawrence Erlbaum Associates (Wiley).

Bodenhausen, G., Sheppard L., & Kramer, G. (1994). Negative affect and social judgment: The differential impact of anger and sadness. *European Journal of Social Psychology, 24*, 45–62.

Botella, L., & Herrero, O. (2000). A relational constructivist approach to narrative therapy. *European Journal of Psychotherapy, Counselling, and Health, 3*, 1–12.

Brewer, M. B., & Gardner, W. (1996). Who is this "we"? Levels of collective identity and self representations. *Journal of Personality and Social Psychology, 71*, 83–93.

Cameron, K., Dutton, J., & Quinn, R. E. (2003). *Positive organizational scholarship: Foundations of a new discipline.* San Francisco: Berrett-Koehler Publishers.

Carnevale P. J., & Isen A. M. (1986). The influence of positive affect and visual access on the discovery of integrative solutions in bilateral negotiation. *Organizational Behavior & Human Decision Processes, 37*, 1–13.

Caza, B. B. (2007). Experiences of adversity at work: Toward an identity-based theory of resilience. Unpublished doctoral dissertation, University of Michigan.

Caza, B. B., & Bagozzi, R.P. (2008). *Individual functioning in the face of adversity at work: An identity-based perspective.* Unpublished manuscript.

Cole, P. M., Bruschi, C. J., & Tamang, B. L. (2002). Cultural differences in children's emotional reactions to difficult situations. *Child Development, 73*, 983–996.

Côté, S. (2005). A social interaction model of the effects of emotion regulation on work strain. *Academy of Management Review, 30*, 509–530.

Ekman, P. (1993). Facial expression and emotion. *American Psychologist, 48*, 384–392.

Ekman, P., Friesen, W., & Ellsworth, P. (1972). *Emotion in the human face: Guidelines for research and an integration of findings.* Oxford, England: Pergamon Press.

Ellsworth, P., & Scherer, K. (2003). Appraisal processes in emotion. In R. J. Davidson, K. R. Scherer, & H. Goldsmith (Eds.), *Handbook of affective sciences* (pp. 572–595). Oxford, England: Oxford University Press.

Fisher, R., Ury, W., & Patton B. (1991). *Getting to yes: Negotiating agreement without giving in.* New York: Penguin Books.

Forgas, J. P. (1992). On mood and peculiar people: Affect and person typicality in impression formation. *Journal of Personality and Social Psychology, 62*, 863–875.

Forgas J. P. (1998). On feeling good and getting your way: Mood effects on negotiator cognition and bargaining strategies. *Journal of Personality and Social Psychology, 74*, 565–577.

Forgas J. P. (2001). On being moody but influential: The role of affect in social influence strategies. In J. P. Forgas & K. D. Williams (Eds.), *Social influence: Direct and indirect processes, Vol. 21.* New York: Psychology Press.

Frank, R. H. (1988). *Passions within reason: The strategic role of the emotions.* New York: W. W. Norton.

Fredrickson, B. L. (2003). Positive emotions and upward spirals in organizations. In K. S. Cameron, J. E. Dutton, & R. E. Quinn (Eds.), *Positive organizational scholarship: Foundations of a new discipline.* San Francisco: Berrett-Koehler Publishers.

Friedman, R., Anderson, C., Brett, J., Olekalns, M., Goates, N., & Lisco, C. C. (2004). The positive and negative effects of anger on dispute resolution: Evidence from electronically mediated disputes. *Journal of Applied Psychology, 89*, 369–376.

Frijda, N. (1986). *The emotions.* New York: Cambridge University Press.

Gelfand, M. J., Major, V. S., Raver, J. L., Nishii, L. H., & O'Brien, K. (2006). Negotiating relationally: The dynamics of the relational self in negotiations. *Academy of Management Review, 31,* 427–451.

Gergen, K. J. (1991). *The saturated self—Dilemmas of identity in contemporary life.* New York: Basic Books.

Gergen, K. J., & Gergen, M. M. (1986). Narrative form and the construction of psychological science. In T. R. Sarbin (Ed.), *Narrative psychology—The storied nature of human conduct* (pp. 22–44). New York: Praeger Publishers.

Gergen, K. J., & Gergen, M. M. (1988). Narrative and the self as relationship. *Advances in Experimental Social Psychology, 21,* 17–56.

Gergen, M. M., & Gergen, K. J. (1984). Social construction of narrative accounts. In K. Gergen & M. Gergen (Eds.), *Historical social psychology.* Hillsdale, NJ: Lawrence Erlbaum Associates.

Greenberg, L. S., & Angus, L. E. (2004). The contributions of emotion processes to narrative change in psychotherapy: A dialectical constructivist approach. In L. E. Angus & J. McLeod (Eds.), *The handbook of narrative and psychotherapy* (pp. 331–350). Thousand Oaks, CA: Sage Publications.

Gross, J. J., & Thompson, R. A. (2007). Emotion regulation: Conceptual foundations. In J. J. Gross (Ed.), *Handbook of emotion regulation* (pp. 3–24). New York: Guilford Press.

Hareli, S., & Rafaeli, A. (2008). Emotion cycles: On the social influence of emotion in organizations. *Research in Organizational Behavior, 28,* 35–59.

Hatfield, E., Cacioppo, L., & Rapson, R. (1992). Primitive emotional contagion. In M. S. Clark (Ed.), *Emotion and social behavior: Review of personality and social psychology* (pp. 151–177). Newbury Park, CA: Sage Publications.

Hegel, G. W. F. (1931). *The phenomenology of mind* (2nd ed.). (J. B. Baille, Trans.). Mineola, NY: Dover. (Original work published 1910).

Hochschild, A. (1983). *The managed heart: Commercialization of human feeling.* Berkeley, CA: University of California Press.

Horstmann, G. (2003). What do facial expressions convey: Feeling states, behavioral intentions, or action requests? *Emotion, 3,* 150–166.

Houlgate, S. (2005). *An introduction to Hegel: Freedom, truth and history* (2nd ed.). Malden, MA: Blackwell.

Isen, A. M. (1987). Positive affect, cognitive processes, and social behavior. In L. Berkowitz (Ed.), *Advances in experimental social psychology, Vol. 20.* San Diego, CA: Academic Press, Inc.

Kark, R., Shamir, B., & Chen, G. (2003). The two faces of transformational leadership: Empowerment and dependency. *Journal of Applied Psychology, 88,* 246–255.

Kopelman, S., Gewurz, I., & Sacharin, V. (2008). The power of presence: Strategic responses to displayed emotions in negotiation. In N. M. Ashkanasy & C. L. Cooper (Eds.), *Research companion to emotions in organizations* (forthcoming). Northampton, MA: Edward Elgar.

Kopelman, S., & Rosette, A. S. (2008). Cultural variation in response to strategic display of emotions during negotiations. Special issue on emotions in negotiation. *Group Decision and Negotiations, 17,* 65–77.

Kopelman, S., Rosette, A., & Thompson, L. (2006). The three faces of Eve: Strategic displays of positive, negative, and neutral emotions in negotiations. *Organizational Behavior and Human Decision Processes, 99,* 81–101.

Li, S., & Roloff, M. E. (2006). Strategic emotion in negotiation: Cognition, emotion, and culture. In G. Riva, M. T. Anguera, B. K. Widerhold, & F. Mantovani (Eds.), *From communication to presence: Cognition, emotions and culture towards the ultimate communicative experience* (pp. 166–185). Amsterdam: IOS Press.

Linde, C. (1993). Life stories—the creation of coherence. New York: Oxford University Press.

Linehan, M. M. (1993a). *Cognitive-behavioral treatment of borderline personality disorder.* New York: Guilford Press.

Linehan, M. M. (1993b). *Skills training manual for treating borderline personality disorder.* New York: Guilford Press.

Linehan, M. M., Bohus, M., & Lynch, T. R. (2007). Dialectical behavior therapy for pervasive emotion dysregulation: Theoretical and practical underpinnings. In J. J. Gross (Ed.), *Handbook of emotion regulation* (pp. 581–605). New York: Guilford Press..

Luthar, S.S., Cicchetti, D., & Becker, B. (2000). The construct of resilience: A critical evaluation and guidelines for future work. *Child Development, 71,* 543–562.

Mancuso, J. C., & Sarbin, T. R. (1998). The narrative construction of emotional life: Developmental aspects. In M. F. Mascolo & S. Griffin (Eds.), *What develops in emotional development? Emotions, personality, and psychotherapy* (pp. 297–316). New York: Plenum Press.

Matsumoto, D., Yoo, S. H., & LeRoux, J. A. (2007). Emotion and intercultural adjustment. In H. Kotthoff & H. Spencer-Oatley (Eds.), *Handbook of applied linguistics, Vol. 7: Intercultural communication* (pp. 77–98). Berlin: Mouton – de Gruyter Publishers.

Mauss, I. B., Levenson, R. W., McCarter, L., Wilhelm, F. H., & Gross, J. J. (2005). The tie that binds? Coherence among emotion experience, behavior, and physiology. *Emotion, 5,* 175–190.

McAdams, D. P. (1985). *Power, intimacy, and the life story: Personological inquiries into identity.* New York: Guilford.

Muraven, M., & Baumeister, R. F. (2000). Self-regulation and depletion of limited resources: Does self-control resemble a muscle? *Psychological Bulletin, 126,* 247–259.

Omer, H., & Strenger, C. (1992). The pluralist revolution from the one true meaning to an infinity of constructed ones. *Psychotherapy, 29,* 253–261.

Peng, K., & Nisbett, R. E. (1999). Culture, dialectics, and reasoning about contradictions. *American Psychologist, 54,* 741–754.

Pennebaker, J. W. (2000). Telling stories: The health benefits of narrative. *Literature and Medicine, 19,* 3–18.

Philippot, P., Baeyens, C., Douilliez, C., & Francart, B. (2004). Cognitive regulation of emotion: Application to clinical disorders. In P. Philippot & R. S. Feldman (Eds.), *The regulation of emotion* (pp. 71–100). New York: Lawrence Erlbaum Associates.

Pillutla, M. M., & Murnighan, J. K. (1996) Unfairness, anger, and spite: Emotional rejections of ultimatum offers. *Organizational Behavior & Human Decision Processes, 68,* 208–224.

Potworowski, G., & Kopelman, S. (2008). Developing evidence-based expertise in emotion management: Strategically displaying and responding to emotions in negotiations. *Negotiation and Conflict Management Research, 1,* 333–352.

Rafaeli, A., & Sutton, R. I. (1987). Expression of emotion as part of the work role. *Academy of Management Review, 12,* 23–37.

Rafaeli, A., & Sutton, R. I. (1991). Emotional contrast strategies as means of social influence: Lessons from criminal interrogators and bill collectors. *Academy of Management Journal, 34,* 749–775.

Rothbart, M. K., Ziaie, H., & O'Boyle, C. G. (1992). Self-regulation and emotion in infancy. In N. Eisenberg & R.A. Fabes (Eds.), *Emotion and its regulation in early development* (pp. 7–23). San Francisco: Jossey-Bass.

Sanchez-Burks, J. (2002). Protestant relational ideology and (in) attention to relational cues in work settings. *Journal of Personality and Social Psychology, 83,* 919–929.

Schwarz, N., & Clore, G. (1996). Feelings and phenomenal experiences. In E. Higgins & A. Kruglanski (Eds.), *Social psychology: Handbook of basic principles* (pp. 433–465), New York: Guilford Press.

Simon, H. (1955). A behavioral model of rational choice. *Quarterly Journal of Economics, 69,* 99–118.

Sinaceur, M., & Tiedens, L. Z. (2006). Get mad and get more than even: When and why anger expression is effective in negotiations. *Journal of Experimental Social Psychology, 42,* 314–322.

Sluss, D. M., & Ashforth, B. E. (2007). Relational identity and identification: Defining ourselves through work relationships. *Academy of Management Review, 32,* 9–32.

Spence, D. P. (1982). *Narrative truth and historical truth: Meaning and interpretation in psychoanalysis* (pp. 21–37). New York: Norton.

Staw, B. M., Sandelands, L. E., & Dutton, J. E. (1981). Threat-rigidity effects on organizational behavior: A multi-level analysis. *Administrative Science Quarterly, 26,* 501–524.

Stryker, S. (1980). *Symbolic interactionism: A social structural version.* Menlo Park, CA: Benjamin Cummings.

Sutcliffe, K. M., & Vogus, T. J. (2003). Organizing for resilience. In K. S. Cameron, J. E. Dutton, & R. E. Quinn (Eds.), *Positive organizational scholarship: Foundations of a new discipline.* San Francisco: Berret-Kohler Publishers, Inc.

Thompson, L., & Hastie, R. (1990). Social perception in negotiation. *Organizational Behavior & Human Decision Processes, 47,* 98–123.

Tiedens, L. (2001). The effect of anger on the hostile inferences of aggressive and nonaggressive people: Specific emotions, cognitive processing, and chronic accessibility. *Motivation & Emotion, 25,* 233–251.

Ury, W., Brett, J., & Goldberg, S. (1993). *Getting disputes resolved: Designing systems to cut the costs of conflict.* Cambridge, MA: PON Books.

Van Kleef, G. (2008). Emotion in conflict and negotiation: Introducing the emotions as social information (EASI) model. In N. M. Ashkanasy & C. L. Cooper (Eds.), *Research companion to emotions in organizations* (pp. 392–404). Northampton, MA: Edward Elgar.

Van Kleef G., De Dreu, C. K. W., & Manstead, A. S. R. (2004a). The interpersonal effects of anger and happiness in negotiations. *Journal of Personality and Social Psychology, 86,* 57–76.

Van Kleef, G., De Dreu, C. K. W., & Manstead, A. S. R. (2004b). The interpersonal effects of emotions in negotiations: A motivated information processing approach. *Journal of Personality and Social Psychology, 87,* 510–528.

White, M., & Epston, D. (1990). *Narrative means to therapeutic ends.* New York: W. W. Norton & Co.

13

Creating and Sustaining Cooperation in Interdependent Groups: Positive Relational Identities, Identity Confirmation, and Cooperative Capacity

Laurie P. Milton

CONTENTS

Individuals, companies, and nations are struggling to pool their expertise in situations that challenge their ability to do so (Blair, 2007). As the world becomes more interdependent (Tapscott & Williams, 2006), it is ever-more important for members of the disparate groups involved to cooperate and develop their capacity to leverage each other's unique strengths. Research focused on identity and cooperation has the potential to assist in this endeavor. By embracing a broad, positive, and socialized view of identity and identity relations, I argue that science can contribute unique insights that help groups to achieve worthwhile outcomes, at the peak of their abilities, in tough contexts.

People can succeed in environments that do not respect, understand, or support them—environments within which they cannot easily be authentic—just as swimmers can swim against the tide. But it is much easier for them to excel in contexts within which they can simply be themselves and succeed, as swimmers carried forward with the tide. Gandhi said that happiness exists when a person's thoughts, words, and actions are aligned. This alignment is a state most easily achieved when the social context supports it. In this chapter, I argue that group members engage, cooperate, and collectively excel within groups that confirm their positive relational identities. Identity confirmation serves as a foundation on which to build the cooperative capacity of groups. Although the argument applies across groups, the chapter focuses on groups within which members are interdependent. I am particularly, but not exclusively, interested in those where members have to integrate their disparate perspectives and knowledge bases to meet their objectives.

COOPERATION WITHIN INTERDEPENDENT GROUPS

Achieving highly complex objectives almost always requires that individuals process considerable information (Kelly, Futoran, & McGrath, 1990) using a range of knowledge and skill bases (Wood, 1986) and judgment. The high task interdependence among those involved increases the need to share information, pool efforts, make joint decisions, and otherwise coordinate as they integrate perspectives and behavior (Arrow, McGrath, & Berdahl, 2000; Wageman, 1995, 2001). Whether members of a board of directors, a flight crew, a consortium addressing environmental issues, or another interdependent group, a group's success hinges on the extent to which members cooperate.

Cooperation is an interactive (Chen, Chen, & Meindl, 1998) and relational (Telford-Milton, 1996) behavior. Group members *cooperate* when they work together to achieve their goals (Kohn, 1992). As distinct from cooperative behavior, *cooperative capacity* exists to the extent that group members are willing and able to behave cooperatively within their interdependent context and to the extent that the group itself and the system within which it is embedded make this possible. The cooperative capacity of a group is highest when group members are willing and able to pool their knowledge and capabilities and to align their behavior. Cooperation is maximized to the extent that they employ this capacity, for example, by sharing information and integrating their actions with those of others in the group. Research on identity confirmation has shown promise in explaining when and why people are predisposed and able to cooperate, actually do so, and thus achieve their goals.

IDENTITY CONFIRMATION AND COOPERATIVE CAPACITY

Research suggests that cooperation in work groups increases to the extent that group members confirm one another's positive relational identities, share positive relational identities, or both. Identity confirmation-based networks form and become aligned with high levels of cooperation and performance (Milton & Westphal, 2005). Diverse groups characterized by high levels of identity confirmation perform particularly well on creative tasks (see Polzer, Milton, & Swann, 2002 for a related discussion). Group members are attracted to and preferentially interact with others who see them as they themselves do, which creates opportunities for cooperation in the process. To the extent that their identities are confirmed within their groups, group members become psychologically and socially centered and thus become more capable of cooperating. As they gain experience cooperating and as the expectation to cooperate becomes normalized, cooperation becomes embedded within the group. In each of these ways that are considered in this chapter, *identity confirmation* increases the *cooperative capacity* of groups.

Identity confirmation is a subjective state that exists when an individual's social environment is aligned with his or her identities (i.e., the emotionally valenced, subjective definitions of self) (Milton & Westphal, 2005). Inasmuch as people value being both understood and being worthwhile, their identity (taken as a whole) is confirmed when they are in contexts that they experience as providing this support. These are contexts within which they are perceived to be who they perceive themselves to be, contexts within which they are valued for who they perceive themselves to be, and contexts that they themselves perceive to be aligned with whom they are in other ways. Individuals will experience these contexts as those within which they can simply be themselves and succeed. From their perspective, the social environment confirms individuals' subjective, emotionally valenced self-definitions by supporting their *authentic selves* and the expression of these *authentic selves*.

Group members may derive identity confirmation from multiple sources. Their identities may be confirmed when others in the group validate these by seeing a group member as he or she sees himself or herself (interpersonal congruence), and/or when they value the group member for who he or she is. Identities may be similarly confirmed when the work that a group member does or when the group culture (e.g., ideology, norms, organizational practices) is aligned with his or her identity (Milton, 1998, 2005). Ideally, the sources of identity confirmation provided in a work group will be substantive enough to assuage work group members' concerns about finding identity support, enabling them to focus completely and authentically on the group's work and on contributing to the fullest extent possible. This state of connectedness to an activity or to a moment in which one is completely absorbed (labeled as "flow") enables people to work at the peak of their abilities (Csikszentmihalyi, 1990).

This chapter infers that interdependent groups that rely on cooperation have the potential to be effective and to *achieve their goals optimally* (on par with the best of what the group members can achieve together) to the extent that they are characterized by high levels of identity confirmation. The system becomes *self-reinforcing* as: (a) Optimal achievement reinforces cooperation and develops the cooperative capacity of a group; (b) group members confirm one another's identities, develop identity confirmation-based ties and networks, and cooperate with others who confirm their identities in these networks; (c) identity confirmation and cooperation reinforce one another, and each becomes normalized within the group; and (d) groups gain experience cooperating and develop their capacity to continue to do so. Group members, whose identities are confirmed within a group, may also internalize a group-based identity that further fuels their cooperation with others in the group. The chapter focuses, however, on connections between positive relational identities, identity confirmation, cooperative capacity, and cooperation and bridges to optimal achievement when doing so is illuminating. Figure 13.1 summarizes this conceptualization.

The perspective offered builds on previous research concerning identity confirmation and cooperation in several ways. Whereas previous research has focused largely on identities that pertain either to individuals' definitions of themselves in terms of attributes, characteristics, or abilities (e.g., intelligent, creative, socially competent), or to individuals' social identities, this chapter defines relational identities more broadly. I consider relational identities that are anchored in attributes (e.g., considerate), social groups (e.g., Canadian), and roles (e.g., botanist). Whereas much previous research has examined how validating an individual's (mostly attribute-based) identities (e.g., by seeing them as they see themselves) affects cooperation, this chapter considers the impact on cooperation of both validating and valuing (supporting and thereby confirming) a person's identities.

Examining the impact of confirming identities in isolation as well as together, and considering the interplay between them, has the potential to help unite often isolated (and perhaps competing) research streams. For example, by helping to bridge self-consistency and self-enhancement perspectives on identity, we are poised to illuminate the boundary conditions of each and explore the contexts within which each is relevant. Milton and Westphal (2005) noted that agreement between how individual group members defined themselves and how others defined them predicted identity confirmation-based network formation and cooperation in groups for all save the two identity dimensions related to self-esteem ("likeable in general" and "competent in most things").[1] They suggested that these dimensions of identity did not pass because

> individuals may care about having specific identities confirmed only after they are generally accepted and their self-esteem needs are met. Alternatively, to function in a workplace, they may require workmates to see them positively on each of these general dimensions of identity (p. 209).

---

[1] Refer to Edwards (2002) for a related discussion of difference scores.

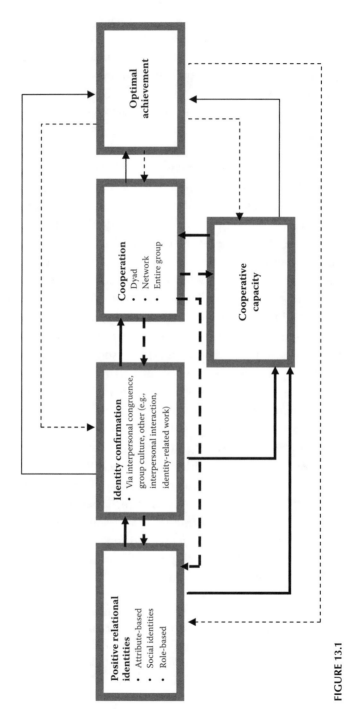

FIGURE 13.1

Self-regenerating cycle of positive relational identities, identity confirmation, cooperative capacity, cooperation, and optimal achievement.

In sharing my perspective, I hope to initiate and contribute to a larger discussion that these possibilities introduce.

POSITIVE RELATIONAL IDENTITIES

Broadly conceived, a person's *self* includes all of the person's thoughts and feelings about himself or herself as an object, that is, as a physical, social, and spiritual or moral being (Rosenberg, 1979). Gecas (1982) provides a simple but useful distinction between

> the content of self-evaluations (e.g., identities) and self-evaluations (e.g., self-esteem). Identity focuses on the meanings comprising the self as an object, gives structure and content to self-concept, and anchors the self to social systems. Self-esteem deals with the evaluative and emotional dimensions of the self-concept. In experience these two aspects of the self-concept are closely interrelated: Self-evaluations are typically based on substantive aspects of self-concept, and identities typically have evaluative components. (p. 4)

The distinction is pivotal to understanding and advancing research on identity. As noted, differences in motivations and in outcomes associated with confirming different dimensions of the self have implications for reconciling current debates.

In a sense, identities—including the self-evaluations embedded in these—are always relational. We come to know ourselves through our interactions with others, and we continue to evolve through human contact (Goffman, 1959; Berger, 1963). Identities and self-evaluations, however social, are subjectively held and experienced—a product of a person's experience and self-perceptions (e.g., Bem, 1972) of how others relate to and perceive him or her (Cooley, 1902; Mead, 1934), and of how the person thinks others perceive him or her (Shrauger & Schoneman, 1979).[2]

---

[2] The idea that the reactions of others provide a basis for our attribute-based identities is widely accepted in the social sciences, having been both theoretically argued (Cooley, 1902; Mead, 1934) and empirically demonstrated (Felson, 1989; McNulty & Swann, 1994). That an individual's social identities are affected by the reactions of others has been similarly established (Ethier & Deaux, 1994). Cooley's (1902) description of the *looking glass self* and subsequent discussions of reflected appraisal (e.g., James, 1890; Lecky, 1945) examine the impact of other's perceptions on individuals' perceptions of themselves. The notion that individuals try to influence what others think of

Relational identities, as distinct from other identities, are social in both their content and orientation. They fundamentally focus on how individuals address the question: "Who am I 'in my relationships with' and 'in relation to' others?" Whether one's relational identities are anchored in characteristics, attitudes, or abilities (*attribute-based relational identities*),[3] in group memberships (*social identities*), or in roles (*role-based identities*),[4] they are indelibly tied to one's conception of self as connected to others. As is the case with other identities, relational identities may be core (relevant to a person across contexts and over time) or they may be working (activated within a particular context at a particular time) (cf., Brewer, 1991; Markus & Kunda, 1986). Individuals may be more certain of and regard particular positive relational identities as more important than others. Those about which they are certain may be especially important to their self-definition. A relational identity may be anchored across relationships (i.e., be generalized) or tied to a specific individual or set of individuals or groups (for a related discussion of role-based relational identities, see Ashforth, 2001).

Attribute-based relational identities are based on characteristics, attributes, or abilities that define who one is in relationships (e.g., kind, considerate, boundary spanner, mediator). Social identity-based relational identities center on the knowledge of and emotional significance attached to one's membership in a social group (or groups) (Tajfel, 1982). Considered together, a person's *social identities* encompass all group memberships that

---

them, for example, by acting in such a way as to elicit self-confirming feedback has also been elaborated conceptually (Swann, 1987) and observed in the field (McNulty & Swann, 1994). Within the symbolic interactionist perspective, the impact of other's views on an individual's self-construed identities is argued to be moderated by what the individual thinks others think of him or her (i.e., via reflected appraisals). Shrauger and Schoneman (1979) provide a theoretical and empirical review.

[3] Attribute-based identities have often been labeled as personal identities, and other-based identities have typically been labeled as social identities. In a sense, all identities are both personal and social. In an effort to be clear about the difference between personal and social relational identities, I label the former as attribute-based relational identities (rather than as personal relational identities). This clearer separation illuminates subsequent discussions about self-verification, self-enhancement, identity confirmation, and cooperation.

[4] Whereas Sluss and Ashforth (2007) define a relational identity "in terms of the nature of one's role relationship" (p. 11) (e.g., manager-subordinate), I include role-, attribute-, and social identity-based identities under the umbrella of relational identities. I recognize that individuals derive a sense of themselves from personal, relational, and collective levels of self-definition (Brewer & Gardner, 1996) and that the importance of these may vary between situations.

are important to his or her self-definition (James, 1910; Tajfel & Turner, 1985).[5]

At a collective level, "*role identities* are socially constructed definitions of self-in-role (this is who a role occupant is)" (Ashforth, 2001, p. 27). When referring to an individual's *role-based identity*, however, I am referring to the person's conception of self within a particular role (e.g., group member, discipline expert, leader). Whereas this self-conception may (and—I would argue—most likely will) include elements of how others define the role, such inclusion is not necessarily the case.

Personal identities (those that individual's define themselves in terms of), including one's relational identities, are subjective. Others may appraise an individual the same as or differently than how the individual sees himself or herself. Others may thereby assign different identities to the individual than the individual does. They may see the person's identities as negative or undesirable at the same time that the person sees them as positive. Although an individual may be aware of this (via reflected appraisals) (Shrauger & Schoneman, 1979), his or her own identities are based on self-definitions, self-appraisals, and the personal emotions attached to these identities. Consistent with this perspective, I define *positive (attribute-, social-, and role-based) relational identities* as relational identities that individuals view as desirable or positive descriptors of themselves.

POSITIVE RELATIONAL IDENTITIES, IDENTITY CONFIRMATION, AND COOPERATIVE CAPACITY

Cooperation is a critical predictor of the performance of interdependent groups—a predictor that confirming the positive relational identities of group members can unleash. The cooperative capacity of work groups increases and becomes more resilient to the extent that the positive relational identities of work group members are supported therein; thus, the group members experience identity confirmation. Identity confirmation: (a) influences the opportunities group members have to cooperate with one another, (b) enhances (or in its absence, diminishes) group members' ability to cooperate, and (c) affects how well group members get

---

[5] Social identification, as distinct from social identity, is a perception of oneness with or belonging to a social category or role (Ashforth, 2001).

to know one another and learn to work together effectively. When positive attribute-based, role-based, and social relational identities are each confirmed within a group, interrelations among these identities can be embraced and further embed cooperation in the group. Each argument is now examined.

Opportunities and Ability to Cooperate

A long line of research finds that people are motivated to create and inhabit social environments that sustain their identities (Lecky, 1945; Goffman, 1955). They preferentially interact (Swann, 1983) and work with others (Milton & Westphal, 2005) who see them as they see themselves (i.e., validate their identities via interpersonal congruence) and with those who validate and who value their identities in other ways (e.g., by relating to them in identity-consistent ways). And, they remain in organizations that are aligned or that they perceive to be aligned with their identities (Dukerich, Golden, & Shortell, 2002; Dutton, Dukerich, & Harquail, 1994). Thus, efforts to sustain identities and identity confirmation-based experiences translate into group members having more opportunities to cooperate with one another.

Beyond opportunity, identity confirmation also renders groups and group members more able to cooperate. When groups reach a working consensus of the identities that group members will assume in their work together, their interaction should become more predictable and coherent (Polzer, Swann, & Milton, 2003); thus, they should be better able to integrate their individual behaviors (Milton, 1995; Telford-Milton, 1996). Group members themselves should be more reliable and focus more effectively on their work when their identities are validated and valued in the group and they experience the identity confirmation as a consequence.

When their working agreements are consistent with group members' own identities, these agreements will be particularly sustainable and effective. Group members, whose identities are confirmed within a group (e.g., via identity-consistent work, group culture, others understanding and valuing these identities and relating to them in ways that demonstrate this), will be able to be authentic and to take for granted the capacity to be their authentic selves. Thus, for instance, a person who defines herself as an adept and careful critical thinker who capably bridges disparate perspectives in a group would be more likely to suggest ways to unite the arguments of her colleagues (and to be successful in doing so) if others in the group perceive and value her "bridging identity" as she does. Diverse individuals with unique perspectives will be more likely to share these in groups when their identities are confirmed in the process. When individuals can simply be themselves and not be concerned about whom others expect them to be, they can simply focus on their work and on performing to the best of their ability (for related discussions of emotional labor, see Hochschild, 1983; Rafaeli & Sutton, 1987). Those who work in groups within which their identities have been confirmed over time may benefit from this history. They may, for example, be able to take it for granted that others in the group will continue to support their identities, relate to them in ways that demonstrate this support, and invest in sorting out relationship issues that develop as they work together. Sorting out relationship issues may be considered as an investment in the group that has the potential to strengthen relations and cooperation therein (for a related discussion refer to Jehn, 1995).

Being centered psychologically in the state of identity confirmation also helps individuals to become centered behaviorally and to be more reliable, constant group members—capable of contributing to and cooperating within the group (as long as the person's identities support this—i.e., the person does not, for instance, define himself or herself in terms of identities that are hostile to the group or its purpose). Self-consistency theory would argue that individuals avoid discrepancies between how others define them and how they define themselves, as well as the dissonance that can be associated with this. Arguing that they become centered through being accepted and valued would be consistent with self-enhancement theory. Inasmuch as group members feel positively about, attracted to, and committed to others who validate and value (confirm) their positive relational identities, they will be more likely to cooperate with them (see Isen & Baron, 1991; Milton & Westphal, 2005). Inasmuch as they feel valued for who they are, they may also be more likely to express their identities and invest these in their work (van Maanen & Schein, 1979) and in cooperating with others involved in this work.

Just as group members preferentially interact with others who validate and value their identities, they will tend to distance themselves psychologically and physically from those who violate these identities. Not confirming a group member's relational identities may erode his or her willingness and ability to cooperate within the group. When members of a group collectively disconfirm—and even violate—another group member's identities, the member will seek confirmation elsewhere (in another group or organization or outside of work) (Telford-Milton, 1996). When the group is hostile to a group member's identities, he or she may experience disintegration anxiety (i.e., anxiety that stems from concerns about not been able to anchor and thus maintain his or her identity and about how this hostility is negatively affecting his or her behavior). In the stress and confusion of this animosity—or even indifference—the group member may be rendered less able to cooperate.

Identity threat is often accompanied by increased stress, loss of self-confidence, self-doubt, and confusion (Zaharna, 1989). Over time, initial misperceptions may become more difficult to correct. Hampering a person's ability to maintain consistent recognizable identities may result in self-shock or "the intrusion of inconsistent, conflicting self-images" (Zaharna, 1989, p. 501), which is accompanied by a loss of communication competence vis-à-vis the self and distorted self-reflections in the responses of others (Zaharna, 1989). Others may collectively judge the person by his or her behavior that, unknown to them, stems from identity threat and (what I have called) the disintegration anxiety associated with this threat. Thus, the perceptions of others may become difficult to change, and the ability of the target to engage in correcting them may be hampered. When group members with high status or high power disconfirm a particular group member's relational identities, others may be more likely to also do so, and it may become more difficult for the group member to resolve the situation and contribute. Alternatively, or in addition

> if an individual perceives a group member with high power to disconfirm their identity, they may perceive others in the group to do so also because they perceive the powerful person to represent the group as a collective. Whether or not the other members of the group actually disconfirm the individual's identity, the damage may already be done because the individual will perceive the group collectively to disconfirm their identity if the high power person does. (B. Caza, personal communication, September 13, 2008)

Together these social forces that contribute to identity threat and disintegration anxiety or simply to nonacceptance may result in a group member becoming less able to cooperate or being excluded from or excluding himself or herself from cooperating within the group. The group may thereby lose the person's expertise and potential to cooperate. In contrast, those whose identities are confirmed in groups will have more opportunities to cooperate and be more capable of doing so.

Identity Confirmation Networks and Cooperation

Just as individuals are more intimate and likely to intend to remain in marriages within which their partners see them as they see themselves (Swann, De La Ronde, & Hixon, 1994), so too it seems that they may invest in and contribute to identity-confirming work groups. Individuals may "date" (or court) groups that see them more positively than they see themselves and "marry" those that confirm their subjectively defined identities. Identity confirmation ties form in groups and are aligned with cooperation. Just as the identity ties between spouses may be unidirectional (when one spouse confirms the other spouse's identity but the other does not) or mutual (when each spouse confirms the other's identities), so too may operate the identity confirmation ties between group members. When an identity confirmation tie between two group members is unidirectional, the group member whose identity is confirmed tends to cooperate with the other even though the other is less likely to reciprocate. When the identity confirmation tie is reciprocal (each confirms the others' identities), each cooperates with the other (the cooperation is mutual). Over and above positions in more commonly studied social networks (based on friendship or social similarity), identity confirmation ties and networks will form and predict cooperation and individual performance within groups.

Even in the high reliability, constantly evolving context of emergency response groups where cooperation is critical (literally life saving) and in the highly scripted protocol-driven context of construction crews, group members cooperated with another group member to the extent that the other confirmed their identities. A study by Milton & Westphal (2005) found that cooperation in these groups was affected by the social structure of identity confirmation relationships among group members. Identity confirmation-based ties formed and dyad members cooperated with one another to the extent that the total level of identity confirmation in their dyad was high and confirmation was reciprocated. Moreover, the social structure of identity and cooperative patterns became aligned beyond dyadic relations. Group members cooperated with others who occupied similar positions in the interpersonal congruence network (i.e., had the same sent and received interpersonal congruence ties to other group members). Their performance increased through higher levels of cooperation, suggesting that identity confirmation ties increased the cooperative capacity of work groups. Group members with more favorable positions in the work group's network performed at a higher level. Those who occupied positions of centrality (had mutual interpersonal congruence ties to other group members who had fewer alternative sources of interpersonal congruence) and were located in a large structurally equivalent subgroup performed particularly well.

The breadth and density of an identity confirmation network within a group should increase further in situations where individual group members adopt a shared positive relational identity that is anchored to their membership in the group. Cooperation among group members will increase as more members of the group internalize this group-based relational identity. Subgroup identities may also form and be positively associated with cooperation among members who share these subgroup identities. When members of one subgroup confirm one another's identities but do not confirm the identities of members of another subgroup, cooperation in the larger group may be fractured. Alternatively, when members of one subgroup confirm the identities of members of another subgroup, cooperation between the two subgroups ensue. In this way, between group cooperation operates similarly to within group cooperation.

Identity confirmation helps group members to collaborate across expertise bases. For example, research finds that diverse groups with high levels of interpersonal congruence outperformed diverse groups with lower levels on creative tasks (Polzer et al., 2002). Moreover, identity confirmation mediated the impact of race-based diversity on performance through its positive impact on cooperation in the groups that Milton and Westphal (2005) studied. Together this and related research highlights the possibility of instilling identity confirmation within relationships as a way to foster cooperation among organizational members who have diverse relational identities. Milton (2008) illustrates the potential of this perspective by arguing that the propensity of incumbents and successors to share knowledge—even when they are not inclined to do so—during successions in family businesses may be strengthened when both parties confirm (validate and value) one another's identities. Identity confirmation ties may foster more effective transitions when, for example, incumbents and successors hold positive relational identities tied to competing family subgroups, or tied to family and nonfamily member status, or when they do not wish to share knowledge for other reasons. Identity disconfirmation may undermine their willingness and ability to cooperate and thereby reduce the cooperative capacity of the succession dyad.

Inasmuch as highly skilled knowledge workers gravitate to, remain within, and perform well in contexts that support their self-defined identities and avoid those that are antithetical to these (Milton, 2003), cooperative groups that embed identity confirmation within them may become a magnet for high-performing interdependent workers. The identity and cooperative dynamics of these groups attract and retain talented individuals and create the conditions that enable them to integrate their information bases.

Knowledge of One Another and Experience Working Together

Group members who confirm one another's identities will get to know one another and gain experience working together. In the process, they will learn about each other's preferences, routines, values, and areas of expertise (Okhuysen, 2001) and become aware of other opportunities to cooperate. They will have opportunities to get to learn about one another's identities and how to support these. Thus, they will develop an understanding of one another that extends beyond knowing one another's surface-level characteristics (for a related discussion, refer to Harrison, Price, & Bell, 1998). This increased knowledge and the identity confirmation that accompanies it may help the group to succeed.

Research has found that familiarity can also buffer against dysfunctional interaction (Gruenfeld, Mannix, Williams, & Neale, 1996) and enable group members to be supportive and engage in critical evaluations without negative repercussions (Shaw & Jehn, 1993). Identity confirmation may foster a sense of psychological safety and openness (a perspective that MacPhail, Roloff, & Edmondson, 2009 develop in Chapter 14 of this book) and promote regenerative interaction (Golembiewski, 1988) in groups. It should then become easier for group members to express disagreement in general (Gruenfeld et al., 1996) and without personal animosity

(Shaw & Jehn, 1993), and to separate task and relationship conflict (Jehn, 1997). Their familiarity would reduce the likelihood that task conflict will morph into relationship conflict and escalate. Increased familiarity also results in members having more latitude on task-related activities (Shaw & Jehn, 1993), latitude that may help them to overcome the often negative effects that diversity on working styles and preferences has on the ability of group members to work interdependently (Okhuysen, 2001). Beyond familiarity, identity confirmation predicts who cooperates with whom in work groups. Familiarity coupled with identity confirmation should facilitate effective interdependent work.

Groups that have developed strong identity confirmation-based networks within them and that have a history of successfully working together may choose to stay together. Group members who support one another's identities may be more likely to invest in their relationship and become committed to one another. Thus, they may work through differences in their preferences and opinions (Jehn & Mannix, 2001) that may otherwise undermine cooperation between them or cause other group members to "divorce" one another.

Positive Social Relational Identities

Much of the research evoked so far has focused primarily on attribute- and role-based relational identities. Drawing substantively on self-enhancement research, the social identity literature argues that people categorize themselves as members of groups and internalize and make value judgments about their social categories or memberships (Tajfel, 1982; Tajfel & Turner, 1985). When individuals identify strongly with a group, the image of the group affects the image they have of themselves (Dutton et al., 1994; Kramer, 1991). When they strongly identify with the group, the person's identity as a group member may be more important than other identities, and the person's identity may share many of the characteristics he or she perceives the group to have (Dutton et al., 1994). Other identities may recede, and individuals may use membership in the group as a basis for self-definition (Kramer, 1991). Research has found that individuals tend to favor and cooperate with others in their in-groups and to neither trust nor cooperate but compete with out-group members (Brewer, 1979). Group members who share social identities (one type of relational identity) will tend to cooperate with one another as they favor members of their social group (Brewer, 1979) and confirm their shared (group-based) social identity in the process. Simultaneously, confirming this group-based social relational identity and the individual identities of group members may help group members to be individuated as a member of the group (for a related discussion of optimal distinctiveness, see Brewer, 1991). Diverse groups that do so may perform particularly well on complex tasks that rely on group members integrating each individual's unique knowledge bases.

Group members who share social identities may cooperate not only because they are similar (i.e., a homophily effect) but also because they internalize social identities associated with the groups that they are in (i.e., an identification effect) (Mael & Ashforth, 1992). In both cases, they may cooperate in part because others in the group support their identities or because doing so is consistent with and perhaps enhances these identities. From the lens of self-consistency theory, individuals who share social category memberships may have a unique advantage in understanding the social-, attribute-, and role-based relational identities of others in the group. As in-group members, they may be privy to experiences and opportunities to learn about one another and help others in the group do the same. Members of social identity-based groups who themselves have positive attribute-based relational identities that motivate them to bridge between others (e.g., by creating opportunities for others to get together or by resolving conflicts) may serve as boundary spanners between social identity-based subgroups, and their presence may encourage cooperation between the subgroups (for a related discussion of faultlines, see Lau & Murnighan, 1998). Group members whose identity confirmation networks bridge individuals who are otherwise isolated from one another may similarly serve as boundary spanners (Milton & Westphal, 2005).

To the extent that they have and share compatible role-based relational identities that embed positive interaction and exchange between group members within their work routines, cooperation will also follow. To the extent that positive relational identities become normalized and embedded in the group, group members may recruit others with these identities and socialize neophytes into a positive relational way of working together. Positive relational identities, identity confirmation, cooperative capacity, and achievement may, in these ways, form a self-regenerating system.

A REGENERATING SYSTEM: IDENTITY CONFIRMATION, COOPERATIVE CAPACITY, AND COOPERATION

I propose that the cooperative capacity of a group will increase over time (a) as the group acquires a history of confirming group member identities and of cooperating and (b) as identity confirmation and cooperation both become embedded within the group. Identity confirmation, cooperation, and achievement will fuel cooperative capacity as the group develops a culture that supports each (e.g., by valuing cooperation, recruiting members who have perspectives and skills that contribute to the team's work and the identities aligned to these, and socializing group members to confirm one another's identities and to cooperate).

As evidenced at SEMATECH, a research consortium within which competitors cooperated to advance the U.S. semiconductor industry, cooperative interaction can breed greater cooperative interaction (Browning, Beyer, & Shetler, 1995) and increase the cooperative capacity of the group overall. Effective cooperation and achievement in which members continue to think and act intelligently—heedfully when required—will fuel continued achievement (cf., Weick & Roberts, 1993). Cooperation should increase and become more resilient as the density of identity confirmation-based networks increases in the group. As noted, this may occur as members get to know one another (e.g., via experience or via other group activities), cooperate, and succeed. It may also occur when group members who occupy structurally advantageous positions in identity confirmation networks (e.g., central positions or positions as members of large subgroups of structural equivalents) help these networks to spread within the group. They may, for example, help group members learn about and support one another's self-defined identities. Some group members who occupy advantageous positions in identity confirmation networks may chose to retain their personal (individual) advantage of their position and connect people only when they themselves benefit. However, as research on identity confirmation networks suggests (Milton & Westphal, 2005), some may share their power and help others to connect when doing so is consistent with or enhances their own self-defined relational identities, for example, when they define themselves as boundary spanners, collaborative institution builders, or as the constant contributors from which Weber and Murnighan (2008) find groups to benefit. By developing identity confirmation networks, these individuals strengthen the cooperative capacity of groups.

SPEAKING OUT ABOUT CONTENT: HIGH-QUALITY CONNECTIONS AND SUPPORTIVE RELATIONAL IDENTITIES

To this point, I have remained silent about the content of attribute-, social-, and role-based relational identities. I have similarly remained silent about the desirability of outcomes that groups achieve by cooperating with others. I would expect connections between identity confirmation and cooperation to hold in groups that others (e.g., organizations and societies) consider as having negative—even deviant—relational identities but that the holders themselves consider as positive. It may in fact be the structure of identity confirmation and disconfirmation that maintains deviant groups and subgroups, deviant forms of cooperation or cooperation toward deviant ends, and the dirty work that Ashforth and Kreiner (1999) consider.

There are, however, reasons to believe that groups will benefit more by confirming positive relational identities of group members that support high-quality connections in the group than by confirming those that do not. *High-quality connections* characterized by vitality, mutual benefit, and high regard (Dutton, 2003; Dutton & Heaphy, 2003) may enhance the cooperative capacity of groups in multiple ways. Their higher emotional carrying capacity (which supports expressing positive and negative emotions), greater tensility (or strength in the face of strain), and higher capacity for connectivity (which supports openness to new ideas and the ability to cull behaviors that interfere with generative processes) (Ragins & Dutton, 2007) may each contribute. High-quality connections may in fact be the bedrock on which groups build their thinking capacity and develop their ability to work effectively in contexts that challenge their ability to do so. I would argue that such connections are pivotal to developing the resilience in groups that enables them to consistently achieve desirable outcomes when they are faced with adversity, strain, and other barriers, and to engage in flexible rather than rigid thinking (refer to Sutcliffe & Vogus, 2003 for a related discussion).

In my opinion, the content of the relational ties among group members should be added to factors that influence employee interaction and give rise to cooperation. Group members with positive relational identities that include providing support and care to team members and not tolerating toxic behavior may help group members to remain psychologically healthy and capable of cooperating (cf., Frost, 2003; Sutton, 2007). To the extent that group members hold identities that cause them to interact cooperatively, expect themselves and one another to do so, and value cooperation within the group, cooperation may become normalized and thereby embedded in the culture of the group (Telford-Milton, 1996). Positive relational identities will be reinforced and strengthened in the cycle through which confirming these identities increases cooperative capacity and cooperation within the group is strengthened.

FUTURE RESEARCH

Confirming positive relational identities has implications for cooperation and optimal achievement in groups beyond those discussed herein. As noted in the introductory comments to this chapter, the implications have the potential to help organizations and societies address substantive issues that concern us all. It is important that we engage in a careful science-based conversation about issues that often involve emotions and politics. Because the word "positive" can be equivocal, one way we can advance this discussion is to be clear about our definition. Of the many directions that research on positive relational identities can take, I suggest two: examining identity confirmation dynamics that enable minority influence, and investigating the potential of research on relational identities (both positive and negative as defined by the person who holds them) to reconcile self-consistency and self-enhancement arguments within identity research.

Definitions of Positive Relational Identities

I defined positive relational identities as attribute-, social-, and role-based identities that individuals consider to be desirable or positive descriptions of them. Doing so is consistent with viewing identities as subjectively held and identity confirmation as subjectively experienced. I was tempted to narrow my definition of positive relational identities to include only those that support high-quality connections between people. I encourage identity researchers to continue to separate the positivity of relational identities from the positivity of outcomes associated with these.

Minority Members of Groups

Research examining the dynamics of identity confirmation in groups where individuals who could otherwise contribute are structurally isolated would be helpful. Westphal and Milton (2000) found minority members to be more influential on corporate boards when these members had direct or indirect social network ties to majority directors through common memberships on other boards. Minority members were also more influential on boards when the majority members on these boards had previous experience working with other minority members on other boards. In the first instance, minority and majority directors alike may have learned how to confirm one another's identities and developed identity confirmation-based ties that helped the minority member to be more influential on a new board. In the second instance, majority members may themselves have learned how to support the identities of minority members and as a result be more supportive of others on a new board. Both propositions warrant further scrutiny.

Validating and Valuing Identities

Self-consistency research argues that individuals seek opportunities to validate both their positive and their negative relational identities (e.g., Secord & Backman, 1965; Swann, 1987). They gravitate to and preferentially interact with others who see them as they see themselves (interpersonal congruence). Doing so provides them with a sense of security; they feel their interactions are predictable and consistent with their identities, even if these are negative. Identity-consistent relationships are argued to stabilize and create reliable interaction partners. Self-enhancement research argues that people are motivated to, prefer, and seek situations and relationships within which their identities are seen positively (e.g., Banaji & Prentice, 1994; Greenwald, 1980; Hogg & Terry, 2000; John & Robbins, 1994; Steele, 1988; Taylor & Brown, 1988). Thus, self-enhancement and self-consistency theories agree that individuals will seek support for their positive relational identities but disagree on whether they will seek support for their negative relational identities (identities they feel negatively about) (for a comparison of the two theories, see Ashforth, 2001). Evidence considered earlier suggests that each motivation has the potential to increase cooperation in work groups. The boundary conditions of each and the possibility that the two are complementary are worth investigating. Research focused on positive relational identities and on confirming specific identities and identities overall (considered as a constellation) may help to bridge and perhaps reconcile the two perspectives.

Arguing and showing that individuals seek to be both similar to and different from others, Brewer's (1991) research suggests that individuals value both their attribute-based and social identities.[6] It seems they are motivated to preserve and advance each, a point consistent with Crocker and Luhtanen's (1990) observation of the importance of individuals being able to maintain both their social and personal self-esteem. Considering self-consistency and self-enhancement research in tandem offers clues as to how to reconcile these two lines of thinking. Research that jointly examines validating and valuing attribute, social identity, and role-based relational identities may help to assess whether both validating and valuing lead to identity confirmation (always or in particular contexts) and what the limits of self-consistency and self-enhancement theories are.

CONCLUSION

I have argued that group members will tend to cooperate with others who validate and value and thereby confirm their positive relational identities. Identity confirmation networks will form and be aligned with cooperation in work groups. Group members whose identities are confirmed will

---

[6] Refer to Kreiner and Sheep (Chapter 2 of this volume) for a related discussion of optimal distinctiveness.

be more likely and better able to cooperate than others. They will be psychologically and socially centered enough to cooperate and will benefit from being able to be authentic. Their behavior will be more predictable and reliable. The cooperative capacity of groups will increase over time as group members confirm one another's identities (via strong, mutual, and dense identity confirmation ties within the group) and acquire a history of working together. They will become more familiar with one another and learn how to integrate their perspectives and behavior and otherwise cooperate. As identity confirmation networks develop and include more group members, cooperation in the group may become normalized. As a way of advancing cooperation among them, group members may embed cooperation in the structure of the group (e.g., hire cooperative people and create mechanisms to help them to cooperate).

Research suggests that groups with high levels of identity confirmation embedded within them may perform particularly well on tasks that require them to integrate disparate sources of information (Milton & Westphal, 2005; Polzer et al., 2002). The benefits of confirming positive relational identities may be especially pronounced when groups are working in tough contexts that necessitate group members going that extra mile to help out or when the group is dealing with particularly difficult issues that require considerable cooperation. Confirming the identities of members of diverse groups or of members of subgroups that align with conflicting opinions about how to resolve issues may help instill cooperation in the groups involved. Identity research, including that on identity confirmation, may, for example, help disparate parties develop ways to address global environmental sustainability (Milton & Stoner, 2009). Family businesses may be able to develop identity confirmation as a unique, hard to imitate competitive resource that leverages their distinctive relational capabilities (Milton, 2008). Doing so may help them address relational challenges that often undermine them, including knowledge transfer between successors and incumbents, competition between family subgroups, and engaging nonfamily members in the business. To the extent that identity confirmation is embedded in both group interaction and culture, group members may become committed to one another and to the group (Beyer, Hannah, & Milton, 2000; Telford-Milton, 1996) and as a result be more cooperative. To the extent that they develop positive social relational identities anchored to their group, this would be especially true (Brewer, 1979).

However informative research on identity can be, it is important to recognize that structural impediments may block what group members can achieve. Confirming positive relational identities may help group members to work together to obtain resources. They are not, however, a substitute for these resources. Nor do they necessarily substitute for meaningful positive work, which itself is often a powerful source of identity confirmation.

A complete discussion of the consistencies and conflicts in the use of "identity" and "self" terminology in the primary discipline and organizations literature extends beyond this chapter. However, I made conceptual choices in defining positive relational identities with the intent of advancing theory within identity science by helping to clarify constructs that are often loosely defined and defined differently within different research streams. Defining positive relational identities as I have and examining positivity with similar clarity may help to bridge self-consistency and self-enhancement identity theories—each of which has its strengths. This clarity also has practical utility. At this stage of theory development on the self, it is important to avoid making ethnocentric judgments about what is good and what is bad. It is also important to recognize our own biases (arguably, for example, bias resident in my initial inclusion of "high-quality connections" in the base definition of positive relational identities). As scientists, we can then play a unique and pivotal role in contributing to and perhaps informing current debates about identity relations in groups, organizations, and society where the parties involved do not necessarily agree on what is good and what is evil. The importance of doing so is clear and unequivocal.

This chapter has focused on the impact of positive relational identities on cooperation in organizational groups. Interdependence and cooperation are two of the most pressing issues of our time. Identity relations have the potential to be the catalyst that enables us to address the multiple issues that concern us all.

ACKNOWLEDGMENTS

I thank Laura Morgan Roberts and Brianna Caza for their helpful comments on earlier drafts of this manuscript. I also appreciate Blake Ashforth for sharing his insights with me along my writing path. Thank you also to participants in the Exploring Positive Identities and Organizations:

Building a Theoretical and Research Foundation Conference (2008) held at the University of Michigan's Center for Positive Organizational Scholarship. Your contributions to my thinking are etched into this chapter and into my enthusiasm for the work we are pursuing within our relational community. I recognize Jim Westphal for our multiple and continuing conversations about identity confirmation, cooperation, and interdependence. I appreciate Steven Shafer for his engagement in helping me to strengthen and craft my argument effectively. The support of the Social Sciences and Humanities Council of Canada for funding my research on identity is gratefully acknowledged.

REFERENCES

Arrow, H., McGrath, J. E., & Berdahl, J. L. (2000). *Small groups as complex systems: Formation, coordination, development, and adaptation.* Thousand Oaks, CA: Sage Publications.

Ashforth, B. E. (2001). *Role transitions in organizational life: An identity-based perspective.* Mahwah, NJ: Lawrence Erlbaum Associates.

Ashforth, B. R., & Kreiner, G. E. (1999). "How can you do it?": Dirty work and the challenge of constructing a positive identity. *Academy of Management Review, 24,* 413–434.

Banaji, M. R., & Prentice, D. A. (1994). The self in social contexts. *Annual Review of Psychology, 45,* 297–332.

Bem, S. L. (1972). Self-perception theory. In L. Berkowitz (Ed.), *Advances in experimental social psychology* (Vol. 6, pp. 1–62). New York: Academic Press.

Berger, P. L. (1963). *Invitation to sociology: A humanistic perspective.* Garden City, NY: Doubleday.

Beyer, J. M., Hannah, D., & Milton, L. P. (2000). Culture and attachments in organizations. In N. Ashkansay & C. Wilderhom (Eds.), *International handbook of organizational climate and culture* (pp. 323–338). Thousand Oaks, CA: Sage.

Blair, T. (2007, October 26). *Global relations: A conversation with Tony Blair.* Speech presented at the Telus Convention Centre, Calgary, Alberta, Canada.

Brewer, M. B. (1979). In-group bias in the minimal intergroup situation: A cognitive-motivational analysis. *Psychological Bulletin, 86,* 307–324.

Brewer, M. B. (1991). The social self: On being the same and different at the same time. *Personality and Social Psychology Bulletin, 17,* 475–482.

Brewer, M. B., & Gardner, W. L. (1996). Who is this "we"? Levels of collective identity and self representations. *Journal of Personality and Social Psychology, 71,* 83–93.

Browning, L. D., Beyer, J. M., & Shetler, J. C. (1995). Building cooperation in a competitive industry: Sematech and the semiconductor industry. *Academy of Management Journal, 38,* 113–151.

Chen, C. C., Chen, X. P., & Meindl, J. R. (1998). How can cooperation be fostered? The cultural effects of individualism-collectivism. *Academy of Management Review, 23,* 285–304.

Cooley, C. H. (1902). *Human nature and the social order*. New York: Scribner.

Crocker, J., & Luhtanen, R. (1990). Collective self-esteem and ingroup bias. *Journal of Personality and Social Psychology, 58,* 60–67.

Csikszentmihalyi, M. (1990). *Flow: The psychology of optimal experience*. New York: HarperCollins.

Dukerich, J. M., Golden, B. R., & Shortell, S. M. (2002). Beauty is in the eye of the beholder: The impact of organizational identification, identity and image on cooperative behaviors of physicians. *Administrative Science Quarterly, 47,* 507–533.

Dutton, J. E. (2003). *Energize your workplace: How to create and sustain high quality connections at work*. San Francisco: Jossey-Bass.

Dutton, J. E., Dukerich, J. M., & Harquail, C. V. (1994). Organizational images and member identification. *Administrative Science Quarterly, 39,* 239–263.

Dutton, J. E., & Heaphy, E. D. (2003). Coming to life: The power of high quality connections at work. In K. Cameron, J. Dutton, & R. E. Quinn (Eds.), *Positive organizational scholarship* (pp. 263–278). San Francisco: Berrett-Koehler.

Edwards, J. E. (2002). Alternatives to difference scores: Polynomial regression analysis and response surface methodology. In F. Drasgow & N. W. Schmitt (Eds.), *Advances in measurement and data analysis* (pp. 350–400). San Francisco: Jossey-Bass.

Ethier, K. A., & Deaux, K. (1994). Negotiating social identity when contexts change: Maintaining identification and responding to threat. *Journal of Personality and Social Psychology, 67,* 243–251.

Felson, R. B. (1989). Parents and the reflected appraisal process: A longitudinal analysis. *Journal of Personality and Social Psychology, 56,* 965–971.

Frost, P. J. (2003). *Toxic emotions at work: How compassionate managers handle pain and conflict*. Boston: Harvard Business School Press.

Gecas, V. (1982). The self-concept. *Annual Review of Sociology, 8,* 1–33.

Goffman, E. (1955). On face work: An analysis of the ritual elements in social interaction. *Psychiatry, 18,* 213–221.

Goffman, E. (1959). *The presentation of self in everyday life*. New York: Doubleday.

Golembiewski, R. T. (1988). *Organization development: Ideas and issues*. New Brunswick, NJ: Transaction Publishers.

Greenwald, A. G. (1980). The totalitarian ego: Fabrication and revision of personal history. *American Psychologist, 35,* 603–618.

Gruenfeld, D. H., Mannix, E. A., Williams, K. Y., & Neale, M. A. (1996). Group composition and decision making: How member familiarity and information distribution affect process and performance. *Organizational Behavior and Human Decision Processes, 67,* 1–15.

Harrison, D. A., Price, K. H., & Bell, M. P. (1998). Beyond relational demography: Time and the effect of surface- versus deep-level diversity on group cohesiveness. *Academy of Management Journal, 41,* 96–107.

Hochschild, A. R. (1983). *The managed heart*. Berkeley, CA: University of California Press.

Hogg, M. A., & Terry, D. J. (2000). Social identity and self-categorization processes in organizational contexts. *Academy of Management Review, 25,* 121–140.

Isen, A. M., & Baron, R. A. (1991). Positive affect as a factor in organizational behavior. In B. M. Staw & L. L. Cummings (Eds.), *Research in Organization Behavior* (Vol. 13, pp. 1–53). Greenwich, CT: JAI Press.

James, W. (1890). *Principles of psychology*. New York: Holt.

James, W. (1910). *Psychology: The briefer course.* New York: Holt.

Jehn, K. A. (1995). A multimethod examination of the benefits and detriments of intragroup conflict. *Administrative Science Quarterly, 40,* 256–282.

Jehn, K. A. (1997). A qualitative analysis of conflict types and dimensions in organizational groups. *Administrative Science Quarterly, 42,* 530–557.

Jehn, K. A., & Mannix, E. A. (2001). The dynamic nature of conflict: A longitudinal study of intragroup conflict and group performance. *Academy of Management Journal, 44,* 238–251.

John, O. P., & Robbins, R. W. (1994). Accuracy and bias in self-perception: Individual differences in self-enhancement and the role of narcissism. *Journal of Personality and Social Psychology, 66,* 206–219.

Kelly, J. R., Futoran, G. C., & McGrath, J. E. (1990). Capacity and capability: Seven studies of entrainment of task performance rates. *Small Group Research, 21,* 283–314.

Kohn, A. (1992). *No contest: The case against competition.* New York: Houghton Mifflin Company.

Kramer, R. M. (1991). Intergroup relations and organizational dilemmas: The role of categorization processes. In L. L. Cummings & B. M. Staw (Eds.), *Research in organizational behavior* (Vol. 13, pp. 191–228). Greenwich, CT: JAI.

Lau, D. C., & Murnighan, J. K. (1998). Demographic diversity and faultlines: The compositional dynamics of organizational groups. *Academy of Management Review, 23,* 325–340.

Lecky, P. (1945). *Self-consistency: A theory of personality.* New York: Island Press.

MacPhail, L., Roloff, K., & Edmondson, A. (2009). Collaboration across knowledge boundaries within diverse teams: Reciprocal positive identity affirmation as an enabling condition. In L. M. Roberts & J. E. Dutton (Eds.), *Exploring positive identities and organizations: Building a theoretical and research foundation* (289–318). New York: Psychology Press.

Mael, F. A., & Ashforth, B. E. (1992). Alumni and their alma mater: A partial test of the reformulated model of organizational identification. *Journal of Organizational Behavior, 13,* 103–123.

Markus, H. R., & Kunda, Z. (1986). Stability and malleability of the self-concept. *Journal of Personality and Social Psychology, 51,* 858–866.

McNulty, S. E., & Swann, W. B., Jr. (1994). Identity negotiation in roommate relationships: The self as architect and consequence of social reality. *Journal of Personality and Social Psychology, 67,* 1012–1023.

Mead, G. H. (1934). *Mind, self, and society from the standpoint of a social behaviorist.* Chicago: University of Chicago Press.

Milton, L. (1995, August). *Taking the self seriously: Encouraging cooperation within work groups.* Paper presented at the 55th Annual Meeting of the Academy of Management, Vancouver, British Columbia, Canada.

Milton, L. P. (1998). *Managing diversity to improve the bottom-line: Confirming identities to enhance work group dynamics and performance.* Retrieved from ProQuest Digital Dissertations (AAT 9905802).

Milton, L. P. (2003). An identity perspective on the propensity of high-tech talent to unionize. *Journal of Labor Research, 24,* 31–53.

Milton, L. P. (2005, February 24). *How identity affects engagement in our work and lives.* (Invited keynote research-based address). Speech presented at the Annual Meeting of the British Columbia Forestry Association, Prince George, British Columbia, Canada.

Milton, L. P. (2008). Identity confirmation in family firms: Implications for succession, cooperation in family-based subgroups & non-family member engagement. *Entrepreneurship, Theory & Practice, 32,* 1063–1081.

Milton, L. P., & Stoner, J. A. F. (2009). Toward environmental sustainability: Developing thinking and acting capacity within the oil and gas industry. In J. A. F. Stoner & C. Wankel (Eds.), *Innovative approaches to global sustainability* (pp. 123–155). New York: Palgrave Macmillian.

Milton, L. P., & Westphal, J. D. (2005). Identity confirmation networks and cooperation in work groups. *Academy of Management Journal, 48,* 191–212.

Okhuysen, G. A. (2001). Structuring change: Familiarity and formal interventions in problem solving groups. *Academy of Management Journal, 44,* 794–808.

Polzer, J. T., Milton, L. P., & Swann, W. B., Jr. (2002). Capitalizing on diversity: Interpersonal congruence in small work groups. *Administrative Sciences Quarterly, 47,* 296–324.

Polzer, J. T., Swann W. B., Jr., & Milton L. P. (2003). The benefits of verifying diverse identities for group performance. *Research on Managing Groups and Teams, 5,* 91–111.

Rafaeli, A., & Sutton, R. I. (1987). Expression of emotion as part of the work role. *Academy of Management Review, 12,* 23–37.

Ragins, B. R., & Dutton, J. E. (2007). Positive relationships at work: An introduction and invitation. In J. E. Dutton & B. R. Ragins (Eds.), *Exploring positive relationships at work: Building a theoretical and research foundation* (pp. 3–25). Mahwah, NJ: Lawrence Erlbaum Associates.

Rosenberg, M. (1979). *Conceiving the self.* New York: Basic Books.

Secord, P. F., & Backman, C. W. (1965). An interpersonal approach to personality. In B. Maher (Ed.), *Progress in experimental personality research* (Vol. 2, pp. 91–125). New York: Academic Press.

Shaw, P. P., & Jehn, K. A. (1993). Do friends perform better than acquaintances? The interaction of friendship, conflict, and task. *Group Decision and Negotiation, 2,* 149–165.

Shrauger, J. S., & Schoneman, T. J. (1979). Symbolic interactionist view of self-concept: Through the looking glass darkly. *Psychological Bulletin, 86,* 549–573.

Sluss, D. M., & Ashforth, B. E. (2007). Relational identity and identification: Defining ourselves through work relationships. *Academy of Management Review, 32,* 9–32.

Steele, C. M., (1988). The psychology of self-affirmation: Sustaining the integrity of the self. In L. Berkowitz (Ed.), *Advances in experimental social psychology* (Vol. 21, pp. 261–302). New York: Academic Press.

Sutcliffe, K. M., & Vogus, T. J. (2003). Organizing for resilience. In K. Cameron, J. E. Dutton, & R. E. Quinn (Eds.), *Positive organizational scholarship* (pp. 94–110). San Francisco: Berrett-Koehler.

Sutton, R. I. (2007). *The no asshole rule: Building a civilized workplace and surviving one that isn't.* New York: Warner Business Books, Hachette Book Group USA.

Swann, W. B., Jr. (1983). Self-verification: Bringing social reality into harmony with the self. In J. Suls & A. G. Greenwald (Eds.), *Social psychological perspectives on the self* (Vol. 2, pp. 33–66). Hillsdale, NJ: Lawrence Erlbaum Associates.

Swann, W. B., Jr. (1987). Identity negotiation: Where two roads meet. *Journal of Personality and Social Psychology, 53,* 1038–1051.

Swann, W. B., Jr., De La Ronde, C., & Hixon, G. (1994). Authenticity and positivity strivings in marriage and courtship. *Journal of Personality and Social Psychology, 66,* 857–869.

Tajfel, H. (1982). Social psychology of intergroup relations. *Annual Review of Psychology, 33,* 1–39.

Tajfel, H., & Turner, J. C. (1985). The social identity theory of intergroup behavior. In S. Worchel & W. G. Austin (Eds.), *Psychology of intergroup relations* (Vol. 2, pp. 7–24). Chicago: Nelson-Hall.

Tapscott, D., & Williams, A. D. (2006). *Wikinomics: How mass collaboration changes everything.* London: The Penguin Group.

Taylor, S. E., & Brown, J. D. (1988). Illusion and well-being: A social psychological perspective on mental health. *Psychological Bulletin, 103,* 193–210.

Telford-Milton, L. P. (1996). Selves in bunkers: Organizational consequences of failing to verify alternative masculinities. In C. Cheng (Ed.), *Masculinities in organizations* (pp. 130–159). Thousand Oaks, CA: Sage.

van Maanen, J., & Schein, E. J. (1979). Toward a theory of organizational socialization. *Research in Organization Behavior, 1,* 209–525.

Wageman, R. (1995). Interdependence and group effectiveness. *Administrative Science Quarterly, 40,* 145–180.

Wageman, R. (2001). The meaning of interdependence. In M. Turner (Ed.), *Groups at work: Theory and research* (pp. 197–217). Mahwah, NJ: Lawrence Erlbaum Associates.

Weber, J. M., & Murnighan, J. K. (2008). Suckers or saviors? Consistent contributors in social dilemmas. *Journal of Personality and Social Psychology, 95,* 1340–1353.

Weick, K. E., & Roberts, K. H. (1993). Collective mind in organizations: Heedful interrelating on flight decks. *Administrative Science Quarterly, 38,* 357–381.

Westphal, J. D., & Milton, L. P. (2000). How experience and social networks affect the influence of demographic minorities on corporate boards. *Administrative Science Quarterly, 45,* 366–398.

Wood, R. E. (1986). Task complexity: Definition of the construct. *Organizational Behavior and Human Decision Processes, 37,* 60–82.

Zaharna, R. S. (1989). Self-shock: The double-binding challenge of identity. *International Journal of Intercultural Relations, 13,* 501–525.

14

Collaboration Across Knowledge Boundaries Within Diverse Teams: Reciprocal Expertise Affirmation as an Enabling Condition

Lucy H. MacPhail, Kathryn S. Roloff, and Amy C. Edmondson

CONTENTS

INTRODUCTION

Increasingly, work in organizations is performed by individuals from different cultural and functional backgrounds who are joined together to solve problems, deliver services, or design new products and processes—sometimes without even meeting face to face. Such variation in cultural and functional backgrounds within teams at work can complicate productive collaboration by creating intragroup knowledge boundaries, or "faultlines," that separate team members into expertise subgroups (Lau & Murnighan, 1998). Knowledge boundaries can emerge from differences in expertise (e.g., jargon taken for granted in one discipline can be incomprehensible in another), national heritage (e.g., differences in language and local norms can hinder communication), organization (e.g., behavior customary to a flat, informal company may seem inappropriate in a hierarchical, formal company), location (e.g., information and processes available at one site may differ from that available in another), and even age and gender. Unless recognized, thoughtfully managed, and embraced for learning, such knowledge boundaries can undermine the effectiveness of diverse teams.

Consider the example of a cross-functional product development team with eight members in five countries and three continents in which a research scientist located in the United Kingdom concluded that a Japanese manufacturing engineer was acting in ways that obstructed progress on the project.[1] Unfamiliar with business norms in Japan, the British scientist assumed the information she wanted existed and was frustrated when it was not forthcoming from the distant team member. Although the norms of science favor speaking up with tentative ideas and far-fetched possibilities, many engineers assume a reasonable level of evidence supporting a new idea is preferred before taking up a colleague's time with mere speculation. In this example, the scientist later learned that the desired information represented a genuine gap in the engineer's knowledge of his customer and, further, that the engineer had not understood the significance of certain veiled criticisms coming from other team members. In the short term, however, the misunderstanding slowed team progress, and unflattering attributions about motives and commitment to the project eroded satisfaction with the work experience. In this way, when unnoticed and

---

[1] Edmondson and Roloff (2008) incorporated a shorter version of this example, derived from Sole and Edmondson (2002)'s work on knowledge sharing in dispersed teams.

uncorrected, small interpersonal failures—namely, the failure to understand critical aspects of another's identity and to appreciate the influence of that identity on observable behavior—can result in larger organizational failures, such as in this case an underperforming project team that did not achieve its true collaborative potential.

The aim of this chapter is to introduce the concept of *reciprocal expertise affirmation*—defined as the mutual recognition by team members that they respect, value, and affirm each other's expertise identity—as an enabling condition of effective collaboration in diverse teams. Effective collaboration across knowledge boundaries requires that each team member understand the expertise-based contribution of other team members (what another discipline involves, its specialized skills, and the boundaries that separate it from other expertise sets), value their contributions (believe each discipline is useful for the success of the team as a whole), and learn to integrate expertise from these varied sources with their own when appropriate given the demands of the team task. Thus, we propose the new construct, reciprocal expertise affirmation, to describe a process by which such understanding, verification, and integration occur. In expertise-diverse groups, we further anticipate that collaboration, or "the coming together of diverse interests and people to achieve a common purpose via interactions, information sharing, and coordination of activities" (Jassawalla & Sashittal, 1998, p. 239), will promote the development of an organic, unifying team-level identity.

In this chapter, we review the research literature on expertise identity, collaboration, and team identification to establish the state of current knowledge on collaboration in work groups with diverse expertise. We then present a theoretical model of collaboration and team identity that specifies the role of reciprocal expertise affirmation as a process enabling diverse team members to work together across knowledge boundaries. We also describe contributions to theory and practice from a positive identity perspective on collaboration in diverse teams. We conclude with a discussion of directions for future research.

BACKGROUND

Organizations encompass—and must find ways to integrate—multiple realms of expertise. This chapter focuses on expertise as one element of positive identity that is increasingly important in today's knowledge-intensive work organizations. We also focus on teams as a frequent structure used to leverage and combine different areas of expertise. On cross-functional or mixed-expertise work teams, individuals with different knowledge and training are intentionally grouped to perform collaborative work.

Expertise and Identity at Work

Expertise, often an integral part of an individual's work-based role identity (Van der Vegt & Bunderson, 2005), is generally conceptualized as inherently positive and includes (but is not confined to) role identity derived from membership in a formal professional group, self-concept that is shaped by focused education or work experience, and identification with a social group defined by its shared specialized knowledge and common daily work tasks ("occupational community," Van Maanen & Barley, 1984). Specifically, the positive component of an individual's expertise identity incorporates strengths, talents, and skills associated with their functional background that are salient to self-concept (Roberts, Dutton, Spreitzer, Heaphy, & Quinn, 2005). Because we view expertise as an aspect of an individual's identity that is virtually always positive in contemporary work organizations, we use the simpler terms *expertise* and *reciprocal expertise affirmation* to convey the notions of positive expertise identity, and positive expertise identity that is mutually affirmed or reinforced.

Teams with expertise diversity, or member differences in knowledge as a result of education and work experience (Van der Vegt & Bunderson, 2005), possess rich and varied knowledge that can create a competitive advantage in what has been characterized as the "knowledge economy" (Drucker, 1993). Such teams can effectively utilize the collective strengths of their members, increasing the likelihood of both superior performance (Dahlin, Weingart, & Hinds, 2005; Lovelace, Shapiro, & Weingart, 2001) and meaningful, enriching experiences for individuals on the team (Hackman, 1987). For example, Pinto et al. (1993) found that cooperation on diverse expertise teams was associated with team member perceptions that a completed task was worthwhile and personally satisfying (Pinto, Pinto, & Prescott, 1993). Such groups face unique challenges for performance, however, because of intrinsic barriers to communication, trust, and collective identity formation that result from member differences.

Effective interpersonal collaboration on mixed expertise teams is difficult when knowledge boundaries reduce understanding of and appreciation for the contributions of other members (e.g., Edmondson & Nembhard, 2009; Edmondson & Roloff, 2008). When differences between team members are apparent, within-group interpersonal boundaries or "faultlines" may become activated, dividing the team into subgroups according to the compositional attributes of its members (Lau & Murnighan, 1998, 2005). Mixed-expertise teams confront faultlines at knowledge boundaries, fracturing the work team at points of divergent specialized skills, communication styles, or practice norms. When expertise differences between team members mean that each member has his or her own language, acumen, and style, the lack of common ground unifying team members can become paralyzing in the absence of a safe, exploratory environment (Edmondson, 1999). Under the right interpersonal conditions, the presence of such boundaries can increase constructive conflict (e.g., surfacing dissenting opinions during decision-making processes), but in their absence faultlines can increase destructive conflict, producing relationship strife (Jehn, 1995; Jehn, Northcraft, & Neale, 1999), especially when triggered by hot topics (Edmondson & Smith, 2006). To avoid potential problems and utilize collective strengths, team members must work together to build a shared identity as a team.

Team Identity

In this chapter, we examine expertise as a positive individual-level construct. For some, expertise may be a core element of the "reflected best-self" (Roberts et al., 2005); for others, expertise is merely a positive attribute they bring to the group's task. We posit a relationship between the mutual recognition of team member expertise and a positive sense of identity as a team. Previous research has demonstrated the importance of identification with the work team as a crucial aspect of team effectiveness (Cheng et al., 2008; Hogg & Terry, 2000; Van der Vegt & Bunderson, 2005). In identity theory, the group level of analysis typically refers to a categorical group of which an individual is a member. This directly follows from social identity and social categorization theory, according to which individuals define themselves in terms of the social groups to which they belong (Tajfel & Turner, 1979; Turner, 1982). Our concept of a team identity, in contrast, refers to a shared identity held by all members of a team—one that refers to defining features separating their team from other teams and from other identity groups. As above, such a team identity would almost always be positive—cognitively and affectively. To identify with and feel an integral part of a team is likely a positive experience. Finally, for a team identity to exist, a working group must have such features as a shared goal and clearly defined boundaries.[2]

Expertise-diverse groups are frequently formed in organizations to complete a specific task during a particular period of time. How identity formation occurs on such work teams presents new conceptual territory. The process of forming a team-level identity may be impeded by competing individual personal and social identities, some of which may undermine the development of a team identity, especially if they appear to conflict. Recall the globally dispersed product development team described earlier. Members' identification with fellow countrymen, or with functional or site-based colleagues, appeared to interfere with forming a shared identity as a project team. Generally, in mixed expertise teams, multidisciplinary team members may feel more strongly identified with their professional identity than their work team identity (Johnson, Morgeson, Ilgen, Meyer, & Lloyd, 2006).

Previous definitions of team identity have stressed the affective component of the construct (Brewer, Manzi, & Shaw, 1993; Van der Vegt & Bunderson, 2005), conceptualizing it as a positive feeling of "oneness" or "sameness" with team members (Mael & Ashforth, 1992). As a result, measures have been adapted from affective commitment (Allen & Meyer, 1990) and organizational identification scales (Mael & Ashforth, 1992). In our conceptualization, team identification refers to the extent to which group members experience a shared team identity—that is, do they establish a shared "we" that transcends, without displacing, individual-level identity differences? Although team members may vary in level of identification with the team and in level of knowledge of each other's strengths, each must feel a part of the team, recognizing its existence, boundaries, and members, if the team is to have a shared identity. We argue that a team identity is important for enabling and motivating collaboration in the presence of team diversity. In expertise-diverse teams, a team identity

---

[2] Extending work by Alderfer (1987) and McGrath (1984), Hackman (2002) outlines four criteria for a "real team." These four criteria are: (a) a clear team task, (b) knowledge of who is on the team and who is not, (c) delimited authority, and (d) stability over time.

thus allows synergy, rather than mere summation, of existing personal and social individual identities (Chen, Chen, & Meindl, 1998). Consequently, team identity is a unique synthesis of the individuals on the team.

We conceptualize team identity as including an important cognitive component to complement the previous emphasis on affect. Creating a team-level identity requires shared knowledge of who is on the team and what strengths and skills each person brings to bear on the team's work. Such group-level knowledge structures have been called transactive memory systems or shared mental models (Mathieu, Heffner, Goodwin, Salas, & Cannon-Bowers, 2000; Moreland & Myaskovsky, 2000; Wegner, 1987). Establishing cognitive clarity on "who we are" is likely to help team members to develop an organic, unifying positive collective identity as a team. Therefore, we conceptualize team identity as comprising both the emotional significance members attach to their membership in a given group (Van der Vegt & Bunderson, 2005) and team-level knowledge about the strengths, skills, and talents available to the team (Cannon-Bowers & Salas, 2001). What makes a team identity positive is a focus on leveraging individual team member strengths. A positive team identity is one in which members have accurate knowledge about other members' specific strengths and talents related to task performance and also a sense of affective attachment to the team and its goals. In contrast, a team may have a shared, but negative, identity, in which case assignment to the group is mutually deplored, attachment is correspondingly low, and mutual knowledge of each other's strengths is limited or inaccurate.

Recent empirical research found that collective team identification was associated with positive team outcomes, such as team learning behavior, on expertise-diverse teams (Earley & Mosakowski, 2000; Gibson & Vermeulen, 2003; Van der Vegt & Bunderson, 2005). Further, in one study, teams with low and high levels of expertise diversity outperformed teams with moderate levels of expertise diversity. This curvilinear relationship may result from the processes by which team members negotiate norms for teamwork. That is, teams low in expertise diversity have organic norms for communication and work style, and teams high in expertise diversity are forced to develop more formal routines and scripts for working together. Teams with moderate levels of expertise diversity, however, may fail to recognize the need to share knowledge carefully, and thus fail to communicate across the knowledge boundaries contained within the team.

Identity Affirmation in Expertise-Diverse Teams

A large body of research posits that self-verification, or seeking feedback to corroborate one's identity, is motivated by a need to establish consistency and enhance predictability across domains of life (Polzer, Milton, & Swann, 2002; Swann, 1987; Swann, Milton, & Polzer, 2000). Likewise, when teams are initially forming, individual members negotiate their team-relevant identities by searching for where they fit within the new system (London, Polzer, & Omoregie, 2005; Northcraft, Polzer, Neale, & Kramer, 1995; Turner, 1982). Yet validating one's own and others' team-relevant identity is a critical but uncertain process. Team members may hesitate to seek verification for fear of evaluation or possibly of finding a discrepancy that would reduce self-esteem (Higgins, 1987; Swann & Ely, 1984). Research has shown that the urge to verify team-relevant identities may be nevertheless irresistible; in one study, individuals began this process within 10 minutes of group formation (Polzer, Milton, & Swann, 2002). However, leveraging individual expertise identities, as opposed to subverting member difference, is critical for achieving effectiveness in diverse groups (Swann, Polzer, Seyle, & Ko, 2004).

This process of affirming team member identities is important for team identification and collaboration for two reasons: First, research has shown that individuals prefer to interact with others who see them as they see themselves (Byrne & Nelson, 1965; Swann, 1983); second, such teams have accurate shared understanding of the knowledge available to the team, enabling collaboration in interdependent tasks (Mathieu, Heffner, Goodwin, Salas, & Cannon-Bowers, 2000; Moreland & Myaskovsky, 2000; Wegner, 1987). Although the first reason—the desire for self-verification—is thought to apply to all teams, the second is particularly important for diverse teams because the knowledge available to the team is unlikely to be understood or even recognized by members who join the team with different backgrounds and areas of expertise. When the self-verification process works, the end state is identity confirmation or interpersonal congruence (London, Polzer, & Omoregie, 2005; Milton & Westphal, 2005). In this state, individuals feel affectively charged by the consistency between self and other views and by their connection to others, as well as cognitively clear about their role and the roles of others (comprising the new entity, "we").

Summary

We have reviewed previous research to develop support for the idea of developing a team-level identity—despite meaningful differences in individual experiences, knowledge, and identities—in cross-functional or expertise-diverse teams. Our primary motivation is to understand and enable collaboration in such teams, so as improve outcomes such as engagement, learning, and performance. In the next section, we build on and integrate the above ideas to propose a theoretical model of team collaboration.

A THEORETICAL MODEL OF TEAM COLLABORATION

We propose a theoretical model of collaboration in diverse work teams in which reciprocal affirmation of expertise identity enables collaboration across knowledge boundaries. In particular, we identify team psychological safety, or the shared belief that a team is safe for interpersonal risk taking (Edmondson, 1999), as the mechanism by which individual-level affirmations of positive identity promote effective group performance. Within such expertise-diverse teams, we further posit that collaboration will encourage the development of a team identity. We hypothesize that team psychological safety works in tandem with expertise affirmation to enhance group effectiveness by enabling individuals to overcome intrateam barriers caused by diverse expertise—so as to profit from their differences—and to establish a shared or collective identity as a unified team, despite expertise diversity.

Reciprocal Expertise Affirmation and Psychological Safety

Team psychological safety, a group-level construct (Edmondson, 1999), is a shared, often tacit, belief among individuals who work closely together that others' perceptions of them will not be harmed if they report a mistake, ask for help, or seek feedback. Psychological safety does not imply reckless permissiveness of error; it refers to a climate of interpersonal trust in which team members believe that they will not be humiliated or rejected by their peers for being themselves (Edmondson, 1999, 2003). For an individual to feel safe engaging in these otherwise interpersonally risky behaviors, she must perceive *ex ante* that others' positive views of her disciplinary knowledge or expert skills in relation to their own will not be in danger if she exposes her own uncertainty, disagreement, or mistakes.

Previous research has demonstrated that individuals resist engaging in behaviors that they perceive will threaten their own image, even if those behaviors would improve their own performance or that of their team or organization (Brown, 1990; Lee, 1997; Michael, 1973). Furthermore, research on team psychological safety and speaking up has demonstrated that team members develop shared beliefs about the consequences of personal failure, and that tacit assumptions about others' tolerance for uncertainty and mistakes can inhibit them from expressing doubt or error—a response that harms team and organizational learning (Cannon & Edmondson, 2001; Edmondson, 2003).

At the same time, the self-verification literature posits that team members who do not feel that important aspects of their self-perceptions, such as functional expertise, are understood and regarded as important by the team will withdraw from active participation on the team (Swann et al., 2004). However, when self-perceptions about task-relevant skills, knowledge, and talents are recognized and valued by the team, members become engaged, and team outcomes, such as creativity, improve (Polzer, Milton, & Swann, 2002).

Building on this previous work, we hypothesize that reciprocal affirmation of diverse team members' expertise identity promotes team psychological safety. Because reciprocal expertise affirmation involves mutual recognition by team members of the value of other members' knowledge, it allows team members to develop a sense of confidence that others will not humiliate or embarrass them when they ask questions or offer ideas—or even criticisms. Thus, we posit that reciprocal expertise affirmation is essential for each individual to believe that his or her contribution to collective performance is sufficiently recognized within the team such that he or she can admit confusion, seek help, or speak up without fearing potential loss of credibility or esteem from engaging in such interpersonally risky behaviors.

Proposition 1. Reciprocal expertise affirmation is positively associated with team psychological safety.

Psychological Safety and Collaboration Across Knowledge Boundaries

We anticipate that mixed expertise teams will be more likely to collaborate effectively if each member perceives that his or her expertise identity is valued and validated by other members and is thus more willing to cross into the unfamiliar or uncomfortable disciplinary territories of other members when performing a team task. Differences in knowledge-based identities, practice norms, and disciplinary beliefs within interdisciplinary groups have been found to interfere with crucial organizational processes such as information sharing, team learning, and organizational change in a variety of work settings (Brown & Duguid, 2001; Carlile, 2002; Ferlie, Fitzgerald, Wood, & Hawkins, 2005; Nembhard & Edmondson, 2006). In our model, team psychological safety—fostered (and also reinforced) by reciprocal expertise affirmation—moderates the relationship between expertise diversity and team collaboration. On expertise-diverse teams, differing mental models, communication styles, and tacit assumptions about demands of the work task create interpersonal barriers to knowledge sharing and thus to synergistic performance. By enabling individuals to ask questions, speak up, and seek help without fear of reputational harm or career repercussions, team psychological safety reduces identity threats that may otherwise be expected to arise in diverse expertise contexts as a result of such intrinsic disciplinary boundaries between team members.

A psychologically safe team environment enables open discussion among team members across knowledge divides by creating the conditions under which team members are encouraged to seek information about—and acknowledge their lack of knowledge about—others' domains of expertise, as well as modify others' views of their own expertise to be accurate and consistent with their self-beliefs. Such dialogue enhances shared understanding of members' heterogeneous expertise identities, valuation of these identities, and consequently the team's collective ability to access and combine knowledge from these varied sources for productive collaborative work. In this way, psychological safety is not only promoted by reciprocal affirmations of expertise within the work group but also reflexively promotes expertise affirmation among diverse team members whose improved dialogue across functional boundaries enhances understanding of and respect for each other's contribution to collective work. (This

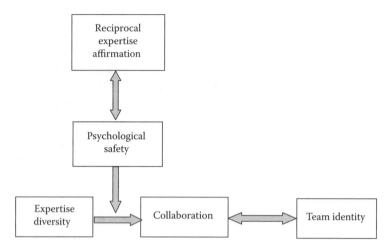

FIGURE 14.1
Proposed model of team collaboration across knowledge boundaries.

argument is represented by a positive feedback arrow in Figure 14.1.) Thus, we propose that psychological safety supports (or, in its absence, impedes) the establishment of consistent self-views within diverse teams and shared understanding of the team's collective knowledge resources by encouraging interpersonal processes that promote collaboration.

These arguments are consistent with previous research on antecedents of intergroup collaboration. Notably, research has demonstrated the importance of common goals and the presence of internal processes for diffusing intergroup conflict and preserving group unity as contributors to effective collaboration across knowledge boundaries. Superordinate goals and team processes for managing intergroup conflict have been identified as critical facilitators of cross-functional cooperation (Pinto et al., 1993). We hypothesize that team psychological safety will moderate the relationship between expertise diversity and team collaboration by enabling team members to establish transparent, mutually respectful routines for resolving intergroup differences and by fostering shared commitment to common group goals. In short, even when team members recognize the potential value of expertise diversity—other members bring knowledge they lack—collaboration may not occur without psychological safety. If individuals in different disciplines fail to speak up for fear that their knowledge might not be valued or might not be relevant, then crucial information will remain unshared.

Proposition 2a. Team expertise diversity is likely to be weakly associated with team collaboration.

Proposition 2b. Team psychological safety positively moderates the weak association between team expertise diversity and team collaboration.

Collaboration and Team Identity

Through repeated interactions during the performance of an integrated task, team members are expected to develop common routines, rituals, and shared mental models that transcend their diverse expertise identities and endow them with a superordinate collective identity. However, individual identities and opinions can become sacrificed for the team when members become overly enmeshed or homogenized (Janis, 1982). Here, we hypothesize that collaboration across knowledge boundaries fosters the development of a positive team identity over time by enabling team members to establish and collectively embrace a unifying image, language, history, and set of norms that leverages the team's diverse, pooled expertise identities. In an expertise-diverse team, collaboration supports building a team identity, in part through self-verification processes (Swann, Kwan, Polzer, & Milton, 2003), which in turn require opportunities for interaction where sharing knowledge salient to members' expertise identity can occur. Such opportunities allow individuals to correct and negotiate their self-images with respect to their expertise, and to coordinate action across knowledge boundaries.

Establishing a collective identity at the team level does not erase or undermine positive affirmation of individual-level identity, but rather enhances it—infusing daily work with shared experiences and beliefs that encourage trust and the development of strong ties among diverse members. In fact, positive perceptions of other team members as part of the identity affirmation process is associated with collective identity formation (Swann et al., 2003). Consistent with existing research on the positive impact of collective team identification on collaboration in diverse work contexts, we acknowledge the bidirectional relationship between collective identity and intrateam work behavior. As group members begin to relate to each other as "we" and establish shared routines, language, and work strategies that transcend their unique individual identities, they are able to access and integrate their collective knowledge more effectively, encouraging increased collaboration. In this way, the association between collaboration and team identity may be mutually reinforcing.

Previous research has shown that cooperative contact among team members, fostered through collaboration to perform interdependent work, can facilitate the development of collective identity by enabling diverse teams to overcome internal intergroup stereotyping and social categorization (Pettigrew, 1998). Allport's (1954) intergroup contact hypothesis specified four conditions under which intergroup contact was anticipated to reduce intergroup stereotyping and prejudice: equal group status within the situation; common goals; intergroup cooperation; and the support of authorities, law, or custom (cited in Pettigrew, 1998). Whereas Allport's initial theory did not specify the mechanisms by which these conditions fostered a change in intergroup attitudes and behavior, recent research in the intergroup contact tradition has proposed four integrated processes that enable diverse groups to overcome internal intergroup boundaries that might otherwise derail effective cooperation: (a) learning about the out-group, (b) repeated contact, (c) generating affective ties through reduced anxiety and increased empathy and friendship, and (d) in-group reappraisal resulting in reshaped norms and beliefs about out-groups with which the in-group interacts (Pettigrew, 1998). Our model reflects these process hypotheses by specifying a direct relationship between collaboration—the productive output of intergroup contact—and team identity—the positive manifestation of new, strong ties that connect previously divided identity groups within the team.

We also build on previous research that examined collective team identification as a moderator between expertise diversity and performance. In their study of 57 multidisciplinary teams in the oil and gas industry in The Netherlands, Van der Vegt and Bunderson (2005) demonstrated that collective team identification moderated the relationship between expertise diversity and team learning behaviors, with low collective team identification engendering a negative relationship between expertise diversity and team learning and high collective team identification fostering a positive relationship between diversity and learning (Van der Vegt & Bunderson, 2005). Rather than examining collective team identification as a static dimension of the team, we posit that expertise diversity can in fact enhance the development of a nascent team identity when interpersonal barriers within the team are reduced, such as by psychological safety, because the diversity of backgrounds creates a need to explain oneself to others.

Under such conditions, team members are more likely to share information about their fields and backgrounds and hence to recognize their disciplinary differences as a collective strength rather than a limitation, promoting collaboration across knowledge boundaries.

> *Proposition 3. Team collaboration is positively associated with team identity.*

The proposed model of team collaboration is shown in Figure 14.1.

DISCUSSION

In this chapter, we propose a model of positive team identity formation within diverse teams, in which reciprocal affirmation of expertise identity among diverse team members fosters collaboration across knowledge boundaries. We argue that such collaboration in turn enables members to build the shared knowledge and routines, strong ties, and mutual trust that are the foundation of a unifying "we" in the presence of individual differences. Team psychological safety is proposed to moderate a weak positive relationship between expertise diversity and team collaboration by reducing communication barriers between individuals with different expertise-based identities. Unencumbered by the subtle fear of embarrassment or the more pragmatic concern about possible harm to one's career, individuals can safely venture out of their own knowledge base into the unfamiliar domains of other experts on the team whose language, priorities, assumptions, and core skills are foreign from (and perhaps even incompatible with) their own. Bridging this distance is critical for the team to leverage its collective expert capital because it allows members to develop a better understanding of the team's internal knowledge resources and how best to deploy them when performing collaborative tasks.

Core Contribution

We extend existing theoretical models of team psychological safety by suggesting a relationship with a new aspect of team functioning, reciprocal expertise affirmation. Introducing expertise affirmation as an interpersonal phenomenon within diverse teams may expand our knowledge of the antecedents to effective group processes for tasks that require individuals with varying identities to work together. Thus, future research examining collaboration and collective identity in diverse teams to explore the roles of reciprocal expertise affirmation and team psychological safety may enhance our understanding of how and under what circumstances diverse teams collaborate effectively, despite knowledge barriers that impede easy communication.

Our conceptualization of team identity as both a relational and a cognitive construct also offers a new perspective on group-level positive identity that positions shared knowledge acquisition as an important antecedent to building a collective identity in a diverse team. Shared knowledge of "what we know" enables the team to establish routines for accessing and integrating its pooled strengths, which we anticipate will facilitate stronger ties among team members across knowledge boundaries (as a product of increased constructive, satisfying interpersonal contact) and therefore greater affective commitment of members to the team as a collective.

Finally, we believe that the processes by which collective identities are formed in teams or work groups are underexplored in existing literature. Our model introduces a process of collective identity formation that we expect to be empirically testable. In particular, our focus on team collaboration suggests that exploring the interactions among team members in a way that leverages individual strengths is an important avenue for understanding positive team identities. Thus, research examining the veracity and strength of the relationships hypothesized in this model may contribute to theory on the mechanisms by which positive work team identities are created and the factors that enhance or disrupt their development.

Limitations and Future Research

Several additional avenues for future research emerge from this chapter. First, we propose that researchers explore team identity, team psychological safety, and team collaboration in "real" organizations across a variety of industries and task contexts. Much existing theory on group behavior has developed from lab-based experimental research, which offers control and allows the researcher to isolate and manipulate variables but may not reflect the true complexity of interpersonal work as experienced by individuals in their jobs. Previous research has identified the need for field research to bridge what has been identified as a gap between group behavior as predicted by existing theory and actual group behavior as manifest in live work teams (e.g., Perlow, Gittell, & Katz, 2004). In-depth, up-close qualitative field work will enhance positive identity scholarship by providing rich insight into the circumstances under which individuals respond positively to diversity in their own work groups and the factors that enable or interfere with effective group performance under varying individual, interpersonal, and organizational conditions.

We also propose that future research on positive identity in organizations should examine the impact of specific types of intrateam diversity, as well as combinations of intrateam diversity types, for team functioning and team identity. We intentionally limit our model to one form of diversity—one that is increasingly relevant to organizational performance—expertise diversity, because of the complexity of team processes, specifically as related to managing the many forms of composition diversity that are possible. By focusing narrowly on expertise diversity, we hope to generate insight into mechanisms and moderating factors shaping the relationship between team identity and effectiveness that could be investigated for subsequent types of diversity as well. Expertise diversity offers the advantage of considerable previous theorizing on navigating knowledge boundaries in teams (e.g., Bechky, 2003; Dougherty, 1992; Edmondson & Nembhard, 2009; Sole & Edmondson, 2002), enabling the development of closely related, theoretically tractable new propositions. As noted, future research may examine the relationships we propose with respect to expertise diversity for other forms of intrateam diversity.

Similarly, we focus on reciprocal expertise affirmation, psychological safety, and collaboration in the context of defined work teams. Although many individuals are members of multiple teams at work, each of which may vary in importance to the individuals' self-image and whose boundaries may be amorphous and overlapping, we start by focusing more narrowly on intact work teams with clear boundaries and well-defined membership. Thus, we develop our model of team identity to apply to groups in which individuals work closely together to accomplish mutual goals, omitting the issue of whether individuals who work with multiple simultaneous teams experience differing levels of identity affirmation. This next level of complexity may be considered in subsequent work.

Lastly, we do not fully consider boundary conditions or moderating factors that may limit the applicability of our model. For example, team structure variables (e.g., size), team composition (e.g., distribution of differences among team members, such as equally distributed heterogeneity versus varying-sized subgroups and status differences), and organizational context (e.g., resources available to the team) likely influence the relationships we propose, but for simplicity at this early stage, we have restricted our model to core variables of theoretical interest only. Exploratory field work is needed to enrich this basic model by identifying additional variables that impact positive identity affirmation processes described in this model and limit the generalizability of the relationships we propose.

CONCLUSION

As organizational performance increasingly depends on an ability to transfer and integrate diverse specialized knowledge effectively to meet multidisciplinary challenges, mixed expertise teams have become a widely popular management structure, yet most organizations may fail to realize the theoretical benefits of these work arrangements. This chapter offers an explanation for the frequent failure of expertise-diverse work teams—the failure to build mutual recognition and understanding of the expertise held by diverse team members, as well as how expertise shapes an individual's identity at work. Building on this explanation, we suggest that mixed expertise teams can leverage their assembled knowledge successfully if their members recognize, understand, and value the unique strengths and contributions of other members; this understanding will allow and encourage team members to collaborate across knowledge boundaries and to build shared learning on how to combine their diverse talents effectively. Further, each individual must believe that his or her own strengths and contributions are recognized by other members, making each comfortable to engage in team learning behaviors, despite the interpersonal threat they present. Thus, we proposed reciprocal expertise affirmation as a crucial process for teams that need to develop shared routines, rituals, and experiences. In this way, a new team identity can emerge, superseding members' unique expertise identities.

Although the emphasis in discussions of expertise-diverse teams has focused on the promise of diverse backgrounds for team performance, we also propose a reinforcing feedback relationship between performance and positive identification. In this way, collaborating across knowledge boundaries enhances a team's ability to construct a unifying, positively charged "we"—a shared team identity that transcends member differences—and to establish the strong ties and shared knowledge that underpin this collective identity. This in turn enhances the team's ability to access and integrate its diverse knowledge. Developing theory on the dynamics of team identity may someday help managers to improve work outcomes while also enriching the work lives of the team members who make it happen.

REFERENCES

Alderfer, C. (1987). An intergroup perspective on group dynamics. In J. Lorsch (Ed.), *Handbook of organizational behavior* (pp. 190–222). Englewood Cliffs, NJ: Prentice Hall.

Allen, N. J., & Meyer, J. P. (1990). The measurement and antecedents of affective, continuance, and normative commitment to the organization. *Journal of Occupational Psychology, 63*, 1–18.

Allport, G. W. (1954). *The nature of prejudice.* Cambridge, MA: Perseus Books.

Bechky, B. A. (2003). Creating shared meaning across occupational communities: The transformation of understanding on a production floor. *Organization Science, 14*, 312–330.

Brewer, M., Manzi, J., & Shaw, J. (1993). In-group identification as a function of depersonalization, distinctiveness, and status. *Psychological Science, 4*, 88–92.

Brown, J., & Duguid, P. (2001). Knowledge and organization: A social-practice perspective. *Organization Science, 12*, 198–213.

Brown, R. (1990). Politeness theory: Exemplar and exemplary. In I. Rock (Ed.), *The legacy of Solomon Asch: Essays in cognition and social psychology* (pp. 23–37). Hillsdale, NJ: Lawrence Erlbaum Associates.

Byrne, D., & Nelson, D. (1965). Attraction as a linear function of proportion of positive reinforcements. *Journal of Personality and Social Psychology, 36*, 659–663.

Cannon, M., & Edmondson, A. C. (2001). Confronting failure: Antecedents and consequences of shared beliefs about failure in organizational work groups. *Journal of Organizational Behavior, 22*, 161–177.

Cannon-Bowers, J. A., & Salas, E. (2001). Reflections on shared cognition. *Journal of Organizational Behavior, 22*, 195–202.

Carlile, P. (2002). A pragmatic view of knowledge and boundaries: Boundary objects in new product development. *Organizational Science, 13*, 442–455.

Chen, C., Chen, X., & Meindl, J. (1998). How can cooperation be fostered? The cultural effects of individualism–collectivism. *Academy of Management Review, 23*, 285–304.

Cheng, C., Sanders, M., Sanchez-Burks, J., Molina, K., Lee, F., Darling, E., & Zhao, Y. (2008). Reaping the rewards of diversity: The role of identity integration. *Social and Personality Psychology Compass, 2*, 1182–1198.

Dahlin, K., Weingart, L., & Hinds, P. (2005). Team diversity and information use. *Academy of Management Journal, 48*, 1107–1123.

Dougherty, D. (1992). Interpretive barriers to successful product innovation in large firms. *Organization Science, 3*, 179–202.

Drucker, P. (1993). *Post-capitalist society.* New York: HarperCollins.

Earley, C., & Mosakowski, E. (2000). Creating hybrid team cultures: An empirical test of transnational team functioning. *Academy of Management Journal, 43*, 26–49.

Edmondson, A. C. (1999). Psychological safety and learning behavior in work teams. *Administrative Science Quarterly, 44*, 350–383.

Edmondson, A. C. (2003). Speaking up in the operating room: How team leaders promote learning in interdisciplinary action teams. *Journal of Management Studies, 40*, 1419–1452.

Edmondson, A. C., & Nembhard, I. M. (2009). Product development and learning in project teams: The challenges are the benefits. *Journal of Product Innovation Management,* forthcoming.

Edmondson, A. C., & Roloff, K. S. (2008). Overcoming barriers to collaboration: Psychological safety and learning in diverse teams. In E. Sales, G. G. Goodwin, & C. S. Burke (Eds.), *Team effectiveness in complex organizations: Cross-disciplinary perspectives and approaches. SIOP Frontier Series.* Mahwah, N.J.: Lawrence Erlbaum Associates.

Edmondson, A. C., & Smith, D. M. (2006). Too hot to handle? How to manage relationship conflict. *California Management Review, 49*, 6–31.

Ferlie, E., Fitzgerald, L., Wood, M., & Hawkins, C. (2005). The nonspread of innovations: The mediating role of professionals. *Academy of Management Journal, 48*, 117–134.

Gibson, C., & Vermeulen, F. (2003). A healthy divide: Subgroups as a stimulus for team learning behavior. *Administrative Science Quarterly, 48*, 202–239.

Hackman, J. R. (1987). The design of work teams. In J. W. Lorsch (Ed.), *Handbook of organizational behavior.* Englewood Cliffs, NJ: Prentice-Hall.

Hackman, J. R. (2002). *Leading teams: Setting the stage for great performances.* Boston: Harvard Business School Press.

Higgins, E. T. (1987). Self-discrepancy: A theory relating self and affect. *Psychological Review, 94*, 319–340.

Hogg, M., & Terry, D. (2000). Social identity and self-categorization processes in organizational contexts. *Academy of Management Review, 25*, 121–140.

Janis, I. (1982). *Groupthink: Psychological studies of policy decisions and fiascoes.* Boston: Houghton Mifflin.

Jassawalla, A., & Sashittal, H. (1998). An examination of collaboration in high-technology new product development processes. *Journal of Product Innovation Management, 15*, 237–254.

Jehn, K. (1995). A multimethod examination of the benefits and detriments of intragroup conflict. *Administrative Science Quarterly, 40*, 256–282.

Jehn, K., Northcraft, G., & Neale, M. (1999). Why differences make a difference: A field study of diversity, conflict, and performance in workgroups. *Administrative Science Quarterly, 44*, 741–763.

Johnson, M., Morgeson, F., Ilgen, D., Meyer, C., & Lloyd, J. (2006). Multiple professional identities: Examining differences in identification across work-related targets. *Journal of Applied Psychology, 91*, 498–506.

Lau, D., & Murnighan, J. K. (1998). Demographic diversity and faultlines: The compositional dynamics of organizational groups. *Academy of Management Review, 23*, 325–340.

Lau, D., & Murnighan, J. K. (2005). Interactions within groups and subgroups: The effects of demographic faultlines. *Academy of Management Journal, 48,* 645–659.

Lee, F. (1997). When the going gets tough, do the tough ask for help? *Organizational Behavior and Human Decision Processes, 72,* 336–363.

London, M., Polzer, J., & Omoregie H. (2005). Interpersonal congruence, transactive memory, and feedback processes: An integrative model of group learning. *Human Resource Development Review, 4,* 114–135.

Lovelace, K., Shapiro, D., & Weingart, L. (2001). Maximizing cross-functional new product teams' innovativeness and constraint adherence: A conflict communications perspective. *Academy of Management Journal, 44,* 779–793.

Mathieu, J. E., Heffner, T. S., Goodwin, G. F., Salas, E., & Cannon-Bowers, J. A. (2000). The influence of shared mental models on team process and performance. *Journal of Applied Psychology, 85,* 273–283.

Mael, F., & Ashforth, B. E. (1992). Alumni and their alma mater: A partial test of the reformulated model of organizational identification. *Journal of Organizational Behavior, 13,* 103–123.

McGrath, J. E. (1984). *Groups: Interaction and performance.* Englewood Cliffs, NJ: Prentice Hall.

Michael, D. (1973). *Learning to plan and planning to learn.* San Francisco: Jossey-Bass.

Milton, L. P., & Westphal, J. D. (2005). Identity confirmation networks and cooperation in work teams. *Academy of Management Journal, 48,* 191–212.

Moreland, R. L., & Myaskovsky, L. (2000). Exploring the performance benefits of group training: Transactive memory or improved communication? *Organizational Behavior and Human Decision Processes, 82,* 117–133.

Nembhard, I., & Edmondson, A. C. (2006). Making it safe: The effects of leader inclusiveness and professional status on psychological safety and improvement efforts in health care teams. *Journal of Organizational Behavior, 27,* 941–966.

Northcraft, G., Polzer, J., Neale, M., & Kramer, R. (1995). Diversity, social identity, and performance: Emergent social dynamics in cross-functional teams. In S. E. Jackson, & M. N. Ruderman (Eds.), *Diversity in work teams: Research paradigms for a changing workplace* (pp. 69–96). Washington, DC: APA Publications.

Perlow, L., Gittell, J., & Katz, N. (2004). Contextualizing patterns of work group interaction: Toward a nested theory of structuration. *Organization Science, 15,* 520–536.

Pettigrew, T. (1998). Intergroup contact theory. *Annual Review of Psychology, 49,* 65–85.

Pinto, M. B., Pinto, J., & Prescott, J. (1993). Antecedents and consequences of cross functional cooperation. *Management Science, 39,* 1281–1297.

Polzer, J., Milton, L., & Swann, W. (2002). Capitalizing on diversity: Interpersonal congruence in small work groups. *Administrative Science Quarterly, 47,* 296–324.

Roberts, L., Dutton, J., Spreitzer, G., Heaphy, E., & Quinn, R. (2005). Composing the reflected best-self portrait: Building pathways for becoming extraordinary in work organizations. *Academy of Management Review, 30,* 712–736.

Sole, D., & Edmondson A. C. (2002). Situated knowledge and learning in dispersed teams. *British Journal of Management, 13,* S17–S34.

Swann, W. (1987). Identity negotiation: Where two roads meet. *Journal of Personality and Social Psychology, 53,* 1038–1051.

Swann, W., Kwan, V. S. Y., Polzer, J. T., & Milton, L. P. (2003). Fostering group identification and creativity in diverse groups: The role of individuation and self-verification. *Personality and Social Psychology Bulletin, 29,* 1396–1406.

Swann, W., Milton, L., & Polzer, J. (2000). Should we create a niche or fall in line? Identity negotiation and small group effectiveness. *Journal of Personality and Social Psychology, 79,* 238–250.

Swann, W., Polzer, J., Seyle, D., & Ko, S. (2004). Finding value in diversity: Verification of personal and social self-views in diverse groups. *Academy of Management Review, 29,* 9–27.

Swann, W. B., Jr. (1983). Self-verification: Bringing social reality into harmony with the self. In J. Suls & A. G. Greenwald (Eds.), *Psychological perspectives on the self* (Vol. II, pp. 33–66). Hillsdale, NJ: Lawrence Erlbaum Associates.

Swann, W. B., Jr., & Ely, R. J. (1984). A battle of wills: Self-verification versus behavioral confirmation. *Journal of Personality and Social Psychology, 46,* 1287–1302.

Tajfel, H., & Turner J. C. (1979). An integrative theory of inter-group conflict. In W. G. Austin & S. Worchel (Eds.), *The social psychology of intergroup relations* (pp. 335–358). Monterey, CA: Brooks/Cole Publishing Co.

Turner, J. (1982). Towards a cognitive redefinition of the social group. In H. Tajfel (Ed.), *Social identity and intergroup relations* (pp. 15–40). Cambridge, England: Cambridge University Press.

Van der Vegt, G., & Bunderson J. S. (2005). Learning behavior and performance in multidisciplinary teams: The importance of collective team identification. *Academy of Management Journal, 48,* 532–547.

Van Maanen, J., & Barley, S. (1984). Occupational communities: Culture and control in organizations. In B. M. Staw & L. L. Cummings (Eds.), *Research in organizational behavior* (Vol. 6, pp. 287–365). Greenwich, CT: JAI Press.

Wegner, D. M. (1987). Transactive memory: A contemporary analysis of the group mind. In B. Mullen & G. R. Goethals (Eds.), *Theories of group behavior* (pp. 185–208). New York: Springer-Verlag.

15

Commentary: The Elusive Search for a Positive Relational Identity—Grappling With Multiplicity and Conflict

Jeffrey Sanchez-Burks and Fiona Lee[1]

CONTENTS

The present volume on positive identities addresses issues that have long preoccupied the minds of humankind. Much of philosophy, psychology, sociology, religion, economics, literature, and the arts are, in one way or another, pursuits of the "good life." Each discipline approaches this intellectual journey in a different way—for example, a psychologist might be interested in facilitators and inhibitors of mental health,

---

[1] Both authors contributed equally to this commentary.

a religious leader might consider how individuals can gain higher levels of intimacy with a deity, an artist might strive to take our perceptions beyond what is ordinary and mundane, or an economist might focus on how resources can be best allocated within a society—but all are concerned with what having a good life entails, and how a good life can be attained. In these various efforts to understand positivity, the question of identity, or how the self is related to others and the world at large, inevitably emerges. In each person's pursuit of a good life, we have to resolve issues such as our purpose in the larger scheme of the world, our place in the history of humankind, our role in the welfare and happiness of others, and ultimately who we are and how we are connected to our fellow human beings.

Our goal in this essay is to examine how positive identities are shaped by and influence dyadic and group processes in organizations. Given the enduring theme of positive identities in our intellectual history, we begin our commentary on some of the earliest explorations of positivity and identity in psychology, philosophy, and the arts. Taking a historical perspective, we examine how classic conceptualizations of positive identity are elaborated and expanded in the chapters within this section.

We begin with William James, who in his 1890 volume *Principles of Psychology* articulated one of the more insightful ways to think about both positivity and identity. James understood these topics well. On the one hand, James's life appears to be an exemplar of positivity—he hailed from one of the most intellectually prominent families of his time, was in the inner circle of the preeminent thinkers in his generation (including his brother Henry James, Ralph Waldo Emerson, John Dewey, W. E. B. Dubois, and Gertrude Stein, just to name a few), and is widely considered the father of psychology. Yet, James's achievements are just as well known as his struggles to attain a positive identity. He suffered extended bouts of depression and mental breakdowns, spent time in institutions for physical and mental rehabilitation, failed at several vocations such as art and medicine before landing in academia, and seriously contemplated suicide many times in his life (Fisher, 2008).

James's personal struggles led him to deeply consider what it means to have a positive identity, and he criticized superficial definitions of what it means to be positive or "good." Particularly he argued that "… if merely feeling good could decide, drunkenness would be the supremely valid human experience." (1905, p. 16). In this commentary, we take up

James's challenge and examine critically what it means to have a positive identity. Through juxtaposing classic conceptualizations with more recent empirical research, we question whether what seems to be good is indeed good, and whether what seems to be bad is indeed bad. In doing so, we explore several questions that emerged as we read the chapters in this section: Who am I in relation to others? How do my identities affect the groups to which I belong? How do my relationships affect my behavior? How do my individual identities relate to my relational and team identities?

> Whenever two people meet there are really six people present. There is each man [sic] as he sees himself, each man as the other person sees him, and each man as he really is.

> —**William James (1890)**

MULTIPLE IDENTITIES AND THE SOCIAL CONTEXT: WHO AM I IN RELATION TO OTHERS?

William James fundamentally challenged the idea that identity, or the sense of self, is a unitary construct. Rather, identity is *multifaceted* (it incorporates different and even conflicting components), *dynamic* (it changes over time), and *relational* in nature (how others see the self is just as important as one's own perceptions). Any discussion of identity must recognize these three characteristics. As several chapters in this volume have already suggested, we all have multiple selves—for example, a person may be simultaneously a woman, a Latina, an engineer, a Catholic, a mother, a Yankees fan, and so on. Having multiple identities is not necessarily problematic; it may be relatively straightforward, for instance, to see oneself as both a Catholic and a Yankees fan. However, when one's multiple identities have conflicting values or norms, challenges may arise. For example, given that Boston and New York baseball teams are archrivals, a woman who identifies with being a Boston Red Sox fan and being a New Yorker at the same time may find herself feeling "split" or conflicted. Or, given that conservative Catholic doctrine typically denounces abortion, it may be problematic to identify with being a Catholic and being pro-choice at the same time.

Most importantly, our relational and social contexts are deeply related to how multiple identities are managed in our everyday lives. First, recent research has shown that which of our many identities becomes salient changes depending on the cues in the environment, the people with whom we are interacting, or the groups we are in at the time (Benet-Martínez, Leu, Lee, & Morris, 2002; Cheng, Lee, & Benet-Martinez, 2006; Hong, Morris, Chui, & Benet-Martínez, 2000). This is particularly important for people with identities that embody conflicting values. In each of their dyadic and social interactions, they have to constantly figure out which identity to embrace and which to abandon, if only for the moment (Phinney & Devich-Navarro, 1997; Roccas & Brewer, 2002). For example, when surrounded by Red Sox fans at Fenway Park in Boston, the Red Sox fan who is a New Yorker may be wise to perceive her Red Sox fan identity as "me" but perceive her New Yorker identity as, temporarily, "not me." As one can imagine, to the extent that this person cannot abandon her New Yorker identity in that social situation and activates both identities at the same time, she will encounter problems relating to the people around her.

Further, this identity-switching dynamic affects how we perceive and feel toward others and who we perceive to be part of our in-group. In a study of biculturals (or individuals who identify with two conflicting cultural identities), Cheng and Lee (2008) experimentally activated Asian Americans' Asian or American cultural identities. When biculturals' Asian identities were activated, they were more likely to see other Asians as their in-group—they rated the outputs of an Asian team more favorably and were more likely to prefer the Asian team to the American team. The opposite trend emerged when their American identities were activated. In short, perceptions of close relationships and group boundaries are associated with our salient identity. All and all, our relational and social context often determines which of our multiple identities are salient, whereas the activation of an identity in turn affects how we perceive, feel about, and relate to others in our social environment.

Consistency and Conflict

Several of the chapters in this section argue, in one way or another, that achieving consistency between one's individual and relational identities is important for engendering positive relational and group dynamics. Particularly, positive outcomes come from activating the salient identity that best matches the immediate social and relational context. For instance, DeRue, Ashford, and Cotton (Chapter 10) suggest that successful leaders need to claim the leader identity for oneself, but this must be consistent with others' granting that person the same identity. Similarly, LeBaron, Glenn, and Thompson (Chapter 9) suggest that our identities emerge from the verbal and nonverbal give-and-take between interactants within a relationship. Implicit in these chapters is the idea that, in addition to the content of one's identity, the *relationship* between one's identity and the expectations of others in our social environment is key—when one's identity matches these relational demands, we find positive dyadic and group dynamics. However, when there is a conflict between the values associated with one's identity and those of the social environment, it can lead to a split, chaotic, or inauthentic sense of the self, which in turn can wreak havoc on our own psychological and relational well-being (Milton, Chapter 13).

Identity Integration and Relational Outcomes

Several prominent theories have outlined how conflicting identities are psychologically managed (see Berry, 1990; Roccas & Brewer, 2002). We focus specifically on recent research that examines individual differences in identity integration (or II), which refers to the degree to which two conflicting identities are perceived as compatible or in opposition to each other (Benet-Martínez & Haritatos, 2005; Cheng, Lee, & Benet-Martínez, 2006; Sacharin & Lee, in press). Individuals high in identity integration (i.e., *high IIs*) do not find it problematic to have two identities at the same time despite their conflicting nature. For example, biculturals who identify themselves as both Asian and American see themselves as "Asian American" rather than an "Asian in America." Or, women in male-dominated professions find that their gender and professional identities, although different, complement each other and can blend together seamlessly. Despite their inherent differences, high IIs perceive the two distinct and contrasting identities as inextricably tied together. In contrast, *low IIs* feel caught between their two identities and prefer to keep them separate. Like individuals who use the compartmentalizing strategy, low IIs believe they can identify with one or the other group at different times or in different contexts but never both at the same time. They suppress one identity when the other is being activated or used and chronically feel torn between the two identities (Benet-Martínez et al., 2002; Hall, Lopez, & Bansal, 2001).

Recent studies show that individuals with high II—for example, academics with joint appointments who perceive compatibility between conflicting disciplinary identities, biculturals who perceive compatibility between conflicting cultural identities, or women in male-dominated professions who perceive compatibility between their gender and work identities—were more productive and more creative (Cheng et al., 2008; Leung, Maddux, Galinsky, & Chiu, 2008). These enhanced individual-level performance outcomes may be a result of better relational and social resources of high IIs. Specifically, people who can integrate multiple identities simultaneously are better at drawing social support from diverse relationships and groups. In a recent study, Mok, Morris, Benet-Martínez, and Karakitapoglu-Aygun (2007) found that high II biculturals who perceive their cultural identities as compatible rather than conflictual have larger, more culturally diverse, and more richly interconnected relationship networks. Such network characteristics have been shown to positively predict individual, relational, and group-level well-being (Ibarra, Kilduff, & Tsai, 2005). Individuals might be able to get more advice and more varied forms of advice in the face of adversity. When one source of social support is unavailable, they can draw support from a nonoverlapping source.

DIVERSITY AND COLLECTIVE IDENTITY: HOW DO MY IDENTITIES AFFECT THE GROUPS TO WHICH I BELONG?

In addition to individuals, having diverse identities can be beneficial for teams as well. As MacPhail, Roloff, and Edmondson argue in Chapter 14, having multiple perspectives within a team is integral to its success. Frequent interaction between team members from diverse backgrounds—be it demographic, functional, or cognitive—exposes team members to a variety of knowledge and perspectives, which promote knowledge synthesis and in turn innovation (Phillips, Mannix, Neale, & Gruenfeld, 2004). Yet, the research evidence supporting this relationship remains inconclusive (Ferlie, Fitzgerald, Wood, & Hawkins, 2005; Gerbert, Boerner, & Kearney, 2006). This is due in part to process losses; for example, the miscommunication, knowledge boundaries, and relationship conflict experienced by diverse teams hamper information sharing and team performance (Bassett-Jones, 2005; De Dreu & Weingart, 2003).

Indeed, MacPhail et al. (Chapter 14) provide vivid illustrations of how these process losses can undermine the effectiveness of diverse teams. For example, they discuss how differences between the norms of scientists and engineers can contribute to miscommunication, a process loss that in turn undermines the team progress and heightens interpersonal conflict within teams.

Understanding how to reap the benefits of diversity while avoiding the associated pitfalls of unproductive team dynamics is a holy grail for team researchers. One approach that has been shown to minimize the friction common in diverse teams is to promote a superordinate collective identity, one that emphasizes a unified team identity and reduces the salience of differences between members (Gaertner, Dovidio, Mann, Murrell, & Pomare, 1990; van Knippenberg & Haslam, 2003). Here, team members find a common identity to which all members collectively embrace, and other identities are abandoned or minimized. In other words, the team focuses on the "us/not us" collective identity rather than individual-level "me/not me" identities. Supporting this idea, Argote and her colleagues have shown that making salient a common, superordinate, collective identity increases knowledge sharing of existing innovations across organizational units (Darr, Argote, & Epple, 1995; Kane, Argote, & Levine, 2005).

Drawing from our research showing that individuals who can simultaneously embrace multiple identities perform better, we suggest an alternative, contrasting approach to enhancing unique knowledge sharing, creativity, and team learning—team dynamics that facilitate the performance of diverse teams (MacPhail et al., Chapter 14). Like MacPhail et al., we suggest that diverse teams should retain the salience of diverse identities within the team while simultaneously fostering perceptions about the compatibility between these distinct identities (Cheng, Sanchez-Burks, & Lee, 2008a; Ely & Thomas, 2001). Our argument is based on recent research showing that knowledge and expertise are tied to our identities, and depending on which of our multiple identities is being activated, different knowledge systems are made accessible for use (Fiske, 1998; Higgins, 1996). For example, activating gender identity among Asian women increases gender-stereotypic performance on academic tests (doing worse on math tests and better on verbal tests). However, activating their Asian identity increases culturally stereotypic performance on these same tests (doing worse on verbal tests and better on math tests) (Shih, Pittinsky, & Ambady, 1999). Even though one might theoretically possess the expertise or know-how to solve a problem, certain knowledge systems may not be accessible because the relevant identity is not made salient.

Drawing from this research, we suggest that keeping diverse identities salient, separate, and distinct within a cross-functional team help team members better access multiple and disparate knowledge sets that are salient to them, which in turn improves team performance and innovation. To illustrate, imagine a cross-functional team with members who represent a diverse set of functional backgrounds such as engineering, design, marketing, and customer service. Rather than shifting the focus toward the team's collective identity, team leaders might emphasize differences between the functional subgroups. In such teams, the engineer has ready access to her engineering expertise and the graphics designer can easily evoke his design-related knowledge, which is essential for knowledge sharing and knowledge synthesis. In contrast, a unified collective identity that de-emphasizes members' diversity can undermine the ability of team members to draw on different identity-related knowledge sets to produce team-level innovations (Adarves-Yorno, Postmes, & Halsam, 2007). For example, to the extent that the engineer and the graphics designer in the cross-functional team suppress their function-specific identities within the team setting, their function-specific knowledge and expertise may well be inhibited or rendered less accessible.

It is important to note that, in addition to retaining differences, effective diverse teams must also create perceptions of compatibility across different identities within a team. MacPhail et al. (Chapter 14) suggest that "reciprocal expertise affirmation" allows diverse teams to retain functional differences while facilitating constructive communication and coordination. Specifically, reciprocal expertise affirmation fosters psychological safety within teams, which in turn facilitates the associated processes of understanding, valuing, and integrating differences within diverse teams. Cheng, Sanchez-Burks, and Lee (2008a) propose additional strategies that would facilitate similar dynamics. For example, in a cross-functional team, a designer might be asked to work intensively on a marketing analysis project, a task typically performed by a marketing expert. In the process, the designer realizes that the goals and priorities of the marketing group (such as making the product cheaper), although different, can be compatible with design goals (such as a cheaper material may make the product lighter and more versatile). This in turn increases the designer's identification beyond his or her own functional group to other functional groups as well.

Further, team cultures can engender whether team members value distinctiveness, a process integral to reciprocal expertise affirmation as described by MacPhail et al. (Chapter 14). In cross-functional teams where talking about function-specific goals and norms is "taboo," unique functional identities will be suppressed, and function-specific expertise and/or perspectives will be inhibited and less likely voiced and applied to the team's task. As Milton (Chapter 13) suggests, such identity-suppression or identity-negation processes can undermine cooperation within groups. Thus, the ability of teams to increase innovation may hinge on the ability to create a culture that retains the two distinct functional social identities.

There is a voice inside which speaks and says: "This is the real me!"

—**William James (1890)**

"AUTHENTIC" IDENTITIES AND RELATIONSHIPS: HOW DO MY RELATIONSHIPS AFFECT MY BEHAVIOR?

Of our many identities, perhaps the one most important to the "good life" is who we *really* are, or what Milton (Chapter 13) calls the authentic self. Three astute observers of human behavior, coincidentally all named William, support Milton's argument. We start again with William James who, as the quote above illustrates, argues that authenticity is critical to a positive identity. William Shakespeare echoes the same sentiment in his play *Hamlet*, where the character Polonius advises his son Laertes in Act I: "This above all; to thine own self be true / And it must follow as the night the day / Thou canst not then be false to any man." Shakespeare, like Milton (Chapter 13), suggests that acting authentically in our relationships is just as important as knowing who you are.

This fundamental motivation to know one's authentic self and behave accordingly is best illustrated by the research of a third William. William Swann, a psychologist, suggests that people are inherently driven to self-verify, or to seek out information that one knows to be true of one's self (Swann, Pelham, & Krull, 1989). In her chapter, Milton provides a detailed discussion of Swann's work on identity verification and confirmation. Briefly, Swann and his colleagues show that people choose interaction partners who are more apt to support their self-views; solicit feedback that confirm their self-views (even if they have to use their personal funds to get it, or even if they think that this feedback will make them depressed); pay more attention to, recall better, and consider more accurate information that is self-confirming (Swann, 1987). Presumably, verification of one's authentic self enables a stable and predictable self-conception that acts like a rudder of a ship in the murky seas of everyday social life.

Although the virtues of authenticity are clear, the road to authenticity has its downsides. As we argue below, research on relational dynamics suggests that true authenticity may not be practical or possible. In addition, there are conditions where authenticity is dysfunctional for relationships and groups, and times where inauthentic behaviors can be beneficial and valuable. We turn to these theories below.

Constructive Inauthenticity: Goffman's Polite Liars

In their chapter, Kopelman, Chen, and Shoshana (Chapter 12) suggest that our relational identities arise from our interactions with others. Similarly, LeBaron et al. (Chapter 9) posit that our identities are crafted through our everyday interactions with others, that what "is me" and what "isn't me" emerge from the verbal and nonverbal behaviors we enact when relating to others. Interestingly, these interactions need not be authentic to contribute to positive relational outcomes. In his seminal paper on facework, Goffman (1967) asserts that much, if not all, of our social interactions involve deceptions we perpetuate about others and ourselves. These seemingly inauthentic behaviors—half truths or downright lies—are not done to deliberately mislead or hurt others. Rather, Goffman asserts that these inauthentic behaviors are the basic "ground rules" of social interactions. They make our everyday interactions with others predictable, manageable, and pleasant. Moreover, these inauthentic behaviors communicate to others the basic respect and consideration we have for our interaction partners. As such, they are indispensable for any "positive" social interactions.

Fundamental to Goffman's (1967) theory is the idea of face, which refers to the "positive social value" each person can claim from an interaction with others. Interactants operate under the basic assumption that each will do what he or she can to save or maintain the face of others. When there is a possibility that another's face may be threatened—for example, when delivering a negative evaluation of another person that would undermine his or her positive image, or when communicating bad news that would lead to negative emotions—we engage in deliberate forms of facework to mitigate against the potential harm to another person's face (Lee, 1993, 1999). Goffman offers many examples of facework that involve inauthentic behaviors in some form or another—this includes reciprocal self-depreciation (e.g., publicly undermining oneself with the expectation that others will in turn compliment oneself), indirectness (e.g., using innuendo and ambiguity to communicate threatening information), avoidance (e.g., staying away from potentially threatening interactions or topics), and even deception (e.g., using false flattery).

Extending Goffman's (1967) analyses of everyday interactions, Brown and Levinson (1987) use social linguistics methodology to examine facework among a varied set of languages, including English from both sides of the Atlantic; Tzeltal, a Mayan language spoken in the community of Tenejapa in Chiapas, Mexico; and South Indian Tamil from a village in the Coimbatore district of Tamilnadu. In this work they found that facework is universally pervasive in our everyday communication. In fact, from modern societies to indigenous civilizations, facework constitutes a vast *majority* of what we say to others. We illustrate this idea using a single line in William Shakespeare's play *King Lear*. In the beginning of Act V, the character Edmund says to Albany: "If e'er your grace had speech with man so poor, hear me one word." Edmund's intention behind this line is clear—he wants Albany to listen to him. This sentence can be economically condensed into a single word "Listen." As such, what are we to make of all the excess verbal language? Why does Edmund waste time and effort saying 14 words when one will suffice to communicate his intention?

Goffman (1967) and Brown and Levinson (1987) would argue that much of what is said by Edmund is inauthentic facework. For example, Edmund flatters Albany by addressing him as "your grace" and deprecates himself by referring to himself as "man so poor." Edmund minimizes his request by characterizing what he wants to say as "one word," even though it is clear to both Edmund and Albany that he will say more than that. (In fact, Edmund goes on for a full seven lines after this.) Much of what is said is inauthentic, yet these words are essential if Edmund and Albany are to continue their relationship—these words are signals that Edmund esteems Albany, that Edmund is considerate of Albany's time, and ultimately that Edmund wants to maintain Albany's face (Brown & Gilman, 1989).

It is important to note that facework is often mutually recognized as inauthentic. In the case of reciprocal self-deprecation, for example, both interactants understand that one's person self-deprecating comments are not to be taken seriously. Rather, the fact that the speaker (or the person who self-deprecates in the relationship) has taken on this facework is a signal to the listener that the speaker highly respects and admires the listener. The listener is supposed to show appreciation for this sentiment by first flattering and complimenting the speaker profusely—thus engaging in another type of inauthentic facework to indicate respect and consideration for the speaker, and then turning around to deprecate oneself. This ritual routine of inauthentic behaviors—self-deprecation and flattery—is in fact an indication of more authentic intentions to show respect and consideration for others. As such, these pervasive and universal forms of inauthenticity are essential to many positive social interactions.

> We want all our [colleagues] to tell us our bad qualities; it is only the particular ass that does so whom we can't tolerate.

> **—William James (1890)**

Destructive Authenticity

Although inauthentic behavior such as facework can be conducive to positive relationships and teamwork, some authentic behaviors can undermine positive outcomes. As Kopelman et al. (Chapter 12) suggest in their chapter, some emotional displays can be counterproductive to positive relational outcomes. Responding reactively, spontaneously, and mindlessly to these emotional displays can lead to further dysfunctions. There is evidence suggesting that, in these situations, regulating and suppressing the expression of one's "true" self may be effective. For example, a critical aspect of emotional intelligence is the ability to harness, inhibit, and manage (rather than express) one's negative emotions (Lopes, Salovey, Côté, & Beers, 2005). When experiencing negative events, disengaging of the resultant negative emotions (while still acknowledging the event) improves individual and relational resilience and outcomes (Leary, Tate, Allen, Adams, & Hancock, 2007).

Beyond emotional experience, there are other aspects of authentic selfhood and identity that can undermine positive relational dynamics, or relationships that are productive, personally fulfilling to the interactants, and able to persist over time (Hackman, 1987). Sutton (2007), for example, recently examined people who persistently oppress, demean, de-energize, humiliate, and belittle others, especially those who are less powerful. For these individuals, authentic behavior is toxic for relationships—Sutton described one individual who went through 250 personal assistants in a span of 5 years; this person's abusive behaviors and attitudes toward others make maintaining a relationship with him impossible. Similar to what Milton (Chapter 13) argues, when others are not valued for who they are, authenticity may not be conducive to positive relationships.

For individuals who chronically fall into these destructive relational patterns, active and persistent efforts to curb authentic behaviors are essential if positive identities of others and relationships are to be realized. Sutton describes a manager who uses a four-step plan to help a coworker overcome his tendencies to oppress and demean others with the help of a roll of duct tape. When the coworker begins to behave in an oppressive manner, she first takes out the roll of tape and puts it beside him. If his behavior continues, she begins rolling the tape on the table. Third, she peels a section of the tape from the roll. Last, she takes the tape and sticks it over her colleague's mouth. This strategy works in part because this coworker has a sense of humor, but more importantly he has a genuine desire to change his ways (Sutton, 2006). This anecdote suggests that deliberate strategies to inhibit one's authentic self may be needed to create an effective and positive relational dynamic.

The great use of life is to spend it for something that will outlast it.

—William James (1890)

HOW DO MY INDIVIDUAL IDENTITIES RELATE TO MY RELATIONAL AND TEAM IDENTITIES?

This volume examines positive identities at different levels of analyses, such as individuals, relationships, groups, and organizations. In reading the chapters across the multiple sections of this book, one inevitably asks how positive identities across multiple levels are related. This essay raises several such propositions. On the one hand, positive identities at the individual level (e.g., integrating multiple conflicting identities) can predict outcomes at the relational level (e.g., richer and more diverse social networks). Or, mechanisms that occur at one level can also occur at a different level—for instance, just as activating different social identities simultaneously can be beneficial for individuals, the ability of teams to affirm the different identities of team members can reduce team process losses such as miscommunication or interpersonal conflict.

In addition, identity dynamics at one level may be necessary to engender identity dynamics at another level. For example, some of the chapters in this section suggest that positive individual identities are inherently products of negotiation with others. DeRue et al. (Chapter 10), for example, suggest that individuals need to claim the role of leadership, but others also have to grant it. In this way, assuming the role of leader must include others. Also, Ragins (Chapter 11) suggests that mentors play a critical role in helping their protégés develop their professional identities, and as such the identity-crafting process is inherently interpersonal. In fact, LeBaron et al. (Chapter 9) suggest that there is no individual identity that is independent of relational dynamics through which ideas of "me/not me" emerge.

Other chapters suggest that effective relationships must first start with a clear identity of the self, one that is defined before the interaction and can exist outside of the relationship. For example, Milton (Chapter 13) suggests that without a clear and preformed authentic identity, effective interactions will be impossible. Along the same vein, Kopelman et al. (Chapter 12) suggest that when relationship conflict occurs, one solution is to increase interpersonal distance—for example, to take a third-person perspective "outside" the relationship or to reduce emotional contagion within a relationship or a group.

A third perspective on this question is offered by the Dutch expression *Gezellig*. Among colleagues, friends, or family, someone will say "*gezellig*" when they sense that a special level of relational comfort or congenial ambience has been achieved. In these moments, individuals feel free to be themselves—*authentic*—in relation to others, and to mutually experience an affirmation of their individual and relational identities. Here, positive relational dynamics are neither consequences nor antecedents of individual identities, but positivity transfers fluidly between interactants in a relationship, blurring the boundaries between individuals. Although there is no direct English translation to *Gezellig*, this relational dynamic is echoed in Ragins's (Chapter 11) description of mentoring relationships where dimensions of the self and the relationship mutually reinforce one another. According to Ragins, such mentoring relationships create a "positive relational identity"—one that is unique to that relationship, and one in which the positivity is undisputed, genuine, and deeply experienced.

CONCLUSION

The quest for positive identities has seen a long history spanning multiple centuries and multiple disciplines. Psychologists such as William James, playwrights such as William Shakespeare, and sociologists such as Erving Goffman have examined many of the same questions around positive identities posed by this essay and the chapters in this book. As we grapple with the meaning of positive relational and group identities, we find that James may be right in claiming that "feeling good" cannot be the criterion for positivity. Indeed, positive relational and group identities can be related to feelings of conflict, ambiguity, and even inauthenticity. For example, a rich and diverse social network is associated with the propensity to simultaneously tap into two conflicting social identities (Mok et al., 2007). Or, a highly functional diverse team requires retaining intragroup differences rather than creating an overarching superordinate team identity (Cheng, Sanchez-Burks, & Lee, 2008b; MacPhail et al., Chapter 14). Or, effective communication of one's fundamental esteem or "positive social value" to others requires manifestly disingenuous facework (Goffman, 1967). This inherently complex and often paradoxical nature of positive identities may contribute in part to why positive identities are often elusive, despite our deep-seated drive to seek them in ourselves, our relationships, and the groups and communities to which we belong.

REFERENCES

Adarves-Yorno, I., Postmes, T., & Haslam, S. A. (2007). Creative innovation or crazy irrelevance? The contribution of group norms and social identity to creative behavior. *Journal of Experimental Social Psychology, 43,* 410–416.

Bassett-Jones, N. (2005). The paradox of diversity management, creativity and innovation. *Diversity Management, Creativity and Innovation, 14,* 169–175.

Benet-Martínez, V., & Haritatos, J. (2005). Bicultural identity integration (BII): Components and psychological antecedents. *Journal of Personality, 73,* 1015–1050.

Benet-Martínez, V., Leu, J., Lee, F., & Morris, M. (2002). Negotiating biculturalism: Cultural priming in blended and alternating Chinese-Americans. *Journal of Cross Cultural Psychology, 33,* 492–516.

Berry, J. W. (1990). Psychology of acculturation. In J. Berman (Ed.), *Cross-cultural perspectives: Nebraska symposium on motivation* (pp. 201–234). Lincoln, NE: University of Nebraska Press.

Brown, P., & Levinson, S. (1987). *Politeness: Some universals in language usage.* New York: Cambridge University Press.

Brown, R., & Gilman, A. (1989). Politeness theory in Shakespeare's four major tragedies. *Language in Society, 18,* 159–212.

Cheng, C., & Lee, F. (2008). *Who is your ingroup? It depends. Biculturalism and ingroup favoritism.* Unpublished manuscript, University of Michigan, Ann Arbor, MI.

Cheng, C., Lee, F., & Benet-Martínez, V. (2006). Assimilation and contrast effects in cultural frame switching (CFS): Bicultural identity integration (BII) and valence of cultural cues. *Journal of Cross Cultural Psychology, 37,* 1–19.

Cheng, C., Sanchez-Burks, J., & Lee, F. (2008a). Taking advantage of differences: Increasing team innovation through identity integration. In K. Phillips, M. Neale, and E. Mannix (Eds.), *Research on managing groups and teams: Diversity and groups* (Vol. 11, pp. 55–74). New York: Elsevier.

Cheng, C., Sanchez-Burks, J., & Lee, F. (2008b). Connecting the dots within: Identity integration and innovation. *Psychological Science, 19,* 1178–1184.

Cheng, C., Sanders, M., Sanchez-Burks, J., Molina, K., Lee, F., Darling, E., & Zhao, Y. (2008). Reaping the rewards of diversity: The role of identity integration. *Social and Personality Psychology Compass, 2,* 1182–1198.

Darr, E., Argote, L., & Epple, D. (1995). The acquisition, transfer, and depreciation of learning in service organizations: Productivity in franchises. *Management Science, 44,* 1750–1762.

De Dreu, C. K. W., & Weingart, L. R. (2003). Task versus relationship conflict, team performance, and team member satisfaction: A meta-analysis. *Journal of Applied Psychology, 88,* 741–749.

DeRue, S., Ashford, S., & Cotton, N. (2009). Assuming the mantle: Unpacking the process by which individuals internalize a leader identity. In L. Roberts & J. Dutton (Eds.), *Exploring positive identities and organizations: Building a theoretical and research foundation.* New York: Psychology Press.

Ely, R., & Thomas, D. (2001). Cultural diversity at work: The moderating effects of work group perspectives on diversity. *Administrative Science Quarterly, 46,* 229–273.

Ferlie, E., Fitzgerald, L., Wood, M., & Hawkins, C. (2005). The nonspread of innovations: The mediating role of professionals. *Academy of Management Journal, 48,* 117–134.

Fisher, P. (2008). *House of wits: An intimate portrait of the James Family.* New York: Henry Holt & Company.

Fiske, S. T. (1998). Stereotyping, prejudice, and discrimination. In D. T. Gilbert, S. T. Fiske, & G. Lindzey (Eds.), *The handbook of social psychology* (pp. 357–414). New York: McGraw-Hill.

Gaertner, S. L., Dovidio, J. F., Mann, J. A., Murrell, A. J., & Pomare, M. (1990). How does cooperation reduce intergroup bias? *Journal of Personality and Social Psychology, 59,* 692–704.

Gerbert, D., Boerner, S., & Kearney, E. (2006). Cross-functionality and innovation in new product development teams: A dilemmatic structure and its consequences for the management of diversity. *European Journal of Work and Organizational Psychology, 15*, 431–451.

Goffman, E. (1967). *Interaction ritual: Essays on face to face behavior.* New York: Anchor Books.

Hackman, J. R. (1987). The design of work teams. In J. W. Lorsch (Ed.), *Handbook of organizational behavior.* Englewood Cliffs, NJ: Prentice-Hall.

Hall, G. C. N., Lopez, I. R., & Bansal, A. (2001). Academic acculturation: Race, gender, and class issues. In H. L. K. Coleman & D. Pope-Davis (Eds.), *The intersection of race, class, and gender: Implications for multicultural counseling* (pp. 171–188). Thousand Oaks, CA: Sage.

Higgins, E. T. (1996). Knowledge activation: Accessibility, applicability, and salience. In E. T. Higgins & A. W. Kruglanski (Eds.), *Social psychology: Handbook of basic principles* (pp. 133–168). New York: Guilford.

Hong, Y., Morris, M., Chiu, C., & Benet-Martínez, V. (2000). Multicultural minds: A dynamic constructivist approach to culture and cognition. *American Psychologist, 55*, 709–720.

Ibarra, H., Kilduff, M., & Tsai, W. (2005) Zooming in and out: Connecting individuals and collectivities at the frontier, *Organization Science, 16*, 359.

James, W. (1890). *Principles of psychology.* Cambridge, MA: Harvard University Press.

James, W. (1905). *The varieties of religious experience.* New York: Longmans, Green.

Kane, A. A., Argote, L., & Levine, J. M. (2005). Knowledge transfer between groups via personnel rotation: Effects of social identity and knowledge quality. *Organizational Behavior and Human Decision Processes, 96*, 56–71.

Kopelman, S., Chen, L., & Shoshana, J. (2009). Re-narrating positive relational identities in organizations: Self-narration as a mechanism for strategic emotion management in interpersonal interactions. In L. Roberts & J. Dutton (Eds.), *Exploring positive identities and organizations: Building a theoretical and research foundation.* New York: Psychology Press.

Leary, M., Tate, E., Allen, A., Adams, C., & Hancock, J. (2007). Self-compassion and reactions to unpleasant self-relevant events: The implications of treating oneself kindly. *Journal of Personality and Social Psychology, 92*, 887–904.

LeBaron, C., Glenn, P., & Thompson, M. (2008). Identity work during boundary moments: Managing positive identities through talk and embodied interaction. In L. Roberts & J. Dutton (Eds.), *Exploring positive identities and organizations: Building a theoretical and research foundation.* New York: Psychology Press.

Lee, F. (1993). Being polite and keeping MUM: How bad news is communicated in organizational hierarchies. *Journal of Applied Social Psychology, 23*, 1124–1149.

Lee, F. (1999). Verbal strategies for seeking help in organizations. *Journal of Applied Social Psychology, 29*, 1472–1496.

Leung, K., Maddux, W. M., Galinsky, A. D., & Chiu, C. Y. (2008). Multicultural experience enhances creativity: The when and how. *American Psychologist, 63*, 169–181.

Lopes, P. N., Salovey, P., Côté, S., & Beers, M. (2005). Emotion regulation abilities and the quality of social interaction. *Emotion, 5*, 113–118.

MacPhail, L., Roloff, K., & Edmondson, A. (2009). Collaboration across knowledge boundaries within diverse teams: reciprocal expertise affirmation as an enabling condition. In L. Roberts & J. Dutton (Eds.), *Exploring positive identities and organizations: Building a theoretical and research foundation.* New York: Psychology Press.

Milton, L. (2009). Creating and sustaining cooperation in interdependent groups: Positive relational identities, identity confirmation and cooperative capacity. In L. Roberts & J. Dutton (Eds.), *Exploring positive identities and organizations: Building a theoretical and research foundation*. New York: Psychology Press.

Mok, A., Morris, M., Benet-Martínez, V., & Karakitapoglu-Aygun, Z. (2007). Embracing American culture: Structures of social identity and social networks among first-generation biculturals. *Journal of Cross-Cultural Psychology, 38,* 629–635.

Phillips, K. W., Mannix, E. A., Neale, M. A., & Gruenfeld, D. H. (2004). Diverse groups and information sharing: The effects of congruent ties. *Journal of Experimental Social Psychology, 40,* 497–510.

Phinney, J., & Devich-Navarro, M. (1997). Variation in bicultural identification among African American and Mexican American adolescents. *Journal of Research on Adolescence, 7,* 3–32.

Ragins, B. (2009). Positive identities in action: A model of mentoring self-structures and the motivation to mentor. In L. Roberts & J. Dutton (Eds.), *Exploring positive identities and organizations: Building a theoretical and research foundation*. New York: Psychology Press.

Roccas, S., & Brewer, M. B. (2002). Social identity complexity. *Personality and Social Psychology Review, 6,* 88–106.

Sacharin, V., & Lee, F. (in press). Identities in harmony: Assimilation and contrast in gender and professional identities. *Gender and Society.*

Shih, M., Pittinsky, T. L., & Ambady, N. (1999). Stereotype susceptibility: Identity salience and shifts in quantitative performance. *Research Report, 10,* 80–83.

Sutton, R. I. (2006). Places and people that use the no asshole rule. Retrieved October 1, 2008, from http://bobsutton.typepad.com/my_weblog/2006/06/the_no_asshole_.html.

Sutton, R. I. (2007). *The no asshole rule: Building a civilized workplace and surviving one that isn't.* New York: Business Plus.

Swann, W. (1987). Identity negotiation: Where two roads meet. *Journal of Personality and Social Psychology, 53,* 1038–1051.

Swann, W., Pelham, B., & Krull, D. (1989). Agreeable fancy or disagreeable truth? Reconciling self-enhancement and self-verification. *Journal of Personality and Social Psychology, 57,* 782–791.

van Knippenberg, D., & Haslam, S. A. (2003). Realizing the diversity dividend: Exploring the subtle interplay between identity, ideology, and reality. In S. A. Haslam, D. van Knippenberg, M. Platow, & N. Ellemers (Eds.), *Social identity at work: Developing theory for organizational practice* (pp. 205–221). New York: Taylor & Francis.

Part IV

Positive Identities and Organizations and Communities

16

Generative Organizational Identity Change: Approaching Organizational Authenticity as a Process

Kevin G. Corley and Spencer H. Harrison

CONTENTS

Plato, quoting Heraclitus, observed that, "everything flows, nothing stands still." A less elegant although more popular rephrasing of the sentiment argues that, "the only constant is change." Although there is certainly some truth underlying these beliefs, especially in the realm of organizations, does it necessarily hold all the time? Take for instance an organization's identity; not only does the original conceptualization of this phenomenon include the notion of enduringness or consistency (Albert & Whetten, 1985), but also several authors have noted the virtues that arise when companies "stick to your knitting" (Peters & Waterman, 1982) or stay true to "timeless core values" (Collins & Porras, 1994). Even when we see an organization undergo some form of identity change, it is often change in the service of not changing, or as Gagliardi (1986) explained it, "organizations must change to remain what they have always been … [they] must change in order to preserve identity."

But what about changes to an organization's identity that are genuinely about change, whether adaptive or transformative? What do we know about organizational identity change that involves a bona fide new understanding of what it means "to be us as an organization?" Much of the previous literature on organizational change, and identity change in particular, paints a bleak picture of significant amounts of organizational resources being devoted to pushing through a new set of identity labels or meanings that often meet fierce resistance and obstacles to implementation when finally presented to the bulk of an organization's membership. In other words, much of our current understanding of organizational identity change is as a degenerative process where, regardless of the ultimate outcomes of the change effort, more energy is spent in the change effort than is created either through the processes or outcomes of the change. This raises the following questions: Is generative identity change even possible in organizations? If so, what might it look and feel like? What is required of an organization to achieve such a generative approach to its identity change? To begin answering these questions, we first must consider our approach to the notion of organizational identity, as well as what we mean by generative change.

ORGANIZATIONAL IDENTITY

When we speak of organizational identity, it is important to note that we refer to it as a collective sense of "who we are as an organization" based in member perceptions, in contrast to other, more social actor conceptions (see Corley et al., 2006 for a discussion of this distinction). In line with this definition, we want to highlight the perspective that organizational identity is a situated and ongoing accomplishment wherein the members of an organization continually undertake to decide who they are as a collective and enact that sense of collective self given the internal and external realities they face as an organization (Carlsen, 2006; Weick, 1979). In this way, change in organizational identity need not be conceived of as a major transformation for the organization (although that is certainly possible; Gioia, Schultz, & Corley, 2000), but rather can include the day-to-day work (Leana & Barry, 2000) necessary to ensure that "who we are" aligns both with "who we want to be" and "who we need to be" as the organization moves through its institutional and competitive environments.

In some ways, this conception of organizational identity as an ongoing accomplishment reverberates with the platonic notion that an organization's identity might be inherently change-based (Tsoukas & Chia, 2002), making the notion of identity change easier to envision. If organizational identity change does not need to involve radical restructuring of how we conceive of ourselves and how others conceive of us, then the various impediments to change often mentioned in the literature (from individual resistance to structural barriers; e.g., Nag, Corley, & Gioia, 2007) can be significantly downplayed, perhaps even removed from the picture. Contrarily, however, the difficulty of change is still present in this socially constructed perspective of organizational identity because it is still change in the most foundational of areas for a collective, its self-definition. However, the difficulties of identity change can be easier to swallow when approached from a generative perspective.

GENERATIVE CHANGE

We are unaware of the explicit use of this term in the organizational sciences literature. Nonetheless, there are several concepts in the field, and specifically in the positive organizational scholarship (POS) area, that can be drawn on to illustrate what we mean by this term. In the broadest sense, generative change simply refers to organizational change that is implemented in such a way that both the process and outcomes of the change result in net positive returns in regard to emotional energy (Collins, 1981; Dutton, 2003; Quinn & Dutton, 2005), or "the feeling that one is eager to act and capable of action" (Baker & Quinn, 2007, p. 1). Participants in the change report "coming through the other side" of the change effort feeling better about themselves, the organization, and the process followed in implementing the change itself. Exemplar outcomes at various levels might include:

- Individuals experience a sense of growth and change in who they are and who they can be (e.g., "reflected best selves"; Roberts, Dutton, Spreitzer, Heaphy, & Quinn, 2005)
- Amplified "lateral thinking" (DeBono, 1970) and self-growth

- Improved resilience of both individuals and collectives (Weick & Sutcliffe, 2001)
- Enhanced collaborative interactions (Luscher & Lewis, 2008)
- Augmented organizational capacity for change (Jansen, 1996)

Building on these foundational concepts, we consider the notion of positive organizational identity for this book by examining a POS perspective on organizational identity *change*. We do so through the consideration of a case example of an organization we believe exhibits generative organizational identity change. Through an extensive field study in this organization over the past 2 years, we have come to understand a heretofore unexamined approach to generative identity change that involves enacting *authenticity as process*—a collective effort that involves an action component (comparison that invites participation) and a reflection component (respecting irony to engender variety). The enactment of these two components sets the conditions for the enabling of generative change as the organization is put in the position of continually seeking answers to the question "what does it mean to be who we are?" We detail the unique components of this form of generative change and explore how the organization goes about achieving it in a manner that has proven effective for them over the years. We conclude with a more general discussion of how this one organization's experiences with generative identity change provide insight into our understanding of identity change from a POS perspective and our understanding of positive identities more broadly.

OUR CASE EXAMPLE

To aid in this purpose, we draw on research we are currently conducting in an organization undergoing continual changes in the face of rapid growth, both in its performance as a company and in its organizing as a collective. Naturally, the organization's identity is implicated in this ongoing change; thus, the organization serves as an example from which we can draw insights on the potential for identity change to be generative in the way it is undertaken.

About the Organization

Over the past 2 years, we have conducted field research in an employee-owned outdoor sports company specializing in the manufacture and distribution of climbing and skiing equipment (to help maintain confidentiality, we use the pseudonym "ACS" throughout the rest of the chapter). ACS is a leader in the climbing and skiing industry—not only does the company's DNA go back to the beginning of the industry, but it is also widely recognized as one of the top manufacturers providing gear for climbing and skiing enthusiasts. This manufacturing prowess, although emblematic of external views of the organization, is not the sole basis for ACS's self-definition—its "anchor ethos statement," a key component of every year's strategic planning process and included in CEO communications, reads "Working to create a company on par, in mission, idealism, style, and action, with the life-defining activities of climbing, skiing, and alpinism that we were founded to serve." This notion of an intimate connection with, and ultimately a passion for, the sports the company serves is critical to how ACS goes about its business, both with external and internal stakeholders.

Closing in on its 20th anniversary as an independent company (it has been manufacturing climbing equipment for more than 50 years, however), ACS has manufacturing centers in both the United States and China and sales people located in more than 20 countries, with its 300 employees spread across locations on three continents. Large (but shrinking) portions of the employee population are considered "core users" of the skiing and climbing equipment for which the company is known. In fact, at any one time, ACS has some of the best climbers and skiers in the world working for them, whether it be in a full-time capacity as a designer or quality control engineer, as an endorsed athlete providing consulting on product or marketing, or as a seasonal worker in the manufacturing center earning enough money to take another extended trip to the slopes/crag.

ACS's growth has been remarkable and consistent, achieving double-digit growth in revenues for more than a decade and almost doubling revenues in the past 5 years. ACS is a relatively flat organization, with only four levels separating the lowest professional employees from the CEO. The senior leadership team consists of eight individuals, each responsible for a functional area of the company and each still very active in day-to-day decisions within that area. This is representative of a still young and vibrant organization living off the energy and chaos most often associated with entrepreneurial startups. Size and complexity have begun to impact operations in the past several years, however, and the company currently finds itself struggling with the transition from a small, nimble organization to a medium-sized firm where boundaries of structure and process play a more important role in day-to-day decisions.

During our time in ACS, we have had the luxury of conducting multiple in-depth interviews with all members of the top management team, as well as a broad and deep swath of the rest of the professional portion of the organization (almost 60 interviews with 41 informants). We have also been non-participant observers during two annual strategic planning cycles, sat in on several sales and manufacturing meetings, toured the manufacturing and distribution centers, and had detailed discussions with members of the marketing team about their sales and marketing strategies (including all customer and employee branding efforts—i.e., brochures, catalogs, web pages). We have helped the organization with its first all-employee culture survey and worked with the CEO to better understand the role employees can play in strategic change. All in all, we have been granted unfettered access to ACS and its members with the intent of gaining insight into how they manage their continued growth and the tensions that arise during such growth.

Growth and Change at ACS

As ACS has continued along its upward trajectory of financial and structural growth, anxiety has arisen about how to maintain growth in a way that continues to embody its heritage and yet still adapt to the new realities the company faces as a larger and more complex organization. In essence, ACS is trying to figure out, in the words of one informant, "how to reconfigure our approach to business without losing sight of who we are"—a seemingly paradoxical statement that nonetheless drives its current change efforts. So although the necessity of change is well accepted throughout the organization, the ultimate impact of that change on its organizational identity is a source of unease. This general anxiety reported throughout the company centers on two areas of conflicting demands: (a) how to continue growing without losing its entrepreneurial spirit, and (b) how to bring in new employees who have skills and experiences in critical business domains without tipping the balance away from having "core users" in key roles throughout the hierarchy.

The first concern is not necessarily unique to ACS; most small firms with entrepreneurial roots that find themselves successful enough to not only survive but also thrive competitively must negotiate the path from "simple and nimble" to "complex and stable" (see Lashinsky, 2008 for a similar phenomenon at Google). Even the desire to remain dynamic and adaptive in its stability is not unique to ACS; many organizations not only strive for this goal but also attain it (Gioia et al., 2000). What is perhaps distinctive about ACS's situation, however, is the intense way this entrepreneurial spirit is intertwined with its identity—not only is it how the company has defined itself for its full 20 years of independent existence, but it is also a key value in the sports by which the company has chosen to define itself. Climbing and skiing are activities that take individuals away from the complexity of modern society and, by contrast, provide a simpler, streamlined experience. At a superficial level, these sports provide enjoyment and entertainment much like any other hobby or recreational activity. However, these activities also often create "human versus nature" scenarios that provoke "human versus self" reflection—a climber caught in an ice cave has a lot of time for retrospective sensemaking. This occurs as individuals test their skills and courage in increasingly more difficult terrain while minimizing opportunities for retreat and thereby sharply reducing any margin for error. This latter form of climbing and skiing embraces an "alpinist ethos," a desire to achieve goals relying more on the technical skills and expertise of the individual or a small team rather than reducing the risk through a heavy reliance on technologically sophisticated gear and large support teams with retreat lines and more prudent levels of supplies. The goal of "alpinism" is to have climbers and skiers rely more squarely on their skills rather than relying on their gear and, in doing so, to create an experience that more fully challenges the individual rather than the equipment.

The differences between an alpinist ethos and a more recreational approach are often evident in climbers' stylistic choices on Mount Everest. For example, the teams that were involved in the famous Everest disaster of 1996 publicized in the Everest IMAX film and John Krakauer's *Into Thin Air* (1997) were not following alpinist ethics. Most of the climbers relied on supplemental oxygen and used "siege tactics," in which their camps were stocked by Sherpas ferrying food, gear, and additional oxygen up the mountain for them, as well as fixing rope lines for the climbers to follow. In contrast, in the same year, Goran Kropp rode a mountain bike from his home in Norway, across Russia and Nepal to the base of Everest. He then climbed Everest solo—without a support team checking the weather, stocking his tents, and preparing his food and without any supplemental oxygen—downclimbed Everest, and rode his bike back home (Kropp & Lagercrantz, 1999). Kropp's efforts epitomize the alpinist ethos: doing the most with the least in an effort to challenge human capability and ingenuity. This same alpinist philosophy pervades ACS's culture and structure, and although having proved successful over the past 20 years of being a small entrepreneurial firm, it is less clear how this philosophy will guide the organization as it grows larger and more complex.

The second area involves not only a key strategic process—recruitment and retention of employees—but also a key assumption within their cultural framework: "We can best serve our focal sports by ensuring that we ourselves are active and passionate participants in those sports." This assumption plays out in key ways in the organization, including:

- Every member of the senior leadership team is an active climber and/ or skier (some with strong reputations in their particular aspect of the sports).
- Most job interviews for key positions in design, engineering, and marketing involve a climbing or skiing session (some lasting several days) with the job candidate to help determine the person's passion for the sport and level of expertise with equipment.
- Employees regularly schedule "dawn patrols" where a group will meet to go climbing or skiing before sunrise and then head into work to put in a full day.
- Employees are regularly given new equipment for testing in the field or brought in as "BS detectors" for marketing materials to ensure quality standards are being met.
- ASC's campus includes a full-service climbing gym so that employees can either work out or learn the sport over lunch or after work (this includes a recently installed climbing wall at the Asian manufacturing/distribution center).

Because serving the sports plays such a prominent part of daily life inside ACS, the possibility of continued growth causing more and more "noncore users" to be brought into the company could create problems—the fewer climbers and skiers employed at ACS, the more likely that sports-based values and ideals will decrease in salience. New skills in areas like human resources, marketing, and computer-aided design and engineering are needed to help the organization keep up with competitors and the marketplace, yet the number of people in these fields that also fit the criteria of being a "core" climber/skier is relatively small. Thus, ACS finds itself faced with the very real scenario of core users becoming a minority in-house because of attrition and the increased hiring of noncore employees.

GENERATIVE IDENTITY CHANGE AT ACS

It is in the context of this growth and its accompanying demands that ACS's identity change process must be understood. The data we report in this section detail our grounded insights into how ACS approaches identity change, with a precise focus on the processes and factors that help explain why its attempts fall under the rubric of generative identity change.

Interestingly, at no time have our informants described a formal organizational identity change process (planned change at the level of identity labels) or even the desire for such an identity change. Yet, there is a general awareness that to keep up with the structural and processual changes occurring throughout the company, as well as those coming down the pipe, its identity must adapt. These adaptations are often subtle; the most prominent seem to focus on embracing an attitude of inclusion and welcoming a sense of professionalism as ACS seeks to attract individuals with more technical skill sets that might not have a climbing or skiing background. As the CFO observed, "I think certainly the organization will continue to evolve as new people come in with different sets of personal goals and priorities."

A key breakthrough in our understanding of ACS's approach to identity change came when we realized that the identity change the company saw as necessary was not based in answering the usual identity questions of "who are we?" or "who do we want to be?"—identity questions often invoked during times of identity ambiguity (Corley & Gioia, 2004) or identity conflict (Pratt & Foreman, 2000) instigated by either a perceived identity/image discrepancy (Dutton & Dukerich, 1991; Gioia et al., 2000) or a perceived temporal identity discrepancy (Corley & Gioia, 2004; Gioia & Thomas, 1996). In fact, ACS knows quite well "who they are" and "who they want to be"—there are no perceived identity discrepancies that we have encountered in our data collection and analysis efforts.

Instead, the change they see as necessary is based on answering the more advanced and complex identity question: "What does it mean to be who we are?" Answering this question represents a form of nondiscrepancy-based identity change because the meanings underlying their identity labels are up for redefinition as they come to better understand what it means "to create a company on par, in mission, idealism, style, and action, with the life-defining activities of climbing, skiing, and alpinism that we were founded to serve." So, for instance, although ACS's executives know confidently that the company is dedicated to advancing the sports of climbing and skiing, they are seeking answers as to what that means for how the company grows via acquisition or how they develop the right succession plan for their top executives. This nondiscrepancy-based form of identity change is best represented as a process involving a proactive effort to be authentic to its core values and beliefs; or, in other words, how ACS enacts identity change from the perspective of *authenticity as process*.

AUTHENTICITY AS PROCESS

The notion of authenticity is slippery, even without trying to establish the basis for applying it to organizations. Most common uses of the notion refer to correspondence with an original or "worthy of acceptance or belief as conforming to or based on fact" (*Merriam-Webster Online Dictionary*, 2008). But in applying the notion to a socially constructed entity like an organization, with no originals for comparison and little "fact" as a basis for conformance, these definitions do not necessarily work well. Perhaps this is why, to date, most applications of authenticity in the organizational sciences are found in discussions of individual authenticity (e.g., "authentic leadership," Avolio & Gardner, 2005), or authentic presentation of emotion (Ashforth & Tomiuk, 2000) or authentic marketing (cf., Grayson & Martinec, 2004).

In contrast to the still developing interest in authenticity in organizations (see Chapter 7 by Roberts, Cha, Hewlin, & Settles in the current volume), philosophers have long wrestled with the notion of authenticity, particularly existentialist philosophers. Much of this literature challenges the Western emphasis on materialism and the need to "have" with the need to "be"—the latter being seen as the more authentic approach to life. An attitude of being emphasizes a process-oriented approach to authenticity (e.g., "she wrestles with issues of authenticity") rather than a static or claim-based view of authenticity (e.g., "she is authentic"); that is, an attitude of being (as opposed to an attitude of having) highlights the differences between impermanence and permanence. Being is an impermanent state; it is generated from moments of action, by challenging the self to do new things, and reflection, by pondering what has happened and why. In contrast, having provides a sense of permanence because the individual receives a material thing rather than a fleeting feeling or thought. Authenticity begins to emerge as individuals realize that the impermanent moments of being provide a greater sense of durability because they breed adaptability and evolution. Moving from having to being necessitates a shift away from permanence to impermanence, which engenders an evolution to a new kind of permanence that embraces the "flowing" undulations of life. In essence, authenticity becomes the constant search for self—by searching one is being (see Pratt & Kraatz, Chapter 17 in this volume for a detailed discussion on the self, especially their explanation of Mead's notion of self at the organizational level).

Another reason for viewing authenticity as a process rather than a state emerges from the realization that claims of authenticity represent pragmatic paradoxes (Watzlawick, Bavelas, & Jackson, 1967). Pragmatic paradoxes create catch-22, no-win scenarios where any action invalidates the purpose of the action. For example, consider the observation "to try to be cool is to not be cool" (Sacks, 2008)—coolness connotes a sense of natural ease, so in trying to be cool the potential of achieving the goal of coolness is nullified. Similarly, claims of authenticity immediately provoke questions such as "if you were authentic, then why would you have to draw attention to it?" Rather than assessing the veracity of a claim of authenticity, approaching authenticity as a process provides the wherewithal to avoid the pragmatic paradox and refocus attention on whether an entity is pursuing authenticity (not whether it has been attained).

Although the philosophy literature contains disagreements about specific definitions and characteristics of authenticity, there is a fair degree of convergence regarding two mechanisms that seem to undergird the process of authenticity, namely, *action* and *reflection*. Action includes notions of vitality and play (Ferrara, 1998), spontaneity (Golomb, 1995), and creation (Chen, 2004), often in the face of systems that might inhibit or forestall these behaviors. In this literature action tends to be inventive and original, as Chen summarizes by opining "authenticity requires constant creativity, not just creativity. An authentic person is constantly more than what the person is now and here" (2004, p. 49).

Reflection is epitomized by the Delphic maxim "know thyself" and includes ideas like questioning and inquiry (Chen, 2004), awareness of one's limits (Guignon, 2004), and approaching the world with a sense of wonder (Trilling, 1980). Furthermore, reflection and action have a rich interplay—reflection promotes action by helping individuals become mindful of their identities, to use deeply held values and personal narratives as resources that enable new enactments of self. Action, particularly the inventive forms listed above, challenges the individual to adopt new frames of seeing and thereby promotes reflection.

In applying this understanding of the dynamics of authenticity as process to organizations, it is necessary to understand how its two components, action and reflection, are enacted in change processes across the organization. We do so by exploring the emergent themes of "comparison inviting participation" (how ACS embodies the action component) and "irony engendering variety" (how ACS embodies the reflection component).

Action: Comparison Inviting Participation

The ACS ethos statement ("Working to create a company on par, in mission, idealism, style, and action, with the life-defining activities of climbing, skiing, and alpinism that we were founded to serve") is notable for several reasons. First, it includes a specific and exacting reference to the sports the company serves and the ideals embodied in those sports. In a very real sense, by basing their identity on external activities (climbing and skiing) and their related ideals, the members of ACS have made themselves accountable to their organizational audience (customers, institutional agencies, and stakeholders that oversee the sports, even land managers that maintain access)—or as one informant explained:

> If we can create a product that inspires someone to go out there and do something they haven't done before and push themselves, then we're being authentic to not only ourselves but to that customer and their expectations.

This stringent level of accountability beckons a comparison between the company and the sport, in essence invoking the question, "does the company uphold the ideals of the sport." But, just as this question mobilizes scrutiny from the external audience, it mobilizes interest from the members of the organization. In effect, the organization's identity affords the opportunity to promote participation in two interconnected ways: participation in the sports themselves and, as a result, greater participation in the company. One informant noted this dual participation in ACS's hiring patterns:

> Obviously to be a designer you had to have some design or engineer knowledge, and it was nice if you had some business knowledge if you were going to work in the planning department and it was good that I had some accounting knowledge, but that was secondary to being a group of like-minded individuals who participated in the sports we serve and care about the environment and the community and the face of our sports within society.

Participation in the sport leads employees to ask the aforementioned question, comparing company and sport. As a result, employees are able to see the organization as customers would, through the lens of the sport. Employees who adopt this perspective gain an additional level of credibility within the organization because they are able to question organizational choices with a level of expertise. For example, individuals who participate in the sports often provide input on new product designs, photographs for advertising, or essays to be included in catalogs, and their opinions, whether accepted or not, are generally respected because of their level of participation in the sports. A clear example comes from one of our informants in the marketing department explaining what it is like when someone outside of marketing disagrees with an idea of his:

> It's usually pretty heated because everybody's got that stake that their holding and they have some pretty passionate ideas about what it should be. So, you know, it never gets to the point where it's defensive or anything because everybody has that understanding that it's part of the style, the management of the company as well as just like the style of climbing. There's a lot of disagreement about style, you know how you should climb this or that or whether you should be using this tool for this purpose, but there's a certain level of respect that goes along with that. Like if you see somebody's innovating in maybe a totally different way than you think is appropriate, you

still have a certain level of respect for them getting out there and pushing those limits. I think a lot of it comes back to that.

The phrases "working to create," "on par," and "that we were founded to serve" in ACS's ethos statement reduce the potential forcefulness of the statement—without these words, the statement would sound almost brazen, suggesting an eventual end point. Indeed, the original version of the statement from the company's genesis read "one with the sports we serve: absolutely indistinguishable from them." Although potentially more inspiring, it is also more rigid and less inviting of participation. By changing the statement and adding the above phrases as hedges, a sense of reverence has been added, thus placing the company below the ideals it is striving for. The vice president of sales noted how this reverence generates additional reflection and inquiry:

As the day-to-day environment here changes, the business requirements here tend to change from what is very directly related to a climbing-skiing ethos. The big challenge is "how do we keep our heads straight?", even here. So we're super aware of it and all we can do is just keep talking and try to exemplify [the mission] in how we run the business and deal with every single situation.

The result of this reverential mindset is a focus on process. As a result, the purpose of the company becomes a "flowing"—a means rather than an end. Durand and Calori emphasize the importance of means versus ends orientations in change, hinting that individuals in a means-oriented environment are able "to gain a deeper understanding of their organization's strengths and weaknesses, to be more alert, and to gather more relevant information useful for conducting change" (2006, p. 100). Because information is more accessible, the organization itself appears more transparent and fluid, connoting a sense of impermanence.

The result is a reversal of Weick's observation that "microstrength shapes macroweakness" (1996, p. 52)—that is, strong personalities produce actions that offer guideposts for coherence and interpretation in novel or weak situations—at ACS, macroweakness invites microstrength, generating spaces for individual voice and improvisation. At ACS, voice and improvisation often look and feel similar to Luscher and Lewis' (2008) notion of sparring. Luscher and Lewis found that individuals often respond to contextual paradox (a form of macroweakness) by engaging in inquiry and debate, which generate coherence by surfacing assumptions and broadening thought repertoires. Likewise, we found that individuals at ACS often feel empowered to offer their opinions on projects that are completely divorced from their department's purview simply because the individual feels a duty derived from their connection to the sports.

The macroweaknesses engendered in the reverent phrases of the ethos statement emerge in other ways throughout the organization. For example, the agenda for the strategic planning process contained a session outlined purely by questions such as, "What is our business and what should it be?" Similarly, a few days later during a breakout session with middle managers the CEO offered, "we need to be open-minded enough to say, 'do our strategic objectives make sense?' Consistency is a virtue of small minds." Another macroweakness is the open office spaces that allow casual observers to see what is on a designer's desk, to look inside the product testing lab to see freshly broken prototypes of upcoming products, or to glance at the screen of a graphic designer and see recent photographs that might be included in advertising collateral. This openness attracts feedback, in a sense provoking individuals to provide more of themselves, helping foster a generative form of change.

Reflection: Irony Engendering Variety

The second aspect of generative identity change at ACS is a respect for the ironic. Consider the observation: "Embedded in the norms of most groups is an awareness that a certain degree of dissent and critical self reflection is desirable" (Postmes & Jetten, 2006, p. 77). Similarly, Benson argues

> at the level of organizations, the multiple levels and divisions form differentiated contexts within which social production proceeds in a partially autonomous manner. As a result the fabric of social life is rent with contradictions growing out of the unevenness and disconnectedness of social production" (1977, p. 5).

The implication is that, although rationality, consistency, and uniformity are often considered hallmarks of organizations, the social reality of existing within an organization is fraught with duality, paradox, and irony. Consider these quotes from our first interview with the CEO:

It's kind of an exciting place to be right now because people realize that and go, again, all humility aside, I don't think ever before in one company in the climbing and back country skiing industry has anybody ever assembled the manufacturing competency, the sourcing competency, the engineering and design competency with passion in one organization and people feel that.

Later in the interview:

Interviewer: "So what values are most important to who ACS is as a company?"

CEO: "I'd say first it's the qualities of an Alpinist, of a climber. Then you ask what are those? And I think, so then I would define them, one is, I mean I think one thing that true climbing, and I'm talking about Alpinism, what Alpinism will teach you is humility—that hubris will kill you. So, that's something—humility."

Although not directly contradicting one another, when read together the two quotes demonstrate conflicting views of elitism and humility— the first explicitly tosses humility aside and pridefully celebrates elitism, whereas the second shows veneration for humility, describing it as one of the primary values of the company. The coexistence of elitism and humility is widespread throughout ACS, and informants were regularly able to seamlessly discuss both without hesitation. This suggests a level of comfort with the ironic and paradoxical.

Another example of respect for irony is the relationship between individuals and the collective. In an industry as individual focused as the outdoor industry (although teams do work together on "big projects," much of climbing and skiing is about individual achievement), it is almost paradoxical for an organization to expect cohesion and teamwork from its outdoor-enthusiast employees. And yet, ACS not only expects it but also excels at it, as evidenced by the complex products the company is known for designing and manufacturing at high-quality levels (products that require significant coordination and teamwork). This is all the more remarkable considering the historical importance ACS has put on hiring accomplished skiers and climbers, most of whom are used to depending on their own skills and experiences for success. Indeed, our initial desire to research individuals in the outdoor industry was guided by a curiosity about how the independent individualists attracted to outdoor sports fare in organizations with strong collective identities. What we have found in ACS is a willingness, almost a passion, for "working through" this paradox (Luscher & Lewis, 2008, p. 234) via the simultaneous embracing of both the individual and the collective in day-to-day work interactions. Consider how the following quote seamlessly meanders from a concern with the group to a concern for the individual:

> But the team, it's about the team. It's collegial, it's collaborative, it's transparent and that's, the best climbing teams are those that work as a real team, understand each other, are accommodating of each other's strengths and weaknesses. It's one of respect, being very respectful of the competency of one's peer and treating them with all due respect.

And this quote about what it takes to be an effective member of ACS:

> I think a lot of times one of the desirable traits in looking for someone to work here is a certain amount of autonomy and a certain amount of willingness to take on things individually. And so, not to generalize, but that oftentimes can lead to strong personalities and some hard-headedness … yet, if there's not some organization and there's not some structure to what we're doing then, the volume alone is just too much to be able to handle. [To be effective here] you need to have that autonomous mentality while still being able to work within a certain structure that the company needs.

Thus, the irony of being strong individuals working within and for the greater good of a strong collective is not lost on most members of ACS, especially those who have shown a commitment to the company beyond just the few years many noncore users put in ("people that come to work for [ACS] are either here for a year or two and gone, or they're here for 5 or 10 years").

Organizations often resolve ironies such as these by emphasizing one end of the spectrum over the other. For example, according to Weiner (1988), a common irony is that organizations often contain both elitist values (e.g., "we are a superior company" or "we are the best") and functional values (e.g., "we provide excellent service"), but they tend to emphasize one or the other. Similarly, reward systems are often structured to emphasize either collective or individual rewards. ACS shuns this conventional solution and maintains these dualities. They exist symbolically throughout the organization. For example, elitism is demonstrated by the multiple awards that sit on the desk next to the front entrance, whereas humility is symbolized in broken pieces of gear embedded in the conference room tables or welded into mobiles hanging from the ceiling. The juxtaposition of awards and broken gear indicates the superiority of ACS's products and their potential fragility—elitism and humility. This juxtaposition also serves as a physical example of Kundera's comment about the function of irony: "[irony] denies us our certainties by unmasking the world as an ambiguity" (1988, p. 134).

The existence of ironies, perhaps, more accurately the maintenance of ironies, inculcates variety by inviting inquiry. Because examples of broken products are proudly displayed, these artifacts serve as cues that trigger the search for better design, better production, and better testing. In turn, rewards and the concomitant sense of elitism confirm a sense of competence and efficacy. Together, the iteration between the competing values that form an ironic duality provides multiple frames that individuals can use to view a situation and thereby increases the possibility for detecting novelty and crafting new puzzles to ponder. The result is a more mindful, curious environment that promotes the reflexivity necessary for generative identity change.

In the end, action and reflection allow individuals to view the organizational identity as resource (rather than a constraint), while also facilitating the production of new resources via engagement with the organization's identity—thus, continually answering the question "what does it mean to be us?" does not necessarily promote the same answers because participation and variety constantly bring new perspectives to the table, affording the organization a form of resilience (Weick & Sutcliffe, 2001) in the face of continual growth and change.

DISCUSSION

We defined generative change in our introduction as "change that is implemented in such a way that both the process and outcomes of the change result in net positive returns in regard to emotional energy." ACS has found a way to approach the prospect of organizational identity change in a generative manner by eschewing the typical approach of "be content with who we are until discrepancies arise that force us to reassess that identity" and instead pursuing a more dynamic sense of self grounded in the notion of "authenticity as process"—a near-continual search for its authentic self based in answering the question "what does it mean to be who we are?" In the former approach, organizational identity exists as a fairly static, inert outcome of collective sensemaking that provides stability yet also produces fear when shocks occur; malleability occurs only under the stress of uncertainty; thus, change is experienced as painful, or at least uncomfortable (Durand & Calori, 2006). The energy necessary to deal with this pain and discomfort, not to mention the energy required to begin moving forward again, is what helps make traditionally approached identity change so degenerative.

On the other hand, identity change based in "authenticity as process" invites members to continually ask what it means to be us during their common work behaviors—designing new equipment, discussing copy for a catalog, debating new hires—without the stress or fear experienced during discrepancy-based shock (indeed, individuals often seem to enjoy these opportunities). The upshot is a relatively continuous level of malleability that provides the organization with a sense of forward momentum in its identity. By creating a positive trajectory of change (as opposed to a trajectory of stability interrupted by change), the organization is able to conserve (and sometimes even build) emotional energy. The result is generative identity change because instead of asking members to react and redefine "who we are" in times of shock and disequilibrium (as a discrepancy model of change implies), a trajectory of positive momentum affords the organization an evenness to its identity change processes that removes much of what members fear and dread about identity change.

Given that ACS has been engaged in its approach to authenticity as a process for at least the 2 years we have been observing the company (and indications are the company was engaged in it before this time as well) and it shows no signs of change fatigue or overload (Corley & Gioia, 2004) when it comes to the organizational identity, it is clear to us that ACS has achieved at least some level of generative change. In fact, the energy levels expressed around understanding what it means to be ACS sometimes surprise us as we observe the passion with which the company pursues action and reflection around its self-definition. Indeed, when we first approached ACS about doing research, our contact took great pains to help us understand the lengths that members of ACS went to in pursuing success in business with a "style" that resonated with success in the sports they support.

A key component to understanding how ACS has been able to accomplish this is found in the details of "authenticity as process." As our empirical narrative described, authenticity as process involves two notions from the classic authenticity literature, action and reflection. Together, action and reflection serve as mutually reinforcing practices that foster a functional awareness of impermanence that becomes embedded in organizational symbols (e.g., broken carabineers, epitaphs to dead employees), narratives (a dedication to means not ends), and strategic plans (play with strange ideas, focus on challenging, big goals). This collective sense of impermanence is functional because it increases requisite variety and thereby dislodges the organization from the potential downfalls of simplicity (Miller, 1990). This increased variety, in turn, fosters adaptation to changing realities and provides a foundation on which the organization can evolve over time. Continued adaptation and evolution demand an equally constant search for understanding of the self, virtually guaranteeing the improbability of "achieving" a state of authenticity, and thus driving the need for more action and reflection.

In this way, authenticity as process represents one possible path to generative identity change, which itself represents one of two possible ways organizational identity change can occur (see Figure 16.1).

GENERALIZING BEYOND OUR CASE EXAMPLE

In many ways, ACS is a unique organization—one with its business focus also being a pastime that engenders passion in its participants, and having those passionate participants not only be core users of the organization's products but also its employees. In other, important ways, however, ACS is like many other organizations in today's hypercompetitive markets— one where progress is sought after but comes with growing pains in both structure and process; one where change has become ubiquitous, to the point that sometimes it seems to simply blend into the day-to-day vagaries of work; and one where the fundamental notion of identity serves as key guide and enabler of future action. In this way, we feel our emergent

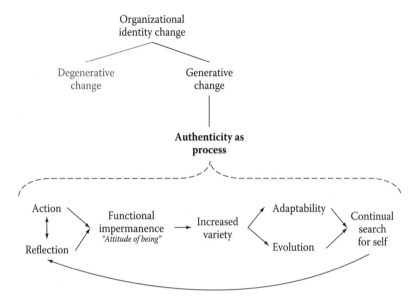

FIGURE 16.1
Generative identity change at ACS: enacting authenticity as process.

findings on how ACS approaches identity change from a positive perspective can be generalized beyond its boundaries.

So, how are these notions and processes of generative change possible in other organizations? We believe that although our report focuses on ACS's specific approach, other approaches to authenticity as a process are possible. Mechanisms of action and reflection other than those reported at ACS can be institutionalized at the organizational level and thereby enable organizations to pursue authenticity as a process for generative identity evolution. We believe it is important for researchers interested in organizational identity change to pay close attention to how their focal organizations deal with questions of authenticity, looking especially for ways in which action and reflection manifest around those authenticity questions. Doing so will not only increase the use of a POS perspective in the study of identity change, but it can also provide valuable insight on the effects of organizational identity change on individual members of the organization, an area of knowledge currently lacking in substance.

It is also possible that some organizations may not be well-suited for approaching authenticity as a process, and thus experiencing generative change in their organizational identity. Research exploring the obstacles and barriers to action and reflection around organizational authenticity will also provide key insights into the boundary conditions of this emergent theory, as well as begin providing more potential for exploring how organizations can proactively change their orientation toward identity change and its generative side. Finally, future research can also explore in depth the individual and collective outcomes associated with generative organizational identity change. We suggested some conceptual possibilities in the introduction, and our observation of ACS's approach supports the potential of many of these, most notably improved resilience, enhanced collaborative interactions, and suggestions of augmented capacity for change.

Ultimately, we return to the questions that launched our inquiry: Is generative identity change possible in organizations? If so, what might it look and feel like? What is required of an organization to achieve such a generative approach to its identity change? In describing how our case organization achieved generative identity change by approaching organizational authenticity as a process through action and reflection, we believe we have provided initial answers to these questions, answers we hope mark the trailhead of a new path toward a greater understanding of organizational identity change.

REFERENCES

Albert, S., & Whetten, D. (1985). Organizational identity. In L. L. Cummings & B. M. Staw (Eds.), *Research in organizational behavior* (Vol. 7, 263–295). Greenwich, CT: JAI Press.

Ashforth, B. E., & Tomiuk, M. A. (2000). Emotional labour and authenticity: Views from service agents. In S. Fineman (Ed.), *Emotion in organizations*. London: Sage.

Avolio, B. J., & Gardner, W. L. (2005). Authentic leadership development: Getting to the root of positive forms of leadership. *Leadership Quarterly, 16,* 315–338.

Baker, W. E., & Quinn, R. E. (2007). *Energy networks and information use.* Ann Arbor, MI: Ross School of Business, University of Michigan.

Benson, J. K. (1977). Organizations: A dialectical view. *Administrative Science Quarterly, 22,* 1–21.

Carlsen, A. (2006). Organizational becoming as dialogic imagination of practice: The case of the indomitable Gauls. *Organization Science, 17,* 132–149.

Chen, X. (2004). *Being and authenticity.* New York: Rodopi.

Collins, J. C., & Porras, J. I. (1994). *Built to last: Successful habits of visionary companies.* New York: HarperCollins.

Collins, R. (1981). On the micro-foundations of macro-sociology. *American Journal of Sociology, 86,* 984–1014.

Corley, K. G., & Gioia, D. A. (2004). Identity ambiguity and change in the wake of a corporate spin-off. *Administration Science Quarterly, 49,* 173–208.

Corley, K. G., Harquail, C. V., Pratt, M. G., Glynn, M. A., Fiol, C. M., & Hatch, M. J. (2006). Guiding organizational identity through aged adolescence. *Journal of Management Inquiry 15,* 85–99.

DeBono, E. L. T. (1970). *Lateral thinking.* New York: Harper and Row.

Durand, R., & Calori, R. (2006). Sameness, otherness? Enriching organizational change theories with philosophical considerations on the same and the other. *Academy of Management Review, 31,* 93–114.

Dutton, J. E. (2003). *Energize your workplace,* San Francisco: Jossey-Bass.

Dutton, J. E., & Dukerich, J. M. (1991). Keeping an eye on the mirror: Image and identity in organizational adaptation. *Academy of Management Journal, 34,* 517–554.

Ferrara, A. (1998). *Reflective authenticity: Rethinking the project of modernity.* New York: Routledge.

Gagliardi, P. (1986). The creation and change of organizational cultures: A conceptual framework. *Organization Studies, 7,* 117–134.

Gioia, D. A., Schultz, M., & Corley, K. G. (2000). Organizational identity, image and adaptive instability. *Academy of Management Review, 25,* 63–81.

Gioia, D. A., & Thomas, J. B. (1996). Identity, image, and issue interpretation: Sensemaking during strategic change in academia. *Administrative Science Quarterly, 41,* 370–403.

Golomb, J. (1995). *In search of authenticity.* New York: Routledge.

Grayson, K., & Martinec, R. (2004). Consumer perceptions of iconicity and indexicality and their influence on assessments of authentic market offerings. *Journal of Consumer Research, 31,* 296–312.

Guignon, C. B. (2004). *On being authentic.* London: Routledge.

Jansen, K. J. (1996). Characteristic level of change: An inherent constraint to organizational action. *The International Journal of Organizational Analysis, 4,* 285–298.

Krakauer, J. (1997). *Into thin air: A personal account of the Mount Everest disaster.* New York: Villard.

Kropp, G., & Lagercrantz, D. (1999). *Ultimate high: My Everest odyssey.* New York: Discovery Books.

Kundera, M. (1988). *The art of the novel* (1st ed.). New York: Grove Press.

Lashinsky, A. (2008). Where does Google go next? Retrieved May 15, 2008, from http://money.cnn.com/2008/05/09/technology/where_does_google_go.fortune/index.htm.

Leana, C. R., & Barry, B. (2000). Stability and change as simultaneous experiences in organizational life. *Academy of Management Review, 25,* 753–759.

Luscher, L. S., & Lewis, M. W. (2008). Organizational change and managerial sensemaking: Working through paradox. *Academy of Management Journal, 51,* 221–240.

Merriam-Webster Online Dictionary (2008). Retrieved May 15, 2008, from http://www.merriam-webster.com/dictionary/authentic.

Miller, D. (1990). *The Icarus paradox: How exceptional companies bring about their own downfall.* New York: HarperBusiness.

Nag, R., Corley, K. G., & Gioia, D. A. (2007). The intersection of organizational identity, knowledge, and practice: Attempting strategic change via knowledge grafting. *Academy of Management Journal, 50,* 821–847.

Peters, T. J., & Waterman, R. H. (1982). *In search of excellence: Lessons from America's best run companies.* New York: Harper & Row.

Postmes, T., & Jetten, J. (2006). *Individuality and the group: Advances in social identity.* London: Sage.

Pratt, M. G., & Foreman, P. O. (2000). Classifying managerial responses to multiple organizational identities. *Academy of Management Review, 25,* 18–42.

Quinn, R. W., & Dutton, J. E. (2005). Coordination as energy-in-conversation. *Academy of Management Review, 30,* 36–57.

Roberts, L. M., Dutton, J. E., Spreitzer, G. M., Heaphy, E. D., & Quinn, R. E. (2005). Composing the reflected best-self portrait: Building pathways for becoming extraordinary in work organizations. *Academy of Management Review, 30,* 712–736.

Sacks, D. (2008, June). Believe it or not, he's a PC. *Fast Company,* 64–73.

Trilling, L. (1980). *Sincerity and authenticity* (uniform ed.). New York: Harcourt Brace Jovanovich.

Tsoukas, H., & Chia, R. (2002). On organizational becoming: Rethinking organizational change. *Organization Science, 13,* 567–582.

Watzlawick, P., Bavelas, J. B., & Jackson, D. D. (1967). *Pragmatics of human communication: A study of interactional patterns, pathologies, and paradoxes* (1st ed.). New York: Norton.

Weick, K. E. (1979). *The social psychology of organizing* (2nd ed.). Reading, MA: Addison-Wesley.

Weick, K. E. (1996). Enactment and the boundaryless career: Organizing as we work. In M. B. Arthur & D. M. Rousseau (Eds.), *The boundaryless career: A new employment principle for a new organizational era* (pp. 40–57). Oxford, England: Oxford University Press.

Weick, K. E., & Sutcliffe, K. M. (2001). *Managing the unexpected: Assuring high performance in an age of complexity.* San Francisco: Jossey-Bass.

Weiner, Y. (1988). Forms of value systems: A focus on organizational effectiveness and cultural change and maintenance. *Academy of Management Review, 13,* 534–545.

17

E Pluribus Unum: Multiple Identities and the Organizational Self

Michael G. Pratt and Matthew S. Kraatz

CONTENTS

Organizational identity research has proliferated in recent years, and the core community of identity scholars has steadily expanded to include institutionalists, ecologists, and strategy scholars. Although this growth and progress are encouraging, several recalcitrant and deep-rooted questions seem to repeatedly emerge in theoretical discussions of organizational identity. These questions, which also spill over into empirical identity research, include the following:

- How can we reconcile the compelling idea that organizations have identities that are unique, internally generated, and self-possessed with the equally powerful observation that organizational identities are externally ascribed and categorical in nature?
- In a similar vein, how can we reconcile the idea that organizational identity is a font of purposive action and a resource for agentic organizational behavior with the observation that it represents a key source of social constraint?
- How can we reconcile the idea that organizational identity represents a shared set of foundational beliefs that serves a socially integrative function with the commonly observed reality of identity multiplicity, fragmentation, and conflict within individual organizations?

The key tensions embedded in these questions have been surfaced and debated within the identity literature (see Corley et al., 2006) but appear to have intensified as our understanding of identity grows. Newer and more distinctly sociological perspectives are revealing and useful in that they clearly position the organization within its societal context and thus draw attention to the social/institutional categories that provide some of the raw materials for determining "who an organization is." Organizational identities, after all, do not materialize out of thin air, and it would appear possible to explain a good part of any organization's identity simply by attending to the larger institutional context of which it is a part. However, this new sociological knowledge seems to come at a substantial cost. To the extent that we see identities as socially ascribed, categorical, and constraining (Hannan, Baron, Hsu, & Kocak, 2006), it becomes more difficult to see them as sources of uniqueness and agency, as well as genuine social integrators of pluralism. Thus, many of the things that organizational identity scholars have historically found valuable about the concept appear to be at risk in light of this newer knowledge.

The reason for these tensions may be that "organizational identity," as a concept, is asked to bear too much weight. Can one term meaningfully capture the societally embedded, categorical, similarity-producing, objective, constrained part of the organization AND the unique, autonomous, self-acting, socially integrative, subjective part of the organization? The purpose of our chapter is to introduce a concept that may help mitigate these tensions and, in doing so, introduce a new way of thinking about organizational identity. The concept that we introduce is the *organizational self.* Although the term "self" in most common usage is merely a synonym for identity, it has a very distinct meaning in sociological theories of the self. The theories to which we specifically refer are those that have been developed in various streams of structural symbolic interactionism, a perspective that traces its roots to Mead's (1934) *Mind, self and society*. This perspective provides a useful conceptualization of the self and an alternative way to think about the integrally related and complementary concept of identity. Specifically, this view sees the self as the "whole" entity that encompasses an actor's multiple socially ascribed identities, and more specifically as an integrative structure that orders these various identities and binds them together. Although these sociological theories have been developed exclusively at the individual level of analysis, we believe that they are readily and fruitfully transferrable to the organizational level of analysis. Our chapter aims to provide this translation, as well as to elaborate some of the theoretical (and ultimately practical) benefits that may be obtained from it.

Because our chapter attempts to break new theoretical ground and to grapple with some very deep-seated tensions, it is appropriate for us to specify a few caveats before we proceed. To begin, we do not propose that our theoretical translation efforts can ultimately "solve" the recalcitrant problems that we identified in the opening paragraph. These tensions are rooted in alternative paradigms, and some might argue that they are inherent in social life and social organizing. Our approach is essentially an ameliorative one. Second, we wish to emphasize that we introduce the notion of the organizational self as a *metaphor*, rather than a literal thing that can be empirically verified and pinned down. We will suggest that it might be *useful* to think of organizations as if they are selves (i.e., as if they are quasi-integrated entities that are made up of multiple, socially ascribed identities), but we will not claim that this is necessarily *the* best way for identity scholars to think about organizations. In light of the goals of this book, we believe that adding an organizational self metaphor to ongoing conversations about organizational identity is especially useful in revealing its role in serving the seemingly paradoxical purposes implied in our questions. In doing so, we hope to reveal the highly generative potential of these concepts for all students of organizations. In particular, an organizational self infuses identity conversations with notions about how organizations can be more agentic, more distinctive, and more unified *while at the same time* recognizing their fundamentally pluralistic and institutionally constrained nature.

Our chapter unfolds as follows. First, we review a prominent sociological perspective on self and identity and further highlight its potential relevance to the theoretical questions that we have identified. Second, we will provide a direct translation of these theories to the organization level of analysis and provide examples that demonstrate its relevance and utility. Third, we discuss the benefits of this translated theoretical perspective and also identify where it falls short in addressing the questions noted above. Finally, we will return to Mead's initial work and pull out some pieces of his theoretical frame that may allow us to more fully examine these questions.

IDENTITY AND SELF: A SOCIOLOGICAL TAKE ON AN INDIVIDUAL'S IDENTITY

Structural symbolic interaction theory, or "identity theory," takes as a central premise the notion that individuals face multiple and competing expectations and demands from others in society. These competing demands, or *roles* (e.g., postal worker, boss, father), are the source for an individual's *identity* (i.e., *role identity*) or internalized social roles. Over a lifespan, an individual can come to possess a multitude of these identities (Thoits, 1983).

Individuals act on various role identities as a function of their salience. According to Stryker and Serpe (1982) and others, salience is determined by *commitments*. Commitment, as used by identity theorists, refers to "the degree to which persons' relationships to others in their networks depend on possessing a particular identity and role; commitment is measurable by the costs of losing meaningful relations to others, should the identity be foregone" (Stryker & Burke, 2000, p. 286). Thus, the salience of one's role as an academic—and thus one's propensity to enact that role—depends on the degree to which others expect, require, or need one to act in that role. Thus, social relationships constrain not only the identities one adopts via roles but also the propensity to enact these roles.

Burke and colleagues (Burke, 1991; Stryker & Burke, 2000) further suggest that individuals hold culturally prescribed "identity standards" that are verified or not verified in particular social situations. Verification serves as a motivator for behavior. This notion of verification harkens back to McCall and Simmons' (1968) emphasis on legitimacy; they note that individuals are strongly motivated to legitimate their role identities. Such verification, as well as all communication between self and society more generally, occurs as individuals share in common language, artifacts, and symbols. Thus, interactions between self and society are symbolic interactions.

To manage these multiple identities—and the commitments and verification processes associated with them—each individual forms a self. Mead's (1934) central dictum was that "self mirrors society" (Stryker, 2008). Self and society are inexorably intertwined: the same social processes that form a society also give rise to an individual's self. The self serves to organize the multiple identities within an individual. Thus, structural symbolic interaction theory is sometimes referred to as a "multiple identities' conceptualization of the self" (MICS), a label we likewise employ as it makes salient the key components of the theory we are discussing (Stryker & Burke, 2000, p. 290). In MICS, the twin forces of verification and commitment help shape the structure of the self. Early work by McCall and Simmons (1968) noted that some identities are clustered and "go together" and some are more antagonistic. Thus, identities that are evoked by a particular audience (e.g., a business professor's teaching and research role identities) would tend to cluster together, whereas other identities (e.g., father) might not. Further, these various identities tend to be hierarchically organized—with different identities varying in prominence or salience (McCall & Simmons, 1968; Stryker, 1987). As discussed in more detail below, having a hierarchy of identities greatly facilitates the management of identity plurality; when an individual activates multiple identities, the hierarchical structure allows the individual to prioritize some identities over others.

Although the influence of social forces on individual identity is strong, individuals are neither cultural dopes nor societal drones. MICS suggests at least three pathways for agency. First, individuals can choose which roles to internalize and thus which become identities. Therefore, the key distinction between role and role identity is individual choice. Second, individuals can, to a degree, choose their communities, and thus increase their chances of having their identities verified and legitimated (McCall & Simmons, 1968) by community members. Third, and perhaps most critically, individuals have agency in their ability to choose among and enact multiple identities. These multiple identities allow individuals the freedom to more fully engage in a complex society (Thoits, 1983). Thus, business school professors who are also soccer dads and amateur astronomers not only have the potential to express "more of their selves," but they can also use multiple role obligations to get out of a specific role obligation. Going to your son's graduation can trump the need to attend a departmental meeting. One could argue, however, that rather than freedom, multiple roles simply mean more constraints. But individuals can avoid being trapped in multiple obligations by ordering the priority of their identities. Thus, by prioritizing some role identities over others, the door is opened for some identities to chronically be superseded by others (e.g., researcher over amateur astronomer for a business school professor).

The pressures facing individuals in this perspective are much like those facing organizations. Organizations, like individuals, have "no place else to be" except for in society (i.e., in social and cultural environments). Organizations, like individuals, are faced with multiple and competing demands from this society. Organizations, like individuals, look to societal institutions for standards of action. Organizations, like individuals, internalize multiple standards for action (i.e., multiple identities). And organizations, like individuals, are bound to some identities more tightly than others. An individual creates a self to manage these competing identity demands—but what does an organization do?

IDENTITY AND SELF AT THE ORGANIZATIONAL LEVEL: A THEORETICAL TRANSLATION

As we have noted, the core of our chapter is its effort to translate a multiple identity conceptualization of self to the organizational level of analysis. We are particularly interested in showing how this translated perspective helps alleviate the deep-seated tensions that we identified in the chapter's opening questions. For example, we hope that it will allow us to reaffirm organizational autonomy and uniqueness without falsely and arbitrarily denying the powerful influence that societal context and overarching institutions play in the construction of organizational identity. We attempt to make our case by forwarding four distinct but integrally related propositions about organizational identities and the organizational self. These are all rooted in the individual-level perspective that we have just summarized.

Organizations possess identities that are anchored in their societal context. The first and most basic insight that emerges from our translation effort is the idea that individual organizations draw their identities from the broader society in which they are embedded. This society, in turn, is built up largely out of cultural categories and established roles that act to *constitute* organizations, defining their very identities. Banks, to provide one tangible example, may vary quite meaningfully in terms of their self-understandings, and they may also possess internal cultures that are highly idiosyncratic. However, they are all fundamentally similar in the simple sense that they are *banks* (e.g., rather than charities, hospitals, or universities). This central and defining aspect of the individual organization's identity is rooted in the larger society, and more precisely in the bank's institutional environment. This environment affects the individual organization both by presenting it with legal imperatives and by surrounding it with cultural "givens." Regulators place strong and identifiable demands on any organization that wishes to call itself a bank. Access to the category is tightly controlled. Further, any self-defining statement that the individual organization within this cultural category can make is sure to prominently include the societally ascribed element of its identity (i.e., "We are a ___ type of a bank"). Most banks are also likely to share certain normative values that are not necessarily cherished by organizations that have different societal roles and which occupy separate institutional categories (e.g., software companies or vegetarian food co-ops). These common values are also inherited from the broader institutional environment that embeds the individual organization.

This basic line of argument obviously parallels the perspective on organizational identity that is favored by institutionalists (e.g., Fox-Wolfgramm, Boal, & Hunt, 1998; Zuckerman, Kim, Ukanwa, & von Rittmann, 2003) and organizational ecologists (Hannan et al., 2006; Polos, Hannan, & Carroll, 2002) who have recently entered the identity arena. It also corresponds directly to Whetten's social actor model of organizational identity that claims, "organizational identity is appropriately conceived as a set of categorical identity claims ... in reference to a specified set of institutionally standardized social categories" (Whetten & Mackey, 2002, p. 397; see also Whetten, 2006). That is, organizational identities are derived from institutional logics and claims in a manner analogous to individuals and roles.

Moreover, analogous to identity commitment, organizations tend to enact identities that are most centrally tied to their core constituencies. Business schools, for example, will enact different identities depending on whether they are being judged by academia, where rigor is a key criterion, or by business leaders, where relevance is critical. These identities represent binding commitments that, if broken, threaten their support (e.g., diminished university allocations) and legitimacy (e.g., lower rankings). In turn, this may ultimately lead to the death of these identities (e.g., business schools ostracized from academic institutions), if not organizational death.

An MICS provides at least two key additions, however, even at this basic level. First, the theory implies that the individual organization needs to internalize its societal role if it is to become an organizational identity. This is not a trivial point. It reminds us that organizations *express choice* about which demands they choose to obey. In a similar way, Selznick (1957) notes that organizations have a choice of actions and define their character by deciding which commitments to make (and not to make). This is analogous to organizations claiming certain identities over others (Glynn, 2002) and selecting some organizational forms over others at founding (Whetten & Mackey, 2002). Identity claiming in this sense, however, means that identities must not only be voiced, but they must also be made manifest in the organization's actions and visible commitments regarding who the organization is. To illustrate, business schools who want to be considered "green" must not simply parrot green values on Web sites and in other publications, but they must take clear, public, and relevant "green" actions—such as changing how they heat their buildings, how they construct new facilities, how they manage their waste, and so on.

Second, an MICS highlights the individual organization's ability to escape a given social category. Organizations can reconstitute themselves by eschewing their existing categorical attachments. However, as noted by Pratt and Foreman (2000), simply "deleting" an identity is exceedingly difficult to do, and escaping all institutional fields is seemingly impossible. Thus, it is more likely that organizations will enter a new category or possibly shuffle the salience of particular identities. With regard to the former, Porac, Thomas, and Baden-Fuller (1989) argue that organizations actively seek out their rivals or comparison groups as a means of creating social categories. With regard to the latter, one advantage of multiple identities is that it provides multiple identity avenues for the organization to escape into. In a similar way, business schools avoid some of the heat from practitioners over relevancy by evoking their need to placate the needs of their educational institution.

Organizations seek to verify their societal identities by exchanging symbols with their institutional environment. Our theoretical translation also implies that organizations, like people, are constantly engaged in *identity verification* processes. They verify their identities by making symbolic offerings (or expressing various images; Gioia, Schultz, & Corley, 2000) to the society of which they are a part. Their symbolic efforts are, in particular, aimed at showing the organization's conformance with various *identity standards* that are derived from the macro level.

As we have noted, structural symbolic theorists posit that identities tend to have well-defined ideals and standards associated with them. These standards, like their associated roles, have their roots in the societal level. These theorists have similarly argued that people strive to verify their claimed identities by embodying these relatively stable standards. A directly analogous process appears to occur at the organization level, and institutionalists have well documented this dynamic. Specifically, they empirically show that organizations attempt to demonstrate their cultural fitness by adopting organizational structures and practices that are symbolically appropriate within their cultural milieu (DiMaggio & Powell, 1983; Meyer & Rowan, 1977). Put differently, the perspective implies that organizations attempt to play their social roles in an *exemplary* fashion. They have further shown that organizations tend to gain social approval (i.e., legitimacy) when they adopt symbolically appropriate structures, and to suffer penalties when they fail to maintain such structures (Staw & Epstein, 2000; Westphal, Gulati, & Shortell, 1997). It is important to note that we assume a very broad conceptualization of the "symbolic" in making this argument. A school can (obviously) be seen as engaging in a symbolic process of identity verification when it adopts "decoupled" structures that serve no technical or operational function but are approved of by its accreditors. Institutionalists have made much of such actions (Meyer & Rowan, 1977). But, a corporation can also be seen as engaging in identity verification when it espouses a commitment to the ideals of efficiency and profitability and adopts practices that demonstrate its commitment to these ideal standards (Staw & Epstein, 2000).

The organization is a self in at least the minimum sense of being a collection of societally anchored identities. Although the preceding two propositions are foundational to an MICS and are necessary starting points in our translation, the perspective's real payoff is apparent when we consider the pluralistic nature of the organization's social context and the multiple identities that inevitably result from this pluralism. The concept of an organizational self, as distinct from organizational identity, would seemingly be unnecessary if an organization inhabited a homogeneous, monistic society and thus had only a single corresponding role to play therein. Pluralism and identity multiplicity are, we believe, what makes the organizational self theoretically possible and worth the trouble of theorizing about and differentiating from organizational identity.

As we previously noted, an MICS conceptualizes the self as the "whole" entity that is composed of the actor's multiple identities. The case that organizations, like people, have multiple, societally ascribed identities is not a difficult one to make. Consider the corporation as an example. All corporations have role identities as producers (a product market identity), as employers (labor market identity), as stocks (capital market identity), and as legal entities (legal identity), among others. These identities are rooted in the firm's pluralistic environment and linked to specific roles that the corporation is called on to play within society (Kraatz & Block, 2008). Different identity standards also exist in the various segments of this pluralistic milieu. The firm typically seeks to embody these disparate ideals in its actions (e.g., by producing products that consumers value, creating an attractive work environment, and providing good benefits to employees, yielding superior returns on investor's assets, and obeying the law). Importantly, these disparate identities are all present "inside" the organization, as well as in its environment. The product market role identity, for instance, is typically represented by marketers, who assume the perspective of the consumer and give voice to his or her ideals. Financial personnel and human resources (HR) managers represent the capital and labor market role identities, respectively. This internal identity pluralism gives rise to persistent internal tensions within the corporation (Ocasio & Kim, 1999). These tensions may be either productive or destructive, but they are the stuff from which organizational selves are made.

It is also important to note that the organizational self that we conceptualize need not be, in its minimal sense, anything more than a loosely coupled and highly differentiated set of tangentially related identities. It may, in other words, be little more than the sum of its parts. March's conceptualization of the American university as an "organized anarchy" is a useful case in point (Cohen & March, 1986; March & Olsen, 1976). Although universities have numerous societally anchored identities that are taken very seriously, these identities do not necessarily or inevitably cohere in any obvious way. Thus, although all organizations may be thought of as selves, these selves may often be fragmented (as with human personalities that are internally divided). The organizational self's actions may thus appear to be reactive, contradictory, or even random rather than purposive, intentional, or cooperatively coordinated.

The organization is also usually a self in the more restrictive sense of being a structure that prioritizes and integrates its constituent identities. Although some organizational selves are only minimally integrated (as in March's organized anarchy), most appear to be more tightly coupled and ordered. Structural differentiation and radical autonomy that allow one part of a research university to operate with little regard for the other parts are lacking in many organizations. As a result, different identities are generally brought into direct relationship with one another. Internal governance structures of some type (whether formal or informal) are necessary to manage the resultant tensions and are likely to emerge in response to them. In considering the nature of these structures, it seems plausible that there would be at least two organizing features. The first feature is *clustering*. It is likely that just as for individuals, some identities are likely to be more closely related to each other (i.e., will cluster) than others (McCall & Simmons, 1968). Pratt and Foreman (2000) address this issue by noting that identity synergy is a key dimension to consider when managing multiple identities (the other being the level of organizational resources). When an organizational identity is very different from the others, it is likely that it will be separated from other identities in some way. For example, hospitals who own insurance companies often run these practices in separate facilities—thus, providing physical compartmentalization.

The second organizing feature is *prioritization*. Organizations are likely to prioritize some of these identities over others. Therefore, it seems plausible that an organizational self would involve the creation of an identity hierarchy, analogous to the hierarchies that structure individual selves. It also seems likely that these identity hierarchies are shaped by analogous processes. Identities that are more successfully verified in the external environment are, for instance, more likely to ascend the hierarchy. An example would be a business school that successfully invests in MBA education and increasingly emphasizes that aspect of its identity in the wake of its success. Such identities are not only validated, but they also increase the dependence of the organization on a specific constituency (e.g., MBA ranking institutions)—thus, forming binding commitments. Identities that are not confirmed, by contrast, are likely to descend or drop out altogether (as when a school invests heavily in the MBA program but fails to gain acclaim in the business school rankings).

We have outlined the key elements of an MICS perspective on organizational identity and self, and have shown in what ways this perspective resonates with, integrates, and extends existing work on organizational identity. We now turn to the utility of such a perspective in understanding and ameliorating the tensions that opened this chapter.

TAKING STOCK OF AN MICS PERSPECTIVE ON ORGANIZATIONAL IDENTITY AND SELF: DOES IT ANSWER OUR QUESTIONS?

At the outset, we identified three questions that are currently being debated by organizational theorists. Specifically, we noted that scholars are divided as to whether organizational identities are: (a) unique and internally developed versus categorical and externally ascribed, (b) fonts of purposive action versus sources of social constraint, and (c) shared and integrative versus pluralistic and fragmented.

Extrapolating from the individual level to the organizational level, it appears that a multiple identity conceptualization of self speaks most strongly to the first tension, but less so to the second and third tensions. Given its emphasis on elaborating the sociological forces that shape identities and self, it is perhaps not surprising that sociological perspectives, such as MICS, align with the issue of identities as imposed and similar versus internally generated and different. In the organizational identity literature, this debate reflects social actor versus social constructivist tensions, or as Whetten and Mackey (2002) note, debates between identity *in* versus identity *of* organizations.

In addressing how organizational identities can be both imposed and self-generated, as well as both unique and different, an MICS perspective comes to a conclusion similar to that reached by Glynn (2008) and Kraatz and Block (2008). Institutions provide raw materials for organizational identities—this is what makes organizations in the same field fundamentally the same (i.e., a bank is a bank, and a business school is a business school). However, there are multiple social demands embedded within a single institution, and a single organization may reside at the intersection of multiple institutions. Thus, organizations have access to multiple institutional demands, which in turn provide numerous social roles from which to choose. Organizational differentiation comes from the unique combination of internalized institutional roles (cf., Whetten & Mackey, 2002). This is analogous to Mead's (1934, p. 201) comment about individual selves:

> The fact that all selves are constituted by or in terms of social processes … is not in the least incompatible with, or destructive of, the fact that every individual self has is own peculiar individuality, its own unique pattern … and thus reflects in its organizational structure a different aspect or perspective of this whole social behavior pattern from that which is reflected in the organized structure of any other individual self within that process.

An MICS perspective also speaks, at least to some degree, to the issue of constraint versus agency in the organizational identity literature. As noted above, population ecologists (Hannan et al., 2006; Polos et al., 2002) and institutionalists (see Glynn, 2008 for a review and critique) primarily view organizational identity as a constraint, and that the destabilization of identity as extremely threatening to the organization. It also speaks of ways—not so much of being agentic—but of escaping some of these constraints. Thus, choosing which social roles to adopt, choosing "audiences" for one's identities, and moving away from (and toward other) social categories are all ways that organizations can express some sort of agency. However, this perspective is limited. Is agency simply limited to escaping or evading certain social forces (Kraatz, in press)? Or do organizational identities also allow organizations to respond to environmental changes and threats (see Dutton & Dukerich, 1991)?

An MICS perspective is also relatively weak at addressing the issue of organizations as "wholes" versus "parts." In the organizational identity literature this tension is played out in the "essentialist" perspective on identity that sees an organizational identity as the organization's "soul" or "fundamental essence" (Corley et al., 2006, p. 91), and those that view organizations as having two or more identities (Albert & Whetten, 1985; Fiol, 2001; Glynn, 2000; Pratt & Foreman, 2000; Pratt & Rafaeli, 1997). The former camp can be seen as recognizing the need for something "whole" in organizations; the latter recognizes the inherent pressures for multiplicity. Viewing organizations as having something akin to a self and identities acknowledges, to some degree, the truth in both "camps"—but more so the latter. As we discussed previously, a self in the MICS perspective may be little more than a "box" where identities are placed. Put another way, it speaks to integration (i.e., hierarchies) of identities, but not of making anything "one": achieving *pluribus* but not *unum*.

A deeper understanding of organizations as wholes, however, is critical because organizations are evaluated as *both* parts and wholes (Kraatz & Block, 2008). It is perhaps easy to see that organizations, as well as organizational identities, are expected to be consonant with the demands of multiple stakeholders (Pratt & Foreman, 2000; Scott & Lane, 2000). However, organizations are not only often viewed as wholes (Levinson, 1965), but also humans are evolutionarily predisposed to view them in this way (Guthrie, 1993). Recent research even suggests that organizations are judged and rewarded for appearing coherent and consistent (Love & Kraatz, in press). But how do organizations facilitate this perception of wholeness? To further flesh out how this and agency issue can be more fully addressed, we return to the intellectual foundation of MICS: Mead's (1934) treatise on *Mind, self and society*.

SELF AND IDENTITY FROM A MEADIAN PERSPECTIVE: ADDING THE SUBJECTIVE "I"

Although we do not promise to do full justice to the complexity of Mead's (1934, pp. 136–137) arguments and work, we do point out a key differentiating feature of his writing from the later MICS: the focus on self as "reflexive … that which can be both subject and object." The self as subject is one's "I". The "I" is knower and actor. The self as object is one's "me." In the MICS perspective, an individual's multiple "me's" are referred to as multiple identities. Mead further argues that the conceptualization of self is "not merely a set of specific roles one is ready to perform. There is a unity or wholeness to the self, transcending the specific roles one is ready to play" (Albert & Ramstad, 1998, p. 14). Thus, the self and identity are tied, but the former is not simply an aggregate of the latter. Rather than seeing the relationship in terms of hierarchy, Mead's view of self and identity is similar to Cooley's (1902/2006, p. 182), who referred to the self as a "nucleus of a living cell, not altogether separate from the surrounding matter, out of which indeed it is formed, but more active and definitely organized."

This subjective (self as knower and initiator of action) and objective (self as known—the collection of identities as responses to social demands) parallel the tensions with which we began this chapter. Self as I—as subject—is unique, agentic, and whole. Self as me—as identities and objects—is common, restricted, and pluralistic. Because of its focus on the empirically observable role identities, the MICS and similar sociological perspectives tend to not focus on "self as subject," but Mead discusses in some detail the reflexive dance between subjective and objective facets of self and identity. We highlight a few of his main arguments about self as subject that we see as most useful to a deeper conceptualization of an organizational self.

Shared language is critical for Meadian self formation. Mead (1934) argues that one's self cannot form in the absence of a shared language. Because Mead believes that the self forms from social interaction, there has to be a mechanism that bridges the individual and others in the collective. Specifically, this bridge is a language of "universal symbols" that allows one to share experiences with others and is a necessary precondition for the self. Particularly, Mead (1934, p. 149) argues that one needs, "symbols which could arouse in herself [or himself] the responses they arouse in other people," before an individual can form a self.

The creation of a "generalized other" is necessary to develop a "complete" Meadian self. To make the self the most developed, Mead further argues that individuals must view all of the social demands placed on them by a community in an integrative way. This occurs in a two-stage process (Mead, 1934, p. 158). The first stage is when an individual simply organizes those expectations of others toward oneself and others in the community as they relate to activities in which the individual participates. This seems roughly analogous to the internalization of role identities in an MICS. Mead (1934, p. 154) further suggests that the individual must then move from individual attitudes to social attitudes of the entire collective—to form a "generalized other":

> The organized community or social group which gives to the individual his unity of self may be called the "generalized other." The attitude of the general other is the attitude of the whole community.

Thus, an individual must know the needs and desires of the entire community and be able to act on those needs.[1] The analogy Mead uses is that of a baseball player. To successfully enact his or her various roles, the individual must know what each person on the field is doing and expects of him or her. This synthesis and integration of external demands allow a complete self to form. That is, by organizing, making sense, and integrating these community needs and desires into a coherent picture, the individual can create a coherent and unified self.

As one comes to not simply understand demands but also to react to them, an "I" is formed. As Mead (1934, p. 175) notes, "The 'I' is the response of the organism to the attitudes of others; the 'me' is the organized set of attitudes of others which one himself assumes."

The development of a complete Meadian self allows the individual and community to influence each other. By internalizing the "organized social attitudes" of the community, the individual and the community are opened to mutual influence. The community or collective shapes the self through the organized demands of others that ultimately structures one's multiple "me's" or identities. But it is through the "I," the spontaneous and agentic part of the self, that an individual can ultimately influence the community. Mead illustrates this point by noting how famous individuals such as Socrates both reflect their community needs, as well as transform their community. As Mead (1934, p. 214) argues:

> The response of the "I" involves adaptation, but an adaptation which affects not only the self but also the social environment which helps to constitute the self; that is, it implies a view of evolution in which the individual affects its own environment as well as being affected by it.

Thus, in Mead's view, the self is a dynamic, reflexive accomplishment between the "I" and the demands of the community embodied in multiple "me's."

---

[1] Mead (1934: 155) notes that one must take this attitude towards the generalized other and apply them to social or community action: "This getting of the broad activities of any given social whole or organized society as such within the experiential field of any one of the individuals involved or included in that while is, in other words, the essential basis and prerequisite of that individual's self." Thus, as with an MICS, "who one is" is tied to what one does. More fully, Mead suggests that "who one is" is tied to how the individual helps the community do what it needs to do.

FROM "I" TO "WE": A THEORETICAL TRANSLATION

As with an MICS, there are parallels between Mead's arguments for individuals and our understanding of organizational dynamics (see also Hatch & Schultz, 2002). As before, we make our case by forwarding propositions about organizational identities and organizational self that are rooted in the individual-level perspective we have just reviewed.

A Meadian organizational self needs common language. Key to Mead's perspective is that individuals and others in society need to share a common language so that the individual can experience things similarly to others around him or her. Similarly, organizations must be able to communicate to stakeholders within their organization and throughout wider institutional fields in such a way that mutual understanding can occur.

If we apply this condition to the organization level most exactly—advocating a "strong case" for the Meadian translation—it would suggest that for an organizational self to form and be sustained there must be a common language and set of shared understandings among actors within and outside of the organization. Of course, commonality of language varies by degree. Most generally, there exists enough of a shared language for the construction of a shared social reality (Berger & Luckmann, 1966). However, there are likely to be "gaps" in understanding and "pockets" of shared meaning in the institutional landscape—social reality is "lumpy." This may be especially true for international organizations, conglomerates, and other organizational types that span multiple institutions, multiple countries (and multiple languages), and multiple markets. What might organizations and their members, who are in these situations, do to create more shared meaning with and across its boundaries?

On the face of it, two approaches seem possible, although not equally likely. First, one could attempt to create an institutional *vision*, akin to an organizational vision, that attempts to create and sustain common meanings to help ensure that all constituents are truly "on the same page." This is perhaps not unlike religious organizations that attempt to create a strong sense of "we" by articulating to all key stakeholders the "true" meanings behind the language and symbols that define and guide the institution. But, this approach is not only difficult to do well (as religious and other institutions have found), but also "too much success" in this arena may lead to the stifling of diverse identities. A second, and probably more likely, approach would be to engage in robust action—creating multivocal symbols that are shared by many but are interpreted differently by different individuals and groups (Eccles, Nohria, & Berkley, 1992; Padgett & Ansell, 1993; Pratt & Foreman, 2000). Robust language could create the semblance of commonality, even where it does not exist. For example, institutional players can rally around the issue of "quality" despite wildly different interpretations of what quality means. Among business schools, for example, some may see quality in terms of student satisfaction, whereas others may pay more attention to recruiters' views or to the starting salary of its graduates.

A Meadian organizational self needs the integration of constituent needs and demands. A complete individual self involves understanding, internalizing, and creating an integrative whole out of a myriad of societal demands. Mead outlines the process for individuals to create an integrated understanding of these demands via the creation of a "generalized other." What might this process look like for organizations?

Building from Mead, to attain an organizational self that is not simply the sum of its individual identities, organizations must be aware of the myriad of stakeholder demands that impinge on it—especially those critical to their identities. To continue with our business school example, individuals in these organizations must learn the demands and needs of students, school administrators, faculty, business personnel, investors (the state or private contributors), accrediting institutions, and the like. The next step is to *integrate* these various demands into a whole—not simply understand them as parts. In organizational identity terms, members must understand, at minimum,[2] the reputational demands placed on it and create a reputational gestalt—an organizational "generalized other." This relationship between "external" demands and identity dynamics is echoed in the work of Hatch, Shultz, Gioia, and others (Gioia et al., 2000; Hatch & Schultz, 2002). However, what is critical here is the necessity of understanding all of these demands, and how they impinge *on each other* as they impinge on the organization. Such a holistic understanding allows organizational members to act effectively to social demands by acting from one's self—to follow, in the words of James March, a logic of appropriateness (March & Olsen, 2004).

---

[2] We use the phrase "at minimum" because organizations, unlike individuals, also have a variety of vocal constituents within its boundaries.

A Meadian organizational self is a gestalt and fluid structure. We use the term *gestalt* to reflect Mead's notion that the self is more than simply the sum of its parts. Returning to Cooley's (1902/2006) depiction, the self is akin to a cell's nucleus, embedded in and nourished by its identities, but also somewhat distinct, dynamic, and organized. We further use the term *fluid* to reflect Mead's notion that self is an ongoing process. For example, as community needs/demands change and identity salience shifts, the organizational structure that embodies these identities changes as well. Fluidity also occurs because once a structure like an organizational self is formed, the self is poised to act as both subject and object in its environment—as both initiator and reactor. As the self acts on the community, the self changes the demands that community places on it, which changes both the community and its very own identities. It is this transcendent and fluid structure that allows organizations to create, even if for brief times, a unity that exists within and along with its identity plurality. Thus, within organizations, the creation of a self-like structure would be a momentary accomplishment. Identities, by contrast, may remain as consistent as the social demands that spawned them (e.g., the educational identities of business schools).

A Meadian organizational self includes a spontaneous and agentic "we." Within individuals, the "I" is actor and knower; it is the spontaneous and agentic force in the self. It is the "I" that updates the self—that creates the momentary accomplishment of wholeness and completeness. In fact, the self is a reflexive interplay between the "I" and the "me." But can organizations be self-reflexive? How might organizations become a "we"?

A "strong" translation of Mead's ideas might lead one to see the organizational self as a collective cognition—akin to a group mind, or to a lesser degree, something like a transactive memory system (Pratt, 2003). Here, the organization as embodied in a collective cognitive structure serves as initiator of action—a literal "social actor." However, such a state may not only be unlikely, it may also be unnecessary. Perhaps a smaller subset of organizational members can act as the "we": acting as an organizational agent to represent the larger organization.

At this point, we wade into an issue that has been festering in the organizational identity literature for some time (see Corley et al., 2006; Ravasi & van Rekom, 2003), although most commonly conceptualized as a methodological issue—who "speaks" for the organization? Put in Meadian terms, if the self is a reflexive process, who in organizations has to be reflexive?

Does any single person or persons have to have a complete picture of external demands to form a "generalized other," or is it enough that this information is somehow distributed in the organization?

Mead appears to suggest that for a given community, it may be enough for a leader to serve as an agent for the organization. Using an example from politics, he argues:

> In politics ... the individual identifies himself with an entire political party and takes the organized attitudes of the entire party toward the rest of the given social community and toward the problems which confront the party within the given social situation; and he consequently reacts or responds in terms of the organized attitudes for the party as a whole (Mead, 1934, p. 156).

Selznick (1957) would seem to suggest a similar stance, highlighting the role of leader as organizational actor and institutional change agent (see Kraatz, in press). This issue we leave unsettled, not having enough extant research to make a more definitive statement. However, given that the managing of external demands is more public in an organization than in an individual, these "we" dynamics in organizations may be amenable to empirical examination.

TAKING STOCK OF A MEADIAN PERSPECTIVE ON ORGANIZATIONAL IDENTITY AND SELF

Although we believe that Mead enriches our understanding of all three of the questions we used to open the chapter, we also argued that an MICS perspective on organizational identity does a good job of explaining organizational identity as both unique and similar. Thus, we turn here to the last two questions and the tensions they embody.

Subjective Self as a Source of Agency

Similar to an MICS perspective on organizational identity, Mead's frame acknowledges the "given" or imposed nature of identity that comes from social institutions. At the same time, it also acknowledges the dynamic and "bottom-up" nature of self-beliefs that are inherent in a social constructionist view (Corley et al., 2006). However, the structuration-like relationship between organization and institution—that they mutually constitute each other—further enriches our understanding of the dance between constraint and agency; in particular, it views organizations on more equal footing with their institutional partners. In doing so, this perspective opens the door for organizations to do more than simply escape institutional constraints. As we elaborated in our discussion of an organizational "generalized other," organizations may be able to modify the demands placed on them, thus changing their constraints, their institution(s), and, ultimately, their organizational self.

Self as a Unifying Whole That Is More Than the Sum of Its Identities

We also believe that a notion of an organizational self provides a more complete and compelling response to the unity/plurality issue. For organizational identity theorists, adding the Meadian "self" along with "identity" more deeply addresses the schism between the "essentialist" single-identity perspective and those who view organizations as having multiple identities (see Corley et al., 2006). More than even an MICS perspective, a Meadian view on organizational self and identity sees the self as truly holistic, coherent, and unifying. It is more like the organization's "soul" that essentialist researchers propose (Corley et al., 2006). However, Mead views this whole as existing with its constituent parts: thus, both perspectives bring a valuable, but incomplete, truth to the table.

By positing a self or self-like process/structure at an organizational level, we can more easily imagine alternatives to how advocates for specific identities in organizations may interact. Mead used a parliamentary metaphor to describe the organization of multiple "me's" within each individual. Although viewing self as a hierarchy might be sufficient for a single individual (as an MICS implies), perhaps a parliament—an image based on a dynamic organizational form—may better reflect the dynamism of a collective. Self as parliament not only recognizes clustering (that identities be complementary, oppositional, or unrelated) and prioritization (that some identities may be more important than others), but it also opens the door to more identity brokering. Identity supporters can form temporary alliances, make deals, and craft solutions for joint action that may not have come from any existing identity "group." This adds a much-needed balance to approaches where multiple identity management is largely viewed as a top-down process (e.g., Cheney, 1991; Golden-Biddle & Rao, 1997; Pratt & Foreman, 2000). It is more akin to Pratt and Rafaeli's (1997) and Glynn's (2000) depiction of bottom-up multiple identity management. However, whereas most treatments of bottom-up identity negotiations involve only a limited number of identities (two in Glynn's and four in Pratt & Rafaeli's), a parliament of identities may involve much more. As a result, we move beyond dialectical approaches to managing multiple identities (largely implicit in hybrid identity approaches) to more dynamic and political approaches.

CONCLUDING THOUGHTS AND FUTURE RESEARCH DIRECTIONS

We believe that the power of concepts is in shaping how we think and act in the world. Looking at organizations as having both a self and multiple identities helps us to ameliorate some deep-seated social tensions at the heart of organizational identity research. In general, it eases the load that "identity" has been asked to carry. Here, identities represent the external, imposed, and similar nature of organizations. The organizational self, by contrast, helps us recognize that organizations are also unique, agentic, and reflect the choices of its members. However, even this perspective is not without limitations. As noted above, we do not know exactly who and what is involved in creating a "we" in organizations. More generally, one must approach with caution moving a theory of an individual—even a sociological one—to the level of the organization. Unlike organizations, individuals can more easily compartmentalize different sets of expectations; they can find "new constituents" and break off contact with the old, and can even move geographically to shed new identities and try on new ones (Pratt & Foreman, 2000). Their entire existence is not observed. However, even acknowledging these limitations, we argue that by integrating structural symbolic and Meadian notions about self and identity, we perhaps may see more than what we have previously.

We end this chapter with two observations and some thoughts about future research in this area. First, we point out that even if it was sociological perspectives that have most clearly raised the inherent limitations of the organizational identity concept, it is another sociological theory and frame that may help to address these issues—a sociological theory and frame, ironically, aimed at understanding individual identity (but may be as or even more applicable to organizations). Second, the Meadian perspective that we propose places certain organizational identity characteristics with different "dance partners." Most top-down sociological perspectives on organizational identity see external forces acting on organizations as a source of wholeness (i.e., the essential core) for the organization. Most bottom-up social constructivist perspectives, by contrast, see those within the organization as being responsible for maintaining and cultivating identity plurality. However, by linking identities to external demands, the institutional environment becomes the source of identity plurality. Integration and unity, by contrast, come from within—via the creation of a self. This inversion provides food for thought to those organizational identity researchers who have eschewed externally driven perspectives of organizations for creating identities that are too isomorphic and homogeneous, as well as for those researchers who have railed against multiple identity approaches for granting individuals within the organization too much say in defining what an organization is.

So where does all this leave organizational identity research, especially as it relates to positive identities? We have posed some of these questions throughout our chapter. But these questions raise others. How do we conceptualize organizational (identity) change when we consider both self and identities? What role do leaders, followers, and other constituents play in self formation, maintenance, and change? In addition to these questions, we hope that identity scholarship will examine more deeply how organizations can create structures, practices, and symbols that not only reflect its diversity but also transcend it to create a sense of wholeness (Fiol, Pratt, & O'Connor, 2009). We noticed in writing this chapter how few organizational exemplars we could readily identify to illustrate self-identity dynamics. Thus, we encourage comparative case studies of organizations that act as if they are a self versus those who do not. Additionally, organizational identity scholars may look more closely at how these issues have been talked about in other arenas (e.g., diversity literature). However, perhaps most importantly, we hope that viewing organizations as having both a self and multiple identities will spark research that looks at issues of *process*—specifically, how organizations and their members deal with the questions we pose at the start of this chapter.

These questions are not simply theoretical concerns but are lived tensions. We live in organizations that reside at the nexus of multiple institutions, that may reside at multiple locations throughout the globe, that are embedded in multiple institutions, that answer to multiple stakeholders, and that are populated by a diverse workforce. However, we argue that to harness the *positive* potential of identity, you must also understand the self—so that distinctiveness can come from various similarities, agency can come from a multitude of constraints, and out of the many can come one.

REFERENCES

Albert, A., & Ramstad, Y. (1998). The concordance of George Herbert Mead's "social self" and John R. Commons's "will." (the social psychological underpinnings of Commons's institutional economics, part 2). *Journal of Economic Issues, 32,* 1–46.

Albert, S., & Whetten, D. A. (1985). Organizational identity. In B. M. Staw & L. L. Cummings (Eds.), *Research on organizational behavior* (Vol. 7; 263–295). Greenwich, CT: JAI Press.

Berger, P., & Luckmann, T. (1966). *The social construction of reality.* New York: Anchor.

Burke, P. J. (1991). Identity processes and social stress. *American Sociological Review, 56,* 836–849.

Cheney, G. (1991). *Rhetoric in an organizational society: Managing multiple identities.* Columbia, SC: University of South Carolina Press.

Cooley, C. H. (2006). *Human nature and the social order.* New York: C. Scribner's and Sons. (Original work published 1902)

Cohen, M. D., & March, J. G. (1986). *Leadership and ambiguity.* Boston: Harvard Business School Press.

Corley, K. G., Harquail, C. V., Pratt, M. G., Glynn, M. A., Fiol, C. M., & Hatch, M. J. (2006). Guiding organizational identity through aged adolescence. *Journal of Management Inquiry, 15,* 85–99.

DiMaggio, P., & Powell, W. W. (1983). The iron cage revisited: Institutional isomorphism and collective rationality in organizational fields. *American Sociological Review, 48,* 147–160.

Dutton, J. E., & Dukerich, J. M. (1991). Keeping an eye on the mirror: Image and identity in organizational adaptation. *Academy of Management Journal, 34,* 517–554.

Eccles, R. G., Nohria, N., & Berkley, J. D. (1992). *Beyond the hype: Rediscovering the essence of management.* Boston: Harvard Business Press.

Fiol, C. M. (2001). Revisiting an identity-based view of sustainable competitive advantage. *Journal of Management, 27,* 691–699.

Fiol, C. M., Pratt, M. G., & O'Connor, E. (2009). Managing intractable identity conflicts. *Academy of Management Review, 34,* 32–55.

Fox-Wolfgramm, S. J., Boal, K. B., & Hunt, J. G. (1998). Organizational adaptation to institutional change: A comparative study of first-order change in prospector and defender banks. *Administrative Science Quarterly, 43,* 87–126.

Gioia, D. A., Schultz, M., & Corley, K. G. (2000). Organizational identity, image and adaptive instability. *Academy of Management Review, 25,* 63–81.

Glynn, M. A. (2000). When cymbals become symbols: Conflict over organizational identity within a symphony orchestra. *Organization Science, 11,* 285–298.

Glynn, M. A. (2002). Chord and discord: Organizational crisis, institutional shifts, and the musical canon of the symphony. *Poetics, 30,* 63–85.

Glynn, M. A. (2008). Beyond constraint: How institutions enable identities. In R. Greenwood, C. Oliver, R. Suddaby, & K. Sahlin-Andersson (Eds.), *Handbook of institutional theory* (pp. 413–430). Thousand Oaks, CA: Sage.

Golden-Biddle, K., & Rao, H. (1997). Breaches in the boardroom: Organizational identity and conflict of commitment in a non-profit organization. *Organization Science, 8,* 593–611.

Guthrie, S. (1993). *Faces in the clouds: A new theory of religion.* New York: Oxford University Press.

Hannan, M. T., Baron, J. N., Hsu, G., & Kocak, O. (2006). Organizational identities and the hazard of change. *Industrial and Corporate Change, 15,* 755–784.

Hatch, M. J., & Schultz, M. (2002). The dynamic organizational identity. *Human Relations, 55,* 989–1019.

Kraatz, M. S. (in press). Leadership as institutional work: A bridge to the other side. In T. Lawrence, R. Suddaby, & B. Leca (Eds.), *Institutional work: Actors and agency in institutional studies of organizations*: Cambridge University Press.

Kraatz, M. S., & Block, E. S. (2008). Organizational implications of institutional pluralism. In R. Greenwood, C. Oliver, R. Suddaby, & K. Sahlin-Andersson (Eds.), *Handbook of organizational institutionalism* (pp. 243–275). London: Sage.

Levinson, H. (1965). Reciprocation: The relationship between man and organization. *Administrative Science Quarterly, 9,* 370–390.

Love, E. G., & Kraatz, M. S. (in press). Character, conformity or the bottom line? How and why downsizing affected corporate reputation. *Academy of Management Journal.*

March, J. G., & Olsen, J. P. (1976). *Ambiguity and choice in organizations,* 2nd ed. Bergen, Norway: Universitetsforlaget.

March, J. G., & Olsen, J. P. (2004). *The logic of appropriateness.* Oslo: Arena Working Paper.

McCall, G. J., & Simmons, R. L. (1968). *Identities and interactions.* New York: Free Press.

Mead, G. H. (1934). *Mind, self, and society.* Chicago: University of Chicago.

Meyer, J. W. & Rowan, B. (1977). Institutionalized organizations: Formal structure as myth and ceremony. *American Journal of Sociology, 83,* 340.

Ocasio, W., & Kim, H. (1999). The circulation of corporate control: Selection of functional backgrounds of new CEOs in large U.S. manufacturing firms, 1981–1992. *Administrative Science Quarterly, 44,* 532–562.

Padgett, J. F., & Ansell, C. K. (1993). Robust action and the rise of the medici, 1400–1434. *American Journal of Sociology, 98,* 1259–1319.

Polos, L., Hannan, M., & Carroll, G. (2002). Foundations of a theory of social forms. *Industrial and Corporate Change, 11,* 85–115.

Porac, J., Thomas, H., & Baden-Fuller, C. (1989). Competitive groups as cognitive communities: The case of the Scottish knitwear industry. *Journal of Management Studies, 26,* 397–416.

Pratt, M. G. (2003). Disentangling collective identities. In J. T. Polzer (Ed.), *Identity issues in groups* (pp. 161–188). Amsterdam: Elsevier Science.

Pratt, M. G., & Foreman, P. O. (2000). Classifying managerial responses to multiple organizational identities. *Academy of Management Review, 25,* 18–42.

Pratt, M. G., & Rafaeli, A. (1997). Organizational dress as a symbol of multilayered social identities. *Academy of Management Journal, 40,* 862–898.

Ravasi, D., & van Rekom, J. (2003). Academic research key issues in organizational identity and identification theory. *Corporate Reputation Review, 6,* 118–132.

Scott, S. G., & Lane, V. R. (2000). A stakeholder approach to organizational identity. *Academy of Management Review, 25,* 43–62.

Selznick, P. (1957). *Leadership in administration.* New York: Harper and Row.

Staw, B. M., & Epstein, L. D. (2000). What bandwagons bring: Effects of popular management techniques on corporate performance, reputation, and CEO pay. *Administrative Science Quarterly, 45,* 523–556.

Stryker, S. (1987). Identity theory: Development and extensions. In K. Yardley & T. Honess (Eds.), *Self and identity: Psychosocial perspectives* (pp. 89–103). New York: Wiley.

Stryker, S. (2008). From Mead to a structural symbolic interactionism and beyond. *Annual Review of Sociology, 34,* 15–31.

Stryker, S., & Burke, P. J. (2000). The past, present, and future of an identity theory. *Social Psychology Quarterly, 63,* 284–297.

Stryker, S., & Serpe, R. T. (1982). Commitment, identity salience, and role behavior: Theory and research example. In W. Ickes & E. S. Knowles (Eds.), *Personality, roles, and social behavior* (pp. 199–218). New York: Springer-Verlag.

Thoits, P. A. (1983). Multiple identities: Examining gender and marital status differences in distress. *American Sociological Review, 51,* 259–272.

Westphal, J. D., Gulati, R., & Shortell, S. M. (1997). Customization or conformity? An institutional and network perspective on the content and consequences of TQM adoption. *Administrative Science Quarterly, 42,* 366–394.

Whetten, D. A. (2006). Albert and Whetten revisited: Strengthening the concept of organizational identity. *Journal of Management Inquiry, 15,* 219–234.

Whetten, D. A., & Mackey, A. (2002). A social actor conception of organizational identity and its implications for the study of organizational reputation. *Business & Society, 41,* 393–414.

Zuckerman, E. W., Kim, T. Y., Ukanwa, K., & von Rittmann, J. (2003). Robust identities or nonentities? Typecasting in the feature-film labor market. *American Journal of Sociology, 108,* 1018–1074.

18

Organizational Identity as a Stakeholder Resource

Shelley L. Brickson and Grace Lemmon

CONTENTS

We seem to be at a critical juncture in history. As innumerable theorists and social commentators point out (e.g., Margolis & Walsh, 2003; Miller, 1999; Ritzer, 2004), the world cries out for repair. Alongside human ills such as war, poverty, and disease exist ever more alarming environmental crises, including global warming, deforestation, and species extinction (Carey & Shapiro, 2004; Malhi et al., 2008; The Scientists Speak, 2007; see also Hamilton & Gioia, Chapter 19). As these social and natural maladies mount, the governmental and nongovernmental sectors are increasingly ill-equipped to handle the burden. Meanwhile, relative to the other sectors, businesses continue to gain prominence and power in the global arena (Kaliski, 2001). Globalization puts business organizations center stage (Cormack & Fitzgerald, 2006). Businesses affect an expanding range of stakeholders in more geographic locations both directly and indirectly through their influence on social policy (Cormack & Fitzgerald, 2006). Therefore, for-profit organizations are particularly capable of exerting widespread influence (Doh & Guay, 2006).

There also seems to be a desire among business leaders to constructively use this influence to address social problems. A recent poll of business leaders suggests that the majority are frustrated by their organizations merely talking about social problems and want them to act on them more strategically (Maitland, 2005). At the same time, business organizations' goals and behaviors depend on what their leaders perceive the role of the firm to be (Ghoshal, 2005; Gioia, 2002). Thus, crucial questions facing us today are (a) how do organizational actors view business organizations in the first place; and (b) what are the implications of different views of the firm for social welfare generation? Each of these questions informs a different branch of stakeholder theory. The first is the purview of descriptive stakeholder theory and the latter of instrumental stakeholder theory (Donaldson & Preston, 1995).

It is our contention that business organizations' influence on society is tightly bound to organizational identity. We apply to the organizational identity construct Feldman's (2004) recent model of resourcing to suggest that organizational identity elicits a chain of organizational goals and actions, which in turn give rise to specific stakeholder resources. Further, we suggest that this cycle is self-perpetuating and that it also spawns new cycles of resource generation. After introducing the stakeholder resourcing model, we then draw on the more specific construct of identity orientation (Brickson, 2000, 2005, 2007) to illustrate how different fundamental assumptions about who the firm is relative to stakeholders—whether it is perceived as an atomized entity, relationship partner, or common group member—likely yield striking distinctions in the types of resource organizations are best equipped to contribute.

DEFINITIONS AND ASSUMPTIONS

Organizational identity is a collectively shared self-reflexive cognitive schema that members draw on to answer the question, "Who are we as an organization?" (Ashforth & Mael, 1996; Corley et al., 2006). It consists of a series of traits and characteristics that members deem definitional to the organization (Albert & Whetten, 1985). Organizational identity enables organizational goals and actions (Ashforth & Mael, 1996; Dutton & Dukerich, 1991). *Organizational identity orientation* refers to the assumed nature of association between an organization and stakeholders as perceived by members and answers the question, "Who are we as an organization vis-à-vis our stakeholders?" (Brickson, 2005, 2007). Specifically, an individualistic identity orientation is one whereby members understand the organization first and foremost as an atomized actor; a relational identity orientation is one whereby they understand it primarily as a dyadic relationship partner to specific others; and a collectivistic identity orientation is one whereby they deem it principally as a member of a larger group or community (Brickson, 2005). Finally, we define a *positive organizational identity* as one that provides the basis for actions that generate a net positive level of socially valuable resources to the earth and its living inhabitants. In other words, according to this view, a positive identity is identified through its outcomes. As such, we take a functionalist perspective (Dewey, 1989; James, 1918) of the value of organizational identity, cautiously proposing that there may be nothing inherently positive or negative about an organization's identity aside from the consequences it fosters.

Applying the resourcing perspective to organizational identity may prove useful for three reasons. First, it helps to develop existing theory on the link between organizational identity and social value generation (e.g., Brickson, 2007) by applying a process perspective to better understand *how* organizational identity can result in socially valuable resources. Ultimately, this process-based understanding may help to elucidate the interconnections between descriptive and instrumental aspects of stakeholder theory. To date, not only have both areas been underdeveloped, with descriptive theory virtually nonexistent (Jones & Wicks, 1999) and with instrumental stakeholder theory focused primarily on economic rather than social value generation (Margolis & Walsh, 2003), but also researchers have not begun to address their relationship to one another.

Second, this chapter may contribute to work on resourcing by showing the relevance of identity schemas. Whereas the story Feldman (2004) draws on to understand resourcing begins with an institution taking certain actions, the present chapter may help to identify one common source of institutional action: organizational identity. Third, the chapter may contribute to a burgeoning literature on identity as a resource.

For example, Caza and Bagozzi (2008) found, at the individual level, that certain identity qualities buffered against the negative effects of adversity at work. Cha and Roberts (2008) describe ways in which members of multivalent social identity groups (e.g., women, Asians) may rely on those identities as a resource for achieving such ends as drawing attention to positive aspects of their selves and building stronger relationships. Meanwhile, Quinn and Worline (2008) describe how hijacking victims on United Airlines Flight 93 drew on personal identities and a common group identity to enable courageous counteraction. The present work may prove complementary to these studies. First, it addresses organizational identity rather than personal and group identity. Second, whereas the research mentioned considers how identity can be used to help a person or group (the entity itself) cope with troubling events or circumstances, the present model is intended to explore how identity produces resources that may benefit other stakeholders in positive or negative circumstances.

This chapter is divided into three sections. In the first, we introduce a general model of organizational identity as a stakeholder resource. This model illustrates the process through which organizational identity sets in motion a chain of organizational goals and actions rendering certain resources available to internal and external stakeholders. These resources then cycle back to inform organizational identity, as well as stakeholders' own self-schemas, enabling further resource generation. After introducing the model, we next employ the identity orientation lens to explore how distinct conceptions of organizational identity vis-à-vis stakeholders may produce markedly different cycles of resource generation. Finally, we end by suggesting some avenues for future research.

ORGANIZATIONAL IDENTITY AND STAKEHOLDER RESOURCE GENERATION

Feldman (2004) recently offered a provocative model of resource generation. In contrast to the view that resources are external to the organization (Pfeffer & Salancik, 1978; Thompson, 1967; Zald, 1970) or are firm specific and relatively immutable (Teece, Pisano, & Shuen, 1997), she takes a view of resources as internally produced and molded through organizational dynamics. By studying a university undergoing institutional change, she develops a model of resourcing whereby distinct organizational actions produce particular patterns of resources. These resources then enable certain cognitive schemas, which in turn continue to influence action and to perpetuate the cycle. In her specific case study, changes in resident staff hiring and training processes (dorm-specific hiring and training versus centralized hiring and training) are organizational actions that produce distinct types of resources (tight within-dorm networks versus connections between individual staff members and an across-dorm topic specialist). These resources then energize different schemas (resident staff as an interconnected unit versus resident staff as individual experts), which ultimately cycle back to taking particular actions in response to events (taking a team-based approach versus taking an individual approach to addressing incidents of bulimia in the residence halls). Feldman's model of resourcing depicts how organizational actions in the form of routines, such as organizational processes, set in motion a cycle whereby certain resources are generated, these shaping future actions and resources.

We suggest that applying Feldman's model of resourcing to the construct of organizational identity may prove useful to understanding organizations' ability to generate resources. Figure 18.1 outlines the basic model we propose. Conceptually, we begin with members' cognitive schema of an organization's identity. Organizational identity guides organizational goals (Ashforth & Mael, 1996). Members serving as organizational agents then enact these goals in organizational actions. Organizational actions give rise to the resources made available to internal and external stakeholders. The constellation of resources generated in turn reinforces or modifies the organization's identity. Although we rely very heavily on Feldman's model, we add organizational goals as an intermediary step between organizational identity and organizational action. Members acting on behalf of their organizations must do so with some sense of what they are trying to move toward (Ashforth & Mael, 1996; Gross, 1969). We also extend Feldman's original model to highlight the impact that these emergent resources have on stakeholder self-schemas and stakeholders' own resourcing cycles.

Organizational Identity Schema → Organizational Goals

Organizational goals are an intention or aim for the organization *as a whole* and need not be output specific (Gross, 1969, p. 291, italics original). Organizational goals are notoriously complex. Simon (1964) suggests

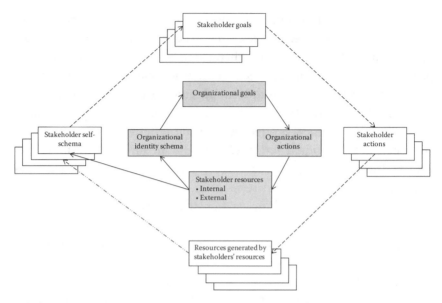

FIGURE 18.1

A model of organizational identity as a stakeholder resource. Dotted lines and white boxes represent additional resourcing cycles emanating beyond the organization and its direct stakeholders to increasingly distal stakeholders. (Derived from Feldman, M. S., *Organization Science*, 15, 295–309, 2004.)

that organizational goals are value premises that serve as constraints on decisions to act. Constraints can either be used to directly generate action alternatives (e.g., the organization aims to increase profits, so perhaps we should raise prices) or to test the acceptability of different alternatives (e.g., if we raise prices, will we turn away an unacceptable number of customers?). Because organizations are complex entities embedded in complex environments, they are subject to a plethora of constraints. In Simon's view, although there may be some level of agreement among members as to the whole set of constraints (goals) facing an organization, members likely vary in which constraints they use to generate alternatives and which they use to test them. We agree that in reality organizations are embedded in extraordinarily multifaceted environments that impose a huge number of minimal requirements on organizational action. To be considered legitimate, organizations need to meet a minimal set of standards on a multitude of fronts.

At the same time, strong organizational identities bring coherence to an otherwise hugely cumbersome and even ambivalent set of organizational goals. For example, although all organizations must arguably meet minimal requirements related to profitability, customer service, employee treatment, and community relations, an organization's identity may indicate which of these dimensions to particularly emphasize and how. An organization's identity infuses the organization with meaning, defining what it fundamentally is at its core (Albert & Whetten, 1985; Ashforth & Mael, 1996). It is a claim that is more internally consistent and simplistic than is strictly warranted by reality. As Ashforth and Mael (1996, p. 30) describe, "consistent with cognitive need for consistency, simplicity, and stability, identity claims are typically shorn of the diffuse inconsistencies, complexities, and ambiguities that would inhibit understanding." They go on to say that strong organizational identities provide a rudder, enabling commitment to goals. Therefore, although all organizational actions must be weighed against many minimal requirement tests, one of the great powers of organizational identity is that it tells members on which dimensions to focus, helping to ensure that the same criteria are used to actively generate action alternatives.

Organizational identity is enacted and expressed via organizational goals (Ashforth & Mael, 1996). Identities are associated with mental models outlining rules for appropriate targets and aspirations, where different rules are elicited by different identities (March & Olsen, 1998; Stephens, Markus, & Townsend, 2007). The organization's identity serves as a cognitive filter for sensemaking among members (Ashforth & Mael, 1996) about the kinds of ends to which the organization is appropriately directed (see Dutton & Dukerich, 1991). This is consistent with Hsu and Hannan's (2005) suggestion that organizational identities are associated with social codes or rules as held by members (and other stakeholders) outlining appropriate organizational actions.

For the purposes of simplicity, we assume here that an organization's identity schema is relatively strong or commonly shared (Ashforth & Mael, 1996) and that there are not prominent within-organization divisions regarding organizational identity (e.g., Glynn, 2000; Pratt & Rafaeli, 1997). Between-member discrepancies in the organization's perceived identity schema would lead to certain actors taking different actions and generating distinct types of resources. Therefore, we view this circumstance as adding complexity to the model but not as beyond its potential scope.

Organizational Goals → Actions

Consistent goals fostered by a strong identity provide the basis for consistent action (Ashforth & Mael, 1996). Generally speaking, possible courses of action are not preexisting, but must be discovered, designed, or synthesized through the use of goals (Simon, 1964, p. 7). Organizational goals focus members' attention by defining what actions are organizationally relevant (Zald, 1963) and appropriate (Balser & Carmin, 2002). Once members acquire a sense for the organizational goals appropriate to the organization's identity, they then, as organizational agents, are tasked with carrying out the actions deemed essential to the organization's sense of self (see March & Olsen, 1998).

Identity informs how organizations go about doing things and the structures set in place, as well as the policies and procedures enacted through those structures (Ashforth & Mael, 1996; Dutton & Dukerich, 1991). Dutton and Dukerich's (1991) Port Authority study illustrates how the organization's identity as a professional organization with technical expertise led to the view that dealing proactively with homelessness was not an organizationally appropriate goal. This influenced organizational action. Whereas proactive actions for handling the problem were constrained, reactive actions such as removing the homeless were enabled.

Actions → Stakeholder Resources

Rather than viewing resources as external and stable, Feldman (2004) offers a perspective of resources as part of the organizational context and as mutable. She views resources as assets (e.g., people, time, money, knowledge, and skill) and relationship qualities (e.g., trust, authority) that enable actors to engage cognitive schemas while constraining their use of others. Resources are sources of energy because they energize particular schemas, making possible new actions and resources (Feldman, 2004). Feldman's case study outlines how routine organizational processes and practices alter both the availability and the meaning of resources.

This perspective is consistent with work on organizational goals and organizational identity. For example, Zald (1963) notes that the organizational practices and processes required to achieve specific goals impose restrictions on members, affecting such phenomena as communication and authority (Zald, 1963, p. 207), viewed here as types of resources. Meanwhile, in the domain of organizational identity, Dutton and Dukerich's (1991) study shows how identity-consistent organizational actions in response to homelessness affected relationships between the organization and outsiders. When the organization took the action of moving the homeless out, strong relationships were developed with the police. In a later era of serving as quiet advocates for the homeless, relationships were instead strengthened with homeless service providers and with other transportation facilities also dealing with homelessness. Importantly, this study shows that organizational actions affect not only the resources of internal stakeholders but also those of external stakeholders.

Stakeholder Resources → Organizational Identity Schema

One important facet of Feldman's model is its recursive nature. The model does not end with resources but highlights the fact that resources themselves, once created, serve as inputs into the resourcing process. In fact, it is the energizing of subsequent schemas that distinguishes mere potential resources from true resources in use (Feldman & Quick, in press). As applied to organizational identity, her model underscores how the resources set in motion through organizational goals and actions help to reinforce or modify the organization's identity. Just as stakeholder resources are shaped by organizational identity, so, too, do they shape organizational identity.

Organizational identity construction and maintenance are socially negotiated (Dutton & Dukerich, 1991; Scott & Lane, 2000). An organization's identity must be validated to be sustained where validation requires that social ends conform to stakeholder needs and social expectations (Ashforth & Mael, 1996; Dutton & Dukerich, 1991; Hsu & Hannan, 2005; Scott & Lane, 2000). Validation strengthens the identity, reinforcing consistent goals and actions (Ashforth & Mael, 1996). However, when the resources generated through organizational action do not conform to stakeholder needs or social expectations, delegitimizing schemas are evoked. For example, when the Port Authority moved the homeless out, the relationship with police became increasingly ineffective at handling the escalating problem. This elicited (or resourced) the schema of the Port Authority among outsiders and insiders as ineffective, clashing with its identity as "committed to quality." The resulting threat to the organization's identity led to a shift in the particular organizational identity characteristics members emphasized to impute goals and direct actions. Rather than focusing on the identity trait of a professional organization with technical expertise, agents drew on other identity traits such as its commitment to quality and its public service ethic. This shift enabled different actions (e.g., working with service providers to create drop-in centers) to address the problem. As such, organizational identity (Scott & Lane, 2000) as well as subsequent organizational goals (Thompson & McEwen, 1958) and actions (Dutton & Dukerich, 1991) reflect stakeholders' needs and preferences.

Stakeholder Resources → Stakeholder Self-Schemas

In addition to their influence on stakeholders' schemas of the organization, the resources generated for stakeholders through organizational actions will also affect their own self-schemas. Among members, the kinds of communication and relationship patterns, for example, that result from organizational routines will influence the qualities and characteristics that members consider central to their own self-views (Brickson, 2000, 2008b; Covaleski, Dirsmith, Heian, & Samuel, 1998). For example, Covaleski et al. (1998) observed that Big Six public accounting firms utilized such practices as *management by objectives*, whereby in communications with partners, supervisors encouraged them to commit to ever-increasing sets of self-expectations. This form of communication transformed partners' identities from autonomous professionals to business entrepreneurs. The identities elicited among members are apt to bear striking similarity to that of the larger organization because they reflect the broader organization's goals (e.g., Covaleski et al., 1998). In Covaleski et al.'s study, for example, partners began to see themselves as profit-maximizing "corporate clones" of the larger profit-maximizing organization. Beyond general self-view, resources will also influence a more specific facet of member self-schema, organizational identification. To the extent that the resources generated meet members' needs and expectations, members are more apt to identify with, or define themselves in terms of, their organization (Ashforth & Mael, 1989; Brickson, 2008a; Dutton, Dukerich, & Harquail, 1994).

Further, just as the self-schemas of internal stakeholders are influenced by the assets and relationship qualities arising from their experience with the organization, so, too, are those of external stakeholders. For example, an organization providing tailored and empathic customer service may make salient in the customer's self-schema qualities of worthiness and dignity. Imagine a physically handicapped patron interacting with a customer service representative. Often, because of preconceptions of handicapped people as incapable victims, service providers address questions about handicapped people to their companions or take a pitying tone (Mayer, Stephens, & Bergman, 1995). Such responses challenge the customer's personhood (Mayer et al., 1995). A more empathic and dignity-eliciting response would set aside the service provider's preconceptions and accept the customer's own version of reality (Mayer et al., 1995).

These emergent stakeholder self-schemas take on life of their own, generating new cycles of resourcing that emanate outward in expanding circles from the focal organization. When members' identities parallel that of the organization, similar goals and actions are elicited at the individual level of analysis (Covaleski et al., 1998). Members' own goals and actions then shape the resources made available to other organizational members, to external stakeholders members engage within the context of work, and even to individuals with whom members interact outside of work. For example, Feldman and Khademian (2003) suggest that organizational practices that empower members lead those members to take actions toward external stakeholders that empower them as well. Meanwhile, altering one's self-schema specifically by identifying with one's organization influences one's goals and actions such that members are more apt to engage in organizational citizenship behaviors (e.g., Tyler & Blader, 2000), influencing resources generated vis-à-vis coworkers and external stakeholders.

At the same time, changes to external stakeholders' self-schemas will also affect their goals and behaviors vis-à-vis their own stakeholders. These in turn will ultimately mold the resources conferred on them. For example, with a worthy and dignified self-schema, the customer noted on the previous page is more apt to demonstrate patience and empathy for his or her own clients.

THE MULTIPLE RESOURCE GENERATIVE POTENTIALITIES OF ORGANIZATIONAL IDENTITY

Having outlined a basic model of organizational identity as a stakeholder resource, we now apply the lens of identity orientation to illustrate specific examples of how different types of organizational identity vis-à-vis stakeholders may lead to the generation of distinct forms of stakeholder resources. Table 18.1 outlines the distinct organizational goals, actions, and emergent stakeholder resources hypothesized to be associated with each identity orientation. Organizational identity orientation is not a

TABLE 18.1

Stakeholder Resourcing by Identity Orientation

Organizational Self-Schema	Individualistic	Relational	Collectivistic
Organizational goals	Self interest	Other interest	Collective interest
	• Improve corporate image • Grow market share • Increase employee performance	• Maximize client care • Better serve suppliers • Help employees live more satisfying lives	• Ensure consumer safety • Advance a cause • Provide members with a sense of community
Organizational actions	• Transactional psychological contracts • Calculative HR practices • Arm's reach external relationships	• Relational psychological contracts • Relational HR practices • Intimate connections with external stakeholders	• Ideological psychological contracts • Collective HR practices • External relationships based on common mission
Stakeholder resources	Relationship qualities	Relationship qualities	Relationship qualities
	• Information-rich • Opportunity-rich • Inspirational	• Trust • Compassion	• Community • Camaraderie
	Assets	Assets	Assets
	• Financial benefits • Bravery virtues • Inexpensive goods and services	• Time • Caring virtues • Personalized care • Organizational capacity building	• Transcendent meaning • Just virtues • Social capital • Resource and information sharing

These are meant to serve as illustrative examples and are not exhaustive.

Source: Derived in part from Brickson, S. L., *Academy of Management Review*, 32, 864–888, 2007.

taxonomy, meant to categorize organizations into three camps, but is rather a typology that outlines three pure types with which organizations can be compared (Brickson, 2005). Both pure and hybrid identity orientation organizations exist (Brickson, 2005), although we focus here on pure types for simplicity.

Identity Orientation → Organizational Goals

Embedded within identity orientation are different loci of organizational self-definition (see Brewer & Gardner, 1996; Brickson, 2007). These implicate distinct organizational roles vis-à-vis stakeholders, sole entity, dyadic partner, or collective member. Each role of the firm is associated with a primary social goal, self-interest, other-interest, and collective interest, respectively (Brickson, 2007). In each case, members will deem that overarching goal as appropriate to the organization's sense of self (March & Olsen, 1998).

High-level goals, such as those related to self, other, or collective interest, serve to guide meaning, indicating the purpose and implications of actions (Vallacher & Wegner, 1987). As such, they make action sustainable, protecting against other competing goals (Vallacher & Wegner, 1987). Meanwhile, however, lower-level nested goals are necessary for members to know how to go about achieving and implementing the more abstract goals (Vallacher & Wegner, 1987). Therefore, nested within this meta-goal of self, other, or group interest lie a number of more specific organizational goals. For example, organizations can achieve the goal of enhancing their own welfare through several means, including improving corporate image, growing market share, and securing higher employee performance. Organizations may advance the other's welfare through such directives as maximizing client care, seeking to better serve suppliers, and helping their employees to live more satisfying lives. And organizations may improve the welfare of some larger group through such specific goals as ensuring consumer safety, working to advance a cause, and providing members with a sense of community. Although high-level goals afford sustainability to action, they also foster action flexibility as specific circumstances change (Vallacher & Wegner, 1987). As such, more microlevel goals nested within the higher-level basis of social motivation will vary both between organizations sharing the same orientation and within a given organization over time.

Organizational Goals → Organizational Actions

One particularly compelling aspect of identity is that it enables the basis for distinct action relative to other organizations, serving as a counter-weight to institutional pressures to imitate widely accepted practices (Ashforth & Mael, 1996). Distinct identity types, such as different identity orientations, set the course for markedly different forms of organizational action through their influence on higher level and nested organizational goals. With the particular meta-goal of self, other, or collective interest as the compass, organizations engage, through their members, in actions aimed at achieving the more specific nested goals that serve as focal points. According to this view, organizational action is not only a function of what is appropriate to organizational identity but is also a function of what organizational agents deem to be most consequential in terms of meeting identity-derived organizational goals. Although a logic of consequences, typically painted in self-interested terms whereby an entity seeks outcomes that maximize its own lot, is usually contrasted with a logic of appropriateness, whereby an entity does what is appropriate to its sense of self (e.g., Meglino & Korsgaard, 2004), the two are not mutually exclusive. March and Olsen (1998) point out that the logic of consequences can be a special case of the logic of appropriateness when identity elicits its use. Each identity orientation renders different forms of consequences as appropriate measures of successful action.

Although specific organizational practices and procedures will vary between organizations sharing the same identity orientation as a function of nested organizational goals (see Brickson, 2007, for more examples), they should also bear some strong similarities. Organizations' perceived role of the firm and higher order goal of self, other, or collective interest will heavily influence their approach to managing internal and external stakeholder relationships (Brickson, 2007). Individualistic organizations tend to institute transactional psychological contracts (based on each party advancing its own welfare; Rousseau & McLean Parks, 1993), employ calculative human resource (HR) practices (e.g., strong individual performance-based incentives; Gooderham, Nordhaug, & Ringdal, 2004), and form arm's reach external relationships (e.g., writing checks to relatively few, highly visible nonprofits). Relational organizations tend to initiate relational psychological contracts (based on a socioemotional dyadic bond; Rousseau & McLean Parks, 1993), introduce relational HR practices (e.g., incentives based on meeting developmental goals), and seek and maintain intimate connections with external stakeholders (e.g., devoting top management time and attention to a nonprofit partnership). Collectivistic organizations tend to enact ideological psychological contracts (based on a common ideological purpose; Thompson & Bunderson, 2003), engage in collective HR practices (e.g., group-based performance incentives), and forge external ties based on commonly shared ends (e.g., engaging in joint activities with a number of nonprofits sharing a similar mission).

Although nested organizational goals and the specific actions taken to address them may change with varying circumstances, organizational agents will act with relative consistency toward the overarching goal of self, other, or collective interest. Once a high-level goal, such as these, is identified to explain one's actions, people tend to act consistently with that purpose in the future (Wegner, Vallacher, Kiersted, & Dizadji, 1986, experiment 1).

Organizational Actions → Stakeholder Resources

Organizational action has a profound influence on the resources made available to internal and external stakeholders. In addition to the direct influence it has on both types of stakeholders, it also has an indirect impact on insiders through shaping members' relationships with one another and resources resulting from those relationships. Resources consist of both relationship qualities and assets (Feldman, 2004). In addition to the things Feldman notes as assets, including money, information, and time, we suggest that personal virtues, which imbue individuals with a moral compass (Walker & Hennig, 2004), are another type of asset. We also mention other assets relevant to external stakeholders, such as goods and services and customer care.

Relationships forged with and within individualistic organizations are apt to be weaker in nature, so as to minimize switching costs should more instrumental alternative relations arise (Brickson, 2007). Such weak ties are particularly effective for maintaining relationships with diverse networks of individuals or bridging the gap between two separate networks (Granovetter, 1973) so as to be rich in information and opportunity. Relationships with individualistic entities may also have an inspirational quality as the organization or individual is likely striving to achieve excellence (see Lockwood & Kunda, 1997). With respect to assets, internal stakeholders of individualistic organizations are apt to benefit financially. Their relationship with the organization is built on a foundation of instrumentality, while the organization's HR practices likely emphasize financial performance-based incentives. Individualistic assumptions underlying organizational action and individualistic processes advanced by it also may instill "bravery" virtues such as intrepidity, dedication, and confidence (Brickson, 2007; see Walker & Hennig, 2004). Meanwhile, among external stakeholders, consumers are likely to benefit from a wide array of inexpensive goods and services (Brickson, 2007). These resources are enabled by actions directed at maximizing efficiency and innovation, likely goals in individualistic organizations. As another potential external stakeholder, nonprofits with which businesses choose to align themselves for public relations purposes stand to make significant economic gains (Brickson, 2007).

Resources contributed to stakeholders associated with relational businesses would look strikingly different. Close dyadic ties extended toward both internal and external stakeholders engender the relationship qualities of trust and compassion. With regard to assets, insiders may also benefit from increased time. Whereas organizations' employee relationships in individualistic and collectivistic organizations are a means to an end, self-interest or collective interest, they are an end in themselves among relational firms. The organization is invested in the welfare of the employee per se, likely resulting in greater concern for and attention to employees' need for work-life balance. Whereas employees of collectivistic and especially individualistic organizations may be subjected to a time famine (Perlow, 1999), those within relational organizations may be granted a greater degree of flexibility. Because of the personalized bonds of attachment generated by organizational actions, insiders also likely benefit from the elicitation of "caring" virtues, such as empathy, altruism, and dependability (Brickson, 2007; see Walker & Hennig, 2004). Among external stakeholders, organizational clients probably benefit from highly personalized care, whereas nonprofits or other organizational partners may receive tailored advice and capacity building (Brickson, 2007).

Finally, stakeholders of collectivistic organizations are likely to benefit from different relationship qualities and assets. Because these organizations seek and maintain ties based on a common overarching purpose, those connected to the organization's cliquish network structure (Brickson, 2007) probably enjoy the relationship qualities of community and camaraderie. Assets may be equally distinct. Insiders are apt to experience a special kind of knowledge, transcendent meaning (see Ashforth & Vaidyanath, 2002). Systems of shared meaning, provided by group life, facilitate sensemaking and understanding (Pratt, 2000; Weick, 1995). Further, collectivistic assumptions and processes are also associated with the elicitation of "just" virtues, such as conscientiousness, fairness, and principle (Brickson, 2007; see Heine et al., 1999; Walker & Hennig, 2004). External stakeholders are apt to gain through their affiliation with collectivistic organizations' assets such as social capital and information (Brickson, 2007). Collectivistic organizations, by virtue of their actions to build and maintain ties with others having parallel missions, are uniquely apt to unite people within and across organizations. The resulting networks are high in social capital because of shared sense of purpose. This in turn encourages greater resource and information sharing (Uzzi, 1999).

Stakeholder Resources → Organizational Identity Schema

Resources generated through organizational action can either reinforce or modify organizational identity. Assuming important stakeholders were involved in negotiating the organization's identity orientation, generally speaking, resources derived from those actions should reinforce the existing identity orientation. Even if involved stakeholders deem the resulting resources inappropriate or insufficient, they will likely take efforts to crystallize the organization's identity orientation such that subsequent organizational actions are more in keeping with the negotiated identity. On the other hand, if key stakeholders were left out of the identity formation process, they may not be able to accurately discern what the organization's identity *is*, or they may not buy into that identity (Scott & Lane, 2000). Thus, they may view the resources enabled by organizational action as inappropriate relative to expectations. As a result, they may try and renegotiate the organization's identity orientation altogether (see Scott & Lane, 2000).

Stakeholder Resources → Stakeholder Self-Schemas

Along with their influence on organizational identity, stakeholder resources also facilitate certain self-schemas among stakeholders themselves. Organizational processes and practices (Covaleski et al., 1998), as well as the relationship qualities and assets they engender, tend to align stakeholders' identities with that of the focal organization. Despite between-entity differences (Brickson, 2005; Gabriel & Gardner, 1999), identity orientation is also situationally primed (e.g., Brewer & Gardner, 1996; Brickson, 2008b). Although this effect is arguably stronger among internal stakeholders, identities can also spread through populations of organizations (March, 1996). Organizations imitate others perceived as relevant, successful, and legitimate (DiMaggio & Powell, 1983; March, 1996; Meyer & Rowan, 1977). Given that business schools and the popular press have in recent years endorsed shareholder wealth maximization, consistent with an individualistic orientation, as the only legitimate model (DiTomaso, Parks-Yancy, & Post, 2003; Ghoshal, 2005; Gioia, 2002, 2003), associating with relational and collectivistic organizations legitimated by stakeholders may be especially important in fostering those orientations among business organizations.

Once elicited, stakeholder self-schemas then begin new cycles of resourcing. Members' goals and actions toward other members and toward outsiders will reflect the identity orientation elicited by their organization. External stakeholders' goals and actions toward their own internal and external stakeholders will also be influenced. Further, as noted above, another facet of member self-schema to consider is their identification with the organization. Although organizations of any identity orientation can secure identification (Brickson, 2008a), increasing organizational citizenship behaviors (Rioux & Penner, 2001), the nature of the behaviors elicited by identification depends on what the organization's goals and interests are perceived to be (van Knippenberg, 2000). For example, members of individualistic organizations may exert particular effort in doing their own job well; those in relational organizations may extend extra efforts to help colleagues in need; and those in collectivistic organizations may go to extra lengths to advance a positive group atmosphere. A recent study (Coleman & Borman, 2000) shows that these three sets of organization citizenship behaviors do cluster together. Whether the product of the stakeholder's elicited identity orientation or of members identifying with organizations with different identity orientations, the actions and resources generated from stakeholder self-schemas will set in motion new cycles of resourcing emanating outward beyond the organization in ever-expanding circles of influence or contagion.

FUTURE RESEARCH DIRECTIONS

Identity enables action (Ashforth & Mael, 1996; Freese & Burke, 1994; Stryker & Burke, 2000). Yet we still know very little about the relationship between organizational identity, organizational action, and the outcomes of those actions. This suggests a wealth of opportunities ahead for exploring these connections. Given the challenges facing the world today, along with the enormous potential of business organizations to help address these issues, bringing the positive organizational scholarship lens to the study of organizational identity may help to focus our attention on the more specific question of how organizational identity can serve to generate actions leading to socially beneficial outcomes.

In the current model, we tried to illustrate how organizational identity can serve as a resource to internal and external stakeholders through the elicitation of organizational goals and actions. We cautiously propose that a positive organizational identity is identifiable through its creation of a "net positive" level of socially valuable resources. Although theoretically convenient, this begs for more conceptual work around its meaning. Further, finding a means of empirically measuring such a standard would be both enormously helpful and challenging.

We suggest that distinct types of organizational identities, because of their influence on organizational goals and actions, are uniquely well-qualified to produce certain forms of stakeholder resources. This leads to a whole string of potentially important questions. Is this claim true? Does diversity in the resources provided by business organizations contribute to a healthy society? Is diversity in organizational identity decreasing with the rhetoric of shareholder wealth maximization? How might we increase diversity in organizational identity so as to broaden the array of stakeholder resources generated?

One strength of applying the resourcing model to organizational identity is that it enables one to simultaneously view organizational identity as a source of agency and the product of social construction. Questions confront each view. From an agency perspective, how challenging is it for businesses to negotiate and maintain relational and collectivistic identities? Is it mostly a matter of finding stakeholder relationships that support these identities (e.g., Thompson & McEwen, 1958), or are there broader significant institutional blockages? How can different types of identities be leveraged to address society's most pressing problems, such as our environmental crisis? Does each have a role to play (e.g., finding more efficient means of using natural resources and inventing innovative green technology—individualistic; caring for victims of natural disasters through fair lending, etc.—relational; working collectively with others in the industry and the government to change standards—collectivistic)? From a social constructionist perspective, what role can internal and external stakeholders play in negotiating organizational identities with net positive outcomes? More diverse organizational identities? Finally, given that organizational identities must be legitimized by stakeholders, what forces currently constrain our hopes and expectations of organizations?

Societal need, corporate resources, and business leaders' interests all suggest that the time may be ripe for business organizations to significantly and positively contribute to society. But academics and practitioners alike are grappling with questions about *how* they can affect positive change. We provide one view of this process here. The present model suggests that an organization's identity directs organizational goals and actions, in turn enabling certain kinds of stakeholder resources. The particular resources made available to stakeholders then serve to energize self-schemas among the stakeholders themselves, creating new cycles of resourcing. As such, we view the positive potential of business organizations as expansive.

We hope that the model serves to advance work on organizational identity by making a stronger connection between organizational identity, organizational actions, and implications for actions on insiders and outsiders. We hope that it contributes to stakeholder theory by drawing a connection between descriptive and instrumental branches, illustrating how distinct views of the firm, as held by organizational actors, inform the kinds of noneconomic and economic effects that organizations have on society. On the practice side, we hope that this line of thinking may ultimately help to direct managers' attention toward ways of successfully addressing societal needs. In a world that cries out for so much, leaders may often feel overwhelmed and unsure of where to begin. Some may worry that efforts to contribute to society may pull them away from their organizations' identities. It may be, however, that organizational identity can itself serve as an inspirational guidepost helping leaders identify effective means of contributing.

REFERENCES

Albert, S., & Whetten, D. A. (1985). Organizational identity. In L. L. Cummings & B. M. Staw (Eds.), *Research on organizational behavior* (Vol. 8, pp. 263–295). Greenwich, CT: JAI Press.

Ashforth, B., & Mael, F. (1989). Social identity theory and the organization. *Academy of Management Review, 14*, 20–39.

Ashforth, B. E., & Mael, F. A. (1996). Organizational identity and strategy as a context for the individual. *Advances in Strategic Management, 13*, 19–64.

Ashforth, B. E., & Vaidyanath, D. (2002). Work organizations as secular religions. *Journal of Management Inquiry, 11*, 359–370.

Balser, D. B., & Carmin, J. (2002). The interpretive basis of action: Identity and tactics in environmental movement organizations. *Academy of Management Proceedings*, B1–B6.

Brewer, M. B., & Gardner, W. (1996). Who is this "we"? Levels of collective identity and self-representations. *Journal of Personality and Social Psychology, 71*, 83–93.

Brickson, S. L. (2000). The impact of identity orientation on individual and organizational outcomes in demographically diverse settings. *Academy of Management Review, 25*, 82–101.

Brickson, S. L. (2005). Organizational identity orientation: Making the link between organizational identity and organizations' relations with stakeholders. *Administrative Science Quarterly, 50*, 576–609.

Brickson, S. L. (2007). Organizational identity orientation: The genesis of the role of the firm and distinct forms of social value. *Academy of Management Review, 32*, 864–888.

Brickson, S. L. (2008a). *Athletes, best friends, and social activists: Modeling multiple paths to organizational identification*. Unpublished manuscript.

Brickson, S. L. (2008b). Re-assessing the standard: The expansive positive potential of relational identity in diverse organizations. *Journal of Positive Psychology, 3*, 1–15.

Carey, J., & Shapiro, S. R. (2004). Global warming. *Business Week, 3869*, 60–69.

Caza, B., & Bagozzi, R. P. (2008). *Individual functioning in the face of adversity at work: An identity-based perspective*. Unpublished manuscript.

Cha, S. E., & Roberts, L. M. (2008). *Steering identity: Mobilizing a multivalent identity as a resource in organizations*. Unpublished manuscript, McGill University and Harvard Business School.

Coleman, V. I., & Borman, W. C. (2000). Investigating the underlying structure of the citizenship performance domain. *Human Resources Management Review, 10*, 25–44.

Corley, K. G., Harquail, C. V., Pratt, M. G., Glynn, M. A., Fiol, C. M., & Hatch, M. J. (2006). Guiding organizational identity through aged adolescence. *Journal of Management Inquiry, 15*, 85–99.

Cormack, M., & Fitzgerald, N. (2006). *The role of business in society: An agenda for action*. Cambridge, MA: Harvard University. (Report CSR-06-Citizen)

Covaleski, M. A., Dirsmith, M. W., Heian, J. B., & Samuel, S. (1998). The calculated and the avowed: Techniques of discipline and struggles over identity in big six public accounting firms, *Administrative Science Quarterly, 43*, 293–327.

Dewey, J. (1989). In John J. McDermott (Ed.), *The philosophy of John Dewey*. Chicago: University of Chicago Press.

DiMaggio, P. J., & Powell, W. W. (1983). The iron cage revisited: Institutional isomorphism and collective rationality in organizational fields. *American Sociological Review, 48,* 147–160.

DiTomaso, N., Parks-Yancy, R., & Post, C. (2003). Structure, relationships, and community responsibility. *Management Communication Quarterly, 17,* 143–150.

Doh, J. P., & Guay, T. R. (2006). The role of multinational corporations in transnational institution building: A policy network perspective. *Human Relations, 59,* 1571–1600.

Donaldson, T., & Preston, L. E. (1995). The stakeholder theory of the corporation: Concepts, evidence, and implications. *Academy of Management Review, 20,* 65–91.

Dutton, J. E., & Dukerich, J. M. (1991). Keeping an eye on the mirror: Image and identity in organizational adaptation. *Academy of Management Journal, 34,* 517–554.

Dutton, J. E., Dukerich, J. M., & Harquail, C. V. (1994). Organizational images and member identification. *Journal of Management, 17,* 191–206.

Feldman, M. S. (2004). Resources in emerging structures and processes of change. *Organization Science, 15,* 295–309.

Feldman, M. S., & Khademian, A. M. (2003). Empowerment and cascading vitality. In K. S. Cameron, J. E. Dutton, & R. E. Quinn (Eds.), *Positive organizational scholarship* (pp. 343–358). San Francisco: Barrett-Koehler Publishers.

Feldman, M. S., & Quick, K. S. (in press). Generating resources through inclusive public management. *International Public Management Journal.*

Freese, L., & Burke, P. J. (1994). Persons, identities, and social interaction. In B. Markovsky, K. Heimer, and J. O'Brien (Eds.), *Advances in group processes* (Vol. 11, pp. 1–24). Greenwich, CT: JAI.

Gabriel, S., & Gardner, W. L. (1999). Are there "his" and "hers" types of interdependence? The implications of gender differences in collective versus relational interdependence for affect, behavior, and cognition. *Journal of Personality and Social Psychology, 77,* 642–655.

Ghoshal, S. (2005). Bad management theories are destroying good management practices. *Academy of Management Learning & Education, 4,* 75–91.

Gioia, D. A. (2002). Business education's role in the crisis of corporate confidence. *Academy of Management Executive, 16,* 142–144.

Gioia, D. A. (2003). Business organization as instrument for societal responsibility. *Organization, 10,* 435–438.

Gooderham, P., Nordhaug, O., & Ringdal, K. (2004). Institutional context and HRM: US subsidiaries in Europe. In F. McDonald, M. Mayer, & T. Buck (Eds.), *The process of internationalization. Strategic, cultural, and policy perspectives* (pp. 135–148). New York: Palgrave Macmillan.

Glynn, M. A. (2000). When cymbals become symbols: Conflict over organizational identity within a symphony orchestra. *Organization Science, 11,* 285–298.

Granovetter, M. (1973). The strength of weak ties. *American Journal of Sociology, 78,* 1360–1380.

Gross, E. (1969). The definition of organizational goals. *British Journal of Sociology, 20,* 277–294.

Hamilton, A. E., & Gioia, D. A. (2009). Creating sustainable organization identities. In L. M. Roberts & J. Dutton (Eds.), *Exploring positive identities and organizations: Building a theoretical and research foundation.* New York: Psychology Press, Taylor & Francis Group.

Heine, S. J., Lehman, D. R., Markus, H. R., & Kitayama, S. (1999). Is there a universal need for positive self-regard? *Psychological Review, 106,* 766–794.

Hsu, G., & Hannan, M. T. (2005). Identities, genres, and organizational forms. *Organization Science, 16*, 474–490.

James, W. (1918). *The principles of psychology*. New York: Holt.

Jones, T. M., & Wicks, A. C. (1999). Convergent stakeholder theory. *Academy of Management Review, 24*, 206–221.

Kaliski, B. (2001). Social responsibility and organizational ethics. In B. Kaliski (Ed.), *Encyclopedia of business and finance* (2nd ed., Vol. 1). New York: Macmillan Reference.

Lockwood, P., & Kunda, Z. (1997). Superstars and me: Predicting the impact of role models on the self. *Journal of Personality and Social Psychology, 73*, 93–103.

Maitland, A. (2005, June 1). A responsible balancing act. *The Financial Times*.

Malhi, Y., Timmons Roberts, J., Betts, R. A., Killeen, T. J., Li, W., & Nobre, C. A. (2008). Climate change, deforestation, and the fate of the Amazon. *Science, 319*, 169–172.

March, J. G. (1996). Continuity and change in theories of organizational action. *Administrative Science Quarterly, 41*, 278–287.

March, J. G., & Olsen, J. P. (1998). The institutional dynamics of international political orders. *International Organization, 52*, 943–969.

Margolis, J. D., & Walsh, J. P. (2003). Misery loves companies: Rethinking social initiatives by business. *Administrative Science Quarterly, 48*, 268–305.

Mayer, R. N., Stephens, D. L., & Bergman, K. (1995). The Americans With Disabilities Act: A mandate for marketers. *Journal of Public Policy & Marketing, 14*, 164–168.

Meglino, B. M., & Korsgaard, M. A. (2004). Considering rational self-interest as a disposition: Organizational implications of other orientation. *Journal of Applied Psychology, 89*, 946–959.

Meyer, J. W., & Rowan, B. (1977). Institutionalized organizations. *American Journal of Sociology, 83*, 340–363.

Miller, J. (1999). *Egotopia: Narcissism and the new American landscape*. Tuscaloosa: University of Alabama Press.

Perlow, L. A. (1999). The time famine: Toward a sociology of work time. *Administrative Science Quarterly, 44*, 57–81.

Pfeffer, J., & Salancik, G. R. (1978). *The external control of organizations: A resource dependence perspective*. New York: Harper and Row.

Pratt, M. (2000). The good, the bad, and the ambivalent: Managing identification among Amway distributors. *Administrative Science Quarterly, 45*, 456–493.

Pratt, M. G., & Rafaeli, A. (1997). Organizational dress as a symbol of multilayered social identities. *Academy of Management Journal, 40*, 862–898.

Quinn, R. W., & Worline, M. C. (2008). Enabling courageous collective action: Conversations from United Airlines Flight 93. *Organization Science, 19*, 497–516.

Rioux, S. M., & Penner, L. A. (2001). The cause of organizational citizenship behavior: A motivational analysis. *Journal of Applied Psychology, 86*, 1306–1314.

Ritzer, G. (2004). *The McDonaldization of society: An investigation into the changing character of contemporary social life*. London: Sage Publications Inc.

Rousseau, D. M., & McLean Parks, J. (1993). The contracts of individuals and organizations. *Research in Organizational Behavior, 15*, 1–13.

Scott, S. G., & Lane, V. R. (2000). A stakeholder approach to organizational identity. *Academy of Management Review, 25*, 43–62.

Simon, H. A. (1964). On the concept of organizational goals. *Administrative Science Quarterly, 9*, 1–22.

Stephens, N. M., Markus, H. R., & Townsend, S. S. (2007). Choice as an act of meaning: The case of social class. *Journal of Personality and Social Psychology, 93,* 814–830.

Stryker, S., & Burke, P. J. (2000). The past, present, and future of identity theory. *Social Psychology Quarterly, 63,* 284–297.

Teece, D. J., Pisano, G., & Shuen, A. (1997). Dynamic capabilities and strategic management. *Strategic Management Journal, 18,* 509–533.

The scientists speak. (2007, November 20, late edition). *New York Times.*

Thompson, J. A., & Bunderson, J. S. (2003). Violations of principle: Ideological currency in the psychological contract. *Academy of Management Review, 28,* 571–586.

Thompson, J. D. (1967). *Organization in action.* New York: McGraw-Hill.

Thompson, J. D., & McEwen, W. J. (1958). Organizational goals and environment: Goal setting as an interaction process. *American Sociological Review, 23,* 23–31.

Tyler, T. R., & Blader, S. L. (2000). *Cooperation in groups: Procedural justice, social identity, and behavioral engagement.* Philadelphia: Psychology Press.

Uzzi, B. (1999). Embeddedness in the making of financial capital: How social relations and networks benefit firms seeking financing. *American Sociological Review, 64,* 481–505.

Vallacher, R. R., & Wegner, D. M. (1987). What do people think they're doing? Action identification and human behavior. *Psychological Review, 94,* 3–15.

van Knippenberg, D. (2000). Work motivation and performance: A social identity perspective. *Applied Psychology: An International Review, 49,* 357–371.

Walker, L. J., & Hennig, K. H. (2004). Differing conceptions of moral exemplarity: Just, brave, and caring. *Journal of Personality and Social Psychology, 86,* 629–647.

Wegner, D. M., Vallacher, R. R., Kiersted, G., & Dizadji, D. (1986). Action identification in the emergence of social behavior. *Social Cognition, 4,* 18–38.

Weick, K. E. (1995). *Sensemaking in organizations.* Thousand Oaks, CA: Sage.

Zald, M. N. (1963). Comparative analysis and measurements of organizational goals. *The Sociological Quarterly, 4,* 206–230.

Zald, M. N. (1970). Political economy: A framework for comparative analysis. In *Power in organizations* (pp. 221–269). Nashville, TN: Vanderbilt University Press.

19

Fostering Sustainability-Focused Organizational Identities

Aimee Hamilton and Dennis A. Gioia

CONTENTS

In this chapter, we conceptualize the essential aspects of organizations that have the idea of sustainability at the core of their identities. *Sustainability* is a multifaceted concept that presumes a dynamic balance among economic, environmental, and social goals. This sort of balance is admittedly difficult to achieve—for most organizations today it is more an aspiration than a reality and will require a shift in, and possibly even a thorough reconsideration of, current beliefs, values, and practices. Sweeping change of this nature is far more likely to take hold and become permanent when new thinking and acting express a deeply held commitment to sustainability on the part of the organization. In other words, an enduring shift toward sustainable organizational practice requires that sustainability become a fundamental, indispensable part of an organization's identity. As we will explain, we view an organizational identity that is sincerely sustainability focused as one that has an important element of a positive identity, in terms of the content and structure of that identity, as well as the outcomes that it engenders.

In the following sections we provide our key definitions and core assumptions. We then conceptualize the content and structure of sustainability-focused organizational identities and illustrate our ideas with examples drawn from actual organizations. We believe that sustainability-focused identities can take many forms and can manifest in various expressions, practices, and outcomes. We also make some preliminary suggestions about the general and essential characteristics of such identities to stimulate further theorizing and research on the topic. In the subsequent section, we suggest the theoretical means through which sustainability-focused identities might be developed. In particular, we outline two distinct but related processes, one involving identity-image relationships and one involving institutional discourse about identity, that have the potential to shape sustainability-focused identities in organizations. We conclude the chapter with a discussion of the research implications that a positive organizational identity perspective presents for scholars interested in sustainability.

KEY DEFINITIONS AND ASSUMPTIONS

Sustainability

In the 1980s, the United Nations defined the concept of *sustainable development* as societal advancement that "meets the needs of the present without compromising the ability of future generations to meet their own needs" (WCED, 1987, p. 25) and called for international cooperation to achieve this type of development on a global scale. At the organizational level, we define *sustainability* as achieving a balance among environmental responsibility, social equity, and economic capability (Bansal, 2005; WCED, 1987). We prefer "sustainability" to the related concept of "corporate social responsibility" (CSR) for several reasons. First, sustainability reflects a balance among economic, social, and environmental objectives without privileging any one of the three. Second, sustainability is to us an inherently *positive* word; it suggests creation rather than remediation, the striving toward an affirmative situation rather than the counteracting of societal ills and problems. Third, traditional organizational CSR research has tended to concentrate on the link between CSR and financial performance (e.g., Orlitzky, Schmidt, & Rynes, 2003). This is undeniably valuable work, and our comments are not intended to diminish its importance. Rather, we believe that the "business case" for sustainability can and should encompass other conceptions of organizational performance. For that reason, we seek a broader research agenda that connects sustainability to multiple forms of organizational effectiveness and success.

We must note that sustainability and sustainable development are contested concepts in the global "green" discourse. For one thing, sustainability advocates fall into two general camps—the preservationist (i.e., Earth first) and the instrumentalist (i.e., people first)—that frequently disagree on the ends of sustainability (cf., Gladwin, Kennelly, & Krause, 1995; Purser, Park, & Montuori, 1995). The former camp views people as a part of the ecosystem with no greater claim to natural resources than any other species on the planet. The latter views the ecosystem as the servant of humankind. Further, there is ongoing and strenuous debate about what sorts of activities constitute sustainable development. For example, nuclear energy has been championed as a boon—a green and renewable energy source by some (Cohen, 1990; Moore, 2006) and condemned as a bane and, therefore, vehemently opposed by others (Berger, 1998; Greenpeace, 2007).

Although there is no widespread agreement about the definition of "green," there is a growing international consensus about the *non*sustainability of traditional models of economic development and an acceptance of anthropogenic (i.e., people caused) sources of ecological problems (cf., Intergovernmental Panel on Climate Change, 2007). Setting aside disputes about the means and ends of environmental protection and climate change, ecocentric and anthropocentric factions do share one practical and urgent conclusion: as developing economies continue to grow dramatically and demand an ever larger share of the world's resources, the current levels of consumption in the developed nations simply cannot continue. "If everyone in the world were to live like an average person in the high income countries, we would need 2.6 additional planets to support us all" (United Nations Commission on Sustainable Development, 2007). Whether the consequences of global progress are dire or manageable depends largely on the discovery and dissemination of sustainable development solutions.

Unfortunately, the widespread adoption of sustainable development practices involves nothing short of a radical turn for civilization. The developed economies of the world have been built to a large extent on strategies that have brought financial rewards but have been environmentally and socially questionable. Humans are depleting the world's nonrenewable resources at an alarming rate and changing the natural environment in unintended and possibly disastrous ways. As competition for natural resources increases, the subsistence of impoverished and indigenous groups is being threatened by their more powerful neighbors who want to build on their land or take what is on or under it. Businesses have achieved financial success by selling products that contribute to poor well-being, often actively encouraging consumers to substitute unhealthful choices for better ones. In their quest for economic sustainability, many organizations have demonstrated little or no concern for social or environmental sustainability. Yet, for the same reasons that they have contributed to the crises that the world faces, organizations can play an important role in turning things around.

The Critical Role of Organizations

Even if there were broad agreement about sustainability's means and ends, one cannot assume that consensus is enough to spur a necessary "new ecological order." Some actors (both individual and organizational), in fact, profit from prolonging the unsustainable (cf., Newton, 2002). In this context, organizations are the social actors best positioned to catalyze global sustainability.

Organizations are "centers of human relatedness" (Cooperrider & Sekerka, 2003, p. 231) in all its glorious manifestations. To be forthright about it, we as authors are unabashed "fans" of organizations because of the potential that the act of *organizing* presents for humankind. Through organizing, collective effort can coalesce into something greater than the sum of the individual contributions put into the effort. In the organizational context, organizing becomes supercharged by the social and legal status that society grants to organizations. This status as a social actor enables organizations to take actions (such as entering contracts and owning property) with significant ramifications for the social spaces that they inhabit. We do not intend to dismiss the influence and importance of *non*-organizational actors (e.g., individuals, communities, coalitions of organizations) in the shift toward sustainable development practices. Rather, because organizations embody a critical mass of capital (human and otherwise), we view them as societal pressure points with tremendous potential to influence and be influenced by other social actors.

Paul Hawken, an environmentalist and successful entrepreneur wrote that "business is the only mechanism on the planet today powerful enough to produce the changes necessary to reverse global environmental and social degradation" (1993). We live in an age dominated by business organizations (cf., Gioia, 2003). Thirty-eight of the world's 100 largest "economies" are public corporations. Wal-Mart Stores, the world's largest company in terms of 2007 sales, generates annual revenues on the order of $387 billion (DeCarlo and Zajac, 2008). This figure exceeds the 2007 gross domestic product of all but 27 nations (Central Intelligence Agency, 2008). Clearly, as Hart (1999) contends, corporations have both the resources and reach to address the challenge of sustainability. We would add that corporations and other types of organizations also have the incentive to act before other social actors coerce or regulate them into action. Organizations, unlike the people who constitute them, have the potential to sustain existence indefinitely, and, indeed, virtually all organizations have attempted to achieve sustainability in this (limited) sense of the word. This is one of the reasons why Albert and Whetten (1985) declared "enduringness" as one of the three definitional pillars of organizational identity and why Gioia, Schultz, and Corley (2000) argued that "continuity" was a key attribute of organizational identity. We should emphasize, however, that in this chapter we are not talking about whether organizational identity is "enduring" or "continuous." Rather, we are addressing the need for organizations to develop identities that feature a deep commitment to environmental and social sustainability—in addition to economic sustainability—as a central element.

Organizational Identity

We define *identity* as the answer to the self-referential question, "Who am I?" ("Who are we?") by an entity. It is "a *self*-construction *by an actor* in social space that is associated with a pattern of thinking, feeling, *expressing, and* doing that enables purposeful action." The words in italics reflect our additions to a definition developed jointly during the Ann Arbor conference of January, 2008. The key point we wish to make here is that "identity" is an extended metaphor when applied to any level of analysis other than the individual level. Any metaphor likens one concept to another in terms of some putatively (or functionally) shared essential attributes. As an extended metaphor, "organizational identity" must retain some of the essential elements of individual identity. There is nothing more fundamental about individual identity than the fact that it is *self-referential, self-constructed, self-defined,* and/or *self-attributed.* Simply put, *I* define who I am. Of course my definition of myself is very much involved with a social process, wherein I engage in the social construction of myself (cf., Gergen & Davis, 1985) as influenced by others' images, opinions, statements, actions, and so on. The most germane point, however, is that although I attend to all these external influences, *I* decide my identity. In other words, the locus of attribution for my identity is *internal to me.* A similar argument pertains to organizational identity as well.

The notion of *organizational* identity is a very engaging concept. Scholars from many different perspectives have begun to explore the idea of an organizational identity and even the ideas of field-level and societal identities (see, for example, the chapter on positive community identity by Marquis & Davis in this volume). Field-level analysis offers an intriguing perspective on organizational identity, but researchers must take care to avoid granting the assignment of organizational identity to external agents (e.g., rivals, regulatory bodies, customers). Identity is not bestowed on an organization by outsiders. Those attributions of identity are images of an organization, not its identity. Of course, such externally based opinions and images are influential for the construction of organizational identity—they might even be constitutive of identity—but they are not *the* organizational identity. That prerogative is reserved for the members of the organization via their own claims—claims that are socially constructed and obviously influenced by the organization's standing, roles, and practices, and so on, but that members nonetheless make on behalf of their organization. The locus of organizational identity lies within the organization itself. As social actors, organizations, just like individuals, retain the privilege of deciding "who they are."

This issue parallels the definitional problem encountered by Dutton and Dukerich (1991) in their study of organizational identity and image. In that work, they defined organizational image as "the way insiders think outsiders view them"—in other words, they defined image as an internal phenomenon. A number of readers of that classic article thought that this was a rather curious and constrained definition of image, which many organizational and marketing scholars view as predominantly an external perception. Interestingly, these authors subsequently made a small but significant adjustment by employing the label *construed external image* to describe the phenomenon of insiders' beliefs about outsiders' perceptions of them (Dutton, Dukerich, & Harquail, 1994). This is a much more descriptive and accurate label for the phenomenon they were trying to describe. Likewise, when scholars consider external entities' views of another organization's identity, they are not describing an identity per se. Rather, they are portraying an ascribed or attributed organizational identity. As awkward as those labels might be, they are more accurate descriptors of the phenomenon under consideration. Attributions made about another's identity by external agents are just that: *construed* organizational identity, not organizational identity per se.

A contributor to this book said during the Ann Arbor conference, "'Who you are' is a story you tell yourself [about yourself]." In the case of organizations, "who you are" is a reflexive understanding harbored by the members themselves—an understanding about which they also make public claims. Identity, however, is also a relational notion, as we suggested above, because entities define themselves in relation to the other entities in the social space around them. Therefore, both social construction and social actor views are necessary to understand and explain the construction of identity (cf., Corley, Harquail, Pratt, & Glynn, 2006; Ravasi & Schultz, 2006).

SUSTAINABILITY AS POSITIVE ORGANIZATIONAL IDENTITY

Identity would seem to be, almost by definition, a "positive" concept. People and organizations almost invariably define who they are in positive terms (cf., Cornelissen, Haslam, & Balmer, 2007). Still, a "positive organizational identity," in the context of positive organizational scholarship (POS), brings a more nuanced meaning to the concept of "positive." How does this perspective inform the way we understand sustainability-focused organizations? The lens of positive organizational identity draws our attention to the following set of related ideas. First, sustainable practices require deep-seated change in the way most organizations today conduct themselves. Second, this sort of fundamental change requires a transformation in the way organizations see themselves—that is, in their conceptualizations of *who they are*. In other words, a change of this magnitude in organizational practices requires a profound change in organizational identity. We can think of no more positive a change in identity than a shift to incorporate sustainability as a core element.

Our perspective on sustainability-focused identity has a positive or "affirmative bias" (Cameron, Dutton, & Quinn, 2003, p. 5) because we want to emphasize the constructive content and outcomes associated with a sustainability-focused identity. Sustainability can be conceived as a core value that qualifies as an "organizational-level virtue" in which satisfaction or "fulfillment is part and parcel of the actions that manifest virtue" (Park & Peterson, 2003), that is, virtue is its own reward. We would also argue that sustainability now is as widely valued as other organizational-level virtues suggested by Park and Peterson (2003), such as fairness, humanity, and dignity. In the words of one manager, "it's the right thing to do from our standpoint and the right thing to do from the consumer's standpoint" (Bansal & Roth, 2000, p. 728).

Further, a deep commitment to sustainability can trigger "upward spirals" (Fredrickson, 2003, p. 163) and can nourish exceptional (positive) outcomes. What we mean by this is that sustainability and other organizational characteristics can be mutually reinforcing and lead to (positive) results not predicted by linear process models. For example, sustainability and the organizational qualities of hope and patience can be mutually reinforcing. Hope, a "future oriented quality of experiencing" (Carlsen, 2006; Carlsen & Pitsis, Chapter 4) sets the stage for aspirations toward sustainability by focusing organizational members on what the organization has the potential to become. Hope and patience may both be necessary for organizations to take the longer-term view of performance that is needed if sustainability (as engendered by a sustainability-focused identity) is to take root and ultimately lead to sustainable organizational practices.

As sustainable practices take effect and show results, they in turn can bring about more hope and greater reserves of patience. Thus, sustainability can trigger upward spirals of positive action—which is somewhat paradoxical because sustainability entails an aspiration for equilibrium (by balancing the economic, environmental, and social aspects of organizational practice). Yet sustainable activities can set off a chain reaction of transformations (for the organization and for other actors) such that the equilibrium point keeps shifting toward ever-increasing levels of system-wide abundance (as the snowballing effects of the increasing use of wind power technologies would seem to demonstrate).

Sustainability facilitates growth and well-being within the organization (e.g., of employees) while contributing to the sustainability of the global social, economic, and natural environment. Within the organization, sustainability as a core value can be especially generative because it can strengthen the relationship between employee and organization. Alvesson (1990) has noted that the link between worker and organization has become weaker because the meaning of work is less apparent in modern organizations. Sustainability as an aspect of organizational identity has the potential for fostering both meaning *in* and meaning *at* work. Pratt and Ashforth (2003) define this as "transcendence," an optimal state in which individuals feel connected to something greater than themselves. Workers achieve transcendence in organizations when they find meaning "from both doing and being in the organization" (Pratt et al., 2003, p. 315). In sustainable organizations, individuals derive meaning from *doing* activities that they consider important (and perhaps even consider to be a calling) and from *being* part of an organization that they believe possesses virtuousness. Research by Rhee, Dutton, and Bagozzi (in press) provides some empirical support for the connection between organizational virtue and member well-being. In their case study of an organization dealing with the aftermath of September 11, 2001, the authors found that individuals who saw their organization as virtuous also experienced higher levels of organizational attachment (i.e., affective commitment to and emotional involvement with the organization; Rhee et al.). With respect to sustainability as an organizational virtue, there are indications that workers desire a shift toward sustainability in their workplaces: increasing numbers of job applicants are showing a preference for green companies, and a recent Harris poll indicated that a majority of employees want their organizations to do more to foster environmental sustainability (Adecco, 2007).

Content and Structure of Sustainability-Focused Organizational Identities

Sustainability is never fully attained; there is never an end point at which an organization can assert incontrovertibly that it has achieved sustainability. This is true for two reasons: First, sustainability implies a focus on future generations. Thus, sustainability is necessarily a moving target, and there is always an aspirational quality to the concept. Second, although there is general agreement regarding what are *individually* sustainable organizational practices (e.g., waste reduction, recycling, using renewable energy and local materials), there is no agreed-on metric for deciding whether an organization's practices *collectively* can be deemed sustainable. Granted, numerous nonprofit and for-profit organizations (e.g., Green Seal, GreenTick, the Sierra Club) have launched sustainability certification programs and promote the value and soundness of their own methods for determining whether a given company is certifiably "green." Still, given that notions of sustainability have shifted and will continue to shift as a result of technological progress and societal change, we doubt whether one standard can ever prevail. It is worthwhile, however, to consider, as an ideal, what a sustainability-focused identity might look like. To that end, we suggest that sustainability as a core element of an organization's identity can be ascertained by evaluating an organization's official claims, the values and beliefs of its members, its organizational practices, and also the degree of alignment between these three facets of the organization.

Official Claims

An organization's official claims are among the most readily observable indicators of what the organization, as a social actor, believes itself to be (Whetten, 2006). A sustainability-focused identity is reflected in the organization's public statements, oral (by people speaking on behalf of the organization) and written (by representatives articulating the beliefs, values, and practices of the organization). For example, Method, the innovative manufacturer of green household products, describes its approach to product development in this way:

> The Cradle to Cradle environmental design approach is our guiding vision—we strive to make products that are healthy for people and the environment, not just "less bad." We like to say we believe in reincarnation—that

every product has a past, a present and a future. This means we seek ingredients that are responsibly sourced from nature, that are healthy when they are used, and can be safely returned to nature (biodegradable) to grow again. (Method Products, 2008)

By contrast, note the following rationale reported for Clorox's Greenworks line of natural cleaners:

Clorox says it believes that consumers will pay more for natural products. So, while they may be more expensive to produce, they will also be more profitable. Clorox research recently found that 53 percent of consumers planned to buy more eco-friendly products this year and that 47 percent were willing to pay 20 percent to 25 percent premiums for them. (Story, 2008)

Noticeably absent are any references to an interest in being socially responsible or practicing sustainability for its own sake.

Mission statements are another telling form of official claim. Consider, for example, the contrasts between the following the statements made by three competitors in the wine industry.

At Fetzer, we strive everyday to ensure that the wines you enjoy are of exceptional quality and value, while managing our impact on the environment. Working in harmony with nature and with the utmost respect for the human spirit, we are committed to the continuous growth and development of our people, the quality of our wines, and the care of our planet. (Fetzer Vineyards, 2008)

Robert Mondavi started in his family's wine business and eventually broke away to pursue a singular and, at the time, radical vision: to build a winery that would craft Napa Valley California wines that would stand in the company of the world's finest. (Robert Mondavi Winery, 2008)

At Columbia Crest we pride ourselves on delivering handcrafted, superior-quality small-lot wines, as well as affordable everyday wines. Our winemakers make it their mission to deliver wines that beat expectations year after year (Columbia Crest, 2008).

All three statements emphasize quality, although only the first mission statement suggests an accompanying commitment to environmental and social sustainability. Careful examination of a variety of written and verbal claims made by the organization can be a very strong indicator of the content and structure of a sustainability-focused identity. Focusing on claims alone, however, is not enough (because, as any media-savvy person knows, these kinds of claims are only too easy to make for the sake of having one's company be seen as fashionable or consistent with socially desirable orientations). In addition, one must also examine the collective beliefs and values held by organizational members.

Member Beliefs and Values

Organizational identity is a social construction constituted by the collective beliefs and values held by members about "who we are" as an organization. Researchers have developed rich understandings of organizational identity by simply asking members what they believe are the defining features and principles of their organizations (e.g., Corley, 2004; Ravasi & Schultz, 2006). Thus, one way to assess the degree to which sustainability is part of the organizational identity is to ask members to describe the central values of the organization or to inquire about the organization's beliefs about environmental and social issues. There are, however, challenges in terms of defining what can be rightly considered to be "collective," particularly when different groups within the organization appear to hold conflicting or different beliefs about what they take to be an essential feature of their organization. This is all the more reason why researchers must compare evidence from both public claims and members' beliefs when attempting to develop an accurate picture of a sustainability-focused identity. A commitment to sustainability should be a strong theme that runs through both.

Organizational Practices

We suggested earlier that not only do member beliefs and values about identity influence organizational practices but also that organizational practices influence members' beliefs about the identity. Other authors have gone further, suggesting that there is a reflexive, mutually constitutive relation between organizational practices and identity (Carlsen, 2006; Nag, Corley, & Gioia, 2007). For example, in their case study of a failed organizational change attempt, Nag et al. (2007) found that organizational identity infused the daily practices of organizational members to such an extent that it thwarted the effort to transform those practices. Playing off this idea, we believe that by observing organizational practices, one can gather evidence to validate or refute the sustainability referents that one has detected in the public claims and expressed beliefs of organizational members—a form of the old folk wisdom that actions speak louder than words. In addition, the extent and variety of sustainability-oriented procedures found throughout the organization may be a useful indicator of whether organizational practices reflect a sustainability-focused identity or whether they are the result of other exigencies. For example, an organization that applies sustainable practices on the production line, in raw materials sourcing, in human resources procedures, and in the handling of office supplies may be more likely to be expressing a sustainability-focused identity than one that touts sustainability but only applies sustainable practices in one or two of these areas.

Does Size—and Ownership Structure—Matter?

Organizations face both constraints and enablers as they develop sustainability-focused identities. Two important potential constraints to consider are size and ownership structure. PepsiCo CEO Indra Nooyi has said, "Companies today are bigger than many economies. We are little republics. We are engines of efficiency. If companies don't do [responsible] things, who is going to? Why not start making change now?" (Morris, 2008, p. 57). Under Nooyi's leadership, PepsiCo has adopted a new motto, "performance with purpose," and has expanded its line of "good for you" snacks; 70% of PepsiCo's revenues, however, still derive from products it euphemistically describes as "fun for you" (and others would describe as junk food). Contrast PepsiCo's $38 billion operation with that of Clif Bar Inc., a company generating $88.5 million in revenues (both figures are 2007 sales; Hoovers, 2008) through the manufacture and distribution of organic snacks, such as CLIF and LUNA bars. By all appearances, Clif Bar Inc. possesses an identity with sustainability at its core. For example, Clif Bar Inc.'s Web site is covered with statements that explicitly connect its business to sustainable practices. On the main pages, the company proclaims, "We like food. Natural and organic foods aren't just good for your body; they're good for the planet" and "food, made right, can make the world a better place" (Clif Bar Inc., 2008). The site also has a page entitled "Who we are" that features "Five Aspirations: Sustaining our Planet, Sustaining our Community, Sustaining our People, Sustaining our Business, Sustaining our Brands." For each of these aspirations, the company provides detail on how they are working to achieve it. We might note, by way of foreshadowing, that when a company engages in this degree of public declaration of adherence to sustainable values and practices, the public image created by these declarations serves to shape and reinforce the ideals that further contribute to a sustainability-focused organizational identity (see below).

We suspect that large public corporations like PepsiCo will find it much more difficult to adopt sustainability as a central feature of their identities precisely because they are large and publicly held. First of all, the competitive business model in which success is measured in terms of above-market returns and ever-increasing growth rates is more deeply ingrained in their beliefs and practices. Second, they tend to be focused on short-term results like the next quarter's earnings. Again, PepsiCo's Nooyi: "The fact of the matter is we operate within the stock market, which has a certain psyche, which has a certain approach to everything, and we can't ignore that" (Morris, 2008, p. 66). Incidentally, taking (or keeping) a company private may be one way for companies—perhaps smaller ones, at least—to find the longer-term time frame they need for exploring sustainable practices. One CEO who recently took his firm private said the move was "to get away from Wall Street. The public markets never got our business, and we were tired of worrying about earnings every quarter" (Miller, 2008).

Size and public ownership may make it more difficult to become green, but other deeply held aspects of the organizational identity may help a company to overcome these barriers. Johnson & Johnson (J&J), the diversified health care company with 2007 sales of $61 billion (Hoovers, 2008), may be one example of such a firm. Collins and Porras (1994) note that J&J (established in 1886) has been guided since inception by a strong ideology embodied in its "credo." The credo recites a list of stakeholders to whom the company is responsible. It begins with customers, then employees, then communities (including the "world community"), and finally shareholders, who "should realize a fair return when we operate according to these principles" (Johnson & Johnson, 2008).

Although J&J has periodically reviewed and slightly revised the wording of the credo since 1943, the essential ideology—the hierarchy of responsibilities descending from customers down to shareholders and the explicit emphasis on a *fair* return rather than maximum return—has remained consistent. (Collins et al., 1994, p. 58)

J&J's ideology does not necessarily reflect our definition of sustainability as its central feature, but it clearly envisions a corporate philosophy that goes beyond maximizing shareholder wealth, and it also reflects patience as a deeply held value. As suggested above, we believe that patience must be part of the identity structure if sustainability beliefs are to be manifested in sustainable organizational practices.

We would also like to make a passing comment about another important potential constraint on organizations developing more sustainable identities: There might be "built-in limits to green honesty in a wealthy materialist culture ... [because] genuinely going green would mean giving up most of the products and services that clutter our consumer culture" (Roberts, 2008, p. 70). The implication here is that organizations cannot truly become sustainable unless and until the communities of which they are a part become less wealthy, less materialist, or both. This is a provocative idea, but exploring it further is beyond the bounds of this chapter.

TOWARD A CONCEPTUALIZATION OF SUSTAINABILITY-FOCUSED IDENTITY CHANGE

We believe that the path to sustainability-focused identity change involves the interaction of both internal enablers and external pressures. Both are likely to be important for sustainability to become a deep and abiding part of an organization's identity, and both are likely to be inextricably intertwined. For purposes of advancing the conceptualization of a sustainability-focused organizational identity, however, it is useful to consider them separately.

Internal Enablers

When the identity is not already sustainability-focused, internal change processes are initiated when an organization adopts (for whatever reason) aspirations toward sustainability in terms of environmentally and socially responsible goals. In working toward these aspirations, members rely on other key traits that they believe to be *already true* about the organization to leverage the change process. Corley and Harrison's (Chapter 16) case study of identity change in one organization suggests important mechanisms through which such change can proceed via generative processes. They found that organizational members drew on what they believed to be "authentic" about their organization (e.g., respect, passion; we would call these core identity elements) as enablers of balance between tensions brought about by the identity change (e.g., growth versus stability). We would argue that similar processes can enable some organizations to leverage existing identity elements to achieve greater sustainability. For example, J&J's core identity already embodies important enablers of sustainability (e.g., a balance between competing stakeholders' interests and commitment to a fair, rather than maximized, return to shareholders) that might help the corporation manage the tensions inherent in a change toward an identity that incorporates sustainability as a central feature. Other core beliefs that might foster identity change include a commitment to employee empowerment and safety; the valuing of innovation; an emphasis on flexibility and responsiveness; and a dedication to quality in products and services. We think it likely that, all other things being equal, the more internal enablers possessed by an organization (*especially* if they are increasingly expressed as core values), the quicker and easier it will be to change identity even more toward inclusion of those features that we would characterize as associated with sustainability. The process here is an organizational enactment of the old folk wisdom that "the rich get richer." In the organizational analogy, however, the process takes the form of a virtuous recursive cycle wherein existing enablers breed the ability to inculcate yet more sustainability-associated enablers. This process leads to a self-perpetuating cycle wherein increasing sustainability beliefs (as part of organizational identity) foster increasingly sustainable practices, which in turn foster even stronger sustainability beliefs as components of identity.

External Forces

Two broad categories of external forces that might prompt identity change are competitive pressures and institutional pressures. For example, Bansal and Roth (2000) noted that competitiveness motivates firms to reduce energy use and adopt more efficient waste management techniques. Xerox's strategic goal of becoming a "waste-free company" (Maslennikova & Foley, 2000, p. 226) is an example of this sort of ecological responsiveness. Competitiveness also motivates firms to develop green products and launch green marketing campaigns, sometimes referred to as "greenwashing" because these green claims often "hype some narrow eco-friendly quality (say, recycled content), while omitting mention of more significant drawbacks, such as manufacturing intensity or travel costs" (Roberts, 2008, p. 70). Colgate's 2006 acquisition of Tom's of Maine and Clorox's 2008 purchase of Burt's Bees and launch of its own Green Works line are examples of this sort of ecological response. Clorox also provides an example of ecological responsiveness brought about by institutional pressures. Clorox sought legitimation of its Green Works products via certifications by the Sierra Club. The Green Works product packages feature the logos of both Clorox and the Sierra Club. In an interesting contrast, Colgate has kept its name off Tom's of Maine packaging and does not mention the all-natural toothpaste company on Colgate's Web site. Legitimation motives can also lead companies to undertake voluntary reporting of their green behavior (e.g., reports of sustainability performance in accordance with Global Reporting Initiative guidelines; GRI, 2008).

The Role of Image in Identity Change

Acts of ecological responsiveness are often met with skepticism by external observers, especially when the organization has a questionable environmental record. "I want to believe, but when you see brands like Clorox going green, it's hard to believe," said one consumer (Adler, 2008). Whether these behaviors are authentic expressions of organizational identity or attempts at corporate impression management through greenwashing, we would argue that they nonetheless provide potentially powerful mechanisms to create positive identity change and the adoption of an identity with sustainability at its core. Greenwashing may be intended to change an organization's image with customers and other stakeholders, but organizational practices can have unintended consequences for the focal organization itself. The interrelation of image and identity and the destabilizing effect that image has on identity have been noted by a number of authors (Dutton et al., 1991; Elsbach & Kramer, 1996; Gioia & Thomas, 1996; Gioia et al., 2000). Gioia et al. developed a model of identity change in which image was key. In that model, an organization projects an image in an attempt to influence outsiders. The organization then looks for feedback regarding how outsiders perceive it and how well it is meeting their expectations. Any discrepancies between the construed and intended image can prompt changes in identity or further changes in projected image. The power of image to result in more societally beneficial identity change is exemplified by Royal Dutch Shell (Livesey, 2001). Attempts to improve the company's image led to what some observers deemed to be a more genuine "eco-identity" (Coupland & Brown, 2004). Thus, even inauthentic projected images like those intended by greenwashing can be hopeful signs of a process of positive identity change. More important, positive projected images have the potential for motivating companies to change so that they can conform to the images they are projecting.

Discourse and Identity Change

The example of Royal Dutch Shell also is germane to another theoretical process we propose for how sustainability-focused identities can develop: through discourse or "practices of writing and talking" that collectively constitute how a concept is understood by a given community of social actors (Phillips, Lawrence, & Hardy, 2004, p. 636). When organizations engage in greenwashing they produce texts that become embedded in the discourse of sustainability. Discourse sets the rules for acceptable and unacceptable ways for actors to talk, write, and conduct themselves in relation to a topic. One powerful example of how the sustainability discourse can be changed is the term coined by Elkington (1994) of "the triple bottom line" for businesses. Elkington used the term to indicate the need for businesses to demonstrate not just a net profit but also a net positive contribution to society and to the environment as well. The term elegantly captured the multiple facets of sustainability as outlined by the United Nations' WCED (1987) and became centrally embedded in the sustainability discourse. Discourse shapes the institutional norms that enable and constrain the actions of organizations (Phillips et al., 2004). All texts on sustainability, including greenwashing efforts and debates over who is greenwashing and who is not, expand the discourse on sustainability, contribute to its sharper definition, and increasingly make sustainability a normative expectation. As sustainability becomes more and more normative, it will be seen as more and more positive or valuable and will be more readily reinforced or adopted as an aspect of positive identity.

Image and discourse present two different yet related means for triggering identity change that harbors more of the features associated with sustainability, and with more socially virtuous organizations in general. Research in each of these areas has the potential to shed light on how the move toward sustainability in organizations can be fostered and accelerated. Regarding the role of image in sustainability, compelling research questions include, "What factors determine how an organization responds to a discrepancy between its projected and construed image of sustainability?" and "What internal and external pressures lead an organization more in the direction of identity change instead of simply attempting to change the projected image?" Regarding sustainability discourse, we know very little about the process through which discourse "rules-in" some modes of sustainability talk, writing, and action and "rules-out" others. Why, for example, was Clorox's purchase of Burt's Bees met with disdain ("just slap some bleach on your lips, it'll all be good"; Story, 2008), when the Danone Group's 80% ownership stake in Stonyfield Farm did not seem to raise such controversy? Below, we elaborate a bit further on some specific lines of inquiry that might make significant contributions to the connection between positive identity change and sustainability.

DIRECTIONS FOR FUTURE RESEARCH

We preface our suggestions for future research by noting that there has been a call to balance the rigor of organizational research with relevance to real world problems (Bennis & O'Toole, 2005). Sustainability-focused organizational identity is an unexplored domain with the potential for both rigor and relevance. Below, we highlight four main areas that we think may be especially fruitful for researchers interested in sustainability and positive organizational identity.

Process-Oriented Research and Longitudinal Studies

First and foremost, we see great need for more inquiry that focuses on processes of identity adaptation and change. As noted above, sustainability is never fully attained. Terms in the organizational literature such as "sustained competitive advantage" (Barney, 1991) have been difficult to grapple with empirically for this very reason. Is an advantage "sustained" if it exists for only 1 year? Ten years? One hundred years? Because of the aspirational quality inherent in sustainability, it is better characterized as a process than a state. Longitudinal close observation of evolving organizations is essential if research claims regarding key processes are to be substantiated. Longitudinal observation allows the researcher to examine "beliefs, artifacts, … and routines before they become impervious to scrutiny" and to "avoid the 'retrospective rationality trap'" (Garud & Rappa, 1994, p. 348). In the case of sustainability, process research can bring a focus to the paths through which sustainable organizational practices evolve. This type of research can shed light on the reflexive relationship between image and identity that we suggest is an important mechanism for bringing about sustainability in organizations.

Narrative and Discourse Analysis

As touched on above, analysis of the sustainability discourse could foster an empirical understanding of the processes underlying positive identity change and, as part of the discourse, might also produce socially, environmentally (and even economically) beneficial changes on the discourse itself. Relatedly, a narrative approach (Brown, 2006) would complement the picture of sustainability-focused identity that is presented by the written and formal claims (such as those found in Web sites, press releases, and annual reports) made by organizations. "Identity-relevant narratives are stories about organizations that actors' author in their efforts to understand, or make sense of, the collective entities with which they identify" (Brown, 2006, p. 734). As an organization adopts sustainability as a core element of identity and as this identity develops and changes, narratives offer a way of understanding the points of fragmentation and cohesion in members' definitions of sustainability and its salience to the organizational identity.

Multiple Identity Research

A narrative approach implies that organizations may be multivoiced or harbor competing and conflicting conceptions of sustainability-focused identity. Indeed, it is easily conceivable that the three primary domains of sustainability (economic, environmental, and social) might appeal to different groups within an organization and lead to "identity fault lines" within organizations. Researchers have provided case studies of organizations with multiple identities that do not necessarily harmonize with each other (e.g., Foreman & Whetten, 2002; Glynn, 2000). Pratt and Foreman (2000) theorized that there are several possible ways in which organizations might seek to manage the opportunities and challenges presented by multiple identities, noting that these management approaches may or may not be generative. The organizational self (Pratt & Kraatz, Chapter 17) provides a conceptual mode for integrating multiple identities and achieving a sense of wholeness and organizational well-being. We also believe that Appreciative Inquiry (Cooperrider & Sekerka, 2003) presents a very productive approach for conducting research on multiple identities and multiple conceptions of sustainability. "Appreciative Inquiry is a process of search and discovery designed to value, prize and honor. It assumes that organizations are networks of relatedness" (Cooperrider & Sekerka, 2003, p. 226). We believe that Appreciative Inquiry can facilitate dialogue between stakeholders with different conceptions of sustainability (e.g., the ecocentric and anthropocentric factions) and with differing conceptions of the organizational identity itself. By asking positive questions and encouraging dialogue between parties, Appreciative Inquiry leads to shared understanding (not necessarily agreement) that can enable greater cooperation and more positive outcomes.

Multilevel Studies

There are several important cross-level effects and interdependencies between social actors at the individual, organizational, and supraorganizational level. Government regulation, for example, exerts a significant influence on the actions of individual and organizational actors alike. Likewise, the actions of a small group or even a single individual can have profound effects on other levels of the system, for better or worse (on the one hand think of Mother Teresa and on the other, Captain Hazelwood of Exxon Valdez notoriety). Network analysis and multilevel analysis are two potential methods for investigating how factors at different levels of analysis contribute to positive identity change in organizations. For example, these methods may shed light on the nature of "high quality connections" (Dutton & Heaphy, 2003) and how they might enable organizational identity change toward sustainability. High-quality connections are defined by their strength, mutuality, resilience, multifunctionality, and ability to convey and withstand the expression of intense and wide-ranging emotion

(Dutton et al., 2003). Such ties are assumed to "encourage actions that are the seed corn for revising one's identity in the direction of a desired and valued possible self" (Dutton et al., 2003, p. 270). These connections undoubtedly exert cross-level influences and might thereby foster sustainability as a core element of organizational identity.

Further, Brickson (2007) and Brickson and Lemmon (Chapter 18) have theorized that organizations differ in terms of their relational orientation, that is, that organizations tend to approach stakeholder relationships from either an individualistic, relational (dyadic), or collectivistic perspective. This orientation might have profound structural implications for how sustainability becomes incorporated into an organization's identity and how it interacts with other core features of that identity. For example, it would be useful to understand whether collectivistic organizations are able to adopt sustainability beliefs more quickly than individualistic or dyadic organizations. Also, are sustainability beliefs manifested in different organizational goals, practices, and outcomes depending on the relational orientation of an organization? Research into these questions requires analytical techniques that span multiple levels of analysis for the antecedents and consequences of sustainability-focused identity.

CONCLUSION

We see a natural connection between sustainability and positive organizational scholarship (POS) with its focus on thriving, resilience, and virtuousness (Cameron et al., 2003, p. 4). The time has come for sustainability to be added to the list of core POS concepts. POS draws on ideas grounded in positive psychology, a field that examines how positive experiences, positive individual traits, and positive institutions contribute to the well-being of individuals (Cameron et al., p. 7). By extending these concepts to the organization level, positive scholarship necessarily invokes the question, "*Whose* well-being is at issue in a given inquiry?" A tacit possibility is that the thriving of the focal entity (be it a society, community, organization, group, or individual) may come at the expense of another entity whose well-being is held outside the given boundaries of consideration. By explicitly linking the concept of sustainability with POS, we bring attention to the fact that all social actors are interconnected within a series of systems that at the highest level of aggregation includes the entire planet. Sustainability assumes concern for the well-being of all social actors and systems.

It is imperative that organizations develop the wherewithal to become sustainable enterprises and to present themselves as sustainable entities to their constituents and stakeholders. Our basic premise is that organizations are the social actors best positioned to be change agents for sustainability and that lasting organizational change of this magnitude depends critically on an organization's identity—that is, the answer to the basic existential question, "Who we are, as an organization?" We believe that the fundamental changes necessary to achieve the level of sustainability we envision require that sustainability be "woven into the fabric" of organizational identity and that such sustainability be conceived and enacted as a triumvirate of economic, environmental, and social sustainability. Sustainability as a core identity referent can instigate a virtuous cycle of positive outcomes that not only reinforce an organization's commitment to sustainability but also stimulate other organizations to adopt these principles as well. The outcome of such a collective pursuit would be a fundamental shift away from an unsustainable business model toward a more positive one, in which pursuit of the triple bottom line is the generally accepted mode of organizational conduct.

REFERENCES

Adecco (2007). Earth Day 2007: Are American workers going green? Retrieved July 31, 2008 from http://www.harrisinteractive.com/news/newsletters/clientnews/2007_Adecco.pdf.

Adler, E. (2008, April 20). Many on "green" overload as marketplace responds. *McClatchy Newspapers*, Kansas City, MO.

Albert, S., & Whetten, D. A. (1985). Organizational identity. In *Research in organizational behavior* (Vol. 7; pp. 263–295). Greenwich, CT: JAI Press, Inc.

Alvesson, M. (1990). Organization: from substance to image? *Organization Studies, 11,* 373–394.

Bansal, P. (2005). Evolving sustainably: a longitudinal study of corporate sustainable development. *Strategic Management Journal, 26,* 197–218.

Bansal, P., & Roth, K. (2000). Why companies go green: A model of ecological responsiveness. *Academy of Management Journal, 43,* 717–736.

Barney, J. (1991). Firm resources and sustained competitive advantage. *Journal of Management, 17,* 99–120.

Bennis, W. G., & O'Toole, J. (2005). How business schools lost their way. *Harvard Business Review, 83,* 96–104.

Berger, J. J. (1998). *Charging ahead: The business of renewable energy and what it means for America.* Berkeley: University of California Press.

Brickson, S. L. (2007). Organizational identity orientation: The genesis of the role of the firm and distinct forms of social value. *Academy of Management Review, 32,* 864–888.

Brown, A. D. (2006). A narrative approach to collective identifies. *The Journal of Management Studies, 43,* 731–753.

Cameron, K. S., Dutton, J. E., & Quinn, R. E. (Eds.). (2003). *Positive organizational scholarship: Foundations of a new discipline.* San Francisco: Berrett-Koehler.

Carlsen, A. (2006). Organizational becoming as dialogic imagination of practice: The case of the indomitable Gauls. *Organization Science, 17,* 132–149.

Central Intelligence Agency (2008). *The world factbook.* Retrieved July 31, 2008, from https://www.cia.gov/library/publications/the-world-factbook.

Clif Bar Inc. (2008). Retrieved July 31, 2008, from http://www.clifbar.com.

Cohen, B. L. (1990). *The nuclear energy option.* New York: Plenum Press.

Collins, J. C., & Porras, J. I. (1994). *Built to last.* New York: Harper Collins.

Columbia Crest (2008). Retrieved July 31, 2008, from http://www.columbia-crest.com.

Cooperrider, D. L., & Sekerka, L. E. (2003). Toward a theory of positive organizational change. In K. S. Cameron, J. E. Dutton, & R. E. Quinn (Eds.), *Positive organizational scholarship: Foundations of a new discipline* (pp. 225–240). San Francisco: Berrett-Koehler.

Corley, K. G. (2004). Defined by our strategy or our culture? Hierarchical differences in perceptions of organizational identity and change. *Human Relations, 57,* 1145–1177.

Corley, K. G., Harquail, C. V., Pratt, M. G., & Glynn, M. A. (2006). Guiding organizational identity through aged adolescence. *Journal of Management Inquiry, 15,* 85–99.

Cornelissen, J. P., Haslam, S. A., & Balmer, J. M. T. (2007). Social identity, organizational identity and corporate identity: Towards an integrated understanding of processes, patternings and products. *British Journal of Management, 18,* S1–S16.

Coupland, C., & Brown, A. D. (2004). Constructing organizational identities on the web: A case study of Royal Dutch/Shell. *The Journal of Management Studies, 41,* 1325–1347.

DeCarlo, S., & Zajac, B. (Eds.). (2008, April 2). The world's biggest companies. *Forbes.* Retrieved July 31, 2008, from http://www.forbes.com/business/2008/04/02/worlds-largest-companies-biz-2000global08-cx_sd_0402global_land.html.

Dutton, J. E., & Dukerich, J. M. (1991). Keeping an eye on the mirror: Image and identity in organizational adaptation. *Academy of Management Journal, 34,* 517–554.

Dutton, J. E., Dukerich, J. M., & Harquail, C. V. (1994). Organizational images and member identification. *Administrative Science Quarterly, 39,* 239–263.

Dutton, J. E., & Heaphy, E. D. (2003). The power of high-quality connections. In K. S. Cameron, J. E. Dutton, & R. E. Quinn (Eds.), *Positive organizational scholarship: Foundations of a new discipline* (pp. 263–278). San Francisco: Berrett-Koehler.

Elkington, J. (1994). *Cannibals with forks: The triple bottom line of 21st century business.* Stony Creek, CT: New Society Publishers.

Elsbach, K. D., & Kramer, R. M. (1996). Members' responses to organizational identity threats: Encountering and countering the Business Week rankings. *Administrative Science Quarterly, 41,* 442–476.

Fetzer Vineyards (2008). Retrieved July 31, 2008, from http://www.fetzer.com/fetzer/wineries/philosophy.aspx.

Foreman, P., & Whetten, D. A. (2002). Member's identification with multiple-identity organizations. *Organization Science, 13,* 618–635.

Fredrickson, B. L. (2003). Positive emotions and upward spirals in organizations. In K. S. Cameron, J. E. Dutton, & R. E. Quinn (Eds.), *Positive organizational scholarship: Foundations of a new discipline* (pp. 163–175). San Francisco: Berrett-Koehler.

Garud, R., & Rappa, M. A. (1994). A socio-cognitive model of technology evolution: The case of cochlear implants. *Organization Science, 5,* 344–362.

Gergen, K. J., & Davis, K. E. (Eds.). (1985). *The social construction of the person.* New York: Springer-Verlag.

Gioia, D. A. (2003). Business organization as instrument of societal responsibility. *Organization, 10,* 435–438.

Gioia, D. A., Schultz, M., & Corley, K. G. (2000). Organizational identity, image, and adaptive instability. *Academy of Management Review, 25,* 63–81.

Gioia, D. A., & Thomas, J. B. (1996). Identity, image, and issue interpretation: Sensemaking during strategic change in academia. *Administrative Science Quarterly, 41,* 370–403.

Gladwin, T. N., Kennelly, J. J., & Krause, T.-S. (1995). Shifting paradigms for sustainable development: Implications for management theory and research. *Academy of Management Review, 20,* 874–907.

Glynn, M. A. (2000). When cymbals become symbols: Conflict over organizational identity within a symphony orchestra. *Organization Science, 11,* 285–298.

Greenpeace (2007). Climate change: nuclear not the answer. Retrieved July 31, 2008, from http://www.greenpeace.org/international/press/reports/briefing-nuclear-not-answer-apr07.

GRI (2008). Retrieved July 31, 2008, from http://www.globalreporting.org.

Hart, S. L. (1999). Corporations as agents of global sustainability: Beyond competitive strategy. In D. L. Cooperrider & J. E. Dutton (Eds.), *Organizational dimensions of global change: No limits to cooperation* (pp. 346–362). Thousand Oaks, CA: Sage.

Hawken, P. (1993). *The ecology of commerce: A declaration of sustainability.* New York: Harper Collins.

Hoovers (2008). Retrieved July 31, 2008, from http://www.hoovers.com.

Intergovernmental Panel on Climate Change (2007). *Climate change 2007—Synthesis report.* Retrieved July 31, 2008, from http://www.ipcc.ch/pdf/assessment-report/ar4/syr/ar4_syr.pdf.

Johnson & Johnson (2008). Retrieved July 31, 2008, from http://www.jnj.com.

Livesey, S. M. (2001). Eco-identity as discursive struggle: Royal Dutch/Shell, Brent Spar, and Nigeria. *Journal of Business Communication, 38,* 58–91.

Maslennikova, I., & Foley, D. (2000). Xerox's approach to sustainability. *Interfaces, 30;* 226–233.

Method Products (2008). Retrieved July 31, 2008, from http://www.methodhome.com/#formulation.

Miller, M. (2008, May 5). Ultimate cash machine, *Forbes.*

Moore, P. (2006, April 16). Going nuclear: A green makes the case. *The Washington Post,* p. B1.

Morris, B. (2008). The Pepsi challenge, *Fortune, 157,* 54–66.

Nag, R., Corley, K. G., & Gioia, D. A. (2007). The intersection of organizational identity, knowledge, and practice: Attempting strategic change via knowledge grafting. *Academy of Management Journal, 50,* 821–847.

Newton, T. J. (2002). Creating the new ecological order? Elias and actor-network theory. *Academy of Management Review, 27,* 523–540.

Orlitzky, M., Schmidt, L. F., & Rynes, L. S. (2003). Corporate social and financial performance: A meta-analysis. *Organization Studies, 24*, 403–441.

Park, N., & Peterson, C. M. (2003). Virtues and organizations. In K. S. Cameron, J. E. Dutton, & R. E. Quinn (Eds.), *Positive organizational scholarship: Foundations for a new discipline*. San Francisco: Berrett-Koehler.

Phillips, N., Lawrence, T. B., & Hardy, C. (2004). Discourse and institutions. *Academy of Management Review, 29*, 635–652.

Pratt, M. G., & Ashforth, B. E. (2003). Fostering meaningfulness in working and at work. In K. S. Cameron, J. E. Dutton, & R. E. Quinn (Eds.), *Positive organizational scholarship: Foundations of a new discipline* (pp. 309–327). San Francisco: Berrett-Koehler.

Pratt, M. G., & Foreman, P. O. (2000). Classifying managerial responses to multiple organizational identities. *Academy of Management Review, 25*, 18–42.

Purser, R. E., Park, C., & Montuori, A. (1995). Limits to anthropocentrism: Toward an ecocentric organization paradigm? *The Academy of Management Review, 20*, 1053–1089.

Rhee, S. Y., Dutton, J., & Bagozzi, R. (2006). Making sense of organizational actions in response to tragedy: Virtue frames, organizational identification and organizational attachment. *Journal of Management, Religion and Spirituality, 3, 1&2*, 34–59.

Ravasi, D., & Schultz, M. (2006). Responding to organizational identity threats: Exploring the role of organizational culture. *Academy of Management Journal, 49*, 433–458.

Robert Mondavi Winery (2008). Retrieved July 31, 2008, from http://www.robertmondaviwinery.com.

Roberts, D. (2008). Another inconvenient truth: the reason why companies greenwash their products. *Fast Company, 123*, 70.

Story, L. (2008, January 6). Can Burt's Bees turn Clorox green? *The New York Times*, p. 3.1.

United Nations Commission on Sustainable Development (2007). Sustainable production and consumption: fact sheet. Retrieved July 31, 2008, from http://www.un.org/esa/sustdev/media/SustProd_ConsFactSheet.pdf.

WCED. (1987). *Our common future: Report of the World Commission on Economic Development*. New York: United Nations.

Whetten, D. A. (2006). Albert and Whetten revisited: Strengthening the concept of organizational identity. *Journal of Management Inquiry, 15*, 219–234.

20

Organizational Mechanisms Underlying Positive Community Identity and Reputation

Christopher Marquis and Gerald F. Davis

CONTENTS

Why does civic and public commitment thrive in some communities and wither in others? Why has Minneapolis-St. Paul come to be known for the civic spirit of its populace, whereas Silicon Valley has cultivated an identity as the home of the "cyber stingy?" In this chapter we propose that local corporations and nonprofits play an essential role in the development and maintenance of such community identities and reputations and that once developed, these intertwined processes have a self-reinforcing function. Communities become known for being more or less desirable places, which serves as an internal signal to shape the behaviors of existing corporations, and further, an external signal to attract new firms and residents (Marquis, Glynn, & Davis, 2007). Having a positive identity and reputation yields many benefits, yet because these processes are complex and durable, community identity and reputation may be resistant to purposeful change. In this chapter we discuss how geographical communities and their identities and reputation still matter in a globalized corporate world, focusing on some of the organizational mechanisms underlying positive community processes.

To understand community identities and reputations, we focus on how both internal and external perceptions of geographically defined units take on a positive shape based on actions of their organizational constituents. We follow Romanelli and Khessina (2005) in arguing that historical features and ongoing organizational activities foster lasting impressions of communities that inform audience perceptions. We focus on both internal and external audiences, examining the intertwined concepts of positive community identity (i.e., how members within a community define themselves) and positive community reputation (i.e., how others define and perceive the community).

Further, whereas Romanelli and Khessina theorize about the industrial identities that developed for places such as Silicon Valley (technology) and Pittsburgh (steel making) as a result of concentrated economic activities, our discussion focuses more on what we are describing as positive identity and reputation, or how geographies become known for the existence (or absence) of positive social phenomena, such as social cohesion, generalized trust, and reciprocity. Thus, our concept of positive community identity is similar to Putnam's (2000) idea that communities vary in their stock of "social capital." But a key difference is that whereas Putnam focused on the norms and networks connecting individual residents of a community, we focus on *organizations* as the most consequential constituents of communities. It is the actions of organizational decision makers that have the greatest impact on positive community identity and reputation.

Our focus on community identity and reputation in this chapter specifically relates to how local corporations contribute to positive social phenomena through their engagement with the civic sector. We detail how such activities shape both internal and external perceptions of communities. Specifically, businesses vary substantially across cities in whether and how they engage with the nonprofit sector, which in turn is a critical element of positive social phenomena, such as social cohesion, generalized trust, and reciprocity. Active support of local nonprofits serves as a visible symbol of this commitment on the part of corporations and residents, shaping how both insiders and outsiders perceive the community. We suggest there are two important mechanisms by which local corporations enact and maintain their community identity, and we term these the *hardware* and *software* of creating and maintaining positive community identity. We further suggest that these activities have an influence on how the community is perceived by outsiders. First, local corporations contribute to the social infrastructure (i.e., hardware) of their community through the networks connecting their decision makers and the norms that guide their actions. Cohesive relations among local organizations encourage trust and reciprocity and can embody templates for successful cooperation. Second, local corporations can be a vehicle for community involvement for the local populace (i.e., software)—aiding in the aggregation of individuals for volunteering and other community-oriented activities, which has positive spillovers for a community's identity and reputation.

In this chapter, we explore the underlying theoretical mechanisms standing between corporations and positive community identity and reputation, and we provide illustrative examples of these processes from our fieldwork in a major U.S. metropolitan area.[1] We begin with a discussion of the enduring importance of geographic location to firms, discuss how community identities and reputation can be more or less positive, and finally describe how corporations and other social actors in a locale shape and maintain these internal and external perceptions.

DO LOCAL COMMUNITIES STILL MATTER?

It is an irony of recent times that as business and public attention have identified globalization processes as the dominant social feature of our era (e.g., Fiss & Hirsch, 2005), the effects of local communities endure. Several studies have shown that as globalization has proceeded, the forces of community still matter for corporations (see Marquis & Battilana, 2009 for a review). For example, in a study of U.S. bank foundings, Marquis and

---

[1] We interviewed 19 civic leaders in a major metropolitan area as part of a research project on corporate involvement in local nonprofits.

Lounsbury (2007) showed that a broad group of community actors were motivated to maintain a local financial infrastructure as a reaction against more global pressures. As outsider banks expanded into communities, local bankers and other residents perceived their communities' financial infrastructure to be at risk and responded by founding new banks.

Studies have also demonstrated that the prevalence of contemporary corporate practices varies by city, ranging from taken-for-granted traditions of corporate governance (Marquis, 2003) to controversial strategies like golden parachutes (Davis & Greve, 1997). Modern industrial districts vary in their norms and networks, resulting in divergent outcomes for firms in the same industries depending on where they are headquartered (Saxenian, 1994). Ironically, the success of Silicon Valley—the place most charged with causing the "death of distance" in economic affairs—has led to a search for the factors enabling municipal economic vibrancy, encouraging governors and mayors across America to better nurture a "creative class" of mobile workers (Florida, 2002).

A characteristic of these studies is the finding that local communities have enduring effects on firms by providing traditions and reference groups for firms. Norms and ideologies about appropriate action develop along diverse paths across communities, creating characteristic variation in organizational behaviors, from the appropriate composition of a corporate board (Marquis, 2003) to the level of contribution to the local art museum (Ostrander, 1984). For example, a norm has developed around giving to children-oriented causes among companies headquartered in Columbus, Ohio, perhaps a result of the legacy of Wendy's founder Dave Thomas (Marquis et al., 2007).

The idea of community and its influence on social actors has a long tradition in the social sciences, dating back to Tönnies (1887) and his distinction between *Gemeinschaft* (community) and *Gesellschaft* (society). Community for Tönnies relates to the interpersonal connections and social cohesion that frequently occur when individuals are collocated. In studies of corporations, community is typically defined as the metropolitan area (e.g., Marquis, 2003; Marquis et al., 2007; Stuart & Sorensen, 2003), although this definition is mainly a result of convenience because many potential variables of interest are reported at the metropolitan level. Although physical boundaries are an important part of such definitions, broader regions, such Silicon Valley (Saxenian, 1994), could also be considered communities to the extent that there is common identification and similar cultural and social elements that unite residents.

In earlier work, we conceptualized the community as an institutional field and identified the mechanisms that maintain the local community focus and identification for firms (Marquis et al., 2007). Paralleling Scott's (2001) approach, we examined how three sets of institutional forces (i.e., three pillars) affect community actors. First, the social and corporate infrastructure includes features of organizational populations (e.g., corporations and nonprofits), social networks, and local connecting institutions such as social clubs. These forces create an enduring social infrastructure for a community that is highly resistant to change (Marquis, 2003). Second, local political and governmental factors, including governmental size, spending, and leadership ideology, create variation across communities because of variation in incentives and coercive processes such as laws and regulations. Finally, cultural-cognitive factors reflect enduring belief systems in communities about the appropriate way things are done in the locale. These three broad types of mechanisms ensure that variation between communities remains even in an age of globalization.

Glynn (2008) shows the fruitfulness of taking a community-based approach in her study of the Olympic Games in Atlanta in 1996. Organizing and staging the Olympics brought the relational and symbolic systems underlying the Atlanta organizational community into relief and shows how the elite "clubbiness" and insularity documented by Hunter (1953) over 40 years earlier still existed. Importantly, Glynn shows that cities are conscious of their reputations and how they are perceived by the broader public, and the importance of these perceptions in establishing a normative environment that influences how corporations act and undertake community-oriented events. Others have noted that the Atlanta business community is highly focused on image building through visible public works (Burbank, Andranovich, & Heying, 2001). For example, the local *Atlanta Journal-Constitution* reported that "even a hundred years ago, Atlanta was the city of big horn-tooters," and that the same underlying interest in promoting the city that led Atlanta vying to host the 1895 Cotton States Exposition also led to its pursuit of the 1996 Olympics (Chambers, 1998).

Glynn's focus on image building in Atlanta is important because it shows not only how organizational actions are idiosyncratic across cities but also that cities are focused on promulgating an image or identity of the locale to external audiences. Glynn (2008, drawing on a quote from Putnam, 1993) argues this is about "common symbols, common leaders, and perhaps common ideals." Ideas about the identity and reputation of Atlanta mobilize action and thus connect research on organizations and their communities back to an older stream of organizational sociology that focused on interorganizational fields of communities (Warren, 1967). Hunter's earlier portrayal of Atlanta is clearly important in this stream of research, as well as earlier studies such as Baltzell's (1958) study of Philadelphia and Dahl's (1961) study of New Haven. But this earlier tradition had been lost in the ensuing decades. Scott (2001) postulates that modern transportation and communication systems developed such that geographical boundaries became meaningless, and so researchers abandoned the community in favor of geography-independent units such as the industry or field. More recently, as globalization processes have come to occupy even more importance, the community level has been even further neglected (Marquis & Battilana, 2009; Sorge, 2005).

COMMUNITY IDENTITY AND REPUTATION

Given this variation across communities in organizational actions, it should not be surprising that communities and their identities and reputation continue to shape the actions of corporations. In his influential work on economic geography, Storper (2005, p. 34) views common identity as central to unpacking how communities influence economic activities, and even defines community as a "wide variety of ways of grouping together with others with whom we share some part of our identity, expectations, and interests." More generally, it is well established that organizations derive their social identity from membership in groups and strive to maintain a positive social identity (Rao, Davis, & Ward, 2000; Tajfel & Turner, 1986). Socially oriented identities reflect the meaning that members derive from being part of a social collective; for instance, firms' identities are shaped in part from the stock market on which they list their shares (Rao et al.), their industry, and their market.

Although community identity is salient for some firms (Marquis et al., 2007), it need not be in competition or conflict with other sources of identity for corporations, such as industry. Early social scientists such as Cooley (1902) theorized that individuals had multiple identities and drew on different components of their identity depending on the broader social context. Informants in our fieldwork also verified that industry and community were the two main reference groups for large corporations. For example, a corporate philanthropy manager of a large U.S. company told us that when looking for examples when setting their giving levels, they typically look to two sets of firms—those in their industry and those headquartered in the same locale.

Having a positive identification with a community refers to a greater feeling of belonging to that community on the part of residents, which then has spillovers to community well-being more generally, reflected in activities such as nonprofit support and citizen volunteering rates. To the extent that cities become known for such behavior, this engenders further commitment. The best-known example of this dynamic is the development of the "5-Percent Club" in Minneapolis in the 1960s by local business leaders there (Galaskiewicz, 1985). All members donate 5% (or a reduced level of 2%) of their income to charitable causes. The current membership includes more than 200 Minneapolis businesses, and the club has become a visible symbol of the community. The example set by the Minneapolis tithing club has been imitated by other cities (Navarro, 1988). The epigraph from Galaskiewicz's 1997 article on the organization of the Minneapolis community shows how businesses in the city have crafted a unique positive identity as a result of their creation and involvement in the club, and this has significant influence on a community's reputation.

> I heard so much about the City of Minneapolis, about its Chamber of Commerce, about the public spirit of its business community, about your remarkable Five Percent Club—that I feel a bit like Dorothy in the Land of Oz. I had to come to the Emerald City myself to see if it really exists.
> —Speech delivered by John D. Rockefeller, III to the Minneapolis Chamber of Commerce, June 30, 1977

This example shows the power of organizations and associations both as substance and symbol for a community. Corporations in Minneapolis developed a 5-Percent Club to encourage corporations to give more to charity, and this club and the spirit underlying it then became a durable symbol of the community.

HOW LOCAL CORPORATIONS CONTRIBUTE TO POSITIVE COMMUNITY IDENTITY AND REPUTATION

The description of Galaskiewicz's research above highlights two important aspects that are missing from the broader literature on community social infrastructure (e.g., Putnam, 1993, 2000). Most research on civic infrastructure only examines direct effects, such as how levels of association membership lead to concrete positive outcomes for communities. For example, in a study of Italian communities and their success in implementing governmental programs, Putnam (1993) contrasts how the rich civic and social traditions of northern Italy made them more receptive to democratic reforms than their disconnected neighbors to the south.

But as discussed above, such behavior also has important symbolic value, influencing how the local population is engaged and outsiders view the city. For example, the 5-Percent Club becomes a symbol of what it means to be a Minneapolis corporation, which encourages other local corporations to belong and therefore give greater amounts to local charities (Galaskiewicz, 1991). This has the effect of creating greater awareness and recognition outside Minneapolis.

A second missing feature from most work on communities is a systematic consideration of how corporations influence internal and external perceptions of communities. This is also ironic because corporations are perhaps the dominant social actors of our time (Davis & Marquis, 2005). Perrow (1991) argues

> organizations are the key to society because *large organizations have absorbed society.* They have vacuumed up a good part of what we have always thought of as society, and made organizations, once a part of society, into a surrogate of society.

Aldrich (1999) makes a similar point and connects corporations to their communities by suggesting that even the definition of what is a community is constructed in a bottom-up process, resulting from relations between organizations. To understand a community requires an understanding of the organizations of which it is constituted.

Below, we identify two mechanisms by which corporations and their leaders reinforce a community's positive identity and reputation: the creation and maintenance of local social infrastructure (i.e., hardware), and mobilizing citizen involvement in the community (i.e., software). Although both of these mechanisms are internally focused activities, and hence mainly strengthen communities' identities, we believe they further have important spillovers to the reputation of the community. We provide illustrative examples from our fieldwork in a major U.S. metropolitan area.

Local Corporations and Social Infrastructure: The Hardware of Positive Community Identity and Reputation

One of the primary ways that local corporations contribute to a positive community identity is through their support and engagement in building and maintaining local foundations and nonprofits within a community. Below we discuss how the presence of corporate headquarters influences the well-being of local nonprofits. Second, we also address how the density of network connections between local corporate decision makers influences their commitment and degree to which they agree on the nature of their community's identity. Underlying our examples is the idea that such social infrastructure takes on a symbolic function, which increases the positive external perception of a community, that is, reputation.

Previous studies suggest that, even in an age of globalization, the location of corporate headquarters is an important component in determining where and how generously corporations support social programs and infrastructure (Guthrie, 2003). For example, a study of companies in Miami, Boston, and Cleveland described how locally headquartered companies identified more with their headquarters city and so contributed considerably more than nonlocal companies to the community, in addition to being much more involved in local civic leadership than nonlocally based companies (Kanter, 1995). Galaskiewicz (1985) also found that the philanthropic efforts of local corporate leadership in Minneapolis-St. Paul resulted in an institutional support tying corporations to their community, as in the creation of a symbolic tithing club where local companies gave 5% of after-tax profits to charity.

The relationship between Cummins Engine and its headquarters city—Columbus, Indiana—illustrates the positive influence corporations can have on local social infrastructure and how identity and reputation issues are particularly salient for local firms. As described by Whitman (1999, p. 113), Cummins Engine "functioned as the mainstay of local charities, entered into imaginative partnerships with local public schools, and once even lobbied for a higher state corporate income tax so as to pay more of what it regarded as its fair share." Integral to this mission was creating visible markers of support through buildings of architectural significance. Cummins, for instance, created a social program where they would pay the architects' fees for any building that used an architect from a list of prestigious architects, ensuring that buildings of note would rise in this small city of 30,000. As a result, the city has become known as an architectural mecca. For example, in a ranking of cities with the greatest amount of architecturally significant buildings, the American Institute of Architects ranked Columbus sixth behind the much larger cities, such as Chicago, New York City, Washington D.C., San Francisco, and Boston. Thus, this program by Cummins and its leaders had the dual benefit of creating a more aesthetically pleasing city, and in the process creating a more positive identity for the community, which then impacts its broader reputation.

Conversely, the loss of local corporate headquarters has detrimental effects on the community that had formerly benefited from its support, with negative implications for community identity more generally. Jay Lorsch describes the cost to Boston's status brought about by a string of lost headquarters:

> A company headquartered in Boston does give the city a certain amount of prestige, so you can't ignore it, I think anytime a city begins not to have any of them, people can look at it and say it's a second-class place. That's the danger. So having a few of them around is not a bad thing, at least symbolically. (Appelbaum, 2008)

The cost of lost headquarters is not merely symbolic because local corporations are often among the most generous supporters of local nonprofits. When Pittsburgh lost Gulf Oil, more than $2 million in local giving evaporated from the community. "[C]ivic organizations that lost money and volunteer support on account of Gulf's sale include hospitals, colleges, museums and the world renowned Pittsburgh Symphony" (Hirsch 1987, p. 68). These examples indicate that having locally headquartered firms is not only positive symbolically, as such institutions enhance the reputation and standing of the community, but also that they directly contribute to the civic health of their communities through their local spending and leadership.

Consistent with the research on corporations and communities described above, interview subjects in our fieldwork asserted that locally based businesses promoted social infrastructure in at least two ways: through the leadership of corporate personnel and through direct financial support. Almost all of the representatives of civic organizations that we interviewed indicated the importance of electing members from local corporations to nonprofit boards to have the right names on the letterhead and to ensure financial support. The executive director of a local nonprofit said:

> While there are many reasons why we invite people to our board, for example, diversity and expertise, one of the key factors is willingness for their company to support our group financially. We think for most non-profits that is the case—features of the person and their corporation are important, but it is also essential that they be active supporters as well.

Moreover, corporate involvement with nonprofits is overwhelmingly focused on the company's "home town." One interviewee, the president of the corporate foundation for one of the largest corporations in the United States, indicated that "80% of corporate spending is typically in the headquarters city." Galsakiewicz (1997) similarly found that about 70% of corporate philanthropy stayed within his focal city of Minneapolis-St. Paul. Another respondent indicated that "Just about all of our funding of cultural activities is in [headquarters city], because it is in the HQ city." Thus, the mere presence of local headquarters is likely to help the social infrastructure of a city simply through the local spending of the corporation.

A particular type of corporation—the commercial bank—has historically held a distinctly central place in the social organization of local elites in the business and nonprofit sectors. Part of the appeal of bank leaders for nonprofits is symbolic, as informants cited the importance of having bank managers on their board for legitimacy, even if those individuals do not contribute. Idiosyncrasies of U.S. federal and state banking laws tightly restricted the geographic growth of banks for much of American history, and as a result they established deep roots within their communities and typically have a greater commitment to their locale, which is shown not only through civic commitment such as greater philanthropic donations but also by local banks and bankers creating community-oriented business services (Marquis et al., 2007; Marquis & Lounsbury, 2007). Thus, banks have long been perceived as the center of community social and economic life (Ratcliff, 1980) and are particularly important in geographically based intercorporate networks (Mintz & Schwartz, 1985). The importance of banks to communities is illustrated by the response of San Francisco firms to an attempted takeover of Bank of America, the leading local bank. As reported in the local newspapers, this takeover was prevented because other corporations felt that a locally headquartered financial institution was important to regional well-being and identity.

Finally, it is not just the existence of businesses but the social organization of their leaders, as well as the links between business leaders and the non-profit community, that can shape a community's identity and reputation. Our respondents stated that the tighter the ties between corporate leaders and those directing nonprofits in a community, the more likely those leaders were to give money and time (cf., Galaskiewicz, 1997). Cities vary substantially in how well-connected their local corporate elites are, reflecting long-standing local traditions around corporate governance (Marquis, 2003). Business leaders with memberships on more corporate boards and in elite social clubs are more prone to participating in local policy-related groups (Ratcliff, 1980). Corporate connections to nonprofit organizations generated greater local charitable giving in the Minneapolis-St. Paul area (Galaskiewicz, 1997). This suggests that the density of social networks connecting local business leaders contributes to greater commitment to, and development of, the local social infrastructure and thus by extension provides a more positive community reputation.

Local Corporations and Citizen Involvement: The Software of Positive Community Identity and Reputation

There is more to having a city develop a positive identity and reputation than simply the support of the social infrastructure by corporations and their leaders. Our informants also suggested that a grassroots element is also necessary, and in the community we studied corporations were influential in mobilizing and aggregating citizen involvement. Below, we discuss how the presence of and connections between corporations and nonprofits can increase grassroots volunteering (i.e., the software in our model). This involvement of broader elements of the society we argue has the effect of building individuals' attachment to the locale and hence maintaining and strengthening communities' positive identity. A similar process has also been documented by Feldman and Khademian (2003) in their study of how city governmental organizations, through their empowerment of their individual employees, strengthen connection to the community for members of the general public.

Corporations' aggregation of local volunteering efforts was described by several of our informants. A community relations manager for a Fortune 500 retailer we interviewed described her company's contributions to the leadership of local nonprofits:

> We encourage our employees to participate in non-profit activities. For instance, one of our regional managers is taking the non-profit board member development program run by the local Chamber of Commerce. This is a program where they take up-and-coming corporate leaders and teach them what they need to know to serve on a board of directors. It is a rigorous program and we sponsor that person. Then they try to set that person up with an appointment to a board.

Corporations also provide a venue for aggregating rank-and-file volunteer labor. A respondent from a Fortune 500 manufacturer described how the company gave two paid days off to all employees to volunteer for nonprofit activities, and some companies provide executive-on-loan programs to help local nonprofits.

These programs can be extensive. For example, an executive of a major U.S. corporation whom we interviewed noted that the company had a centralized infrastructure that:

> coordinates (volunteering) activities and ... provide[s] a venue where that is possible. We had a clean-up day last May where employees were encouraged to help clean areas of the communities where they worked. In addition we fund a huge retiree volunteer association. They logged almost 100,000 hours of volunteer time last year. We provide them with a budget, but aside from that, it is entirely employee-run.

These activities, which result in civic involvement by greater numbers of citizens, contribute to a more positive community identity by the promotion of the community as a good place to live and further strengthen individuals' ties to the community.

CONCLUSIONS AND IMPLICATIONS
FOR THEORY AND PRACTICE

Building on previous research regarding how communities vary in the identities and reputations that they portray internally and to the outside world (Romanelli & Khessina, 2005) as well as research that shows how communities vary on positive social phenomena such as social cohesion, trust, and reciprocity (Putnam, 2000), in this chapter we have proposed that the internal and external perceptions of cities vary on how they develop a more or less positive identity and reputation. Our extended discussion of the previous research on Minneapolis and Atlanta, as well as other anecdotal examples from our fieldwork in a major U.S. city, bears out this distinction. Local corporations and a community's identity and reputation are intimately intertwined, and we have focused on two mechanisms that help make these connections. Corporations help build the community "hardware," whereby they contribute to the establishment of local social infrastructure, and further a "software" component, whereby they enable the more effective aggregation of individuals to community-oriented activities, generating higher levels of attachment and commitment. We illustrated these two mechanisms with examples from our fieldwork in a major U.S. city. Below we discuss contributions to theory, possible areas for future research, and finally how some of our insights can aid business and policy makers interested in creating more positive identities for their communities.

One of our larger theoretical concerns is how, despite globalization, geographically based communities are still an essential organizational environment. Although there is a growing interest in the influence of communities on organizations, the processes of how organizations contribute to community identity have been relatively unexplored. We see our discussions above as a first step in this direction and see a number of avenues for future research. For example, although identity at the community level may be durable, the corporations that enact that identity come and go with the processes of founding and death, as well as merger and acquisition. This raises a number of interesting questions at a variety of levels of analysis. At the organizational level, there are a number of interesting questions that could be examined: How are new firms socialized and made aware of a community's identity? What happens when firms are acquired? And at the community level, how can these mechanisms explain how communities can change their identities?

We also believe that understanding positive community identity processes may be relevant to understanding the levers available to municipalities seeking to build their own social and civic infrastructures, and hence well-being. If organizational scholars want to have something to say in the debate on how corporations "affect the distribution of privilege and disadvantage in society" (Hinings and Greenwood, 2002, p. 411), our discussion suggests that the community and community identity may be an appropriate and useful site for doing so. The vibrancy of local social infrastructure within a community represents one of the most direct indicators of the quality of life in that community, from the availability of education and the arts to the nature of the social safety net (Putnam & Feldstein, 2003; Saegert, Thompson, & Warren, 2001). Our theorizing above suggests that the corporate sector—its size, its composition, and the ways its constituents interact within a community—is perhaps the most proximate factor behind the vibrancy of the nonprofit sector and hence how positive identity is created and maintained within communities. Thus, there is a relatively straight path from corporations to quality of life within communities, and this path merits further study.

ACKNOWLEDGMENTS

We thank Jane Dutton and attendees of the Positive Identity conference for feedback on an earlier version of this chapter.

REFERENCES

Aldrich, H. (1999). *Organizations evolving.* Thousand Oaks, CA: Sage.

Appelbaum, B. (2008, April 24). Corporate headquarters are overrated, mayor says. *The Boston Globe*, p. 3.

Baltzell, E. D. (1958). *Philadelphia gentlemen: The making of a national upper class.* Glencoe, IL: Free Press.

Burbank, M. J., Andranovich, G. D., & Heying, C. H. (2001). *Olympic dreams: The impact of mega-events on local politics.* Boulder, CO: Lynne Rienner Publishers.

Chambers, R. (1998, July 20). Century old story has flavor of modern Atlanta, *Atlanta Journal-Constitution*, p. E-01.

Cooley, C. H. (1902). *Human nature and the social order.* New York: C. Scribner's Sons.

Dahl, R. A. (1961). *Who governs?* New Haven, CT: Yale University Press.

Davis, G. F., & Greve, H. R. (1997). Corporate elite networks and governance changes in the 1980s. *American Journal of Sociology, 103,* 1–37.

Davis, G. F., & Marquis, C. (2005). Prospects for theory about organizations in the early 21st century: institutional fields and mechanisms. *Organization Science, 16,* 332–343.

Feldman, M. S., & Khademian, A. M. (2003). Empowerment and cascading vitality. In K. S. Cameron, J. E. Dutton, & R. E. Quinn (Eds.), *Positive organizational scholarship: Foundations of a new discipline* (pp. 343–358). San Francisco: Berrett-Koehler.

Fiss, P. C., & Hirsch, P. M. (2005). The discourse of globalization: Framing and sensemaking of an emerging concept. *American Sociological Review, 70,* 29–52.

Florida, R. L. (2002). *The rise of the creative class: And how it's transforming work, leisure, community, and everyday life.* New York: Basic Books.

Galaskiewicz, J. (1985). *Social organization of an urban grants economy: A study of business philanthropy and nonprofit organizations.* Orlando, FL: Academic Press.

Galaskiewicz, J. (1991). Making corporate actors accountable: Institution-building in Minneapolis-St. Paul. In W. W. Powell & P. J. DiMaggio (Eds.), *The new institutionalism in organizational analysis* (pp. 293–310). Chicago: University of Chicago Press.

Galaskiewicz, J. (1997). An urban grants economy revisited: corporate charitable contributions in the twin cities, 1979–1981, 1987–1989. *Administrative Science Quarterly, 42,* 445–471.

Glynn, M. A. (2008). Configuring the field of play: How hosting the Olympic Games impacts civic community. *Journal of Management Studies, 45,* 1117–1146.

Guthrie, D. (2003). *Survey on corporate-community relations.* New York: Social Sciences Research Council.

Hinings, C. R., & Greenwood, R. (2002). Disconnects and consequences in organization theory. *Administrative Science Quarterly, 47,* 411–421.

Hirsch, P. M. (1987). *Pack your own parachute: How to survive mergers, takeovers, and other corporate disasters.* Reading, MA: Addison-Wesley.

Hunter, F. (1953). *Community power structure: A study of decision-makers.* Chapel Hill, NC: University of North Carolina Press.

Kanter, R. M. (1995). *World class: Thriving locally in the global economy.* New York: Simon & Schuster.

Marquis, C. (2003). The pressure of the past: Network imprinting in intercorporate communities. *Administrative Science Quarterly, 48,* 655–689.

Marquis, C., & Battilana, J. (in press). Acting globally but thinking locally? The influence of local communities on organizations. *Research in Organizational Behavior.*

Marquis, C., Glynn, M. A., & Davis, G. F. (2007). Community isomorphism and corporate social action. *Academy of Management Review, 32,* 925–945.

Marquis, C., & Lounsbury, M. (2007). Vive la resistance: Consolidation and community-level professional counter-mobilization in US banking. *Academy of Management Journal, 50,* 799–820.

Mintz, B., & Schwartz, M. (1985). *The power structure in American business.* Chicago: University of Chicago Press.

Navarro, P. (1988). Why do corporations give to charity? *The Journal of Business, 61,* 65–93.

Ostrander, S. A. (1984). *Women of the upper class.* Philadelphia: Temple University Press.

Perrow, C. (1991). A society of organizations. *Theory and Society, 20,* 725–762.

Putnam, R. D. (1993). *Making democracy work: Civic traditions in modern Italy.* Princeton, NJ: Princeton University Press.

Putnam, R. D. (2000). *Bowling alone: The collapse and revival of the American community.* New York: Simon & Schuster.

Putnam, R. D., & Feldstein, L. M. (2003). *Better together: Restoring the American community.* New York: Simon & Schuster.

Rao, H., Davis, G. F., & Ward, A. (2000). Embeddedness, social identity and mobility: Why firms leave the NASDAQ and join the New York Stock exchange. *Administrative Science Quarterly, 45,* 268–292.

Ratcliff, R. (1980). Banks and corporate lending: An analysis of the impact of the internal structure of the capitalist class on the lending behavior of banks. *American Sociological Review, 45,* 229–249.

Romanelli, E., & Khessina, O. M. (2005). Regional industrial identity: Cluster configurations and economic development. *Organization Science, 16,* 344–358.

Saegert, S., Thompson, J. P., & Warren, M. R. (2001). *Social capital and poor communities.* New York: Russell Sage Foundation.

Saxenian, A. L. (1994). *Regional advantage: culture and competition in Silicon Valley and Route 128.* Cambridge, MA: Harvard University Press.

Scott, W. R. (2001). *Institutions and organizations* (2nd ed.). Thousand Oaks, CA: Sage Publications.

Sorge, A. (2005). *The global and the local: Understanding the dialectics of business systems.* Oxford, NY: Oxford University Press.

Storper, M. (2005). Society, community, and economic development. *Comparative International Development, 39,* 30–57.

Stuart, T., & Sorensen, O. (2003). Liquidity events and the geographic distribution of entrepreneurial activity. *Administrative Science Quarterly, 43,* 175–201.

Tajfel, H., & Turner, J. C. (1986). The social identity theory of intergroup behavior. In S. Worchel & W. G. Austin (Eds.), *The psychology of intergroup relations* (pp. 7–24). Chicago: Nelson-Hall.

Tönnies, F. (1887). *Gemeinschaft und Gesellschaft: Abhandlung des Communismus und des Socialismus als empirischer Culturformen.* Leipzig, Germany: Fues.

Warren, R. L. (1967). The interorganizational field as a focus for investigation. *Administrative Science Quarterly, 12,* 396–419.

Whitman, M. v. N. (1999). *New world, new rules: The changing role of the American corporation.* Boston: Harvard Business School Press.

21

Commentary: Finding the Positive in Positive Organizational Identities

Mary Ann Glynn and Ian J. Walsh

CONTENTS

This book, and especially the five chapters in this section, signals a growing interest in the study of positive *organizational* identities. The preceding chapters build a solid theoretical foundation, demonstrating that a focus on the positive can cultivate the kinds of collective identities that mobilize collective action toward valued outcomes for organizations and communities. Importantly, the authors theorize about not only the nature of positive identity at this higher level of analysis but also *how* positive identities function. Each chapter makes contributions that advance our conceptualization of positive identity at the organizational and collective levels. Together, they lay the groundwork for rich and rigorous future scholarship that can map how positive identities are constructed, maintained, and important to broader aspects of organizations and communities.

In this commentary, we reflect on some of the thematic ideas that have emerged for us from the preceding chapters and use these to address questions of import: What is so *positive* about positive identities at this higher level? What does it mean for organizations and communities to have a positive identity? And, in what ways does it matter? Drawing on the insights advanced by the preceding chapters suggests that answering these questions will focus on three core elements: positive or valued identity *attributes*, positive *processes* of identity construction and maintenance, and positive or socially beneficial *outcomes* that flow from an organizational or community alignment with a positive identity. We elaborate and discuss each of these three aspects of positive identities—attributes, processes, and outcomes—for organizations and collectives in the next sections.

POSITIVE IDENTITY ATTRIBUTES

Broadly speaking, the chapters in this section are concerned with defining and clarifying the construct or nature of positive identity attributes. The authors offer conceptualizations that are rich, varied, complex, and multifaceted. Taken together, the chapters suggested for us that at least four characteristics are "central and distinctive" (Albert & Whetten, 1985) elements of positive identities for organizations and communities: Positive identities tend to have attributes that are inspirational, generative, authentic, and adaptive.

First, positive identities are *cognitively and emotionally inspiring* to the collective; organizational and community members see these identities as attractive and aspirational. Marquis and Davis (Chapter 20), in examining the community level, show that geographically defined regions can have idealized identities that incite public commitment to local businesses and can overflow to increase the social good. Moreover, such identities are not only attractive to the community residents but also other municipalities; thus, positive identities can inspire a broader diffusion of these attributes. Hamilton and Gioia (Chapter 19) focus on the case of a positive organizational identity that embodies a primary organization-level virtue of sustainability; such a "green" positive identity can ensure a flourishing, longer-lived habitat for all the inhabitants of our planet. Strikingly, the chapter authors do not shy away from the normative implications of these identities. Instead, they illuminate explicitly those aspects of positive identity that are evaluated as "good" and typically link this to the creation of a high level of emotional energy among stakeholders (Corley & Harrison, Chapter 16).

Second, positive identities are *generative*, enabling increased resource capabilities and enhanced well-being for the collective. Brickson and Lemmon (Chapter 18) theorize how positive organizational identities can enrich and cultivate stakeholder relationships and in turn advantageous resource flows to the corporation. Marquis and Davis (Chapter 20) show how a positive identity for a geographic region can invigorate and sustain the civic health of communities to the benefit of its citizens and its organizations.

Third, positive identities are *authentic*, faithfully and realistically representing the foundational character of organizations and collectives. Identities in general are grounded in the central, distinctive, and enduring elements of the collective identity (Albert & Whetten, 1985); thus, positive identities veridically describe this fundamental character of the collective. Positive identities are authentic in the sense that they offer credible and accurate accounts of "who we are as an organization" both to members and to outsiders. For instance, Hamilton and Gioia (Chapter 19) contrast the plausibility of the positive identity claim to sustainability of Method company from others with less compelling environmental missions (e.g., Clorox) that engage in the apparently less than authentic "greenwashing." This authenticity carries implications for collective action; positive identities function as a kind of rudder for steering organizational or community behaviors toward the kinds of positive goals that align with this identity and establish continuity over time, even under stormy conditions. Corley and Harrison (Chapter 16) clearly recognize that action and reflection are equally important in the pursuit of authentic organizational identities. Pratt and Kraatz (Chapter 17) show how organizational identities can be reflexive and in turn how this enables consistency and coherence across a plurality of selves.

Finally, positive identities are *agile and adaptive*, charting new courses of change for organizations or communities while still remaining authentically true to their character and espoused values. Positive identities function as collective mechanisms that enable successful change for an organizational entity. Corley and Harrison (Chapter 16) demonstrate how the ACS company adapted to changing market and consumer needs as a way of fostering the authenticity of its identity. Pratt and Kraatz (Chapter 17) model the collective as specifically agentic and capable of authoring an identity that is complex and multifaceted. Importantly, too, although they note that this is not unbounded; clearly, organizations operate in complex economic, social, and institutional environments that can curb an exuberant—or excessively positive—definition of the organizational self. Identity claims are disciplined by organizational actions apperceived by relevant audiences.

In summary, the authors of the five chapters in this section seem to suggest that positive identities can be described as inspiring, generative, authentic, and agile. Although these attributes may be at the core of positive identities, they do not presume a collective fixedness; attributes can be interpreted and reinterpreted (e.g., what does it mean to be green?) over time and in response to changing environmental conditions. Thus, positive identities can potentially be both enduring and adaptive over time. More generally, it seems that positive organizational identities embed paradoxes of stability and change; they promote and respect the collective history while also providing necessary tools and capabilities for future action. Understanding how these underlying tensions are resolved requires an examination of the underlying collective processes that shape and sustain positive identities, which we discuss next.

POSITIVE IDENTITY PROCESSES

Theorizing positive identities at higher levels of analysis invokes critical questions about the nature of the collective (organizational or community), its membership, and the processes by which members collectively create, sustain, or change the positive character of its identity. Here, we shift gears from understanding what is so *positive* to what is so collective about a positive identity. Thus, we turn to the question of "we" in identity processes ("who *we* are as an organization") and the collective organizing that defines it. As the authors in this section demonstrate extensively, positive identities are socially constructed by members of collectives. So we consider: What is so organizational (or collective) about positive identities?

The foregoing chapters point to the underlying and complex social processes that mobilize collective beliefs and action in service of identity formation and transformation. Understanding these collective processes sheds light on how positive organizational identities evolve or change to remain positive even when environments change or when the identity itself becomes threatened in ways that render it less positive or outright negative. In particular, the chapters in this section draw our attention to three collective processes that underlie the construction of a positive identity at the organizational or community level: resourcing, relationship building, and meaning making.

First, positive identity processes involve *resourcing and resourcefulness.* Resourcefulness is the "power to originate and propagate something that would not exist otherwise" (Rousseau & Ling, 2007, p. 3), thereby increasing the capacities and capabilities of the collective. Resourcefulness is the companion to the generativity attribute (discussed above) and focuses on how a positive identity can be a collective resource. Brickson & Lemmon (Chapter 18) explicitly detail how positive identities represent a critical resource from which organizations derive goals and plans of action that produce a broader array of resources for stakeholders. Similarly, Marquis and Davis (Chapter 20) relate a comparable role for positive community identities, which attract civic involvement and philanthropy from local organizations to enrich the overall resources of the community. For instance, the "5-Percent Club" in Minneapolis has fostered a vibrant civic identity that has encouraged higher levels of charitable donations from Minneapolis-based corporations, thereby fortifying a social infrastructure, itself a critical and generative resource for the local community.

Second, positive identity processes involve *relationship building* that creates, connects, and strengthens the social structure of a collective. Such positive relationships (e.g., Dutton & Ragins, 2007) seem intimated in positive identities. Marquis and Davis (Chapter 20) show how grass roots involvement of organizational members in volunteering activities and leadership involvement on corporate boards develops ties that create a positive identity for a community. Hamilton and Gioia (Chapter 19) detail how a positive organizational identity is grounded in relational processes that evolve from the connections among social actors. Brickson and Lemmon (Chapter 18) focus on how the relational orientation of an organization can develop a positive identity and foster connections with stakeholders; these connections in turn influence shared identity schemas. As Pratt and Kraatz (Chapter 17) highlight, organizations exist in a pluralistic context that serves up multiple identities, implying perhaps that a positive perspective on identity can unify diverse constituencies. Across all the chapters, building effective relationships with actors both internal and external to the collective seemed vital to cultivating a positive identity.

Third, positive identity processes involve *meaning making* that matters to members of the collective. Hamilton and Gioia (Chapter 19) define organizational identity as "a social construction constituted by the collective beliefs and values held by members about 'who we are' as an organization" and focus on how meaning is derived from doing and being in the organization. Corley and Harrison (Chapter 16) point to the need for organizational vigilance in attending to the symmetry of identity labels and their meanings, which in turn serves as a guide for action. Pratt and Kraatz (Chapter 17) focus on how the metaphor of the "organizational self" reflects an intentional effort by the organization to prioritize and rationalize differences among multiple (and possibly competing) identities. Whether meaning arises through collective beliefs, values, causes, coherence, or aspirational attributes (such as those discussed earlier), it nevertheless appears to be dynamic, ongoing, and engaging for the collective in crafting a positive identity.

In summary, the five chapters in this section suggest that positive identities for organizations and communities likely involve three interrelated collective processes: resourcing, relating, and meaning making. Taken together, these processes can undergird the social system of the collective so as to craft a positive identity that connects a broad set of actors and that can yield outcomes of positive benefit; we take up the issue of positive identity outcomes next.

POSITIVE IDENTITY OUTCOMES

Arguably, the most salient feature of positive identities at the organizational and community levels is its creation of beneficial or valued outcomes for the collective. If positive identities encapsulate positive attributes and positive processes, then their functionality lies in generating positive outcomes. A consideration of outcomes speaks to the potency of positive identities and their inherent capacity to better the collective that they define. The authors in this section articulate a broad range of outcomes associated with positive identities, ranging from local benefits of a particular organization or regional community, to a truly global effect of the sustainability of the entire planet. At the local level, Marquis and Davis (Chapter 20) focus on how a geographic community's positive identity enhances the vibrancy, social cohesion, trust, and reciprocity of its organizations and civic infrastructure. Corley and Harrison (Chapter 16) show how positive organizational identity can direct "organizational change that is implemented in such a way that both the process and outcomes of the change result in net positive returns in regard to emotional energy." At the global level, Brickson and Lemmon (Chapter 18) define a positive organizational identity as one that yields "a net positive level of socially valuable resources to the earth and its living inhabitants." Hamilton and Gioia (Chapter 19) link positive organizational identities to environmental sustainability, social responsibility, and the "triple bottom line."

Together, the chapters in this section suggest several outcomes that may be characteristic of positive identities at the organizational and community levels. Noticeable is the casting of these as *net positive* in two of the chapters (16 and 19) and the enormous reach of these effects, from organizations through communities and ultimately perhaps to the world. It struck us that the notion of organization in society figured more prominently in these conceptualizations of *positive* organizational identity than in existing research on organizational identity. Allowing that organizational and community identities may be unabashedly positive seemed to widen scholars' lens in examining just how far-reaching a collective's impact might be, and that it adds value above and beyond that which might ordinarily be expected, that is, the returns of positive identities should be net positive. Vivid to us was the prominence of the interface between the firm and its embedded society in these chapters.

Characteristically, the authors linked positive identities to their societal value or "social welfare generation" (Brickson & Lemmon, Chapter 18). Hamilton and Gioia (Chapter 19) broaden organizational sustainability beyond an ecological focus, suggesting that organizations with sustainable positive identities achieve a "balance among environmental responsibility, social equity, and economic capability." The importance of social value may be most evident in those municipalities that have lost corporate headquarters, as Marquis and Davis (Chapter 20) describe. Pittsburgh's loss of Gulf Oil as a member of the community and the subsequent effects of lower financial support for local nonprofit organizations echoes the experience of many other cities in an era of corporate consolidations and acquisitions; this suggests that the notion of positive identities may well apply to a broad spectrum of organizations and other collectives. Importantly, the loss or lack of a positive identity may adversely affect community life and well-being.

In summary, the hallmark attributes and processes of positive identity seem to generate a resourcefulness that can yield "net positive" effects. What surprised us is the potential for these effects to ripple outward from the organization in far-reaching ways to affect broader social audiences that may be worldwide. Underlying this, perhaps, is the generative engine of resourcefulness and the compelling nature of identities that inspire, energize, and authenticate one's identity. Although some of the resources generated by positive identities may be tangible, in terms of their organizational or social benefits, they need not be. Intangible effects on a collective's actors, values, beliefs, emotions, aspirations, and motivation were also evident in the foregoing chapters. Given the centrality of authenticity and meaning making to positive identities, important outcomes are often represented in the ideals, symbols, representations, and meaning of the identity itself. Pratt and Kraatz (Chapter 17) argue that, in a pluralistic society, identities may foster coherence among multiple organizational selves; their work suggests the possibility that identities claimed and internalized as the organizational self direct action that may seem more authentic, as, for instance, when universities not only "talk the talk" of environmentalism but act on it. The authenticity of a positive identity may yield compatibility between an organizational identity's labels and meaning (Corley & Gioia, 2004) and its practices and action, as Corley and Harrison (Chapter 16) reveal. Finally, given the reflexive and self-reinforcing nature of identities, sustaining positive identities requires validation through alignment with, or social conformity to, stakeholder interests and audience expectations (Brickson & Lemmon, Chapter 18), as well as community needs (Marquis & Davis, Chapter 20).

POSITIVE IDENTITY ATTRIBUTES, PROCESSES, AND OUTCOMES: AN INTEGRATION

For the sake of discussion, we have parsed positive identities into three elements or factors—attributes, processes, and outcomes—but clearly these are interrelated. Moreover, their ultimate potency—to define the collective, to shape and mobilize collective action, and to generate outcomes of collective benefit—may derive from their gestalt. Identities are reflexive, self-reinforcing, and dynamic, even at the more macro level (Pratt & Kraatz, Chapter 17); thus, once defined, they tend to endure over time and over changes in the organization or community. It follows then that positive identities for organizations and communities are perhaps best defined not in terms of a singular characteristic, but instead in how the collective understanding of "who we are" coalesces into "what it means to be who we are."

Positive identities also mobilize action ("being and doing who we are"), which in turn feeds back to sustain the collective understanding of "who we are." Thus, we see these factors as linked recursively in ways that may echo the enduringly positive character of a collective; however, recursivity—and continual performance of identity—introduces some variations in attributes, processes, or outcomes that can reinterpret identity in new or creative ways. This was evident in the case of the Clorox company, for instance, which tried to reframe itself in terms of a "greener" identity (Hamilton & Gioia, Chapter 19). Although such variations may define or reinforce a positive identity, they may also edit, question, or reinterpret identity in ways that are not uniformly positive. Hamilton and Gioia hint at this, suggesting that Clorox's newly branded "green" identity was viewed by some as inauthentic, faddish, or an advertising ploy to grab market share.

What was striking to us as we read these five very thoughtful chapters was how they squarely locate positive identities within the broader environment that envelopes organizations and communities. Using this wider angle, we easily see that societies put expectations and pressures on organizations—to be authentic, to be socially responsible, to be meaningful—and, to the extent that organizations succeed in doing so, their identities may be judged by internal and external audiences, to be more "positive." Research at the individual level has demonstrated cross-cultural differences in identity, self-construals, and subjective well-being across societies (e.g., Diener & Diener, 1995; Erez & Earley, 1993; Kitayama & Markus, 2000) and in geographic regions within societies (e.g., Plaut, Markus, & Lachman, 2002). This evaluative aspect—in judging identities as being appropriate, good, or right—lends a distinctly normative tone to *positive* identities that can complement the cognitive and affective approaches that are so prominent in identity research. An illustration of the cognitive approach at the organizational level is Dutton and Dukerich's (1991) study of homelessness at the Port Authority of New York, in which they showed how rethinking the organization's identity shifted its attentiveness to social needs. Glynn and Dowd (2008) showed how "emotive leadership" was evident under identity threat precipitated by a CEO's scandalized image.

This concern about the distinctly "positive" outcomes or effects of a collective identity expands the frontier of identity research. This model of organization in society offers a unique and important unit of analysis for positive organizational scholarship more generally. It is a view that seems to redound to the open-system models of organizations that interact with, and are consequent for, their environment. Marquis and Davis' (Chapter 20) investigation of positive identities at the level of the geographic community or region reminds us that organizations' identities function beyond competitive markets, fields, or industries. Organizations are embedded in larger systems of actors, collectivities, and their associated expectations, which critically affect identities. Thus, a positive lens on collective identities offers a new set of dependent variables that may have more social or idealistic referents. We take up such possibilities for future scholarship in the next section.

INTO THE FUTURE: A POSSIBLE RESEARCH AGENDA

As important as the work on positive psychology has been to positive organizational scholarship, this section of the book highlights what can be distinctly organizational (or collective) about positive identities. The preceding chapters sketch a starting agenda for research in this area but also raise some questions to be addressed by future scholars. We outline a few of these here.

As with any theoretical construct that crosses levels of analysis, identity raises questions about its composition or similarity across different levels of analysis: Does identity mean the same thing for individuals and collectives? Are identity processes functionally similar (or different) across levels of analyses? Do macro-level organizational processes parallel microlevel individual processes? The answers that we draw from the preceding chapters are yes and no! Yes, in that positive identities at the collective level have attributes that are central, distinctive, and enduring, while they are also adaptive and changing to meet revised audience expectations, beliefs, or needs. The reflexivity and reinforcing nature of identity seemed to operate in functionally similar ways for organizations and individuals, as Pratt and Kraatz describe. Moreover, authenticity and coherence characterized collective identities in ways that seemed to correspond to individual identities. Of course, the "positive" essence of their identity embeds a value system that contains an evaluative element of what is good, right, or proper. However, even with this similarity, all the authors suggest aspects of positive identities at the collective level that imply differences between the individual and the collective.

On the other hand, this research also suggests that collective identities may operate in different ways than the self-concepts of individuals. At the aggregate level of the collective, positive identities have greater carrying capacity for resources, meaning, and generativity and, as a result, have far greater impact than individuals because of their size and scope. Carrying capacity refers to the number of entities that can be supported or sustained without detrimental effects. In ecological and strategic theories of the firm, carrying capacity refers to the maximum number of organizations that an environment (or market) can support effectively (e.g., Zammuto & Cameron, 1985). Here, we propose that positive collective identities have greater carrying capacity because their inherent resourcefulness and generativity typically expands what can be supported; moreover, the aggregated quality of organizational and community identities expand the pool of cognitive, emotional, and normative resources beyond that which can be sustained by a lone individual's identity. Issues of sustainability, community vitality, stakeholder interests, and, more generally, audience needs figured prominently in the preceding chapters. The model of the collective was one that not only had a core set of identity attributes (like individuals) but also was firmly implanted in, and affected by, the world around it. Thus, organization in society was a focal unit of analysis that brought a wider angle to the lens of positive identities.

At the level of the collective, the processes of identity formation and transformation may be far more complex than that for individuals. Taking on a cause like sustainability requires not only a claim of a "green" identity but also the mobilization and concerted action of a large cast of actors, both internal and external to the collective. Thus, the identity-action link for collectives can often involve high coordination costs, political interaction, resource allocation decisions, and divergent audiences in a pluralistic society (Pratt & Kraatz, Chapter 17) that complicate the possibility of following the logic of appropriateness that is governed by one's identity (March & Olsen, 2004).

Positive identities at the collective level can often be very visible and public, subjecting organizations to added environmental pressures to endure or change. Corley and Harrison (Chapter 16) show how one organization tried to do both—to be authentic to their original mission but to adapt to changes in markets, technologies, consumers, and products. In meeting such identity challenges, organizational stumbles, intentional or not, may garner public and media attention. Thus, organizations may face the struggle of transforming negative identities into more positive ones; a look at the recent spate of corporate scandals in the United States suggests that the perceptions of identities may fluctuate considerably but that there is much to be gained in redeeming a tainted identity (Glynn & Dowd, 2008). Moreover, such environmental shifts raise interesting questions about the mechanisms, rate, and possibility of identity change and its evaluation as good or bad.

Together, these five insightful chapters offer a rich representation of positive organizational identity that spans its core attributes, processes, and outcomes. Simultaneously, they raise questions about the implications of positive identity in terms of its potential effects on organizational performance or community benefits, as well as its endurance over the longer term. How sustainable are positive identities for the collective? Could there be decomposition effects such that the energy and inspiration of positive identities wane or dilute over time? Can significant and adverse events adversely affect a positive identity and its authenticity? Do organizations with positive identities achieve higher and longer periods of success than those with identities that are negatively or neutrally valenced? Although we raise the possibilities of such inquiries here, we leave it to future researchers to articulate the theoretical linkages between positive identities and exceptional levels of organizational performance (Cameron, 2003), as well as their emergence, growth, decline, or recovery over time. Rigorous empirical studies that measure these relationships offer an opportunity to embed the theorized role of positive collective identity more fully in organizational studies and to tie it explicitly with other theoretical perspectives.

Finally, these chapters draw our attention to the processes by which positive identities change and adapt over time. In light of recent debates about the endurance of organizational identity (Gioia, Schultz, & Corley, 2000; Whetten, 2006), future research might examine the long-term trajectories of positive identities. In their work on resilience, Allenby & Fink (2005, p. 1034) discuss "the capability of a system to maintain its functions and structure in the face of internal and external change and to degrade gracefully when it must." Organizations that radically change or even go out of existence through bankruptcy, merger, or acquisition may carry legacy organizational identities, or shared understandings of "who we *were* as an organization" (Walsh & Glynn, 2008), that persist even when the organizations themselves are gone. Positive identities, or specific elements of them, may offer great survival potential in the face of organizational change and demise, fostering the ongoing, "deep structure" identification of former members (Rousseau, 1998; Walsh, 2008). Longitudinal research that examines the strength, adaptation, and persistence of positive identities over time may illuminate the identity dynamics that promote such durability and the consequent (positive or negative) effects on communities, organizations, and their members.

CONCLUSION

The chapters in this section draw attention to the attributes, processes, and outcomes from which organizations and communities can construct positive identities. This research illuminates what it means for an identity to be positive, the means by which such identities are constructed and sustained, and the robust benefits that may accrue for members, stakeholders, and broader society. These three core aspects represent interrelated components of an upward, recursive spiral that further strengthens the positive character of organizational and community identities, much like the deviation-amplifying loops that Weick (1979) describes. Collectively, the authors advance a clear and credible perspective on positive collective identities that brings a deeper and more accessible meaning to this concept and breaks open new avenues for research. Through further study, the definitively constructive effects of positive identities on organizational life, and, more broadly, social and global functioning, may become more transparently understood in ways that bring them within reach of a broad range of contemporary organizations. We are confident that this volume will be influential in advancing this work.

REFERENCES

Albert, S., & Whetten, D. A. (1985). Organizational identity. In L. L. Cummings & B. M. Staw (Eds.), *Research in organizational behavior* (Vol. 7; pp. 263–295). Greenwich, CT: JAI Press.

Allenby, B., & Fink, J. (2005). Toward inherently secure and resilient societies. *Science, 309,* 1034–1036.

Cameron, K. (2003). Organizational virtuousness and performance. In K. Cameron, J. Dutton, & R. Quinn (Eds.). *Positive organizational scholarship: Foundations of a new discipline* (pp. 48–65). San Francisco: Berrett-Koehler.

Corley, K. G., & Gioia, D. A. (2004). Identity ambiguity and change in the wake of a corporate spin-off. *Administrative Science Quarterly, 49,* 173–208.

Diener, E., & Diener, M. (1995). Cross-cultural correlates of life satisfaction and self-esteem. *Journal of Personality and Social Psychology, 68,* 653–663.

Dutton, J., & Dukerich, J. (1991). Keeping an eye on the mirror: The role of image and identity in organizational adaptation. *Academy of Management Journal, 34,* 517–554.

Dutton, J., & Ragins, B. R. (2007). *Exploring positive relationships at work: Building a theoretical and research foundation.* Mahwah, NJ: Lawrence Erlbaum Associates.

Erez, M., & Earley, P. C. (1993). *Culture, self-identity and work.* New York: Oxford University Press.

Gioia, D. A., Schultz, M., & Corley, K. G. (2000). Organizational identity, image and adaptive instability. *Academy of Management Review, 25,* 63–81.

Glynn, M. A., & Dowd, T. (2008). Charisma (un)bound: Emotive leadership in Martha Stewart Living magazine, 1990–2004. *Journal of Applied Behavioral Science, 44,* 71–93.

Kitayama, S., & Markus, H. R. (2000). The pursuit of happiness and the realization of sympathy. Cultural patterns of self, social relations, and well-being. In E. Diener & E. M. Suh (Eds.), *Subjective well-being across cultures* (pp. 113–161). Cambridge, MA: MIT Press.

March, J. G., & Olsen, J. P. (2004). *The logic of appropriateness.* Oslo: Arena Working Paper.

Plaut, V. C., Markus, H. R., & Lachman, M. E. (2002). Place matters: Consensual features and regional variation in American well-being and self. *Journal of Personality and Social Psychology, 83,* 160–184.

Rousseau, D. M. (1998). Why workers still identify with organizations. *Journal of Organizational Behavior, 19,* 217–233.

Rousseau, D. M., & Ling, K. (2007). Commentary: Following the resources in positive organizational relationships. In J. E. Dutton & B. R. Ragins (Eds.). *Exploring positive relations at work: Building a theoretical and research foundation* (pp. 373–387). Mahwah, NJ: Lawrence Erlbaum Associates.

Walsh, I. J. (2008). A model of deep structure identification: Antecedents, components and consequences. Paper presented at the Academy of Management annual meeting, Anaheim, CA.

Walsh, I. J., & Glynn, M. A. (2008). The way we were: Legacy organizational identity and the role of leadership. *Corporate Reputation Review, 11,* 262–276.

Weick, K. (1979). *The social psychology of organizing* (2nd ed.). Reading, MA: Addison-Wesley.

Whetten, D.A. (2006). Albert and Whetten revisited: Strengthening the concept of organizational identity. *Journal of Management Inquiry, 15,* 219–234.

Zammuto, R. F., & Cameron, K. S. (1985). Environmental decline and organizational response. *Research in Organizational Behavior, 7,* 223–262.

Part V

Conclusion

22

Forging Ahead: Positive Identities and Organizations as a Research Frontier

Laura Morgan Roberts, Jane E. Dutton, and Jeffrey Bednar

CONTENTS

We opened this volume with the question: When and how does applying a positive lens to the construct of identity generate new insights for organizational researchers? In responding to this question, the contributors to this volume have made substantial progress toward addressing the six goals that inspired this book. In addition, the contributors to this volume have started us on a journey into a new frontier of identity research by motivating the pursuit of new research questions, charting the course toward relevant identity research, and paving the way with new approaches to identity research. In this conclusion, we provide an initial roadmap of this new research frontier by highlighting new insights that can be gleaned from the chapters in this volume regarding the positivity of identity content, identity processes, and outcomes of identity for individuals, dyads, groups, organizations, and communities. We also demonstrate how several themes that emerge across the levels of analysis build conceptual and empirical pathways toward a deeper and broader understanding of identity and organizational studies that we hope enriches both theory and practice. We close with an invitation for others to join us in exploring this exciting new frontier.

MOTIVATING THE PURSUIT OF NEW RESEARCH QUESTIONS

The chapters in this volume serve an "opening-up" function (adopted from Carlsen & Pitsis, Chapter 4), in that each chapter, both explicitly and implicitly, uncovers numerous questions that have been prompted by each contributor's perspective on positive identity. The commentators—Ashforth (Chapter 8), Sanchez-Burks and Lee (Chapter 15), and Glynn and Walsh (Chapter 21)—open up even more questions to explore in this new research frontier across the levels of analysis. We highlight several new questions for identity research that cut across all three levels of analysis: (a) How does an identity become more positive; (b) What role does agency play in positive identity construction; (c) How are positive identities interdependent with their relational and institutional contexts; and (d) How can positive outcomes emerge from identity conflict, tension, and threat?

Positive Trajectories of Identity Development: Pathways Toward Becoming

Ashforth (Chapter 8), in his commentary, observes that "individuals and groups are constantly in a state of becoming" (p. 174). Many of the chapters in this volume examine identity in process; there are various accounts of how identities are constructed or transformed into more positive identities. These dynamic, rather than static accounts of identity encourage scholars to locate their investigations of identity within a trajectory of identity development. They also provide new answers to a fundamental question of identity construction, namely, *how does an identity become more positive?*

Corley and Harrison's Chapter 16 approaches this question by examining how ACS corporation (pseudonym used to maintain confidentiality) continually searches for authenticity by understanding "what it means to be who we are" and aligning its identity with its core values and strategic goals. Through a perpetual learning process, the organization sustains the clarity and relevance of its identity and evolves (i.e., changes in a positive, generative direction) to meet new demands from internal growth and external pressures. In their model, Corley and Harrison emphasize that generative change is not prompted by internal or external discrepancies between current and desired states or by external threats to core values or reputation. Instead, the quest for authenticity pushes organizational identities along a trajectory of becoming more positive.

Milton's Chapter 13 also captures a dynamic process of development in work groups. She proposes a regenerating cycle of identity confirmation in teams. Identity confirmation is a subjective state that exists when an individual's social environment is aligned with his or her identities. Identities are confirmed when they are validated and valued and can be confirmed in multiple ways (e.g., within interpersonal interaction, via meaningful work, via work group culture). According to her model, the confirmation of team members' relational identities creates the social fabric necessary to build cooperative capacity in work groups. This cooperative capacity fuels cooperation that then strengthens existing positive relational identities, creates new positive relational identities, and increases confirmation of those identities within the group, ultimately moving the group toward optimal achievement. Ragins' Chapter 11 about mentoring identity also emphasizes development along a positive trajectory. Her discussion of the formation of a mentoring identity emphasizes how positive mentoring experiences and established expectations of the mentor role increase and motivate one's capacity to incorporate mentoring into the future possible self and continue involvement in current (and future) mentoring relationships.

Other chapters explain how disruptive or problematic identity dynamics motivate shifting toward the development of more positive identities. Maitlis' Chapter 3 discussion of individual growth from trauma is one such example. Roberts, Cha, Hewlin, and Settles (Chapter 7) describe how people can become more authentic by peeling away masks or challenging others' simplistic or stereotypic expectations for how they should behave. These views of identity in progress raise interesting questions about identity trajectory or development: what differentiates those identities (and their possessors) that are capable of shifting toward an upward path of growth and vitality from those that remain ensnared in a downward spiral of despair or detachment? What constitutes progress or positive identity change at different levels of analyses, and how would we study these patterns?

Illuminating the Agency in Positive Identity Construction

Several chapters in this volume address the question, "*What role does agency play in positive identity construction?*" Agency is central to the accounts of positive identity construction in this volume, as individuals and collectives are seen as initiators and/or shapers of identity creation, identity work, or identity change. Ashforth (Chapter 8) comments on the prominence of agency in the volume, reminding readers that, "so important is agency or control that it is frequently regarded as a fundamental psychological need. As Gecas (1986, p. 140, his emphasis) wrote, 'the *experience* of agency… seems to lie at the very heart of the experience of self.'" For instance, Kreiner and Sheep (Chapter 2) emphasize the central role of proactivity in identity work as individuals choose to engage their world in a way that enhances their experience of competence, resilience, authenticity, holism, and transcendence. Rothbard and Ramarajan (Chapter 6) focus on the control that individuals and organizations have over the coactivation of work and nonwork identities as a key variable in fostering compatibility between multiple identities. Kopelman, Chen, and Shoshana (Chapter 12) posit that positive relational identities are a product of concentrated attempts to regulate the experience and expression of counterproductive negative or positive emotions, emotional displays that produce a threatening interpersonal encounter. DeRue, Ashford, and Cotton (Chapter 10) explain how individuals attempt to claim a leadership identity by engaging in verbal or nonverbal acts that are intended to reflect the characteristics that are considered unique and essential to leaders (e.g., "taking the seat at the head of a meeting table or asserting one's expertise in a particular domain" [p. 216]). Pratt and Kraatz (Chapter 17) also highlight agency in their description of the organizational self, suggesting that organizations modify and change their constraints, the institutions in which they are embedded, and ultimately the organizational self. In Carlsen and Pitsis' Chapter 4 account of the interplay between hope and positive identity construction, agency is implied as individuals open up to the possibility of attaining, transforming, and becoming stronger or more capable in some way. In their account, the mobilizing force of hope gains momentum as it resonates with an entity's present and future narrative of becoming. Viewing oneself as hopeful, and subjectively experiencing hope, promotes goal achievement, legacy building, and flourishing.

A focus on agency in identity construction opens a host of new questions for organizational scholars. For example, what are the different ways that individuals or collectives exercise agency in identity construction? What motivates the expression of agency in identity construction? Further, what are the important enablers and constraints within interpersonal relationships, groups, organizations, or within institutional fields that close down or open up opportunities for exercising agency in identity construction? This last question leads us directly to our next core theme.

Mapping the Interdependencies Between Positive Identities and Their Relational, Organizational, and Institutional Contexts

Another line of questioning that this volume raises is: "*How are positive identities interdependent with their relational and institutional contexts?*" Contextual understanding is necessary to explain the form, functions, and relevance of positive identities. Positive identities are embedded in relational, organizational, and institutional contexts that play a critical role in determining their evolution. In some contexts, agency is met with validation, and positive identities are solidified and strengthened.

Descriptions of the social construction of identity make this evident, as individual, relational, and collective identities are cocreated through the dynamic processes of claiming, verifying, and validating.

LeBaron, Glenn, and Thompson's Chapter 9 makes strong claims regarding the essential role of the relational context in identity construction. They argue that positive relational identities are interactive accomplishments that only exist in the context of interactions when moment to moment communications (verbal and nonverbal) call forth positive constructions of the self and other. DeRue et al. (Chapter 10) suggest that a leader identity is developed by claiming and granting, whereby people employ behaviors to signal their possession of leadership qualities, which, when validated by others, results in the internalization of a leader identity into one's self concept. Roberts et al. (Chapter 7) also use the example of leader identity to illustrate how authentication (i.e., validation from others regarding one's own identity claims) enhances experienced authenticity and generates more positive feelings about oneself. Both Milton's Chapter 13 and MacPhail, Roloff, and Edmondson's Chapter 14 propose that identity validation (i.e., having one's identities recognized and affirmed) enhances members' willingness and ability to cooperate and collaborate within a team. These studies suggest that relational contexts, characterized by mutual verification *and* affirmation of identities, are important for positive identity construction.

Organizational identities are validated by members and stakeholders when their actions align with stakeholder expectations or preferences (see Brickson & Lemmon, Chapter 18) and community or societal needs (see Hamilton & Gioia, Chapter 19; Marquis & Davis, Chapter 20). Pratt and Kraatz (Chapter 17) suggest that organizations verify their identities by "making symbolic offerings to the society of which they are a part ... aimed at showing the organization's conformance with various *identity standards* that are derived from the macro level." Hamilton and Gioia give examples of "greenwashing" (i.e., potentially disingenuous or purely instrumental attempts to brand oneself with a "green" identity through products, practices, mission statements) in response to institutional pressures. For example, when Clorox attempted to brand itself with a green identity, these identity claims were met with skepticism by those who considered it to be an inauthentic advertising scheme. Colgate, on the other hand, has not experienced such skepticism toward its unpublicized ownership of Tom's of Maine toothpaste (p. 442). Hamilton and Gioia also note that although "greenwashing may be intended to change an organization's image with customers and other stake-holders, ... organizational practices can have unintended consequences for the focal organization itself" (p. 443) by promoting positive identity change (i.e., becoming more green).

Glynn and Walsh (Chapter 21) remind readers that, for organizational scholars, the idea of contextual embeddedness is key (Dacin, Ventresca, & Beal, 1999; Granovetter, 1985). When applied to the construct of identity, researchers must take into account the varying levels of the situation that enable, mold, shape, and alter the processes, structures, and contents of identities. Brickson and Lemmon (Chapter 18) focus on how the relation-ships that organizations build with stakeholders, based on the organiza-tion's identity orientation (e.g., individualistic, relational, or collectivistic), provide a set of goals and actions that enable the organization to pro-duce valued resources for itself and its stakeholders. Marquis and Davis (Chapter 20) explain how geographical communities shape firms through the provision of traditions and reference groups, while at the same time local firms' actions importantly contribute to a geographical community's identity. Glynn and Walsh (Chapter 21) also comment that "the notion of organization in society figured more prominently in these conceptualiza-tions of positive organizational identity than in existing research on orga-nizational identity" (p. 477).

A close consideration of context raises new questions about how posi-tive identities form and function, and why they matter. Context offers a lens through which researchers can study the embeddedness of identity processes and dynamics with a multilevel analysis that takes into account geographic, institutional, organizational, and relational features.

Finding the Positive in Unexpected Places

The invitation to apply a positive lens seemed to liberate our colleagues from certain assumptions about how identities are conceptualized and function. Many of the authors chose to reevaluate whether what has often been construed as "bad" might, under certain conditions, in fact be "good." Specifically, these chapters pose the question: *"How can positive outcomes emerge from identity conflict, tension, and threat?"* Two areas of identity research illuminate how a positive lens can recast identity dynamics that have often been considered problematic into possibilities for contribution, connection, and growth: identity threat and multiple identities.

Identity Threat as a Catalyst for Growth

Identity threat is typically cast as a negative challenge to the significance, status, or distinctiveness of an identity. Yet, several chapters in this volume recast identity threat as a catalyst for growth or generative change. Several authors explain how entities (e.g., individuals, groups, organizations) can become stronger, more capable, and more connected to others when they respond to identity-threatening experiences constructively. For example, Maitlis' Chapter 3 on growth shows how people challenge their former assumptions about their own professional goals and relationships after experiencing a career-altering injury. This process of reflection infuses one's professional and personal identities with new meaning and broadens one's aspirations beyond the career he or she previously pursued (e.g., teaching, conducting, writing music instead of performing, playing a different instrument for pleasure). According to Maitlis, this experience of trauma also fosters growth and positive identity development as people come to see themselves as more capable of thriving in the midst of traumatic experiences. Kreiner and Sheep (Chapter 2) describe identity work tactics such as identity jujitsu (i.e., using the very power of the threat to catalyze increased self-awareness and positive identity change), which enable people to transform identity threats into opportunities. As a consequence of reframing identity threats and improving relationships with people who pose identity threats, people experience identity growth and develop identities that are more resilient. A third example of growth resulting from identity threat can be found in Kopelman et al.'s Chapter 12. They propose that as individuals respond to threatening interpersonal encounters in resilient ways, they can conarrate a positive relational identity that is viewed as constructive and able to overcome relational challenges and threats.

These chapters point to new directions for research that specify the conditions under which threatened identities can promote growth. They also raise important questions regarding the types and degrees of identity threat that can build personal and collective capacity compared with those that diminish performance and well-being.

Positive Outcomes of Multiple Identities

In their commentary, Sanchez-Burks and Lee (Chapter 15) challenge the assumption that multiple identities create tension, distraction, and dissonance. Instead, they review research on how multiple identities lead to positive psychological and performance outcomes when they are framed as compatible. Following this same line of reasoning, Rothbard and Ramarajan (Chapter 6) propose that cognitive reframing and routine coactivation of work and nonwork identities (i.e., making one's work and nonwork identities salient at the same time) facilitate an individual's ability to experience both identities as compatible and to engage both identities at work in ways that enhance creativity and reduce intrapsychic conflict. Caza and Wilson's (Chapter 5) data on certified nurse midwives support these claims. They reveal how complex (i.e., multifaceted, compatible) role and social identities provide cognitive, social, and behavioral resources that enhance professionals' ability to respond to patient crises with resilience. They present additional data that link identity complexity to positive discretionary behaviors (organizational citizenship behavior) among professionals. At the macro level, Pratt and Kraatz (Chapter 17) embrace the metaphor of the organizational self as an agent of discovery, prioritization, and rationalization of differences among multiple (and perhaps) competing identities to explain how unity or wholeness exists alongside pluralism in organizational identities. Each of these chapters points to the value of embracing multiple facets of identification to harness cognitive, social, and instrumental resources that enhance individual and institutional performance and well-being.

Questions such as these can inspire new lines of research on identity and organizations. In this way, the chapters in this book take important steps toward meeting one of our stated goals:

- *Developing diverse perspectives on how individuals, dyads, and collectives can construct, sustain, and change positive identities*

CHARTING THE COURSE: HIGHLIGHTING THE SIGNIFICANCE OF POSITIVE IDENTITIES

The importance of positive identities in the current world of work calls for relevant research. Chapters in this volume take up the issue of why identity matters. They do so by moving beyond a descriptive account of who I am, toward an account of "what it *means* to be who I am" (adopted from Corley & Harrison, Chapter 16) and why it matters that I am who I am. We highlight two ways that the chapters in this volume explain why positive identities are important for individuals, groups, organizations, and societies. First, many chapters detail how identities positively impact entities and their constituents. Second, several chapters discuss the processes by which identities grant meaning, order, and adaptability in a complex, interconnected, changing world of work. Both of these lenses help to reveal even more of the interplay between positive identities and the social context.

The Functional Significance of Positive Identities

There are several explanations of how and why identities generate favorable outcomes for individuals, collectives, and their constituents. In these accounts, identities are central engines in dynamic cognitive and social processes that expand possibilities for how entities engage with and contribute to their social world. Glynn and Walsh (Chapter 21) note the normative stance that underlies several of the chapters in this volume with respect to the importance of identity in generating positive outcomes for others (e.g., benefiting society in a meaningful or valuable way). Hamilton and Gioia (Chapter 19) put forth a call for organizations to harness identities that promote sustainability by balancing environmental responsibility, social equity, and economic capability. Brickson and Lemmon (Chapter 18) claim that positive organizational identities provide the basis for actions that "generate a net positive level of socially valuable resources to the earth and its living inhabitants" (p. 404) by building stakeholder resources and enhancing stakeholders' self-schemas. In Marquis and Davis' Chapter 20, they offer a compelling account of how corporations shape community identities and reputations sustaining local foundations and nonprofits and by mobilizing citizen involvement in the community. They discuss how such actions ultimately contribute to a community's well-being.

This volume also reveals how, within work groups, identities serve to enhance connections, contributions, and group outcomes. For example, MacPhail et al. (Chapter 14) discuss how individual identities (e.g., expert identity), when validated and affirmed, can motivate actions that contribute to a positive team identity and group performance outcomes (e.g., knowledge sharing, creativity, group learning). Ragins' Chapter 11 on mentoring identity proposes that relational identities also produce important outcomes, such as the formation and maintenance of high-quality connections at work. She claims that as mentoring becomes internalized into the mentor's self-structure, the quality of mentoring relationships and the motivation to pursue future mentoring relationships increase. These are just a few of the many positive outcomes that are associated with identity content and processes in this volume.

Positive Identity Processes in the Contemporary Work Environment

Ashforth (Chapter 8) points out in his commentary:

> a positive identity is not only instrumental to organizational effectiveness—in these chapters, through organizational citizenship behaviors, creative problem solving, and organizational change, to name a few—but also is desirable as an end in itself ... for the edification of self and others that they provide. (p. 173)

The edifying and organizing properties of identities are especially important in our fast-paced global society where organizational boundaries are becoming increasingly permeable. As we mentioned in the introduction, this focused inquiry into positive identity reveals various ways organizations and their members can construct and maintain identities that are appropriately meaningful, legitimate, and stable yet also dynamic, flexible, and adaptable. Here we offer a few examples of ways that identity construction contributes to favorable outcomes in the contemporary organizational environment.

One of the principal functions of identity is to provide order and meaning to social life. Several chapters illuminate how and why positive identities are especially important for helping entities make sense of and derive meaning from their existence, actions, and aspirations. For instance, we glean from Carlsen and Pitsis' Chapter 4 illustrations of personal and organizational change that hope serves to anchor and validate the persistent drive to progress beyond apparent constraints in pursuit of a higher potential. In accordance with LeBaron et al. (Chapter 9), positive identities are also the conduit through which connections are forged and sustained during boundary moments in social life. The mutual accomplishment of positive identities involves bridging past, present, and future relational selves and cohering one's file self (objectified self as represented in written record) with one's embodied self. Kopelman et al. (Chapter 12) draw on a narrative framework of relational identity to explain the "means by which people make themselves intelligible within the social world." In their account, people develop a story of their relationship with another person that is constantly refined to incorporate emerging interactions. The construction of an organizational self is also a means for providing order and cohesion among an organization's multiple identities. In a complex institutional environment, Pratt and Kraatz (Chapter 17) advocate for the conceptualization of organizations using a multiple identity conceptualization of the self (MICS) to embrace the paradoxical coexistence of an organization's unifying and fragmenting properties.

This volume also provides new ways to think about facilitating the benefits of diversity in a global marketplace. Several authors, in their discussions of positive identity, call attention to the individual, relational, and organizational dynamics that promote inclusion and allow entities to engage their varied backgrounds and orientations in a positive way. MacPhail et al. (Chapter 14) emphasize that reciprocal expertise affirmation is a key mechanism for enabling workgroups to overcome the faultlines that often emerge when members do not recognize or appreciate each others' respective expertise. Ragins (Chapter 11) invites scholars to consider how gender influences the internalization and enactment of mentoring identity to enhance the quality of same and cross-gender mentoring relationships. Roberts et al. (Chapter 7) explain how underrepresented minorities and women can become more authentic by peeling away masks of identity suppression and countering stereotypical expectations. They also note that a diverse workplace climate creates a context that welcomes authenticity from diverse employees. Sanchez-Burks and Lee review several studies that show how work groups that fully engage their diversity (i.e., maintain salience and foster compatibility among multiple identities that exist within the group) increase knowledge sharing and knowledge synthesis. Brickson and Lemmon (Chapter 18) invite scholars to consider the diversity in organizational identity orientations to appreciate various resource-generating relationships between organizations and stakeholders.

A better understanding of how positive identities form and function can broaden the ways that identity is used as a vehicle for generating beneficial or desirable outcomes within and for organizations and communities. Together, these chapters point scholars toward relevant research on the functions and formation of identity, which aligns with another goal for the book:

- *To provide individuals and collectives with ideas, concepts, and resources that will aid them as they strive to construct and to engage positive identities*

PAVING THE WAY: DEMONSTRATING VARIED APPROACHES TO IDENTITY RESEARCH

A third way that we see this volume advancing research is by offering varied theoretical and empirical approaches that pave the way for others to join in this focused inquiry on positive identity.

Revisiting Frequently Trodden Conceptual Paths

Some of the preceding chapters reexamined familiar identity topics through a positive lens, deepening our understanding of generative mechanisms and valued outcomes associated with identity processes. In addition to identity change, multiple identities, and diversity, which we have discussed in previous sections of the Conclusion, here we mention just two of many other possible examples where traditional identity topics have been expanded through consideration of positive identity: identity categorization and identity work.

Identity categorization has been a core idea in identity research for both macro and micro scholars. Researchers have focused on both the causes and consequences of categorization into social groups. Consideration of positive identity content, processes, and outcomes focuses attention on certain types of identity categories that have inherent value in certain social contexts and to an expanded repertoire of outcomes associated with categorization into particular social groups. For example, DeRue et al. (Chapter 10) draw attention to the category of leader, Ragins (Chapter 11) the category of mentor, and MacPhail et al. (Chapter 14) the category of expert as being categories that are charged with a particular positive valence. Other chapters broaden consideration of the consequences from certain forms of identity categorization, drawing attention to the generative consequences from an individual's or collective's defining themselves in terms of specific traits, such as authentic (e.g., Roberts et al., Chapter 7), sustainability focused (e.g., Hamilton & Gioia, Chapter 19), or charitable (Marquis & Davis, Chapter 20).

Identity work directs attention to the efforts and practices deployed to create, sustain, or change a particular identity. Much of the research on identity work has focused on individual and collective efforts expended in the wake of identity threats. This volume offers a view of identity work that is inspired by an entity's desire to grow and evolve rather than a need to maintain social status or self-worth in the face of threat. Corley and Harrison (Chapter 16) describe a form of organizational identity work that guides organizational change absent identity threats or discrepancies. Kreiner and Sheep's (Chapter 2) five positive identity work tactics differ from many other studies of identity work that emphasize coping with stigma or identity threat. LeBaron et al. (Chapter 9) capture yet another form of identity work by coding verbal and nonverbal enactments (e.g., statements in context, tone, enthusiasm, silence) that mutually constitute positive relational identities. They emphasize the importance of knowing and relating (i.e., indicating a knowledge of and appreciation for the other) in identity work.

These descriptions of identity work differ from the threat-induced accounts of coping via cognitive reframing or behavioral expressions that have been featured in traditional studies of identity work. In reviewing one definition of identity work as "being engaged in forming, repairing, maintaining, strengthening or revising the constructions that are productive of a sense of coherence and distinctiveness" (Sveningsson & Alvesson, 2003, p. 1165), we believe this volume offers several new descriptions of forming, repairing, maintaining, and strengthening identities.

Creating New Conceptual Paths

Other chapters used the positive lens to expand the scope of future identity research and build new bridges between positive dynamics and identity theories. Authenticity receives a great deal of attention in this volume as it relates to positive identity. Corley and Harrison, Hamilton and Gioia, Kopelman et al., Milton, and Roberts et al. (Chapters 16, 19, 12, 13, and 7) all point to authenticity as a core element of a positive identity for individuals, dyads, and collectives. All three commentaries highlight authenticity as a theme in their reviews, which suggests that this remains a central issue for identity research. A review of these chapters and commentaries also suggests that the bridge between authenticity and positivity is paved with contingencies. Several contributors question whether authenticity is inherently positive from an identity perspective. Ashforth (Chapter 8) cautions against idealizing the authentic self and presuming that when one behaves authentically, idealized traits and virtues are displayed rather than character flaws. Sanchez-Burks and Lee (Chapter 15) invite scholars to consider that inauthenticity might also generate desirable identity outcomes by ensuring smoother social interactions.

Resilience is explicitly mentioned in Caza and Wilson's Chapter 5 discussion of how identity complexity generates resources that professionals draw on to respond to workplace challenges in a resilient manner. Resilience is also a theme in Maitlis' Chapter 3 study of musicians who transcend the pain and disappointment of career-altering injury by constructing a resilient self-narrative. Kopelman et al. (Chapter 12) propose that a resilient response to a counterproductive emotional display promotes the formation of a positive relational narrative identity. Kreiner and Sheep (Chapter 2) include resilience as one of five characteristics that are core to the development of a positive individual identity.

Carlsen and Pitsis (Chapter 4) join hope with positive identity and, in so doing, reveal how hope serves as a future-oriented quality of experiencing that motivates people to narrate themselves in terms of goal pursuit, expanding possibilities, and escaping or transforming hardship. The formation of hoped-for possible selves (i.e., visions of whom one wishes to become) is also linked to identity growth (Kreiner & Sheep, Chapter 2), motivation to build high-quality work relationships (Ragins, Chapter 11), and generative change (Corley & Harrison, Chapter 16). However, Ashforth (Chapter 8) reminds us to take note of how false hopes might encourage engagement in futile action and forestall more efficacious action.

The theoretical grounding of these chapters makes headway on another goal:

- *To facilitate the integration of a positive identity perspective into new and established areas of organizational behavior and organizational theory*

Empirical Investigations of Positive Identity

It is interesting to note the predominance of conceptual frameworks, case studies, and qualitative analyses, as well as the relative absence of survey and laboratory studies in this volume. Contributors have forged into this territory of positive identity with rich, descriptive accounts of identity content, processes, and outcomes. This is likely an artifact of the novelty of a focused inquiry on positive identity. Although identity has been a central topic in organizational studies and related disciplines for decades, the application of a positive lens to identity requires that scholars revisit core assumptions and build new theories about the form and function of positive identities. As such, it is appropriate that this early-stage research is pursued through inductive, theory-building studies of positive identity rather than deductive, theory-testing studies.

Contributors do point to the need for additional empirical studies to test the claims that have been raised in their chapters. These chapters also encourage the study of organizational contexts that enable the formation and functioning of positive identities. For example, Carlsen and Pitsis (Chapter 4) invite scholars to consider how human resource practices and job practices cultivate and sustain positive identity construction via the generation of hope. Hamilton and Gioia (Chapter 19) raise the issue of how organizational size and public versus private ownership influence the adoption of sustainability into an organizational identity. Caza and Wilson (Chapter 5) note that certain organizational contexts embrace identity complexity (e.g., welcoming the varied professional approaches of certified nurse midwives), which better enables professionals to draw on their multiple identities as a resource.

Mobilizing a Cross-Disciplinary, Multilevel Inquiry Into Positive Identity

These chapters are also imbued with an energizing, mobilizing quality that is fostered by multilevel, multidisciplinary dialogue. Our book-building conference, which took place on a wintry (January) weekend in Ann Arbor, literally brought together scholars from around the world, at different stages of their careers, with different theoretical takes on identity, to engage one another in this conversation about naming the positive in, of, and from identity. Together, we probed into each other's research questions and considered the theoretical implications of our claims for individuals, dyads, groups, organizations, and communities.

As a result, this process for collectively pursuing the study of positive identity yielded a wide range of theoretical approaches to identity, including identity as narrative (e.g., Maitlis, Chapter 3; Carlsen & Pitsis,

Chapter 4; Kopelman et al., Chapter 12), identity as object or schema (e.g., Ragins, Chapter 11; Roberts et al., Chapter 7; DeRue et al., Chapter 10; Brickson & Lemmon, Chapter 18), and identity as subject (e.g., LeBaron et al., Chapter 9; Carlsen & Pitsis, Chapter 4; Corley & Harrison, Chapter 16; Pratt & Kraatz, Chapter 17). Some chapters span levels of analysis, such as Marquis and Davis' Chapter 20 discussion of the interplay between organizational and community identities, Carlsen and Pitsis' Chapter 4 attention to how hope mobilizes identity construction for individuals and collectives, and MacPhail et al.'s Chapter 14 propositions that reciprocal affirmation of individual expert identities strengthens the team identity. Interesting questions emerge from this multilevel volume regarding the extent to which "positive qualities and processes are isomorphic across levels of self and across levels of analysis?", as Glynn and Walsh (Chapter 21) stated.

We have pushed one another to own and articulate our assumptions, sharpen our insights, and bolster our claims—generating a renewed energy for identity scholarship. The process of creating this volume, as well as the chapters that were produced, help to address two of our goals:

- *To establish positive identity as a multidisciplinary, multilevel field of inquiry, and to facilitate and encourage cross-fertilization and interdisciplinary linkages*
- *To offer a foundation for building a community of scholars in all stages of their careers and from various disciplines to pursue research that identifies antecedents, outcomes, processes, and mechanisms associated with positive identities*

CONCLUSION

As we continue to explore this new frontier of identity research, we are excited by the possibilities that lie ahead. The chapters herein point to various ways in which scholars can help to accomplish our sixth and final goal for this book:

- *To bring positive identity to the forefront of organizational research by establishing, deepening, and broadening the link between the positive organizational scholarship perspective and identity research*

Positive organizational scholarship endeavors to understand the generative dynamics and processes the underlie individual, group, and organizational flourishing (Cameron, Dutton, & Quinn, 2003; Dutton & Glynn, 2008; Roberts, 2006). A focus on identity processes helps to shed light on how different forms of positive meaning applied to different levels of entities (individuals, relationships, groups, organizations, and communities) deepens understanding of the conditions and processes that cultivate individual or collective flourishing. By examining what is positive about identity, this volume adopts an appreciative stance toward the content, processes, and outcomes of identities. Just as we conclude from a POS perspective on relationships (Dutton & Ragins, 2007), we are reminded that remedying the negative (e.g., negative identity content, processes, or outcomes) is not the same as cultivating the positive. By focusing on the different meanings of positive identities at different levels of analysis, the authors in this volume have helped us to see new possibilities for understanding the generative possibilities of identity as a topic in organizational studies.

As we forge ahead into this terrain of research on positive identity, we recognize those scholars who heed us to keep sight of the interplay between the positive and negative (and all of their variations) in understanding and researching identity content, processes, and outcomes. We hope that as researchers carefully examine the generative insights from serious consideration of positive identity (in all of its various forms), they develop and test theories that also attend to the potential pitfalls and limits derived from an explicit focus on the positive (e.g., Fineman, 2006; Hackman, in press). Our commentators remind us of the value in understanding the interplay between positive and negative dynamics as they relate to identity, such as the sustainability of positive outcomes of identities for individuals and collectives, and the contingent nature of many of the relationships proposed in this volume.

We conclude this volume inspired by newly sparked conversations about identity; we enthusiastically direct our attention toward understanding new mechanisms and new consequences that are revealed at the intersection of identity and positive organizational scholarship. The conceptual frameworks and empirical findings presented in the chapters illuminate the impact of positive identity across levels of analysis. In turn, we hope that forging ahead into this domain will catalyze research that increases the capacity for organizational studies to foster hope, growth, resilience, connections, and contributions for individuals, dyads, and collectives.

REFERENCES

Cameron, K. S., Dutton, J. E., & Quinn, R. E. (2003). *Positive organizational scholarship: Foundations of a new discipline.* San Francisco: Berrett-Koehler Publishers.

Dacin, T., Ventresca, M. J., & Beal, B. (1999). The embeddedness of organizations: Dialogue & directions. *Journal of Management, 25,* 317–356.

Dutton, J., & Ragins, B. (Eds.). (2007). *Exploring positive relationships at work: Building a theoretical and research foundation.* Mahwah, NJ: Lawrence Erlbaum Associates.

Dutton, J. E., & Glynn, M. (2008). Positive organizational scholarship. In C. Cooper & J. Barling, (Eds)., *Handbook of organizational behavior* (pp. 693–712). London: Sage Publications.

Fineman, S. (2006). On being positive: Concerns and counterpoints. *Academy of Management Review, 31,* 270–291.

Gecas, V. (1986). The motivational significance of self-concept for socialization theory. *Advances in Group Processes, 3,* 131–156.

Granovetter, M. (1985). Economic action and social structure: The problem of embeddedness. *American Journal of Sociology, 91,* 481–510.

Hackman, J. R. (in press). The perils of positivity: "Counterpoint" of point-counterpoint section. *Journal of Organizational Behavior.*

Roberts, L. M. (2006). Shifting the lens on organizational life: The added value of positive scholarship. *Academy of Management Review, 31,* 241–260.

Sveningsson, S., & Alvesson, M. (2003). Managing managerial identities: Organizational fragmentation, discourse and identity struggle. *Human Relations, 56,* 1163–1193.

Author Index

Subject Index